CONSTITUTIONAL LAW

CONSTITUTIONAL LAW

An Outline of the Law and Practice of the Constitution including Central and Local Government the Citizen and the State and Administrative Law by E. C. S. Wade and G. Godfrey Phillips

EIGHTH EDITION

by

E. C. S. WADE

Q.C., F.B.A., LL.D.

Emeritus Downing Professor of the Laws of England;
Fellow of Gonville and Caius College, Cambridge

and

A. W. BRADLEY

M.A., LL.B.

Professor of Constitutional Law in the University of Edinburgh;
Solicitor of the Supreme Court (England and Wales)

LONGMAN

LONGMAN GROUP LIMITED
London
Associated companies, branches and representatives throughout the world

First Edition 1931
First Edition, Revised 1933
Second Edition 1935
Third Edition 1946
Fourth Edition 1950
Fifth Edition 1955
Sixth Edition 1960
Seventh Edition 1965
Eighth Edition 1970
Second Impression 1973

ISBN 0 582 48823 0 Cased
ISBN 0 582 48824 9 Paper

Printed in Great Britain by
Lowe & Brydone (Printers) Ltd., Thetford, Norfolk

PREFACE TO EIGHTH EDITION

The machinery of central and local government throughout the United Kingdom and the Islands has over the past five years been subjected to strains and stresses which have been made known to the public to a greater degree than in the past by the use of modern (as well as the old established) means of communication. This does not mean that as a matter of constitutional law the time is ripe for re-writing the past or indeed as yet for recording major changes in the machinery, although such changes are likely to take place in the near future. The student, whose primary interest is to learn how the constitution functions at the present time, wants to know what is the present law and practice, how Government, Parliament and courts operate in 1970 in the setting of the oldest parliamentary constitution, which has extended far and wide in the Commonwealth and the New World.

This edition of a book first published forty years ago takes the story to the end of 1969. Topics which receive emphasis include the call for a written constitution, the enactments resulting from racial discrimination, immigration, fugitive offenders in the Commonwealth, departmental organisation, reform of the Civil Service and changes in the procedure of criminal courts. In more detail the office of the Parliamentary Commissioner for Administration (the so-called Ombudsman) is examined as well as the changing attitude of the higher courts to administrative problems. There has been some reduction in the space devoted to Commonwealth relations. Enough remains to enable the story of the constitutional advance to independent status to be told. This will always be a landmark in the achievements of British government, although it is no longer for an imperial role that any lawyer is trained. There is, perhaps surprisingly, less change to record in Part II, which deals with the liberty of the subject. Demonstrations, whereby grievances are currently aired, result in isolated and occasionally massive breaches of the peace; these can be an onerous burden for an over-worked police force. Yet the means of dealing in the courts with such outbreaks, at all events in public places, do not seem to call for any radical amendment of the substantive law, which remains unchanged.

Publishers' requirements have meant that the text was delivered in December 1969. We have deliberately not indulged in speculation as to prospective changes in the law. Even if space had permitted, confusion between present law and the law of the future has to be avoided. This preface, however, is written six months later when the United Kingdom has elected a new Parliament and a new Administration has taken office. Both inherit a wealth of material in the form of reports (published or forthcoming) of Royal Commissions, including one on the constitution itself, of departmental and parliamentary committees and other public inquiries; advice is also available from a wide variety of standing and *ad hoc* advisory organs which have become essential aids to the formation of policy. Blue Books, White Papers and Green Papers are available in plenty; of these a small selection relate to the constitution, particularly parliamentary practice.

If guidance is wanted, there follows a list of topics which may be the subjects for action in the lifetime of the present Parliament.

(1) The Royal Commission on the Constitution, whose terms of reference are printed in Appendix D, may report within the next two years. It is uncertain whether the Commission will interpret its function broadly or will confine its attention to the problems of legislative and administrative devolution within the United Kingdom against a background of nationalist and regional aspirations. The report of the Conservative Party's Scottish Constitutional Committee, entitled "Scotland's Government", was published in March 1970; with two dissentients, it recommended the creation of a directly elected Scottish Convention to undertake some of the work of Scottish legislation at present conducted solely at Westminster. In view of the Conservative party's relative lack of success in Scotland in the General Election 1970, it is doubtful whether this limited proposal will be given high priority by the new Government.

(2) The breakdown of public order in Northern Ireland in 1969 and 1970 is probably the most acute current constitutional problem within the United Kingdom. It is not yet possible to be confident that the reform programme of the Northern Ireland Government will form a sufficient long-term solution, unaccompanied by more fundamental constitutional changes.

(3) Although in February 1970 the Labour Government announced its intention of implementing the main recommendations of the Redcliffe-Maud Commission on English local government (pp. 341–2 and Cmnd. 4276) the new Conservative administration is to re-examine the subject and may decide in favour of a two-tier system rather than the essentially one-tier system favoured by the Commis-

sion. A decision is also awaited on the recommendations of the Wheatley Commission on Scottish Local Government (p. 366).

(4) In the judicial sphere implementation has already begun of the main recommendations of the Report of the Royal Commission on Assizes and Quarter Sessions (summarised in Appendix D at pp. 740–2). Royal Assent was given in May 1970 to an Administration of Justice Bill which establishes a Family Division of the High Court and transfers the remaining jurisdiction of the Probate and Admiralty Division to the Chancery and Queen's Bench Divisions respectively.

(5) In the parliamentary sector important changes in the law and practice relating to privilege recommended by the Select Committee on Parliamentary Privilege (H.C. 34, 1967–68) await formal approval, partly by legislation; they were favourably received in a debate in the last House of Commons. The Report from the Select Committee on the Declaration of Members' Interests (H.C. 57, 1969–70) has yet to be adopted. As regards the financial business of the House of Commons, the report from the Select Committee on Procedure on the scrutiny of public expenditure and administration (H.C. 410, 1968–69) has in part been implemented. On 21 and 22 January 1970, the House held the first of a proposed series of annual debates on a White Paper outlining projected public expenditure over the next five years. But the proposal for the conversion of the Estimates Committee into a Committee on Expenditure, with eight specialised sub-committees, is still under consideration. Earlier proposals for a new structure of relationships between the Government and the nationalised industries (outlined at p. 293) may be reconsidered by the new Government.

(6) The Civil Service is already in process of re-organisation (see chapter 18 for the tasks of the new Civil Service Department), but it will be some years before the full effects of the change-over from Treasury control are appreciated.

(7) Consideration by the six member States of the application of the United Kingdom to enter the European Economic Community opens at the end of June 1970. If the application for membership succeeds, obligations under the Treaty of Rome will be accepted, some of which are of such a character that the authority of Parliament in certain spheres of municipal law must be surrendered. Earlier official views of the legal and constitutional implications of United Kingdom membership (Cmnd. 3301, 1967) will be closely scrutinised and there may be further re-examination of the orthodox view of the sovereignty of Parliament, such as resulted with less impact on the law of the

United Kingdom from the enactment in 1931 of the Statute of Westminster.

(8) Entry into the European Community may, having regard to the political and legal nature of the constitutional arrangements, strengthen arguments for the enactment of a written constitution for the United Kingdom. Moreover there is a school of political thought which favours such a step as an attempt to stabilise rights of personal liberty in a time of increasingly complex and far-reaching public controls. The new Government has stated that it will be its special duty more effectively to safeguard the freedom of the individual under the law.

(9) Although the Labour Government in December 1969 rejected the recommendation by the English and Scottish Law Commissions for the appointment of a Royal Commission on administrative law (pp. 595, 715), the Law Commissions were in 1970 asked to review existing remedies for the judicial control of administrative acts and omissions with a view to evolving a simpler and more effective procedure.

(10) An Industrial Relations Bill will almost certainly figure in the programme of the new Government.

In a book which has passed through several editions it is fitting to remember the help and advice of many colleagues and former pupils who have made suggestions for improvements and helped the editors to avoid errors. On this occasion, as always, there have been newcomers to their ranks; as some of these hold public offices, mention of names must be avoided, but our appreciation is none the less warm. Nor do we forget the clerical help so ungrudgingly offered which we have each of us enjoyed.

June, 1970.

E. C. S. WADE
A. W. BRADLEY

For this edition, compiled under conditions which have prevented the closer personal contact at Cambridge hitherto enjoyed with my colleague, I, as always, accept responsibility for the whole book. Professor Bradley shares this responsibility only in respect of the editorial revision of Part III (Administrative Law) and the chapters on local government, to which he has again given his special skills. But on many other matters I have enjoyed the benefit of his advice.

Fakenham,
Norfolk.

E.C.S.W.

TABLE OF CONTENTS

TABLE OF STATUTES

PAGES

STATUTES OF OTHER PARLIAMENTS

Ceylon

Dominion of Canada

Ireland

India

Pakistan

Union of South Africa

TABLE OF CASES

D

PAGES

K

N

O

PAGES

P

Q

R

S

ABBREVIATIONS

C.B.R.	= Canadian Bar Review.
C.L.C.	= Constitutional Laws of the Commonwealth, Vol. I, by Sir Ivor Jennings. (Clarendon Press.)
C.L.J.	= Cambridge Law Journal.
H.C.	= House of Commons Paper.
H.E.L.	= *History of English Law*, by Sir William Holdsworth. (Methuen.)
H.L. or H.C. Deb.	= House of Lords (or Commons) Debates. (Hansard.)
I.C.L.Q	= International and Comparative Law Quarterly.
K. & L.	= *Cases in Constitutional Law*, by Sir David Keir and F. H. Lawson. 5th Edition. (Clarendon Press.)
L.Q.R.	= Law Quarterly Review.
M.L.R.	= Modern Law Review.
M.P.R.	= Report of Committee on Ministers' Powers, 1932. (Cmd. 4060.)
S.I.	= Statutory Instrument.
S.R. and O.	= Statutory Rule and Order.

PART I: General Constitutional Law

INTRODUCTION

Law of the Constitution, 10th edn., pp. 1–35, by A. V. Dicey (Macmillan).
English Constitutional History, pp. 526–39, by F. W. Maitland (Cambridge University Press).
The Law and the Constitution, 5th edn., by Sir Ivor Jennings (University of London Press).

CHAPTER ONE

DEFINITION AND SOURCES OF CONSTITUTIONAL LAW

A. What is a Constitution?

By a constitution is normally meant a document having a special legal sanctity which sets out the framework and the principal functions of the organs of government of a State and declares the principles governing the operation of those organs. Such a document is implemented by decisions of the particular organ, normally the highest court of the State, which has power to interpret its contents. In addition there are gradually evolved a number of conventional rules and practices which serve to attune the operation of the constitution to changing conditions and thereby to avoid, in the main, alterations to a written document which is designed to be permanent in its operation. It is thus that a document framed in 1787 remains in force today, with few important amendments, as the constitution of the United States of America.

A constitution does not necessarily or usually contain the detailed rules upon which depend the working of the institutions of government. Legal processes, rules for elections, the mode of implementing services provided by the State, so far as these are matters for enactment, are to be found, not in the constitution, but in ordinary statutes made by the legislature within the limits set by the constitution itself. Such statutes can be altered by the same method as that by which they were originally enacted, whereas changes in the constitution call for a more elaborate process. This is to ensure that it shall not be in the power of those who for the time being can command control of the legislative organ to vary without special consultations and, may be, direct reference to the electors, the system and principles of government which have been set up with solemn formalities by agreement between all major political interests in the State.

Written Constitutions

A documentary constitution will normally reflect theoretical beliefs. It is, therefore, not surprising that in our own country, where progress has been achieved less by adherence to philosophical concepts than by the process of trial and error, no written formulae have been embodied in a code of rules for government. Hence there is no constitutional document which can form the starting-point of a student's instruction in the constitutional law of the United Kingdom, and it is said that there exists no written constitution. Nevertheless, without abandoning our instinctive dislike of declaring our political philosophy in terms of law, written constitutions have been framed for British communities overseas, whether as colonies or as members of the Commonwealth, in terms of organs and general rules for their operation. Such constitutions formerly stopped short of attempting to enact fundamental concepts in terms of law. Not only did they contain no definition of responsible government but they offered no guarantee of the primary rights of the subject. Some of these constitutions have stood the test of time virtually unchanged, e.g. the Commonwealth of Australia. Canada, the oldest dating from 1867, has lately added a Bill of Rights, though this was not enacted as part of the British North America Act 1867 which contains the constitution, but as ordinary legislation. In recent years dating in particular from the Federal Constitution of India in 1948, and again in the case of Nigeria in 1960, guarantees of constitutional rights have been included in the constitution, and this has now become in the case of practically all the independent States of Africa within the Commonwealth the accepted method of safeguarding the rights of minorities. The older pattern provided little more than the machinery of government but served to show the student that the "unwritten" Constitution of the United Kingdom could be reduced at all events in part to written, *i.e.* specifically enacted, form.

An important consequence of the absence of a written constitution is that there is no part of the machinery of government, whether organs or functions, which is protected against change by the special requirements for altering a written constitution. This gives Parliament, and in particular the House of Commons, where the Government normally has an adequate majority, a special responsibility not to use its power of changing the law for the purpose of altering those parts of the machinery of government which have acquired through long usage a special value for preserving the accepted form of political institutions. Equally the power is available for the purpose of achieving constitutional amendment with the minimum of formality where it is desired on all sides, as for example when war conditions demand the sacrifice of a well-established rule for the time being. Such flexibility then has its advantages as well as its dangers.

Of late there has been a movement of opinion in favour of a written constitution for the United Kingdom. One reason for this is the growth of nationalism in Scotland and Wales which calls for a far greater measure of independence from Westminster and Whitehall than has hitherto been granted to Edinburgh or Cardiff by administrative devolution. It proved feasible fifty years ago to grant Northern Ireland [1] separate executive, legislative and judicial organs by the Government of Ireland Act 1920 enacted by the Parliament of the United Kingdom. This Act may rightly be regarded as a constituent Act, but on the prevailing view of legal sovereignty of the Westminster Parliament it could be expressly repealed, however reluctant a court might be to presume implied repeal in interpreting its provisions. The main purpose of a constitution in written form is to secure that changes shall not be enacted without special safeguards to secure entrenchment for constitutional rights, such as joint sessions of the houses of the legislature with special majorities for decision, or referenda of the electorate, and therefore the aims of Scottish and Welsh nationalists are unlikely to be satisfied with ordinary, *i.e.* repealable, legislation. It is doubtless on that account that a Royal Commission on the Constitution [2] embarked in 1969 on a thorough inquiry into the relationship between the various parts of the United Kingdom, including the Channel Islands and the Isle of Man, and the central government.

But apart from the desire to change the machinery of government there is a growing demand that certain fundamental rights of individual liberty of action should be secured, even against the government of the day with its control over the legislative machine. This can best be achieved in the view of its advocates by a formal guarantee

[1] Ireland became part of the United Kingdom on the formation of the latter by the Acts of Union 1800 passed by the Parliaments of Great Britain and Ireland. Since the Ireland Act 1949 the union has applied only to Northern Ireland, since Ireland is construed as exclusive of the Republic of Ireland.

[2] Appendix, p. 742, *post*.

in a written constitution. As will be seen[1] the protection of minorities has been attempted by this method in the case of newly independent territories in the Commonwealth during the past twenty-five years.

Whether there is a clash of interests between regional and central governments as to the limits of the powers of each, or between individual citizens and government agencies as to rights guaranteed by the constitution, the task of interpretation can best be undertaken by a constitutional court specifically charged with the duty of upholding the provisions of the constitution.

What is Constitutional Law?

There is no hard and fast definition of constitutional law. In the generally accepted use of the term it means the rules which regulate the structure of the principal organs of government and their relationship to each other, and determine their principal functions. These rules consist both of legal rules in the strict sense and of usages, commonly called conventions, which without being enacted are accepted as binding by all who are concerned in government. Many of the rules and practices under which our system of government is worked are not part of the law in the sense that their violation may lead directly to proceedings in a court of law. Though the constitutional lawyer is concerned primarily with the legal aspects of government, there is required for an understanding of constitutional law some knowledge of the chief features of constitutional history and of the working of our political institutions. The constitutional lawyer should also be conversant with the relationship between the citizen and the State, and more particularly with what may be called political relationship, though nowadays the term, political, is apt to embrace economics as well as politics.

Scope of Text-books

Logically it is difficult to justify the selection of subjects which are normally covered in text-books on constitutional law. Generally speaking the books deal with the functions of the State in relation to the maintenance of order and the defence of the realm rather than with its expanding activities in the social and economic sphere. It is in regard to the latter that the average citizen comes face to face with the official, in the course of day-to-day administration, but his fundamental freedoms, to use a topical expression, are more likely to be infringed in relation to the maintenance of order. It is in this sphere that the courts are likely to be in conflict with the Executive, and it is

[1] Chap. 32. C.

to the courts rather than to Parliament that the citizen resorts for the redress of his individual grievances. Accordingly the constitutional lawyer has always had a particular interest in the means which the law provides for safeguarding individual liberty, whether of the person or of speech. Included in this category are subjects like freedom from arrest and unlawful imprisonment, freedom of expression of opinion, whether by spoken word or writing, by meetings and processions or by exercising free choice as an elector. Nowadays it is also essential to include something about the impact made on a citizen by the administration of the various public services which are the feature of the welfare State. The lawyer is chiefly concerned with the sources of administrative power and with the adjudication of disputes, particularly when the requirements of a public service, such as housing, or the use of land generally, affect the proprietary rights of the private individual.

Constitutional Law and Administrative Law

The exclusion from a work on constitutional law of all but the major features of administrative law [1] is based upon convenience rather than upon principle. Some limit must be placed upon the contents of a text-book concerned with outlines. The constitutional lawyer can cover only part of the vast field of governmental activities. Thus he will discuss the organisation of government departments and the constitutional status of Ministers and civil servants, but not the details of services such as education or housing. He will discuss the office of Secretary of State and the principal functions of the Home Secretary, including the preservation of order, but not the detailed regulations which govern the police forces. Under foreign affairs it is necessary to refer briefly to such topics as the treaty-making power and immunities from court process which are more fully covered by writers on public international law. The structure of the principal organs of government will be described, but only principal functions can be treated in any detail in a work on general principles.

B. Sources of Constitutional Law [2]

Meaning of Sources

Reference has been made to those rules of the constitution which lack the direct force of law. These extra-legal rules complicate the task of stating the sources from which constitutional law is drawn.

[1] For meaning of administrative law, see Chap. 41.

[2] For a concise account of the sources of English law, including custom, see Part II of O. Hood Phillips, *A First Book of English Law*, 4th edn. (Sweet and Maxwell).

By sources are meant here—though the term is sometimes used to indicate historical origins—the means whereby force and expression are given to law.

Summary of Sources

The sources of constitutional law are:

(1) *Rules of Law:*

(*a*) *Legislation, i.e.* Acts of Parliament and the enactments of other bodies upon which Parliament has conferred power to legislate and more particularly statutory instruments.

(*b*) *Judicial precedent, i.e.* the decisions of the courts expounding the common law or interpreting statutes.

(*c*) *Custom*, for example, the source of many of the usages of Parliament.

(2) *Conventional rules, i.e.* rules not having the force of law but which can nevertheless not be disregarded since they are sanctioned by public opinion, and perhaps indirectly by law proper.

(3) *Advisory, i.e.* the opinions of writers of authority.

I. LEGISLATION

Meaning of Law

Rules of law may be defined as "rules of civil conduct recognised by the courts." Such rules may be divided into two categories: (*a*) those prescribed by legislation, and (*b*) those to be deduced from the decisions of courts of authority.

Unwritten Constitution of Great Britain

When in the late eighteenth century the constitution of the United States of America was drawn up, definition of the powers of government was regarded as all important and was embodied in a formal document, which was, and is, unalterable save by a process which differs entirely from the method of enacting ordinary legislation. The provision of a constitutional code is a *sine qua non* of every new State, and the principal States of the world have adopted constitutions in the form of definite and comprehensive enactments. Great Britain is still without a constitution in this sense. Those statutes which are properly regarded as part of constitutional law are not sections of a code. If a collection were made of all the extant enactments (from the Coronation Charter of Henry I to the present day) which deal with the form and functions of government, the result would present a most imperfect description of the constitution. Moreover, these enactments can each and all of them be repealed by the simple expedient of an Act of Parliament, unlike formal constitutions, which are expressed to be more or less immutable, contemplate no radical changes and usually can only be varied by processes more elaborate than that of amending ordinary statutes.

Some Principal Statutes

None the less, although Great Britain has no written constitution, a large part of our constitutional law is based on statutes. The importance of this source of constitutional law can be illustrated by reference to a few statutes of major importance, which, though in law in no different position from any other Acts of Parliament, have always been regarded with peculiar veneration by constitutional lawyers and historians.

Magna Carta

The importance of the first of them, Magna Carta 1215 and its numerous confirmations in later years, lies not so much in the actual contents, since it preceded the era of representative government, as in the fact that it contained a statement of grievances the settlement of which was brought about by a union of important classes in the community. The Charter set out the rights of the various classes of the mediaeval community according to their different needs. The Church was to be free; London and other cities were to enjoy their liberties and customs; merchants were not to be subject to unjust taxation. The famous clauses which laid it down that no man should be punished except by the judgment of his peers or the law of the land, and that to none should justice be denied, have been described as the origin of trial by jury and the writ of habeas corpus. Trial by jury is, however, to be traced to another source, and the writ of habeas corpus had not yet been devised. But these clauses embody a protest against arbitrary punishment and assert the right to a fair trial and to justice which need not be purchased. The observance of the Charter came to be regarded both by lawyers and politicians as a synonym for constitutional government. It was the first attempt to express in legal terms some of the leading ideas of constitutional government.[1]

Petition of Right

Another document, enrolled on the statute book as 3 Car. 1 c. 1, is the Petition of Right 1628 which contained protests against taxation without consent of Parliament, arbitrary imprisonment, the use of commissions of martial law in time of peace and the billeting

[1] H.E.L., Vol. III, p. 215.

of soldiers upon private persons. To these protests the King yielded, though the effect of the concessions was weakened by the view Charles I held that his prerogative powers were not thereby diminished.

Bill of Rights and Act of Settlement

Close attention must be paid to the enactments arising from the Revolution of 1688 which embodied the terms of the settlement which the Lords and the remnants of Charles II's last Parliament arranged with William III and Mary. The principal provisions of the Bill of Rights 1688 which laid the foundations of the modern constitution by disposing of most of the more extravagant claims of the Stuarts to rule by prerogative right, were:—

> That the pretended power of suspending of laws or the execution of laws by regal authority without consent of Parliament is illegal.
>
> That the pretended power of dispensing with laws or the execution of laws by regal authority as it hath been assumed and exercised of late is illegal.
>
> That the commission for erecting the late court of commissioners for ecclesiastical causes and all other commissions and courts of like nature are illegal and pernicious.
>
> That the levying money for or to the use of the crown by pretence of prerogative without grant of Parliament for longer time or in other manner than the same is or shall be granted is illegal.
>
> That it is the right of the subjects to petition the king and all commitments and prosecutions for such petitioning are illegal.
>
> That the raising or keeping of a standing army within the kingdom in time of peace unless it be with consent of Parliament is against law.
>
> That the subjects which are Protestants may have arms for their defence suitable to their conditions and as allowed by law.
>
> That election of members of Parliament ought to be free.
>
> That the freedom of speech and debates or proceedings in Parliament ought not to be impeached or questioned in any court or place out of Parliament.
>
> That excessive bail ought not to be required nor excessive fines imposed nor cruel and unusual punishments inflicted.
>
> That jurors ought to be duly impanelled and returned and jurors which pass upon men in trials for high treason ought to be freeholders.
>
> That all grants and promises of fines and forfeitures of particular persons before conviction are illegal and void.
>
> And that for redress of all grievances and for the amending, strengthening and preserving of the laws Parliaments ought to be held frequently.

The Scottish Parliament enacted the Claim of Right in 1689. The contents of this measure followed those of the Bill of Rights of the English Parliament with certain modifications, *e.g.* the distinction between the suspending and dispensing powers was not made, but all proclamations asserting an absolute power to "cass, annul or disable laws" are illegal.

The Act of Settlement 1700 not only provided for the succession to the Throne, but added certain important provisions complementary to those contained in the Bill of Rights, especially—

> That whosoever shall hereafter come to the possession of this crown shall join in communion with the Church of England as by law established.
>
> That in case the crown and imperial dignity of this realm shall hereafter come to any person, not being a native of this kingdom of England, this nation be not obliged to engage in any war for the defence of any dominions or territories which do not belong to the crown of England, without consent of Parliament.
>
> That no person who has an office or place of profit under the king or receives a pension from the crown shall be capable of serving as a member of the House of Commons.
>
> That after the said limitation shall take effect as aforesaid, judges' commissions be made *quamdiu se bene gesserint*, and their salaries ascertained and established, but upon the address of both Houses of Parliament it may be lawful to remove them.
>
> That no pardon under the great seal of England be pleadable to an impeachment by the Commons in Parliament.

The Bill of Rights and the Act of Settlement mark the victory of Parliament. In the place of Kings who claimed to govern by the prerogative was developed a constitutional monarchy with the result that government is by and through Parliament. It is, however, to be noted that there is nothing in these statutes to secure the responsibility of the King's Ministers to Parliament and indeed the exclusion of all holders of office under the King from membership of the House of Commons quickly proved a stumbling block to the recognition of that responsibility and was modified early in the next reign.

It is not intended to catalogue other principal statutes that form part of constitutional law. To illustrate that statute law is a vital and important source of constitutional law it is sufficient to mention the Act of Union with Scotland 1706, the Parliament Act 1911,[1] the Supreme Court of Judicature Act 1925, the Statute of Westminster 1931.[2]

II. CASE LAW

The other source of rules of law is the decisions of courts of authority, *i.e.* the superior courts of record, which are stated in

[1] Pp. 135–7, *post.* [2] Chap. 32.

authoritative form in the law reports. Judge-made, or judiciary, law is derived from two sources:

(1) The common law proper. This consists of the laws and customs of the realm which have received judicial recognition in the reasons given from early times by the judges for their decisions in particular cases coming before them. In the reports of these cases governing the particular set of facts before the court are to be found authoritative expositions of the law. In the sphere of constitutional law here are to be found much of the law relating to the prerogatives of the Crown,[1] the ordinary remedies of the subject against illegal acts by public officers,[2] as well as the remedies by way of judicial order of prohibition, certiorari and mandamus [2] and the writ of habeas corpus,[3] which affords protection against unlawful invasion of personal liberty by the Executive.

Examples of judicial decisions are *The Case of Impositions*,[4] which defined the scope of the arbitrary power of the Crown to impose duties for the regulation of trade, or the modern case which decided how the discretionary powers of the Crown (the royal prerogative) are limited by a statute conferring similar powers: *Attorney-General* v. *De Keyser's Royal Hotel, Ltd.*[5] Again, it is a rule of the common law that the Crown can do no wrong, a rule which long enabled government departments to a large extent to escape legal liability for the wrongful acts of their employees. This rule depended for its validity on the decisions of the courts and it was not until 1947 that the Crown Proceedings Act removed this immunity of the Crown, subject to important limitations where the common law rule still prevails.[6]

(2) Interpretation of statute law. The task of the judge is in theory confined to an exposition of the meaning of the enacted law, and in the case of subordinate legislation (statutory instruments made under the authority of Acts of Parliament) also to an enquiry into the validity of the enactment. In practice, however, judges make law by interpretation. Thus in the case of *Eton College* [7] the court was called upon to interpret the second article of the Bill of Rights, the dispensing power "as it hath been assumed and exercised of late," and decided that the expression did not apply to a general dispensation for which there was a precedent in the time of Elizabeth I. In *Cooper* v. *Wandsworth Board of Works* [8] a statutory power of demolition was

[1] Chap. 11, C. [2] Chaps. 44–45. [3] Chap. 35, A.
[4] (1606), 2 St. Tr. 371; K. & L. 78; pp. 40–1, *post*.
[5] [1920] A.C. 508; K. & L. 118; p. 191, *post*.
[6] Chap. 46.
[7] (1815) Philip Williams' Report 53 and p. 42, *post*.
[8] (1863), 14 C.B. (N.S.) 180; K. & L. 518.

qualified by the court asserting the right of the owner first to be heard in objection to the exercise of the statutory power. Since most of the powers of government departments and local government authorities are derived from statute, this type of judge-made law is of greater importance in the sphere of public law to-day than the common law. Indeed, generally speaking, as legislation increases in volume—and in the nineteenth and twentieth centuries the output of general legislation has been stupendous—the tendency is to confine the work of the courts more and more to the interpretation of statute law.

The task of interpretation for the courts is based "on the principle that a court's duty is to ascertain the true meaning of the words used by Parliament and that the policy of the Act and the intentions of Parliament are irrelevant except in so far as they have been expressed in the words so used". But there is another method of approval "based on the principle that a court should endeavour to give effect to the policy of a statute and to the intentions of those who made it."[1] Professor de Smith relates this to the well-known case of *Heydon*.[2] The constitutional lawyer must lay emphasis on the common-law presumption that it is not the intention of Parliament to take away the rights of the subject by implication, as distinct from by express words.[3] This presumption is a factor in modifying the exercise by Parliament of its legal supremacy to enact any law whatsoever.

III. CONVENTIONS OF THE CONSTITUTION AS A SOURCE OF LAW

There are many rules and precepts to be mastered by men and women engaged in public life, as well as by students of constitutional law, which are not, at all events directly, part of the law of England in the sense that their validity can be the subject of proceedings in a court of law. In particular, breach of such rules will not result in a civil action or criminal prosecution being directed against the offender. Dicey named these rules conventions of the constitution. Can they properly be called law at all? If the answer is yes, he argues that they are a source of constitutional law. But other writers regard them as no more than practices which experience shows to be necessary for developing, within the law, existing political institutions. As such they are practices which are regarded as binding.

[1] S. A. de Smith, *Judicial Review of Administrative Action* (2nd edn.), p. 87.
[2] (1584) 3 Co. Rep. 71.
[3] *Op. cit.*, pp. 88–9.

Conventions are numerous and vary in character from a rule which is as invariably observed as if it was enforceable by legal process to a practice which will be abandoned when there is a change in the circumstances from which it arose.

There are many important conventions which govern the exercise of the royal prerogative, and in particular the whole system of cabinet government has been evolved without changes in the rules of law (in the narrow sense) by building up a body of rules of conduct which prescribe within the legal framework what is and is not constitutionally proper.[1] Other examples are to be found in the sphere of political relationship between the members of the British Commonwealth, especially the rules governing the relations between the United Kingdom and the other States. The law and custom of Parliament contains much that is based on precedent alone and has never been the subject of formal promulgation either by Parliament (itself the highest court of law) or by the Supreme Court of Judicature.

The existence of conventions is due to the need for rules to supplement the legal framework of the constitution. Sometimes an Act of Parliament, as did the Statute of Westminster 1931, may recognise or even reduce to legal form conventional rules. Conventions form a series of rules and practices for the guidance of those who run the machine of government. They are not to be found in the statute book or the law reports. Judges may from time to time recognise their existence, *e.g.* that a Minister of the Crown is answerable to Parliament, but they are not directly required to adjudicate upon their validity or to enforce them by a legal sanction.

The claim of conventions to be considered as part of constitutional law rests largely upon the regularity with which they are in practice followed, and the lawyer must consider the consequences of disregarding them. These consequences are, in the case of Ministers, loss of office or at least of reputation, and in the last resort fear of revolution. In the sphere of Commonwealth affairs secession is the ultimate sanction. But none of these consequences really explain why the conventional rule is normally followed. The explanation lies in the desire to maintain orderly government. Thus the resolve of Ministers to carry with them the House of Commons, as reflecting public opinion, is the principal factor in securing obedience to those conventions which govern the conduct of Ministers.

Conventions are a mixture of rules based on custom and ex-

[1] The terms "constitutional" and "unconstitutional" are not in practice confined to describing obedience to or disregard of conventions as the case may be. The conduct of a Minister is sometimes condemned as being unconstitutional when it involves a breach of law in the narrow sense, *e.g.* acting in excess of authority conferred on him by an Act of Parliament.

pediency, but sometimes their source is express agreement. Students must turn to a wealth of material to trace conventions to their source; for example, the letters of Queen Victoria, biographies, such as Sir Harold Nicolson's *George V*, the memoirs of Cabinet Ministers, parliamentary debates, leading articles in the press. Here it will suffice to give three illustrations of conventions as a source of constitutional law.

1. In the sphere of ministerial conduct a Government whose policy in a major matter ceases to command the support of the House of Commons must either resign or seek to reverse opinion in the House by obtaining a dissolution of Parliament so that there can be an appeal to the electorate to renew their confidence in the Government. In practice the decision to resign or to seek a dissolution is one peculiarly for the Prime Minister who may seek to avoid his own resignation or a General Election by reconstructing his Government.

2. In Commonwealth relations the Sovereign in all matters appertaining to a State of the Commonwealth of which she is Head (as distinct from the Presidential States) acts on the advice of the Cabinet Ministers in that State, to the exclusion of seeking other advice in particular from the Ministers in the United Kingdom Government.

3. In the parliamentary sphere the House of Commons will not allow any amendment of a financial provision in a Bill to be made by the House of Lords without its express consent.

It will be seen that there is common to each of these three rules the desire to take the course which ensures that the will of the electorate shall prevail. Such is the nature of responsible government in the democratic way of life.

IV. TEXT-BOOK WRITERS

Before leaving the subject of sources, reference must be made to text-book writers. The authority of a legal text-book as a source of law is confined to the extent to which it reproduces the law as enacted by the legislature or decided by the courts. But the lack of interpretation of legislation and the absence of anthoritative pronouncements by the courts on matters not covered by legislation are often remedied by the opinions of text-book writers of established reputation; these opinions are not law until accepted as such by the courts. Nevertheless in the field of constitutional law the scope for pronouncement by text-book writers is larger than in any other branch of law with the exception of international law. This is due partly to the existence of conventions which do not require enforcement through the courts, and partly to the fact that many of the problems of constitutional law are not in practice the subject-matter of litigation, even though they relate to law proper. Thus the duty of the Speaker of the House of Commons in regard to the certification of money Bills is defined by the Parliament Act 1911, but it is probably safe to predict that the courts will never be called upon to interpret these provisions. It is left to text-book writers to pronounce upon their effect. More reliance, then, may be placed upon text-books as a quasi-authoritative source than is the case, for example, with the law of contract. It must, however, be borne in mind that unanimity is not to be expected in the views expressed upon controversial topics. Nevertheless, such works as Erskine May's *Parliamentary Practice* or the critical accounts of the government of the country, such as that given in Bagehot's *The English Constitution*—a masterpiece in its day, and still in many respects not out of date—or Sir Ivor Jennings' *Cabinet Government*—are consulted with a confidence which the practitioner of law cannot afford to give to text-books on branches of private law, where conclusions must be supported by the authority of a statute or a judicial decision.

Historians

Writers of text-books on the constitution fall into three classes, namely, historians, political scientists, and lawyers. The historian, to quote Dicey, "is primarily occupied with ascertaining the steps by which a constitution has grown to be what it is." [1] He is mainly concerned with the value of past experience. While it is not to be suggested that the past does not contain many lessons for the present, particularly in an age when respect for tradition is at a discount, it is equally true that, for example, we can find little that is helpful in understanding the position and working of the present House of Commons in an historical account of the Witenagemot or of the Commune Concilium Regni. On the other hand it is essential for an understanding of the constitution to study the development of its organs and, for example, a clear appreciation of the seventeenth-century constitutional struggle is necessary for mastering the subject of the royal prerogative as it exists to-day.

Political and Social Sciences

The political scientist is concerned with the problems of government, as the lawyer is with the rules. The former is naturally

[1] *The Law of the Constitution*, p. 15.

attracted by the possibility of deducing abstract principles in relation to the science of government. The task of the student of constitutional law is to master the nature and operations of the existing organs of government rather than to attempt generalisations. Nevertheless, the relation between the theory of government and constitutional law is a close one.

The rapid growth in the study of social sciences has generally developed without close association with the study of law, though there are signs, in particular in the programmes of universities of recent foundation, that law as a general educational subject is best classed as a social science. The requirements of the legal profession for graduate qualifications for entry are such that even academic lawyers are reluctant to enter into this association. The question may be asked by students of the constitutions which have been framed by Whitehall or locally to initiate independence in former colonial territories—would not the attempt to imitate the Westminster model have been modified, had those responsible been trained in social sciences which included law?

Lawyers

Lawyers who attempt the task of depicting the law of the constitution are handicapped by the unreality of many of the legal terms which they must of necessity employ. For example, it is a correct statement of law to say that the Queen is the fountain of justice, or that the Queen can do no wrong. Yet everybody knows that the Queen does not sit as judge in her own courts, and that illegal acts are sometimes done in the name of the Queen by her servants. The training of the lawyer accustoms him to respect rules of law, irrespective of their political background. He may be impatient with the actions of politicians, but he cannot disregard the activities of the legislature; its processes are of concern to him as affording the means of amending the law. Without his assistance policy could not be transformed into terms of law. Traditionally he is suspicious of executive government with its wide discretionary powers and he watches jealously each attempt to oust the jurisdiction of the courts. The study of constitutional law is vital to an understanding of these matters and it is as well to approach the subject without stressing too much the origins portrayed by the historian or the speculative thinking of the political scientist. So the lawyer may claim to be a guide to the student, provided that he avoids a too legalistic approach to those matters which lie in the field of political conventions.

CHAPTER TWO

THE NATURE OF THE CONSTITUTION

Does the Constitution exist?

It has been said that the constitution has no separate existence since it is part of the ordinary law of the land. It is true that there is no special source giving expression to the rules of the constitution in the form of a code which is unalterable save by the act of a special constituent assembly or a specific reference to popular vote. There is, however, a body of law which forms the constitution, partly statutory, partly common law and partly conventional. It would be possible to enact this body of law in the form of a code. Even conventions are capable of enactment. Thus the Republic of Ireland gives statutory authority to the doctrine of ministerial responsibility which in the United Kingdom and the older States of the Commonwealth continues to rest upon convention.

Capacity for Development

The British constitution is flexible, not in the sense that it is unstable but in that its principles are alterable and constitutional rules can be changed by the ordinary process of an Act of Parliament or the establishment by general acceptance of a new convention. Despite, or perhaps because of, this flexibility the constitution has so far escaped those radical changes and convulsions which so frequently occur in countries with rigid constitutional codes.

Process of Evolution

For nearly three hundred years the constitution has been adapting itself to new conditions, usually a little behind the trend of expressed contemporary opinion. In the result there has been a complete change almost imperceptible at any given stage, so gradual has been the evolution from the personal supremacy of the monarch to the collective ascendancy of the political executive—a change which has been marked by the retention of existing forms and organs. Much of the structure is now mere form which is tolerated and indeed venerated because it represents historic continuity. The form is, however, remote from the practical working of the constitution.

Constitutional Monarchy and Parliamentary Government

In the place of kings who governed by the prerogative we have a constitutional monarchy. The Queen is the head of the State and government is carried on in her name, but it is government by an Executive answerable to and dependent for its office upon Parliament. After the Revolution Settlement of 1688 the King could govern only through Ministers who had the confidence of Parliament. This, though it was not at first realised, was the result of the Bill of Rights and Act of Settlement. The prerogative of the Crown came to be exercised by responsible Ministers. Successive extensions of the franchise have made the House of Commons more representative, while social and economic changes have involved widespread development effected by statute in the organisation and functions of government. This process of political evolution has avoided becoming a revolution. But parliamentary government is not to be explained solely in terms of law and convention. To quote from the Report of the Joint Committee of Parliament on Indian Constitutional Reform, 1934:

> Parliamentary government, as it is understood in the United Kingdom, works by the interaction of four essential factors; the principle of majority rule; the willingness of the minority for the time being to accept the decisions of the majority; the existence of great political parties divided by broad issues of policy, rather than by sectional interests; and finally the existence of a mobile body of political opinion, owing no permanent allegiance to any party and therefore able, by its instinctive reaction against extravagant movements on one side or the other, to keep the vessel on an even keel.

Nowadays the concentration of political power in the hands of the Executive, including as it does the direction of much of the economic life of the community, makes it more important than ever to emphasise that majority rule is only tolerable because of the dependence of the rulers upon the last of these factors. Free elections, guaranteed by law to occur at least every five years, and by force of public opinion at a lesser interval, ensure free expression for the mobile body of political opinion whose reactions are watched by every Government, no matter the size of the majority it presently commands in the House of Commons. The principle of majority rule emphasises the need for an organised opposition and as will be seen parliamentary government works best when the opposition is able to take concerted action.[1]

[1] Pp. 130–1, *post*.

Functions of Government

It is customary to divide functions of government into three classes, legislative, executive (ministerial and administrative) and judicial. It is not always easy, or indeed possible, to determine under which head an act properly falls, but the organs which mainly perform these functions are distinguishable. While the classification of functions is a vital matter of law in a written constitution, it is often relevant to the interpretation of statutory functions by an organ of government in the United Kingdom, *e.g.* to what functions of government do the rules of natural justice, such as the right to a hearing, apply.[1]

The Legislative Function and the Legislature

The legislative function primarily involves the enactment, after proper scrutiny, of general rules of conduct usually proposed to Parliament by the Executive, but there are types of legislation which determine administrative organisation or procedure rather than prescribe rules of conduct. In the United Kingdom the Legislature consists of the Queen in Parliament, and Parliament sits in two Houses, the House of Lords and the House of Commons. Since the passing of the Parliament Act 1911,[2] which enables legislation to be enacted in spite of its rejection by the House of Lords, legislative supremacy is in fact exercised by the House of Commons. The Queen is an integral member of the Legislature and her assent is required to all Acts of Parliament. As, however, she only acts on the advice of her Cabinet, her assent has been a formality since the development of the principle of ministerial responsibility. A Ministry which has successfully piloted a measure through both Houses of Parliament will never, it may be assumed, advise Her Majesty to withhold her assent to that measure becoming law. The power of the House of Lords to reject measures passed by the House of Commons is limited. There is no power to reject money Bills, and other public Bills, with the exception of a Bill to prolong the duration of Parliament, can only be delayed for a period of one year. Nevertheless, the House of Lords is still an active part of the Legislature. Important Bills which do not involve political controversy are often introduced in that House. As a revising chamber the relief which it affords to a Government which has embarked upon a heavy programme of legislation is considerable, especially when it becomes necessary to limit debate on a Bill in the House of Commons.

[1] de Smith, *Judicial Review of Administrative Action* (2nd edn.). Chap. 2 contains a full discussion of the importance and difficulties of classification.

[2] P. 135, *post*.

The amount of time devoted by Parliament to the legislative programme seldom exceeds half the number of days in a session, for the Legislature has other functions to perform. There is the grand inquest of the nation where policy and administration are debated. Indeed the primary function of Parliament is the redress of grievances and thus results its pressure on the Executive. It maintains the Executive in power by endorsing, not without amendment of detail, its legislative programme, and it is ever watchful of administration.

The Executive Function and the Executive

Although some writers attempt to distinguish between the executive and administrative function by confining the first to matters of policy and the second to administration, there is in practice no true distinction. Administration necessarily raises questions of policy, just as policy can only be implemented by administrative action.

The executive function embraces the direction of general policy. This includes the initiation of legislation, the maintenance of order and the promotion of social and economic welfare, and indeed all administration, though some public services are administered not by the departments of the Central Government, but by local authorities [1] and independent statutory bodies.[2] The majority of the powers of the Executive are to-day derived from statutes, though some of the most important are prerogative powers of the Crown [3] based on common law, *e.g.* the conduct of foreign affairs, the summoning and dissolution of Parliament, appointments to the public services, and the control of the armed forces of the Crown. The Sovereign is in law the head of the Executive. The prerogative powers and some statutory powers are vested in the Sovereign or the Sovereign in Council,[4] but, like those many statutory powers conferred directly upon Ministers, they are in fact exercised by the Government. The Government consists of Ministers who are by convention members of one or other House of Parliament.

The Party System

The political party having a majority in the House of Commons is entitled to form a ministry. This presents little difficulty when the House of Commons is divided into two parties. The two-party system "has been the normal type to which after occasional interludes we have regularly reverted, for the very reason that it has always

[1] Chap. 25. [2] Chap. 21. [3] Chap. 11, C.
[4] Chap. 11, B.

centred round the business of maintaining a majority in Parliament for a Government or securing its displacement by another Government." [1] Twice in the present century the substantial representation in the Commons of three political parties has resulted in the leaders of a party holding ministerial office without that party obtaining a clear majority of seats, and, therefore, of supporters in the House of Commons, over the other two parties.[2] The great advantage of the two-party system is to ensure that the Government is vigilantly criticised by an Opposition which is waiting to succeed to office and therefore criticises with a sense of responsibility. Under the two-party system minority government in the sense of government by a party which cannot command a majority in the House of Commons is impossible.[3]

Recent Trends

Experience in the twentieth century has shown that it is by no means unusual for the party system not to work according to rule. National Governments composed of members of all or more than one of the major political parties have held office on five occasions since 1918. Their formation has been due to grave emergencies in foreign or economic affairs, which caused party differences to be sunk in the interests of national unity. However inevitable and advantageous this form of government has been, it has resulted in depriving the House of Commons of an effective opposition ready to succeed the Government, and this has undoubtedly weakened the control of Parliament over the Executive. In 1945 the Government which was returned to power at the end of the war with Germany commanded so large a majority in the House of Commons that the role of the Opposition was difficult to maintain; as a result of the general election of 1950 this majority declined to a mere handful. In the next year after another election there was a change of government but the Conservatives were maintained in office only by a majority of less than twenty. In theory neither very large nor very small majorities are favourable to the working of the two-party system. The latter in particular militates against the execution of whatever policy the Government thinks is best, while the former

[1] *Thoughts on the Constitution*, by L. S. Amery, 2nd edn., at p. 43 (Oxford University Press).

[2] In the nineteenth century it was not unusual for the Government not to have a majority, *e.g.* Lord John Russell's Ministry in 1846, and Mr. Gladstone's Ministry in 1892–4.

[3] A majority party may under the electoral system prevailing in the United Kingdom nevertheless represent a minority of the total votes cast at a General Election; see p. 117.

encourages irresponsibility in the Opposition since it has no early prospect of reversing the policy of its opponents in office. "We are the masters now" is not a cry which is appropriate to our constitutional system, no matter how much it may reflect the views of the electorate.

The Cabinet System

By convention the Queen is advised on all matters by the Cabinet. The acts of the Queen become the acts of her Ministers. The Cabinet consists of the principal Ministers of the Crown, who are invited to sit in the Cabinet by the Prime Minister. A few Cabinet Ministers have no departmental responsibilities, but the majority are entrusted with a particular branch of governmental activity and preside over the government departments which are staffed by civil servants. Thus as members of the Cabinet the principal Ministers advise the Sovereign collectively, while individually they are responsible to the Queen and to Parliament for the conduct of a department. Junior Ministers have departmental duties but are not members of the Cabinet. The Cabinet decides major questions of policy. The departments carry out that policy by administering the law and devising measures to be presented to Parliament for enactment as law. Routine matters are decided in the department without reference to the Cabinet. Inasmuch as the Legislature rarely legislates without the guiding hand of the Government, the Cabinet in practice can prevent any legislation being passed by Parliament which it, or even the Minister chiefly concerned, does not wish to see passed.

Local Authorities

A great deal of administration is shared between central and local authorities. All locally elected authorities derive their powers from statutes of the central Parliament. This means that, apart from the enactment of local byelaws in form approved by the central government, legislating plays no part in the work of the elected bodies. Even in the administration of public services where in theory there is still some room for local initiative, the requirements of consultation with the central government coupled with the need to seek financial assistance from the Exchequer have served to make the local authorities unequal partners with the central government departments.

Independent Authorities

In the twentieth century there has been a number of experiments of entrusting a public service to an independent authority set up by Parliament but not directly responsible to the House of Commons through a Minister of the Crown. The most controversial of these authorities have been the public corporations which administer the nationalised industries of coal, gas, electricity and iron and steel, and some spheres of transport, especially the railways.[1]

The Judicial Function and the Judiciary

The judicial function is to declare what the law is and to apply the law with a view to its observance. It usually involves also the ascertainment of facts. The judicial function must be invoked by the subject or by the Executive before it can be exercised. The judges declare the common law and interpret statutes. It is no part of their function to give advice on hypothetical cases, but only to resolve the disputes of litigants. Nor are they concerned to debate the policy of the legislature, but only to interpret what has been decreed by its enactments.

Certain legislative and administrative functions are also performed by the Judiciary, *e.g.* the enactment of rules of court and the administration of the estates of deceased persons. The courts are the Queen's Courts, but the Queen does not exercise justice in person. The final court of appeal in the United Kingdom is the House of Lords. The principal court of first instance with general civil jurisdiction is the High Court of Justice, from which an appeal lies to the Court of Appeal and thence by leave to the House of Lords. From the criminal courts of Assizes and Quarter Sessions, where all serious cases are triable on indictment by judge and jury, an appeal lies to the Court of Appeal and thence on important points of law only to the House of Lords.[2] The vast majority in number of criminal cases are tried by summary adjudication in the magistrates' courts. Judges of the Superior Courts are independent of the Executive. They are appointed by the Crown, but they hold office during good behaviour, being removable by an address from both Houses of Parliament. While, however, the independence of the higher Judiciary is strictly preserved, many justiciable issues are referred to administrative tribunals; the composition, procedure and degree of independence of such tribunals have often been criticised, but they have become an established part of the machinery of justice and in general they operate subject to the supervision of the High Court which can restrain excesses or abuses of jurisdiction, unless such supervision is expressly excluded by statute.[3]

[1] Chap. 21.

[2] For organisation of the Courts, see Chap. 22; at County Quarter Sessions a bench of justices presided over by a chairman with legal qualifications takes the place of the single judge.

[3] Chap. 47.

PART I: General Constitutional Law

GENERAL PRINCIPLES

Law of the Constitution, 10th edn., by A. V. Dicey (Macmillan).
Part I—The Sovereignty of Parliament.
Part II—The Rule of Law, Chaps. IV, XI and XIII.
Part III—The Law and Conventions of the Constitution.
Introduction by E. C. S. Wade.
The Law and the Constitution, 5th edn., by Sir Ivor Jennings (University of London Press).
Thoughts on the Constitution, 2nd edn., by L. S. Amery (Oxford University Press).
History of English Law, by Sir William Holdsworth, Vol. X (Methuen).

CHAPTER THREE

THE DOCTRINE OF THE SEPARATION OF POWERS

BEFORE examining more closely the organs of government it will be convenient to study four topics which throw light upon every branch of constitutional law. In this Chapter there will be examined the doctrine of the separation of powers. Convenient though it is to divide the main organs of government into three, the doctrine in its application to modern government does not mean that a rigid threefold classification of their functions is possible. Its value lies in the emphasis placed upon those checks and balances which are essential to prevent an abuse of the enormous powers which are in the hands of rulers.

In Chapter 4 there will be discussed the supremacy of Parliament, the organ of government which exercises the legislative function; under a system of parliamentary government the House of Commons politically is supreme in that it can in the last resort dismiss the Government which exercises the executive function. Moreover Parliament makes and can repeal the laws which the Judiciary can only interpret. In Chapter 5 there will be discussed the rule of law. We shall observe the effect upon the constitution of the extension of functions of government since 1885 when Dicey first published *The Law of the Constitution* and gave his threefold interpretation of the rule of law as a characteristic of the constitution. In Chapter 6, under the title, Conventions of the Constitution, there will be explained more fully the nature of the constitutional conventions which have already been mentioned as one of the sources of constitutional law.

Meaning of Separation of Powers

It has been seen that it is customary to divide the powers of government into three, legislative, executive and judicial. The doctrine of separation of powers has played a prominent part in the theory and practice of constitution making and particularly influenced the framers of the constitution of the United States. To avoid confusion of thought it is important to note that separation of powers may mean three different things: (*a*) that the same persons should not form part of more than one of the three organs of government, *e.g.* that Ministers should not sit in Parliament; (*b*) that one organ of government should not control or interfere with the exercise of its function by another organ, *e.g.* that the Judiciary should be independent of the Executive or that Ministers should not be responsible to Parliament; (*c*) that one organ of government should not exercise the functions of another, *e.g.* that Ministers should not have legislative powers. In considering each of these three aspects of separation of powers we shall consider two quite different questions: (i) How far is there separation of powers in the British constitution to-day? (ii) How far is separation of powers desirable?

Montesquieu

The doctrine of the separation of powers was first formulated by the French jurist, Montesquieu,[1] who based his exposition on the British constitution of the first part of the eighteenth century as he understood it. His division of powers did not closely correspond except in name with the classification which has become traditional; for, although he followed the usual meaning of legislative and judicial powers, by executive power he meant only "the power of executing matters falling within the law of nations," *i.e.* making war and peace, sending and receiving ambassadors, establishing order, preventing invasion. His statement of the doctrine has been thus interpreted: If the Executive and the Legislature are the same person or body of persons, there must be a danger of the Legislature enacting oppressive laws which the Executive will administer to attain its own ends. Particularly is this true of a personal Executive, not responsible in law to the courts, or politically to a representative assembly. For

[1] *Esprit des Lois*, Book XI, Chap. 6.

laws to be enforced by the same body that enacts them results in arbitrary rule and makes the judge a legislator rather than an interpreter of the law. If the one body or person could exercise both executive and judicial powers in the same matter, there would be arbitrary power which would amount to complete tyranny, if legislative powers also were added to the powers of that person or body. Montesquieu did not, it may be surmised, mean that Legislature and Executive ought to have no influence or control over the acts of each other, but only that neither should exercise the whole power of the other.[1]

Separation of Powers practised in U.S.A. rather than in England

Though the doctrine was based on a study of the constitution of the United Kingdom, it is in the constitution of the United States rather than our own even in the eighteenth century that its influence can best be seen. Montesquieu, viewing the constitution as a foreign observer, saw the triumph of Parliament in 1688 and its achievement of legislative supremacy with the passing of the Bill of Rights. He saw too that the King still exercised executive power and that the independence of the Judiciary was solemnly declared. A provision of the Act of Settlement which was repealed before it came into force had attempted to exclude Ministers from the House of Commons. Before the eighteenth century was over, however, there had been established in England the Cabinet system under which the King governed only through Ministers who were members of and responsible to Parliament. George III exercised personal rule, but this took the form of influencing Parliament through the distribution of offices and by the control exercised by the Crown and the Crown's supporters over membership of the House of Commons. With the redistribution of seats, including the abolition of rotten boroughs, and the extension of the franchise by the Reform Act of 1832, there began to disappear government by influence and parliamentary government was securely established.

Checks and Balances

In many continental constitutions separation of powers has meant an unhampered Executive; in England it means little more than an independent Judiciary. It is in the United States that there is a real division of powers between the three organs and strict adherence to the doctrine of separation of powers. The framers of the American Constitution intended that the balance of powers should be attained

[1] Sir Ivor Jennings, *The Law and the Constitution*, 5th edn., App. 1; Sir Carleton Allen, *Law and Orders*, Chap. 1; *Separation of Powers*, by J. Finkelman, 1 Toronto Law Journal 313.

by checks and balances between separate organs of government. They imitated the form of the English constitution. But by this time in England executive power was passing from Crown to Cabinet. They were influenced too by the form of colonial charters under which separation of executive and legislative functions was a prominent feature, executive functions being under the control of the Crown, legislative being strictly limited.

Executive in U.S.A.

In the United States executive power is vested in the President. The so-called Cabinet consists of the heads of the chief departments (eleven in number), each being personally responsible to the President alone for his own department, but not to Congress (Senate and House of Representatives) or to his colleagues. The President holds office for a fixed term; he is not necessarily of the same political party as the majority in either or both Houses of Congress; he is not removable by an adverse vote; his powers are declared by the Constitution.

Legislature in U.S.A.

Neither the President nor members of his Cabinet can sit or vote in Congress; they have no direct power of initiating Bills or securing their passage through Congress. The President may recommend legislation in his message to Congress, but he cannot compel it to pay heed to his recommendations. He can, however, veto legislation which has been passed by Congress. Treaties are negotiated by the Executive, but require the approval of a two-thirds majority of the Senate (Upper House). The Senate, though elected, is an undying body since only one-third of its membership falls vacant every two years. The House of Representatives is elected for a fixed term of two years and cannot be dissolved in the interval. As in all countries with federal constitutions, there are in the United States fundamental laws which cannot be altered by a simple vote of the Legislature. Amendments must be proposed by a majority of two-thirds in both Houses or by a convention called by two-thirds of the States; ratification is required by a majority of three-quarters of the States. The Judiciary is not only independent of the Executive, but acquired at an early date the power to declare laws invalid as being contrary to the constitution. The Federal Supreme Court may declare the actions either of the Executive or the Legislature to be unconstitutional. Despite this rigid demarcation of functions it may be remarked that in practice separation tends to break down.

Contrast between Presidential and Cabinet Systems

A clear description of the difference between the Presidential System and the Cabinet system is given in the following extract from the pen of the first Earl of Balfour in Bagehot's *The English Constitution* (Introduction to 1928 edition):

> "Under the Presidential system the effective head of the national administration is elected for a fixed term. He is practically irremovable. Even if he is proved to be inefficient, even if he becomes unpopular, even if his policy is unacceptable to his countrymen, he and his methods must be endured until the moment comes for a new election.
>
> "He is aided by Ministers, who, however able and distinguished, have no independent political status, have probably had no congressional (*i.e.* parliamentary) training, and are by law precluded from obtaining any during their term of office.
>
> "Under the Cabinet system everything is different. The head of the administration, commonly called the Prime Minister (though he has no statutory position), is selected for the place on the ground that he is the statesman best qualified to secure a majority in the House of Commons. He retains it only so long as that support is forthcoming; he is the head of his party. He must be a member of one or other of the two Houses of Parliament; and he must be competent to lead the House to which he belongs. While the Cabinet Ministers of a President are merely his officials, the Prime Minister is *primus inter pares* in a Cabinet of which (according to peace-time practice) every member must, like himself, have had some parliamentary experience and gained some parliamentary reputation. The President's powers are defined by the Constitution, and for their exercise within the law he is responsible to no man. The Prime Minister and his Cabinet, on the other hand, are restrained by no written Constitution: but they are faced by critics and rivals whose position, though entirely unofficial, is as constitutional as their own; they are subject to a perpetual stream of unfriendly questions, to which they must make public response, and they may at any moment be dismissed from power by a hostile vote."

Lord Balfour proceeds to emphasise the weakness of the President's position through his narrow prerogatives defined by the constitution. The President is unable to influence legislation or taxation in face of a hostile Legislature which he cannot dissolve.

The constitution of the Fifth French Republic preserves the separation of the legislature and executive, as well as the independence of the judiciary. The circumstances in which a Government can be compelled to resign are restricted in order to encourage governmental stability, but the powers of the President to rule by decree without Parliament are enlarged.

Legislature and Executive

Enough has been said of the organs of the constitution and the working of the Cabinet system to attempt to answer in relation to the Legislature and the Executive the three questions that may be asked in ascertaining whether there is in the constitution of the United Kingdom a separation of powers:

(*a*) *Do the same persons or bodies form part of both the Legislature and Executive?* The form of the constitution shows the Sovereign as the head of the Executive and also an integral part of the Legislature.[1] More important, however, is the convention so essential to the working of Cabinet government which secures that Ministers should be members of one or other House of Parliament. Their presence in Parliament makes a reality of their responsibility to Parliament and facilitates co-operation between them and the Legislature, both features which are vital to parliamentary government. Only those who are prepared to abandon the Cabinet system and parliamentary government, as we understand it, will criticise this departure from a strict separation of powers.

Parliamentary Supremacy

(*b*) *Does the Legislature control the Executive or the Executive control the Legislature?* Here again there is no separation of powers. The House of Commons ultimately controls the Executive. Strong government has been combined with responsible government by ensuring that Parliament, while leaving the task of governing to the Government, can insist on the dismissal of a Government which does not obtain parliamentary support for its general policy. Even in the eighteenth century Montesquieu's interpretation was inapplicable in practice. Once it had been established that Parliament alone could make laws and vote taxes, it became recognised, gropingly at first in the reigns of William III and Anne, more clearly under the early Hanoverian Kings, that a Government could only act with strength and speed if it could command the support of Parliament. That support was obtained by entrusting the exercise of the powers of the Crown to Ministers who could command a majority in Parliament. This ensures co-operation between the Government and the Commons.

Influence of Cabinet over Parliament

To emphasise, however, that Parliament is supreme is not to give the whole picture of the relationship between Legislature and Executive. So long as the Cabinet retains the confidence of Parliament, it exercises a decisive voice in regard to the passage of legislation. Major Acts of the Legislature must in practice originate with the approval, and normally nowadays on the initiative of a Minister

[1] P. 18, *ante*.

of the Crown who acts in important matters of policy with the support and prior approval of the Cabinet. Since the House of Commons is divided into only two main political parties, the leaders of the majority party who form the Cabinet exercise real control over the House. Parliament can dismiss a Ministry, but a political party is unwilling to vote against its leaders. The defeat of a Ministry involves a dissolution of Parliament and the risk that a general election will result in power passing to the opposition party. Thus while Parliament is supreme in that it can make or unmake a Government, a Government once in power tends to control Parliament. In truth there is no separation of powers, but rather a system which can only work if there is co-operation between Legislature and Executive. If the legislative business of a modern State is to be transacted with speed and efficiency, Parliament must accept the lead of the Government and consent to inroads upon the time of private members. Moreover, modern government has become a business for experts. Parliament cannot perform its legislative functions without the assistance of civil servants to whom are available fuller sources of information than to the ordinary public or even to members of Parliament. The officials work out the details of a policy which the Cabinet or a Minister has approved. When concrete proposals have been prepared, the parliamentary machine is employed to put the proposals into the form of law. The speeches of Ministers in Parliament and memoranda published before or contemporaneously with a Bill explain the objects of important measures and the methods by which those objects are to be achieved. The public may have been prepared for important legislative changes by the programme put before the electorate at a general election by the party which subsequently forms the Government. Particularly is the idea of a mandate from the electorate relied upon by Governments in the early sessions after their accession to power. Just as Parliament must accept direction from the Government, so the Government must remember that Parliament represents the electorate. A Government which does not take care that its general policy retains the confidence of the public risks defeat either in Parliament or when it faces the electorate, which it must do at least every five years. But its task is to govern; this is its general mandate and may well justify legislation or other action which was not contemplated at the time of the election.

The ascendancy of the Cabinet over the House of Commons, coupled with the legal and conventional checks upon the suspensory powers of the House of Lords, makes it difficult to maintain that the Legislature in enacting laws exercises a function separate from the

Executive. Rather it is the case that the Executive in performing the tasks of governing uses the Legislature as a means of securing those changes in the law which it desires. That there is a risk in the Executive enjoying the power to have enacted any legislation that it wishes is not to be denied. It is one of the outstanding political problems to reach agreement on what safeguards should exist to prevent abuse of this power by the Executive. We may note that a Bill to prolong the life of Parliament beyond the statutory limit of five years is exempted from the provisions of the Parliament Acts 1911 and 1949[1] and, therefore, still requires the assent of both Houses and can be rejected by the House of Lords outright. It is not, therefore, possible for the Government to use the House of Commons to postpone a general election by extending the five-year limit, unless, of course, the House of Lords also passes the Bill.

Three Political Parties

Where there are more than two main political parties, the Government is less sure of its control over Parliament. It may be necessary in order to secure a majority to form a Government which will consist of members of more than one political party. Experience shows that parties to a coalition tend sooner or later to break up into their component parts. When this happens each party is bidding for the support of another party at present in opposition. This makes it more likely that a Government will be defeated by a hostile vote in Parliament whenever serious differences of opinion emerge within a coalition. The Cabinet system has been built up on a two-party system. If for any lengthy period there were, as has happened in the past, more than two main political parties with adequate representation in Parliament, there might develop a new relationship between the Government and Parliament, which would inevitably weaken the control of the Government over the Commons.

Delegated Legislation

(*c*) *Do the Legislature and the Executive exercise each other's functions?* Here we are on debatable ground. The mass of detail involved in modern administration and the extension of the functions of the State to the economic and social sphere has rendered it essential for Parliament to delegate to Ministers the power to make statutory instruments. So long as the main principles of the legislation are laid down in an Act of Parliament, there is little objection in theory to Ministers being given the power to implement those principles by detailed regulations. But it is not easy to decide what is a matter of principle and what is detail which can safely be left to ministerial

[1] P. 135, *post*.

discretion. Few would deny that delegated legislation [1] is inevitable. It is, however, generally held that, unless it is subject to effective parliamentary scrutiny, there is a real threat to liberty from undue expansion of the power of the Executive. The process of legislation by departmental regulations saves time, can deal with local variations and is more flexible than legislation by Act of Parliament. It can also be used when a Minister requires a wide discretion, to give him freedom to experiment in the administrative field without seeking new powers from Parliament. The power to legislate by statutory instrument is conferred by Parliament and can be taken away by Parliament. Unless, however, the exercise of the power is effectively controlled by Parliament, there is lost that safeguard of liberty which depends upon the law-making power being exercised by the elected representatives of the people who will be affected by the laws that are made. Self-government is endangered when the representatives of the people do not effectively control the making of the laws which the people must obey. This does not, however, mean that Parliament should attempt to supervise every detail of day-to-day administration for which Ministers are responsible. It must, moreover, be borne in mind, when it is said that legislation is the function of Parliament, that the line between legislation and administration is not always easily drawn. The legislative function is the making of general rules. Some Acts of Parliament, especially private and local Acts, decide particular issues, such as authorising the construction of a new length of railway, and do not lay down general rules. Here Parliament may claim to be exercising an administrative function using legislative forms.

Executive and Judiciary

There must now be examined the relationship between the Judiciary and the other two organs of government. Again the three questions may be asked:

(*a*) *Do the same persons form part of the Judiciary and the Executive?* The courts are the Queen's Courts, but the Queen only exercises her judicial functions through her judges. The Judicial Committee of the Privy Council,[2] the highest court of appeal from some Commonwealth States and from the Colonies, is in form a committee of the Privy Council, an executive organ, but in fact it is an independent court of law. The Lord Chancellor, who is invariably a Minister of Cabinet rank, is also the senior member of the judiciary and therefore when he sits, which nowadays is but seldom on account of his

[1] For a full discussion of this topic, see Chap. 42.

[2] Chap. 33.

other duties, he presides over the Appellate Committee of the House of Lords, which is the final court of appeal from the courts of the United Kingdom. Neither, however, of these apparent exceptions to the separation of powers is of constitutional importance. Only persons with high judicial qualifications in practice can adjudicate on these tribunals.

Independence of Judiciary

(*b*) *Does the Executive control or influence the Judiciary or the Judiciary control or influence the Executive?* In this field the separation of powers is strictly observed. Judicial independence is secured by law and by public opinion, and the standard of conduct maintained by both Bench and Bar. The Act of Settlement[1] determined that the judges of the superior courts should have fixed salaries and hold office during good behaviour subject to a power of removal by the Crown exercisable on an address from both Houses of Parliament. It can be stated with confidence that there is no interference by the Executive with the exercise of their judicial functions by the judges of the Supreme Court and the House of Lords. Similarly the courts take no part in the formulation of policy, but simply administer the law as it is, leaving it to the Executive to propose whatever changes in the law may be decided upon if a particular decision of the courts shows the need for such change. That the independence of the Judiciary is desirable no one will deny. An independent Judiciary is the surest protection against abuse of power, but its control cannot operate unless set in motion by a litigant. It is an essential function of the Judiciary, if application is made to the courts, to check administrative authorities from exceeding their powers and to direct the performance of duties owed by public officials to private citizens.[2] Only an independent Judiciary can impartially perform these tasks.

Administrative Courts

(*c*) *Do the Executive and Judiciary exercise each other's functions?* It is idle to boast of an independent Judiciary if major justiciable issues are excluded from the jurisdiction of the courts and entrusted to administrative authorities. Statutes sometimes prescribe that orders made by Ministers shall be final and not subject to appeal to the courts but, as will be seen,[3] there is a growing tendency for the courts to investigate the validity even of orders expressed to be final.

[1] P. 9, *ante*.
[2] For full discussion of the control of public authorities by the Courts; see Chaps. 44 and 45.
[3] Pp. 673–6, *post*.

Justiciable issues are given by statute to administrative tribunals or even to the decision of individual Ministers as final arbiters. The reasons for this latter practice, which will be examined later,[1] are many: the expense of litigation; the belief that judges are by their training at the Bar and outlook unfitted to decide issues involving administrative policy; dissatisfaction with the judicial method of interpreting statutes; the unsuitability of court procedure for the decision of complicated technical issues. These are powerful arguments in favour of the reference of many disputes involving questions of public law to administrative courts. On the other hand, it is when the citizen has a dispute with the State that he most needs the protection of an independent tribunal. There is general agreement that except in times of grave emergency disputes involving freedom of the person and freedom of speech should always be heard by the ordinary courts. In regard to those administrative disputes which arise from the entitlement of individuals to statutory benefits, *e.g.* pensions and all forms of national insurance, the solution has been found in the establishment of administrative courts which preserve the best features of normal judicial procedure, *i.e.* publicity, reasonable certainty through adherence to precedent, the publishing of reasons for decisions, and yet are more appreciative of the problems of administration and cheaper for the citizen. It is generally accepted that there should be a right of appeal to an impartial tribunal where an administrative decision rejects a claim to the payment of benefits or deprives an individual of his property. There is no agreement as to whether the courts or an *ad hoc* administrative tribunal is to be preferred. The problem is not a simple one. Moreover it is not easy to decide what is a justiciable issue, the determination of which should lie, at all events ultimately, with the ordinary courts of law. Just as it is sometimes difficult to draw a line between legislation and administration, so it is often difficult to distinguish between judicial and administrative decisions. Many decisions given by judges involve the exercise of discretion, *e.g.* the passing of sentences for crimes or the award of damages. Many administrative decisions involve the settlement of disputes. Primarily the judicial function involves the application of settled law to facts, while an administrative decision is primarily determined by the discretion of the administration in applying policy, but the line is often blurred, and frequently the distinction appears one of form rather than of substance.[2] Judges of the High Court perform certain purely administrative functions, *e.g.* the administration of the estates of deceased persons and the winding-up of companies. Justices of

[1] Chap. 47. [2] For discussion, see Chaps. 43 and 47.

the peace still have a few administrative duties surviving from the age when the justices in Quarter Sessions were the principal local administrative authority.[1] The exercise of such administrative functions by the Judiciary is, however, simply a matter of organisation and does not involve those questions of principle which arise from the exercise of judicial functions by the Executive which may have a direct interest in securing that the decision does not conflict with the policy of the department.

Judiciary and Legislature

Finally there must be examined the relationship between the Judiciary and the Legislature:

(*a*) *Do the same persons exercise legislative and judicial functions?* Generally speaking all the higher judicial appointments disqualify for membership of the House of Commons. The House of Lords, the Upper House of Parliament, is the highest court of appeal in the United Kingdom and once exercised original jurisdiction over those impeached by the House of Commons.[2] Formerly it also tried peers accused of treason or felony. The Lord Chancellor presides over the House of Lords sitting in both its legislative and judicial capacities. The Lords of Appeal in Ordinary[3] who sit as judges in the Appellate Committee of the House of Lords occasionally take part also in the legislative business of the House. There is, however, here no substantial infringement in practice of separation of powers. The House of Lords sitting as a court is in substance a court of law with only a historic and formal connection with the House of Lords sitting as a chamber of the Legislature. Lay peers by long established convention do not take part in the hearing of appeals.[4]

(*b*) *Is there any control by the Legislature over the Judiciary or the Judiciary over the Legislature?* It has been stated that judges of the superior courts may be removed by an address from both Houses of Parliament. Such an address would, however, never be accepted if it interfered with judicial independence. The judges interpret the laws which Parliament enacts and Parliament can alter the law, should the decisions of the courts in interpreting statutes or in expounding the common law be contrary to the policy of the Legislature. These, however, are the normal functions of both Legislature and Judiciary.

(*c*) *Do the Legislature and Judiciary exercise each other's functions?* The judicial functions of the House of Lords have already been discussed. Each House of Parliament too has the powers of the High Court of Parliament of enforcing its own privileges and

[1] P. 356, *post*. [2] P. 312, *post*.
[3] Pp. 101 and 313, *post*. [4] P. 82, *post*.

punishing those who offend against them.[1] In prescribing rules of court the judges of the High Court, as members of the statutory committee for this purpose, exercise a legislative function, but it is limited to procedural details for the administration of justice. These instances involve no real departure from the separation of powers.

Since the controversies associated with the name of John Wilkes there have been few occasions when Parliament has encroached on the sphere of the courts. Ministers, however, have put forward a novel interpretation of ministerial responsibility to Parliament as a justification for the withdrawal from the courts of issues involving civil liberties. Needs of security during the Second World War made it necessary to give to Ministers powers over individual liberties, and in particular a power to detain on suspicion, which could not be questioned in the courts.[2] The grant of such powers was, however, from time to time defended on the ground that it was the duty of Parliament to safeguard liberty and that an individual aggrieved by a ministerial decision should rely upon his Member of Parliament to put forward his grievance. Ministers claimed that being responsible to Parliament they should be judged by Parliament and not by the courts of law. The mere plea of the interests of the State in time of war was reinforced by the plea that the House of Commons was the judge. The danger of this plea lies in the fact that parliamentary criticism of a Minister may and indeed frequently does result in the issue being made one of confidence in the Government. The Minister relies upon the doctrine of collective responsibility to rally the support of his colleagues and the House of Commons hesitates to defeat a Government because of an unjust decision on a point affecting only one individual. It would be a poor day for liberty if Parliament ceased to protect individual freedoms, but an appeal to Parliament cannot take the place of a right to appeal to the courts and an independent Judiciary. This was no mere war-time danger. The arguments used to justify withholding an appeal to the courts from those detained in war time in the interests of the State have been used to withhold an appeal to the courts from those denied permission to sell milk. There are arguments, as has been shown, for the reference of administrative disputes to specially qualified administrative courts, but disputes involving fundamental issues of liberty should be referred to tribunals that are independent of political influence. Access to an independent Judiciary must not be

[1] Chap. 10.
[2] Chap. 48, B; this power was among the first to be revoked on the cessation of active fighting in Europe in 1945.

barred on the ground that Ministers are responsible not to the courts but to Parliament.

Conclusion

There is no separation of powers in the strict sense between Executive and Legislature. Parliamentary supremacy involves ultimate control of the Executive. The practical necessities of parliamentary government make it necessary for Parliament to trust the Government to govern and accept the direction of the Cabinet in regard to the legislative programme, though retaining the right to amend, to criticise, to question and in the last resort to defeat. Practical necessity again demands a large measure of delegation to the Executive of power to legislate by rules, regulations and orders. The independence of the Judiciary has been strictly preserved, but many justiciable issues are referred not to the ordinary courts, but to administrative authorities. Where such reference is expedient, machinery has been devised to secure that reference is made to tribunals which are impartial and, as a general rule, preserve the essential features of a fair trial.

How far is Separation of Powers desirable?

No direct answer has been given to the question—how far is separation of powers desirable? Nor is it easy to say dogmatically that a doctrine which has been subject to widely differing interpretations is or is not desirable.[1] It is not difficult to agree with Montesquieu that monopoly of power in any government is dangerous. So far as his exposition failed to admit that the legislature should act as a check on the executive power, *i.e.* in his day the prerogative of the King, his opinion is unacceptable to the modern conception of parliamentary government, even in the field of external affairs. Nor does he take much account of the part played by the common law in moulding constitutional principles and checking royal power. His classification has indeed been used to sustain the argument that execution and adjudication are only aspects of the single function of administration. Sir Carleton Allen has pointed out that Montesquieu does not himself use the term, separation, or suggest that the three powers of government should not touch at any point but rather that they should be subject to mutual restraints—the checks and balances which have come since to be recognised as fully developed in our eighteenth-century constitution. If this be so, there is no

[1] *Cf.* for example Sir Carleton Allen, *Law and Orders*, Chap. 1, and Sir Ivor Jennings, *The Law and the Constitution*, pp. 18 ff. and App. I.

need to strive to fit separation of powers into the functional organs of our constitution.

Should the constitution be enacted, as a growing number of advocates propose, separation of powers would be an important element in defining the functions and powers of the executive, even if the supremacy of Parliament was retained.

CHAPTER FOUR

PARLIAMENTARY SUPREMACY

A. History of Parliamentary Supremacy

We have seen that a system of parliamentary government involves the supremacy of Parliament. Before discussing the legal meaning of legislative supremacy, its practical limitations and how far Parliament in fact exercises its legislative powers, we shall give a brief account of the stages by which Parliament established itself as the sole legislative authority, and how it has come to exercise political supremacy by controlling the Executive. Legislative supremacy was established by the end of the seventeenth century. The responsibility of the Executive to Parliament was not clearly established till after the Representation of the People Act 1832 (the Reform Act).

Middle Ages

It was recognised in the Middle Ages that an Act of Parliament could change the common law. With the Reformation there disappeared the idea that there were certain ecclesiastical rules and doctrines that Parliament could not touch. Henry VIII and Elizabeth I made the Crown of England supreme over all persons and causes and used Parliament to attain this end. Even in the seventeenth century it was contended that there were certain natural laws which were immutable,[1] but the common lawyers were the allies of Parliament in the seventeenth-century struggle with the Crown and in order to defeat the Crown's claim to rule by prerogative were forced to concede that the common law could be changed by Parliament.[2]

The Struggle for Supremacy

Legislative supremacy involves not only the right to change the law but also that no one else should have that right. In many spheres the King's prerogative at the beginning of the seventeenth century was undefined and the King exercised through the Council a residue of judicial power which enabled him to enforce his prerogative powers. Acts of Parliament which purported to take away any of

[1] K. & L., pp. 1, 2.
[2] Dicey, *op. cit.*, Introduction by E. C. S. Wade, p. c.

the inseparable prerogatives of the Crown were held invalid.[1] The struggle for legislative supremacy is closely connected with the royal prerogative to be discussed in Chap. 11.

(1) *Ordinances and Proclamations*

There was a lack of any clear distinction between the Statutes of Parliament and the Ordinances of the King in Council long after the establishment of the Model Parliament at the end of the thirteenth century. The Lex Regia or Statute of Proclamations 1539 gave the King wide but not exclusive powers of legislating without reference to Parliament by proclamation which had replaced the ordinance as a form of legislation. This statute did not give to the King and Council power to do anything that they pleased by royal ordinance, but was a genuine attempt by the King and Parliament to deal finally with the obscure position of the authority possessed by proclamations. It safeguarded the common law, existing Acts of Parliament and rights of property, and prohibited the infliction of the death penalty for a breach of a proclamation.[2] Despite the repeal of this statute in 1547, both Mary and Elizabeth continued to resort to proclamations as a means of governing. The judicial powers of the Council, and in particular of the Court of Star Chamber, were available to enforce proclamations. The scope of the royal prerogative was largely undefined. It is a most difficult task for the constitutional historian to say at any given period prior to 1689 exactly what must be enacted by Parliament alone and what could be achieved by prerogative ordinance. Nor is this surprising when it is remembered that legislative power originally lay with the King in Council, and that the influence of the Council varied with the ability of the monarch to choose his counsellors. James I made full use of this power, with the result that in 1611 Coke was consulted by the Council, along with three of his brother judges who were added at his request, for an expression of opinion on the legality of proclamations. The result of their considerations is to be found in the *Case of Proclamations* [3] and may be regarded as final.

> 1. The King by his proclamation cannot create any offence which was not one before; for then he might alter the law of the land in a high point; for if he may create an offence where none is, upon that ensues fine and imprisonment.
>
> 2. The King hath no prerogative but what the law of the land allows him.

[1] K. & L., p. 2; "No Act of Parliament can bar a King of his regality."—*The Case of Ship Money* (1637), 3 St. Tr. 825, *per* Finch, C.J., at p. 1235; K. & L. 81.

[2] H.E.L., Vol. IV, pp. 102–3.

[3] (1611), 12 Co. Rep. 74; K. & L. 110.

> 3. But the King for the prevention of offences may by proclamation admonish his subjects that they keep the laws and do not offend them upon punishment to be inflicted by law; the neglect of such proclamation aggravates the offence.
>
> 4. If an offence be not punishable in the Star Chamber, the prohibition of it by proclamation cannot make it so.

A definite limit is thus put upon the exercise of the prerogative, the full force of which was only effective when the Court of Star Chamber and other conciliar tribunals were abolished in 1640. But the existing prerogative powers were left undefined except that in Coke's opinion proclamations could no longer increase them. The gist of the *Case of Proclamations* is that the King is the Executive and his business the enforcement of the existing law; his prerogative is under the law, and Parliament can alone alter the law which the King is to administer.[1]

(2) *Taxation*

The imposition of taxes is a matter for legislation. Inevitably taxation was a major issue between the Stuart Kings and Parliament. If the Crown could not levy taxes without the consent of Parliament, the will of Parliament must in the long run prevail. It had been conceded by the time of Edward I that the consent of Parliament was necessary for direct taxation. The history of indirect taxation is more complicated, but it was established by the time of the Wars of the Roses that parliamentary consent was required for taxes on specific commodities. The regulation of foreign trade was, however, a part of the royal prerogative in relation to foreign affairs. There was no clear distinction between the imposition of taxes by way of customs duties and the prerogative powers in relation to foreign trade. There was a conflict of authorities. Parliament was feeling its strength and each side appealed to the law to decide what was really a political issue that had lain dormant so long as Tudor Kings worked in harmony with Parliament. "If it was no part of the Tudor theory of government that emergency powers should be used for the raising of revenue, neither was it a bonâ fide use of the power of the purse to attempt to remove foreign policy or the defence of the realm from the hands of the Crown." [2]

> In the *Case of Impositions* (*Bate's Case*),[3] John Bate refused to pay a duty on imported currants imposed by the Crown on the ground that its imposition was contrary to the statute 45 Edw. 3 c. 4 which prohibited indirect taxation without the consent of Parliament. The

[1] Anson, *Law and Custom of the Constitution* (5th edn., Gwyer), Vol. I, p. 343.
[2] K. & L. 95.
[3] (1606), 2 St. Tr. 371; K. & L. 78.

> Court of Exchequer unanimously gave a decision in favour of the Crown. The King could impose what duties he pleased for the purpose of regulating trade, and the court could not go behind the King's statement that the duty was in fact imposed for the regulation of trade.
>
> In the *Case of Ship Money* (*The King* v. *Hampden*),[1] John Hampden, Knight of the Shire for Buckinghamshire, refused to pay ship money, a tax levied for the purpose of furnishing ships in time of national danger. Counsel for Hampden conceded that sometimes the existence of danger will justify taking the subject's goods without his consent, but only in actual as opposed to threatened emergency. The Crown conceded that the subject could not be taxed in normal circumstances without the consent of Parliament, but contended that the King was the sole judge whether an emergency justified the exercise of his prerogative power to raise funds to meet a national danger.
>
> A majority of the Court of Exchequer Chamber gave judgment for the King.[2]

The decision was reversed by the Long Parliament,[3] and this aspect of the struggle for supremacy was concluded by the Bill of Rights:

> That the levying money for or to the use of the Crown by pretence of prerogative without grant of Parliament for longer time or in other manner than the same is or shall be granted is illegal.

(3) *Dispensing and Suspending Powers*

The power of the Crown to dispense with the operation of statutes within certain limits seems to have been a necessary one having regard to the form of many ancient statutes and the irregular meetings of Parliament. So long, however, as the limits upon the dispensing power were not clearly defined, there was here a threat to the legislative supremacy of Parliament. It could be contended that the dispensing power was one of the inseparable prerogatives which could not be curtailed, but violations of the common law or statutory enactments of the common law were probably not within the scope of the royal dispensation. In the leading case of *Thomas* v. *Sorrell*[4] a distinction was drawn between dispensing with laws which are not for the particular benefit or safety of third persons and laws which are for such benefit or for the benefit of the public as a whole. In *Godden* v. *Hales*[5] the court upheld a dispensation from James II to Sir Edward Hales excusing him from taking the oaths and fulfilling the other obligations imposed by the Test Act. It can be argued that

[1] (1637), 3 St. Tr. 825; K. & L. 81.

[2] For analysis of the arguments of Counsel and the judgments, see *The Case of Ship Money*, by Sir D. L. Keir, 52 L.Q.R. 546.

[3] Shipmoney Act 1640.

[4] (1674), Vaughan 330.

[5] (1686), 11 St. Tr. 1165; K. & L. 96.

the decision could have been given without impairing the distinction indicated in *Thomas* v. *Sorrell*. The judgment was, however, based on wider grounds and it was held that it was an inseparable prerogative of the Kings of England to dispense with penal laws in particular cases and upon necessary reasons of which the King is sole judge.

Fortified by the favourable decision in the latter case, James II proceeded to set aside statutes as he pleased. Hard though it may be to define the dispensing power, there is no doubt that James overstepped all limits of legality in granting a suspension of the penal laws relating to religion in the Declaration of Indulgence. The validity of his act only came before the courts in an indirect way at the trial of the Seven Bishops for seditious libel arising out of their petitions to James against reading the declaration from church pulpits. The Bill of Rights abolished the Crown's alleged power of suspending laws.

Comparison should be made with the provision relating to the dispensing power:

> (1) That the pretended power of dispensing with laws, or the execution of laws by regal authority, as it hath been assumed and exercised of late, is illegal.
>
> (2) That from and after this present session of Parliament, no dispensation by *non obstante* of or to any statute, or any part thereof, shall be allowed, but that the same shall be held void and of no effect, except a dispensation be allowed of in such a statute, and except in such cases as shall be specially provided for by one or more Bill or Bills to be passed during this present session of Parliament.[1]

It is apparent from these provisions that, while James II's dispensations were regarded as illegal, earlier dispensations were not called in question. Further it was recognised that the power might be required by the Executive in future. For this provision was to be made by Parliament. Actually no such provision was made. In the *Case of Eton College*,[2] there was upheld a dispensation granted by Queen Elizabeth to enable Fellows of the College to hold benefices up to a certain value in conjunction with their fellowships, notwithstanding College statutes which forbade this type of plurality.

(4) *The Independence of the Judiciary*

So long as the tenure of judicial office depended upon the royal pleasure there was a risk of the subservience of the Bench. Judicial independence is, therefore, closely connected with parliamentary

[1] No attempt was made to curtail the prerogative of pardon or the Attorney-General's power to enter a *nolle prosequi* (pp. 321–3, *post*).

[2] (1815) Philip Williams' Report 53; for an account of this case, see Broom, *Constitutional Law*, 2nd edn., pp. 503–5, and p. 10, *ante*.

supremacy. No doubt some of the decisions, such as the *Case of Impositions* and *Thomas* v. *Sorrell*, should be accepted without accusing the Judiciary of bias. But it is more difficult to absolve the judges who favoured the Crown in *Hampden's Case* or in *Godden* v. *Hales*.

Act of Settlement 1700

It was left to the Act of Settlement, enacting a provision which was originally intended to have taken its place in the Bill of Rights, to ensure the independence of the Bench

> "that . . . judges' commissions be made *quamdiu se bene gesserint*, and their salaries ascertained and established; but upon the address of both Houses of Parliament it may be lawful to remove them." [1]

Earlier the executive power had been checked by the abolition in 1640 of all jurisdiction of the Council in common law matters, and of the Court of Star Chamber which had been used for the enforcement of prerogative powers.

Position at end of Seventeenth Century

The result of the seventeenth-century conflict between the Executive and Parliament was that the Bill of Rights and the Act of Settlement gave to Parliament the supremacy on all points, while preserving the prerogative rights of the Crown in matters which had not been called in question. But as yet there was absent the recognition of the principle that the King's Ministers could best be controlled by their presence in Parliament as members, and so responsible to Parliament. It was not until early in the eighteenth century that this began to be recognised and it was indeed essential if the will of Parliament was to prevail. The process of impeachment was too cumbrous and drastic to be used as the everyday method of ensuring that a Minister should not disregard the will of Parliament, but the ultimate solution of the collective responsibility of the Cabinet was not at first perceived. The Bill of Rights was the first great victory of Parliament. The Act of Settlement by attempting to exclude Ministers from the House of Commons showed how far from realisation was the solution of the problem of co-ordination between the Executive and Parliament. Thus in the eighteenth century the nature of the struggle changes. The absolute discretion of the Crown, which the events of the closing years of the seventeenth century had still left in many respects unimpaired, could not be left with the Crown and its Ministers in such a way as to enable them to govern without

[1] Repealed by Statute Law Revision Act 1881. See for similar provisions Supreme Court of Judicature Act 1925, ss. 12, 13; Appellate Jurisdiction Act 1876, s. 6. For interpretation of these provisions, see p. 329, *post*.

responsibility in those matters which still fell within the royal prerogative. The significance of the period from 1688 until after the Reform Act 1832 lies in the development of ministerial responsibility to Parliament.

Growth of Ministerial Responsibility

The first step was to ensure the individual responsibility of Ministers of the Crown to Parliament for their actions, and, secondly, collective responsibility for general policy and for the actions of other Ministers.[1] This responsibility is political, and not legal, though for his individual acts contrary to law each Minister was, and is, responsible to the courts. *Danby's Case*[2] went a long way towards establishing the principle that a Minister cannot shelter himself from legal responsibility by a plea of obedience to the command of the Sovereign.

But the collective responsibility of the Cabinet could not be developed until that body had emerged as the effective executive organ. Anne, like her predecessors, retained a personal initiative in the Councils of the Crown, frequently presiding at meetings of the Cabinet, a body which had as yet no regular composition.[3] Even in the reign of George III membership of the Cabinet did not by itself entitle a Privy Councillor to take part in decisions on policy. There was a distinction between the efficient or confidential Cabinet, all the members of which received papers, and the outer circle of the Cabinet Council, the titular or external Cabinet.

Exclusion of Office holders

It has been seen that the Act of Settlement at the end of the previous reign excluded the Ministers of the Crown, as holders of offices of profit, from membership of the House of Commons. At the same time it attempted to impose personal responsibility for executive acts on Privy Councillors. It is true that neither of these provisions came into operation, as they were repealed before the death of Anne, but they serve to illustrate the lack of appreciation of the modern solution.

Transition to Cabinet Government

The real point of transition to Cabinet Government came with the accession of the House of Hanover. The absence of George I from meetings of the Cabinet made it essential that a Minister should

[1] For fuller treatment of Ministerial Responsibility, see Chap. 6.
[2] (1679), 11 St. Tr. 599. *Cf. Somers' Case* (1701), 14 St. Tr. 234.
[3] Anson gives three such bodies under titles of: (1) The Cabinet, or Lords of the Cabinet Council. (2) The Committee of Council. (3) The Privy Council or Great Council. Anson, *op. cit.*, 4th edn., Vol. II, Part I, p. 104.

be selected to preside at these meetings. Here is to be found the beginning of the office of Prime Minister. Henceforth the leaders of the two great parties of State, Whigs and Tories, control the direction of policy by maintaining a majority of supporters in the House of Commons. The methods to which both the Whigs and the Tories freely resorted included the acquisition of pocket boroughs, the grant of pensions and the gifts of sinecure offices and government contracts. The long Whig supremacy illustrates the effectiveness of these weapons. When George III tried through the King's friends to re-establish personal government, he did so on parliamentary lines. Since the Bill of Rights it was impossible for the Executive to govern without the support of Parliament. As long, however, as Parliament was unreformed, that support could be secured by the use of bribery and patronage, except in times of great popular feeling, as on the occasion of the loss of the American Colonies and the fall of Lord North's Ministry.

Reform Act 1832

With the coming of parliamentary reform in 1832 it was no longer possible to govern by these means, and indeed steps had been taken earlier on the initiative of Burke to purge the Commons of corrupt supporters of the Ministry by means of Bills abolishing old offices and disqualifying contractors and other placemen from membership. The necessity of parliamentary support which had existed since 1689 meant that the Executive must hold the same political views as the majority in Parliament. Gradually there was evolved an Executive responsive to the will of the majority of the electorate. It is true that at first "the electorate" meant principally owners of land. To-day it means every adult male and female.

Conclusion

Thus executive power has become impossible without the support of Parliament, which support is only obtainable by winning the confidence of a vast electorate. In the twentieth century the House of Commons has the final voice in legislation, as in taxation and expenditure, and a Ministry can be forced to resign by defeat or by the defection of some of its supporters in the House of Commons. In the past Parliament could not dismiss a King without a revolution. The Commons can now dismiss the Ministry which advises the Sovereign and ensure its replacement by another pledged to give effect to a policy approved by a majority of the electorate.

B. Meaning of Legislative Supremacy

Legal Power Unlimited

From this brief historical summary we turn to an examination of the practical results of parliamentary supremacy. Dicey, after examining several illustrations from history and showing that there existed no competing authority, concluded that within the limits of physical possibility Parliament could make or unmake any law whatever. The courts can only interpret and may not question the validity of Acts of Parliament. No Parliament can bind its successor; otherwise the supremacy of succeeding Parliaments would be limited. So far as constitutional law consists of statutes, there is no Act which Parliament could not repeal. The Bill of Rights could be cast overboard by the same process as a Prevention of Damage by Pests Act, namely by a repealing measure passed in ordinary form. Parliament can override the decisions of the courts, if need be with retrospective effect. It could restore to the Executive unfettered power to legislate as freely as if the *Case of Proclamations* had never been accepted as representing the law. The most firmly established convention could be declared illegal by statute.

Supremacy Illustrated

That Parliament can pass any law whatsoever and that no one Parliament can be bound by an Act of its predecessors nor bind its successors may be illustrated both by His Majesty's Declaration of Abdication Act 1936 (this changed the succession to the Throne which had been secured by the Act of Settlement), and by the statutes which have from time to time fixed or prolonged the duration of Parliament's own life. The duration of Parliament has been fixed by successive Acts which each repealed its predecessor, the Meeting of Parliament Act 1694,[1] the Septennial Act 1715 and the Parliament Act 1911 which is still in force. The Parliament elected in December 1910 was dissolved in 1918, having five times renewed its own existence, which was limited to five years by its own enactment, the Parliament Act 1911. The Parliament elected in 1935 five times renewed its own existence by Prolongation of Parliament Acts.[2]

Indemnity Acts and Retrospective Legislation

Parliament alone possesses the power to legalise past illegality. This power denies supremacy to the courts and has been used by an Executive which has a secure majority in Parliament to reverse

[1] Formerly entitled the Triennial Act 1694.
[2] Such Acts require the assent of both Houses; see p. 135, *post*.

inconvenient decisions of an impartial Judiciary.[1] The conclusion of the First World War, in the course of which a number of illegal acts were inevitably committed by an over-zealous Executive in the interest of the prosecution of the war, was marked by the passage of two Indemnity Acts, the Indemnity Act 1920 and the War Charges Validity Act 1925. There are many other instances of retrospective legislation, *e.g.* the Enemy Property Act 1953, ss. 1–3, relating to the making or withholding of payments and other dealings with property since the outbreak of war in 1939, Acts validating void marriages, the Building Societies Act 1939, s. 3, validating advances made by building societies in excess of their powers.

> Retrospective laws are, however, "*prima facie* of questionable policy and contrary to the general principle that legislation by which the conduct of mankind is to be regulated ought, when introduced for the first time, to deal with future acts and ought not to change the character of past transactions carried on upon the faith of the then existing law. Accordingly the court will not ascribe retrospective force to new laws affecting rights unless by express words or necessary implication it appears that such was the intention of the legislature." [2]

Retrospective laws may not only confirm irregular acts but also make void and punish what was lawful when done. In this category fell Acts of Attainder and in modern times taxation is occasionally imposed with retrospective operation to penalise widespread evasion which, though lawful when practised, has violated the general intention of the legislature.

Parliamentary Supremacy and the Commonwealth

Legislative supremacy means that the validity of an Act of Parliament cannot be questioned by the courts which are bound to accept as law the validity of all parliamentary enactments.[3] If Parliament made it a criminal offence for a Frenchman to smoke in the streets of Paris, the Act would not be enforced by the French courts, but an English court could enforce it against a Frenchman who came to this country and was prosecuted under it. The legislative supremacy of the Parliament of the United Kingdom (the Imperial Parliament) formerly extended throughout the King's dominions (the Dominions and the Colonies) and was applied by British courts in protectorates

[1] See Provisional Collection of Taxes Act 1913, p. 149, *post.;* War Damage Act 1965, p. 269, *post*.

[2] Willes, J., in *Phillips* v. *Eyre* (1870), L.R. 6 Q.B. 1; K. & L. 31.

[3] "If an Act of Parliament has been obtained improperly, it is for the legislature to correct it by repealing it; but, so long as it exists as law, the courts are bound to enforce it."—*Lee* v. *Bude and Torrington Rly. Co.* (1871), L.R. 6 C.P. 577, at p. 582.

and those foreign countries in which the Crown exercised jurisdiction. There was, however, a convention that Parliament should not legislate for a self-governing Dominion except at the request and with the consent of that Dominion. This convention was enacted as law by section 4 of the Statute of Westminster 1931.[1] Does this enactment limit the legislative supremacy of Parliament? The question may be framed differently: Would the courts recognise the validity of a statute passed in contravention of section 4 of the Statute of Westminster? Or can Parliament repeal the section? In strict legal theory an affirmative answer can be given to both these questions so far as the courts of the United Kingdom are concerned.

> It is doubtless true that the power of the Imperial Parliament to pass on its own initiative any legislation that it thought fit extending to Canada remains unimpaired; indeed the Imperial Parliament could, as a matter of strict law, repeal section 4 of the Statute. But that is theory and has no relation to realities.[2]

The Statute of Westminster did not purport to abrogate the supremacy of the Imperial Parliament. Indeed it expressly preserved the right of the Imperial Parliament to amend the British North America Acts (which contain the Canadian constitution) and to pass legislation affecting the States of Australia.[3] It is, however, open to doubt whether the courts of either Canada or Australia would recognise as part of Canadian or Australian law legislation passed in contravention of section 4. South Africa, while still a member of the Commonwealth, had long ceased to recognise the supremacy of the United Kingdom Parliament and enacted that no Act of the United Kingdom Parliament passed after December 11, 1931, should extend, or be deemed to extend, to the Union as part of the law of the Union unless extended thereto by an Act of the Parliament of the Union.[4] In *Ndlwana* v. *Hofmeyer N.O.*[5] the Supreme Court of South Africa described the Union Parliament as the supreme and sovereign law-making body of the Union and characterised as absurd the suggestion that section 4 of the Statute of Westminster could be repealed. "Freedom once conferred cannot be revoked."[6]

[1] Chap. 32, B.
[2] *British Coal Corporation* v. *The King*, [1935] A.C. 500, at p. 520.
[3] Pp. 444–5, *post*.
[4] Status of the Union Act 1934, s. 2.
[5] [1937] A.D. 229.
[6] [1937] A.D. 229, at p. 237. This case was overruled by the same Court in *Harris* v. *Minister of the Interior*, [1952] (2) S.A. 428; but the latter case expressly upheld the sovereignty of the Parliament of the Union.

Territorial Jurisdiction

The supremacy of Parliament is not limited so far as British courts are concerned by the rules of international law. The courts have nothing to do with the question whether the legislature has or has not done what foreign States consider a usurpation. Neither are they concerned whether an Act of Parliament is null and void on the ground that it contravenes generally accepted principles of international law.[1] No statute will, however, be held to apply to aliens with respect to transactions outside British jurisdiction unless the words are perfectly clear.[2] In practice Parliament only enacts legislation which can be enforced and, in accord with international law, attempts to exercise authority only within its own territories,[3] or over its own citizens when abroad.[4] As an example of legislation which is intended to operate outside the territory of the United Kingdom the Continental Shelf Act 1964 vests in the Queen the rights of exploration and exploitation of the continental shelf. The shelf is a new concept which is acquiring recognition under public international law and confers jurisdiction in relation to the seabed and subsoil and the natural resources thereof on the State adjacent to the underwater shelf. The Act is therefore a striking illustration both of the process of making a new rule of public international law by agreement and of the exercise of the supremacy of Parliament extending beyond territorial waters. The Act incidentally makes provision for the application of criminal and civil law in respect of acts or omissions taking place around any installations which may be placed with the authority of the relevant Minister in the surface waters above a continental shelf area. The Tokyo Convention Act 1967 applies the criminal law including piracy, to acts or omissions taking place on board British-controlled aircraft, while in flight elsewhere than in or over the United Kingdom. In the United Kingdom the territorial conception of law is stronger than that of most other countries and the extent to which citizens of the United Kingdom and Colonies are affected by English law while in foreign countries is small. A few serious crimes committed in a foreign State by citizens of the United

[1] *Mortensen* v. *Peters* (1906), 8 F. (Ct. of Sess.) 93.

[2] *Cail* v. *Papayanni* (1863), 1 Moo. P.C. (N.S.) 471, at p. 474. For an example of prohibiting an activity abroad by whomsoever committed (election broadcasts), see Representation of the People Act 1949, s. 80.

[3] Including British ships wherever they may be.

[4] And not over the citizens of other States of the British Commonwealth for offences committed outside the United Kingdom, unless such offences are punishable when committed by an alien: British Nationality Act 1948, s. 3. A citizen of a Commonwealth State, however, like an alien, is subject to English or Scots law when resident in the United Kingdom.

Kingdom and Colonies are justiciable in this country, such as treason, murder, manslaughter, bigamy, piracy.[1] Any British subject employed by the Government of the United Kingdom in the service of the Crown who commits in a foreign country, when acting in the course of his employment, any offence which, if committed in England, would be punishable on indictment, can be proceeded against in England for that offence.[2] The National Service (Foreign Countries) Act 1942, which was repealed after the end of hostilities, empowered the Crown to impose military service on British subjects in foreign countries. The Marine Broadcasting (Offences) Act 1967, which is based upon an agreement by a number of States to control off-shore broadcasting, prohibits acts by British subjects connected with broadcasting outside the United Kingdom.

Future Parliaments cannot be bound

No Parliament can bind its successors. Otherwise succeeding Parliaments would not be sovereign or supreme.

This rule is illustrated by *Vauxhall Estates* v. *Liverpool Corporation*,[3] where it was held that provisions contained in a later Act (Housing Act 1925, s. 46, which related to compensation for land compulsorily acquired), repealed by implication the provisions of an earlier Act (Acquisition of Land (Assessment of Compensation) Act 1919, s. 7 (1)) which attempted to invalidate subsequent legislation so far as it might be inconsistent.

In *Ellen Street Estates Ltd.* v. *Minister of Health*,[4] Maugham L.J. said: "The legislature cannot according to our constitution bind itself as to the form of subsequent legislation, and it is impossible for Parliament to enact that in a subsequent statute dealing with the same subject matter there can be no implied repeal. If in a subsequent Act Parliament chooses to make it plain that the earlier Statute is being to some extent repealed, effect must be given to that intention just because it is the will of the legislature."

Sovereign and Non-Sovereign Legislatures

A distinction must be drawn between Parliament and a colonial legislature. Nowadays the policy has been adopted of granting independence to all colonial territories if their size permits a separate political and economic existence. In the few small territories which remain of colonial status the powers of the local legislature are subject to statutes of the Parliament at Westminster as well as to

[1] Lord McNair, *Legal Effects of War*, 4th ed., p. 435 (Cambridge University Press). Kenny, *Outlines of Criminal Law*, 19th edn., chap. xxix, especially p. 550.

[2] Criminal Justice Act 1948, s. 31 (1).

[3] [1932] 1 K.B. 733.

[4] [1934] 1 K.B. 590.

legislation under the royal prerogative.[1] Colonial legislatures are sovereign within the limits of their powers,[2] but they are bound by the Colonial Laws Validity Act 1865 [3] and other Acts of the Imperial Parliament which apply to the colonies, such as the British Nationality Act 1948 and merchant shipping legislation. The Colonial Laws Validity Act requires any amendment of a colonial constitution to be made "in the manner and form" required by imperial or colonial legislation in force at the time. The Privy Council held invalid an Act of the New South Wales Parliament which purported to abolish the Upper House of New South Wales in contravention of a previous Act of the same Parliament. That Act had provided that the Upper House might only be abolished by a Bill which before being presented for the royal assent had been approved by the electors at a referendum, and the requirement of a referendum could only be abolished by the same process.[4] In the High Court of Australia [5] it was suggested that if a similar provision were enacted in England and a subsequent Bill received the royal assent without a referendum having been held, the courts might be called upon to consider whether the supreme legislative power had in fact been exercised in the manner required for its authentic expression and by the elements in which it had come to reside. This suggestion, it should be noted, came from a court which was investigating the powers of a legislature which by reason of s. 5 of the Colonial Laws Validity Act was a subordinate legislature. It was further suggested that it would be an unlawful proceeding to present such a Bill for the royal assent before it had been approved by the electors and that, if before the Bill received the assent of the Crown it was found possible to raise for judicial decision the question whether it was lawful to present the Bill for assent, the courts would be bound to hold it unlawful to do so. It is, however, submitted that the courts in the United Kingdom would never question the validity of an Act of Parliament which had been duly promulgated. The courts will certainly not consider whether or not prescribed forms have been followed in passing a Bill:

> All that a Court of Justice can do is to look at the parliamentary roll; if from that it should appear that a Bill has passed both Houses and received the royal assent, no court of justice can inquire into the

[1] *E.g. Madzimbamuto* v. *Lardner-Burke*, [1969] A.C. 645 where the Judicial Committee of the Privy Council held that the sovereignty of the Queen in Parliament of the United Kingdom prevailed in Rhodesia after its unilateral declaration of independence.

[2] P. 427, *post*.

[3] Pp. 435-7, *post*.

[4] *Attorney-General for New South Wales* v. *Trethowan*, [1932] A.C. 526; see p. 437, *post*.

[5] 44 C.L.R. 394, *per* Dixon, J., at p. 426.

> mode in which it was introduced into Parliament, nor into what was done previous to its introduction, or what passed in Parliament during its progress in its various stages through both Houses.[1]

Nor will the courts enforce an agreement preventing the submission to Parliament of matters which may be relevant to the passage of a Bill.[2] But in *Harris* v. *Minister of the Interior*[3] it was sought to challenge the validity of a South African Act to alter the rights of coloured voters on the ground that the procedure prescribed by the constitution had not been followed; the Supreme Court of South Africa held that the Union Parliament was a sovereign legislature but that the courts had power to declare invalid an Act passed by both Houses of Parliament and duly promulgated and published by the proper authority on the ground that the Act had not been passed by the special machinery required by the Constitution Act of the Union. Thus the Union Parliament was sovereign, but must comply with its constitutional procedure when asserting that sovereignty.[4]

No rival Authority

It has been shown in discussing the struggle for supremacy in the seventeenth century that legislative supremacy requires that there should be no rival legislative authority. Neither the Crown[5] nor one House of Parliament[6] can change the law. Neither devolution nor delegation of legislative authority infringes the supremacy of Parliament. Legislative supremacy does not require that only Parliament should legislate, but it means that other bodies should only legislate with the authority of Parliament.[7] Until the past decade there has been little enthusiasm in this country for devolution, whether regional (*e.g.* separate legislatures for Scotland and Wales)

[1] *Edinburgh and Dalkeith Rly. Co.* v. *Wauchope* (1842), 8 Cl. and F. 710, *per* Lord Campbell, at p. 725.

[2] In *Bilston Corporation* v. *Wolverhampton Corporation*, [1942] 1 Ch. 391; K. & L. 15, the court refused to grant an injunction to prevent the defendants from opposing a local Act in breach of an agreement not to oppose which had itself been embodied in another local Act; see note by Sir William Holdsworth in 59 L.Q.R. 2.

[3] [1952] (2) S.A. 428. This case preceded by several years the departure of South Africa from the Commonwealth, a step which, however, was taken without overthrowing the main provisions of the existing Constitution.

[4] The Court overruled on the latter point its earlier decision in *Ndlwana* v. *Hofmeyr N.O.*, [1937] A.D. 229. For later examples of *ultra vires* legislation by a sovereign legislature see *Bribery Commission* v. *Ranasinghe*, [1965] A.C. 172; K. & L. 17 where the Ceylon legislature failed to pass the legislation by the majority laid down in the constitution; in *Liyanage* v. *The Queen* [1967] A.C. 259, at p. 287 legislation was disallowed as infringing provisions of the Ceylon constitution intended to secure the independence of the judiciary.

[5] Pp. 39–40, *ante*.

[6] Pp. 149 and 158, *post*.

[7] For prerogative legislation see pp. 599–600, *post*.

or functional (*e.g.* an economic legislature elected by trade and professional organisations). That devolution can be reconciled with parliamentary control is shown by the procedure devised for the consideration and passage of measures of the General Synod of the Church of England.[1] It is recognised that a substantial delegation of legislative powers is inevitable in the modern State. Apart from minor legislative powers exercised by local authorities and other bodies with statutory powers to enact byelaws, wide powers of legislation are delegated to government departments. Such delegation may in the absence of proper safeguards lessen control by Parliament of legislation, but it does not impair supremacy. Parliament may take away the powers that it has given. Moreover, unless Parliament excludes the jurisdiction of the courts, delegated legislation will be held invalid if the powers conferred by Parliament are exceeded.[2]

If the United Kingdom enters the European Economic Community (the Common Market), legislation by Parliament will be necessary to give effect in United Kingdom law to some of the obligations under the Treaty of Rome thereby accepted. Would such legislation be subject to repeal or amendment on the initiative of Parliament alone?

Foreign Legislation

We have considered the territorial limitations upon parliamentary sovereignty and how far the laws passed by Parliament have extra-territorial effect. It is also necessary to consider how far foreign laws are enforced or recognised in the United Kingdom. The courts refuse to investigate the validity of the acts of a foreign State done within its own territory,[3] and will recognise a transfer of property situated in that territory by a decree of that State, should the question of its ownership be raised in litigation here. The meaning and effect of a foreign decree is a question of fact to be determined by evidence. The courts do not recognise the validity of a decree of a foreign State

[1] Chap. 34.
[2] Chap. 44.
[3] *A. M. Luther Co.* v. *James Sagor and Co.*, [1921] 3 K. B. 532; *Princess Paley Olga* v. *Weisz*, (1929) 1 K.B. 718. Lord McNair suggests (*op. cit.*, pp. 438–40) that the courts may investigate the constitutionality as opposed to the validity of the act of a foreign State, but it is submitted that such an investigation will only be made in most exceptional circumstances, *e.g.* where there is involved the freedom of a person living in the United Kingdom: *In re Amand* (No. 2), [1942] 1 K.B. 445. Nor, it is suggested, would an English court investigate a question of constitutionality which by the foreign law is reserved for a special constitutional court.

or a foreign law purporting to affect property situated outside the territory of that State.[1]

Second World War

It is only with the authority of Parliament that foreign jurisdiction can be exercised in this country. Such jurisdiction was granted during the Second World War to Allied Governments in London over their armed forces stationed in this country.[2] In the case of members of the United States forces Parliament surrendered its own jurisdiction over crimes committed in the United Kingdom.[3] Similarly Parliament gave authority to the Crown to allow the exiled Netherlands Government to legislate in the United Kingdom for its own subjects.[4] International law recognises that a State may legislate in respect of its own subjects wherever they may be, and it mattered not whether such legislation was enacted in Holland or in the United Kingdom. It could, however, only be enforced in the United Kingdom through the authority of Parliament.

> Amand, a Netherlands subject, was called up for military service by a Netherlands decree made in the United Kingdom. He was arrested in pursuance of an Order in Council made under the Allied Forces Act 1940 which gave to the Netherlands authorities jurisdiction over their armed forces in the United Kingdom and lent assistance in enforcing that jurisdiction. The Divisional Court recognised that a valid Netherlands decree could apply to Netherlands subjects in the United Kingdom; but it was an Act of the United Kingdom Parliament and an Order in Council made thereunder that made Amand liable to arrest and detention and thus gave enforceability to the Netherlands decree.[5]

Interpretation of Statutes

The seventeenth-century struggle for supremacy left its mark upon the interpretation of statutes by the courts. Lawyers are traditionally suspicious of any encroachment by the Executive and this is reflected in the attitude of the courts to the interpretation of penal statutes, and statutes imposing taxation or conferring new powers on the Executive.

[1] *The Jupiter* (No. 3), [1927] P. 122, at p. 144. Possible exceptions are laws affecting the transfer of ownership of foreign ships (McNair, *op. cit.*, pp. 441–5) and requisitioning the property of nationals in time of war (McNair, *op. cit.*, p. 445).

[2] Pp. 390–1, *post*.

[3] United States of America (Visiting Forces) Act 1942 which remained in force until 1954. See now Visiting Forces Act 1952, pp. 391–2, *post*.

[4] *In re Amand* (No. 2), [1942] 1 K.B. 445.

[5] McNair, *op. cit.*, p. 437.

In *Attorney-General* v. *Wilts United Dairies* [1] a charge imposed by the Food Controller during the First World War as a condition of the grant of a licence to deal in milk was held invalid. The Food Controller entered into agreements with the dairy company by which the company was permitted to buy milk in certain areas outside its registered area on condition that a payment of a sum of 2*d.* per gallon was paid for the licence. The licence was issued under statutory orders which themselves were authorised by the Defence of the Realm (Consolidation) Act 1914. The High Court referred to the "historic struggle of the legislature to secure for itself the sole power to levy money upon the subject," and held that express words were required for any delegation of the power to tax.[2] There was no direct authority to require the payment of the levy as in the case of an ordinary tax. Nor could Parliament be taken to have authorised such a charge by implication. The court was unable to distinguish between a payment of this character and a tax. Since the Bill of Rights 1688 which forbade the levying of taxation without the consent of Parliament, nothing but the direct authority of Parliament could authorise a charge of this character.

The courts will not question the supremacy of Parliament, but it was understood by the lawyers when they allied themselves with Parliament that the common law should be preserved, and this understanding has influenced the interpretation of statutes to the present day.[3] Judicial interpretation of discretionary powers will be discussed in Chap. 44, but some leading principles of interpretation may be mentioned here to illustrate how loath the Judiciary has hitherto been to construe a statute as changing the basic principles of the common law.[4] There is thus a presumption against the alteration of existing law. As we have already seen [5] a court will not ascribe retrospective force to legislation except at the specific command of the legislature. In the absence of express provisions to the contrary the Crown and the rights of the Crown are deemed not to be affected by any enactment.[6] Express terms are required to take away the legal right of the subject to compensation in respect of property compulsorily acquired.[7] There is a presumption that Parliament

[1] (1921), 37 T.L.R. 884; K. & L. 55.

[2] For an instance of a wide delegation of taxing power, see p. 132, *post*. Though the Crown may not without parliamentary sanction levy a charge in return for the performance of a public duty, the courts will enforce payment for the performance of a service which cannot be demanded as of right, *e.g.* the provision of protection by armed forces for merchant vessels trading in peace time in foreign waters which were infested with pirates: *China Navigation Co.* v. *Attorney-General*, [1932] 2 K.B. 197; K. & L. 146.

[3] K. & L. 9–14; Dicey, *op. cit.*, Introduction, p. c and note 1.

[4] "That principle of construction is now, I apprehend, discredited," *Liberty and the Common Law*, by Lord Wright, 9 C.L.J. 3.

[5] P. 47, *ante*.

[6] P. 686, *post*.

[7] *Per* Lord Atkinson in *Central Control Board (Liquor Traffic)* v. *Cannon Brewery Co. Ltd.*, [1919] A.C. 744, at p. 752.

does not intend to deprive a subject of his right of access to the courts in respect of his common law rights.

In *Chester* v. *Bateson* [1] during the First World War it was held that a regulation debarring any person from applying to the courts without the consent of the Minister of Munitions to recover possession of premises occupied by a munitions worker was not validly made under a statutory power to issue regulations for preserving the public safety and the defence of the realm.

Express and clear words are required to effect any major constitutional changes.

In *Nairn* v. *University of St. Andrews* [2] at a time when women were not enfranchised generally it was held that express words were required to confer the vote on women graduates of a Scottish university, and that they could not be enfranchised simply by the use of the words "every person" in connection with the statutory right to be registered as an elector.

Political Limitations

We have hitherto considered territorial limitations on parliamentary supremacy and the legal meaning of the term. There are also practical political limitations. It is essential to the working of a parliamentary democracy that the laws made by the representatives of the people should be obeyed. It follows that laws must not be enacted that would prove unenforceable owing to their being repugnant to the moral sense of the people. In theory, but not in practice, Parliament could enact a law condemning all red-haired males to death or making attendance at public worship illegal.

Consultation of Interests affected

The immense complexity of the business of government makes it necessary that, while preserving its supremacy, Parliament should exercise it only after the major interests affected have been consulted. The modern State regulates the whole life of the community. The initiation of legislation is the function of the Executive, but prior consultation with major interests affected is an essential part of the legislative process. Indeed it is not uncommon in the case of delegated legislation for Parliament expressly to provide for consultation between a Minister and the organisations representing interests to be affected by the making of regulations. Legislation affecting industrial life is not passed without consultation with the major industrial organisation of employers and employed—the Confederation of British Industries and the Trade Union Congress. Such

[1] [1920] 1 K.B. 829; K. & L. 44.
[2] [1909] A.C. 147.

consultation ensures that legislation is passed with adequate knowledge of the problems involved and that Parliament is aware in advance how far it will secure the co-operation essential for its enforcement. It is of the highest importance that the persons or bodies consulted should be truly representative of the interests concerned, but not all interests—especially domestic consumers—are organised. Similar consultation takes place before the passage of legislation directly affecting the professions, *e.g.* the medical profession had to be consulted before the initiation of the National Health Service; the Bar Council and the Law Society before the introduction of measures changing legal procedure. Numerous measures necessitate the co-operation of local authorities which is secured in advance by consultation between the Ministry of Housing and Local Government and the Associations of Municipal Corporations and of County Councils. There is a tendency for the Executive to face Parliament with "agreed measures." But consultation does not mean that the bodies whose advice is sought can dictate policy. It is for the Minister to weigh up that advice and to present the policy of the Government to Parliament. Consultation must not be allowed to hamper Parliament in reaching final decisions. No dictation to Parliament must be tolerated. Parliamentary democracy would not work if a minority attempted to influence national action, *e.g.* in the sphere of foreign policy, by organised obstruction or strikes. The practice of consultation is one of the factors which have stood in the way of the establishment of any rival to Parliament by means of functional devolution. An economic Parliament elected by sectional interests might easily become a rival claimant for supremacy.

Parliament and the Electorate

Finally there must be mentioned the responsibility of Parliament to the electorate, the political sovereign. Some constitutions provide that constitutional changes shall only take effect with the consent of the electorate obtained by a referendum (a poll of the electorate). The referendum need not be confined to constitutional issues. Other constitutions provide for the Initiative—a device to enable the electorate to instruct Parliament to proceed with a measure. Our constitution does not find a place for any machinery of direct democracy, but the view that the party which has come into power after a general election has a mandate from the electorate to implement by legislation the whole of its election promises has been increasingly urged of late. Equally any departure from the mandate is apt to be criticised by the Opposition. There is danger in the doctrine of the mandate, especially when election programmes are settled largely by reference to the views endorsed by large gatherings at party political conferences; it is the duty of a Government to govern and it can hardly be the case that decisions on foreign relations or on the elementary duty of maintaining order can only be taken with reference to action authorised beforehand by an electoral mandate. Power gained and held by consent may well be stultified by too rigid reliance on the mandate. Legislative supremacy is not shared with the electorate. None the less, though the power exists, no Parliament, save in an emergency, would prolong its own life, and at regular intervals the electorate exercises its political supremacy by the choice of representatives. Parliament accordingly exercises its legislative supremacy with its responsibility to the electorate in mind. History has shown that Parliament is always sensitive to public opinion. Even in the eighteenth century when Parliament was not a truly representative assembly, public opinion made itself felt in times of national crisis, *e.g.* the dismissal of the Fox-North coalition and the call to power of the younger Pitt. Experience of direct democracy shows that the voter when confronted by an isolated issue on a referendum is slow to favour any change in the *status quo*. Parliamentary government makes for more flexible government and probably for truer and more effective concern for the public interest of the community as a whole.

Recent Controversy

The foregoing account of parliamentary supremacy, apart from a number of references to parliamentary supremacy and the Commonwealth [1] and to sovereign and non-sovereign legislatures [2] has not dealt with the challenge which has emerged in recent times to Dicey's interpretation of sovereignty. This book is concerned, as was Dicey,[3] with the supremacy or sovereignty of the Parliament of the United Kingdom. There are, however, difficulties which the application of the doctrine has caused in Commonwealth States with in every case a formally enacted constitution. The question whether or not the Sovereign can bind himself cannot be answered by a mere assertion of supremacy. It may be relatively easy in the case of a State with a unitary constitution to answer the question, who is the legal Sovereign? Even this may be obscure where the constitution is a federal one. But the questions, why is he Sovereign? and, who

[1] Pp. 47–8, *ante*.
[2] Pp. 50–2, *ante*.
[3] *The Law of the Constitution* 10th edn., Part I.

made him Sovereign?, are matters which fall outside the sphere of courts. The answers are to be found not in law so much as in history or political philosophy.

Even in the case of the United Kingdom where the doctrine has not been seriously questioned in the courts, it is not easy to point to legal authority for the doctrine of parliamentary supremacy, but a case like *Ellen Street Estates Ltd.* v. *Minister of Health* [1] may now be cited as authority for the proposition that Parliament cannot bind itself as to the form or substance of subsequent legislation, and therefore that each succeeding Parliament is omnipotent. There is also modern authority to prove that the judicial process does not lie where Parliament has exclusive jurisdiction and that the court will not examine the procedure in Parliament which precedes the enactment of an Act.[2] It has been argued [3] that a skilful draftsman could protect—or entrench—an Act by providing that no Bill purporting to repeal it should have effect unless approved by referendum. This statement was suggested by a passage in the judgment of Dixon, J. (as he then was), in *Attorney-General for New South Wales* v. *Trethowan*,[4] but the case which gave rise to this statement *obiter* related to the legislation of a subordinate legislature, the powers of which were limited by the constitution. Today it is certainly true that Parliament does not acknowledge the priority of any existing statute on any legal ground whatever.

Basis of Sovereignty

Dicey has shown that political expediency in practice operates to limit the working of the legal rule. To the lawyer, however, there ought to be an explanation of why the courts enforce without question all Acts of Parliament. No one can point to any statute which says that this is the rule. The answer then would seem to be found in the common law. Yet the common law is not infrequently changed by statute. Can Parliament change this rule of the common law like all other such rules? At first sight the answer would seem to be that there is no difference between this rule and all others. Is there something in the rule requiring judicial obedience to statutes which makes it sacrosanct? For this we must turn to history rather

[1] [1934] 1 K.B. 590; p. 50, *ante*.
[2] P. 51, *ante*.
[3] Keir and Lawson, *Cases in Constitutional Law*, 4th edn., p. 7. This is omitted in the current edition.
[4] (1931), 44 C.L.R., at p. 425; p. 51, *ante*.

than to the law reports. An authoritative view [1] is that the source of the rule is historical only and not legal; but no statute can confer this power upon Parliament; that would be to assume and to act on the very power that is to be conferred. If no statute can confer, similarly no statute can abolish the rule; it must then be a rule of the common law but unlike all other rules of the common law, it is an ultimate political fact upon which the whole system of legislation hangs. This means that if there is a change, that change can only be brought about by political events and not by legislation. There is plenty of evidence in the history of the seventeenth century of the courts recognising the authority of Parliament, although the very character of Parliament underwent radical changes as in 1649, 1660 and 1689.

The English doctrine of parliamentary sovereignty was criticised by the Lord President in the Court of Session in *MacCormick* v. *Lord Advocate*,[2] the case which unsuccessfully challenged the Queen's title as Elizabeth II in Scotland. Lord Cooper doubted *obiter* whether the new Parliament of Great Britain must have inherited in 1707 the attribute of sovereignty which the Parliament of Scotland preceding the union had not enjoyed. The answer to this would seem to be that the former Parliament of England could not to be understood to have given up at the union the attribute of sovereignty which it already had.

Sovereignty in the Commonwealth

Turning to the other States of the Commonwealth, discussion naturally centres around the Statute of Westminster 1931 [3] and particularly that provision of the Statute, s. 4, which enacted that no future Act of Parliament of the United Kingdom should extend to a State of the Commonwealth as part of the law of that State unless it contained an express declaration that that State had requested and consented to its enactment. As will be seen later, the Statute was concerned only with the exercise of legislative power, and this in practice had ceased to be exercised by the United Kingdom Parliament some time before the Statute of Westminster except at the request of the State concerned. In relation to the supremacy

[1] Sir John Salmond, *Jurisprudence*, 11th ed., p. 137; H. W. R. Wade, *The Basis of Legal Sovereignty*, [1955] C.L.J. 172; for the possible application of a new view of sovereignty to Parliament in the United Kingdom, see R. F. V. Heuston, *Essays in Constitutional Law*, 2nd edn., pp. 23–30; this distinguishes between rules governing composition and precedure of a sovereign legislature and those relating to the area of its power.

[2] 1953 S.L.T. 255

[3] Pp. 48, *ante*, and pp. 438–45 *et seq.*, *post*.

of the United Kingdom Parliament, the view which has the support of the Judicial Committee of the Privy Council is that Parliament could as a matter of abstract law repeal or disregard s. 4. This is dismissed with the statement "but that is theory and has no relation to realities." [1] On another view s. 4 may be regarded as an abdication by Parliament of its supremacy—a contingency which Dicey himself recognised when he wrote that "the impossibility of placing a limit on the exercise of sovereignty does not in any way prohibit either logically, or as a matter of fact, the abdication of sovereignty." [2]

Where the legislature is governed by a written constitution, it is the constitution which must be regarded as fundamental. The legislature is sovereign in the sense that it may have the power derived from the constitution to repeal or amend existing legislation. But if the constitution prescribes the manner of legislating and in particular entrenches, *e.g.* requires a special majority of both chambers sitting together to change, certain constitutional rights, then there is no limitation on the power of the Parliament to amend the constitution, but the manner of legislating must obey the fundamental statute which contains the constitution.[3]

By analogy with the proposition that the rule which ordains that Acts of Parliament shall have the force of law is legally ultimate but that its source is historical, the fact that the courts in other States in the Commonwealth are competent to challenge the validity of constitutional enactments may be explained by treating the Act containing the constitution as a fundamental statute. This does not mean that the Act may not provide for its own amendment by subsequent legislation, but only that whatever it does provide is binding on the courts. Put in another way, in the United Kingdom no statute has succeeded in enacting the effect of fundamental political events. In the Commonwealth each constituent Act, preceded as it normally has been by constitutional conferences, embodies the fundamentals upon which the new State rests its basis.

[1] *British Coal Corporation* v. *The King*, [1935] A.C. 500; C.L.C. Vol. I. 160; *Copyright Owners Reproduction Society* v. *E.M.I.* (*Australia*) *Pty Ltd*, (1958) 100 C.L.R. 597, as a rule of construction to be applied by the courts no statute of the Parliament of the United Kingdom is intended to extend to a State of the Commonwealth.

[2] Dicey, *op. cit.*, p. 68, note 1.

[3] Pp. 50–2, *ante*.

CHAPTER FIVE

THE RULE OF LAW

THE supremacy or rule of law has been since the Middle Ages a principle of the constitution. It means that the exercise of powers of government shall be conditioned by law and that the subject shall not be exposed to the arbitrary will of his ruler.[1] There is much truth in the contention that "principles of the constitution" are only "political principles." The rule of law had a different interpretation under weak Lancastrian monarchs than under the Tudors. It has been said that "unconstitutional" may mean merely "contrary to tradition," but "the principles of 1689 have become part of the accepted theory of democracy" and "in the political sphere there is much in the Whig philosophy with which any democrat will agree, and which is, therefore, an accepted and, one might almost say, permanent part of the constitution." [2] But the rule of law is a concept of greater antiquity, although admittedly it had to be reconciled with the doctrine of parliamentary supremacy in the course of the seventeenth-century contest with the Crown.

History of the Rule of Law

In the Middle Ages the theory was held that there was a universal law which ruled the world. Bracton, writing in the first half of the thirteenth century, deduced from this theory the proposition that rulers were subject to law. We have seen [3] how the alliance between common lawyers and Parliament had a decisive effect upon the contest between Crown and Parliament. That alliance had its roots in the later Middle Ages. Mediaeval lawyers never denied the wide scope of the royal prerogative, but the King could do certain things only in certain ways. It was not until the seventeenth century that Parliament established its supremacy, but Fortescue, C.J., writing in the reign of Henry VI, had applied what later became the two major principles of the constitution—the rule of law and the supremacy of the Parliament—and relied upon the rule of law to

[1] For historical summary, see M.P.R., pp. 71–73.
[2] Jennings, *The Law and the Constitution*, 5th edn., p. 314.
[3] Pp. 38–44, *ante*.

justify the contention that taxation could not be imposed without the consent of Parliament. With the rise in the sixteenth century of the modern territorial State the mediaeval conception of a universal law which ruled the world gave place to the conception of the supremacy of the common law. The abolition in 1640 of the Court of Star Chamber ensured that the principles of the common law should apply to public as well as private law. The rule of law meant the supremacy of all parts of the law of England, both enacted and unenacted. The supremacy of the law together with the supremacy of Parliament were finally established by the Bill of Rights in 1688.

Dicey's exposition of the Rule of Law

Of all writers on the constitution since Blackstone the most influential has been the late A. V. Dicey, whose lectures delivered as Vinerian Professor of English Law at Oxford and first published in 1885 under the title *Introduction to the Study of the Law of the Constitution* [1] have been studied by successive generations of statesmen, lawyers and a large section of those interested in public life. The constitutional law of today differs in many respects from that of 1885, but the influence of Dicey remains a real force. There is no better way of distinguishing between the permanent and impermanent features of our constitution than by examining the principles of the constitution as expounded by Dicey and determining how far they hold good to-day. Of those principles which Dicey expounded that which has had most influence and at the same time has received most modern criticism is his exposition of the rule of law.[2]

Committee on Ministers' Powers

One of the terms of reference of the Committee on Ministers' Powers appointed by the Lord Chancellor in 1929 [3] was to report what safeguards were desirable or necessary in respect of the legislative and judicial powers of Ministers in order to secure the constitutional principles of the sovereignty of Parliament and the supremacy of the law. It was understood that what was meant by the supremacy of the law was the principle expounded by Dicey.

[1] 10th ed., with Introduction by E. C. S. Wade (Macmillan), 1959.

[2] The reader should study Dicey, *op. cit.*, Chaps. IV, XII and XIII, and Introduction, pp. xcvi to cli; Jennings, *The Law and the Constitution*, 5th ed., Chap. II and App. 2; and "Constitutional Government and the Rule of Law," by G. Godfrey Phillips, *Journal of Comparative Legislation*, 3rd series, Vol. XX, pp. 262 *et seq.*

[3] Pp. 593–4, *post.*

First of Dicey's three meanings of the Rule of Law: Absence of Arbitrary Power

Dicey gave to the rule of law three meanings:

> It means in the first place, the absolute supremacy or predominance of regular law as opposed to the influence of arbitrary power, and excludes the existence of arbitrariness, of prerogative, or even of wide discretionary authority on the part of the government . . . a man may be punished for a breach of law, but he can be punished for nothing else.[1]

This interpretation conveyed that no man is punishable or can be lawfully made to suffer in body or goods, except for a distinct breach of law established in ordinary legal manner before the ordinary courts of the land. In this sense the rule of law is contrasted with systems of government based on the exercise by persons in authority of wide arbitrary or discretionary powers of constraint.

Second meaning of the Rule of Law: Subjection of Officials to the Ordinary Courts

The rule of law—

> means, again, equality before the law or the equal subjection of all classes to the ordinary law of the land administered by the ordinary law courts.[2]

In this sense the rule of law conveys that no man is above the law; that officials like private citizens are under a duty to obey the same law, and (though this does not necessarily follow) that there are no administrative courts to which are referred claims by the citizen against the State or its officials.

Droit Administratif

Dicey contrasted the rule of law with the *droit administratif* of France. He was at pains to contrast the disadvantages involved in a system of administrative law and administrative courts to judge disputes between officials and citizens with the advantages enjoyed by Englishmen through the absence of such a system. He did not properly appreciate the working of the French system of *contentieux administratif* by the *Conseil d'État*.[3] This was indeed the chief part of *droit administratif* with which he dealt. Nor did he pay much attention to the wide powers of the Executive which existed in

[1] Dicey, *op. cit.*, p. 202.
[2] Dicey, *op. cit.*, pp. 202–3.
[3] Dicey, *op. cit.*, 10th edn., App. I. For the *Conseil d'État*, see C. J. Hamson, *Executive Discretion and Judicial Control* (Stevens) 1954.

England even in his day.[1] The law which regulates the powers and duties of public authorities and officials in this country is as much administrative law as the *droit administratif* of France even though its enforcement or supervision may be controlled by the same courts as the rest of English law.[2] But, although Dicey misinterpreted the meaning of *droit administratif*, his emphasis upon equality before the law served to stress that fundamental liberties can be protected by the common law—that police law is not law, and that freedom requires a legal system which protects essential liberties.

Third meaning of the Rule of Law: Constitution the result of the ordinary Law of the Land

Finally the rule of law as expounded by Dicey means—

> that with us the law of the constitution, the rules which in foreign countries naturally form part of a constitutional code, are not the source but the consequence of the rights of individuals, as defined and enforced by the courts, that, in short, the principles of private law have with us been by the action of the courts and Parliament so extended as to determine the position of the Crown and of its servants; thus the constitution is the result of the ordinary law of the land.[3]

By this is meant that the legal rights of the subject, *e.g.* his freedom of action and speech, are secured not by guaranteed rights proclaimed in a formal code but by the operation of the ordinary remedies of private law available against those who unlawfully interfere with his liberty of action, whether they be private citizens or officials. A person libelled may sue his defamer. Free access to courts of justice is an efficient guarantee against wrongdoers.

Each of these three meanings of the rule of law will be examined. How far Dicey's exposition was true of Dicey's time is primarily a question for the legal historian. We shall consider how far Dicey's exposition is true to-day in order to ascertain how far, if at all, the conception of the rule of law has a permanent value as a principle of the constitution.

Arbitrary Power and Discretionary Authority distinguished: Absence of Arbitrary Power

In considering Dicey's first meaning of the rule of law a distinction must be drawn between arbitrary power and discretionary authority.

[1] But see Introduction to 8th edn. and his article *Administrative Law in England*, 31 L.Q.R. 148, which is reprinted in 10th edn. App. 2.

[2] Chap. 43.

[3] Dicey, *op. cit.*, p. 203.

It is still an essential principle of constitutional government in the United Kingdom that there should be no arbitrary power to arrest or punish. It may be argued that, provided the law authorises the punishment of those who in the opinion of the Judiciary, or even the Executive, have acted in a manner contrary to the interests of the State, there is nothing contrary to the rule of law in inflicting such punishment. This, however, is to deny any real meaning or value to the conception of the rule of law. What is authorised by law cannot be illegal, but it may be contrary to the rule of law as a principle of constitutional government.[1] The essential feature of Dicey's first meaning of the rule of law remains a feature of the constitution to-day, viz. that, so far as punishment for offences is concerned, the citizen can foresee the consequences of his conduct and will not be punished save for a breach of the ordinary law. He will, moreover, be tried in the ordinary courts. The law of England knows nothing of exceptional offences punished by extra-ordinary tribunals. There are no special courts for the trial of crimes against the State. Judges have power to adjust sentences to the gravity of offences and the circumstances and past records of offenders. Maximum sentences for specific crimes are, however, laid down by law for nearly every criminal offence. The common law crime of public mischief provides dangerous scope for judicial discretion,[2] but in general so far as major crimes are concerned the definition of an offence—whether by common law or statute law—is fixed and can be ascertained.

"*The Ordinary Law*"

When Dicey referred to "ordinary law," he had in mind the common law or law enacted in Acts of Parliament. To-day criminal law includes innumerable offences which are created by statutory regulations. It is important that the individual should have the assurance that the law can be ascertained with reasonable certainty. A person who takes the trouble to consult his lawyer ought to be able to ascertain the legal consequences of his actions. The bulk and detail of the regulations enacted by government departments undoubtedly creates uncertainty.[3] The power to create offences must be delegated because the needs of the modern State require that

[1] See review by Sir William Holdsworth of E. C. S. Wade's Introduction to Dicey, 9th edn., in 55 L.Q.R. 585.

[2] *The King* v. *Manley*, [1933] 1 K.B. 529; see *Public Mischief*, by W. T. S. Stallybrass, 49 L.Q.R. 183; *The Queen* v. *Newland*, [1954] 1 Q.B. 158; *Shaw* v. *Director of Public Prosecutions*, [1962] A.C. 220 (conspiracy to corrupt public morals), and Chap. 39, *post*.

[3] Dicey, *op. cit.*, 10th edn., Introduction, pp. cx–cxi.

innumerable regulations be made and enforced. In order, however, to secure as far as practicable conformity with the rule of law provision must be made for simplicity, publication and accessibility.[1] The drafting of regulations is primarily the task of the legal staffs of the separate departments, but statutory instruments which (a) impose or vary taxation, *e.g.* Purchase Tax Orders, (b) apply or amend Acts of Parliament under general powers, *e.g.* the Visiting Forces Act 1952 or the Nigeria Independence Act 1960 consequent on the colony becoming independent, (c) deal with constitutional matters of a general character, *e.g.* Aliens Orders, are understood to be drafted by Parliamentary Counsel.[2] This is a safeguard that there will be no violation of the accepted principles of criminal liability under pressure of administrative expediency. In another way the growth of delegated legislation touches upon the principle of the rule of law. There is a close connection between the rule of law and parliamentary supremacy. So long as criminal law was based on either common law or statute law a man was only punishable for a breach of law which was based on the ancient custom of the country or was enacted by the representatives of the people. If offences are to be created by regulations made by government departments or subordinate bodies, it is essential that there should be scrutiny by Parliament to ensure conformity with the will of the people as expressed by its representatives. The need of such scrutiny is recognised by the appointment each session of a select committee of the House of Commons to scrutinise those classes of delegated legislation which are required to be laid before Parliament.[3]

Group Law

While as a citizen a man is subject only to the ordinary law, he may also be subject to the special law affecting his particular calling which may be enforced by special tribunals. But no man can be judged by his fellow citizens except so far as Parliament has authorised it or, as in the case of domestic tribunals, the parties agree upon it.[4] The armed forces are subject to statutory codes of discipline as well as to the ordinary law of the land. Offences against the codes are triable at courts-martial.[5] The clergy are subject to ecclesiastical law enforced by the ecclesiastical courts.[6] Solicitors are subject to the

[1] See Statutory Instruments Act 1946; Chap. 42, *post*.
[2] P. 143, *post*.
[3] Pp. 614–5, *post*.
[4] *Lee* v. *Showmen's Guild*, [1952] 2 Q.B. 329, 341.
[5] Chap. 28.
[6] Chap. 34.

disciplinary powers of a statutory body composed of members of the profession, with a right of appeal to the High Court. The General Medical Council, which is also a body set up by statute, has power to try by a Disciplinary Committee, which sits with a legal assessor, members of the medical profession for unprofessional conduct and, as the one penalty which it may impose, has power to remove a doctor's name from the Medical Register. An appeal by the person whose conduct is investigated lies to the Judicial Committee of the Privy Council.[1] The General Dental Council has similar powers. Provided that there is no imposition of arbitrary punishments and that ordinary judicial methods are observed, "group law" is not inconsistent with the rule of law. Courts-martial follow legal forms and observe strict rules of procedure. One extension of "group law" is, however, open to criticism. Provision has been made by statute [2] to enable a substantial majority of persons engaged in a particular branch of agriculture to frame a scheme for the organisation of their industry which has the force of law and is binding on all producers in the industry concerned whether they voted for or against the proposal. Schemes provide for the establishment of marketing boards elected by the industry which are given powers of control over the production and marketing of a particular commodity. These powers include the power for the board itself to punish for a breach of the provisions of a scheme. Marketing boards have been criticised on the ground that they are in the position of prosecutor, judge and jury in their own case; that their chairmen are usually without legal qualifications; and that they do not follow normal rules of procedure and evidence. In 1939 a departmental committee recommended [3] that allegations of offences should be heard by small disciplinary committees presided over by an independent chairman with legal qualifications, and that provision should be made for an appeal from a disciplinary committee to the High Court on a point of law; both of these recommendations were accepted.[4]

Discretionary Authority

We must now consider discretionary authority as opposed to arbitrary power. If it is contrary to the rule of law that discretionary authority should be given to government departments or public officers, then the rule of law is inapplicable to any modern constitu-

[1] Medical Act 1956, ss. 32–39, and Fourth Schedule.
[2] Agricultural Marketing Acts 1931–33; *cf.* Herring Industry Acts 1935–44.
[3] *Report of the Departmental Committee on the Imposition of Penalties by Marketing Boards and Other Similar Bodies*, 1939, Cmd. 5980.
[4] Agricultural Marketing Act 1958, ss. 9 and 12.

tion. When Dicey wrote the first edition of his *Law of the Constitution*, the primary functions of the State were the preservation of law and order, defence and foreign relations. The exercise of discretionary authority in these spheres did not touch directly upon the citizen's daily life, nor did it frequently give rise to cases in the courts. To-day the State regulates the national life in multifarious ways. Discretionary authority in every sphere is inevitable. A citizen can still so regulate his conduct that he can in general foresee whether he is likely to appear as a defendant in a criminal court. A citizen cannot foresee how far the State will interfere with his freedom to enjoy his property. A piece of land may be compulsorily acquired for some vital national purpose not known at the time when the land was purchased. Discretion to determine when the time for compulsory acquisition has come must be given to someone —in this case the local authority. Again, a borough may have too many public houses and some must be closed as redundant. No one can with certainty foresee which houses the licensing justices will classify as redundant; it is a matter for their discretion exercised bonâ fide and in the public interest, but none the less it is a discretion which may result in injury to the existing rights of a licence-holder. It is this absence of foreseeability which has caused a critic to suggest that planning in the sense of control of private enterprise by the State is inconsistent with the rule of law.[1] His view is that the rule of law means that "government in all its actions is bound by rule, fixed and announced beforehand—rules which make it possible to foresee with fair certainty how the authority will use its concise powers in given circumstances, and to plan one's individual affairs on the basis of this knowledge." Such certainty is not attainable in modern conditions. The rule of law, however, demands that, so far as is practicable, where an individual plans his affairs reasonably with due regard for public welfare, he shall receive compensation, if he suffers damage as the result of a change in the law or the exercise of a discretionary authority granted in the public interest. To enable the citizen to foresee as far as possible the consequences of his actions and as a safeguard against arbitrary official conduct the grant of discretionary authority should prescribe as a minimum the general lines on which it should be exercised and fix precisely its limits. In this way the exercise of power can be challenged for excess or abuse in the courts. Discretionary power should not mean arbitrary power, *i.e.* power exercised by an agent responsible to none and subject to no control.

[1] *The Road to Serfdom*, by F. A. Hayek (Routledge), Chap. VI, *Planning and the Rule of Law*.

Powers of Public Officers

Dicey's second meaning of the rule of law also requires careful examination. "Equality before the law" does not mean that the powers of the private citizen are the same as the powers of the public official. Here it will suffice by way of illustration to mention that the powers of arrest possessed by police constables are, and always have been, somewhat wider than those of private citizens.[1] It is not contrary to the rule of law that special powers should be given to public officers to enable them to perform their public duties.[2] What the rule of law requires is that powers should be defined by law and that any abuse of power or other wrongful act by public officers should be subject to control by the courts in the same way as any wrongful act committed by a private citizen. The orders of the Crown or of a superior officer are no defence to a prosecution for a crime or a civil action in respect of a tortious injury.[3] This is what Dicey meant by "equality before the law." [4]

It is not inconsistent with the principle of "equality before the law" that, as we have seen, certain groups of the community, *e.g.* soldiers [5] and clergy [6] are subject to laws which do not affect the rest of the community, because those laws apply to all members of a particular calling. They are subject like others to the general law, though they incur additional liabilities as well as privileges by reason of their calling.

Qualifications to Dicey's Second Meaning

But the second meaning attributed by Dicey to the rule of law requires some qualification under current conditions. In the first place there remain, even after the operation of the Crown Proceedings Act 1947, a few privileges and immunities (as distinct from powers of government) which are open to public authorities and their officers. So far as judicial authorities enjoy protection from being sued,[7] their immunities are conferred solely to ensure the

[1] See *Christie* v. *Leachinsky*, [1947] A.C. 573; K. & L. 320, and Chap. 35, at pp. 482–4, *post*.

[2] Powers are sometimes conferred directly upon officials, but more frequently the powers exercised by officials are conferred either upon the Crown or upon Ministers or other public authorities. They are inevitably exercised through officials of the department or authority concerned.

[3] For the position of soldiers acting under orders, see Chap. 28.

[4] Dicey, *op. cit.*, p. 194.

[5] Chap. 28.

[6] Chap. 34.

[7] Chap. 23.

impartial administration of the law and these cannot be regarded as qualifications of the rule of law. So far as these privileges relate to the position of the Crown as litigant they are mainly concerned with the conditions of service in the armed forces. But the Crown also enjoys a wide privilege of refusing to disclose relevant documents or to answer relevant questions which arise in the course of litigation.[1]

Secondly, in common with all civilised States, the United Kingdom affords immunities to the persons and the property of other States, their rulers and diplomatic agents, in the form of exemption from process in the courts, but not from legal liability as such.[2] The significance of those immunities, which on the authority of the International Organisations (Immunities and Privileges) Act 1950 have been made capable of a wide extension in favour of recognised international agencies and their officers, lies not so much in the licence to commit offences with impunity on the part of respectable diplomats who can be certain of other sanctions in that event, as in their possible extension to the trading activities of modern States. In this connection it may be noted that, although the immunity from process extends to State property destined for the public use since it rests upon the dignity of national States,[3] the House of Lords has left open the question of its application to State-owned trading ships.[4]

In the third place there are one or two instances where internal political expediency has required the conferment of special immunities. The most important of these immunities is contained in the Trade Disputes Act 1906. Section 1 provides that an act done in combination by two or more persons shall, if done in contemplation or furtherance of a trade dispute, not be actionable unless the act, if done without such combination, would be actionable. This provision standing by itself is important if intimidation is actionable only if committed by more than one person. But the Act goes further and by s. 4 (1) prohibits the bringing of any action against a trade union in respect of a tort. This rule applies whether the trade union is sued in its own name or through its officers. It has always been impossible to bring an action against an unincorporated body as such, *e.g.* social clubs and many charitable institutions, though individual members or officers are, of course, liable for wrongful acts in which they take part,[5] but it was held (prior to the Trade Disputes Act 1906) that an action could be brought against trade

[1] Chap. 46. [2] *Dickinson* v. *Dei Solar*, [1930] 1 K.B. 376.
[3] *The Parlement Belge* (1880), 5 P.D. 197.
[4] *Companía Naviera Vascongado* v. *SS. Cristina*, [1938] A.C. 485; p. 275, *post*.
[5] *Hardie and Lane Ltd.* v. *Chiltern*, [1928] 1 K.B. 663.

unions, which were given special statutory privileges not enjoyed by other unincorporated associations but were also subject to important disabilities.[1] A trade union can, to a limited extent, sue and be sued on its contracts,[2] and an action for tort can be brought against individual members, unless acts normally wrongful are protected by some other statutory provisions, *e.g.* section 3 of the Trade Disputes Act 1906 which removes liability for inducing a breach of contract, provided the act done is in contemplation or furtherance of a trade dispute. This section was interpreted by the House of Lords in *Rookes* v. *Barnard*[3] as enabling individual officials of a trade union to be sued for the tort of intimidation notwithstanding the admitted existence of a trade dispute. The immunity conferred by section 1 was excluded because each individual acted tortiously in threatening to withdraw labour in breach of contract between the members of the union and their employer, the nationalised British Overseas Airways Corporation. The officials had induced the Corporation to dismiss a former member of the union. The Trade Disputes Act 1965 reversed this interpretation and restored the immunity.[4]

The immunity of trade unions is an immunity from all actions for tort and is not confined to acts done in contemplation or furtherance of a trade dispute.[5] The trustees of a union may be sued in relation to union property vested in them provided that the action does not relate to a tortious act committed by or on behalf of a union in contemplation or furtherance of a trade dispute. An action for a declaration[6] is sometimes available to obtain relief against a trade union or one of its members.

Specialised Courts

It is as true to-day as when Dicey wrote that officials are not exempted from the jurisdiction of the ordinary courts and that, as we have seen, the law of England knows nothing of exceptional offences

[1] *Taff Vale Railway* v. *Amalgamated Societies of Railway Servants*, [1901] A.C. 426; see Trade Union Act 1871 which provided that the purposes of a trade union should not be deemed unlawful merely because they might be in restraint of trade and gave to trade unions a limited legal capacity.

[2] Thus a member who has been expelled in breach of the rules of his union can recover damages from the union: *Bonsor* v. *Musicians' Union*, [1956] A.C. 104.

[3] [1964] A.C. 1129

[4] For the tort of intimidation see Winfield, *Torts*, 8th edn., pp. 546–51.

[5] *Vacher* v. *London Society of Compositors*, [1913] A.C. 107

[6] Pp. 671–3, *post*.

punished by extra-ordinary tribunals. There are no special courts for the trial of crimes against the State or of civil claims against officials. There are, however, as has been mentioned in discussing the separation of powers, many special courts for the decision of issues which may affect vitally the proprietary rights of citizens or their entitlement to benefits. Special tribunals appointed by Ministers, or even Ministers themselves acting through civil servants may determine questions of insurability; what compensation shall be paid for the compulsory acquisition of land; whether a dairy farmer may sell milk. How far is the existence of such special courts contrary to the rule of law? It is submitted that the rule of law is satisfied, provided that the tribunals are impartial and independent; that every man is heard before a decision is given affecting his rights; that reasons are given for decisions and reasonable regard is paid to precedent. It is inconsistent with the rule of law that a judicial issue (as distinct from a purely administrative decision) should be decided by a Minister interested in carrying out a policy affected by the issue.[1] Judicial decisions not referred to the ordinary courts should generally be entrusted to a tribunal with a chairman with legal qualifications, and on points of law there should be provision for an appeal to the courts, *e.g.* whether or not an individual comes within the definition of an insured person. The essential requirements are, however, that decisions should be impartial and that those who give them should not be liable to pressure from the Executive.

That these requirements are accepted as standards of what should be the normal procedure is important. It will be seen later that the number of tribunals is considerable and that their creation has been piecemeal. To expect absolute uniformity of procedure in such circumstances would be unreasonable, but there remains the need for vigilance particularly on the part of Parliament, lest the grant of statutory powers of adjudication be accompanied by a laxity of procedure so as to defeat the ends of justice under cover of administrative convenience.

Dicey's Third Meaning of the Rule of Law explained

Finally there must be examined the third meaning of the rule of law, viz. that private rights depend not upon a constitutional code, but on the ordinary law. Dicey is here referring not to the mass of rights derived from statutes, *e.g.* pensions, insurance, or free educa-

[1] The whole question of special tribunals is discussed in Chap. 47, and see Chap. 3 of W. A. Robson, *Justice and Administrative Law*, 3rd edn. (Stevens & Sons).

tion, but to the fundamental political freedoms—"the common law of the constitution "—freedom of the person, freedom of speech, freedom of association. The citizen whose fundamental rights are infringed may seek his remedy in the courts and will rely, not upon a constitutional guarantee, but on the ordinary law of the land. The right to personal freedom is protected by the writ of habeas corpus, the right of self-defence and the right to bring an action or a prosecution for wrongful arrest, assault or false imprisonment.[1] The writ of habeas corpus existed at common law, but was made effective by the Habeas Corpus Acts of 1679 and 1816. The right to arrest is governed partly by common law, partly by statutes, *e.g.* the Criminal Law Act 1967, s. 2. Freedom of speech means that a man may write or say what he pleases provided that his words are not treasonable, seditious, obscene or contrary to the law of defamation (libel and slander).[2] The law of libel is primarily common law, but various statutes give special privileges to the Press, *e.g.* the Defamation Act 1952 which extends the defence of qualified privileges to reports of proceedings of a large number of public bodies. The Public Order Act 1936 is an important part of the law of public meeting, but the basis of that law is the common law relating to trespass and nuisance.[3] The ordinary law may prove a more effective protection than constitutional guarantees contained in a written constitution which may be suspended in times of emergency.[4] "The unwritten constitution of England consists of a set of legal principles gradually evolved out of the decisions of our Courts of Justice in individual cases." [5] For this reason there must be watched jealously any encroachment upon the jurisdiction of the courts and any restriction on the subject's right of access to them. "By any such encroachment the principal safeguard provided by the constitution for the maintenance of the subject's rights is impaired."[5]

Modern Conception of the Rule of Law

The principle of the rule of law has since the end of the Second World War been a matter of universal discussion and endeavour to formulate the basic elements of the rule. So far from the principle being confined to the common law jurisdictions, the rule of law is now considered as a basic idea which can serve to unite lawyers of many differing systems, all of which aim at protecting the individual from arbitrary government. In this way the rule has come to be

[1] Chap. 35. [2] Chap. 36. [3] Chap. 38.

[4] Note the very limited effect of the so-called Habeas Corpus Suspension Acts; Dicey, *op. cit.*, pp. 229–32.

[5] M.P.R., p. 73.

identified with the concept of the rights of man. Most countries, outside the Communist world, accept that the rule has a positive content, no matter how much that content may differ in the various countries. If justice is to be done in the process of harmonising the opposing notions of individual liberty and public order, that is achieved ultimately but not exclusively by the ordinary courts. There are, however, other methods of making a government submit to the law, such as adjudication by administrative tribunals and action in the legislature at the instance of private members, and even in the case of action by subordinate authority by higher administrative control. As will be seen later,[1] all these methods play their part in securing the observance of the law and orderly government in the United Kingdom.

Universal Application

In one sense the acceptance of the rule of law as a feature of the positive law of the land is an international obligation which has been accepted by all States, including the United Kingdom, which are parties to the European Convention on Human Rights. This Convention has recognised that a citizen is entitled to redress against his own State if certain basic rights are violated. It is therefore a prerequisite to adherence to the Convention that the law of each State should contain provisions to maintain administration on lines which recognise its submission to that law.

With this in view the International Commission of Jurists, an international organisation with consultative status under the United Nations, has undertaken a series of studies which have been discussed at successive congresses in various parts of the world. A congress was held in Delhi in 1959, where representatives of no fewer than fifty-three countries, judges, lawyers and teachers of law, affirmed in a formal declaration their recognition that the rule of law is a dynamic concept which should be employed to safeguard and advance the political and civil rights of the individual in a free society.[2] Moreover, the congress for the first time associated the concept with the establishment of social, economic, educational and cultural conditions under which the individual could realise his legitimate aspirations and dignity. Admittedly this goes much further than the English practising lawyer or administrator would normally claim. But the congress, through four committees, reported on the practical safeguards required for the maintenance of the rule of law.

[1] Part III, *post*.

[2] Subsequent congresses have been held in West and East Africa, South America, and South-East Asia.

(1) Thus the committee which was concerned with the legislature and the rule of law emphasised that the legislature must not pass discriminatory laws in respect of individuals, classes of persons or minority groups, nor interfere with religious beliefs, nor place restrictions on freedom of the person, freedom of speech, or freedom of assembly. Such safeguards should, of course, depend for their efficacy on the constitutional arrangements within each State. So far as the United Kingdom is concerned, so long as the sovereignty of Parliament is accepted there can be no absolute legal guarantee, but the climate of political opinion can ensure the acceptance by the legislature of the requisite standards.

(2) Another committee examined the executive and the rule of law and recorded that the rule depended not only on the existence of adequate safeguards against abuse of power by the executive, but also on the existence of effective government capable of maintaining law and order and of ensuring social and economic conditions of life for the society. Safeguards against the abuse of executive power are familiar ideas to the English lawyer; the arrival of the Welfare State is proof of the recognition within the United Kingdom of the second requirement.

(3) More closely linked with the actual administration of the law were the findings of the third committee which reported on the criminal process and the rule of law. Here reference is to be found to existing provisions of English law which we have come to regard as axiomatic, such as the presumption of innocence; restrictions on power of arbitrary arrest and detention; provision of legal advice and the right to a fair hearing, including the calling of witnesses; the elimination of evidence collected by discreditable means; the requirement of public trial; the provision of a right of appeal.

(4) Finally, a fourth committee stressed the importance of an independent judiciary with security of tenure, free from legislative and executive interference. The committee examined certain considerations with regard to methods of appointment and removal for stated cause. They would extend these considerations to appointment of members of administrative tribunals. The ethics of legal practice were also examined, since the maintenance of the rule of law necessitates an independent legal profession.

Conclusion

The rule of law remains a principle of our constitution. It means the absence of arbitrary power; effective control of and proper publicity for delegated legislation, particularly when it imposes penalties;

that when discretionary power is granted the manner in which it is to be exercised should as far as is practicable be defined; that every man should be responsible to the ordinary law whether he be private citizen or public officer; that private rights should be determined by impartial and independent tribunals; and that fundamental private rights are safeguarded by the ordinary law of the land. If this be accepted, it is only necessary to contrast the state of affairs in the totalitarian States, with their apparatus of secret police and people's courts administering not law, but the orders of those who can dictate what is the people's will, in order to answer affirmatively the question —does the rule of law to-day remain a principle of the constitution? This does not mean that it is a fixed principle of law from which there can be no departure. Since Parliament is supreme, there is no legal sanction to prevent the enactment of a statute which violates the principle of the rule of law. The ultimate safeguard then is to be found in the acceptance of the principle as a guide to conduct by any political party which is in a position to influence the course of legislation.

This chapter opened with a short passage on the history of the rule of law in England. Even as late as Dicey's time, most English-speaking people assumed that such a rule was characteristic of constitutions in the common law world. To-day there is striking evidence of the universal interest which the subject invokes. Commissions of jurists, including even some from Communist States, have striven to formulate the elements of the rule. It is no longer a question of drawing an unfavourable comparison between the common law of England and the jurisprudence of European States. On the contrary, there is a striving to reach agreement on the institutions and procedures which are regarded as essential to protect the individual from arbitrary government. Nor has this inquiry been limited to the Western World. The rule of law has come to be regarded as the mark of a free society. Admittedly its content is different in different countries, nor is it to be secured exclusively through the ordinary courts. But everywhere it is identified with the liberty of the individual. It seeks to maintain a balance between the opposing notions of individual liberty and public order. In every State the problem arises of reconciling human rights with the requirements of public interest. Such harmonising can only be attained by the existence of independent courts which can hold the balance between citizen and State and compel Governments to conform to the law.

In this discussion of general principles of the constitution of the United Kingdom priority has been given to the supremacy of Parliament as the source of positive law. The reconciliation of the rule of law with such supremacy is achieved through an independent judiciary. But just as there is a difference between legal and political supremacy, so the rule of law may be explained not merely in terms of positive law and legal institutions but also as meaning a climate of legality which the states of Western Europe, North America and Australasia value so highly that they wish to preserve it.

CHAPTER SIX

CONVENTIONS OF THE CONSTITUTION

"Constitutional law creates obligations in the same way as private law, but its reactions as to persons possessed of political power are extra-legal: revolutions, active and passive resistance, the pressure of public opinion. The sanction is derived from the threat of these consequences."—Vinogradoff, *Outlines of Historical Jurisprudence*, Vol. I, p. 120 (Clarendon Press).

What is a Convention of the Constitution?

In discussing conventions as a source of constitutional law it is desirable first to examine the nature of the obligation and then to consider what compels obedience in the absence of the ordinary means of enforcing a legal rule through the orders of a court. The term "convention" has been accepted, largely through the influence of Dicey,[1] to describe this kind of obligation, whether it derives from custom, agreement or expediency. There is, however, no necessary connection with the notion of express agreement in the sense in which the term, convention, is used by international lawyers. Dicey discussed the rules for the exercise of the royal prerogative by Ministers of the Crown and those governing the relations between the two Houses of Parliament, rules based on custom or expediency rather than resulting from any formal agreement. Nowadays conventional rules have a wider ambit and govern (*inter alia*) the relations between the various member States of the British Commonwealth. Since the Statute of Westminster 1931 the rules governing the full competence of their Parliaments to legislate are statutory, though the Statute gave effect to much that had hitherto rested on agreement. But otherwise the relations between the various States including the United Kingdom are conventional, *i.e.* based on agreements reached at conferences which have been subsequently adopted by the various Governments.[2] More recently agreement has been reached at less formal conferences, usually at meetings attended by Prime Ministers

[1] *Law of the Constitution*, 10th ed., Chap. XIV and see Introduction, pp. cli to cxci.

[2] *Report of Conference on Operation of Dominion Legislation*, 1930, pp. 19, 20, Cmd. 3479.

or Ministers for Finance or External Affairs.[1] With the attainment of independence over most of the former British Empire, the scope for agreed action has become less and it is improbable that new conventions will be formulated.

Inadequacy of Legal Rules

As well in the sphere of high policy as in the work of routine administration modern government demands a high degree of flexibility. In the case of an enacted constitution changes can be achieved by constitutional amendment, but amendment is normally difficult to procure, and in practice many changes are brought about without formal modification. In this process interpretation by the courts of the written law plays its part, though not always in the direction of adapting the law to present needs, but evolution by conventional rules is equally important. In the United Kingdom the legal framework of executive government has been adapted to other ends than those which it formerly served without any change in the law, not by judicial interpretation, for which opportunity seldom occurs where there is no enacted constitution, but by the growth of conventional rules. In this way has the Executive, the servant in law of the Crown, became subject to Parliament and through the House of Commons to the electorate, its political overlord. The whole conception of constitutional monarchy was thus developed without destroying the legal powers of the Crown, other than those doubtfully claimed by the Stuarts. Again parliamentary government means not merely that there is a legislature with capacity to enact all laws, but that co-operation between Ministers and Parliament is secured by rules which are largely conventional and are enforced by political rather than legal sanctions. Fear of loss of office or of reputation is the ultimate sanction which causes Ministers to observe this part of constitutional law, rather than fine or imprisonment. Equally, expectation of office and regard for their political reputations ensure observance on the part of the Opposition.

Scope of Conventions

"Conventions are rules for determining the mode in which the discretionary powers of the Crown (or of Ministers as servants of the Crown) ought to be exercised." [2] So wrote Dicey eighty-five years ago. He was concerned to establish that conventions were "intended to secure the ultimate supremacy of the electorate as the true political

[1] *E.g.* in 1965 the Agreed Memorandum on the Commonwealth Secretariat (Cmnd. 2713).

[2] Dicey, *op. cit.*, pp. 422–3. See Introduction, 10th edn., pp. cli–clvii.

sovereign of the state." He was therefore mainly concerned with rules governing the use of the prerogative. The complexity of modern government has caused innumerable statutory duties to be entrusted to the Executive. The older powers are still exercised in the name of the Queen, though convention entrusts them to Ministers. Modern statutes recognise the convention and confer the powers expressly on individual Ministers in many, but not in all cases. When Parliament gives a Minister discretionary power, that power is exercised by him as a matter of law, but it will none the less be a discretionary power exercised on behalf of the Crown. The conventions which impose individual and collective responsibility upon Ministers operate to secure that in the exercise of legal powers conferred upon him by statute a Minister shall be as responsible to Parliament as if he were exercising a prerogative power which is in law the sole responsibility of the Crown. But it is not only in the sphere of the discretionary powers of the Executive that conventions are an important source of constitutional law, and a fuller examination of their contents and application is required.

In the pages which follow reference will be made to some of the more important conventions which govern the exercise of her powers by the Sovereign, the working of cabinet government, with particular reference to ministerial responsibility to Parliament, the relationship between a Minister and the civil servants in his department, the relationship between the two Houses of Parliament, and finally, Commonwealth relations. It is important to emphasise that conventions operate not merely in these specific spheres but over the whole range of governmental activity. There is what has been called "the climate of opinion" which influences the working of our constitution to an extent which no legal text-book can hope fully to describe. It may, however, be convenient at this point to refer to other chapters in the book where constitutional law and convention intermingle. Thus in Chapter 9, A. there will be found reference to the importance of Her Majesty's Opposition in Parliament, which has been described as proof of the British genius for inventing political machinery. This machinery in no way depends on the sanction of law. In the same chapter is discussed the interaction between convention and law which culminated in the enactment of the Parliament Act 1911 without affecting some of the still operative conventional rules such as that which prohibits the Lords from amending a financial provision in a Bill. Turning to the Executive, the attempt to discuss the duties of the Sovereign in Chapter 11 is concerned almost exclusively with constitutional propriety rather than law. The fuller discussion of cabinet government which follows in Chapters 13 and 14 is concerned solely with conventional rules. The civil service too (Chapter 16) is regulated as much by practices prescribed by the Treasury as by the law of the civil service contained in Orders in Council. In the novel sphere of the public boards, which include the nationalised agencies, there are signs that these creations of statute are developing conventional practices. It is, therefore, necessary to discuss in Chapter 21 how far the exercise of the ministerial power to give directions to a statutory corporation which is associated with his department can be tempered in practice by an agreed compromise between the Minister and the board.

The chapters on the Judiciary do not disclose any important conventions. Nevertheless tradition plays an all-important part in the administration of justice, and it would be difficult to justify by reference to legal authority many of the established customs of Bench and Bar. The composition of the House of Lords when sitting as a final court of appeal is governed by convention so far as the exclusion of lay peers is concerned. Although Commonwealth relations are only dealt with briefly in Chapter 32, the part played by conventions in developing the self-governing status of what are now the independent States of the Commonwealth will be obvious.

The Sovereign; choice of Prime Minister

The Queen acts upon the advice of her Ministers in each of her realms in the Commonwealth. At home she receives advice from United Kingdom Ministers; elsewhere her Governors-General, to whom are entrusted most of her powers, act on the advice of the Ministers who form the Cabinet of each State. But there are some matters which fall to be determined by the exercise of her independent judgment, and in particular the appointment of a Prime Minister,[1] and in some circumstances the dissolution of Parliament. There are conventional rules which limit her range of choice of a new Prime Minister. The support of the party or coalition which may be expected to command a majority in the House of Commons is a condition precedent to acceptance of the office. It is perhaps safe to say that membership of the House of Commons is another. At all events no peer has held the office since Lord Salisbury resigned in 1902, and the choice of Mr. Baldwin (as he then was) in preference to Lord Curzon in 1923 was regarded by some as establishing that no peer could again accept the office, so long as the House of Lords is constituted as at present. When it became

[1] Sir Ivor Jennings, *Cabinet Government*, Chap. II, where all the precedents are discussed. The Sovereign may, of course, seek advice, but it is not ministerial advice in the constitutional sense. The choice is the personal responsibility of the Sovereign.

clear in May 1940 that a National Coalition Government could not be formed by the Prime Minister in office (Mr. Neville Chamberlain), it is on record that King George VI's first and personal preference was Lord Halifax.[1] The King's diary shows that he suggested the name of Lord Halifax to the outgoing Prime Minister and considered that his peerage should be placed in abeyance for the time being. His biographer states that none of those who had previously expressed a preference for Lord Halifax as Prime Minister, including Mr. Chamberlain, saw any constitutional objection to a Prime Minister in the House of Lords, and that Lord Halifax's own doubts on accepting the Premiership did not include this. In the event the choice fell upon Mr. Winston Churchill. The recent enactment of the Peerage Act 1963 [2] enabled the Earl of Home to accept appointment after informing the Queen of his intention to renounce his peerages and seek immediate election to the Commons.

The practice of the Sovereign first consulting the leader of the Opposition when a Government tenders its resignation on defeat in the Commons is well established and ensures the impartial position in politics which a constitutional monarchy should occupy. Yet the ultimate decision is the personal responsibility of the Sovereign, and in the task of selection precedent is not conclusive, and therefore the conventions lack the binding force which they possess in other fields. This does not mean that they can normally be disregarded, but that unforeseen circumstances may deprive them of their force on a particular occasion.

As a result however of these precedents the position of the Sovereign seems clear. At all events it stood the test to which it was subjected in 1963 when on the resignation of Mr. Harold Macmillan under stress of an urgent operation, the Conservative Party were deprived of their leader at the same time as the Queen accepted the resignation of her Prime Minister. To quote a leading authority: [3]

> "No one is in a position to give her (the Queen) advice in the constitutional sense that she must follow it. She can, either directly or through her Private Secretary, whose role is very important on these occasions, seek advice in the ordinary sense of the word from such persons as she thinks fit. She could seek none, but this would be unlikely to happen today. In the case of a Labour Prime Minister resigning, the Queen's effective choice would be limited to his elected

[1] Sir Harold Nicolson, *George V*, pp. 377 ff.; Sir John Wheeler-Bennett, *George VI*, pp. 443–4; *cf.* Sir Winston Churchill, *The Second World War*, Vol. I, at pp. 523–4. for an account of Lord Halifax's views on this point.

[2] P. 102, *post*.

[3] Robert Blake, Feature Article, *The Times*, 19 October, 1963.

> successor as party leader. When the Conservatives are in power she will endeavour to find the person whom the party wants by less formal methods. Among those consulted will almost certainly be the retiring Prime Minister, but his advice, however weighty, cannot be binding. The decision is in the end that of the Monarch, and the Monarch alone."

In 1945 Mr. Churchill felt it to be his duty to the Sovereign to safeguard the latter against unforeseen circumstances, for it is on record that he advised King George VI to appoint Mr. Anthony Eden, the Foreign Secretary, to succeed him in the event of his death, and further, before he and Eden left the country for a conference in the Crimea, he wrote a letter to the King advising that Sir John Anderson (later Lord Waverley) be offered the Premiership in the event of both Churchill and Eden being killed.[1]

Dissolution of Parliament

The other important personal prerogative of the Sovereign is the power to grant to a Prime Minister a dissolution of Parliament. In this, as in other matters, the Sovereign will normally accept the advice of the Prime Minister since to refuse would be tantamount to dismissal and involve the Sovereign in the political controversy which inevitably follows the resignation of a Ministry. There can never be any justification for the dismissal against the advice of the Prime Minister of a Ministry which commands a majority in the House of Commons. A Prime Minister is entitled to choose his own time within the statutory five-year limit prescribed by the Parliament Act 1911 for testing whether his majority in the House of Commons still reflects the will of the electorate. No Sovereign could constitutionally refuse to grant him a dissolution of Parliament at the time of his choice. Indeed, it is doubtful if the Sovereign is free to seek advice on such an issue from anybody other than the Prime Minister. Admittedly, when a minority Government holds office the position is more complicated, but here again it is for the Prime Minister rather than for the Sovereign to choose the occasion for appealing to the electorate. Only if a break up of the main political parties took place could the personal discretion of the Sovereign become the paramount consideration. There are, however, circumstances when a Sovereign may be free to seek informal advice against that of the Prime Minister. If the Sovereign can be satisfied that (1) an existing Parliament is still vital and capable of doing its job, (2) a general election would be detrimental to the national economy, more particularly if it followed closely on the last election, and (3) he could rely on finding another Prime Minister who was willing

[1] *George VI*, pp. 544–46.

to carry on his Government for a reasonable period with a working majority, the Sovereign could constitutionally refuse to grant a dissolution to the Prime Minister in office. It will be seldom that all these conditions can be satisfied. Particularly dangerous to a constitutional Sovereign is the situation which would arise if having refused a dissolution to the outgoing Prime Minister he was faced by an early request from his successor for a general election. Refusal might be justified if there was general agreement inside and outside the House of Commons that a general election should be delayed and clearly it would be improper for a Prime Minister to rely on defeat on a snap vote to justify an election. This prerogative is one which in Commonwealth States is delegated to the Governor-General (except, of course, in the republican States). It is perhaps more difficult for such an officer to maintain a position of political impartiality. Moreover, it is in the Commonwealth where in most cases the numbers in Parliament are much smaller than in Westminster that there is more likely to be doubt about reliance on an incoming Prime Minister carrying on his Government without a general election. In 1939 all the three conditions were satisfied when the Governor-General of South Africa refused a dissolution to his Prime Minister. But in Canada in 1926, when all the conditions appeared to be satisfied, the third quickly proved not to be so.[1]

The Cabinet

A number of the conventional understandings which Dicey, quoting from Freeman's *Growth of the English Constitution*, cited as belonging to "the code by which public life in England is (or is supposed) to be governed" are closely connected with the prerogative of dissolution which has just been mentioned.[2] For example, "a Cabinet when outvoted on any vital question may appeal once to the country by means of a dissolution," or "If an appeal to the electors goes against a Ministry, they are bound to retire from office and have no right to dissolve Parliament a second time." There is, however, one convention upon which rests the whole doctrine of ministerial responsibility—"The Cabinet are responsible to Parliament as a body for the general conduct of affairs," as Freeman put it. It is impossible to exaggerate the importance of understanding the consequences of this rule, which is the foundation of parliamentary government as it is known throughout the British Commonwealth.

[1] See J. W. Wheeler-Bennett, *George VI*, at p. 775, reproducing an anonymous letter to *The Times* of 2 May, 1950, attributed to a former Private Secretary to His Majesty.

[2] Dicey, *op. cit.*, 10th edn., p. 416.

For this reason it is selected as the single illustration of the operation of conventions in relation to Cabinet government.

Meaning of Ministerial Responsibility

Ministerial responsibility has for the constitutional lawyer two distinct meanings, the one strictly legal, the other, which is under consideration here, purely conventional in the sense that it is no part of the law as applied by the courts. It is as well first to explain the former meaning, which is an integral part of the law. Holders of office under the Crown (and Ministers all have this status) are personally liable in law for their acts. Since convention requires that a Minister shall be responsible for an act of the Crown, every such act must be done through a Minister whose Department may under the Crown Proceedings Act 1947 be sued in respect of it if an issue of tort or breach of contract should arise. Acts requiring the Sovereign's participation must be authenticated by a seal for the custody of which a particular Minister is responsible or be recorded in documents bearing the counter-signature of a Minister. The use of the various seals on forms for recording the royal assent is regulated partly by statute and partly by custom.[1] When it is said that Ministers are personally liable in law for their acts, this means that they are responsible for acts which they commit or sanction in their individual capacity. In early times liability was confined to officers of low status. Impeachment was used against the holders of the great State offices, though for a while under the Tudors it fell into disuse, as responsibility was regarded as being solely to the King and not to the law. By the end of the seventeenth century it was firmly established that no official, high or low, could plead the orders of the Sovereign when charged with a breach of the law. The rule of responsibility to the law has not been successfully challenged since the Act of Settlement provided that a royal pardon could not be pleaded in bar of an impeachment *i.e.* to prevent a person being brought to trial by this procedure. The Sovereign can do no wrong, but those who commit wrongs in the course of executing the Sovereign's business are personally liable and since 1948 can make the Crown, which is represented for this purpose by a Department or the Attorney-General [2] responsible in law for illegal acts or omissions.

Development of Collective Responsibility

To return to the conventional meaning of ministerial responsibility, it is not the fear of legal liability, but the desire to operate the

[1] Anson, *op. cit.*, 4th edn., Vol. II, Part I, pp. 62–72.
[2] See Crown Proceedings Act 1947, s. 17.

machinery of government on constitutional lines which influences Ministers in their conduct of affairs and their relationship with Parliament. Accordingly there has been evolved since 1688 the rule of collective responsibility which rests upon convention alone. During the greater part of the eighteenth century the Cabinet was still a body of holders of high office whose relationship with one another was ill defined, and thus the body as a whole was not responsible to Parliament. The Government was the King's Government in fact as well as in name, and the King acted on the advice of individual Ministers. The advice tendered by a Minister might, or might not, agree with that acceptable to his nominal colleagues, some of whom were seldom, if ever, consulted by their Sovereign. Apart from the relatively homogeneous Ministries under Walpole's pre-eminent leadership Cabinets were formed of different groups with many different aims. This made collective responsibility impracticable. Moreover, the King sometimes consulted those who were out of office without the prior approval of his Ministers. Eventually the Representation of the People Act 1832 (the great Reform Bill), brought realisation that for the future the Executive must hold the same political views as the majority in Parliament. The support of Parliament could no longer be secured by the expedients of sinecure offices, pensions, the gift of seats in rotten boroughs, and such-like devices which had not shocked eighteenth-century political morality. The Cabinet, all its members united by party ties, became the definite link between the King and Parliament and so acquired the whole control over the direction of public affairs. Thus collective responsibility developed later than the political responsibility of individual Ministers. Just as it became recognised that a single Minister could not retain office against the will of Parliament, so later it became clear that all Ministers must stand or fall together in Parliament, if the Government was to be carried on as a unity rather than by a number of advisers of the Sovereign acting separately.

What Collective Responsibility involves

By the middle of the nineteenth century collective responsibility as it is understood to-day, was firmly established. Lord Salisbury said in 1878: [1]

> For all that passes in Cabinet every member of it who does not resign is absolutely and irretrievably responsible and has no right afterwards to say that he agreed in one case to a compromise, while in another he was persuaded by his colleagues. . . . It is only on the principle that absolute responsibility is undertaken by every member of the Cabinet, who, after a decision is arrived at, remains a member

[1] *Life of Robert, Marquis of Salisbury*, Vol. II, pp. 219–20.

of it, that the joint responsibility of Ministers to Parliament can be upheld and one of the most essential principles of parliamentary responsibility established.

This statement explains why it is essential to draw the veil of secrecy over all that passes in Cabinet even in times when the requirements of security do not necessarily impose the ban of silence. It is impossible to preserve a united front, if disclosures are permitted of differences which have emerged in arriving at a decision. The fate of the minority of Ministers on the occasion of the single departure from the rule of unanimity reinforces its validity. In 1932 a coalition Cabinet issued an announcement to the effect that they had agreed to differ over the tariff issue, while remaining united on all other vital matters of national policy. The dissenting Ministers were given leave to oppose in Parliament the majority view by speech and by vote. The convention of Cabinet unanimity was, however, reinforced when those Ministers decided a few months later to resign on the cognate issue of imperial preference.[1]

Collective responsibility does not require that every Cabinet Minister must take an active part in the formulation of policy, nor that his presence in the Cabinet room is essential whenever a decision is taken. His obligations may be passive rather than active when the decision does not relate to matters falling within his own sphere of administrative responsibility. He must, however, be informed beforehand of what the proposal is and have an opportunity of voicing his doubts and objections. The size of modern Cabinets (in peace time) would alone seem to preclude active participation by each Minister in forming conclusions. A body of some twenty or more is too large for effective committee work, but in the nature of things Ministers in Cabinet are, or should be, concerned more with decisions of principle rather than detail.[2] Collective responsibility does, however, mean that a Cabinet Minister, and his Parliamentary Secretary, must vote with the Government in Parliament and, if necessary, be prepared to defend its policy. Neither in Parliament nor outside can a Minister be heard to say that he is in disagreement with a Cabinet decision, or for that matter with a decision of a colleague taken without reference to the Cabinet.

Individual Responsibility

The individual responsibility of a Minister to Parliament is more positive in character. Each in his own sphere bears the burden of

[1] Jennings, *Cabinet Government*, pp. 260–62; Dicey, *op. cit.*, Introduction, pp. clxxxix–cxc.

[2] The number was 23 both before and after the change of Government in 1964. It fell to 21 in 1969.

speaking and acting for the Government. When a Minister announces that Her Majesty's Government have decided that they are prepared to take a certain course of action, it does not follow that the decision has been referred to the Cabinet. No doubt it would have been on an important issue of policy; but if the decision relates exclusively to the sphere for which the Minister is responsible, it must be at his discretion whom he chooses to consult beforehand; it is in the exercise of that discretion that he may decide to act without previous reference to his Cabinet colleagues. Nowadays so complex are results of governmental action that it is safe to assume that the practice of prior inter-departmental consultation is firmly established at all levels, and the experience of war should serve to ensure that there is no relapse into departmental isolationism. Moreover a Minister knows that he will ultimately have to rely upon the support of his Cabinet colleagues if political criticism becomes vocal, and he must temper his decisions by reference to that consideration.

Ministers and the Civil Service

While collective responsibility ensures that the Queen's Government presents a united front to Parliament, individual responsibility in its political meaning ensures that for every act or neglect of his department a Minister must answer. Hence the rule of anonymity in the Civil Service is important. For what an unnamed official does, or does not do, his Minister alone must answer in Parliament and the official, who can not be heard in his own defence, is therefore protected from attack. This positive liability of a Minister is essential to the performance by Parliament, and more particularly by the House of Commons, of its rôle of critic of the Executive. No Minister can shield himself by blaming his official. "It would be new and dangerous constitutional doctrine if Ministers of the Crown could excuse the failure of their policies by turning upon the experts whose advice they have taken or upon the agents whom they have employed." [1]

Ministerial responsibility to Parliament was debated in the House of Commons in 1954. A public enquiry conducted by a Queen's Counsel had been ordered by the Minister of Agriculture and Fisheries to enquire into the circumstances of the disposal of land which was no longer needed for the purpose for which it had been acquired by the State.[2] The enquiry had resulted in the exposure of

[1] *The Times*, Leading Article, 21 November, 1949. In 1963 the Prime Minister named a former Secretary to the Cabinet as responsible for not informing him of a warning given in the interests of State security as to private conduct which he had thought fit to give to a Minister of Cabinet rank.

[2] *Crichel Down Enquiry*, Cmd. 9176, 1954.

a number of civil servants to severe public criticism. Speaking in the debate the Home Secretary reaffirmed that a civil servant is wholly and directly responsible to his Minister and can be dismissed at any time by the Minister—a "power none the less real because it is seldom used." He went on to give a number of categories where differing considerations apply:

(1) A Minister must protect a civil servant who has carried out his explicit order.

(2) Equally a Minister must defend a civil servant who acts properly in accordance with the policy laid down by the Minister.

(3) "Where an official makes a mistake or causes some delay, but not on an important issue of policy and not where a claim to individual rights is seriously involved, the Minister acknowledges the mistake and he accepts the responsibility although he is not personally involved. He states that he will take corrective action in the Department."

(4) "Where action has been taken by a civil servant of which the Minister disapproves and has no previous knowledge, and the conduct of the official is reprehensible, there is no obligation on a Minister to endorse what he believes to be wrong or to defend what are clearly shown to be errors of his officers." He remains, however, "constitutionally responsible to Parliament for the fact that something has gone wrong," but this does not affect his power to control and discipline his staff.[1]

Nor can a Minister throw responsibility on a ministerial colleague, once it is established that the matter under consideration is the responsibility of his own department. This responsibility under modern conditions may not be easy to determine, and there are many arguments in favour of rationalising the machinery of government, so that the lines of demarcation of functions, and therefore of responsibility, may be more clearly marked. Those who see virtue in associating standing committees of Parliament with the work of government departments are faced with the argument that the existence of such committees, even though in theory their functions are advisory and not executive, detracts from ministerial responsibility and hinders the exercise of criticism in Parliament itself.[2]

Ministerial Responsibility in War

Thus far the doctrine of ministerial responsibility has been discussed without reference to what has happened twice in the present century to meet the exigencies of the two World Wars. The institution late in 1916 and again at the outbreak of war in 1939 of a War

[1] 530 H.C. Deb., cols. 1289 ff.

[2] See also the effect of the creation of a Parliamentary Commission for Administration on ministerial responsibilities; Chap. 47, *post*.

Cabinet has raised some interesting questions. What has been said about collective responsibility has assumed the existence of a body of Ministers all sharing equally, whether their number be twelve or twenty-four, responsibility for the direction of public affairs and acting together under the stimulus of an effective Opposition in Parliament. What happens then to the doctrine when the Cabinet consists of some five to nine senior Ministers, while other Ministers (including in the First World War all the Ministers with departmental responsibilities, except the Chancellor of the Exchequer) have no seat in the Cabinet, though they are invited to attend when matters affecting their departments are considered? On both occasions the normal number of departmental Ministers was considerably increased by the necessity for setting up new departments arising out of the demands of war.

On one view it can be maintained that only the members of a War Cabinet are collectively responsible, together with such other Ministers as may have been called into consultation for a particular decision. Against this it may be said that the Ministers who are not members of the War Cabinet have delegated for the time being the power to take decisions to their colleagues in the War Cabinet and thereby pledged themselves to stand or fall by what the Cabinet decides, although they may have had no right or opportunity of voicing their point of view beforehand.

The question is perhaps of academic interest only. In war a Government must take rapid decisions. A team of as many as forty Ministers, some of them stationed abroad, others chosen not on account of political experience, but by reason of business capacity for a war job entrusted to a highly specialised department, could not conceivably function as a supreme executive sitting together on every occasion. Unity is secured by the urgency of the danger; political differences may be suppressed for the time being. The absence of regular opposition in Parliament reduces to a minimum the chances of effective challenge. In these circumstances it is unlikely that a clear definition of the position of Ministers outside the War Cabinet can emerge. The question would only become one of practical importance if and when a similar type of Cabinet held office in times when the parties were divided on traditional lines.

Ministers not in the Cabinet

Despite the return to larger Cabinets in 1945 there remains the category of senior Ministers, some of them with full departmental responsibilities, who are not in the Cabinet, others who are Ministers of State to assist the Minister or Secretary of State in charge of a department. In 1960 they numbered sixteen against the nineteen in the Cabinet and under modern conditions no substantial reduction seems probable. In 1964 the number rose to twenty-eight. Since Ministers who are not in the Cabinet have been so classified on appointment, it cannot be said that they have agreed to delegating their authority to Cabinet colleagues It is clear that they are bound by Cabinet decisions and must refrain from criticising or opposing them in public. But on matters outside their departmental responsibilities they are not consulted in advance. It may be said that such Ministers share the consequences of collective responsibility, but that their actual responsibility is not the same. Their rôle is negative, that of the Cabinet is positive.

The Civil Service

It is the law that all servants of the Crown can be dismissed at the pleasure of the Crown. This rule is only enforced against civil servants in cases of misconduct or gross inefficiency, for convention requires that civil servants shall remain in office, despite a change of Government. There is thus ensured continuity in the operation of the administrative machine, and without it something like chaos might follow with each change of Ministry. Ministers, who so far as their legal status is concerned are, like civil servants, servants of the Crown, may in the last resort be dismissed on political grounds, though they normally go out of office only on the Prime Minister tendering his resignation, unless they resign on account of a difference of opinion with their colleagues. Political considerations do not justify the dismissal of a civil servant, but such a step, though unconstitutional, would undoubtedly be legal. Here then is an example of the way in which a convention can restrict the operation of a rule of law. It is a corollary of this convention that any civil servant who, however remotely, may be regarded as the agent of (or in contact with) a Minister must abstain from active participation in politics, lest his loyalty to his party should bring him into conflict with his loyalty to his Minister.[1]

The rules which govern the conduct of a civil servant do not often come before the courts, since in a matter which is at the discretion of the Crown the aggrieved civil servant has no legal remedy. They are to be found in Treasury Minutes. The contents of these rules closely resemble rules of law proper and are enforced as such by the

[1] Chap. 16, for a discussion of the extent to which political activity may be allowed. Since 1947 a limited number of civil servants have been removed or transferred on account of membership of the Communist party, to ensure that they do not have access to confidential State papers.

heads of departments, but their character is largely determined by the need for securing continuity of administration and the exclusion of individual participation in political activity. The enforcement of such rules is not a matter for the courts, as it is the prerogative of the Crown to regulate the conditions upon which its servants are employed. There are, however, some rules relating to Crown servants which derive from statute law, for example, disqualification from sitting in the House of Commons rests upon the House of Commons Disqualification Act 1957.[1] Resignation on adoption as a parliamentary candidate is required by an Order in Council.[2]

Parliament

The law and custom of Parliament may be said in some respects to occupy a position midway between law, in the narrower sense of rules applied by the courts, and convention. Some part of the law of Parliament is contained in statutes; for example, the composition of the House of Commons is determined by the Representation of the People Acts; the powers of the House of Lords to reject Bills passed by the Commons are limited by the Parliament Acts 1911 and 1949. Another part is contained in decisions of the courts, though it does not follow that Parliament will accept these as conclusive; under this head comes a parliamentary privilege when it is in conflict with the legal rights of the subject.[3] Much else, including all matters relating exclusively to internal procedure and discipline of members, is determined by each House for itself. Under this heading comes the rule which excludes peers who have no judicial qualifications from sitting in the House of Lords to determine appeals from the courts. This is purely conventional. The Standing Orders of the House of Commons are determined by the House itself. In form they are not readily distinguishable from a code of law, but no judge is concerned with their enforcement. Standing Orders provide for the course of legislation, for rules of debate, for safeguarding the rights of the House, especially with regard to supplies (money) and taxation. They are not comprehensive; other matters of ordering proceedings can only be ascertained by reference to precedents recorded in the Journals of the House. Standing Orders embody much that is important to the constitutional lawyer, such as the principle that the expenditure of public funds can only be proposed by a Minister of the Crown, a provision which, as has happened elsewhere in the Commonwealth, would be included in a written constitution.

[1] P. 112, *post.*
[2] Servants of the Crown (Parliamentary Candidature) Order 1960.
[3] Chap. 10.

Privilege and Prerogative

If the narrow view of the distinction between law and convention be accepted, namely that law is limited to those rules which are applied by the courts, much of the law and custom of Parliament is properly included under conventions. But in so far as Parliament itself enforces this law and custom by requiring compliance with its procedural code and maintaining its privileges, the distinction is a thin one. Perhaps the answer is to be found in comparing the privileges of Parliament with the royal prerogative since both confer rights and grant immunities. There are many matters of prerogative, such as the conduct of foreign affairs, the dissolution of Parliament (otherwise than by efflux of time), the disposition of the Armed Forces, which cannot be challenged in the courts. So too with privilege, and generally with the unwritten law of Parliament, the evidence of what is part of the ancient law of Parliament is only to be found in declarations made by that body, and not in decisions of the courts. As will be seen later,[1] the subject of parliamentary privileges lies in a field where the relations between the House of Commons and the courts are not yet clearly determined.

Commonwealth Relations

There is still room for conventions in the rules and practices which influence and govern relations between the members of the Commonwealth. There is a prevalent but erroneous belief that the Statute of Westminster removed dominion status from the realm of convention to that of law. The Statute, however, conferred legal autonomy only in the exercise of the legislative function. It marked the end of a long period of evolution of inter-imperial relations by means of conventions which still apply in the executive sphere of government. Two well-established conventions are recited in the preamble to the Statute and section four, which prohibits the Parliament of the United Kingdom from legislating for another State within the Commonwealth without its express request and consent, merely gives legal sanction to an existing convention. This again serves to emphasise how slender may be the distinction between convention and law.[2]

It is in this field that conventions derive from express agreements

[1] Chap. 10; and see especially May, *Parliamentary Practice*, 17th edn., Chap. IX.

[2] For an example of conventions being enacted as law and yet excluded from enforcement by action in the courts, see s. 4 (2) of Ceylon Constitution 1947 cited in 65 L.Q.R. 469 in Sir Ivor Jennings' article, *The Making of a Dominion Constitution*. The conventions are those relating to the exercise of the powers of the Crown on ministerial advice.

which in the past have been reached at periodic meetings of Imperial Conferences. But it must be emphasised that such agreements have no sanction behind them, and indeed there have been occasions when no convention has resulted simply because one or other of the Governments represented at a conference has gone out of office before any step had been taken to implement the decisions reached which have not proved acceptable to its successor. In place of such conferences, the recent practice has been to hold meetings of Prime Ministers or of other Ministers concerned with common problems, such as finance and external affairs. Their deliberations help to fix policy, but are less likely to result in new conventions.

Local Government

Lastly, even in the field of local government, practices which are without strict legal authority are regularly followed and accordingly qualify for description as conventions. The absence of anything which corresponds closely to Cabinet government inevitably narrows the scope. There is, however, at least one clear example. When negotiating for the acquisition or sale of land local authorities employ the District Valuer of the Commissioners of Inland Revenue as an independent valuer. This practice has been more or less forced upon local authorities because they are disabled from entering into such a transaction or from borrowing money to finance it without the consent of the appropriate Minister.[1] To this perhaps may be added the practice of adopting departmental models for local byelaws and regulations. This practice, which ensures the necessary ministerial consent, contradicts the autonomy of the local authority which the byelaw-making power confers.

Why Conventions are observed

Dicey concluded that the reason why conventions are observed was that a breach would almost immediately bring the offender into conflict with the courts and the law of the land.[2] Other writers find the answer less easy and criticise Dicey's reasoning, even in its application to the limited field of conventions governing the use of the royal prerogative. Sir Ivor Jennings in particular makes the point,[3] that the emphasis upon the courts is misplaced, because much modern law is created by statute and enforced by administrative authority. The same writer points out that the absence of a written constitution is responsible for the difficulty of dividing law and convention by a

[1] E. S. Walker, *Conventions in Local Government*, 123 J.P. 234.
[2] Dicey, *op. cit.*, pp. 445–6; Introduction, pp. clxxix *et seq.*
[3] See *The Law and the Constitution*, 5th edn., Chap. III, sect. 2.

clear line which would separate rules within and without the constitution. With us all institutions of government have been established by custom or convention or by the authority of an institution so established, and this is the case with Parliament itself. He argues that, since this is so, the explanation that a breach of convention may result in a breach of the law is unacceptable.

Effective Sanction

It was Dicey's argument that a breach of the law would usually follow from disregard of the usages by which ministerial responsibility to the House of Commons is maintained, but he was also mindful of political sanctions, as evidenced by his discussion of the so-called external limitations upon the sovereignty of Parliament. Breach of a convention in any case is far more likely to lead to political action than to proceedings in court being brought against the offender. The refusal of a defeated Ministry to resign, though ultimately it could lead to administrative action which Parliament would refuse to sanction or condone and thus lead to illegal acts for which the courts would give redress, would have much more rapid repercussions in the political field. It may safely be said that the effective sanction against defaulting Ministers is to be found in political censure rather than the force of the law as an immediate consequence.

Conclusion

It is of more importance to consider the motive which induces obedience in each field where conventions operate. The Sovereign is guided in the exercise of personal prerogatives by a recognition of the tradition of impartiality which has grown up round the throne and is the real safeguard to ensure a continuance of the monarchy. Ministers fear lest they may be compelled to resign by force of public opinion manifested by an adverse vote at the polls, or, even apart from an election, by estranging some or all of their supporters in the House of Commons. They may also be credited with the desire to govern in accordance with the traditions of representative government. There is in fact a standard of political authority which commands obedience. Those who govern submit to the judgment of public opinion, which they may seek to influence, but cannot ultimately control.

PART I: General Constitutional Law

PARLIAMENT

Parliament, 2nd edn., by Sir Ivor Jennings (Cambridge University Press).
An Introduction to Procedure of the House of Commons, 2nd edn., by Lord Campion (Philip Allan).
Parliamentary Practice, 17th edn., by Sir T. Erskine May (Butterworth). The standard work of reference.
Parliament: a Survey (George Allen & Unwin, 1952).
Parliament at Work, by A. H. Hanson and H. V. Wiseman (Stevens & Sons).
Questions in Parliament, by D. N. Chester and N. Bowring (Oxford University Press).

CHAPTER SEVEN

THE COMPOSITION OF PARLIAMENT

PARLIAMENT consists of the Queen, the House of Lords and the House of Commons. The two Houses sit separately and are constituted on entirely different principles. They must, therefore, be considered separately. The process of legislation is, however, a matter for both Houses and it is important to appreciate at the outset that the two-chamber system is an integral part of the constitution. The Parliament Act 1911 reduced the powers of the House of Lords and the Parliament Act 1949 curtailed still further the powers of that House to exercise a temporary veto on legislation, nor does the House play any part in making or unmaking Governments; for the control of the Executive is the function of the House of Commons. Nevertheless its power of holding up the passage of legislation may be an effective check on hasty legislation and its rôle as a revising chamber is important, especially for securing amendments to Bills which have been subjected to closure[1] in the House of Commons.

A. The House of Lords

The House of Lords consists of (i) over a thousand temporal, and (ii) twenty-six spiritual Lords of Parliament. The temporal peers are:

(*a*) Hereditary peers and peeresses in their own right of the United

[1] P. 142, *post*.

Kingdom,[1] who include holders of titles created in the peerage of England before the Union with Scotland in 1707 and in the peerage of Great Britain from 1707 to 1801 when the Union of Great Britain and Ireland, which lasted until 1922, took effect; they account for the bulk of membership. In March, 1963, there were 672 peers who sat by virtue of succession and 157 hereditary peers of the first creation. No hereditary peerages have been created since November 1964.

(*b*) Hereditary peers of Scotland who were created before the Act of Union of 1706 and who are not also members of the peerage of the United Kingdom.

(*c*) Not more than eleven Lords of Appeal in Ordinary appointed by the Crown on the authority of the Appellate Jurisdiction Acts 1876–1947 to perform the judicial duties of the House of Lords and holding their seats in the House for life.

(*d*) Life Peers: by the Life Peerages Act 1958 the Crown may confer a life peerage upon a man or a woman without limitation as to the number of creations. By 1968 over 150 such peerages had been created.

Creation of Peers

Hereditary peerages are created by the Queen on the advice of her Ministers. They are peerages of the United Kingdom and carry with them the right to a seat in the House of Lords. A hereditary peerage can be created either by the issue of a writ of summons to the House of Lords, followed by the taking of his seat by the recipient of the writ, or by letters patent, the latter method being invariably adopted since very early times.[2] A peerage created by letters patent descends according to the limitation expressed in the letters patent, which is almost always to the heirs male of the body of the grantee, *i.e.* to and through the male line in direct lineal descent from the grantee. A peerage created by writ of summons descends to the heirs general of the grantee, *i.e.* to his heirs male or female, lineal or collateral. Thus in the absence of a special limitation in the letters patent, it is only a peerage created by writ of summons which ever devolves upon a female. Where there is only one female heir, she becomes a peeress in her own right. Where, however, there are two or more female descendants of equal degree, the elder is not preferred to the younger,

[1] Princes of the Blood Royal only sit in the House by virtue of hereditary peerages conferred upon them by the Sovereign, with the exception of the heir apparent, who, unless a minor, sits as Duke of Cornwall.

[2] See specimen Letters Patent in App. C.

and both or all inherit as co-parceners. In such cases a peerage falls into abeyance. Such an abeyance may on the advice of the Committee of Privileges of the House of Lords, which on reference from the Crown decides claims to existing peerages, be terminated by the Crown in favour of one co-heir, or in process of time may become vested in one descendant of the last holder of the peerage. The House of Lords has during the present century resolved to restrict drastically the practice of advising the termination of abeyances. A dispute as to the right of a newly-created peer to sit is determined by the House itself, acting through the Committee of Privileges.

Special Remainders

Where a grantee has no direct male heir of the body, the letters patent, in order to preserve a peerage from extinction, may limit the peerage to the daughter of the grantee and the heirs male of her body, in default of heir males of the body of the grantee.

Restrictions

A peerage cannot be alienated nor, apart from disclaimer for life, be surrendered,[1] nor has a peerage any connection with the tenure of land. This last point was finally decided by the *Berkeley Peerage Case*.[2] A peerage cannot be created with a limitation of descent which is unknown to the law relating to real property.[3] It was decided in the *Wensleydale Peerage Case*[4] that the Crown, although able to create a life peerage, could not create such a peerage carrying with it any office of honour—a term which includes the right to a seat in the House of Lords. The view which prevailed was that, as the issue of a writ of summons followed by the taking of his seat by the recipient created a hereditary peerage, it was therefore impossible to allow one whose peerage was by letters patent limited to his life to take his seat. With the passage of the Life Peerage Act 1958 this restriction has been removed.

Disqualifications

An alien cannot receive a writ of summons to the House of Lords

[1] The Titles Deprivation Act 1917 provided for peers and princes being deprived of their dignities and titles on account of their adherence to the enemy during the First World War.

[2] (1861), 8 H.L.C. 21.

[3] *Wiltes Peerage Case* (1869), L.R. 4 H.L. 126.

[4] (1856), 5 H.L.C. 958.

nor may a writ of summons be issued to a bankrupt peer or to an infant. It was decided in the case of *Viscountess Rhondda's Claim* [1] that the Sex Disqualification (Removal) Act 1919 gave no right to a peeress in her own right to receive a writ of summons to Parliament. The Peerage Act 1963 reversed this decision by allowing a peeress in her own right to take her seat. Such a peeress may disclaim her title for life.[2] A peer who is a civil servant is debarred by Treasury Minute from speaking or voting, though he may take his seat in the House.

Creation of Peers to coerce the Lords

The right of the Crown to create new peers was an important weapon to enable the Crown on the advice of the Prime Minister of the day to compel the House of Lords to give way to the House of Commons in case of conflict. The Peerage Bill of 1719 attempted to limit the power of the Crown to create new peers, but the proposal was rejected. The passing of the Reform Bill in 1832 and the Parliament Bill in 1911 was procured by a statement that the King had consented to create peers in sufficient numbers to secure a majority for the Government in the House of Lords.[3] It seems improbable that this prerogative will again be invoked; the passing of the Parliament Act 1911 was thought at the time to reduce the likelihood of this.[4]

The Peers of Scotland

No new Scottish peerages can be created since the Act of Union of 1706. The Peerage Act 1963 admitted all surviving Peers of Scotland to seats in the House of Lords. Formerly when a new Parliament was summoned the Scottish peers elected sixteen of their number to represent them in the House of Lords. It was at one time thought that the Crown could not confer upon a peer of Scotland a peerage of the United Kingdom entitling him to a hereditary seat in the House of Lords, but this view was rejected by the judges in 1782 in advising the House upon the claim of the Duke of Hamilton and Brandon.

The Peers of Ireland

The Act of Union with Ireland 1800 provided that the Irish peerage might be maintained to the number of a hundred. There has

[1] [1922] 2 A.C. 339.
[2] P. 102, *post*.
[3] Sir Harold Nicolson, *George V*, pp. 184 ff.
[4] Pp. 130–2, *post*.

been no new creation since 1898. Formerly the Peers of Ireland elected 28 of their number to represent Ireland in the House of Lords for life; the last surviving elected Peer died in 1961.[1] All holders of Irish peerages are entitled to sit in the House of Commons and to vote at parliamentary elections anywhere in the United Kingdom.

The Lords of Appeal in Ordinary

The eleven judicial peers appointed by virtue of the provisions of the Appellate Jurisdiction Acts 1876–1947 and the Administration of Justice Act 1968, to perform the judicial functions of the House of Lords are styled Lords of Appeal in Ordinary. They have the right to sit and vote for life, notwithstanding resignation from their judicial appointment. They are entitled to a salary of £11,250 per annum, so long as they perform their judicial work and must have held for two years high judicial office,[2] or have practised at the Bar for fifteen years.

Life Peers

The Life Peerages Act 1958 gave effect to the only reform in the composition of the House of Lords upon which there had been any general measure of agreement in the present century up to that date. The Act enabled the Queen by letters patent to confer a peerage for life with a seat in Parliament upon a man or woman. It did not restrict the power of the Crown to confer a hereditary peerage upon a man. The object of the legislation was partly to enable the representation of the then Opposition to be increased, and partly to secure for the House the experience of distinguished men and women, particularly from outside the ranks of active party politicians.

The Lords Spiritual

The Lords Spiritual are twenty-six bishops of the Church of England; they hold their seats in the House of Lords until they resign from their episcopal office. The Archbishops of Canterbury and York and the Bishops of London, Durham and Winchester have the right to a seat in the House of Lords. The remaining twenty-one spiritual lords are the twenty-one other diocesan bishops having seniority of date of appointment.[3] When such a bishop dies or resigns, his place in the House of Lords is taken not by his successor, but by

[1] *Earl of Antrim's Petition*, [1967] A.C. 691, which decided against any new election since Ireland had as a whole ceased to exist politically under the legislation of 1922 which created the Irish Free State (now the Republic of Ireland).

[2] Chap. 22.

[3] The Bishop of Sodor and Man is excepted and cannot take a seat.

the next senior diocesan bishop. The Lords Spiritual take their seats in Parliament by ancient usage and by statute. In 1847 on the creation of the Bishopric of Manchester it was enacted that the number of bishops sitting in Parliament should not be increased in consequence; similar provision has been made on the creation of subsequent new Bishoprics.[1]

Disclaimer of Titles

The Peerage Act 1963 enables hereditary peers other than those of the first creation to renounce their titles for life by disclaimer. The primary purpose of granting such a right was to enable hereditary peers to sit in the House of Commons. This enactment was the direct result of the action of Mr. Anthony Wedgwood Benn, then Viscount Stansgate by succession, in challenging the existing law which disqualified members of the House of Lords from standing for election to Parliament.[2] Disclaimer binds a wife, but the courtesy titles of children are not affected as these are not matters of law, nor has a disclaimer any effect on the succession of the heir. If a sitting member of the House of Commons succeeds to a title he has one month after the death of his predecessor in which to disclaim, or, if the death occurs during an election campaign, one month from the declaration of the poll in favour of a successful peer. Existing peers were given twelve months from the Royal Assent to the Act, 31 July, 1963, in which to exercise their power to disclaim; peers who succeed thereafter have twelve months from succession or their coming of age. These time limits are extended to cover any period when Parliament is not sitting or a peer is disabled by sickness from making his choice. Subsequent to a disclaimer there can be no restoration of an hereditary peerage, but there is nothing in the Act to prohibit a peer who has disclaimed from subsequently being created a life peer under the Life Peerages Act 1958.

The Summoning of Peers

A summons to Parliament cannot be withheld from a peer who is entitled to it, and individual writs of summons are drawn up for both the temporal and spiritual lords of Parliament. Although peerages are now invariably created by letters patent, a writ of summons must be issued for each Parliament before a peer is entitled to take his seat. The writ addressed to a bishop contains the praemunientes clause which instructs the bishop to warn the clergy of his

[1] Clergy Act 1661 which gave back their seats to the bishops after the Restoration; Ecclesiastical Commissioners Act 1847, s. 2; Bishoprics Act 1878, s. 5; and *e.g.* The Bishoprics of Southwark and Birmingham Act 1904.

[2] P. 109, *post*.

diocese to be present and consent to whatever Parliament ordains. This clause is a reminder of the time when the clergy attended Parliament as a separate estate. The clergy always attended reluctantly and preferred to grant taxes in Convocation. Since the fourteenth century they have not, except for the spiritual peers, attended Parliament, and since the seventeenth century they have ceased to tax themselves. Writs of attendance are also issued to the High Court Judges and the Attorney-General and the Solicitor-General. It is in fulfilment of this summons that the Judges have, in the past, performed the duty of advising the House of Lords on points of law in particularly difficult cases.

Attendance

In order to secure that only those peers who are interested in the work of Parliament shall in practice attend and record their votes the House of Lords adopted in June 1958, a new Standing Order relating to leave of absence.[1] This order emphasised the obligation on Lords of Parliament to attend the sittings of the House in accordance with the writ of summons, but provided for a peer to apply for leave of absence for a session or part of one at any time during a Parliament. A peer who has been granted leave of absence is then expected not to attend the sittings of the House during the period of his leave. In this way it is presumably expected to eliminate the influence of the so-called "backwoodsman". Provision is made for a peer who wishes to terminate his leave of absence to give a month's notice.

B. The House of Commons [2]

The Constituencies

The Representation of the People Act 1948 distributed the par-

[1] S.O. 21.

[2] The law relating to elections is contained in three consolidating statutes, of which the Representation of the People Act 1949 dealing with (*inter alia*) the franchise and the conduct of elections is the most important. This Act repeals and re-enacts in a single statute previous legislation relating to the franchise, the conduct of elections and corrupt and illegal electoral practices. The other Acts are the House of Commons (Redistribution of Seats) Act 1949 as amended in 1958, and the Election Commissioners Act 1949. In the text reference is made to the original statutes which introduced important changes into the law, such as the Ballot Act 1872, the Representation of the People Acts 1918 and 1948 and the Corrupt and Illegal Practices Prevention Act 1883.

To cite only the consolidating Acts of 1949 would prevent an intelligible presentation of the development of the law relating to elections, but students who are concerned with the administration of this branch of law should consult the text of the Acts of 1949, and later amendments, for both parliamentary and local government franchise and elections.

liamentary seats in the House of Commons into 625 single-member territorial constituencies. The House of Commons elected in 1945 contained 640 members; the new composition applied to the Parliament elected in February, 1950, in which the representation of the universities by 12 members ceased. By the House of Commons (Redistribution of Seats) Acts 1949 and 1958 there are constituted four permanent boundary commissions, for England, Scotland, Wales and Northern Ireland. The Speaker is the chairman of each of the four commissions. A High Court judge is Deputy Chairman of the Commissions for England, Wales and Northern Ireland respectively, and a judge of the Court of Session of the Commission for Scotland. The Acts provided for an initial general review by each of the commissions of the representation of the whole of that part of the United Kingdom with which they are concerned; and a periodical review of constituencies by the commissions at intervals of not less than ten or more than fifteen years from the date of the submission of the Commission's last report with a view to recommending redistribution in accordance with changes in the number of electors. Redistribution is effected by Orders in Council which require an affirmative resolution of each House of Parliament for their approval. The review in 1954 resulted in the abolition of six constituencies and the creation of eleven new ones, all in England. This brought the membership of the House of Commons up to 630.[1]

In 1969 reports by the Boundary Commissions were presented to Parliament; the recommendations affected some two-thirds of the constituencies in the United Kingdom. The Government decided that by reason of the proposed radical revision of local government boundaries consequent upon a series of inquiries into the reform of local government it would be inexpedient to act upon the Boundary Commissions' reports until legislation could be introduced after an interval of up to three years to give effect to this reform. This left unaltered a large number of parliamentary constituencies which had increased or diminished substantially since the review of 1954; it also involved the holding of the next general election on the existing distribution. Legislation was necessary to give effect to the Government's decision; the Bill, which proposed to give effect only to such of the recommendations as related to Greater London (where local

[1] An attempt to challenge the validity of one of the draft Orders in Council, after it had been approved by both Houses, was rejected by the Court of Appeal on the merits; *Harper* v. *Secretary of State for Home Department*, [1955] Ch. 238. There seems no reason why delegated legislation proposed by, the Boundary Commission should not be challenged in the courts as *ultra vires* by an action for a declaration. The Act itself forbids such review, once the Order in Council has been made, but cf. Dicey, *op. cit.*, p. xlv; 71 L.Q.R. 336 and p. 687, *post*.

government reorganisation took place in 1963) and a few abnormally large constituencies elsewhere, was drastically amended in the Lords and finally dropped. Whereupon the Home Secretary introduced the necessary Orders in Council to give effect to the reports of the Boundary Commissions and invited the House of Commons to reject them—a course of action which the government majority secured. In this way the necessity for a second series of changes consequent on later local government Acts was defeated for the time being.[1] There is a strong case for retaining the system of conducting parliamentary and local elections on the same register and this in the Government's view justified retaining the unbalance in parliamentary constituencies for a few years longer, despite the near approach of a general election.

The periodic review is intended to ensure that so far as is practicable the electorate of a constituency will not exceed or fall short of the electoral quota by more than approximately a quarter of the quota. The electoral quota means a number obtained by dividing the electorate for that part of the United Kingdom by the number of constituencies in it existing on the enumeration date. The quota in practice is varied in each part of the United Kingdom by the requirement that the total number of seats in Great Britain must not be "substantially greater or less than 613" and that there shall be not less than 71 seats in Scotland and not less than 35 in Wales; the number of seats for Northern Ireland is fixed at 12.[2] The duty of Boundary Commissions is to give effect to the rules set out in the Second Schedule to the Act of 1949, but also to take into account inconveniences attendant on alterations of constituencies and of any local ties which would be broken by such alterations.[3]

Provision is also made for objections to proposed recommendations being investigated by a local enquiry if the objector is an interested local authority or a body of at least 100 electors.

History of the Franchise (England and Wales)[4] *—the County Franchise*

Since 1929 every adult person has, apart from certain disqualifications, possessed the franchise, or the right to vote. Before 1832 the

[1] *The Queen* v. *Secretary of State for the Home Department, ex parte McWhirter, The Times* 21 October 1969; an application for mandamus to compel the Home Secretary to give effect as a statutory duty to the reports of the Commissions was dismissed in view of the action of the Home Secretary.

[2] The quota for England at present is approximately 60,000.

[3] Constituency boundaries must as far as practicable be left in line with local government boundaries.

[4] For the history of the franchise in Scotland and Ireland before 1918 see Anson, *Law and Custom of the Constitution*, Vol. I, 5th edn., pp. 118–21.

franchise in county constituencies was exercised only by those males possessing freehold property worth 40*s.* a year. By the Representation of the People Act 1832 the county franchise was extended to long leaseholders and copyholders of property of the annual value of £10, and to all male leaseholders for terms of not less than twenty years and to occupiers of property of £50 annual value. The county representation was increased from 82 to 139 seats. Various further changes were made in the county franchise by the Representation of the People Act 1867 and the Representation of the People Act 1884 enfranchised all male householders and lodgers occupying rooms of the annual value of £10 unfurnished. The latter Act enfranchised many agricultural labourers.

The Borough Franchise

The borough franchise before 1832 varied from borough to borough.[1] The most common qualifications were: tenure of land, membership of a corporate body, tenure of particular tenements, and in certain cases merely residence. The Act of 1832, in addition to disfranchising many boroughs and transferring the seats to counties and large towns, established for the boroughs a uniform occupation franchise for any male who occupied as owner or tenant any house, shop or other building of the annual value of £10. The Act of 1867, which enfranchised the artisan class, extended the franchise to any male householder occupying a separate dwelling-house, and to lodgers occupying lodgings of the annual value, unfurnished, of £10. The borough franchise was substantially unaffected by the Act of 1884. This Act was followed by a further redistribution of seats, based on the general principle of equal electoral districts, each returning a single member.

Representation of the People Acts 1918–45

The Representation of the People Act 1918 established a uniform franchise for county and borough constituencies. This Act also redistributed seats, increasing the total membership of the House, which was 658 in 1832 and 670 in 1885, to 707. The creation of the Irish Free State in 1922 reduced the membership to 615. The franchise was given to all adult males possessing the qualifications either of residence or of the occupation of business premises. The franchise was also given to women of thirty years of age who, or whose husbands, occupied, in accordance with the requirements as to occupation for local government franchise, land or premises of the annual value of not less than £5 or a dwelling-house. In the university con-

[1] See Ilbert and Carr, *Parliament*, Chap. II (Home University Library.)

stituencies[1] all male graduates were entitled to vote, and all women of the age of thirty who were either graduates, or would have been graduates, if their university had admitted women to degrees. Disqualification by reason of receipt of outdoor poor relief was abolished by the Act of 1918 for both the parliamentary and local government franchise.

A uniform qualification for men and women was introduced by the Representation of the People (Equal Franchise) Act 1928. The effect of this Act, which amended the Representation of the People Act 1918, was that the franchise could be exercised by all adults possessing one or more of the following qualifications:

(*a*) Residence for a qualifying period of three months ending on June 1.
(*b*) Occupation of land or premises for business purposes of the annual value of £10 for the same period.
(*c*) Being the husband or wife of an occupier of such land or premises.
(*d*) Graduate membership of a university in the United Kingdom.

Further changes were made by the Representation of the People Act 1945 following on the recommendations of the Speaker's Conference which reported in the summer of 1944. The qualification of the spouse to be registered as a business premises voter was abolished. The qualification for the parliamentary franchise automatically carried qualification for the local government franchise, which had hitherto been restricted to occupiers of land and premises.

This Act also contained novel provisions to enable the greater part of the armed forces stationed in theatres of war and elsewhere abroad to vote by post at a general election. Only those in the most distant or isolated stations were restricted to voting by proxy.

The Present Franchise

By the Representation of the People Act 1948 the qualifications based on business premises and a university degree were abolished and so the last elements of plural voting in parliamentary elections disappeared; an elector can have only one vote. The sole qualification is residence in a particular place on the qualifying date, 10 October[2];

[1] The Universities of Oxford and Cambridge returned burgesses to Parliament since the time of James I. All the universities in the United Kingdom were represented in the House of Commons elected in 1945.

[2] In N. Ireland, 15 September.

the old requirement of a qualifying period of residence is no longer operative. The separate registration of service electors remains in force.

The Register of Electors

It is a condition precedent to exercising the vote that the elector should be placed upon the register of electors. The register is prepared once a year by the registration officer of each parliamentary borough and county. The registration officers in England and Wales are in the case of the county constituencies the clerks of the county councils, in the case of borough constituencies the town clerks. A new register comes into force on February 16 each year.[1] The register is prepared after a house to house canvass of residents and is published first in a provisional form to allow of claims and objections. A separate register which is compiled on information obtained from declarations contains the names of members of the forces and of the merchant navy whether serving at home or abroad and of other Crown servants who are abroad on service, together with those of their wives resident abroad with them. The principle of registration is that a service voter shall be registered as if he was living at the address at which but for his service he would be normally resident.

Any person may claim to be placed upon the register, and anyone may object to such claims. An appeal lies from the decision of a registration officer to the County Court, and on a point of law from the County Court to the Court of Appeal. Once placed upon the register, any person not suffering from any legal incapacity imposed by common law or statute, such as infancy or insanity, is entitled to vote, even though not qualified for inclusion on the register by reason of residence or service under the Crown. The register is conclusive on the questions whether or not a person registered therein was on the qualifying date resident at the address shown; and whether or not a person registered is registered as a service voter. But such a person if under a legal incapacity may incur penalties if he records a vote. Additions or alterations may be ordered by mandamus issued by the High Court, and may now also in certain circumstances, *e.g.* printing errors, be made by the registration officer or the Home Secretary without such an order.[2]

[1] Electoral Registers Act 1953.
[2] Representation of the People Act 1969, s. 7 (2).

Disqualifications for the Franchise

The following are the various disqualifications for the franchise. The franchise may not be exercised by:

(*a*) Aliens, but citizens of the Republic of Ireland are not disqualified.

(*b*) Infants, *i.e.* a person who has not attained the age of 18 by the date of the poll.[1]

(*c*) Mental Patients. The right to vote seems to depend in the case of a mental patient, likewise a drunkard, a childish person, a deaf and dumb or infirm person, on capacity at the moment of voting to understand what he is about to do. It is for the presiding officer at the poll to take the decision of refusing to allow such a person to vote.

(*d*) Peers and Peeresses in their own right.[2] Irish peers can exercise the franchise.

(*e*) Convicted persons during the time of detention in a penal institution in pursuance of a sentence are legally incapable of voting.

(*f*) Persons convicted of corrupt and illegal practices at elections, suffer a temporary disqualification which is universal in its incidence in the case of a corrupt practice; local in the case of an illegal practice.[3]

Disqualifications for Membership

The following are the main categories of persons who are disqualified from sitting and voting as members of the House of Commons:

(*a*) Aliens, but citizens of the Republic of Ireland are not disqualified.

(*b*) Infants and adults under 21.

(*c*) Mental Patients. By the provisions of the Mental Health Act 1959 s. 137, amending the Lunacy (Vacating of Seats) Act 1886, the detention of a member must be reported to the Speaker. The Speaker obtains a medical report, followed by another report after an interval of six months, and, if the member is still of unsound mind, his seat is vacated.

(*d*) Peers and Peeresses in their own right. Peers of Ireland are eligible for membership.

[1] See Representation of the People Act 1969, s. 1, for the voting rights of certain persons coming of age during the currency of the electoral register.

[2] They may vote at local elections.

[3] Pp. 368 and 507–8, *post*.

(*e*) Clergy ordained in the Church of England and Church of Ireland,[1] Ministers of the Presbyterian Church of Scotland, and Priests of the Roman Catholic Church.

(*f*) Bankrupts. The disqualification lasts until five years after discharge, unless the discharge is accompanied by a certificate that the bankruptcy was not caused by the bankrupt's misconduct.

(*g*) Persons guilty of corrupt or illegal practices, as provided by Parts II and III of the Representation of the People Act 1949 which reproduces with amendments the law enacted by the Corrupt and Illegal Practices Prevention Act 1883. The disqualification which is universal for a corrupt practice, but limited to a particular constituency in the case of an illegal practice, is for five years.

(*h*) A member sentenced to imprisonment may be expelled by the House of Commons, but such expulsion does not amount to a disqualification.[2] Formerly a member vacated his seat on expulsion by the House if sentenced to more than twelve months imprisonment for a felony (a category now abolished).

(*i*) Formerly a person who held or undertook certain contracts or commissions for the public service was disqualified from membership and consequently was liable to incur a penalty of £500 for every day on which he sat or voted. In 1931 this disqualification was restricted to contracts for the supply of money to be remitted abroad or for goods to be used or employed in the service of the public. The House of Commons Disqualification Act 1957 repealed this disqualification as well as that which formerly attached to the holding of any pension from the Crown, *e.g.* Civil List pension. Although the legal disqualification has been removed, there is a convention which is regarded as absolutely binding that a Member of Parliament should disclose his interest and abstain from voting on any issue where he, or a firm of which he is a member or substantial shareholder, is in contractual relationship with the Government.

Disqualification of Office-holders

(*j*) The disqualification arising from the holding of specified offices requires some detailed discussion. Until recently the law on this subject was in a condition which could only be described as "archaic, confused and unsatisfactory." [3] This description was

[1] *Re MacManaway*, [1951] A.C. 161; *Report of Select Committee on Clergy Disqualification*, H.C. 200 (1953).

[2] P. 164, *post*.

[3] *Report from the Select Committee on Offices or Places of Profit under the Crown*, H.C. 120 of 1941, and *The Times*, 13 December, 1949, *Candidates and Members*, by G. Bing.

justified by the fact that, when Parliament achieved a major reform in a process which inevitably had been gradual, it was found necessary to repeal one hundred and thirty-one statutory provisions, of which twelve were complete Acts. During the first half of the seventeenth century the House of Commons had secured recognition of the right to control its own composition. The principle underlying the decisions made by the House was that a position, the duties of which inevitably entailed prolonged absence from attendance at Westminster, was incompatible with the duties of a member. Many of the decisions of this period were confirmed by subsequent statutes.

After the Restoration the House was concerned more with its relations with the Crown than with the desire to ensure that its members performed their duties. Moreover, whereas the earlier decisions of the House purported to declare existing law, it was now seeking to make new law and recognised the necessity of legislation. Fear of undue influence through the presence in the House of Commons of office-holders led to a series of Place Bills and in 1700, by a provision in the Act of Settlement, there was enacted the complete exclusion of the holders of offices of profit to take effect after the accession of the House of Hanover. This provision, which would have prevented the development of the Cabinet system, as we understand it, by excluding Ministers from sitting in the House of Commons, was repealed before it took effect.

The Succession to the Crown Act 1707

The Succession to the Crown Act 1707, which was to remain for two hundred and fifty years the basis of the law relating to the disqualification of office-holders, was intended to enable Ministers to retain their seats in the House of Commons, subject to re-election on appointment, but at the same time to exclude the great majority of the holders of offices of a non-political character. This was achieved by disqualifying persons who accepted an office created since 1705, while leaving eligible for re-election those who accepted an office created before that date unless it was one to which disqualification had been attached by statute. But a considerable volume of subsequent legislation was necessary in order to convert the distinction between "old" and "new" offices into a distinction between ministerial offices, the holders of which were eligible for membership, and non-political offices, the holders of which were excluded. In particular a series of statutes disqualified or suppressed a great many old offices. Another series provided that the ministerial heads of newly-created departments should be eligible, subject until the twentieth century to re-election.[1] The Ministers of the Crown Act 1937 in fact replaced the Act of 1707 so far as it applied to the ministerial offices in existence at the time of its enactment. The Act of 1937 placed numerical limits on the number of Ministers of different groups who could sit simultaneously in the House of Commons. The present law is contained in the Ministerial Salaries Consolidation Act 1965.[2] The effect of the legislation as a whole was to secure a permanent civil service which was politically neutral and a sufficient number of Ministers in the House of Commons to ensure co-operation between Parliament and the Executive, while placemen, *i.e.* those who were indebted to the Government of the day for a means of livelihood in return for giving their support, had been excluded from the House of Commons.

Present Law

The House of Commons Disqualification Act 1957 replaced disqualification which derived from the holding of "an office or place of profit under the Crown" under the Act of 1707 by a disqualification attached to the holding of specified offices. These offices fall into six categories.

(1) A great variety of judicial offices, extending from a judgeship of the High Court of Justice or Court of Appeal to a resident magistrate in Northern Ireland. Broadly speaking, this category covers all major judicial posts. It is not comprehensive; for example, chairmen and deputy chairmen of quarter sessions and recorders are subject to disqualification limited to constituencies to which the jurisdiction of their courts extends.

(2) Employment in the civil service of the Crown, whether in an established capacity or temporarily, and whole-time or part-time. In addition to the home civil service the disqualification extends to members of the civil service of Northern Ireland and the diplomatic service.

(3) Membership of the regular armed forces of the Crown, which includes the Women's Royal Naval Service since this is not otherwise a "regular force." Members of the reserved and auxiliary forces are not, as formerly, disqualified on embodiment for active service. Nor are officers on the retired or emergency lists of any of the regular forces or those who hold emergency commissions. An Admiral of the Fleet, a Field Marshal in the Army, or a Marshal of the Royal Air Force, all of whom remain on the active list, is not

[1] See Anson, *Law and Custom of the Constitution*, 5th edn., Vol. I, p 101; Re-election of Ministers Acts 1919 and 1926.

[2] Pp. 114–15, *post*.

disqualified unless in addition he holds an appointment in the naval, military or air force service of the Crown, *e.g.* is employed as Chief of Staff. Members of the Services may apply for release in order to contest parliamentary elections from which the above disqualification excludes them. A spate of such applications in 1962 caused the appointment of a Select Committee on Parliamentary Elections, whose recommendations resulted in the appointment of an Advisory Committee of seven members to examine the credentials of applicants and to test the sincerity of their desire to enter Parliament as it had become apparent that numerous applicants desired release from the Services rather than membership of the House of Commons.

(4) Membership of any police force, *i.e.* a person employed as a full-time constable. This includes membership of the Metropolitan Police and the Northern Ireland constabulary.

(5) Membership of the legislature of any country or territory outside the Commonwealth. By inference the term "Commonwealth" is used here to include all the realms and territories which acknowledge the Queen as their head. This disqualification was first imposed by this Act.

(6) A great variety of disqualifying offices arising from membership of commissions, boards, administrative tribunals, chairmanship or membership of a number of public authorities and undertakings; in a few cases the disqualification only attaches to particular constituencies (s. 1 and First Schedule).

Provision is made for amendment by way of addition or omission or the removal of any office from one part of the Schedule to another or by change of description by Order in Council pursuant to a resolution approved by the House of Commons. This is an important safeguard because it obviates the need for further legislation by statute as and when new offices are created (s. 5).

For one purpose alone acceptance of an office of profit continues to disqualify. From early times a member of the House of Commons has been unable to resign his seat, and acceptance of an office of profit under the Crown was the only legal method of release from membership. The offices commonly used for this purpose were the office of Steward or Bailiff of the Chiltern Hundreds or of the Manor of Northstead. Prior to 1957 these were in recent times the only "old offices" under the Succession to the Crown Act 1707 which continued to involve resignation of membership. Under the Act of 1957 these offices are treated as disqualifying offices under the First Schedule.

There is no obligation on a person who is a member of the House of Commons or who has been nominated for election to that House to accept any office which would disqualify him from membership, but this does not affect any obligation to serve in the armed forces of the Crown whether such obligation is imposed by an enactment, such as the National Service Act 1948 or otherwise. Thus appointment to the office of Sheriff, which disqualifies in the county concerned, may be refused by a sitting member or nominated candidate. This office is otherwise obligatory upon the person duly nominated and chosen.

Relief from Disqualification

In the past, mainly on account of the ambiguity which has always attached to the meaning of "any office or place of profit under the Crown," it has been the practice to seek an Act of Indemnity in favour of individuals who have unwittingly been elected to membership while disqualified. In future the House of Commons is empowered to direct by order that a disqualification which existed at the material time may be disregarded if it has been removed. No such order can affect the proceedings on an election petition, but the House itself is empowered to dispense with the consequences of a disqualification, once the disqualification itself has been removed. If an order is made, a new election is unnecessary (s. 6).

Limitation of number of Ministers in Commons

The law in regard to the number of Ministers who may sit in the House of Commons is governed by the Ministerial Salaries Consolidation Act 1965. The Schedule names the ministerial offices, the holders of which may sit and vote in the House of Commons at any one time to a maximum number of ninety-one. They include the Prime Minister and First Lord of the Treasury, Secretaries of State, four traditional offices with few, if any, permanently assigned duties, *i.e.* the Lord President of the Council, the Lord Privy Seal, the Chancellor of the Duchy of Lancaster and the Paymaster-General, Ministers of Cabinet rank of the existing government departments not presided over by any of the above and Ministers of State and Parliamentary Under-Secretaries. The principle underlying this legislation is that a ministerial office as such shall be no bar to membership of the House of Commons, but that there ought to be a limit to the maximum number of Ministers and Parliamentary Under-Secretaries in that House; this incidentally, ensures, in view of the size of modern Ministries, that there will be a nucleus of Ministers in the House of Lords; for convention requires the presence of political office holders in one or other House.[1] In the event of an infringement of these provisions disqualification does not apply to any who were both members and holders of ministerial office before the excess occurred. The limitation of the total number of office holders cannot be regarded as ungenerous, especially as there are other government posts, *i.e.* parliamentary private secretaries, who hold no scheduled office but are close supporters of the administration. There are, moreover, some offices of the Royal Household which are filled by political appointments. Only three of these are scheduled offices. The result is that even if there are no more than twenty parliamentary private secretaries, a Prime Minister has at his disposal more than a hundred ministerial posts to offer to his supporters, and in practice relatively few of these posts are given to members of the House of Lords.

Determination of Claims

Disputes as to qualification for membership are determined by the House after consideration by a Select Committee. In 1961 the Committee of Privileges reported adversely on the claim of Lord Stansgate, who had succeeded to his father's peerage while a member of the House of Commons, to retain his membership.[2]

To the Judicial Committee of the Privy Council, which by s. 4 of the Judicial Committee Act 1833 has power to advise on references to it, is entrusted jurisdiction to determine upon whether a person has incurred a disqualification from membership. The application takes the form of one for a declaration and may be made by any person, but the applicant must give security for costs not exceeding £200. Issues of fact may, on the direction of the Judicial Committee, be tried by the High Court or the corresponding courts in Scotland or Northern Ireland. No declaration may be made if an election petition is pending or one has been tried in which disqualification on the same grounds was in issue, nor can a declaration be made if the House of Commons has given relief by order [3] (s. 7). This procedure takes away the right of a common informer to sue a disqualified member for the £500 penalty.[4] This right, which was not taken away when the common informer lost his other rights to sue

[1] The Act of 1965 repealed the previous division which fixed maxima for senior and junior Ministers, thus making it now possible for a Government to have no senior Ministers, except the Lord Chancellor, in the House of Lords.

[2] H.C. 142 (1961).

[3] P. 114, *ante*.

[4] P. 116, *ante*.

for a penalty,[1] still survives against clergy who are disqualified by the House of Commons (Clergy Disqualification) Act 1801.[2]

Illegal Expenditure on Election Campaign

Chief among the prohibitions on corrupt and illegal practices in the conduct of an election are the provisions which prohibit expenditure on advancing candidature unless it is specifically authorised by a candidate or his duly appointed election agent.[3] It has been held that an advertisement in a national newspaper which condemned the policy of Ministers in the Government and thus tended to disparage all the candidates who supported the Government at a current general election was not expenditure incurred in breach of the section.[4] The use of broadcasting and television in connection with election campaigns has raised interesting questions particularly at a general election when it is clearly impracticable to offer equal facilities to all the candidates. At a bye-election, provided that all the candidates agree to the use of whatever facilities are offered, *e.g.* a television interview, the resulting expenditure is not attributable to advancing the cause of any particular candidate, and therefore does not come within the prohibition of unauthorised expenses. But at a general election whatever facilities are offered must in the nature of things be restricted to a very limited number of the total candidates. It is arguable that the money expended in the broadcast or television production would seem to be an expense incurred with a view to promoting the election of those candidates, and accordingly should be included in the expenditure authorised by the candidate or his agent and form part of the total expenses of candidature, the total of which is restricted by law.[5] There is no limit on the number of motor vehicles which a candidate or his agent may use at a parliamentary election for taking voters to and from the poll.[6]

Voting Methods

In single-member constituencies each elector can vote for only one candidate. When there are more than two political parties seeking the votes of the electorate, this system of election makes little provision for the representation of minorities, and can lead to

[1] Common Informers Act 1951.

[2] P. 110, *ante*.

[3] Representation of the People Act 1949, s. 63. A candidate is required by law to have an agent but may appoint himself to act in that capacity (s. 55 (2)).

[4] *The Queen* v. *Tronoh Mines Ltd.*, [1952] 1 All E.R. 697.

[5] Cf. *Grieve* v. *Douglas-Home*, 1965 S.C. 315. The maximum expenditure is laid down by the Representation of the People Act 1969, s. 8. See also s. 9 for restrictions on broadcasting during elections.

[6] Pp. 163–4, *post*, for election petitions to the High Court.

strangely anomalous results. It is mathematically possible for one party to obtain the largest aggregate of votes in the country and yet not win a single seat in the House of Commons. In 1922 the Conservative Party polled 38 per cent. of the votes cast in the election and obtained 347 seats in Parliament. In 1929 the Conservative Party again polled 38 per cent. of the votes cast, but obtained only 253 seats.

Alternative Vote

Various systems of voting have been suggested with a view to securing a better representation of minorities and a distribution of seats corresponding more nearly to opinion in the country. The most notable of these are the alternative vote and proportional representation. If the alternative vote were adopted, single-member constituencies would be retained, but the elector would be allowed to express his choice of candidates in order of preference. If no candidate obtained a clear majority, the lowest on the list would be eliminated, his votes being distributed according to the second preferences shown on the voting papers. While making it more probable that in each particular constituency the final choice would be the real choice of the electors, the alternative vote would not provide adequately for the representation of minorities in the country.

Proportional Representation

Under proportional representation, a form of which, known as the single transferable vote, was formerly used in the university constituencies returning more than one member, the country would be divided into large constituencies, each returning several members. The elector would vote for the candidates in order of preference, and any candidate obtaining a certain quota of first preferences would be immediately elected. His surplus votes would be distributed to other candidates according to the second preferences expressed, and again any candidate then obtaining the quota would be returned and a similar distribution of his surplus would take place. This system would undoubtedly provide adequate representation of minorities, but the drawback to any such system is that the more variety of opinion is represented, the more difficult it becomes to secure a Government of any one party with a reasonable working majority in the House of Commons. The Speaker's Conference on Electoral Reform and Redistribution of Seats rejected by large majorities proposals for proportional representation and for the alternative vote.[1] A similar conference in 1967 recommended by 19 votes to 1

[1] Cmd. 6534 (1944).

against any change in the present system; no reasons were published in the report.

Most European countries have adopted some form of proportional representation. But it is only fair to say that this method of election sometimes produces results which hamper the formation of governments following on elections. So mathematically accurate is the system of proportional representation at present in force in the Netherlands that it may take weeks, and sometimes months, before a government commanding a majority can be formed after a general election. It has proved difficult to rouse any real enthusiasm in favour of a change in the present voting methods in this country. It seems unlikely that either the Conservative or the Labour Party would favour a change in the voting methods which might deny to one or other of them supremacy in the House of Commons and bring about government by coalition with a third party.

CHAPTER EIGHT

THE MEETING OF PARLIAMENT

The Crown and Parliament

PARLIAMENT is summoned by the Queen by royal proclamation,[1] and it is by the Queen that it is prorogued and dissolved.[2] The modern practice is that the same proclamation both dissolves Parliament and summons a new one. The old Parliament is first prorogued [3] and the dissolution immediately follows. The new Parliament can be summoned to meet not less than twenty clear days after the date of the proclamation.[4] Parliament cannot meet without a summons from the Crown. There is no express rule of law requiring an annual meeting of Parliament, though the Meeting of Parliament Act 1694 requires Parliament to meet every three years. But in practice legislation relating to the essential business of governing the country, including taxation and the expenditure of public funds, is only passed for one year and must be renewed annually, thereby ensuring that there is a session of Parliament at least once a year. For some years past it has been the practice for the parliamentary session to be prorogued in the autumn after a short resumption of sittings following the summer recess. The new session is then after a short period of prorogation opened in November.[5]

Elections to House of Commons

After the summoning of Parliament by royal proclamation, individual writs are issued to the members of the House of Lords, and writs are issued to returning officers commanding them to cause an election of members of the House of Commons to be held. The returning officer gives notice of the place and times at which nomination papers are to be delivered and the date of the poll in the event of a contest. Nomination papers must be delivered by the eighth day after the date of the proclamation and the poll held on the ninth day

[1] See Form of Proclamation in App. C, pp. 732–3.

[2] Pp. 122 and 120–1, *post*.

[3] The Crown may, as in 1922 and 1964, dispense with the prorogation meeting of Parliament.

[4] Representation of the People Act 1918, s. 21 (3), which has survived the repeal of the remainder of that Act by the Representation of the People Act 1948.

[5] In 1949 the session which opened in November 1948 was not prorogued until mid-December; that of April 1966 was not prorogued until October (end) 1967.

thereafter. A candidate must be proposed and seconded by an elector, and eight other electors must sign his nomination paper. If there are more candidates than vacancies, a poll is ordered. Voting is by secret ballot, and each elector indicates his choice by placing a mark against the name of the candidate whom he favours. There are provisions enabling a person registered as a service voter to vote by post or by proxy.

Conduct of Parliamentary Elections

Responsibility for the conduct of an election rests upon the returning officer, who in the case of a county constituency is the sheriff, in a borough constituency the mayor. Most of the duties of the returning officer are, however, discharged as statutory duties by the registration officer[1] or by a deputy appointed by him. From these duties are excepted any duty of the returning officer relating to the delivery of the writ and matters connected therewith, and such duties, as for example, the declaration of the poll, as the returning officer may reserve to himself. The cost of an election, as distinct from the election expenses of the candidates, which are limited by statute and subject to scrutiny after the election, is paid out of public funds in accordance with a scale prescribed by the Treasury.

Bye-elections

When a vacancy occurs in the House of Commons during the course of a Parliament, the Speaker issues a warrant for the issue of a writ for the holding of a bye-election. A motion for the issue of the writ is normally moved by the Chief Whip of the party which held the seat before the vacancy occurred. There is no time limit in filling the vacancy; as long as nine months is not unknown, *e.g.* to await the revised register each February.

Dissolution

Parliament endures for five years, unless it is sooner dissolved by the Sovereign.[2] The Sovereign will not exercise the prerogative of dissolution without the advice of the Prime Minister; Ministers may be dismissed, though dismissal would only be justified under modern conditions by wholly abnormal circumstances.[3] It has for some time been a convention of the constitution that the Sovereign will dissolve Parliament at the request of the Prime Minister. The right to request

[1] P. 108, *ante*.
[2] See *Cabinet Government*, by Sir Ivor Jennings (Cambridge University Press), pp. 412 ff. For prolongation of the life of Parliament by legislation, see p. 46, *ante*.
[3] Chap. 6.

a dissolution is a powerful weapon in the hands of a Prime Minister, who may use it to threaten recalcitrant supporters with the expenses of an election, and to compel the House of Lords to give way to the House of Commons, unless they are prepared to face the unfavourable result of an appeal to the country. A Prime Minister, whose Government is defeated in the House of Commons on a major issue, is expected either to resign or to request a dissolution. Whether the convention as to the right to a dissolution would survive the presence of three parties, each with a fair proportion of seats, it is difficult to determine. It may be that the Sovereign would refuse, should the occasion arise, to grant a dissolution at the request of a Prime Minister who had never had a clear majority in the House of Commons. But what happened in 1924 is a precedent to the contrary; King George V granted a dissolution to the Labour Prime Minister who had taken office without a majority, but with the support of the Liberals who subsequently withdrew that support. Another situation, more probable under existing conditions, might raise the question of the right of a Prime Minister to request a dissolution. If, after a general election, particularly one which followed a dissolution granted at his own request, a Prime Minister found himself with a very small majority in the new House of Commons, as actually happened in 1950, it may be that the Sovereign ought to satisfy himself that no alternative Ministry could be formed before granting a second dissolution. In practice no doubt the Prime Minister would himself so advise. If he did not, there is some authority, including that of Lord Oxford and Asquith, for the view that the Sovereign would be entitled to seek advice from other Privy Councillors who might be willing to form a second Government. The dilemma is that, if a new Prime Minister took office, he might himself have to seek an early dissolution. If this was granted to him after it had been refused to his predecessor, the political impartiality of the Sovereign would be endangered.[1]

Demise oj the Crown

Until 1867 the death of the Sovereign affected the duration of Parliament. Since the Representation of the People Act 1867 the duration of a Parliament has been independent of the life of the Sovereign. Similarly should Parliament be prorogued or adjourned at the time of the death of the Sovereign, it meets at once without

[1] A letter to *The Times* (Senex, the writer, was understood to be a former Private Secretary to the Sovereign) dated 2 May, 1950, confirmed the view that the problem of granting or refusing a dissolution is entirely personal to the Sovereign who is free to seek informal advice from anybody whom he thinks fit to consult.

summons. Should the Sovereign die after a dissolution, but before the day fixed for the meeting of the new Parliament, the old Parliament would assemble and sit for six months or until sooner dissolved.[1]

Prorogation

Prorogation brings to an end, not the existence, but a session of Parliament. Prorogation is effected either by the Sovereign in person or by a Royal Commission, the latter being the normal method, and operates until a fixed date. Parliament may be recalled by proclamation at one day's notice during a prorogation, if an emergency occurs.[2] Prorogation terminates all business, and any public Bills which have not passed through all the stages in both Houses lapse. In the case of private Bills a resolution may be passed before the end of a preceding session directing that a particular Bill be held over till the next session, but public Bills have not hitherto been carried over in this way.

Adjournment

An adjournment of Parliament is effected by either House of Parliament for such time as it pleases, but does not put an end to any uncompleted business. The Sovereign may call upon Parliament to meet before the conclusion of an adjournment intended to last for more than fourteen days. In practice arrangements are made for terminating the adjournment of either House at short notice, should the Lord Chancellor or the Speaker be satisfied that the public interest requires it.

Opening of Parliament

Parliament, after a dissolution or a prorogation, is opened either by the Sovereign in person or by Royal Commissioners. As soon as the Houses have assembled, the Commons are summoned to the House of Lords to hear the Speech from the Throne, and, at the opening of a new Parliament, are first bidden to choose a Speaker. After choosing the Speaker the House adjourns until the following day, when the election of the Speaker is announced to the Lord Chancellor in the House of Lords. When a new Parliament meets, the Lords take the oath of allegiance as soon as Parliament has been opened, and the Commons as soon as the Speaker has been approved by the Sovereign and has himself taken the oath.

The Speech from the Throne

The first business of a new session of Parliament is the debate on

[1] Meeting of Parliament Act 1797, s. 3.
[2] Parliament (Elections and Meetings) Act 1943, s. 34.

the Speech from the Throne. The Speech, for which the Cabinet is responsible, announces in outline the Government's plans for the principal business of the session. It is delivered in the House of Lords either by the Sovereign or, when Parliament is opened by Commission, by the Lord Chancellor. In each House an address is moved in answer to the Speech, and the debate on this address provides an opportunity for a general discussion of the political situation. It is in this role that Parliament acts as the grand inquest of the nation and the private member has the chance of contributing to the debate without undue fear of the party whip. Before the address is moved, the ancient right of Parliament to deal with matters not brought before it by the Crown (the rule of redress of grievances before supply) is asserted by the formal first reading of an obsolete Bill; in the Lords usually a Bill for the better regulation of "Select Vestries"; in the Commons a Bill for the better preventing of "Clandestine Outlawries."

Lord Chancellor

The Lord Chancellor presides over the House of Lords. This office may be, but in practice is not, held by a commoner, and the Woolsack on which the Lord Chancellor sits as Speaker of the House is technically outside the precincts of the House. In contrast with the impartial position occupied by the Speaker of the House of Commons, the Lord Chancellor is free to take part in the deliberations of the House of Lords. Indeed he may often be the principal spokesman for the Government, and then he vacates the Woolsack temporarily by stepping aside while speaking; he returns to stand in front of the Woolsack to put the question to the House. Only in his absence does a Deputy-Speaker preside.

The Speaker

The chief officer of the House of Commons is the Speaker. Except when the House is in committee he is its Chairman and is responsible for the orderly conduct of debates. It is through the Speaker that the House communicates with the Sovereign. He issues writs for the filling of vacancies. He has the statutory duty of determining whether a Bill is a money Bill within the meaning of the Parliament Act 1911.[1] He is chairman of each of the four boundary commissions which periodically review the distribution of seats.[2] The Speaker is appointed at the beginning of each Parliament. The party with a majority in the House selects a candidate for the Speakership. Such

[1] P. 136, *post*.
[2] P. 104, *ante*.

selection is usually made after consultation with the other parties, in order that the selection may be the unanimous choice of the House. It is customary for the previous holder of the office to be re-elected, if he is again willing to serve. The Speaker's seat was until recently not contested at an election, but it has become clear that at all events the Labour Party is not prepared to continue this convention. One suggestion which has not yet been adopted is that a special constituency of St. Stephen's (part of the Palace of Westminster) should be created and always held without opposition by a Speaker in office. The result of the convention coupled with the nature of the duties of the office is to deprive the Speaker's constituency of active representation in the House. If a Speaker dies in office, all business comes to an end until a successor is appointed.

Chairman of Ways and Means

When the House of Commons is in committee, the chair is taken by the Chairman or Deputy-Chairman of Ways and Means, or by one of a Chairmen's panel of not less than ten members nominated by the Speaker for the purpose of providing Chairmen of Standing Committees.[1] These officers preside when a Bill is taken in committee by the whole House.[1] The Chairman or Deputy-Chairman of Ways and Means presides over the House in the absence of the Speaker. Unlike membership of the Chairmen's panel, the Chairmanship and Deputy-Chairmanship of Ways and Means are party appointments. New appointments are made with every change of Government. By custom the holders of these two offices do not take an active part in debates in the House itself.

Permanent Officers of the House of Lords

The chief permanent officer of the House of Lords is the Clerk of the Parliaments appointed by the Crown and removable only by the Crown on address from the House of Lords. The Gentleman Usher of the Black Rod enforces the orders of the House, and the Serjeant-at-Arms attends on the Lord Chancellor. Under the Clerk of the Parliaments are a Clerk Assistant and Reading Clerk appointed by the Lord Chancellor and removable only by an address from the House.

Permanent Officers of the House of Commons

The Clerk of the House of Commons or Under-Clerk of the Parliaments is appointed by the Crown; two Clerk Assistants are appointed by the Crown on the nomination of the Speaker. These

[1] P. 140, *post*. The offices remain, though Ways and Means business is no longer taken in the Committee of the whole House sitting under that title.

officers are removable only by an address from the House. The Serjeant-at-Arms appointed by the Crown is responsible for attending upon the Speaker and enforcing the orders of the House, including warrants issued by the Speaker for commitment for contempt or breach of privilege. The question was raised in 1962 whether the Crown was under a duty to consult the House of Commons before making an appointment to the office of Serjeant-at-Arms. After consultation with the Queen the Prime Minister announced that on any future occasion when the office of Serjeant-at-Arms should fall vacant the Queen would, before exercising her prerogative of appointment, initiate informal discussions with the Speaker as had been done in the past. It is for the Speaker to take soundings at his discretion to inform the Sovereign of any feelings there may be in the House before the prerogative appointment is exercised.[1]

[1] 669 H.C. Deb., cols. 209–10.

CHAPTER NINE

THE FUNCTIONS OF PARLIAMENT

A. Control of the Executive

It has been shown in discussing the transition to Cabinet Government [1] that it is Parliament that makes and unmakes the Executive. In order to retain office and to secure the passage of legislation and the grant of supplies a Government must command support in the House of Commons, and the choice of a Prime Minister depends upon the ability to secure such support. Normally the Prime Minister is the leader of the party which has the largest number of supporters returned to the House of Commons, though sometimes two or more groups have combined to keep in office a Government either based on a coalition or on a party which could not alone command a majority. It is through their representatives in Parliament that the electorate controls the Executive. The growth of the party system and the increase in the size of constituencies and the number of the electorate has resulted in votes being cast more for a party and its leaders than for local representatives on their own merits. An elector votes as much to choose a Prime Minister as to choose his local member.

Control by the Electorate

It is chiefly since the Reform Act of 1832 that there has been any control of the Executive by the people, and the degree of that control as well as the method of its exercise are still matters of dispute and subject to changing conventions.[2] It has become the custom for a Ministry defeated in the House of Commons to appeal to the electorate rather than to resign at once, and it has also become an established convention that, should a Ministry decide to offer its resignation rather than to ask for a dissolution, its successors should take the earliest opportunity to appeal to the electorate. A defeat at a general election involves in normal circumstances immediate resig-

[1] Chap. 4.

[2] *Thoughts on the Constitution*, by L. S. Amery, 2nd edn. pp. 13 ff, (Oxford University Press), *The People and the Constitution*, by C. S. Emden (Clarendon Press).

nation. These conventions might, however, quickly become obsolete, should the two-party system give place to a combination of groups or even to three or four parties. With more than two main parties there is a real risk of frequent defeat in Parliament, and parties tend to come together and break away again. It would be impossible for government to be carried on, should every change of Ministry due to a re-shuffling of parties be followed by a general election. It has been pointed out that, though a group system gives more accurate representation of opinion, it lessens the ultimate control of the electorate.[1] Not only do Parliaments tend to last their full time, but it is impossible with more than two parties for the electorate to express its opinion upon a definite issue. The degree to which the electorate can determine policy depends upon the honesty and skill with which the parties frame the issues at a general election. Some elections seem merely to involve a choice between two possible Prime Ministers. Others involve a clear verdict for or against a proposed legislative change. There is a tendency to regard as a convention the rule that no radical change of policy should be undertaken unless the issue has been before the electors at a general election. Whether the difficulty of framing particular issues at a general election will lead to the adoption of the referendum is a problem of the future, but hitherto the advocates of this device have received little support in this country. A series of bye-elections held together or at short intervals may give a fairly accurate idea of any shift of party allegiance in the constituencies. Generally they tend to favour the Opposition without any guarantee that support for the Government will change at the next general election. In this connection it should be remembered that it is not only at an election that opinion can be tested. It is more and more becoming the custom for a Government to sense the feeling of the House and of the public by publishing in advance of a Bill its proposals in the form of a statement of policy as a White Paper.

Members and their Constituents

Under adult suffrage a member represents about 60,000 electors. Political organisation on a scale which only a nation-wide machine can operate is essential to secure election. One reason for the disappearance of independent members was because none of them could command such an organisation without which no candidate could hope to-day to succeed. Candidates are thus necessarily selected because of their acceptability as members of a party. Members of

[1] C. S. Emden, *op. cit.*

Parliament represent the whole community, responsible in the last resort, as Burke pointed out, to their own consciences. They are not mere delegates of their constituents. Neither legally nor morally has a constituency a right to recall its member. But a member who changes his party may be expected to offer his resignation, unless he has strong local support for retaining his seat.

Power of the Cabinet

A further consequence of the party system is the submission of Parliament to the Cabinet. A Cabinet with a clear majority in the House of Commons can usually secure the passage of its legislation in substantially the form that it proposes, subject to the now restricted powers of the House of Lords to delay the passage of a measure. It can also take the whole of the available time for government business, to the exclusion of the private member. In former times Governments were frequently defeated in the House of Commons, and still more frequently were forced to withdraw measures by threats of revolt among their followers. To-day members are returned to Parliament with the assistance of their party; without this assistance they cannot hold their seats. The threat of a dissolution involving the expense of an election, and still more the threat of the withdrawal of the support of the party organisation, will, except in rare cases, ensure the maintenance of the Government in office, until a dissolution is sought at a time chosen by the Prime Minister, whose power to advise such a course can act as a deterrent to dissentient back-bench members of the party in office.

Parliamentary Control

Although the real power to promote legislation rests with the Cabinet and, as will be shown, it is difficult for Parliament to keep any real control over expenditure, it must not be assumed that Parliament has no control over Ministers. The defeat of the Government in the Commons in practice seldom occurs, even in the case of one which commands only a small majority. Moreover, it is only defeat on a major issue which constitutionally compels resignation. Parliament, however, is a deliberative as well as a legislative assembly. Debates of real value may take place during discussions on expenditure which, though failing to alter immediate programmes, may influence subsequent policy. Motions can be moved asking for papers, or for the appointment of commissions or committees of inquiry. The daily question hour, during which questions are addressed to Ministers, provides an opportunity for concentrating public attention on topics of current concern. Parliamentary questions are also of value in securing the redress of individual grievances. The use of question hour for this purpose is a real constitutional safeguard. Civil servants are aware that departmental action for which they are responsible to their Minister may result in a parliamentary question which may embarrass him in the House. Important debates arise on the Address in reply to the Speech from the Throne at the opening of a session; on the Budget speech of the Chancellor of the Exchequer; on a formal motion of censure and on other occasions apart from the ordinary legislative business, *e.g.* on a motion to adjourn. Debates unconnected with the passage of legislation are particularly useful in the House of Lords for the discussion of defence and foreign affairs. Forty members may at the end of question time move the adjournment of the House of Commons in order to discuss specific and important matters which should have urgent public consideration. If the Speaker accepts the motion, it is taken later the same day. The debates on the estimates, taken on Supply days, serve the purpose of providing occasions for general debates on administration and policy, although the scope of debate is limited by the rule that proposals for legislation may not be discussed. There is usually an interval of half an hour every day between the close of public business and the time fixed for the adjournment of the House. An adjournment motion is moved and the ensuing half-hour may be used for raising matters which cannot easily be dealt with by question and answer, though no division can be taken. Ministers inevitably pay attention to general feeling in Parliament as giving valuable indication of general feeling in the country. Parliament does not however exercise detailed supervision of the administrative services of Government. Public administration is a highly technical matter and the ordinary member of Parliament, even if he possesses the qualifications for the task, has not at his disposal all the information available to the departments or the means of collecting such information. Moreover, proposals for the establishment of greater parliamentary control are resisted on the ground that they would interfere with ministerial responsibility and the right and duty of the Government to govern. As the parliamentary system works to-day, the composition of the House of Commons determines the choice of a Government. To that Government is entrusted the determination of matters of policy and general responsibility for administration through the various departments.

For many years it had been suggested that selected departments or groups of departments should have attached to them specialist parliamentary committees chosen from members of the House of Commons who had appropriate qualifications and interests. Such committees would examine in detail departmental estimates and to them would be committed all Bills introduced by the relevant departmental Minister. Such proposals had met with opposition as likely to interfere with ministerial responsibility to the House and to encroach upon the task of a government to govern. In 1967 the House of Commons, which had as far back as 1956 approved the setting up of a select sessional committee to examine the reports and the accounts of the nationalised industries, approved the appointment of two specialised committees, one to consider the activities of the Ministry of Agriculture, Fisheries and Food, the other to consider those of the Department of Education and Science. In the 1968–9 session these committees completed their task and were replaced by others. That they should so soon be dissolved is considered a weakness in the value of the experiment. Other committees, intended to be permanent, have been appointed to deal with subjects, *e.g.* Race Relations rather than the activities of a department. A feature of this experiment is that the terms of reference given to the committees are wide enough to allow the detailed examination of an estimate in advance of its approval by the House. They are empowered to send for persons, papers and records; this enables them to question a Minister. They may sit in public, if they so decide, during the examination of witnesses; this in itself is an innovation for a select committee, as evidence has had to be restricted until reported to the House by the Committee. In 1968 a member of a Committee on Science and Technology was held to be guilty of breach of privilege for disclosing to the press evidence taken by the Committee in private session; he had been warned beforehand of the duty not to disclose the evidence which was taken in relation to a Ministry of Defence research establishment. A Select Committee to receive the reports of the Parliamentary Commissioner for Administration was first established in the Session 1967–8.

Her Majesty's Opposition

That the party system has strengthened the system of modern government is undeniable. But it has also increased the importance of the Opposition in the House of Commons. To the Opposition nowadays falls the greater part of the work of criticising the exercise of executive power, which is the traditional function of the House.

Back-bench supporters of a Government may exert much influence in meetings of the parliamentary party but they will normally support the Government in the division lobbies. The Opposition, the main and perhaps the only minority party, can exert pressure through its leaders, some of whom will already have had experience in office, and most of whom are likely in due course to form a future government. The Leader of the Opposition forms a Shadow Cabinet. Thus is ensured the criticism of leaders who are responsible for alternative policies. They are backed by supporters who are disciplined more or less satisfactorily by the party machine. The constitutional importance of an official Opposition has been recognised by the grant of a salary from public funds to its leader; [1] by the grant to-day under the rules of procedure of a certain precedence for its business in the House of Commons, but more particularly by its adoption in the Parliaments of the member States of the Commonwealth. To quote a former Clerk of the House, Lord Campion,

> The "Official Opposition" is a standing proof of the British genius for inventing political machinery. It has been adopted in all the Dominion Parliaments; the lack of it is the chief weakness of most of the Continental systems. It derives, of course, from the two-Party system; but in its developed form it represents a happy fusion of the parliamentary spirit of toleration with the democratic tendency to exalt party organization. The system involves the discouragement of individual initiative almost as much on the Opposition back benches as on those of the Government Party, for party organization seems more adapted to frontal attack in mass formation than to individual sniping. While admitting the loss to parliamentary life resulting from the sacrifice of the independent private Member, it cannot be denied that under modern conditions the concerted action of the Opposition is the best means of controlling a Government—by criticizing defects in administration loudly enough for the public to take notice.[2]

B. Legislation [3]

Private Members' Bills

When we speak of parliamentary supremacy [4] we mean that the courts recognise that Parliament has the right to legislate on every topic and that no other body may legislate except with the authority of Parliament. We have seen [5] that there are many practical limita-

1 Ministerial Salaries Act 1965, s. 4.
2 *Parliament; a Survey*, p. 30 (1952).
3 App. A contains specimens of legislative forms.
4 Chap. 4, B.
5 *Ibid.*

tions to the legislative power of Parliament. The real power to legislate rests with the Cabinet, which is under the constant pressure of organised opinion of all kinds seeking redress or relief through legislation. A public Bill, *i.e.* a Bill of general application, as opposed to one affecting particular local or private interests, may be introduced by a private member, but has little chance of becoming law unless the Government will allot sufficient time to it later in the session, or adopt the measure as its own after the second reading. The Government can use its majority to secure priority for government business. Private members, if they are successful in a ballot, may move motions and introduce Bills on certain Fridays in the earlier part of a session,[1] unless, owing to pressure of business, private members' time is annexed by the Government. Certain days are also allotted for private members' motions. There is no difference in procedure in regard to introduction between a government Bill and a private member's Bill. Any public Bill [2] may be introduced without leave, in which case no discussion takes place until the second reading. The second and third reading of private members' Bills are taken on Fridays in the first part of a session, and members ballot for the opportunity to move the second reading of their Bills. A Bill may also be introduced under the "Ten Minutes Rule." This method is usually employed when the object of introducing a private member's Bill is to secure publicity for the subject-matter rather than to secure the passage of the Bill. A motion for leave to bring in the Bill is set down for consideration immediately after question time. Short speeches are made by the mover and one oppcser and then the question is put. Private members' time was suspended by sessional orders from 1939 to 1949.

Delegated Legislation [3]

The increasing complication of the business of governing the country has led to ever-growing readiness to delegate legislative powers, though it must always be remembered that these powers are conferred by Parliament and can be annulled or restricted by Parliament. The power to legislate, when delegated, is normally confined to matters of detail relating to administration, though in a sudden emergency power may be delegated to legislate on major matters. The latter is well illustrated by legislation of 1931 when there were

[1] For questions of procedure, see *An Introduction to the Procedure of the House of Commons*, by Lord Campion (Philip Allan).

[2] P. 140, *post*.

[3] Chap. 42.

enacted by Parliament during the administration of a National Government a number of statutes which delegated power to legislate on matters of principle, subject to a time limit as to the exercise of the delegated powers. The Gold Standard (Amendment) Act empowered the Treasury to legislate for the control of the exchange. The National Economy Act empowered the King in Council to effect reductions, including salary cuts, in certain public services. The Foodstuffs (Prevention of Exploitation) Act authorised the Board of Trade, subject to an annulling resolution by either House of Parliament, to control the supply and price of certain foodstuffs, while two other measures which were designed to check abnormal importations of manufactured articles and horticultural products delegated to government departments the power to impose duties, subject to affirmative resolutions by the Commons.[1] Modern Finance Acts have used the method of delegation to authorise changes in purchase tax.

The Import Duties Act 1932 (now replaced by the Import Duties Act 1958) was a striking example of delegation in relation to taxation. This Act delegated to the Treasury the power to legislate on matters of taxation without fixing any time limit for the exercise of the power. The Act established a general *ad valorem* duty on all goods imported into the United Kingdom apart from certain specified exempted articles. The Treasury, after receiving a recommendation from the Import Duties Advisory Committee, who were removable from office by the Treasury, but otherwise independent of parliamentary or executive control, might by order direct that goods should be added to or removed from [2] the list of exempted articles. Similarly the Treasury might, on the recommendation of the Committee, impose or remove by order additional duties on luxury articles or articles of a kind which are produced or likely to be produced in substantial quantities in the United Kingdom.[3] On the recommendation of the Board of Trade the Treasury might by order give preference to goods from particular countries. The Act arranged for preferential tariffs for goods imported from the Dominions and Colonies.[4] The Board of Trade might with the concurrence of the Treasury impose additional duties on goods from those foreign countries which discriminated against United Kingdom

[1] The Abnormal Importations (Customs) Duties Act 1931; Horticultural Products (Emergency Customs Duties) Act 1931.

[2] Finance Act 1932, s. 7.

[3] Since 1939 the requirement of previous recommendation by the Committee has been suspended.

[4] See also Ottawa Agreements Act 1932 giving effect to agreements reached at the Imperial Conference, 1932.

goods. All orders made under the Act had to be laid before the House of Commons. Orders imposing customs duties expire after twenty-eight days, unless approved by resolution of the House of Commons. Other orders cease to have effect, if within twenty-eight days the House by resolution determine that they should be annulled. A more recent example of wider application is to be found in the economic regulation which was introduced by s. 9 of the Finance Act 1961. This empowers the Treasury by statutory instrument [1] to increase or to reduce by up to 10 per cent customs duties, most excise duties and purchase tax.

The Royal Assent

Parliament cannot legislate without the concurrence of all its parts, and therefore the assent of the Sovereign is required. The Sovereign not only summons Parliament and can dissolve Parliament, but must give her consent before any legislation can take effect. After a Bill has passed through all its stages in both Houses of Parliament, it awaits the royal assent by the Sovereign which traditionally has been given in the House of Lords by commissioners and not in person. By the Royal Assent Act 1967 the assent is notified to each House by its Speaker in order to obviate the interruption of the business of the Commons to attend the Lords for this purpose. The traditional procedure is preserved for Bills assented to at the prorogation ceremony and also on at least one other occasion each session. In giving the royal assent ancient forms are used. A public Bill, unless dealing with finance, as also a private Bill other than one of a personal nature, is accepted by the words "La Reine le veult." The formula for the veto was "La Reine s'avisera." A Bill of a personal nature, *e.g.* a divorce Bill in former times, is assented to by the words "soit fait comme il est desiré.". A financial Bill is assented to with the words "La Reine remercie ses bons sujets, accepte leur benevolence et ainsi le veult." The right of veto has not been exercised since the reign of Queen Anne. It may be said to have fallen into disuse as a consequence of ministerial responsibility. The veto could only be exercised on ministerial advice, and no Government would wish to veto Bills for which it was responsible or one for the passage of which it had afforded facilities through Parliament. The consent of the Sovereign is requested before legislation which affects any matter relating to the royal prerogative is debated. Such consent ensures that the ensuing legislation will not be subject to veto.

[1] Chap. 42.

The House of Lords; Parliament Act 1911

Except as provided by the Parliament Act 1911 all legislation needs the assent of both Houses of Parliament. A Bill, other than a Bill relating to the imposition or application of taxes, may be introduced in either House and must pass through all its stages in both Houses. In 1963 the Lord Chancellor withdrew after the third reading a Government Legal Aid Bill which had been introduced in the Lords because it infringed the privilege of the House of Commons as being a Bill dealing with the application of public funds. Important Bills which do not raise acute political controversy are frequently introduced in the House of Lords, but the majority of Bills originate in the House of Commons. It had for long been part of the customary law of Parliament that the House of Lords might reject, but not amend a Bill which related to public finance (other than charges of local authorities). To amend such a Bill would be to trespass upon the exclusive right of the Commons to grant or refuse supplies to the Crown. Though constitutional convention demanded that, when the will of the people was clearly behind the Commons, the Lords must give way in the event of a deadlock between the two Houses, the right of the Lords to reject legislation proposed by the Commons was until 1911 undisputed. The rejection by the House of Lords of the annual Finance Bill in 1909 led to the passing of the Parliament Act 1911 which was amended in 1949. By the provisions of that Act legislation may in exceptional circumstances be effected by the Queen and Commons alone. A Bill may be presented for the royal assent without the concurrence of the Lords:

(1) If the Lords fail within one month to pass a Bill which, having passed the Commons, is sent up at least one month before the end of the session endorsed by the Speaker as a money Bill; or

(2) If the Lords refuse in two (formerly three) successive sessions to pass a public Bill, other than a Bill certified as a money Bill, and if one year (formerly two years) has elapsed between the date when it was read a second time in the House of Commons in the first and the date when it was read a third time in that House in the second (formerly third) of those sessions.[1]

A Bill to extend the duration of Parliament is exempted from the provisions of the Parliament Acts, and in view of the increased power given to the House of Commons a provision was embodied in the Act of 1911 limiting the duration of Parliament to five, instead of seven, years.[2]

[1] The changes were made by the Parliament Act 1949, p. 136, *post*.
[2] For Acts prolonging Parliament, see p. 46, *ante*.

A money Bill is a public Bill which in the opinion of the Speaker contains only provisions dealing with either the imposition, repeal, remission, alteration or regulation of taxation; the imposition of charges on the Consolidated Fund, or on money provided by Parliament for the payment of debt or other financial purposes or the variation or repeal of such charges; supply; the appropriation, receipt, custody, issue or audit of public accounts, or the raising or guarantee or repayment of loans. Bills dealing with taxation, money or loans raised by local authorities or bodies for local purposes are not certifiable as money Bills. It is curious that the annual Finance Bill has not always been endorsed with the Speaker's certificate, nor are many Bills which are on their face within the definition.[1] The only Bills which have passed into law under the operation of the Parliament Act 1911 are the Welsh Church Act 1914, the Government of Ireland Act 1914 and the Parliament Act 1949. The Government of Ireland Act was repealed before it became operative; the Welsh Church Act, subject to later minor modifications, operated after a postponement caused by World War I.

There are no statutory restrictions on the power of the House of Lords to reject such statutory instruments as require their assent.[2]

Parliament Act, 1949

In October, 1947, the Parliament Bill was introduced. It proposed to amend the Parliament Act 1911 by limiting the suspensory veto of public Bills (other than money Bills) to two sessions and one year's interval between the second reading in the Commons on the first occasion and the third reading in the same House on the second occasion. The Bill, after passing the lower House, was rejected by the Lords towards the end of the 1947–48 session, after a delay during which the second reading in the Lords was adjourned for the purpose of holding a conference of party leaders drawn from both Houses. The purpose of the Conference was to find out whether agreement could be reached on the reform both of the composition and of the powers of the second chamber. Agreement was reached for the further consideration by the parties of proposals for the composition of such a chamber. These involved a constitution which would secure that there should be no permanent majority for any one political party, that heredity alone should not constitute a qualification for admission, that women should be admitted, and

[1] See Hills and Fellowes, *The Finance of Government* (Philip Allan), 2nd edn., App. I.

[2] Chap. 42.

that life members whether drawn from hereditary peers or from commoners created life peers should be drawn from persons appointed on grounds of personal distinction or public service and styled lords of Parliament. No agreement was reached on the powers of the proposed second chamber to delay the passage of legislation. The Government offered to recommend that the interval of one year from the second reading should be extended, if the period should prove in a particular case to be longer, to nine months from the third reading of a Bill on the first occasion of its passage through the Commons. The Opposition favoured eighteen months from the initial second reading but might have accepted twelve months from the third reading. They refused to accept the nine months' proposal because it might not have left the Lords adequate time to consider a Bill, in view of the length of time which is taken in the Commons to pass a controversial measure.[1] After the rejection of the Bill by the Lords on second reading, a step which followed the breakdown of the Conference, the Government wound up the session in July, 1948. Parliament reassembled in September for a short session solely for the purpose of again passing the amending Bill through the Commons and presenting it in the Lords where it was rejected for a second time under the Parliament Act procedure. The third session started late in October. It was not until this session had run for twelve months that the Parliament Bill was again passed through the Commons. It was in due course rejected by the Lords and received the Royal Assent on December 16, 1949, being thus the third measure to become law in this way since the enactment of the original Parliament Act in 1911.

Proposals for Amendment

The effect of the Parliament Acts is to leave the House of Lords with a suspensory veto over non-financial Bills, but with no power to prevent legislation proposed by the House of Commons. There have been innumerable proposals both for the reform of the House of Lords and for the amendment of the Parliament Acts. In particular it has been urged that the duty of certifying a Bill to be a money Bill should be transferred from the Speaker to an impartial committee, and that there should be excepted from the provisions of the Parliament Acts a Bill to abolish or alter the constitution of the House of Lords. Those who believe in the necessity of a second chamber with power to revise and insist on its revisions, and with power to

[1] See Cmd. 7380 for *Agreed Statement on Conclusion of the Conference of Party Leaders, 1948.*

compel the democratically chosen first chamber to appeal to the electors before introducing any drastic changes in the law, would welcome the repeal of the Parliament Acts, but any such proposal would involve reform of the composition of the House of Lords.

House of Lords Reform

It is agreed that it is not desirable as a matter of political expediency to give new powers or to restore old powers to the House of Lords as at present constituted on the hereditary principle. At one time no agreement could be reached on any proposals for reforming either the composition or powers of the House. In recent years the enactment both of the Life Peerages Act 1958 and the Peerage Act 1963 shows that some progress has been made with regard to reforming the composition, but as yet there is no agreement as to any change in the powers of a second chamber. But the Conference held in 1948 nearly reached agreement on proposals which retained the power to delay legislation and suggested no corresponding increase of power in other directions. The House of Lords as at present constituted performs competently the task of revising legislation which is not regarded as sacrosanct by the Government and of debating matters of public importance. A reformed House of Lords, if based upon the elective principle, would inevitably come into conflict with the House of Commons, while, if based on any other principle, its composition would in all probability incline to be predominantly conservative. A similar Conference was on the point of reaching agreement in 1968, but ceased to meet after the House of Lords had rejected a contentious Statutory Instrument. Nevertheless the Government introduced, but later withdrew under pressure from back-bench members on both sides of the House of Commons, a Parliament Act Bill which in principle had the support of the party leaders, Government and Opposition, in both Houses. The Bill offered as a solution a chamber of some 250 Life Peers with voting rights and restricted powers of delaying legislation by Bill for up to nine months. The scheme proposed gave the Government a small majority of peers with voting rights over the Opposition in each Parliament. It also provided for a small number of cross-bench peers together with some of the bishops and all the law lords to sit and vote. Other Life Peers were given the right to attend and to speak, but not to vote. The exercise of the Royal Prerogative as regards the creation of Life Peers was to be, as now, in the hands of the Prime Minister of the day; by this means the necessary majority of voting peers to support the Government of the day was assured for each Parliament.

It is noticeable that in those countries where a second chamber proves of most value the constitution is federal. The Lower House is elected on a population basis, while the Upper House normally represents the component parts of the federation and thus secures that the point of view of the component States is put forward.

Conflicts between Lords and Commons

Since the Parliament Act 1911 the knowledge that the House of Commons can usually enforce its will upon the House of Lords has rendered less important the older methods for the solution of conflicts between the two Houses, though the opportunities for a conflict between Lords and Commons between 1912 and 1945 were few. In 1947 there was a direct conflict on the issue of the Parliament Bill which was subsequently enacted as the Parliament Act 1949. On the other hand, in the following year the Government did not resist a vital amendment to the Criminal Justice Bill by which the Lords restored to the Bill the death penalty after the Commons had approved a clause suspending its operation for five years. If the Lords accept without amendment a Bill sent up to them by the House of Commons, they announce to the Commons that they have agreed to the Bill. If they amend a Bill, they return it with a message that they agree to the Bill with amendments to which they desire the consent of the Commons. Apart altogether from the provisions of the Parliament Act, for the Lords to amend a financial provision is a breach of the privileges of the Commons. This rule is sometimes waived owing to the fact that so many Bills containing financial provisions raise issues of general political, as much as financial, importance. If the Lords amend a financial provision (not being a money Bill certified under the Parliament Act), the question of privilege is raised when the Bill is returned to the House of Commons, but the House may waive privilege and consider the amendments made by the Lords on their merits.

In the past if the Commons disagreed with the amendments made by the Lords, there were two methods for attempting to effect an agreement. A formal conference could be held.[1] Alternatively a Committee of the House which was disagreeing with amendments could send to the other House a statement of their reasons, together with the amended Bill. A settlement would probably be reached by informal conferences between the party leaders.

[1] As to conferences, see Anson, *op. cit.*, Vol. I, p. 298.

Public Bills

The process of legislation is complicated. A distinction must be drawn between public and private Bills. The object of a public Bill is to alter the general law. A private Bill is a Bill relating to some matter of individual, corporate or local interest.[1] A private Bill must not be confused with a public Bill introduced by a private member. It will be convenient to state in outline the process by which a public Bill becomes an Act of Parliament.[2] It is presented and receives a formal first reading. It is then printed. Then follows a second reading. The debate on the second reading is a debate on the general merits of the Bill.[3] After receiving a second reading it is referred either to one of the Standing Committees nominated by the Committee of Selection, or, if the House so resolves,[4] in the case of measures affecting constitutional rights to a Committee of the whole House. Since this matter is decided by motion, the Government can successfully resist the Opposition's demand that the importance of a Bill justifies its being committed to a Committee of the whole House. In committee members may move relevant amendments, and may speak any number of times in support of or in opposition to such amendments. When a Bill is committed to a Committee of the whole House, the Speaker leaves the Chair, and his place is taken by the Chairman of Committees—the Chairman of Ways and Means—or his Deputy. Standing Committees, formerly limited to five, are now constituted as business requires. At the beginning of each session there is appointed a Committee of Selection of eleven members drawn from all the main parties. The Committee of Selection nominates the members of the Standing Committees. Parties are represented as nearly as possible in proportion to their representation in the House itself, a rule which prevented use being made of Standing Committees in the Parliament elected in 1950 when the Government had a majority of only six, and restricted the use of such Committees in the subsequent Parliament where the new Government had a majority of less than twenty. For each of these Standing Committees there is a nucleus of at least

[1] Private Bills are of two kinds, Local, *e.g.* those affecting a particular locality, and Private (in the strict sense), *e.g.* those affecting a particular body or individual.

[2] The procedure described is that of the House of Commons.

[3] The second reading debate on Scottish Bills may take place in the Scottish Grand Committee unless this course is opposed by ten or more members.

[4] Whether or not a constitutional Bill is taken in Committee of the Whole House depends on practice. Possibly the test should be that Bills should be classified as constitutional which contain material that would be contained in written constitutions: 648 H.C. Deb. 1170-76.

twenty members and from ten to thirty others may be added by the Selection Committee for the consideration of a particular Bill; the quorum is fifteen. The Scottish Grand Committee, to which may be committed for consideration in principle Bills dealing exclusively with Scotland, consists of all the members for Scottish constituencies with not less than ten nor more than fifteen other members. There is a similar Committee for Wales. After the committee stage the Bill as amended is reported to the House and is again discussed. Further amendments and alterations may be made in the report stage, and, if necessary, the Bill may be recommitted to the Committee. Finally the Bill is submitted to a third reading. During the third reading debate only verbal alterations may be made.

Crown's Recommendation and Financial Resolutions

The recommendation of the Crown, which is a guarantee that the Government accepts responsibility for the charge, is required by Standing Orders dating from the early eighteenth century before the House of Commons will proceed upon any motion for a charge upon the public revenue. It is nowadays signified in writing and the fact is recorded on the Order Paper. Once the recommendation has been signified, the proposed charge cannot be increased by amendment. The rule is in the United Kingdom embodied in a Standing Order, but it is of fundamental importance and is expressly enacted in the constitutions of several Commonwealth States which accept the sovereignty of the Queen. Similarly the Constitution of India requires the recommendation of the President. National expenditure is the responsibility of the Government, which must provide means to meet all approved expenditure. Moreover private members are by the existence of this rule saved from temptation to suggest expenditure for the benefit of their constituents or particular interests. A Bill of which the main object is the creation of a public charge can only be introduced in the House of Commons. Wherever a Bill (and most modern Bills include some incidental expenditure) authorises any expenditure, a financial resolution of the House is necessary. There was formerly an important distinction of procedure between Bills primarily concerned with expenditure and those only incidentally involving expenditure. In the former case, but not in the latter, it was necessary that a financial resolution in Committee of the whole House should precede the introduction of the Bill. The distinction is now of little practical importance, as Bills primarily concerned with expenditure follow the same procedure as Bills incidentally involving expenditure, provided that they are presented, or brought in upon an order of the House, by a Minister of the

Crown.[1] In that event, or when expenditure is only subsidiary to the main object of a Bill, the financial resolutions may follow the second reading of the Bill. The financial clauses are printed in italics, and after the second reading the necessary financial resolutions must be agreed to before any clause authorising a charge can form part of the Bill. Written instructions were given in 1938 to all departments and to the parliamentary counsel to draft financial resolutions in wide terms in order that discussion might not be unduly limited by being confined by the terms of the financial resolutions introduced by the Government. The House then goes into Committee on the Bill or sends it to a Standing Committee. When a Bill is introduced in the House of Lords, the financial clauses are printed, but are only moved in the Commons at a later stage. They are left out of the Bill to avoid questions of privilege, but are inserted in brackets to make the rest of the Bill intelligible.

Closure

The complicated stages through which a Bill must go and the amount of time involved have led, with the increase of the amount of business to which Parliament must attend and of the number of members who wish to speak, to the adoption of various methods of curtailing debates. The simplest method is that known as the "closure," first introduced to check obstruction by the Opposition. Any member may, either in the House or in Committee, move "that the question be now put." The chairman may refuse to put the motion on the ground that it is an infringement of the rights of the minority, but, if the motion is put and carried, it brings to an end the debate which is in progress. The motion "that the question be now put" is voted upon without debate. It can only be carried in the House itself if the number voting is not less than 100. Another method is known as the "kangaroo" closure. The Speaker has the power, when a Bill is being discussed on the report stage, to select from among the various amendments proposed those which shall be discussed. The chairman of a Committee of the whole House may exercise similar power, as since 1934 may the Chairmen of Standing Committees. More drastic still is the "guillotine." By resolution of the House, various periods of time are allotted to each stage of a Bill. At the end of each period the portion of the Bill in question is voted upon without further discussion. The guillotine can also be employed in Standing Committees by a Time Order passed by the

[1] Other than a Bill imposing taxation, which must be preceded by a financial resolution; see p. 149, *post*.

House; this empowers a Business Sub-Committee of the relevant Standing Committee to allocate a time-table for the Bill within the period allowed and fixes the date on which the Bill has to be reported back to the House.[1] An allocation of time by agreement was substituted for the guillotine to deal with the Government of India Bill in 1935, and may be followed in other cases.[2]

Drafting of Bills

Almost all important Bills are brought forward by the Government of the day and are the result either of decisions of policy taken in the Cabinet or of the recommendations of departments. They are drafted by Parliamentary Counsel to the Treasury on instructions framed by the departments. In spite of the skill of these highly trained experts modern legislation becomes increasingly obscure. The problems which the draftsman is called upon to solve by legislative formulae increase in complexity as Parliament tries more and more to regulate social and economic conditions. Moreover pressure on parliamentary time, and even more the desire not to renew debate in Parliament on a former controversial issue, result in legislation by reference to existing statutes. Then too amendments may be hastily introduced at the last moment in order to facilitate the passage of a Bill. On the other hand, the production of numerous consolidation Acts has long been materially assisting to elucidate the Statute Book, Since 1949 a number of Consolidation Bills have been passed into law each year and a wide range of topics has been covered. Outstanding examples are the Magistrates' Courts Act 1952, the Highways Act 1959 and the Town and Country Planning Act 1962. The first of these Acts resulted in the repeal, in whole or in part, of sixty-four earlier statutes.

C. Financial Procedure [3]

Parliament, and more particularly the House of Commons, has two main functions in relation to public finance, the grant of supply and the raising of revenue. No payment out of the Exchequer may

[1] This procedure, first authorised in 1945, was applied to the Transport and Town and Country Planning Bills in 1947 and resulted in a large part of each Bill not being considered at all in committee. The result was that the Government, as well as the Opposition, tabled a very large number of amendments in the Lords; 996 amendments were made to Government Bills sent up from the Commons in the session 1946–7.

[2] The Select Committee on Procedure, 1959, recommended a formal timetable for all Public Bills, H.C. 92 (1959), para. 7. This has not been accepted.

[3] The reader should refer to J. W. Hills and E. A. Fellowes, *The Finance of Government*.

be made without the authority of an Act of Parliament, and then only for the express purpose for which it has been appropriated by the statute. No taxation, charges or loans can be authorised except by or under the authority of an Act.

Supply

In advance of the opening of the financial year on April 1 the requirements of the departments in the form of estimates of the expenditure required for the public services for the coming year are presented to Parliament and published about the end of February. Previous to presentation the estimates are revised by and agreed with the Treasury, whose function is to adjust the competing claims of the various services, so far as the expenditure is capable of adjustment. A great part, however, of the requirements of the civil departments is fixed by statutes which determine the scale of expenditure, except the expenses of actual administration. Thus the Treasury cannot by revision of the estimates scale down the rate of insurance benefits, or of pensions, or the grants-in-aid of public services where the expenditure incurred, though voted annually, is determined by the scale enacted in the Act which created the charge. In the event of disagreement between the Treasury and a department the final arbiter is the Cabinet.

Resolutions approving the various votes into which the estimates are divided are passed by the House of Commons. Each vote can be discussed separately and is separately passed. The number of days allotted for consideration of the annual estimates, including votes on account and supplementary estimates, is regulated by standing orders. The number has been fixed at twenty-nine, all of which must be taken before August 5. The estimates for the separate departments for Scotland are referred to the Scottish Grand Committee, with a limit of six days for debate. The Opposition choose which of the departmental estimates they desire to discuss. Discussions on supply afford an opportunity for discussing the general policy of the Government. In modern form the ancient rule holds good that redress of grievances must come before supply. No subject may be discussed that would require legislation. On the last day but one of the days allotted for supply all outstanding votes are taken, and on the last day there is taken the report stage of all outstanding resolutions. The resolutions when agreed to are embodied in the annual Appropriation Act which authorises the issue from the Consolidated Fund of the grants appropriating the amounts required for the Supply services of the year.[1] The Act also limits the expenditure of each department to the sums set out against each item in a schedule to the Act, thus ensuring not only that expenditure does not exceed the sum voted but that it is only incurred for authorised purposes.[2] Before the Appropriation Act can be passed there must be also voted and agreed to resolutions authorising the withdrawal of moneys from the Consolidated Fund.[3]

Votes on Account and Consolidated Fund Acts

It has been said that no expenditure can be incurred without parliamentary authorisation, but the Appropriation Act is not passed until July or August. Each financial year is a water-tight compartment. It follows that money must be provided for the Government between April 1 and the passing of the annual Appropriation Act. There are submitted to the House of Commons early in March votes on account of the civil and defence departments and there is enacted a Consolidated Fund Bill[4] authorising the withdrawal from the Consolidated Fund of the necessary sum. The sum formally authorised by the Appropriation Act is the total of the expenditure voted for the year less the sum already authorised to be withdrawn by Consolidated Fund Acts.

Supplementary Estimates

Where a department later considers that it will need to exceed its estimated expenditure, a supplementary estimate must be introduced. The resolutions authorising the withdrawal from the Consolidated Fund of the sums so voted are usually embodied in the Consolidated Fund Act which authorises the issue of the next year's vote on account and the sum is appropriated to specific objects in the next year's Appropriation Act. Except when a supplementary estimate relates to a change of policy or a new service, the policy of the service concerned can only be debated in so far as it is brought into question by the excess. These debates have been criticised as time wasting; but the fact that a supplementary estimate must be justified in debate does operate as a check on the departments in framing their original estimates.

[1] Chap. 17, and specimen Vote of Supply scheduled to the Act in App. A pp. 727–9, *post*.

[2] For the functions of the Comptroller and Auditor-General and his reports to the Public Accounts Committee of the House of Commons, see Chap. 17.

[3] The resolutions are treated as formal.

[4] It is sometimes necessary for more than one Consolidated Fund Act to be passed in anticipation of the annual Appropriation Act.

Votes of Credit

In times of grave emergency there may be voted a lump sum not allocated to any particular object. Such votes are known as votes of credit. By this means the extra-ordinary expenditure in time of war is in the main voted. The method involves relaxation of the usual methods of Treasury control, and in consequence the estimates of the departments concerned with expenditure in time of war are presented with a token figure inserted instead of the actual expenditure proposed.

Appropriations in Aid

There must also be mentioned appropriations in aid, the estimates for which appear side by side with the estimates of expenditure, though only the net amount of the latter is voted. Appropriations in aid are sums received by departments and retained to meet departmental expenditure. For example, the net vote on account of the Public Trustee is £10, a token figure for the purpose of preserving parliamentary control, the whole of his expenditure being met by appropriations in aid in the form of fees.

Procedure for Supply

The financial procedure of the House of Commons in relation to sanctioning expenditure is adequate for the purpose for which it came into being, namely to ensure that money should only be spent with the authority of Parliament and for the purposes authorised by Parliament, but it provides no opportunity for real control of expenditure. Debates on Supply afford an opportunity for a general discussion on the work of a department, but not for a detailed examination of departmental expenditure A member may move to reduce, though not to increase a vote, but such motions are invariably treated by the Government as votes of confidence and are invariably withdrawn or rejected. The accounts are not presented in a form which is easily understood by members, nor are they well adapted for the ascertainment of comparative costs.[1] The passing of outstanding votes on the last two days of Supply may involve the approval without discussion of large items of public expenditure.

The Estimates Committee

There was until the outbreak of the Second World War a Select Committee on Estimates drawn from all parties which could examine

[1] See Chap. 17, and Hills and Fellowes, *op. cit.*, p. 33.

estimates already presented and suggest economies, but could not discuss policy. It did not have an opportunity to discuss estimates till after they had been presented and only dealt with a limited number of estimates each year. During the First and Second World Wars there were appointed Select Committees of the House of Commons on National Expenditure. The committee appointed during the Second World War was confined to investigating expenditure directly connected with the war. Nevertheless, it covered a wide range of departmental expenditure and interpreted its terms of reference as enabling it to criticise freely the policy of the departments. Its frequent reports to Parliament received wide publicity in the press, and the resulting action of departments was also reported on by the committee. It also addressed a number of representations to the Prime Minister where on grounds of security it was precluded from issuing a public report. This committee repeated the previous recommendation for closer co-ordination between committees examining estimates and the Public Accounts Committee. They also criticised the form of the national accounts which are kept on a cash basis described by the committee as "the penny note book system."[1] The Select Committee on Procedure reported in 1946 in favour of amalgamating the Public Accounts and Estimates Committees into a Public Expenditure Committee entrusted with the whole task of examining with the assistance of sub-committees the field of public expenditure.[2] But the Government declined to ask the House to adopt this recommendation.

The terms of reference of the Estimates Committee still only allow consideration of how the policy implied in the estimates can be carried out more economically, but the manner of working has changed. Drawing on the experience of the wartime National Expenditure Committees the Estimates Committee appoints investigating sub-committees including one which investigates supplementary estimates. The result has been that as many as fourteen separate reports have been presented by the full Committee to the House in a single session. Evidence is taken from officials, and not only from one or two high officials as formerly, but from those actually responsible for the details of expenditure as well as from non-official witnesses, such as trade associations on the occasion of examination of the estimates of the Ministry of Food. Since 1945 there have been several debates on reports from the Committee on Supply Days. The Committee is concerned to see that the sums voted are well spent within the permitted maxima approved by the

[1] H.C. 122 of 1944.
[2] H.C. 189 of 1946, paras. 42 and 43.

House. It can suggest economies which may be reflected in the estimates of succeeding years. It may be claimed that, subject to the limitation that it is ineffective to secure a reduction of a current estimate, the Committee now functions more effectively than in the inter-war period, despite the mounting size of public expenditure which cannot be curtailed except by legislation since it is largely due to statutory items which reflect accepted policy. The specialised Select Committees,[1] first appointed in the Session 1967–8, were given terms of reference, "to consider" the activities named and "to report". This appears to be wide enough to empower them to examine departmental expenditure.

Ways and Means

Revenue, like expenditure, is raised partly under statutes that continue until repealed, partly under the authority of annual statutes. The bulk of revenue is raised by the former method, though income tax and sur-tax, since the rates are fixed annually, are in theory exceptions. In contrast the bulk of expenditure is sanctioned annually. Shortly after the opening of the financial year in April, the Chancellor of the Exchequer "opens his Budget" in the House of Commons. The traditional Budget statement falls into two parts. The first is a retrospect of the past year, comparing yield of revenue with estimated yield, and actual with estimated expenditure. The second part deals with (1) the estimated expenditure of the new year, which is already known to members and the public through the publication by March of the new year's estimates, and (2) the Chancellor's proposals for meeting it out of taxation on the existing basis, together with his intentions as to the imposition of new or the remission of existing taxation. These matters are closely guarded secrets until the Budget is opened, in order that steps may not be taken to forestall them, *e.g.* by dumping of goods or speculation on the Stock Exchange. In recent years as a result of the increased interest in and importance to the Government of economic affairs there has been published contemporaneously with the opening of the Budget by the Chancellor of the Exchequer a White Paper containing an analysis of the national income of the past year. From this practice, which may well be extended to include other information, such as a statement of capital expenditure, there has resulted a change in the character of the Chancellor's statement in the direction of making it as much a statement of financial policy as a mere review of the actual finance of the period.

[1] P. 130, *ante*.

Budget Resolutions

After the annual Budget resolutions agreeing to the Chancellor's proposals are passed by the House of Commons. These cover the rates of income-tax and new customs and excise duties. Other taxes, such as death duties, which endure until varied or abolished by a Finance Act, do not require the Budget resolutions. The taxing resolutions are later embodied in the annual Finance Act, just as the resolutions authorising supply grants are embodied in the annual Appropriation Act. The effect of any changes made by the Finance Act may be made retrospective to the date of the Budget or any selected date. It was for long the practice to begin at once to collect taxes under the authority of resolutions. This practice was challenged in *Bowles* v. *The Bank of England*,[1] in which Mr. Gibson Bowles sued the Bank of England for a declaration that it was not entitled to deduct any sum by way of income-tax from dividends, until such tax was imposed by Act of Parliament. The decision given in favour of the plaintiff illustrates the fundamental principle maintained in *Stockdale* v. *Hansard* [2] that no resolution of the House of Commons can alter the law of the land. In 1913, however, there was passed the Provisional Collection of Taxes Act, which gives statutory force for a limited period to a resolution of the House varying an existing tax or renewing a tax imposed during the preceding year. An Act confirming such resolutions must become law within four months from the date of the resolution or by August 5 in the same year if voted in March or April, the latter being the usual month for the Budget speech. The Act which was re-enacted in 1968 only applies to resolutions for the variation or renewal of customs and excise duties, income-tax and purchase tax. Though the collection of other new duties may not be started until the Finance Act is passed, the Treasury may make regulations to ensure that they shall be paid in the event of their being given retrospective operation.[3] It should be noted that the control of the House of Commons over taxation is far more real than is its control over expenditure. The raising of moneys by loan charged on the public revenue (Consolidated Fund) also requires the authority of an Act of Parliament; examples may be found in the War Loan Acts 1914–19 and the National Loans Acts 1939–45.

[1] [1913] 1 Ch. 57.
[2] P. 158, *post*.
[3] Finance Act 1926, s. 6, *e.g.* regulations authorising customs officers to record the names of importers.

D. Private Bills

A private Bill is a Bill to alter the law relating to some particular locality or to confer rights on or relieve from liability some particular person or body of persons (including particularly local authorities and statutory undertakers, *e.g.* water companies).[1] After preliminary advertisement of the objects of the Bill, deposit of plans and other documents in Parliament, with local authorities and in other specified places, a petition for the Bill together with a printed copy of the Bill must be deposited with Parliament by November 27 each year. There is thus only one opportunity a year for the promotion of a private Bill. Provided that the other elaborate formalities required by the Standing Orders of the House in which the Bill is introduced have been complied with, the Bill receives a first reading. The second reading of the Bill does not determine, as in the case of a public Bill, its desirability, but merely that, given that the facts stated in its preamble are true, it is unobjectionable from the point of view of national policy. If read a second time, the Bill is committed to a Committee of four members in the Commons or of five members in the Lords. The functions of the Committee are to examine the Bill from the point of view of national policy and to hold the balance as between competing local and private interests. The Committee stage is a quasi-judicial proceeding at which after certain formalities the opponents of the Bill may appear. The promoters and opponents of the Bill are heard, usually by counsel, and may call evidence. It is first decided whether or not the facts stated in the preamble, which sets out the special reasons for the Bill, have been proved. If the preamble is accepted, the clauses are then taken in order. If the preamble is rejected, the Bill is dead. After the committee stage the Bill is reported to the House, and its subsequent stages are similar to those of a public Bill. A private Bill may be opposed in committee in both Houses. Private Bill procedure when a Bill is opposed is both expensive and necessarily takes time. This method of seeking statutory powers is of great importance to progressive local authorities who may seek for powers wider than those conferred by the Acts from which they derive the powers common to local authorities in general. There are, however, other means of obtaining statutory authority for the exercise of special powers, and in particular ministerial orders made under statute may be mentioned as of im-

[1] For history of private Bill procedure, see O. C. Williams, *History of Private Bill Procedure*, Vol. I, 1949, H.M. Stationery Office.

portance to-day both to local authorities and statutory undertakings as sources of their powers.[1]

E. Miscellaneous Functions

Judicial Functions

The judicial functions of Parliament—the appellate jurisdiction of the House of Lords and the process of impeachment—are discussed elsewhere.[2]

Petitions

Another function of Parliament is the receiving of petitions. Any subject may petition the House of Commons, even if he seeks to impose a new charge upon the public funds, and the House decides whether or not to receive such petitions. Petitions must be presented by a member. They are referred to a select committee, which may direct their circulation among members. They may be, but very seldom are, debated.[3]

Committees of Inquiry

Either House may set up a committee to inquire into any matter of public importance, and a resolution to set up such an inquiry may be an expression of no confidence in the Government of the day. Such committees may be composed solely of members of Parliament or may have a wider composition. Under the Tribunals of Inquiry (Evidence) Act 1921 both Houses of Parliament may resolve that it is expedient that a tribunal be appointed to inquire into a matter of urgent public importance. In pursuance of such a resolution a tribunal may be appointed by Her Majesty or by a Secretary of State. The instrument of appointment may confer all the powers of the High Court with regard to the examination of witnesses and production of documents. The tribunal can accordingly require a witness to answer any question which it deems relevant. This power resulted in the imprisonment of two journalists who refused to disclose their sources of information which the tribunal deemed relevant.[4] A tribunal was appointed under this Act in 1936 to inquire into allegations of a leakage of Budget secrets. In 1948 such a tribunal investigated allegations of improper approaches to

[1] Chap. 26, at p. 375, *post*, for the procedure hereon.
[2] Chap. 22.
[3] Petitions are also occasionally presented to the House of Lords.
[4] P. 541, *post*.

certain members of the Government. In 1957 the premature disclosure of a change in the Bank Rate was investigated by another such tribunal and, somewhat surprisingly, in 1959 a tribunal in Scotland was called upon to investigate a minor assault inflicted by a constable upon a youth. In 1962 a tribunal presided over by a Lord of Appeal inquired into allegations concerning security at the Admiralty resulting from the conviction of an employee for espionage. The Aberfan Tip disaster in 1966 was the subject of another inquiry which received much publicity on account of the number of victims, mainly children in schools, and the finding of negligence against the National Coal Board. Although these tribunals are normally presided over by a High Court judge who is assisted by two prominent independent members, not always lawyers, there has been considerable criticism as to the character of the inquiry. The presence of the judge suggests a trial, but there are no accused. The case to be inquired into is presented to the tribunal by a Law Officer or counsel of equivalent status who calls witnesses, whether or not suspicion has fallen upon them. At the discretion of the tribunal legal representation is allowed to witnesses who thus are enabled to cross-examine one another. In the case of the tribunal in 1962 the costs of witnesses in whole or in part were allowed by the Treasury. But normal facilities for answering an accusation are not available to any party appearing at the tribunal. This may result in condemnation of a party who is never called upon to meet a formal charge and so has no opportunity of answering his accusers. So far as the procedure is designed to remove suspicions of discreditable conduct, it is of questionable value and lacks the safeguards which are available to meet a charge properly framed at a trial in court.

Royal Commission 1966 [1]

A Royal Commission which reported before the Aberfan inquiry recommended that these statutory tribunals should only be used in cases of vital public importance, but otherwise did not favour any changes such as a preliminary inquiry or an appeal. Sittings in private were to be discouraged. Emphasis was laid upon the protection of persons whose reputations might be involved, *e.g.* a witness to be called should be told beforehand of any allegations in which he was involved and should be entitled to legal representation and the right of cross-examination. The dual rôle of the Attorney-General as adviser to the Government and independent counsel to the tribunal should be avoided by the appointment of another Queen's Counsel in the latter rôle.

[1] Cmnd. 3121 (1966).

In 1968 the chairman of the Royal Commission (Lord Justice Salmon) was appointed to head a committee on contempt of court in relation to the proceedings of these tribunals.

The Report [1] of this departmental committee recommends that the law of contempt of court [2] should continue to apply to tribunals of inquiry in a modified form, namely that there should be no prohibition on comment at any time on the subject-matter of the inquiry. But after the actual appointment of the tribunal it should continue to be contempt if anyone says or does anything "in relation to any evidence relevant to the subject-matter which is intended or obviously likely to alter, distort, destroy or withhold such evidence from the tribunal". Thus the press could at any time put forward theories as to the cause of a disaster, like that at Aberfan, but could not publish an interview with a witness (actual, as distinct from potential) just prior to his appearance.

Addresses of Removal

Certain officers, such as Judges of the Supreme Court, are removable upon the presentation of an address to the Crown by both Houses of Parliament. The proceedings in relation to such an address are of a judicial character.[3]

[1] Cmnd. 4078 (1969).
[2] Chap. 37, *post*, esp. p. 542.
[3] P. 329, *post*.

CHAPTER TEN

PRIVILEGES OF PARLIAMENT

Nature of Privilege

PRIVILEGES are an important part of the law and custom of Parliament. They concern the relations of both Houses with the Queen, the courts, the public, and with one another. Except so far as it has been made statutory, a privilege is part of the common law and, therefore, neither House can create any new privilege, but must justify its claim on the authority of precedent. The courts, while reluctant to enquire into the exercise of privilege, so far as it concerns the internal proceedings of either House or their relations with one another, will not admit of its extension at the expense of the rights of the subject. For to do so would involve recognising that one House could change the law by its own resolution.

A. House of Commons

In order that neither the House collectively nor members individually may be obstructed in the performance of their duties, there have from earliest times been attached both to the House itself and to members thereof certain privileges and immunities.

Demand of Privileges

At the opening of each session of Parliament the Speaker formally claims from the Crown for the Commons "their ancient and undoubted rights and privileges." Those particularly mentioned are: "that their persons may be free from arrests and molestations; that they may enjoy liberty of speech in all their debates and may have access to Her Majesty's royal person whenever occasion shall require; and that all their proceedings shall receive from Her Majesty the most favourable construction." The right of access is a collective privilege of the House exercised through the Speaker. The grant of these privileges is formally conveyed through the Lord Chancellor.

Freedom from Arrest

The privilege of freedom from arrest protects a member of Parliament from civil arrest in proceedings for a period of from forty days before to forty days after a meeting of Parliament. It does not protect from arrest on a criminal charge nor from preventive detention by order of the executive authority under statutory powers, *e.g.* regulations made under Defence Acts in time of war.[1] A subpoena addressed to a member probably cannot be enforced by the High Court while the House is in session, but in practice the House grants leave of absence for attendance as a witness in courts of justice. Members are entitled to exemption from jury service. Parliament has always maintained the right of receiving immediate information of the imprisonment or detention of any member, together with the reasons for his detention. In cases of imprisonment the House passes without debate a motion for expulsion of the convicted member. In the various Habeas Corpus Suspension Acts of the eighteenth and early nineteenth centuries [2] provision was always made that before a member was committed to prison or detained, there must be obtained the consent of the House of which he was a member. The general history of the privilege shows that the tendency has been to narrow its scope; it does not protect from proceedings under the Bankruptcy Acts nor probably from arrest on a criminal charge for a non-indictable offence nor from proceedings for contempt of court. There is no protection in cases of refusal to give surety to keep the peace or security for good behaviour. In the case of John Wilkes the Court of Common Pleas held [3] that the privilege protected from arrest for seditious libel, but both Houses of Parliament ruled to the contrary. Since the abolition of imprisonment for civil debt (except where it is shown that a debtor has means to satisfy a judgment, but has neglected to do so) [4] the privilege has become of small importance. The privilege applied to members' servants until the passing of the Parliamentary Privilege Act 1770.

Freedom of Speech

The privilege of freedom of speech, though so well established as to be unquestioned, is manifestly of the first importance. It is to-day the only substantial privilege.

[1] *Report from the Committee of Privileges*, H.C. 164 (1940). Detention as the result of words spoken in Parliament would be a violation of the privilege of freedom of speech; see p. 156, *post*.

[2] P. 719, *post*.

[3] *The King* v. *Wilkes* (1763), 2 Wilson 151.

[4] P. 482, note 2, *post*.

Haxey's Case

As early as 1397 one Haxey, about whose status as a member of Parliament doubt has been thrown, was prosecuted for treason. The treasonable act was his sponsorship of a petition (Bill) for the curtailment of the King's household expenses. On his accession in 1399 Henry IV caused the judgment to be reversed. This is sometimes regarded as the first recognition of parliamentary freedom of speech.[1]

Strode's Case

In Henry VIII's reign one Strode was imprisoned by the Stannary Court of Devon for invading the province of that court by introducing a Bill in Parliament to regulate the tin mines of that county which were within that court's jurisdiction. He was fined and imprisoned, but an Act [2] was passed declaring that any legal proceedings "for any bill, speaking, reasoning, or declaring of any matter or matters concerning the Parliament should be utterly void and of none effect."

Strode's Case was a conflict between Parliament and the Stannary Court, not a conflict between the Crown and Parliament. Until the seventeenth century privilege meant little more than the assertion of freedom to choose subjects of discussion (*e.g.* Elizabeth's marriage) in face of objection by the Crown.

Sir John Eliot's Case

In the next century the right to criticise the King's Government came to a head when in 1629 Eliot, Holles and Valentine were convicted for seditious words spoken in the House of Commons and for tumult in the same place.[3] The judgment was subsequently reversed in the House of Lords on the ground that words spoken in Parliament could only be judged in Parliament.

Bill of Rights

Finally it was enacted by the Bill of Rights 1688 "that the freedom of speech and debates or proceedings in Parliament ought not to be impeached or questioned in any court or place out of Parliament." No action will lie against a member of Parliament for words spoken by him in the course of parliamentary proceedings, and similarly no action will lie for any publication among members of Parliament by order of the House or in the ordinary course of parliamentary business. It was held in *Lake* v. *King* [4] that an action would not lie

[1] See J. R. Tanner, *Tudor Constitutional Documents* (Cambridge University Press), p. 555; T. F. Tout, *Chapters in Mediaeval Administrative History* (Manchester University Press), Vol. IV, pp. 18–19.

[2] 4 Hen. 8 c. 8; Statutes of the Realm iii. 53.

[3] *Eliot's Case* (1629), 3 St. Tr. 294.

[4] (1667), 1 Saunders 131.

for defamatory matter contained in a petition printed and delivered to members.

Official Secrets Acts

Disclosures made in Parliament either by speeches or questions may not be made the subject-matter of a prosecution under the Official Secrets Acts 1911–39.[1] Unless there are express words in a statute overriding parliamentary privilege, no member may be proceeded against as the result of words spoken in the performance of his duty as a member of Parliament. The privilege of freedom of speech extends to words spoken outside the House of Commons if spoken in the essential performance of duty as a member, *e.g.* a conversation on parliamentary business in a Minister's private house. Conversely it does not extend to a casual conversation in the House of Commons on private affairs. A member may not without the consent of the House give evidence in a court of law concerning what passes in Parliament.[2]

Privacy of Debate

In connection with the privilege of freedom of speech it is convenient to consider also the right of the House to secure privacy of debate, and to control publication of its debates and proceedings outside Parliament. By resolution of 3 March 1762, any publication of speeches made by members is a breach of privilege. The resolution has never been renewed, but breach of privilege is occasionally raised in cases of misreporting of speeches in the press; this aggravates the breach, of which usually no notice is taken in order that publicity may be given to proceedings of the House.[3] Until the eighteenth century the House resented and prevented any publication of accounts of its proceedings, but since the famous conflict between the House of Commons and John Wilkes, this privilege has not been insisted upon. The House, however, may at any time resolve that publication is a breach of privilege. The House has always enjoyed the right to exclude strangers. In time of war each House occasionally asserts its right to exclude strangers in order to go into secret session for security reasons.

Publication of Debates and Speeches

The right of the House to publish accounts of its proceedings otherwise than among its own members was at common law restricted by

[1] *Report of Select Committee on Official Secrets Acts*, H.C. 101 (1939).

[2] *Ibid.*

[3] There is a proposal under consideration to rescind this resolution and replace it by one adapted to current practice (December 1969).

the ordinary law of defamation (libel and slander) despite the Bill of Rights protection to proceedings in Parliament.

In the case of *Stockdale* v. *Hansard*,[1] Stockdale sued the printer of certain reports containing defamatory matter, which were published by order of the House of Commons and were available for sale to the public. Improper books published by the plaintiff were said to be permitted in Newgate prison. This was the second of a series of actions between the parties arising out of the repeated publication of the reports. The defendant was ordered by the House to plead that he had acted under an order of the House of Commons, a court superior to any court of law, whose orders could not be questioned; and further that the House of Commons had declared that the case was a case of privilege; that each House of Parliament was the sole judge of its own privileges; and that a resolution of the House declaratory of its privileges could not be questioned in any court of law. The Court of Queen's Bench rejected the defence, holding that only the Queen and both Houses of Parliament could make or unmake laws; that no resolution of any one House of Parliament could place anyone beyond the control of the law; and that, when it was necessary in order to decide the rights of private individuals in matters arising outside Parliament, courts of law should determine the nature and existence of privileges of the House of Commons. It was held further that there was no privilege of the House of Commons which permitted the publication outside the House of defamatory matter.

Similarly, although a member of Parliament may speak freely within Parliament, he may be liable to proceedings for defamation if he publishes his speech outside Parliament.[2] The decision of the Queen's Bench showed that there can be no finality on the issue of legality of a privilege so long as the House of Commons asserts exclusive jurisdiction and the courts deny it.

The sequel to the case of *Stockdale* v. *Hansard* was the attempt of the sheriffs to recover for the plaintiff by lawful process of execution on the property of Hansard the £600 damages which the court had awarded to Stockdale in the third action of the series. The House had previously decided that Hansard should not plead and that the plaintiff should suffer for his contempt of the resolutions and authority of the House. The money recovered from Hansard was in the hands of the sheriffs when the parliamentary session of 1840 opened; they were aware of the resolutions of the Commons. The House first committed Stockdale and then, on the sheriffs refusing to refund the money to Hansard, also committed the two sheriffs for contempt, without expressing the real cause for the committal. In habeas corpus proceedings it was held in the *Case of the Sheriff of Middlesex* [3] that the court had to accept the statement by the House that the sheriffs had been committed simply for contempt.

[1] (1839), 9 A. & E. 1; K. & L. 280.
[2] *The King* v. *Creevey* (1813), 1 M. & S. 278.
[3] (1840), 11 A. & E. 273; K. & L. 283.

Thus it would seem that the power to commit for contempt of court which the High Court can exercise for whatever conduct it adjudges to amount to contempt cannot be denied to the House of Commons itself a part of the High Court of Parliament.[1]

As will be seen later,[2] the right of the House of Commons to commit for contempt is not limited to the enforcement of accepted privileges. The House is thus in a position to adjudicate independently of the courts. What it cannot do is to legislate by resolution to create a new parliamentary privilege of which the courts must take notice. That can only be done by Act of the whole Parliament.

Parliamentary Papers

The case of *Stockdale* v. *Hansard* was followed by the Parliamentary Papers Act 1840 which enacted that any proceedings in respect of defamatory matter contained in a publication made by authority of the House of Lords or the House of Commons must be stayed on the production of a certificate from an officer of the House. Thus Parliament as a whole made the law to conform with what the House of Commons had attempted, unsuccessfully so far as the courts were concerned, to declare lawful by its own resolution. This Act also protected in the absence of malice the publication of fair and accurate extracts from papers published under the authority of Parliament. Although not strictly connected with parliamentary privilege, it may be added that, unless a plaintiff can prove malice, a fair and accurate unofficial report of proceedings in Parliament is privileged, as is an article founded on proceedings in Parliament, provided that it is an honest and fair comment on the facts.[3] The interest of the public in the publication of parliamentary proceedings is of more importance than occasional inconveniences to individuals. This decision does not protect reports of detached parts of proceedings published with intent to injure individuals, nor does it protect the publication of a single speech which contains libellous matter.[4] It has been suggested[5] that a similar privilege attaches to the bona-fide publication of a speech by a member for the information of his constituents, but it is difficult to ascertain whether a speech is circulated only to constituents.

[1] P. 165, *post*. It is otherwise if the committal warrant discloses a separate cause of action available to the person committed by the House.

[2] P. 164, *post*.

[3] *Wason* v. *Walter* (1868), L.R. 4 Q.B. 73; K. & L. 295; and see Chap. 36, *post*.

[4] *The King* v. *Creevey* (*ante*).

[5] *Davison* v. *Duncar* (1857), 7 E. & B. 229.

Right to control Internal Proceedings

The House of Commons has the right to control its own proceedings and to provide for its own proper constitution. Except in cases of crimes committed within the precincts of Parliament, the courts will not interfere with what takes place inside Parliament. The House lays down its own rules for the regulation of its proceedings and has the power to enforce those rules. This question will be discussed more fully in considering the relations between the House of Commons and the courts.

Questions on Parliamentary Privilege

Among the many questions of privilege which have been canvassed in the House of Commons in recent years the following is a selection taken from the year 1956.[1]

(1) A question was put down concerning the reappointment of a colonial Chief Justice. The questioner, by supplementary question, complained that his correspondent's house in the Colony had been searched and his papers seized on the ground that by writing to the member he was guilty of contempt of court.[2] The House was later told that the search warrant had been signed by the Chief Justice whose reappointment was challenged by the question "upon sworn information of contempt of court," a form unknown in the law of the colony. An act or omission which obstructs or impedes the House in the exercise of its functions or which obstructs or impedes any member or officer of the House in the discharge of his duty or which has a tendency to produce such results may be treated as a contempt even in the absence of precedent.[3] The Speaker was not prepared to give a *prima facie* ruling which would have extended privilege to cover the correspondence of members.

(2) A member of Parliament was bombarded with telephone calls after the publication of an article in the *Sunday Graphic* which drew attention to a question which he had tabled in the House and invited readers to ring up the member about it; his telephone number was given in the paper. The article had probably appeared in some 700,000 copies. The editor of the paper was clearly responsible for the treatment to which the member had been subjected. The finding of the Committee of Privileges was that molestation of a member on account of his conduct in Parliament is a breach of privilege. The Committee thought the case very different from that of correspondence between a constituent and his member because the invitation was to all the readers of the paper.[4]

[1] See *Applications of Privilege*, 1956, The *Journal of the Society of Clerks at the Table in Commonwealth Parliaments*, pp. 105–16.

[2] 557 H.C. Deb., cols. 417, 422–4.

[3] May, *Parliamentary Practice*, 17th edn., p. 109.

[4] 561 H.C. Deb., cols. 239–43; H.C. 27 (1956).

(3) *Pressure on Members in regard to votes in the House.* A newspaper allegation of pressure to force the Government supporters to vote was held to disclose no *prima facie* case of privilege against the member who was alleged to have made the statement. Attacks on the conduct of Whips are common and have never been treated as breaches of privilege of the whole House.[1]

(4) *Reflections on Members with regard to petrol rationing.* Two allegations that members of Parliament were receiving excessive supplementary allowances of petrol were referred to the Committee of Privileges. In each case the Committee found that a breach had been committed since an attack on members is calculated to diminish the prestige of the House and so to limit its authority.[2] The editor responsible for one allegation was heard in his own defence at the bar of the House. He apologised and the matter was dropped.

Member's Correspondence with Minister

In 1957 the outstanding case was that relating to the London Electricity Board, which, through its solicitors, threatened a member of the Opposition Front Bench with libel proceedings.

The member had written to the Minister responsible in the House of Commons for the nationalised electricity industry (the Paymaster-General, the Minister of Power being in the Lords) complaining of the methods of disposal of scrap cable followed by the board, a regional unit of the Central Electricity Board. The board complained vigorously to the member of the contents of the letter, demanding through its chairman an unqualified withdrawal. Finally the solicitors to the board informed the member that they had instructions to institute proceedings for libel against him unless he withdrew and apologised. On these facts the comment may be made that the correspondence would seem to have been written on occasions which attracted qualified privilege, *i.e.* was protected in the absence of express malice. The member, however, drew the attention of the House to the communications between himself and the Paymaster-General, the London Electricity Board, and the solicitors to the board, and the matter was referred to the Committee of Privileges. The most important question was whether the original letter from the member to the Paymaster-General was a "proceeding in Parliament" within the meaning of the Bill of Rights 1688. Article 9 declared and enacted that "the freedom of speech and debates or proceedings in Parliament ought not to be impeached or questioned in any Court or Place out of Parliament." The conclusion of the Committee was that the writer of the letter was engaged in a proceeding in Parliament, and accordingly the threat on the part of the board and their solicitors to commence proceedings for libel was in respect of statements made by the member in Parliament and therefore threatened to impeach or question his freedom in a court or place outside Parliament. Accordingly both the board and their solicitors had acted in breach of privilege. A subsidiary issue, namely, whether the Parliamentary Privilege Act 1770 afforded protection to the

[1] 562 H.C. Deb., col. 225.

[2] H.C. 28 and 29 (1956).

board, was referred as a special reference to the Judicial Committee, under s. 4 of the Judicial Committee Act 1833 and was answered in the negative. The Committee of Privileges repeated their earlier conclusions but recommended the House to take no further action in the matter.[1] On a motion to agree with the report, the House decided on a free vote (218 to 213) to disagree with the Committee, and thereupon resolved that the original letter was not a proceeding in Parliament and therefore nothing in the subsequent correspondence constituted a breach of privilege. The threat to sue for libel was then withdrawn.

There has been no decision since 1689 in which a court has recognised that the institution of proceedings for defamation against a member of Parliament in respect of a matter which is a proceeding in Parliament within the meaning of the Bill of Rights amounts to a breach of parliamentary privilege. There can be no doubt in view of the leading case of *Stockdale* v. *Hansard*[2] that the High Court would claim to determine the extent of the alleged privilege of Parliament, and would certainly feel at liberty to reject a resolution passed by the House of Commons that the continuance of the litigation would be a breach of its privileges. Had the House of Commons accepted the recommendations of the Committee of Privileges in 1958, the London Electricity Board and its solicitors could have challenged the decision in the courts, despite the risk of their suffering the fate of the Sheriffs of Middlesex[3] and being committed for contempt by the House.

In support of the minority view, *i.e.* that of the Committee of Privileges, members were clearly influenced by the difficulties of raising complaints about those activities of nationalised industries for which a Minister has been made responsible in the House of Commons. Particularly if the complaint made relates to day-to-day administration which is outside the general responsibility of a Minister, a member would seem to be in some peril if he passed on to the Minister without further enquiry a defamatory letter from a constituent. There is no doubt that a complaint addressed by a member of Parliament to a Minister on an issue of public concern has the protection of qualified privilege in the law of defamation, and a member of the public enjoys that privilege in writing to a member of Parliament alleging misconduct by a person holding a public position, such as a justice of the peace. But qualified privilege can be rebutted by proof of malice and it might be held to constitute malice in this technical sense if a member passed on to a Minister without any enquiry a letter from a constituent containing defama-

[1] H.C. 305 (1957); *Re Parliamentary Privilege Act 1770*, [1958] A.C. 331; H.C. 227 (1958).

[2] (1839) 9 A. & E., p. 1, especially at p. 203.

[3] *Sheriff of Middlesex Case* (1840), 11 A. & E. 273; K. & L. 283.

tory allegations. If, instead of passing on the letter, the member used it to frame a question he would enjoy absolute protection under the Bill of Rights. Tabling questions is in practice preceded by preliminary correspondence with a Minister, and therefore there is an argument in favour of according the same absolute privilege as a question enjoys to such correspondence. It would be unreasonable to expect members of Parliament to investigate every complaint which reaches them by letter, and therefore there is something to be said for the view that members in passing on complaints from their constituents should enjoy absolute privilege. This could perhaps take the form of a defence of unintentional defamation.[1] The advantage of this would be to enable the person aggrieved to obtain an offer of amends in the form of a published apology or contradiction. On the other hand, it was stated in the House of Commons by the Leader of the House in the debate on the London Electricity Case that he had been advised that a member forwarding a constituent's allegations would be protected, provided that he had himself acted in good faith. Perhaps the conflict of views is such that the matter could only be clarified by legislation. The danger of such action is that Parliament might be tempted to enlarge its immunities and so deprive the courts of their essential function of interpreting the powers, privileges and jurisdiction even of the High Court of Parliament.[2] It does not seem too much to ask of members of Parliament that they should exercise their functions as members without malice, *e.g.* in the conduct of their correspondence and in their speeches on the public platform, and so leave the operation of the Bill of Rights to the actual conduct of business of the floor of the House. It was some such view which found favour with the majority in the debate in July, 1958.[3]

Disputed Elections

It was for long doubtful as to whether or not the House had the right to determine questions of disputed elections. A dispute arose upon this question between James I and the House of Commons in 1604, when one Goodwin, an outlaw, was elected for Buckinghamshire. A compromise was effected, but the Commons exercised the right to determine such questions from 1604 to 1868. They were first determined by committees, but from 1672 were determined by the whole House. The growth of party government resulted in disputed

[1] See Defamation Act 1952, s. 4.

[2] See generally *Parliamentary Privilege and the Bill of Rights*, by S. A. de Smith, 21 M.L.R. 465–83.

[3] 591 H.C. Deb. col. 809; 592 H.C. Deb., cols. 1370 ff.

election returns being settled purely by party votes. In 1770 the Parliamentary Privilege Act, commonly known as Grenville's Act, transferred the decision of these questions to a committee chosen by lot. In 1868 Parliament entrusted the duty of deciding disputed elections to the courts. The procedure is regulated by the Parliamentary Elections Act 1868.[1] A petition against an election is presented to the High Court of Justice, and the trial of such petition is conducted by two judges [2] of the High Court sitting in the borough or county in which the election took place. The determination of the court is notified to the Speaker, and is entered upon the journals of the House of Commons. The judges determine whether the member whose return is complained of was duly elected, and report to the Speaker whether any corrupt practice by anybody at the election has been proved. The House of Commons gives the necessary directions for confirming or altering the return or for issuing a writ for a new election. Of recent years there has been an almost total disappearance of election petitions, a feature which reflects the improved standard of public morality and the political intelligence of the electorate, though no doubt the large number on the electoral roll of a modern constituency has also contributed to the disappearance of attempts to bribe the electors. The lack of qualification for membership may be raised on an election petition, *e.g.* that a candidate was disqualified by reason of holding a peerage.[3]

Expulsion

The House of Commons still retains the right to pronounce upon legal qualifications for membership, and to declare a seat vacant on such ground. The House may, however, as in the case of *Mitchel*,[4] refer such a question to the courts. The House of Commons cannot, of course, create disqualifications unrecognised by law, but it may expel any member who conducts himself in a manner unfit for membership. A constituency may re-elect a member so expelled, and there might, as in the case of John Wilkes, take place a series of expulsions and re-elections. Expulsion is the only method open to the House of dealing with a member convicted of an offence. In 1947 a member was expelled by the House after the Committee of Privileges had reported that he had been guilty of gross contempt in accusing his fellow members of disclosing for reward the proceedings of confidential party meetings held in the precincts of the House,

[1] Now replaced by the Representation of the People Act 1949, Part III, without change in the law.
[2] Representation of the People Act 1949, s. 110.
[3] *Re Parliamentary Election for Bristol South East*, [1964] 2 Q.B. 257.
[4] (1875), I.R. 9 C.L. 217.

but not forming part of the formal business of Parliament. It was disclosed to the Committee that the member himself had been guilty of the misconduct in question and, except for a single case, could not substantiate any of the charges against his fellow-members which he had published in a periodical circulating among journalists.[1]

Committal for Contempt

The House of Commons has the right to enforce its privileges and to regulate its proceedings by punishing those who offend against the House. A member guilty of disorderly conduct, who refuses to withdraw, may on being named by the Speaker be suspended from the service of the House either for a specified time or for the remainder of the session. Punishment may also take the form of an admonition by the Speaker, or in more serious cases of a reprimand by the Speaker, or of commitment to prison by order of the House. The House of Commons may, in virtue of its inherent and essential right to control its own proceedings and maintain its dignity, commit any person for contempt. Such commitment can be for a fixed term, but a prisoner is automatically entitled to release when the House is prorogued. In parliamentary language the term, breach of privilege, is sometimes used as synonymous with contempt, in the same sense as in contempt of court.[2] But it is clear that a member of the House or other person may be adjudged by the House of Commons to be guilty of contempt without the actual infringement of any parliamentary privilege. Thus in *Allighan's Case*[1] the Committee of Privileges reported that the unfounded imputation in regard to the proceedings of party meetings held in private within the precincts of the Palace of Westminster involved an affront to the House as such. But information about such meetings was not in itself a breach of privilege. This confusion of language is particularly unsatisfactory to a lawyer, because the issue cannot readily be tested in a court of law. If it arises in relation to the internal proceedings of the House, as is most likely, the High Court will decline to intervene. Similarly there is no power in the Court to enquire into the validity of a committal for contempt, as such, by the House. Only if the actual cause of the committal is disclosed and is proved to be unlawful can the court give redress.[3]

Payment of Members

The right of the House of Commons to the exclusive control of financial measures,[4] and the right of impeachment [5] are more appro-

[1] H.C. 138 (1947), *Allighan's Case*.
[2] Chap. 37.
[3] P 168, *post*.
[4] Chap. 9.
[5] P. 314, *post*.

priately discussed when considering the financial and judicial functions of Parliament. It is convenient to refer here to the question of the payment of members of Parliament. Since 1911 every member not in receipt of an official salary has received a salary, which was raised from £400 to £600 a year by the Appropriation Act 1937 and in 1946 to £1,000.[1] This was supplemented in 1957 by the right to claim a tax-free expenses allowance not exceeding £750 per annum. In 1965 the salary was raised to £3,250 and expenses (including £500 for secretarial purposes) may be claimed for tax purposes. Free travel between Westminster and a member's constituency may be claimed. Members, too, are sometimes paid by private bodies, *e.g.* trade unions. Lord Shaw expressed the view that a contract to pay a man in return for his support in Parliament of the views of a particular person or party would be unenforceable as contrary to public policy.[2] It is improper for a member to enter into any contractual agreement with an outside body limiting his complete freedom of action in Parliament. So the House decided in 1947 on a motion to approve a majority report from the Committee of Privileges.[3] Members of the House of Lords receive an allowance (at present £4 14s 6d) for each day of attendance. There is a contributory pension scheme for Members of the House of Commons. This is governed by the Remuneration of Ministers and Members of Parliament Act 1965.

The Courts and Parliamentary Privilege

Questions of privilege have been a source of conflict between the House of Commons and the courts. Parliament has always held the view that whatever matter arises concerning either House of Parliament ought to be discussed and adjudged in that House to which it relates and not elsewhere; and that the existence of a privilege depends upon its being declared by the High Court of Parliament to be part of the ancient law and custom of Parliament.[4] It has been seen that the courts, in the case of *Stockdale* v. *Hansard*,[5] maintained the right to determine the nature and limit of parliamentary privileges, should it be necessary to determine such questions in adjudicating upon disputes between individuals. In *Eliot's Case* [6] the question whether or not the court could deal with an assault on the Speaker

[1] P. 194, *post*, as to members of the Commons who are in receipt of ministerial salaries.

[2] *Osborne* v. *Amalgamated Society of Railway Servants*, [1910] A.C. 87, at p. 110 ff.

[3] H.C. 118 (1947), *W. J. Brown's Case*.

[4] May, *op. cit.*, Chap. IX.

[5] P. 158, *ante*.

[6] P. 156, *ante*.

committed in the House of Commons was expressly left open when the judgment was declared illegal by resolutions of both Houses, but there is no authority showing that crimes committed in the precincts of Parliament cannot be punished by the ordinary courts.[1] In civil cases the test is whether the act alleged took place in the course of parliamentary business and as part thereof.[2] An act which is criminal can hardly form part of such business. The present relationship between the High Court and Parliament is made clearer by the cases centring round Mr. Bradlaugh.

Bradlaugh, a free thinker, was elected to Parliament as member for Northampton on successive occasions. The House of Commons took the view that as an atheist he could not sit or vote, as he could not properly take the oath as required by existing statute law. At one stage Bradlaugh was allowed to affirm, instead of taking an oath, but in an action against him for penalties for sitting and voting without taking the oath it was held by the Court of Appeal that the Parliamentary Oaths Act 1866 and the Promissory Oaths Act 1868 did not authorise him to affirm.[3]

On a subsequent occasion following his re-election to Parliament Bradlaugh required the Speaker to call upon him to take the oath. The Speaker refused to do so. This was followed by a resolution of the House of Commons authorising the Serjeant-at-Arms to exclude Bradlaugh from the House. In an action which he brought against the Sergeant-at-Arms seeking an injunction to restrain him from carrying out this resolution it was held that, this being a matter relating to the internal management of the procedure of the House of Commons, the Court of Queen's Bench had no power to interfere; *Bradlaugh* v. *Gossett*.[4] For the House of Commons had the exclusive power to regulate its own proceedings and no court could interfere with the exercise of such right. The Act of 1866 permitted certain persons to affirm instead of taking an oath. The dispute in *Clarke* v. *Bradlaugh* was whether or not Bradlaugh was a person entitled to affirm; any person making an affirmation otherwise than as authorised by the Act could be sued for certain penalties. It is emphasised in the judgment of Stephen J. in *Bradlaugh* v. *Gossett*[5] that, should the House of Commons have attempted by resolution to state that Bradlaugh was entitled to make the statutory declaration, such a resolution would not have protected him against an action for penalties:

"We should have said that for the purpose of determining on a right to be exercised within the House itself, the House, and the House only, could interpret the statute; but that as regarded rights to be exercised

[1] An attempt to convict members of the Kitchen Committee of the House of Commons of breaches of the licensing law failed, primarily on the ground of the right of the House to regulate its internal affairs: *The King* v. *Graham-Campbell, ex parte Herbert*, [1935] 1 K.B. 594; p. 156, *ante*.

[2] See H.C. 101 (1939); p. 159, *ante*.

[3] *Clarke* v. *Bradlaugh* (1881), 7 Q.B.D. 38.

[4] (1884), 12 Q.B.D. 271; K. & L. 287.

[5] At p. 282.

out of, and independently of, the House, such as a right of suing for a penalty for having sat and voted, the statute must be interpreted by this court independently of the House."

Bradlaugh v. *Gossett* is not a case of the House of Commons attempting to alter the law by resolution as it tried unsuccessfully to do in *Stockdale* v. *Hansard*.[1] All that the resolution of exclusion did was to give effect to the course of proceedings authorised by the Parliamentary Oaths Act.

In *Paty's Case*,[2] where electors sued returning officers for the malicious refusal of their votes, Chief Justice Holt, in a minority judgment, held that a writ of habeas corpus would go to release anyone committed for contempt by the House of Commons where the cause of committal stated in the return to the writ was insufficient in law. This view of the law is accepted to-day. If, however, no cause for committal other than contempt of the House is shown in the return, the High Court is powerless. As it was said by Lord Ellenborough in *Burdett* v. *Abbot*: [3]

> If a commitment appeared to be for contempt of the House of Commons generally, I would neither in the case of that court nor of any other of the superior courts enquire further.

This opinion prevailed in *The Sheriff of Middlesex Case*.[4] Thus the House possesses an arbitrary power of committal for contempt which cannot be enquired into by the courts, provided that the cause of the contempt is not stated. Such a power is not available to the Executive, both by reason of the Statute 16 Car. 1 c. 10 s. 8, which guarantees the writ of habeas corpus against committal by the King and his Council, and because the common law holds arbitrary imprisonment unlawful and does not recognise the plea of act of State as justifying imprisonment of a British subject by a Minister.

It appears, therefore, that there may be two views laid down as to the privileges of the House of Commons. The House may act upon one view when regulating its own proceedings and committing for contempt, while the court may act upon another view when privileges arise in civil disputes. It has, however, been pointed out many times by judges that the court will naturally pay the greatest attention to the views and customs of the House of Commons in deciding what are the privileges of that House. There is none the less a possibility of conflict which may affect the liberty of the subject.

[1] P. 158, *ante*.
[2] (1704), 2 Lord Raymond 1105.
[3] (1811), 14 East 1.
[4] (1840), 11 A. & E. 273; K. & L. 283.

B. House of Lords

The privileges of the House of Lords are:

(*a*) Freedom from civil arrest for peers for a period of forty days before and after a meeting of Parliament, as in the case of members of the House of Commons. In *Stourton* v. *Stourton* [1] a peer was held to be privileged from a writ of attachment consequent on his failure to send to his wife her property under a court order. The privilege was held to apply whether or not Parliament was sitting.

(*b*) Freedom of speech.

(*c*) Freedom of access to the Sovereign for each peer individually.

(*d*) The right to commit for contempt. The House of Lords can commit a person for contempt for a definite term, and the imprisonment is not terminated by prorogation of Parliament.

(*e*) The right to exclude disqualified persons from taking part in the proceedings of the House. The House itself decides, through the Committee of Privileges, the right of newly created peers to sit and vote.[2] Claims to old peerages are referred by the Crown to the House of Lords, and are also decided by the Committee of Privileges. That body is not bound by its own previous decisions.

[1] [1963] P. 303.
[2] P. 99, *ante*.

PART I: General Constitutional Law

THE EXECUTIVE

Cabinet Government, 3rd edn., by Sir Ivor Jennings (Cambridge University Press).
The British Cabinet, 2nd edn., by John P. Mackintosh (Stevens & Sons).
Central Administration in Britain, by W. J. M. Mackenzie and J. W. Grove (Longmans).
George V; His Life and Reign, by Sir Harold Nicolson (Constable).
George VI, by Sir John Wheeler-Bennett (Macmillan).
Government and Parliament, 3rd edn., by Lord Morrison of Lambeth (Oxford University Press).
The New Whitehall Series (George Allen & Unwin).
Nationality and Citizenship Laws of the Commonwealth, by Clive Parry (Stevens & Sons).

CHAPTER ELEVEN

THE CROWN

To study the organs of State which exercise the executive and administrative functions is the most difficult task that a student of constitutional law has to perform. He is, of necessity, without that acquaintance with what takes place in Cabinet meetings or within government departments which could alone give him an intimate knowledge of the machine in operation. When dealing with the Legislature and the Judiciary he is studying organs which work in the public eye. Proceedings both in Parliament and in the High Court can be followed by readers of at most three national newspapers. What happens in the departments and how they work is unknown to the general public. True that from time to time questions in Parliament or strictures from the Bench remind the public that Whitehall is encroaching on their liberty. Public relations officers do their best to explain the more glaring examples of individual hardship which result from a too rigid administrative machine. Occasionally a retired civil servant gives the world a glimpse behind the scenes, but convention normally forbids any active member of that service from writing of his work. For the average lawyer acquaintance with Whitehall is limited to interviews with subordinate officials, while others perhaps get no further than interviews with a local inspector of taxes or a national insurance officer.

Terminology

There is too another difficulty. Terms are used which have no precise legal significance. Differences of form do not always represent differences of substance. The term, the Crown, represents the sum total of governmental powers and is synonymous with the Executive. In the exercise of some of the powers of the Crown the Sovereign may be called upon to exercise a personal discretion;[1] others are exercised by the Sovereign on the sole responsibility of Ministers; in the exercise of others the Sovereign plays no part, for the majority of statutory powers are conferred upon Ministers as such and are exercised by them in their official capacity, though they are none the less exercised on behalf of the Crown. There is only a formal difference between a power conferred upon the Queen in Council which is exercised on the advice of the responsible Minister concerned and a power conferred directly upon that responsible Minister, though exceptionally the exercise of the latter may be enforceable against the Minister in the courts.[2] The Queen, the Queen in Council [3] and the titles of the several Ministers of State are legal titles. It is only comparatively recently that the terms, Government and Prime Minister, have appeared in statutes,[4] and then only in a context which assumes their meaning to be known. The terms, Executive,[5] Cabinet, Ministry and Administration are extra-legal. The Cabinet [6] is the body of principal Ministers with whom rests the real direction of policy. We speak of the Ministry or the Administration of a particular Prime Minister with reference to the full body of political office holders who from time to time hold the reins of government, *i.e.* the Ministers of the Crown and their Parliamentary Secretaries.

A. The Sovereign

Title to the Crown

Title to the Crown is derived from the Act of Settlement 1700: "The Crown . . . shall remain and continue to the said most excellent Princess Sophia" (the Electress of Hanover, granddaughter of

[1] Pp. 82–5, *ante*.
[2] *Padfield* v. *Minister of Agriculture, Fisheries and Food*, [1968] A.C. 997.
[3] P. 179, *post*.
[4] *E.g.* Statute of Westminster 1931 (Government); Ministerial Salaries Consolidation Act 1965, s. 3.
[5] P. 19, *ante*. [6] Chap. 13.

James I) "and the heirs of her body being Protestant."[1] The title to the Crown follows the hereditary principle, but the Queen in Parliament may alter the succession. The limitation to the heirs of the body means that the Crown descends, with certain exceptions, as did real property under the law of inheritance in force before 1926. This branch of property law recognised (*inter alia*) the right of primogeniture and preference for males over females. There are disqualified from the succession to the Throne Roman Catholics and those who marry Roman Catholics, and the Sovereign must join in communion with the Church of England. On the death of King George V he was succeeded by his eldest son, the Prince of Wales and heir apparent [2] who became Edward VIII. On the abdication of Edward VIII it was provided by His Majesty's Declaration of Abdication Act 1936 that the member of the Royal Family then next in succession to the Throne (King George VI), then Duke of York and heir presumptive [3] should succeed and that Edward VIII, his issue, if any, and the descendants of that issue should not thereafter have any right, title or interest in or to the succession.

Style and Titles

The style and titles of the Crown in the reigns of George V and VI were determined by Royal Proclamation under the Great Seal which was issued on the authority of the Royal and Parliamentary Titles Act 1927. The Preamble to the Statute of Westminster 1931 declared that it would be in accord with the established constitutional position that any alteration in the law touching the succession to the Throne or the Royal Style and Titles shall also require the consent of the Parliaments of all the Dominions.[4] By Royal Proclamation the King in 1948 omitted the title, Emperor of India, the assent of Parliament of the United Kingdom having been given thereto by the Indian Independence Act 1947, s. 7 (2); the Dominions

[1] See *Attorney-General* v. *Prince Ernest Augustus of Hanover*, [1957] A.C. 436, for the construction of the Princess Sophia Naturalisation Act 1705 which entitled to British nationality all lineal descendants born before the British Nationality Act 1948 (pp. 247–53, *post*).

[2] The eldest son of a reigning monarch, who is Duke of Cornwall by inheritance and is invariably created Prince of Wales. There is no precedent for the latter title being conferred upon an eldest or only daughter who is the heiress presumptive.

[3] The person at any time next in succession, *e.g.* an only daughter is heiress presumptive, unless and till a son is born to the Sovereign. So, too, before his accession the late King was heir presumptive to his brother, Edward VIII, but would have ceased to be so on the birth of a child (male or female) to his brother.

[4] P. 441, *post*.

passed their own enactments. Before Queen Elizabeth II succeeded her father, the form of royal style and titles was

> George VI by Grace of God of Great Britain, Ireland and the British Dominions beyond the Seas, King, Defender of the Faith.

The Accession Council [1] acknowledged Queen Elizabeth

> Queen of this Realm and of all Her other Realms and Territories, Head of the Commonwealth, Defender of the Faith.

A new Royal Titles Act was necessary to give legal effect to this change, as the Royal and Parliamentary Titles Act 1927 which had authorised the changes made by royal proclamation of that year had expired. Several constitutional developments had made a change in the legal title desirable; in particular the royal title had hitherto rested on the doctrine of the indivisibility of the Crown throughout the Commonwealth. That indivisibility had by 1952 ceased to be the fact, and in the case certainly of the Republic of India the law. Accordingly the Royal Titles Act 1953 gave the assent of the Parliament of the United Kingdom to the adoption by the Queen by royal proclamation of her title for use only in relation to the United Kingdom and all other territories for whose foreign relations the Government of the United Kingdom is responsible, *i.e.* Colonies, Protectorates and certain trust territories. The title is:

> Elizabeth II By the Grace of God of the United Kingdom of Great Britain and Northern Ireland and of Her other Realms and Territories Queen, Head of the Commonwealth, Defender of the Faith.

It was left to the other States within the Commonwealth to enact their own form of title, as they had proclaimed it at the time of the accession. In the result the only description common to all States is "Head of the Commonwealth," though in each case there is reference to the Queen's Headship of her other realms and territories. India, in accordance with her republican form of constitution, issued no decree of proclamation, although she continued to recognise the Queen's Headship of the Commonwealth as her link with the rest of the Commonwealth.

Royal Marriages

The Royal Marriages Act 1772, by placing certain restrictions upon the right of a descendant of George II to contract a valid marriage without the consent of the Sovereign, guards against undesirable marriages which might affect the succession to the Throne. Until the

[1] P. 174, *post*.

age of twenty-five the Sovereign's assent is necessary (except in respect of the issue of princesses who have married into foreign families). After that age a marriage may take place without consent after a year's notice to the Privy Council, unless Parliament expressly disapproves.

Accession and Coronation

Accession to the Crown is a coming of a person into the position of the Sovereign, whereupon all subjects owe personal allegiance. There are two ceremonies which mark the accession of the new Sovereign. Immediately on the death of his precedessor the Sovereign is proclaimed, not by the Privy Council[1] as such, but by the Lords Spiritual and Temporal and other leading citizens, a body which is a survival of an old assemblage, which met to choose and proclaim the King. The Proclamation is afterwards approved at the first meeting of the new King's Privy Council. After an interval of time follows the Coronation, the ancient ceremony which gave religious sanction to title by election and brought to a close the interregnum, when no King reigned, between the death of one King and the election of his successor. Anson noted that, as the recognition of hereditary rights strengthened, the importance of the election and coronation dwindled, while the great practical inconvenience of the interregnum, the abeyance of the King's Peace, was curtailed.

The modern coronation ceremony is full of historical interest. There are three stages:

(1) The acceptance of their Sovereign by the people and the taking of the oath of royal duties by the Sovereign.

(2) The purely religious ceremony which includes the anointing and crowning.

(3) The rendering of homage in person by the Lords Spiritual and Temporal.

It should be noted that the oath illustrates the contractual nature of the sovereign power and has survived both the extravagant prerogative claims of the Stuarts and the Revolution of 1688. The form of the Coronation oath was prescribed by the Coronation Oath Act 1688 as amended by the Acts of Union. In place of the formal declaration against transubstantiation, the Accession Declaration Act 1910 substituted a modified declaration of adherence to the Protestant faith. The oath taken by the Sovereign in 1937 and in 1953 was varied without statutory authority in order to recognise the equal status of Kingship of the various States of the Commonwealth.

[1] P. 179, *post*.

Infancy and Incapacity

The Regency Acts 1937–53 made, for the first time, standing provision for the infancy, incapacity and temporary absence of the Sovereign from the realm. The Sovereign comes of age at eighteen; until he reaches that age, the royal functions are to be exercised by a Regent who will also act in the event of total incapacity of an adult Sovereign. Normally the Regent will be the next person in the line of succession who is not excluded by the Act of Settlement and is a British subject domiciled in the United Kingdom. The Regent, if the heir-apparent or heir-presumptive, must have attained the age of eighteen; if another person, the age of twenty-one. If a Regency should become necessary on the succession of a child of Queen Elizabeth II and her husband, while under the age of eighteen, the Duke of Edinburgh, if living, will be the Regent. He will also become Regent in the event of a Regency during the present reign, until a child or grandchild of the Queen and the Duke can become Regent on attaining the age of eighteen. Regency is automatic on the succession of a minor; but in the case of total incapacity a declaration has to be made to the Privy Council by the wife or husband of the Sovereign, the Lord Chancellor, the Speaker, the Lord Chief Justice and the Master of the Rolls, or any three of them, that they are satisfied by evidence (including that of physicians) that the Sovereign is by reason of infirmity of mind or body incapable of performing the royal functions, or that for some definite cause he is not available for the performance of those functions. Such a declaration must be made to the Privy Council and communicated to the other Governments of the Commonwealth. A Regency may be ended by a similar declaration. A Regent may exercise all the royal functions, except that he may not assent to a Bill for changing the order of succession to the Crown or for repealing or altering the Act of Anne made in Scotland and entitled an Act for securing the Protestant Religion and Presbyterian Church Government.

The Regency Act 1937 did not apply to those Dominions which at that date had accepted the main provisions of the Statute of Westminister, namely Canada and the Union of South Africa, nor to the Irish Free State. While the declaration leading to the appointment of a Regent has to be communicated to the other Governments of the Commonwealth, separate legislation by each Parliament is necessary to make the Act applicable. Presumably the necessity, which arises from section 4 of the Statute, does not extend to Australia or New Zealand by reason of the later dates at which they adopted this part of the Statute, nor to the newer States of the Commonwealth of which the Queen is Head, but all are competent to enact their own legislation.

Illness and Temporary Absence

In the event of illness which does not amount to total incapacity or of absence or intended absence from the United Kingdom, the Sovereign may appoint Counsellors of State to exercise such of the royal functions as may be conferred upon them by letters patent. There may not be delegated the power to dissolve Parliament otherwise than on the express instructions of the Sovereign (which may be conveyed by telegraph), or to grant any rank, title or dignity of the peerage. The Counsellors of State must be the wife or husband of the Sovereign, the four persons next in line of succession to the Crown (excluding any persons (*a*) disqualified from being Regent, or (*b*) being absent or intending to be absent from the United Kingdom during the period of delegation) and Queen Elizabeth, the Queen Mother. The heir apparent or heir presumptive may be a Counsellor of State, if not under eighteen years of age.

The functions of Counsellors of State during absence of the Sovereign from the United Kingdom do not extend to those functions which in relation to a Dominion are normally exercised by the King. Thus when the King visited the Union of South Africa, at that time a Commonwealth State, in 1947 the Canadian Government announced that His Majesty had notified the Governor-General that he would continue to exercise personally in South Africa such functions in relation to Canada and the announcement made it clear that the Council of State was a body set up on the authority of an Act of the United Kingdom Parliament and therefore exercised no authority in Canada.

Demise of the Sovereign

Formerly the death of the Sovereign involved the dissolution of Parliament and the termination of the tenure of all offices under the Crown, since Parliament meets on the personal summons of the Sovereign, and all offices are in theory held at his will and pleasure. The duration of Parliament is now independent of the demise of the Sovereign.[1] The Demise of the Crown Act 1901 provided that the holding of any office should not be affected by the demise of the Crown and that no fresh appointment should be necessary..

Abdication

Akin to a demise of the Sovereign is his abdication. In 1936 King

[1] P. 121, *ante*.

Edward VIII signed a declaration of abdication to which effect was given by His Majesty's Declaration of Abdication Act 1936. This Act enacted that there should be a demise of the Crown upon the Act receiving the royal assent. Prior to the signature of the declaration of abdication the King's intention had been communicated informally to the Dominion Governments by the Prime Minister of the United Kingdom. Upon signature the declaration was formally communicated to the Dominion Governments.[1]

Duties of the Sovereign

No attempt can be made to list the duties which fall to the Sovereign to perform in person. Many formal acts of government require her participation. Many State papers require her signature and of the contents of others she is required to be informed. The Prime Minister keeps her informed of all conclusions of the Cabinet. As a constitutional monarch she is bound to act on the advice of her Ministers. She may, however, temper their counsel and offer guidance from her own fund of experience in affairs. But she cannot reject the final advice they offer without bringing about their resignation and replacement by other Ministers. Much light has been thrown upon the exact tasks which were performed by the Sovereign in the first half of the twentieth century by Sir Harold Nicolson's biography of King George V and that of George VI by Sir John Wheeler-Bennett. In particular it appears that the Sovereign, even before the days when Cabinet conclusions were first recorded and reported by the Secretariat, could insist upon the advice of the Cabinet being given in written form, if he felt that it was dangerous or opposed to the wishes of the people. This was so that the King could record in writing the misgivings and reluctance with which he followed the advice of his Cabinet.[2] The rôle of the Sovereign is to advise, encourage and warn Ministers in respect of the recommendations which they make. This is a role which increases in importance as experience is acquired in dealing with successive Ministers. How each of these two Sovereigns played his part in this regard is told discreetly by their biographers, but it is impossible not to form the impression that the constitutional monarch of the twentieth century is far from being a cipher or mere mouthpiece of his constitutional advisers. Perhaps the most revealing illustration is to be found in

[1] Pp. 441–2, *post*, for a brief account of the separate action taken by the Dominions.

[2] *George V*, p. 116.

the following extract from the diary of King George VI for 23 August, 1945:

> I asked him (Attlee) whom he would make Foreign Secretary and he suggested Dr. Hugh Dalton. I disagreed . . . and said that . . . I hoped he would make Mr. Bevin take it. He said he would.[1]

Private Secretary to the Sovereign

The Private Secretary to the Sovereign must necessarily play an intimate rôle in conducting communications between the Sovereign and his Ministers. This office is filled on the personal selection of the Sovereign and is not a political one. The choice of the Sovereign naturally falls upon a member of the Royal Household who has grown up in the service of the Court. It is through the Private Secretary that communications from the Government to the Sovereign are sent. It would seem inevitable that the secretarial function demands a great measure of discretion in selecting the information which should be brought to the personal notice of the Sovereign. The Private Secretary must be the confidant of all Ministers, but must never leave the impression that he is "anybody's man." He must, of course, belong to no political party.[2] He is made a member of the Privy Council.

Constitutional propriety forbids consultation by the Sovereign with Privy Councillors or others who are outside the ranks of Ministers in office unless it be with their consent.[3] Equally it is not for the Queen to initiate action of her own accord. She holds formal meetings of her Privy Council, gives audiences, *e.g.* to her Ministers, receives the credentials of foreign diplomatic representatives, holds investitures and confers honours and decorations. Her patronage, exercisable on ministerial advice, is wide. Her consent is needed for all major appointments which are made by the Crown on the advice of the Prime Minister, Lord Chancellor and other Ministers. The Queen and her Consort, and all the members of the Royal Family, play a leading part in the ceremonies of public life and the social life of the nation. Visits and short tours of residence in Commonwealth countries are becoming a normal part of the life of the Royal Family.[4] Finally the Queen is the link which binds together the various States of the Commonwealth. To her is owed allegiance by the peoples of

[1] *George VI*, p. 638.

[2] For an account of the office, see *George VI*, App. B.

[3] See p. 82, *ante*.

[4] App. C includes specimens of some documents which require the royal signature. For a fuller account of the functions of the Sovereign, see Nicolson, *George V*; Wheeler-Bennett, *George VI*; Bagehot, *The English Constitution*, (Oxford University Press), Chaps. II, III; Jennings, *Cabinet Government*, Chaps. II and XII; Sir Sidney Low, *The Governance of England*, (Fisher Unwin), Chap. XIV.

the older States which acknowledge her as Queen. In the case of the States which are republics within the Commonwealth she is acknowledged simply as Head of the Commonwealth.

Private Property

The Sovereign may hold private property in a personal capacity, *e.g.* the Sandringham estate in Norfolk. Such property, unlike Crown property,[1] is liable to taxes and rates, but in a personal capacity the Sovereign cannot be sued [2] or prosecuted.

B. The Queen in Council [3]

The King was formerly the sole repository, in theory of law, of executive power, which he executed by and with the advice of his Privy Council. Despite the many powers conferred by modern statutes on individual Ministers, the Order in Council remains a principal method of giving the force of law to acts of the Government. It has been seen that to-day the Queen executes a large number of documents, under her own hand or a facsimile thereof. But the Order in Council is the document in general use for giving effect to the more important executive orders. A Royal Proclamation is issued when it is desired to give wide publicity to the action of the Queen in Council, as for the purpose of dissolving a Parliament and summoning its successor. Nowadays Orders in Council are approved by the Sovereign at a meeting of the Council to which only four or five members are summoned and are authenticated by the signature of the Clerk of the Council. Constitutional history shows both the decline in the advisory and judicial functions of the Council and its supersession in the former capacity by the Cabinet. To-day the acts of the Privy Council are purely formal and give effect to orders, the contents of which are the responsibility of government departments. These are orders made either under the prerogative,[4] *e.g.* constitutional legislation for a colony, or under an Act of Parliament, *e.g.* orders giving effect to university and college statutes under the Universities of Oxford and Cambridge Act 1923.

[1] P. 233, *post*.

[2] Crown Proceedings Act 1947 s. 40 (1). Some writers suggest that a petition of right (p. 679, *post*) could still lie against the Queen in her personal capacity, *e.g.* O. Hood Phillips, *Constitutional and Administrative Law*, 3rd edn. p. 664 (Sweet & Maxwell).

[3] See Baldwin, *The King's Council in the Middle Ages*, (Clarendon Press), and Dicey, *The Privy Council*, (Arnold Prize Essay) (Macmillan), for historical accounts of the Privy Council.

[4] P. 184, *post*.

Committees of the Privy Council

The Council, having ceased to be an advisory Council of the Crown, is summoned for the purpose of making orders, issuing proclamations or performing formal State acts. A few traces remain of its former advisory functions; the Committee for Channel Islands business is a survivor of the old Standing Committees appointed by the King at the beginning or in the course of his reign. Other committees are the Judicial Committee of the Privy Council [1] and a committee to consider grants of charters to municipal and other corporations. Issues of constitutional importance are sometimes referred to *ad hoc* committees of the Privy Council, as, for example, the legal basis of the practice of telephone tapping.[2] This jurisdiction is additional to references to the Judicial Committee.[3] The Lord President of the Council is invariably a member of the Cabinet. The formal business is transacted by the Privy Council Office under the Clerk of the Council.

Office of Privy Councillor

Membership of the Privy Council is a titular honour. Appointments are made by the Sovereign on ministerial advice. By convention all Cabinet Ministers, in whom are vested the right and duty of advising the Sovereign on all matters of government, become Privy Councillors. Members of the Royal Family and holders of certain high offices of a non-political character, such as Archbishops and Lords Justices of Appeal, are sworn members of the Council. In addition the office is a recognised reward for public and political service, and appointments of this nature usually figure in the New Year and Birthday Honours Lists. The Council numbers about 300 members at the present day. Members are entitled to the prefix, "Right Honourable." They take an oath on appointment which binds them not to disclose anything said or done "in Council," without the consent of the Sovereign. As all members of the Cabinet are members of the Privy Council, it is this oath which, in addition to their obligations under the Official Secrets Acts 1911–39, binds to secrecy all present and past Cabinet Ministers, who may only disclose Cabinet proceedings and other confidential discussions if so authorised by the Sovereign.[4] Alienage is a disqualification, but on naturalisation an alien becomes qualified for membership.[5]

[1] Chap. 33.
[2] Pp. 580–1, *post*.
[3] P. 461, *post*.
[4] *The Times*, 8 August, 1952.
[5] *The King* v. *Speyer; The King* v. *Cassel*, [1916] 1 K.B. 595; [1916] 2 K.B. 858.

Relation of Cabinet to Council

The functions of the Privy Council are distinct from those of the Cabinet. The former is a body which gives formal approval to certain acts of the Government; the latter is deliberative. Although all members of the Cabinet are Privy Councillors, it is not as a Committee of the Council that they meet, but as "Her Majesty's Servants." The Cabinet is summoned by the Prime Minister. The Council is convened by the Clerk of the Council, whose office dates back to the sixteenth century. The only connecting link between the modern Cabinet and the Council is the oath and obligation of secrecy which binds Cabinet Ministers as members of the Council; but it should be remembered that the first use of the term, Cabinet, was to describe inner bodies of the Privy Council.

House of Lords as Council of the Crown

The House of Lords is still in theory a Council of the Crown. It has not been summoned, as such, since 1688, but traces of its former function are preserved in the writ of summons. Moreover, it is the privilege of a peer to seek individual access to the Sovereign, though the privilege may not be used by peers as such for the purpose of tendering advice on their own initiative on matters of government.

C. The Royal Prerogative [1]

At most periods in our history the term, prerogative, has been used to connote rights and capacities of the Crown which have little in common with one another except that in the words of Blackstone they are based on that "special pre-eminence which the King hath, over and above all other persons, and out of the ordinary course of the common law, in right of his regal dignity." [2] This chapter is primarily concerned with those powers which may be exercised by the Crown without the authority of Parliament. It is none the less necessary to explain other uses of the word, prerogative, and to touch briefly on the history of the prerogative, some appreciation of which is essential for understanding the present law.

Middle Ages

The mediaeval King was both feudal lord and head of the State. As chief feudal lord and in theory the owner of all land the King

[1] The student should study both the cases and introductory chapters in Keir and Lawson, *Cases of Constitutional Law* on this subject. We express our obligation to the authors, on whose historical summary we have freely drawn.

[2] Blackstone, *Commentaries*, I, 232.

had all the rights of a feudal lord and in addition certain exceptional rights over and above those of all other lords. Like other lords the King could not be sued in his own courts; as there was no lord superior to the King, there was no court in which the King could be sued. In addition the King as head of the State had powers accounted for by the need for the preservation of the State against external foes and an "undefined residue of power which he might use for the public good." We have already seen [1] that mediaeval lawyers did not regard the King as being above the law. Moreover certain of the royal functions could only be exercised in certain ways. The common law courts were the King's courts and only through them could the King decide questions of title to land and punish felonies. Yet as the fountain of justice the King possessed a residuary power of doing justice through his Council where the courts of common law were inadequate. Normally mediaeval writers used the term, prerogative, only of those rights which appertained to the King as feudal lord, but sometimes it was used to include all those rights, powers and capacities which were derived from the King's pre-eminence.

The Seventeenth Century

The history of the royal prerogative is inseparably connected with the history of parliamentary sovereignty and the alliance between common lawyers and Parliament. In outline that story has already been told.[2] The common lawyers asserted that there was a fundamental distinction between what came to be called the ordinary as opposed to the absolute prerogative. The ordinary prerogative meant those royal functions which could only be exercised in defined ways and involved no element of royal discretion. Thus the King could not himself act as a judge; he must dispense justice through his judges.[3] The King too could only exercise legislative authority through Parliament.[4] The absolute or extraordinary prerogative meant those powers which the King could exercise in his discretion. It was round the absolute prerogative that the seventeenth-century struggle between King and Parliament centred. The King has undoubted powers to exercise discretion in the interest of the State, especially in times of emergency, but the claims of the Stuart Kings in this regard could not be reconciled with the growing claims of Parliament.[5] The absolute prerogative covered a

[1] P. 62, *ante*.
[2] Chap. 4, A.
[3] *Prohibitions del Roy* (1607), 12 Co. Rep. 63; K. & L. 108; p. 318, *post*.
[4] *The Case of Proclamations* (1611), 12 Co. Rep. 74; K. & L. 110; pp. 39–40, *ante*.
[5] P. 43, *ante*.

wider field than the King's rights to take extraordinary action to meet emergencies. It was primarily around the King's emergency powers that the seventeenth-century struggle turned, but the rights to pardon a criminal or grant a peerage were also part of the absolute as opposed to the ordinary prerogative. They could be exercised at the King's discretion. The contest could not be settled as a matter of law and indeed involved the execution of one King and the expulsion of another. None the less the rival theories and very real difficulties involved are best understood by a study of the leading cases, most of which were decided in favour of the Crown. The great taxation cases, *Bate's Case* and *The Case of Ship Money* have already been discussed,[1] so too have the cases relating to the dispensing power, *Thomas* v. *Sorrell* and *Godden* v. *Hales*.[2] Another case of the first importance was *Darnel's* or *The Five Knights' Case*,[3] where it was held that it was a sufficient answer to a writ of habeas corpus to state that a prisoner was detained without cause shown *per speciale mandatum regis* (by the special order of the King). No better example can be given of the problem of the absolute prerogative. It was the law that the King had a right to exercise a power of preventive arrest which could not be questioned by the courts. In *Darnel's Case* this power was used to enforce taxation levied without the consent of Parliament. The right of Parliament to control taxation came into conflict with a prerogative power recognised by law. The arbitrary power of committal was declared illegal by the Petition of Right 1628 and the Statute of 1640 (16 Car. 1 c. 10 s. 8) guaranteed to the subject the writ of habeas corpus against the King and his Council.

The Solution of the Problem

The problem of the prerogative was solved in two stages. The first is that of the seventeenth-century struggle culminating in the Revolution Settlement of 1688. The Bill of Rights declared illegal certain specific abuses of the prerogative. Moreover the Settlement marked the final triumph of the view that there was no extraordinary prerogative above the law. It is in this sense that a prerogative power may be described as a common law power. Derived from this ancient pre-eminence of the Crown it is a power which the common law recognises as exercisable by the King. The powers so recognised are many and important, *e.g.* the right to summon and dissolve Parliament, the right to declare war and make peace. There was, however, even after 1688 scope for conflict between King and

[1] Pp. 40–1, *ante*.

[2] Pp. 41–2, *ante*.

[3] (1627), 3 St. Tr. 1; K. & L. 79.

Parliament. The second stage is the growth of responsible government and the establishment of a constitutional monarchy, as it is understood to-day.[1] The meaning of responsible government has already been explained.[2] It became established that the prerogative powers could only be exercised through and on the advice of Ministers responsible to Parliament.

The Prerogative to-day

The Sovereign is still the personification of the State, and has always enjoyed by prescription, custom and law the chief place in Parliament and the sole executive power. The Act of Settlement affirmed the laws of England to be the birthright of the people and that

> all the Kings and Queens who shall ascend the throne of this realm ought to administer the government . . . according to the said laws; and their officers and Ministers ought to serve them respectively according to the same.

Parliament is summoned and dissolved by the Queen; the powers of Ministers are exercised for and on behalf of Her Majesty; the courts are the Queen's courts. The term, prerogative, is sometimes used to include both the common law and the statutory powers of the Crown. It is, however, preferable to confine it to common law powers. It is also sometimes used in the sense, that is now perhaps archaic, of certain of those attributes of the Sovereign which result from the headship of the State. Thus the term, prerogative of perfection, is used of the rule that the Crown can do no wrong; prerogative of perpetuity, of the rule that the succession of one Sovereign is simultaneous with the death of his predecessor. The living meaning of the prerogative to-day is, however, that group of powers of the Crown not conferred by statute but recognised by the common law as belonging to the Crown.

The Exercise of the Prerogative

The prerogative powers of the Crown are with very rare [3] exceptions to-day exercised by the Government of the day. For their exercise, just as for the exercise of statutory powers, Ministers are responsible to Parliament and may be asked questions relating to those public duties for which the Sovereign is responsible, provided that the duties fall within the province of the particular Minister. To this there are some exceptions and in particular a question with regard to the exercise of the prerogative of mercy in capital sentences is not

[1] P. 17, *ante*.
[2] Pp. 44–45, *ante*.
[3] *E.g.* the choice of a Prime Minister; see p. 82, *ante*.

in order. For the exercise of a prerogative power the prior authority of Parliament is not required. Thus, to take but one example, the Crown may grant a new constitution to a colony which has no representative legislature without first consulting or even informing Parliament. Parliament may criticise Ministers for the consequences which result from the exercise of prerogative; Parliament too may abolish or curtail the prerogative by statute; [1] but in regard to the exercise of the prerogative Parliament has no right to be consulted in advance. Certain prerogative powers could of course only be exercised if the Government were assured of parliamentary support. The Crown may declare war, but no Government could take the risk of declaring war without being assured of popular support, and Parliament alone can vote supplies to enable war to be waged. Although the contents of the prerogative depend largely upon historical causes, it will be found that they can be justified on grounds of convenience and political wisdom. Some prerogative powers are those, the exercise of which is not suitable for discussion beforehand in the House of Commons, *e.g.* the disposition of the armed forces, appointments in the Civil Service, the grant of honours to individuals for public services. Such topics are seldom debated or questioned in Parliament after the event. But prerogative matters in relation to foreign affairs (which in this book are discussed as acts of State) and to general defence policy are the occasion of principal debates in both Houses, although legislation is not usually required, action being taken by the Government on the authority of the prerogative alone. [2]

The Prerogative and the Courts

It has been said that prerogative powers are those powers which the law recognises as belonging to the Crown other than powers conferred by statute. If an individual disputes the validity of an act purporting to be done under the prerogative, the courts will investigate whether or not the alleged prerogative power exists. An important illustration of this is discussed at the end of this chapter. Once, however, the existence and extent of the power are established, the manner of its exercise can only be questioned in Parliament. The mere plea of State necessity will not, however, serve to protect any one accused of an unlawful act towards a subject. This is a cardinal principle of English law.

[1] P. 190, *post*.
[2] Chap. 20, A.

> With respect to the plea of State necessity, or a distinction that has been aimed at between State offences and others, the common law does not understand that kind of reasoning, nor do our books take notice of any such distinction: *per* Lord Camden, C. J., in *Entick* v. *Carrington.*[1]

There is a clear distinction between the mere plea of State necessity and reliance upon a prerogative power recognised by law.

The Prerogative and Acts of State

By virtue of his pre-eminence as head of the State the Sovereign exercises numerous powers in the realm of foreign affairs. Acts done in the exercise of such powers are generally known as acts of State. Whether these powers may rightly be described as prerogative powers is a matter of argument. In this book they will be treated separately and the term prerogative powers will be confined to the power and authority of the Sovereign in relation to her own subjects, and not rights vested in her in relation to persons owing no allegiance.[2] In this connection "it still lies within the prerogative power of the Crown to extend its sovereignty and jurisdiction to areas of land or sea over which it has not previously claimed or exercised sovereignty or jurisdiction. For such extension the authority of Parliament is not required." [3]

Powers relating to the Legislature

We may now consider separately some prerogative powers. By virtue of the prerogative the Sovereign summons, prorogues and dissolves Parliament.[4] The royal prerogative to create peers may be used on the advice of the Government to ensure the passage of a Bill through the House of Lords.[5] The Sovereign has a right as an integral part of the Legislature to assent or refuse to assent to Bills.[6] The Crown may by Order in Council or letters patent legislate under the prerogative for certain colonies.[7]

Prerogatives relating to the Judiciary

Lapse of time does not bar the right of the Crown to prosecute, but there are many statutes which impose a time limit. All criminal prosecutions on indictment are brought in the name of the Crown. The Crown may stop such a prosecution by the entry of a *nolle*

[1] (1765), 19 St. Tr. 1030; K. & L. 312.

[2] See *per* Warrington, L.J., in *In re Ferdinand, Ex-Tsar of Bulgaria,* [1921] 1 Ch. 107, at p. 139.

[3] *Post Office* v. *Estuary Radio Ltd.*, [1968] 2 Q.B. 740 at p. 753.

[4] Chap. 8.

[5] P. 98, *ante*.

[6] P. 134, *ante*.

[7] Chap. 31, A.

prosequi, a power exercised by the Attorney-General.[1] The Crown too may pardon convicted offenders or remit or reduce a sentence on the advice of the Home Secretary.[2] It is by virtue of the prerogative that the Crown grants special leave to appeal from British courts overseas to the Judicial Committee of the Privy Council.[3] But most States of the Commonwealth have abolished all appeals to the Privy Council.

Prerogatives relating to the Armed Forces

The Sovereign is commander-in-chief of all the armed forces of the Crown and has assumed the title of Lord High Admiral under the defence reorganisation of 1964. The Navy, though its recruitment and discipline are regulated by statute (Naval Enlistment Acts 1835 to 1884 and Naval Discipline Act 1957) is a prerogative force maintained without any direct statutory authority. The Bill of Rights prohibits the keeping of a standing army within the realm in time of peace without the consent of Parliament, and this prohibition includes all forces serving on land. Thus the authority of Parliament is required to authorise the maintenance of the Army, the Royal Air Force and, for their employment ashore, the Royal Marines.[4] Their control, organisation and disposition are within the prerogative. All officers hold their commissions from the Queen.

Appointments and Honours

The Sovereign appoints Ministers, Judges and Magistrates and makes appointments to all the principal offices in State and Church and to membership of Royal Commissions to enquire into matters of controversy. Appointments to all posts in the Civil Service are appointments to the service of the Crown, though made by and in the name of ministerial heads of departments. The Sovereign too is the sole fountain of honour and alone can create peers and confer honours and decorations. Honours are conferred on the advice of the Prime Minister or the Ministers of the appropriate Departments, but the Order of the Garter, the Order of the Thistle, the Royal Victorian Order (for personal services to the Sovereign) and the Order of Merit are in the personal gift of the Sovereign.

Immunities from Taxation

Taxation, including local rates, is not payable in respect of income received by the Sovereign as such. Nor is it payable on Crown

[1] Pp. 319–21, *post*. [2] Pp. 321–3, *post*.
[3] Chap. 33.
[4] Chap. 27.

properties or in respect of income received on behalf of the Crown by a servant of the Crown in the course of official duties.[1]

Monopolies

Grants and monopolies by the Crown were bad at common law except in the case of patents for new inventions. In *The Case of Monopolies* [2] there was held void a grant of the sole right to make and import playing cards. The Statute of Monopolies 1624, a declaratory Act, controlled the Crown's power to grant to first inventors the monopoly of working new inventions. This statute formed the basis of modern patent law, now regulated by the Patents and Designs Acts 1907 to 1949. The Statute of Monopolies recognised the rights of corporations, companies and societies of merchants and in 1683 the court held that a grant of the sole right of trading to the East Indies was valid,[3] but in 1694 the House of Commons resolved that, unless prohibited by Parliament, all subjects have an equal right of trading with the King's dominions. Since that date the grant of exclusive rights of trading has been by statute, *e.g.* to the East India Company set up in 1698.[4]

Miscellaneous Prerogatives

Other prerogative powers, many of which are nowadays regulated by statute, relate to the creation of corporations by royal charter; the erection and supervision of harbours; the guardianship of infants [5] and persons of unsound mind; the administration of charities; the right to mine precious metals; coinage; the grant of franchises, *e.g.* markets, ferries and fisheries; the right to treasure trove [6]; the sole right of printing or licensing others to print the Bible, the Book of Common Prayer and State papers.

Modern Usages

The foregoing list of powers which are derived from the royal prerogative, apart from the fact that many of them are nowadays of trivial importance, does not disclose the practice governing the exercise of particular powers. For these one must consult other documents than law reports or the statute book. The Report of the Royal

[1] *Bank voor Handel en Scheepvaart N.V.* v. *Administrator of Hungarian Property*, [1954] A.C. 584.

[2] (1602), 11 Co. Rep. 84.

[3] *East India Co.* v. *Sandys* (The Great Case of Monopolies) (1685), 10 St. Tr. 371.

[4] East India Company Act 1698.

[5] This prerogative is not excluded by the exercise of the duties and powers of local authorities under the Children Act 1948; *In re M.* [1961] Ch. 328.

[6] P. 356, note 1, *post*.

Commission on Capital Punishment [1] revealed the practice of the Home Secretary in advising the Sovereign as to the exercise of the prerogative of mercy in capital cases.[2] The prerogative of pardon is one of the few matters upon which a Minister acts on his individual responsibility and the doctrine of the collective responsibility of Ministers has no application. The exercise of this prerogative has seldom been the subject of direct attack in the House of Commons until the sentence has been carried out.[3] Accordingly previous to the publication of the Report little was known as to its manner of exercise.

The setting up of the International Military Court which tried the principal German war criminals offers a modern example of legislation by prerogative; for it was an instance of the exercise by the Head of the State of a power to act on foreign territory in respect of the conduct of aliens. In other words, it was a good example of an act of State in exactly the same way as the Crown may lawfully authorise its servants in a matter of policy, such as making a treaty, to undertake executive action which cannot be challenged in the courts.[4]

Immunities in Litigation

The position of the Crown in civil litigation is historically a matter of prerogative right. Despite modern legislation, which has assimilated the Crown as defendant to much the same position as a private corporation,[5] important consequences for the Crown's opponent survive. No action lies to enforce a contract of service where a a public office is held at the pleasure of the Crown. Judgments obtained against a government department cannot be enforced by levying execution (it is clearly undesirable that public property should be seized to satisfy a judgment debt). The remedies of injunction and specific performance are not available, as the Crown, *i.e.* Ministers, cannot be committed for contempt of court, the method of enforcing these remedies against ordinary personal dependants.

Orders for restitution do not lie against the Crown. Exemptions from the interlocutory processes of discovery of documents and interrogatories may be allowed by the court.[6]

[1] Cmd. 8932, 1953, paras. 37–41.

[2] Pp. 321–3, *post*.

[3] With the abolition of the death penalty in cases of murder this issue has become of academic interest only.

[4] Pp. 276–8, *post*.

[5] Chap. 46, *post*, for Crown Proceedings Act 1947 which removed the general immunities from suit in tort and contract.

[6] *Conway* v. *Rimmer*, [1968] A.C. 910.

The Prerogative in time of National Emergency

The declaration of war and making of peace will be considered in connection with acts of State.[1] The extent of the prerogative powers in time of grave emergency cannot be precisely stated, and in modern times the Executive takes statutory powers to meet emergencies.[2] That the prerogative powers are wide was admitted by Hampden's counsel in the *Case of Ship Money* [3]; nor save in regard to taxation were they abridged by the Bill of Rights. In time of sudden invasion or formidable insurrection the King may demand personal service within the realm.[4] Either the Crown or a subject may invade the land of another to erect fortifications for the defence of the realm,[5] but this right, like the right to take all necessary measures to repel the King's enemies in time of war or to restore order in time of insurrection, should probably not be regarded as a prerogative power.[6] It is a duty rather than a right and is shared by the Crown with all its subjects.

Requisition

The Crown may under the prerogative requisition British ships in territorial waters in time of urgent national necessity, not restricted to invasion or imminent danger.[7] By the right of angary according to international law and also British municipal law, the Crown may, in time of war, requisition any chattels (not only ships) belonging to a national of a neutral State found within the realm, but compensation must be paid.[8]

Control over Exit and Entry

The movement of citizens of the United Kingdom is subject to certain restrictions which are based on the prerogative.[9] Passport control (though a modern device) is the best known and since no law

[1] Chap. 20.
[2] Chap. 48.
[3] P. 41, *ante*.
[4] Chitty, *Prerogatives of the Crown*, p. 49.
[5] *The Case of the King's Prerogative in Saltpetre* (1607), 12 Co. Rep. 12; K. & L. 108; P. 268, *post* for discussion of the right to compensation when property is taken under the prerogative.
[6] Chap. 28.
[7] *The Broadmayne*, [1916] P. 64, at p. 67; *Crown of Leon* v. *Admiralty Commissioners*, [1921] 1 K.B. 595. The right of requisition probably extends to British ships, wherever they may be: *The Power of the Crown to Requisition British Ships in a National Emergency*, by Sir William Holdsworth, 35 L.Q.R. 12. Compensation is probably payable.
[8] *Commercial and Estates Co. of Egypt* v. *Board of Trade*, [1925] 1 K.B. 271. *The Right of Angary*, by Sir Ivor Jennings, 3 C.L.J. 1.
[9] For such citizens resident outside the U.K., see Commonwealth Immigrants Act 1963, p. 253, *post*.

requires the possession of a passport, a British subject should be free to leave and to enter the country without one. Passports are an administrative device and are granted, withheld or revoked under the prerogative; they are in practice international identity cards and without one a traveller is severely handicapped in movement abroad. Arbitrary withholding or withdrawal are occasionally practised; reasons need not be given. Proof of identification by other means, *e.g.* birth certificate, may be rejected by the roundabout, and legally dubious, device of subjecting a British subject to the strict proof of identity for which provision is made by the Aliens Restriction Act, 1914. This is an example of an abuse of power for which a British subject would appear to have a legal remedy, unless genuine grounds exist for suspecting alien nationality.[1] How to reconcile the use of passports to control the movement of private individuals with the common law right of every man to go out of the realm for whatever cause he pleases without obtaining the Queen's leave is a question which awaits answer from the courts.[2]

At common law the Crown could restrain a person from leaving the realm to evade civil justice by the writ, *ne exeat regno.* This writ has not been issued since 1893, but the court still has power to issue it, but must be satisfied that certain conditions laid down by the Debtors Act 1869 are satisfied; *Felton* v. *Callis* [1969] 1 Q.B. 200. The Crown may probably by virtue of the prerogative restrain a British subject from leaving the realm in time of war, or recall him from abroad, but in modern times entry and exit in time of war are controlled by statutory powers.

Prerogative Powers and Statute Law

Many prerogative rights have been regulated by statute. Thus the care of mental patients is now regulated by the Mental Health Act 1959 and statutory regulations made thereunder. It was not, however, until 1920 that it was clearly established that, where statutory powers are conferred covering the sphere of a prerogative power, the Crown must proceed under the statutory powers and cannot rely upon the prerogative. Acts of Parliament may by express words abrogate a prerogative power; but the fact that a statute covers the sphere of a prerogative power merely suspends its exercise, but does not abrogate it. The relationship between prerogative and statutory powers was clearly laid down by the House of Lords in *Attorney-General* v. *De Keyser's Royal Hotel.*[3]

[1] P. 258, *post*. See cases cited in Notes 2, 3 and 4.
[2] See H. W. R. Wade, *Passports and the Individuals' Rights to Travel. The Times*, 7 August 1968.
[3] [1920] A.C. 508; K. & L. 118.

An hotel was required for the purpose of housing the administrative staff of the Royal Flying Corps during the First World War. The Army Council offered to hire the hotel at a rent, but, negotiations having broken down, possession was taken of the premises under the Defence of the Realm Acts and Regulations made thereunder. A petition of right was brought against the Crown claiming compensation as a matter of right for the use of the hotel by the army authorities. (At the time that the Army Council took possession the Royal Flying Corps had not been superseded by the Royal Air Force and was under the control of the War Office.)

It was argued for the Crown that there was a prerogative to take the lands of the subject in case of emergency in time of war, and that no compensation was payable as of right for land so taken. This argument overlooked the provisions of the Defence Act 1842 which had been incorporated into the Defence of the Realm Acts. These provisions imposed conditions upon the compulsory acquisition of land and provided for payment of compensation *as a matter of right* to persons whose land had been taken.

The argument on behalf of the owners of the hotel was that in fact the Crown had taken possession under the statutes and regulations and so could not fall back on the prerogative right, under which no compensation could be claimed, except as a matter of grace.

Both the Court of Appeal and the House of Lords rejected the argument of the Crown, and held that the prerogative had been superseded for the time being by the statute, and therefore the Crown was not in any event entitled to act under the prerogative. There can be no excuse for reverting to prerogative powers when the Legislature has given to the Crown statutory powers which cover all that can be necessary for the defence of the nation, and which are moreover accompanied by safeguards to the individual which are in agreement with the demands of justice. It may be noted in passing that the courts were prepared to hold, had it been necessary, that the alleged prerogative to requisition land in time of war without paying compensation had not been proved.[1]

The Emergency Powers (Defence) Act 1939 passed immediately before the outbreak of the Second World War expressly provided that the powers which it conferred should be additional to any powers exercisable under the prerogative (s. 9).[2]

[1] See also p. 268, *post*. [2] Pp. 721–3, *post*.

CHAPTER TWELVE

MINISTERS OF THE CROWN

THERE have already been studied the Cabinet system in brief outline;[1] the relationship between the Executive and the Legislature;[2] and the meaning of ministerial responsibility.[3] The story of the gradual development of the Cabinet system has been told.[4] It is now necessary to consider the composition and machinery of the Cabinet and the other organs of central government. The determination of policy and the general supervision and co-ordination of all aspects of government is, as we have seen, the responsibility of the Cabinet. The execution and often the initiation of policy is the task of the various government departments. Departments are presided over by Ministers who may or may not be members of the Cabinet. They are staffed by permanent civil servants. In addition to the government departments presided over by Ministers there are also, as has already been mentioned,[5] certain independent authorities exercising functions of central government, but not directly responsible to Parliament through a Minister of the Crown.

Ministers

Ministers of the Crown are those members of the political party, or coalition of parties, in power who hold political office. They are appointed by the Crown on the nomination of the Prime Minister. The term, Minister, is usually confined to the holders of the chief political offices of State and the heads of government departments, but the Ministry includes also junior Ministers who hold subordinate office in the Government. Each ministerial head of a department has one or more Parliamentary Secretaries[6] and there are other junior ministerial posts, *e.g.* Junior Lords of the Treasury who act as Government Whips.[7] There is no legal limit to the number of Ministers, but salaries are provided by statute for only a fixed number of ministerial posts. To provide a salary for an additional Minister without special legislation necessitates special provision in

[1] Chap. 2.
[2] Chap. 3 and Chap. 9.
[3] Chap. 6.
[4] Chap. 4, A.
[5] P. 21, *ante*. See Chap. 21.
[6] When the Minister is a Secretary of State, the Parliamentary Secretary is entitled Parliamentary Under-Secretary of State.
[7] P. 226, *post*.

the annual Appropriation Act, and such a method of increasing the number of political office-holders is not viewed with favour by the Public Accounts Committee.[1] It was, however, used during the Second World War, for example in the appointment of Ministers resident in the Middle East, Washington and North Africa, and of the Minister of Reconstruction.

Ministerial Salaries

Apart from the Lord Chancellor, whose remuneration is partly charged in the House of Lords Vote as Speaker of that House,[2] the salaries of Ministers and the Law Officers are authorised by the Ministerial Salaries Consolidation Act 1965. The Prime Minister, if, as he now invariably does, he also holds the office of First Lord of the Treasury, receives an annual salary of £10,000 and £4,000 untaxed and an annual pension of £4,000.[3] A salary of £4,500 a year is payable to the leader of the Opposition—the leader of the party in opposition to Her Majesty's Government having greatest numerical strength in the House. The Chancellor of the Exchequer, the Secretaries of State,[4] a maximum of nineteen other senior Ministers and a similar number of Ministers of State may be paid such amount not exceeding £8,500 as the Prime Minister, as First Lord of the Treasury may determine. Three Parliamentary Secretaries may receive up to £5,625 and the remainder up to £3,750; the total number of such paid offices is restricted to thirty six. Salaries are also payable to the Chief Opposition Whip in the House of Commons and to the Leader of the Opposition and the Chief Opposition Whip in the House of Lords.[5] All ministerial salaries are maximum salaries and there is expressly preserved the right of the House of Commons to move the reduction of a Minister's salary in order to call attention to a grievance or censure the conduct of a departmental activity.

The Ministers of the Crown (Transfer of Functions) Act 1946 conferred the power to transfer by Order in Council the functions of one Minister to another and also to dissolve an existing government

[1] P. 227, *post*; see Sir Ivor Jennings in 2 M.L.R., 145.

[2] See p. 328, *post*; he receives £14,500 in all: Judges Remuneration Act 1965.

[3] Provided that he is not in receipt of any salary from public funds.

[4] P. 212, *post*.

[5] The salary, but not the pension provisions, were re-enacted in the Ministerial Salaries Consolidation Act 1965, which repealed the Ministers of the Crown Act 1937. Some later amendments have increased the number of salaried Ministers of State and Parliamentary Secretaries.

department. Functions of one Minister may also be shared by that Minister with another Minister.[1]

Ministers in Parliament

It is a convention that ministerial office-holders should be members of one or other House of Parliament. Indeed such membership is essential to the working of parliamentary government. It ensures contact between the Executive and the Legislature and enables Ministers to expound policy. Moreover, it is essential to the working of the parliamentary system that members should be exposed to parliamentary questions not only from the Opposition, but also from members of their own party. It is not, however, a rule of law that a Minister must be in Parliament, and a Minister who is defeated at an election usually continues in office while seeking election in another constituency. As has been seen,[2] the provisions of the Ministerial Salaries Consolidation Act 1965 limit the number of Ministers in receipt of salaries who may sit at any one time in the House of Commons and thus ensure indirectly that there should be ministerial representation in the House of Lords. It has often been suggested, that Ministers should be able to speak and defend their policy in either House of Parliament, thus enabling the best man, whether peer or commoner, to be appointed to any post.

Ministers and the Civil Service

However technical may be the work of a government department its head is a Minister usually appointed because of his general capacity and political experience as a member of his party and not because of expert knowledge. Nowhere is the practice at first sight so open to criticism as in the case of the Ministry of Defence and the Ministry of Technology where scientific developments make their closest impact upon government. The positions of a solicitor-politician or a trade union leader in control of army affairs and a co-operative expert in charge of defence present more apparent anomalies than those of a university don at the Department of Education, or a financial expert as Chancellor of the Exchequer—to illustrate from office-holders of the present century. There is little doubt that the technical work of government can only be carried on by a permanent civil service (assisted by other expert Crown servants in the case of the Ministry of Defence), enjoying security of tenure, so far as political fluctuations are concerned. The traditions of such service incline to routine methods and a cautious approach is dictated by the

[1] Ministers of the Crown Act 1964, s. 4.
[2] P. 114, *ante*.

obligation to protect the Minister from criticism in Parliament. Again the higher officials have not the business man's expectation of pecuniary gain, nor perhaps the professional man's hope of fame and fortune. For the ministerial head of a department there is the political stimulus, the hope of public advancement, and the publicity afforded by criticism in Parliament, which he must answer, and from the press and public who may, sooner or later, drive him and his colleagues from office.

In the case of the Ministry of Defence in particular, both the Cabinet and Parliament are more likely to acquiesce in the financial demands of a department, if they are presented by a civilian or non-expert who has no particular temptation towards excessive expenditure. Defence Ministers do not become famous on account of the amount of public money they cause to be expended, but a professional soldier, if put in a similar position at the head of the Ministry of Defence in peace time, might be prejudiced from the outset by a desire to maintain his personnel and equipment at the highest margin of security. It is better that the technical advisers of these departments should not come direct to Parliament as the heads of the Service in which they have spent their professional lives, but should voice their demands through the political head of the department. What may be lost in departmental efficiency may be gained by the introduction of outside opinion and incentive.

CHAPTER THIRTEEN

THE CABINET

THOUGH the existence of the Cabinet was recognised by the provision in the Ministers of the Crown Act 1937 and the Ministerial Salaries Consolidation Act 1965 of salaries for those Ministers who are members of the Cabinet, the Cabinet is an organ of government the existence of which rests upon convention. No statute or rule of common law regulates its composition or lays down its powers. The Cabinet consists of those Ministers whom the Prime Minister invites to join him in tendering advice to the Sovereign on the government of the country. Cabinet Ministers are chosen by the Prime Minister from the leading members of his party or in the case of a coalition from the two or more parties forming the coalition.

Composition of the Cabinet

No Minister can claim by virtue of his office to be included in the Cabinet, though in peace time there may be said to be a convention that certain offices carry with them a seat in the Cabinet, *e.g.* the Lord Chancellor, the Chancellor of the Exchequer, the Secretaries of State, the Ministers in charge of departments responsible for the principal services, *e.g.* Labour, Agriculture, Trade and Housing and Local Government. In addition there are usually included in the Cabinet two or three members with few, if any, departmental responsibilities, *e.g.* the Lord President of the Council and the Lord Privy Seal. These Ministers, whose executive duties are very few, are free to assist the Prime Minister on special problems or to co-ordinate different aspects of a single problem.

The Prime Minister

Like the Cabinet the office of Prime Minister is conventional, though its existence has been recognised by statutes.[1] We have seen how the Prime Minister is chosen by the Sovereign.[2] It is customary for the Prime Minister to hold the office of First Lord of the Treasury, though this practice has not been invariable. The Prime

[1] Chequers Estate Act 1917; Ministers of the Crown Act 1937: Ministerial Salaries Consolidation Act 1965, ss. 1, 2, 3: see p. 114, *ante*.

[2] P. 82, *ante*.

Minister may also hold other offices, *e.g.* Lord Salisbury was for a long time Prime Minister and Secretary of State for Foreign Affairs while the leader of the House of Commons was First Lord of the Treasury. Lord Salisbury, who resigned in 1902, was the last Prime Minister to sit in the House of Lords. Since the passing of the Ministers of the Crown Act 1937 which authorised a salary for the Prime Minister, if he also holds the office of First Lord of the Treasury, it is probable that the Prime Minister will always hold the post of First Lord of the Treasury. The statutory association of these two offices gives support to the convention that the Prime Minister should be in the House of Commons in view of the fact that that House exercises financial control. The Prime Minister is head of the Civil Service Department and his approval is required for appointments to the principal civil service posts, *i.e.* those of permanent heads or deputy heads of departments and principal financial and establishment officers. The function of the Prime Minister has been described as primarily one of giving advice, particularly in discussion of policy questions before they come to the Cabinet.[1] He is in specially close relations with the Foreign Secretary in whose department matters of political importance are of continuous occurrence and are of such a nature that they may have to be settled between the two Ministers before being brought to the Cabinet. All the most important Crown appointments are filled on the Prime Minister's nomination, *e.g.* the highest judicial appointments and bishoprics.[2] He also advises the Crown in regard to the creation of peerages, appointments to the Privy Council and grant of honours for political and other general services,[3] and appointments to those university professorships which are in the gift of the Crown. He issues invitations to serve on Royal Commissions. The ascendancy of a Prime Minister over his colleagues must vary with the personality of the particular Prime Minister, but Ministers who are not prepared to accept the Prime Minister's decision must tender their resignation. It is understood to be quite exceptional for a Cabinet decision to be taken by a majority vote, though there have been occasions when this has happened in default of an agreed conclusion.[4] On the other hand a Prime Minister cannot govern without the aid of colleagues who

[1] Sir Ivor Jennings, *Cabinet Government*, pp. 215 ff.

[2] Pp. 312–3, 470, *post*.

[3] Honours are also granted on the advice of other Ministers, *e.g.* the Secretaries of State for Foreign and Commonwealth Affairs and for the Defence Department. Similarly certain appointments are made on the recommendation of other Ministers, *e.g.* High Court judgeships on the recommendation of the Lord Chancellor.

[4] Cf. Jennings, *op. cit.*, p. 262.

command the confidence of Parliament and too many resignations may cause the fall of a Government. The Prime Minister may be described as *primus inter pares* rather than as an autocrat.

Size of Cabinets

Cabinets vary in size. They must not be too large for efficient deliberation, and yet they must not exclude those Ministers who are responsible for major spheres of government. Between 1919 and 1939 the usual size of the Cabinet was twenty to twenty-two. A Minister who is interested in a particular topic can always express his views to the Cabinet and, though not a member, will normally be invited to attend particular meetings at which matters relating to his departmental responsibilities are discussed; it is not, however, always easy to say that an issue of policy may not affect departments other than those directly concerned. A major decision on policy may indirectly affect most aspects of government and in peace time it was usual, up to 1939, to include in the Cabinet all the heads of the major government departments. That this practice resulted in unwieldy Cabinets is now generally agreed. From the start of the Second World War the need for day-to-day decisions demanded a smaller Cabinet. The size of the post-war Cabinet has fluctuated between sixteen and twenty-three. The number of important departments with Ministers in charge is about thirty. There has thus resulted a division in classification of Ministers into Cabinet Ministers and Ministers not in the Cabinet; but the line of division is flexible.[1]

Cabinet Committees

A major problem of government is to secure co-ordination. Cabinet committees and committees of senior officials of the departments are designed to secure this. Most problems concern more than one department and should be presented to the Cabinet after agreement has been reached or at least after differences have been defined by the departments concerned. It is necessary to distinguish between the Cabinet and its ministerial committees which settle issues of policy, and committees of officials which co-ordinate and advise. In theory an official committee advises; the Cabinet or a ministerial committee decides; the department takes the necessary action. This does not mean that it is necessary that every question on which a committee is asked to advise should go subsequently to Ministers. Agreed recommendations may be implemented automatically by the departments concerned on the responsibility and

[1] Pp. 86–8, *ante*, for discussion of collective responsibility.

authority of their respective Ministers—or, if the issue involved is not a major one, without specific ministerial authority. Ministerial committees perform a dual function: they dispose of business which is not important enough to come before the full Cabinet; and they focus the issues for decision if reference to the Cabinet is required. A short account of the organisation of Cabinet committees is given in the next Chapter.

The Cabinet Secretariat

The Cabinet Secretariat was created during the First World War in 1917.

> For the first time in the history of the Cabinet a Secretary was present to record the proceedings and keep the minutes of the Cabinet and of its numerous committees, and orderly methods based on those developed by the Committee of Imperial Defence were introduced, including agenda papers, the distribution (in advance of the meetings) of relevant memoranda and other material, the rapid communication of decisions to those who had to act on them; and the knitting up to the Cabinet, not only of government departments, but also of numerous committees combining a vast range of inter-departmental business.[1]

The conclusions prepared by the Secretary to the Cabinet and circulated to the Queen and all Cabinet Ministers are the only authentic record of Cabinet meetings. All Cabinet committees are served by members of the Cabinet Secretariat. Although the Secretariat has no executive functions like those of a department, it is a highly efficient instrument for securing inter-departmental co-ordination by ensuring that documents are circulated before meetings in a form which presents the issue to be decided, for reporting, distributing and following up decisions taken. There is also a Central Statistical Office, which provides a common and impartial statistical service for all departments.[2]

With the development of the committee system and the creation of the Cabinet Secretariat there has been combined with ministerial responsibility the strong points of the local government system—executive committees and a recording department serving all the various committees (the office of the clerk to the council).[3] The efficiency of any large organisation depends very largely on proper co-ordination of departmental activities. There must be proper co-operation in both the framing of policy and its execution. Under the Cabinet system such co-operation is secured without impairing the

[1] *Haldane Memorial Lecture*, 1942, by Lord Hankey.

[2] P. 210, *post*.

[3] Though the clerk to a council is also an executive officer who himself has responsibility for co-ordination.

responsibility of the individual Minister for the work of his department.[1] An influential committee not only frames policy but by calling for progress reports is able to ensure to a large extent that its policy is carried out. The experience of war led to the retention of a number of standing committees of the Cabinet.

Organisation for War

During both the First and Second World Wars it was found necessary to supersede the normal Cabinet by a small War Cabinet to take responsibility for the conduct of the war. In 1916 the War Cabinet consisted of five, later six, senior Ministers without departmental responsibilities, except the Chancellor of the Exchequer. The War Cabinets of 1939–45 were larger, varying between seven and ten, and included a number of senior departmental Ministers. Thus in 1944 the War Cabinet consisted of the Prime Minister (also Minister of Defence), the Lord President of the Council (Deputy Prime Minister), the Foreign Secretary (and leader of the House of Commons), the Chancellor of the Exchequer, the Minister of Labour and National Service, the Minister of Production, the Home Secretary and the Minister of Reconstruction. Other Ministers were invited to attend meetings for the discussion of matters with which their departments were concerned. As in the First World War, when over 250 persons in all were summoned on occasions, other persons than Ministers might be in attendance. Thus the Chiefs of Staff were frequently summoned. Visiting Prime Ministers or their deputies from the Dominions and representatives of the Government of India attended from time to time. The Secretariat of the Committee of Imperial Defence was merged in the War Cabinet Secretariat of which the military members constituted the staff of the Prime Minister as Minister of Defence.[2]

There was no Ministry of Defence and the constitutional responsibilities of the three service Ministers remained in those spheres for which the Minister of Defence did not accept responsibility. In his task of supervision of the work of the Chiefs of Staffs Sub-Committee the Prime Minister was assisted by a Defence Committee. On the home front the Lord President's Committee was the most important element in the elaborate structure of Cabinet Committees and their attendant official committees. To plan for peace there was appointed later in 1943 a Minister of Reconstruction to co-ordinate the activities of the various departments concerned with civil planning. Like the Minister of Defence the Minister of Reconstruction was a Minister without a department.

[1] Chap. 6. [2] *The Organisation for Joint Planning*, 1942, Cmd. 6351.

CHAPTER FOURTEEN

CABINET ORGANISATION

BRIEF reference has been made in the preceding chapter to Cabinet committees and to the Cabinet Secretariat. But for those readers whose interests lie in the field of government rather than the practice of the law, it is proposed here to discuss more fully the organisation of the Executive at the highest level. It has been said that "the personal responsibility of Ministers and the collective responsibility of the Cabinet supply strong inducements for clearing up all those inefficiencies that inevitably from time to time find lodgment in the complicated government structure." [1] With the experience of two world wars to draw upon much has been done to improve the higher organisation which now works at a very different standard of efficiency as compared with the Cabinets of sixty years ago.

Problem of Co-ordination

There are few problems of government that can be resolved within a single department. It is necessary then to devise machinery to enable agreement to be reached, or at least for differences to be defined clearly before a matter comes before the Cabinet. Only so can a coherent policy be evolved. Moreover, without such machinery decisions at the top level are unlikely properly to be implemented by departments; for they will not be fully understood unless departments have been brought into consultation at an early stage and given opportunity of representing their points of view from the administrative angle through high officials as well as from the policy angle through Ministers who are adequately informed of the administrative implications.

Cabinet Committees

It is the general practice of Governments not to disclose the functions or composition of Cabinet Committees, since decisions are those of the Government as a whole. But more information is avail-

[1] *British War Economy*, by Sir Keith Hancock and M. M. Gowing (H.M.S.O.) 1949, p. 88, and *Cabinet Reform in Britain, 1914–1963*, by H. Daalder (Oxford University Press) 1964.

able to the public about central organisation for defence than for other purposes of government.[1] Yet it is surprising that the public should know more about defence organisation than the organisation which determines other issues; for the former must be adapted to change over from peace to active hostilities when it at once becomes shrouded from public knowledge for the time being from considerations of security. But such is the strength of the tradition of anonymity that, apart from the organisation for defence, Governments are seldom willing to disclose the composition, or even the existence of ministerial committees appointed by the Cabinet, whether as standing committees or as *ad hoc* committees to consider a specific issue, lest the collective responsibility of the Cabinet as a whole be weakened as well as that of the Minister who is principally concerned. We can infer what approximately may be the structure of the peace-time Cabinet organisation by analogy from the defence organisation and the wartime structure as disclosed by the war histories. From time to time the veil is lifted to inform the House of Commons that a particular named or unnamed Cabinet committee is considering a specific issue; the composition of the committee is seldom disclosed. It is known that, in addition to the Committee of Imperial Defence (to be discussed later), there existed before the Second World War the Home Affairs Committee which considered the draft of all Bills promoted by the departments. This committee co-ordinated the views of other departments affected before the Bills went to the Cabinet for approval in the form recommended by the Committee. The Law Officers, who are not members of the Cabinet, attended the meetings, as did senior officials concerned with particular Bills. This machinery proved useful for giving effect to the principle of ministerial responsibility as well as lightening the agenda of Cabinets. This Committee under the War Cabinet became the Legislation Committee and was concerned with programming legislation for the current session of Parliament. It has been retained by post-war administrations and a separate committee for future legislation has been added.

Another valuable source of information is to be found in the addresses of ex-Ministers delivered to academic audiences. These cannot give an up-to-date picture of the current Administration, but they are generally speaking valuable because they reflect the considered judgment of elder statesmen and are the fruit of long and

[1] *Central Organisation for Defence*, Cmnd. 2097, 1963; *British War Economy* (*ante*), Chaps. III and VIII, and Vol. II (*Their Finest Hour*) of Sir Winston Churchill's *War Memoirs*, Chap. I, which describe the organisation of the War Cabinets of 1916–19 and 1939–45.

intimate contact with the working of the machinery of government. Among these may be mentioned the Romanes Lecture for 1946 delivered by Lord Waverley, then Sir John Anderson, a few months after he gave up the office of Chancellor of the Exchequer [1] and the chapter on "Machinery of Government" in Mr. L. S. Amery's *Thoughts on the Constitution*.[2] The young administrator, confused by the organisation into which he is plunged on entry, may usefully compare what is with what was and what should be, as described by former Ministers. Another document to be considered is the Report of the Machinery of Government Committee over which Lord Haldane presided in 1918.[3] This was a departmental committee appointed by the war-time Minister of Reconstruction. Its principal recommendation was the distribution of the business of the departments into ten main divisions by reference to their functions. The war of 1914–18 had drawn attention to the piece-meal growth of departments which had accentuated, at a time when co-ordination of effort was imperative, the illogical and overlapping allocation of duties. The Report divided the business of government into ten heads. Without advocating that each division should be under a single Minister, the Report favoured a small Cabinet not exceeding twelve and the retention of the war-time Cabinet Secretariat.[4] A number of the existing departments reflect the influence of the Report, *e.g.* Agriculture, Fisheries and Food, Social Security, Education and Science, Defence, Employment and Productivity. But no radical reallocation of duties was attempted and the size of the Cabinet (as distinct from the War Cabinet) has only once, and that for a few weeks in 1931, been reduced to twelve or below. One reason for not implementing the Haldane Report lay in the absence of any firm proposals as to ministerial relations within the ten divisions and indeed the main reason was the difficulty of reconciling the recommendations with the doctrine of collective responsibility.

Reconstruction of the central organisation prompted by the experience gained during hostilities was considered from 1943 onwards by a Cabinet Committee of the Coalition Government on the Machinery of Government which, it has been stated, is still in being. But, as with all such committees, its conclusions have been for the information of Ministers and no reports have been published.

There is however a certain amount of public information relating

[1] *The Machinery of Government*, Clarendon Press, 1946.
[2] Chap. III, 2nd edn. (1953).
[3] Cd. 9230, 1918.
[4] Pp. 200–1, *ante*.

to post-war cabinet committees.[1] The Defence Committee replaced the Committee of Imperial Defence in 1940 and was retained by the new Government in 1945. The war-time Lord President's Committee [2] was replaced by an Economic Policy Committee under the Prime Minister and a Production Committee during the Attlee Administration. The economic section of the Cabinet Office under Conservative Governments was transferred to the Treasury. To name these few committees gives an inadequate picture of cabinet organisation which may include as many as thirty committees at one time, of which about half are dealing with financial questions.[3] Not all of these are standing committees; indeed as often as not use is made of *ad hoc* committees, as for example at the time of the Suez crisis in 1956.

Committee of Imperial Defence

We turn then mainly to central organisation for defence to trace developments which are believed to have their counterpart to-day in other spheres of central government. The Committee of Imperial Defence was created in 1904 as an outcome of defects in organisation disclosed by the Boer War; the Committee remained in being until the outbreak of war in 1939, though it was replaced during the First World War on the establishment of the War Cabinet in 1916. A brief account of the functions is retained, since, as a matter of history, from it have developed the various uses to which successive Cabinets have put the committee system. It was an advisory body without executive authority, but, because the Prime Minister was its Chairman, its recommendations carried due weight to such an extent that its agreed proposals were in the majority of cases automatically implemented by the departments concerned, without reference to the Cabinet, on the responsibility and authority of the respective Ministers.[4] The function of the Committee was to frame the fundamental principles which should govern imperial defence and to prepare detailed plans to ensure that all authorities both at home and overseas should in the event of war work to a detailed and co-ordinated plan. The value of the work of the Committee was proved in 1914 and again in 1939 by the existence of detailed plans for

[1] Jennings, *Cabinet Government*, 3rd edn., pp. 313–16; Chester and Wilson, *Organization of British Central Government* 1914–56, Chap. IX (George Allen & Unwin), Mackintosh, *The British Cabinet*, 2nd edn.

[2] P. 207, *post*.

[3] Jennings, *op. cit.*, p. 261.

[4] See *Royal United Services Institute Journal*, May 1939, lecture by General (now Lord) Ismay, who was for many years Secretary of the Committee of Imperial Defence.

the transition from peace to war. Although the Committee was always elastic in its composition, successive Prime Ministers nominated a nucleus of Ministers and senior officials who came to form a panel of regular members. Under the Committee itself was a network of sub-committees with which rested responsibility for working out details of policy. From 1924 onwards the need for inter-Service planning which had become insistent with the advent of the Royal Air Force resulted in the creation of the Chiefs of Staff Committee as a sub-committee of the Committee of Imperial Defence. This laid the foundation of the joint staff organisation for planning and intelligence which was developed in the years before 1939 and on the outbreak of war was incorporated into the War Cabinet organisation.

A body, no matter how well constructed, which has no executive authority is incapable of taking decisions on major questions affecting policy which are properly matters for the Cabinet. Accordingly in 1939 the Committee of Imperial Defence was replaced by the War Cabinet itself, but its network of committees was taken over. Blended with the civil committees, some of which had already been created as part of the structure of the Committee of Imperial Defence, there was thus ready for adaptation to wartime tasks a complicated yet flexible instrument for co-ordination.

Defence Committee, 1940

When Mr. Churchill, as he then was, became Prime Minister in 1940, he assumed the title of Minister of Defence without a separate Ministry and without defining his duties as such Minister; for in war responsibility for the mobilisation and direction of the whole resources of the nation rests primarily on the Prime Minister. Although no Ministry of Defence was created, the Prime Minister was served by a small military Secretariat which had formerly served the Committee of Imperial Defence. The executive organ was the Defence Committee of the War Cabinet, presided over by the Prime Minister in which, in addition to senior Ministers including the three Service Ministers, sat the Chiefs of Staff. The last named also retained their own separate committee structure for inter-Service planning and intelligence. There is no need for present purposes to follow up the effect of this organisation on the dual responsibilities of the Chiefs of Staff, collectively to the Prime Minister as Chairman of the Defence Committee on whose behalf they issued unified operational instructions and directives, and individually to the Service Ministers who remained responsible for the day-to-day administration of the Services. As an experiment in co-ordination of effort the machine enabled the Prime Minister to provide the drive without which successful operations cannot be conducted.

Discussion of the later reorganisation for the purpose of securing unification of defence policy which was achieved in 1964 is postponed until the organisation of the armed forces is discussed.[1]

Sir John Anderson's proposals

It is not surprising that the method of co-ordinating committees both in war and in peace has proved itself in the fields of economic and social policy and indeed whenever a problem which overlaps the bounds of responsibility of a single department is in issue. Equally important is it to determine the relationship with his ministerial colleagues of the Minister chosen to preside over such a committee. Any rigid grouping of functions is unlikely to be acceptable; for Prime Ministers may hold different views on how best to mould together the ministerial team. Nor is it solely a matter of personalities. Problems differ in importance from year to year. Lord Waverley made some tentative suggestions in his Romanes lectures.[2] In addition to Defence he proposed an Economic Relations Committee to cover external economic affairs including import and export policy and commercial and economic relationships with foreign countries and with other members of the British Commonwealth. By the addition of the relevant Ministers such a Committee could be enlarged to cover internal economic problems or alternatively a separate National Development Committee might be established. Other committees should include an External Affairs Committee to consider relationships with foreign countries and within the British Commonwealth which are not primarily of an economic or financial character. There would also be an appropriate committee representing the departments concerned with social services to cover the whole field of social welfare. By 1969 it became evident that the Government had been influenced by these proposals.[3] The suggested plan included the retention of the Legislation Committee with terms of reference enlarged to cover the review of all proposals for legislation whether by Bill, Regulation, or Order at the stage of formal drafting. Such a system was no doubt suggested by the experience of the Lord President's Committee of the War Cabinet which was the principal co-ordinating committee for home front affairs, during the greater part of the Second World War.[4] Flexibility of function can be secured

[1] Chapter 27.
[2] Anderson, (later Lord Waverley), *The Machinery af Government*, pp. 13 ff.
[3] Chap. 15.
[4] Hancock and Gowing, *op. cit.*, pp. 215–23, for a discussion of the War Cabinet system including the Lord President's Committee.

not only by changing ministerial representation on Cabinet Committees, but also by the use of the small *ad hoc* committee to report on specific problems. It is often important that similar committees should exist at the official level not to decide, but to report to Ministers.

Supervising Ministers

With regard to the Minister chosen to preside over a Cabinet Committee the choice would seem to lie between a non-departmental Minister, such as the Lord President of the Council or the Lord Privy Seal, or a departmental Minister who has a predominant interest in the matters allocated to a particular group. Personality and endowments may ensure that such a Minister occupies a commanding position, but in constitutional theory he ought to be on a parity with his Cabinet colleagues. If a group of Ministers within the Cabinet were to exercise by reason of their chairmanship of committees supervisory powers over the departmental Ministers who sit with them on a committee, the responsibility of the latter to Parliament for the conduct of their departments might be weakened.[1] Within the departments it would be impractical to serve two masters in the person of the supervising Minister and the departmental Minister, nor could a Minister in practice supervise without a duplication of staff with those of the departments.[2] Such an expensive expedient could only slow down the machinery of government and from time to time would inevitably cause friction and indecision. Another solution of the difficulty might be to select as chairman for the day the Minister whose department was most closely concerned with the principal item on the agenda. It is clear that if the principle of supervising Ministers were accepted as a regular feature, there would be a much smaller Cabinet and the status of the departmental Ministers as such would be permanently weakened; indeed they might become effectively no more than parliamentary secretaries to the supervising Minister. There is much to be said for a smaller Cabinet, as Lord Haldane proposed as far back as 1919. But the experience of the years from 1940 to 1945 shows that this can be obtained without introducing supervising Ministers. For the existence of the War Cabinet did not, in the opinion of one of its members, involve any derogation from the responsibility to Parlia-

[1] Sir Winston Churchill's Administration which was formed in 1951 contained two co-ordinating Ministers during the first two years of its existence. Both had seats in the House of Lords and there was some confusion as to their effect upon departmental responsibility in the Commons so far as concerned the Ministers whose departments had been placed under a Minister for Co-ordination.

[2] Anderson, *op. cit.*, pp. 12–13.

ment and to the public for matters within their departmental sphere of those Ministers who were not members of the Cabinet.[1]

Decentralisation

On the other hand the increasing complexity of modern government has resulted in too much centralisation with the attendant evils of indecision, delay and even frustration; these evils are felt most on the periphery. It is generally recognised that Parliament cannot be burdened with further tasks and that the load on the parliamentary machine is already excessive. The solution lies in limiting the control to be exercised from the centre, at all events in matters of internal government. The experience of the public corporations entrusted with the administration of the nationalised services and industries suggests this. The greater the measure of dispersal, the easier should be the problem of co-ordination of policy at the highest level; for the Cabinet could be relieved of many problems which at present come before it and confine its attention to major questions of policy. Less emphasis would have to be placed on the doctrine of ministerial responsibility as applied to departmental Ministers. In turn there should be more reliance on the courts, including independent administrative tribunals, for the redress of individual grievances resulting from administrative intransigence.[2] The establishment of a Parliamentary Commissioner for Administration only goes a little way to check acts of maladministration.[3]

Cabinet Secretariat

The Cabinet Secretariat serves all Cabinet Committees whether standing or *ad hoc*. Under the Secretary to the Cabinet are three deputy secretaries. A small body of under-secretaries and assistant secretaries are seconded from the departments for a fixed period to provide the services for the Cabinet Committees. This interchange ensures a steady flow of officials who are trained both in departmental administration and in the work of co-ordination at the top level. Upon technical matters especially in the sphere of economics and science a government needs more guidance than the presence of experts in a single department is likely to provide.

[1] Anderson, *op. cit.*, p. 11.
[2] Chapter 47.
[3] Pp. 708–14, *post*.

The Chief Scientific Adviser and the Head of the Government Statistical Service are on the staff of the Cabinet Office. Other advisers from outside the government service are also employed temporarily on the Prime Minister's staff.

The Central Statistical Office forms part of the Cabinet Office, which also contains an historical section.

CHAPTER FIFTEEN

THE CENTRAL GOVERNMENT DEPARTMENTS

Departmental Organisation

ADMINISTRATION at the centre is carried out principally by departments over which a Secretary of State or a Minister presides as the political head who is answerable in Parliament as well as to the Cabinet, of which in the case of the larger departments he is usually a member. The office of Secretary of State has a long history which is summarised below; a Minister derives his title from the Act of Parliament which is necessary to establish that type of department. Both Secretaries of State and Ministers may be assisted by one or more Ministers of State who are not in the Cabinet. Every department has one or more Parliamentary Secretaries, political appointments. These are not Ministers in the strict sense but officers of the Crown who are exempted by statute from the usual disqualification of Crown servants from membership of the House of Commons, of which House (unless they are peers) they are invariably elected members.[1]

The senior civil servant in a department is the Permanent Secretary; he is generally the accounting officer who is answerable to the Public Accounts Committee of the House of Commons and the Comptroller and Auditor-General for the expenditure incurred. Under him are one or more Deputy Secretaries and a hierarchy of administrative officers who are responsible for executing policy and on them, particularly the higher ranks, the Minister must be able to rely for disinterested and impartial advice.

It is not proposed to summarise, as was done in previous editions, the functions of government entrusted to the various departments. Since the end of the Second World War, and particularly in the last ten years, successive Governments have changed the machinery repeatedly to cover the ever-increasing burden of administration and the new spheres of government control of the economy and the provision of welfare services. Prime Minister Wilson, though so far he has, like his predecessors, failed to reduce the size of the Cabinet below 21, has experimented freely on the lines suggested as far back

[1] Where a Secretary of State is head of a department a Parliamentary Secretary is styled Under-Secretary of State and the chief civil servant Permanent Under-Secretary of State.

as 1918 by Lord Haldane's Committee on the Machinery of Government which sought to limit the main divisions of responsibility. This has resulted in the merger of ministerial departments concerned with analagous services. In most cases a Secretary of State is responsible—Defence, Foreign and Commonwealth Affairs, Education and Science, Health and Social Security and certain industrial responsibilities. In others the retention of separate Ministries under a co-ordinating Chief Minister is the solution. Thus the Secretary of State for Local Government and Regional Planning—a new office in 1969 designed to create responsibility at the top for regional policy—has the overlordship over separate departments of Housing and Local Government and of Transport. This device was invented by Sir Winston Churchill and abandoned after a short trial.[1]

Secretaryships of State

There are nine Secretaries of State, who preside over some of the more important departments.[2] For all but peers and privy councillors the Secretary of State is the only avenue of approach for the subject to the Sovereign, save by petition. Whereas departments may be approached by direct communication, this is not so in the case of approach to the Sovereign. Similarly, authentic communications by the Sovereign to his people are normally countersigned by a Secretary of State. The duties of Secretaries of State are legally interchangeable and independent of any distinction on account of the departments over which they preside. In practice each Secretary of State limits his functions to those traditionally related to his own department and many powers are conferred by statute on a particular Secretary of State, *e.g.* on the Secretary of State for Defence by the Defence Act 1842.[3] Documents signed by a Secretary of State do not indicate that they are signed by any particular Secretary, the signature being followed by the words "One of Her Majesty's Principal Secretaries of State."

A recent practice has been to name one of the Secretaries of State as First Secretary. There is no such office in the legal sense, but it is useful to determine seniority in the Cabinet, *e.g.* for choosing a Deputy to act in the absence of the Prime Minister from the chair.

[1] A list of members of the Cabinet and other Departmental Ministers is given in Appendix D.

[2] The Secretaries of State for Foreign and Commonwealth Affairs (1969), the Home Department, Scotland, Education and Science, Defence (1964), Wales 1964), Employment and Productivity (1967), Local Government and Regional Planning (1969) and Social Security (1969).

[3] The Act speaks of the "principal officers of the Ordnance," whose powers and duties have been vested successively in the Secretaries of State for War and Defence by subsequent enactments.

History

The office of Secretary of State springs from a humble origin, and it is not easy to say at what precise moment in history the King's Secretary became a definite office. In the Tudor period the Secretary became a channel of communication for home and foreign affairs, and the office seems to have grown in importance, largely perhaps on account of the personal rule of the Tudors. From about 1540 two Secretaries of State were appointed, but not at first as an invariable practice. It was when the Privy Council sought to combine deliberative and executive functions that the office assumed its present importance. The Secretaries of State ceased in fact, though not in law, to be servants of the King and his Council and became one of the motive forces in the Cabinet. On two occasions before 1782 a third Secretaryship was added for the time being. It was in that year that the Home Office and the Foreign Office came into existence as separate departments. For some 150 years there had been a Secretary of State for the Northern Department, in charge of business relating to the Northern Powers of Europe, and another for the Southern Department, which embraced France and the Southern countries. Ireland fell to the senior Secretary, while the Colonies and Home Affairs came under either.[1] On March 27, 1782, the Foreign Office came into existence as a result of a circular letter addressed by Fox to the representatives of Foreign Powers in London, to the effect that he had been entrusted with the sole direction of foreign affairs, while his colleague, the Earl of Shelburne, had been appointed Principal Secretary of State for Domestic Affairs and the Colonies. The Home Secretary from that date took precedence over all other Secretaries. At that time he had very few of the statutory powers and duties which subsequent legislation has conferred upon him. The other Secretaryships of State may be said to have been created out of this Secretaryship. In 1794 a Secretary of State for War was appointed, who in 1801 took over the Colonies. In 1854 a separate Secretary of State for the Colonies was appointed on account of the Crimean War. In 1858, as the result of the Indian Mutiny, Indian affairs were entrusted to a Secretary of State for India. It was not until 1918 that another Secretaryship was created, namely, that for Air. In 1925 the Secretary of State for the Colonies was appointed to a separate Secretaryship for Dominion Affairs, the Colonial Office and the Dominions Office being (thenceforth

[1] But compare the account in Anson, *op. cit.* (4th edn.), Vol. II, Part I, pp. 178 ff.

organised in separate departments, though the offices were, until 1930, held by the same holder; this practice was resumed in 1962 with the diminution of territories for which the Secretary of State for the Colonies remained responsible following the implementation of the policy of independence for all but the smaller overseas territories. In 1926 the Secretary for Scotland, who, as head of the Scottish Office, controlled much of the internal government of Scotland, assisted by subordinate departments, was given the status of Secretary of State. In the last forty years various changes, of which the merger of Foreign and Commonwealth Affairs in 1969 is the most important, have been made and to-day there are nine holders of the office.

Advisory Bodies [1]

Why Consultation is needed

A description of the structure of government would be incomplete without reference to the many advisory bodies on which reliance is placed.

To secure observance a law must command consent of the governed. To secure that consent a freely elected House of Commons passes the law. Neither Parliament nor the government department which is charged with the duty of preparing a Bill or regulations are necessarily, or even usually, in a position to decide of their special knowledge what detailed provisions, or in some cases what general policy will command acceptance. It is for a Minister, having consulted the Cabinet when important questions of policy arise, to determine what shall be the contents of a Bill. It is for him to explain and justify the contents, clause by clause, accepting modifications, maybe, in the course of its passage through Parliament. It is, however, but rarely that Parliament rejects a Bill because it cannot accept the general principles which are contained in the legislation. Indeed, no Government could long survive if this happened. It is important therefore, to consider briefly some of the means whereby information is obtained by a Government to enable it to perform its duty of preparing legislation.

Royal Commissions and Departmental Committees

When it is apparent that a change in the law is desirable and the issue is one which the Government considers requires preliminary

[1] Sir Kenneth Wheare, *Government by Committee* (O.U.P.), is a valuable essay on all forms of committee government.

enquiry, it is usual to appoint a departmental committee, or, if the matter is of high import and time is not of the essence, a Royal Commission, to enquire into the matter and to report to the Government on all aspects of the problem. The former method is usually followed, but the latter from a constitutional point of view is independent of any government department. For this reason the Royal Commission may be said to enjoy a somewhat greater prestige than the departmental committee. It is the usual practice of either type of inquiry to invite evidence from outside organisations and individuals. The Royal Commission usually hears evidence in public and copies of this and accompanying memoranda are made available to the public. A departmental committee normally sits in private, but both the Committee on Ministers' Powers (1932) and the Committee on Tribunals and Inquiries (1957) took evidence in public and this was subsequently published. Among examples of Royal Commissions may be found the Royal Commission on Population appointed with the object of devising a long-term policy at a time when the decline in the birth-rate was causing some anxiety. More recent examples are the Royal Commission on the Law relating to Mental Illness and Mental Deficiency which resulted in the Mental Health Act 1959, and that on the Police of which the Police Act 1964 gave effect to the main recommendations. The conditions under which there are cared for children who lack parental care was investigated by a departmental committee. While a Royal Commission is appointed by royal warrant and a departmental committee by a Minister, in either case the personnel to conduct the enquiry is selected by the departments most closely concerned with the proposed legislation. Members are chosen, partly from their record of public service, partly by reason of their knowledge of the problem under investigation. They are drawn mainly from outside the ranks of government servants.

When the investigating body has delivered its report which is published as a Command Paper, it is for the Minister, or the Government as a whole, to decide how far the recommendations are acceptable, and if so, in what form they should be presented to Parliament. The function of an extra-governmental body is purely advisory, and this is equally true of the consultative committees to which reference may now be made. A departmental committee should not be confused with a statutory public inquiry such as those which are held in connection with appeals under town and country planning legislation or *ad hoc* inquiries which are set up to investigate a scandal, for example of misconduct by members of a particular police force.

Consultative Commiitees

The practice of consultation with extra-governmental organisations has grown rapidly in the present century. It is inevitable that the increase in the functions of government should have made the need for expert advice felt by the administrator. Nor is the need confined to projected legislation, though consultative committees have proved particularly valuable in the task of framing regulations. The function of such committees is to enable the Minister to ascertain informed opinion before he comes to a decision, whether that decision involves an executive or a legislative act. In some cases there is a statutory obligation on a Minister to consult a standing committee or named association, though it is seldom that the advisory body can take the initiative without the matter being referred to it by the Minister. The majority of these bodies are, however, appointed at the discretion of a Minister, because he feels the need for advice. Under this heading come most of the committees associated with the Ministry of Health, which between 1919 and 1938 numbered one hundred and twenty-five. By 1949 the total of all advisory bodies had reached about seven hundred.

Examples of Consultation

An illustration of the type of body which a Minister must consult is the Police Council. Regulations relating to conditions of service in the police forces can only be made under the Police Act 1964 after the Home Secretary has consulted the Council, a body constituted under the Act, on which sit representatives of local police authorities and of all ranks of the police.[1] The Education Act 1944 required the Minister of Education to establish central advisory councils for education, one for England and one for Wales, to advise not only on any questions referred to them by the Minister, but also upon any matters of educational theory and practice as the councils think fit. The Education Councils replace the Consultative Committee of the former Board of Education, a body which, though lacking the power to take the initiative, made reports at the request of the President of the Board, upon which were based, first the reorganisation of primary education, and later the expansion of secondary education which was intended to raise the status of modern and technical schools to an equality with grammar schools. The Minister of Health is advised in the central administration of the national health service by a Central Council upon such general matters relating to that service or any services provided by the local health

[1] P. 240, *post*.

authorities as the Council thinks fit and upon any questions which he may refer to them.

The National Insurance Advisory Committee advises upon questions referred to it by the Secretary of State for Social Services in relation to his functions under the National Insurance Act 1946 and also has certain duties given to it by that Act; in particular the Minister must submit to the Committee the draft of any regulations which he proposes to make under the Act before their submission to Parliament. The Committee after due advertisement must consider any objection made to the draft and report on the draft to the Minister who is required, when laying the regulations before Parliament in whatever form he then decides to make them, also to submit the report of the Advisory Committee and the reason (if that be the case) why he has not given effect to the report of the Committee. Thus are secured the independent views of a representative committee whose advice the Minister will not lightly reject and, if he does not accept it, the Minister must inform Parliament of the reason.[1]

Consultative bodies influence fundamental reforms, as well as serve as a source of expert knowledge on technical matters. Research and the collection of information are important functions for which departments need the assistance of outside organisations.[2]

[1] Cf. Council on Tribunals, Chap. 47.

[2] For the application of these functions to law reform see p. 325, *post*.

CHAPTER SIXTEEN

THE CIVIL SERVICE

What is a Civil Servant?

THE departments are staffed by administrative, professional, technical, executive and clerical officers who constitute the Civil Service. Civil servants are all servants of the Crown. Recruitment is by prerogative powers and is subject to a minimum of statutory regulation. It follows that in law the Crown has absolute power to terminate employment but this legal power has no relation to the actual position. It is important that those who are most closely concerned with the higher administration of the public services should in fact enjoy security of tenure, without which it would be difficult to ensure continuity of loyal service to successive Ministers of different political parties. Only Ministers in fact hold office at pleasure since their tenure must end when the electorate turns against their party in the House of Commons. But Ministers resign rather than await dismissal. There is no comprehensive definition of a Crown servant. A person appointed by another Crown servant under the authority of a statute may be a Crown servant as much as one appointed directly by the Crown. The facts of each appointment must be considered.[1] The lawyer is particularly concerned with the definition of an officer of the Crown contained in s. 2 (6) of the Crown Proceedings Act 1947 which limits proceedings against the Crown in tort to the act, neglect or default of an officer who "has been directly or indirectly appointed by the Crown and was at the material time paid in respect of his duties as an officer of the Crown wholly out of" the revenues of the Central Government as there defined.[2]

Structure of the Civil Service

For the past one hundred years the Civil Service has been fundamentally the product of the nineteenth-century philosophy derived from the Northcote-Trevelyan Report 1854. This encouraged the

[1] N. E. Mustoe, *Law and Organization of the British Civil Service* (Pitman), Chap. I.

[2] Chap. 46.

cult of the amateur in the processes of administration. So says the latest report on the Civil Service, the Fulton Committee 1968, upon which the Government took action.[1] Changes are already in process of being made in the structure, recruitment and management of that part of the public service, numbering 470,000, which forms the staff of the government departments; the Diplomatic Service is excluded The main changes will take a number of years to implement and the recommendations of the Committee will necessarily be subject to flexible interpretation. They involve:

(1) The separation of general Civil Service matters from the Treasury.
(2) The establishment of a Department of the Civil Service. This has already been set up. The Prime Minister is head of the Department assisted by a senior Cabinet Minister as his delegate responsible for day-to-day administration. The Permanent Secretary is styled the Head of Her Majesty's Civil Service. The Civil Service Commission is placed within this Department.[2]
(3) The abolition of the present system of classification as administrative, general executive, clerical and the professional, scientific and technical classes. In its place there will be uniform grading from top to bottom in the Service.
(4) The establishment of a Civil Service College for training in management and administration, on entry and at later stages.

The constitutional position of Civil Servants is not altered by these internal changes which are designed to improve efficiency and to offer wider opportunities for advancement to skilled professional and executive classes.

Separate mention is desirable for that part of the public service which secures overseas representation of the Crown—Her Majesty's Diplomatic Service. The scope of the service includes foreign States (embassies and legations), Commonwealth States (high commissions which rank as embassies), the few remaining colonial territories (the former colonial service) as well as consular and trade mission services. The amalgamation of these preceded the merger of the Foreign and Commonwealth Relations Offices in 1968. All now come under the Secretary of State for Foreign and Commonwealth Affairs, whose office is responsible for establishments and organisation, training, promotion and security. The unified control and execution

[1] The Civil Service; Report of the Committee 1966–68, Cmnd. 3638, 1968.
[2] P. 223, *post*.

of external policy was long postponed, lest it should imply a loss of interest in the partnership of the Commonwealth.[1]

Organisation within Departments

The organisation within a department is hierarchical. A department will normally consist of a number of divisions or branches. According to the nature of its functions there will in addition be professional and technical staffs whose services are available to the whole department or to more than one division. Under the permanent secretary, who in the case of a department presided over by a Secretary of State, is called Under-Secretary of State, are one or more deputy secretaries who are in charge of a number of divisions or branches. Each of these in turn is under a senior administrative officer of the rank of under-secretary or assistant secretary. The remaining administrative staff hold the ranks of principal or assistant principal and work directly under the various under-secretaries. With this administrative structure routine matters may be disposed of at the lower levels. Where questions of policy arise the papers go upward through the hierarchy for final decision by the Minister, who will thus have the benefit of the views of a number of officers of varying seniority. In between issues of policy and matters of mere routine will, of course, come a large number of issues for which lower grade officers are unable to accept responsibility and therefore the papers are referred upwards to the assistant secretary or under-secretary level. When decisions of a department are communicated to the outside world by letter the formal method of communication is "by direction of the Secretary of State or Minister." Although the letter will be signed by the administrative or executive officer personally, the decision is that of the head of the department in form, if not in fact.

One reason for this description of the organisation of a department of central government is to emphasise that the method secures the maximum protection for the Minister. This is justified on account of his ultimate responsibility to Parliament for all that happens in his department. It is unnecessary to explain that such a method will normally be unsuitable to the conduct of a commercial or industrial enterprise, if only for the reason that it discourages initiative and makes for excessive caution from top to bottom.

Tenure of Appointment

The Civil Service in its present form dates from 1855. From 1870 patronage as a mode of recruitment for the administrative and

[1] Pp. 455–7, *post*.

executive classes was replaced by entry through competitive examinations of a general character. Professional and technical officers are recruited by special examination or by selection by boards after an interview. Appointments are normally terminable at the pleasure of the Crown and the conditions of employment are regulated by Orders in Council. The Civil Service Commission conducts the entrance examinations under regulations made by the Department for the Civil Service. As we shall see, a servant of the Crown may be dismissed at pleasure and has no remedy,[1] but his tenure is in fact secure. A person who holds a pensionable post is only dismissed for misconduct. Salaries, in the case of a few of the higher appointments, are fixed by statute, but are in general subject to regulations, hitherto issued by the Treasury, or are fixed by Order in Council. Only the total sums required for payment of salaries appear in the annual estimates of the departments laid before Parliament. Pensions and superannuation payments are authorised by statute, but no recourse can be had to the courts to enforce payments of pensions, or to afford a remedy for wrongful dismissal either against the Crown, the Civil Service Department, or the head of the department concerned. Civil servants are not in the employment of their departments, all being equally, from the highest to the lowest, in the service of the Crown. There is however, an appeal against dismissal to the head of the department.

Law of the Civil Service

Orders in Council and regulations made thereunder contain the law of the Civil Service, which is for the greater part a matter of the royal prerogative. Parliament has, however, made provision for superannuation by various statutes. But the Civil Service is also regulated by Treasury circulars and minutes. These instruments, though treated as binding upon those whom they affect, have not the force of law, and therefore do not come before the courts for enforcement. But there are in addition certain Orders in Council such as the Servants of the Crown (Parliamentary Candidature) Order 1960 which contain law in the strict sense.[2]

Negotiations as to conditions of service are in the lower grades conducted through Whitley Councils and arbitration in Industrial Courts; but the Treasury retains final control and embodies the agreements or awards in Treasury circulars. The Whitley Council, which dates from 1919, is composed equally of senior departmental officers (the Official Side) and representatives of civil servants appointed by

[1] Chap. 46.
[2] P. 112, *post*, for cases relating to tenure of office.

the recognised civil service associations (the Staff Side), under the chairmanship, up to the present, of a senior Treasury official. The Council is based on the system of joint councils of workers and employers which were recommended by the Commission presided over by Mr. Speaker Whitley in 1918 for settling disputes in industry. The Official Side represents the Crown as employer.

Political Activities of Civil Servants

Reference has already been made to the prohibition on parliamentary candidature which is imposed upon servants of the Crown by modern legislation.[1] In 1949 a departmental committee reviewed the whole question of the existing limitations on the political activities of civil servants.[2] Its proposals were varied after later discussions with the staff side of the Civil Service National Whitley Council and brought fully into force in 1954. It is recognised that the political neutrality of the Civil Service is a fundamental feature of British democratic (*i.e.* constitutional) government. Accordingly participation in national politics is barred not only for the administrative and professional grades, but for many of the executive and clerical staffs who work with them under changing political Ministers. This restricted category, comprising some 11 per cent. of the whole Civil Service, is in general allowed with permission to take part in local government. A second category, totalling some 26 per cent., may with leave of their department take part in all political activities, except parliamentary candidature, subject to accepting a code of discretion laid down by the Treasury; but all in this category are eligible for permission to undertake national as well as local political activities. The rest of the minor and manipulative grades and the industrial grade are free to engage in political activities, national and local, except when on duty, or on official premises or while wearing uniform, subject, however, to the provisions of the Official Secrets Acts relating particularly to unauthorised disclosure of information acquired from official sources. The restriction on political activity, especially in the first category, is no doubt severe, but public confidence in the integrity of the Civil Service is so important that it is probably better to draw no distinction between those who are in daily touch with Ministers of the Crown and those who work in close contact with them in the Departments.

[1] P. 112, *ante*.

[2] *Report of the Committee on the Political Activities of Civil Servants* (*the Masterman Committee*), Cmd. 7718, 1949 and Cmd. 8783, 1953, recommending with variations the implementation thereof. Establishment Circular 26/53; see 32 *Public Administration*, 324 ff.

Security Measures

The threat to the State from Communist or Fascist activities led in 1948 to the introduction of special security measures which affect those engaged in work vital to the security of the State whether they are employed in the public service or by an independent contractor. These measures were reviewed by a Conference of Privy Councillors appointed to examine the security services in 1955.[1] The persons affected by the procedure are those engaged on work which is vital to the security of the State who are, or who have recently been, members of the Communist Party or Fascists or who are, or recently have been, sympathetic to Communism or Fascism, associated with Communists or Fascists, or who are susceptible to pressure from those influences in such a way as to raise doubts as to their reliability. If a Minister rules that a *prima facie* case has been made out against an individual by the Security Services, the civil servant is to be told and sent on special leave. If the Minister decides that the allegations of political unreliability have been made out, he may either have a civil servant posted to non-secret work or dismiss him from the Service. But before the Minister takes a final decision there is a procedure whereby the accused person can appeal to three advisers against the *prima facie* case which has been made out against him.[2]

Civil Service Commission

The Civil Service Commission was created in 1855 following the Northcote-Trevelyan Report on the Civil Service; this recommended that all posts should be filled by open competitive examination. It was not until 1870 that open competition was introduced as the normal method of recruitment. By this means the original objective of the Commission, namely the avoidance of patronage, has ever since been achieved. The present authority of the Commission is derived from an Order in Council of 22nd July, 1920, which provides that "the qualifications of all persons proposed to be appointed, whether permanently or temporarily, to any situation or employment in any of Her Majesty's establishments shall . . . be approved by the Commissioners. . . ." The main functions of the

[1] Cmd. 9715, 1956. For further discussion, see Special Security Measures. Chap. 40.
[2] 563 H.C. Deb. *W.A.*, cols. 197–202.

Commissioners derive from the royal prerogative and in practice they are independent of control and subject to no influence or pressure, political or otherwise, in testing and selecting candidates. The Commissioners also conduct the examinations for entry into the Armed Forces with a view to regular commissions. The commission became part of the new Civil Service Department established in 1968.

CHAPTER SEVENTEEN

PUBLIC FINANCE[1]

In this Chapter there will be considered the manner of raising and spending the national revenue with particular reference to the administration of the Treasury. Parliamentary control of expenditure and taxation has already been described in Chap. 9.

The Treasury

The Treasury is the central department of government. It is organised under three groups, (*a*) Finance (*b*) Public Sector which deals with all sources of public income and all forms of public outlay and (*c*) the National Economy—the co-ordinating division. From 1964 until the Autumn of 1969 the last function was temporarily entrusted to a Department of Economic Affairs under a Secretary of State; but the experiment was given up. Since 1968 the responsibility of the Treasury for Civil Service management has been given to a new Civil Service Department under the Prime Minister.[2] It is not proposed to discuss the variety of bodies, departmental and non-departmental, executive and advisory, which have emerged since 1964 as a result of the economic pressures. So far as these bodies have legal powers, they are of interest to lawyers, but from the point of view of constitutional law bodies whose recommendations for the most part governments are free to accept, to amend or to reject are less significant, indispensable though some are, or have been, to Ministers of the Crown in formulating policy. The National Economic Development Board, the Prices and Income Board, the Monopolies Commission are among the best known.

Treasury Board

The office of Treasurer was first put into commission in 1616. Since 1714 it has always been in commission. The Treasury Board, as were the Commissioners for executing the office of the Lord High

[1] *The Treasury*, (New Whitehall Series No. 12) by Lord Bridges (Allen and Unwin). For the history of the Exchequer and the office of Treasurer, see Anson, *Law and Custom of the Constitution* (4th edn.), Vol. II, Part II, pp. 172 ff.

[2] Chap. 16.

Admiral, *i.e.* the Admiralty, is a body of Commissioners. The Board is created by letters patent under the Great Seal and is composed of a number of individuals appointed by name. In practice they are the First Lord of the Treasury (an office normally taken by the Prime Minister), the Chancellor of the Exchequer (Under Treasurer) and the Assistant Government Whips (Junior Lords of the Treasury). The Board never meets, individual members being responsible for the business transacted. Treasury warrants are generally signed by two of the Junior Lords.

The Chancellor of the Exchequer and other Treasury Ministers

The responsibilities of the Chancellor of the Exchequer cover the whole range of Treasury business including the control of public expenditure and the direction of economic and financial policy. He is invariably a member of the House of Commons. There are four other Ministers who rank as Secretaries to the Treasury Board, but are not members of it. They are the Chief Secretary, the Parliamentary or Patronage Secretary (the Chief Government Whip), the Financial Secretary and a Minister of State. These posts are regarded as of greater importance and prestige than those normally attaching to a Parliamentary Secretary.[1] The Chief Secretary deals with the whole range of public expenditure including the scrutiny of departmental estimates and the preparing of forward surveys. By long tradition the Financial Secretary to the Treasury is charged with the handling of the Government's general financial procedure in the House of Commons.[2] He also deals with all matters connected with the Civil Service. The Minister's chief field of responsibility is overseas finance and banking matters. The Parliamentary Secretary has had no connection with the work of the Treasury as a Department since patronage in the Civil Service disappeared in the nineteenth century.

The Board of Customs and Excise and the Board of Inland Revenue

The department charged with responsibility for the collection of customs and excise duties is the Board of Customs and Excise, while direct taxation, such as income tax, sur-tax, estate duty and stamp duties, are the responsibility of the Board of Inland Revenue.

[1] Bridges, *op. cit.*, pp. 161 ff.
[2] Bridges, *op. cit.*, pp. 34–6.

These subordinate departments are placed by statute under Treasury direction. The Post Office Corporation is also concerned with the collection of revenue on a large scale.

Comptroller and Auditor-General

In addition to the important function of auditing public accounts, the Comptroller and Auditor-General can alone authorise the Bank of England to give credit to the Treasury for payments out of the Consolidated Fund, which is the account at the Bank of England through which all the public revenue passes. He will only give this authority when satisfied that the requirements of the Treasury have been sanctioned by Parliament. As auditor of the public accounts, this officer examines the accounts of departments annually to ensure that public money is spent for the purpose for which it was voted and reports to a standing committee of fifteen members of the House of Commons, called the Public Accounts Committee, which, in turn, makes its report to the House. The report, though not usually debated by the Commons, assists control by the Treasury. The Comptroller draws attention to any excess of authorised expenditure, as well as to unnecessarily extravagant or irregular items in the accounts of a department. The importance of this office is such that the salary attached to it is not subject to the annual vote of Parliament, but is charged on the Consolidated Fund by an Act which does not require annual renewal. In this respect the Comptroller and Auditor-General is in the same position as the Supreme Court judges, and, like the judges, he holds his office during good behaviour, but can be dismissed by the Queen upon an address presented by both Houses of Parliament. He is ineligible to sit in the House of Commons.[1]

Paymaster General

The office of Paymaster-General is usually held by a junior Minister. Payments on account of the public services are made to the Paymaster-General by the Bank of England, and he pays out the money to the departments and other persons authorised by the Treasury.

There may also be mentioned the Royal Mint, responsible for coinage, and the Public Works Loan Board, which advances money to local authorities for the purpose of authorised capital expenditure.

[1] Exchequer and Audit Departments Acts 1866, 1921 and 1950.

Treasury Reorganisation

In 1961 a Committee under the chairmanship of Lord Plowden made certain recommendations which resulted in a reorganisation of the Treasury in the following year.[1] The theme of the report was threefold:

(1) That expenditure should be surveyed as a whole over a period of years in relation to prospective resources;
(2) Greater attention should be given to the systematic improvement of management throughout the public service; and
(3) Opportunity for constructive parliamentary control.

The reorganisation of 1962 went further than the recommendations in the Plowden Report. Its most important feature was that the distribution of duties between divisions and groups was for the first time based on functions. Although this chapter is concerned with public finance it may be helpful to record the grouping of functions of the Department at that time.

(1) Finance group. This group covers home finance, the accounts branch, the finance of exports and imports, statistics and the general range of international payments and questions concerning the sterling area. It also covers overseas finance and development.
(2) Public sector group. This group deals with the financial aspects of defence and science as well as arts and science, *e.g.* the expenditure of the Scientific Research Councils and national museums and galleries as well as the expenditure on the social services and public enterprise, or, more specifically, the nationalised industries.
(3) The national economic group and economic section. The principal task of this group is economic coordination. The economic section contains a number of academically trained economists led by the economic adviser to the Government.
(4) Pay group. This group is responsible not only for the pay matters of the whole civil service but also the pay, pensions and allowances of the armed forces.
(5) Management group. This group dealt with civil service recruitment, general aspects of promotion policy, establishment of staffs, organisation and methods until 1969.

There are also certain common service branches such as the divisions dealing with information, ceremonial and subordinate staff.

[1] For a full outline of Treasury organisation, see Bridges, *op. cit.*, Chap. 15.

Functions of Treasury

The main functions of the Treasury in relation to public finance are:

(1) The imposition and regulation of taxation, including the preparation of the annual Finance Bill, and the collection of revenue.
(2) The control of public expenditure, including supervision of the departmental estimates.
(3) The provision of funds to meet the public services, including the exercise of borrowing powers.
(4) The management of the public debt.

The whole of the national revenue is Crown revenue, but the raising and spending of revenue is subject to the control of the House of Commons. This, in the first place, means that, with unimportant exceptions, the Crown cannot raise any money except by the authority of an Act of Parliament. Secondly, public money cannot be expended without the consent of Parliament, and it is the rule of the House of Commons to appropriate revenue to specific purposes of departmental expenditure (Supply). The procedure in relation to Supply Bills has already been dealt with in Chap. 9, where some comment will be found on the ineffectiveness of parliamentary control so far as securing economy of expenditure is concerned.

It has long been provided by Standing Orders of the House of Commons that no charge can be placed upon the public revenue except on the recommendation of the Crown signified by a Minister. The same rule prevails with regard to taxation. A private member may move to reduce a tax, but not to increase it. Thus the Government of the day is responsible for all taxation and expenditure, and no private member can propose that the public funds be utilised for any public purpose that is not approved by the Government.

Consolidated Fund

All the revenue collected for the National Exchequer is paid into the Consolidated Fund, and all payments for national purposes come out of this fund. In calculating its supply requirements for the forthcoming year a department has to show in its estimates the amount expected as departmental receipts (appropriations-in-aid).[1] These will reduce the amount of the department's total of supply money to be voted by Parliament out of the Consolidated Fund.

[1] P. 146, *ante*.

But like votes of supply, appropriations-in-aid must receive parliamentary sanction in the annual Appropriation Act, and if the estimate of receipts under this head is exceeded, the surplus is surrendered to the Exchequer. A private member may not move in committee to reduce an appropriation-in-aid.

Expenditure: Consolidated Fund Services

The expenditure of the country is grouped under two heads, namely, Consolidated Fund Services and Supply Services. The Consolidated Fund Services are payments under statutes which make a recurrent grant, either for a fixed number of years or without limitation of time. Payments on account of the Supply Services have to be voted each year by the House of Commons. The principal item of expenditure under the heading, Consolidated Fund Services, is the interest upon, and management of, the National Debt. It is obvious that credit which depended for its security on annual review by Parliament would not prove attractive to lenders. Accordingly government loans are charged under statutes which give permanent authority for meeting the obligations incurred to lenders. The National Debt is reduced by application of (*a*) any surplus of national income over expenditure on March 31, the end of the financial year (the Old Sinking Fund), and (*b*) any saving in the permanent annual charge for interest (the New Sinking Fund).

Civil List

The Queen's Civil List [1] was granted to the Queen by the Civil List Act 1952 for her reign and six months after, and accordingly is a Consolidated Fund Service. The Civil List is the annual income granted to the Sovereign to provide the privy purse and household expenses. It is granted at the beginning of each reign in lieu of the ancient hereditary revenues, including the income from Crown lands, which are on each occasion first surrendered to Parliament by the Crown. The present amount of the Civil List is £475,000. Although a system of appropriations, under which parliamentary grants of supplies were assigned for specific purposes, was adopted for general use from 1689 onwards, many items of public expenditure continued to be met out of the hereditary revenues of the Crown and thus escaped parliamentary control. By 1830 the Civil List had been cut down to the personal requirements of the Sovereign, and other public expenditure came under the control of Parliament. The Act of 1952 also made provision for the Duke of Edinburgh, Her

[1] For history of Civil List, see Anson, *op. cit.* (4th edn.), Vol. 2, Part II, pp. 195 ff.

Majesty's younger children and certain other members of the Royal Family. Others, including the Queen Mother, were provided for in the Civil List Act 1937 on the accession of King George VI. The Prince of Wales enjoys separate provision out of the revenues of the Duchy of Cornwall; the Act of 1952 appropriates the bulk of these to the Queen during his minority, as part of the Civil List Grant of £475,000.

The sum of £2,500 per annum is charged upon the Consolidated Fund by the Act for Civil List pensions awarded each year to distinguished persons or their dependants who are in poor financial circumstances, but despite the name these pensions have nothing to do with the Civil List.

Salaries charged on Consolidated Fund

The salaries of those officials whom it is desired to make more independent of parliamentary control than the ordinary departmental officials are also made by statute Consolidated Fund payments. Whereas the total amount needed for salaries by each government department comes under annual review by Parliament, the salaries of the Lord Chancellor (as a judge),[1] the Speaker of the House of Commons, the Comptroller and Auditor-General, the Lords of Appeal in Ordinary, the judges of the Court of Appeal, the High Court of Justice and the County Courts and the Metropolitan Magistrates are charged on the Consolidated Fund. There is thus no special opportunity of criticising in Parliament each year the work of these officers, as in the case of those who are paid from the Supply Services, and this practice tends purposely to preserve their independent position.

Supply Services

The Supply Services, as we have seen,[2] fall under three main heads, the Armed Forces of the Crown, the Civil Services and the Revenue Services. The financial year runs from April 1 to March 31, except for the purposes of income tax and sur-tax, where the period is April 6 to April 5. Each year in the autumn the government departments submit to the Treasury an estimate of their expenditure for the ensuing year. Each estimate is closely scrutinised by the Treasury and cannot be submitted to the House of Commons until it has received Treasury approval. In this way the Treasury is able to a limited extent to check a tendency to extravagance on the part of the spending departments. No doubt a strong Chancellor of the

[1] Part of the salary is charged to the House of Lords Offices Vote.
[2] Chap. 9, C.

Exchequer can make administration as economical as possible. But it must be remembered that the Treasury must assist in carrying out the policy of the Cabinet. Successive Cabinets by introducing legislation which involves expanding expenditure are really responsible for increasing items. Policy is apt to be synonymous with expenditure, and therefore the opportunities for the Treasury to curtail expenditure are largely confined to curtailing the expenses of administration. If, for example, the Cabinet decides to increase old age pensions by statutory amendment, the estimates of the Department of Social Security, when submitted to the Treasury, must show the increase resulting from the extended benefit. The Treasury may insist that the administrative expenses be restricted—and Treasury control is in this sphere effective—but it has no control whatever over the statutory rate of benefit, once it is approved by Parliament. A strong Chancellor of the Exchequer may, however, as a member of the Cabinet, use his influence with his colleagues by indicating that he is unable to find the money to carry their proposed policy into effect. In the past this has been effective to curtail expenditure on the fighting services, none of which is incurred on the authority of permanent Acts. All capital expenditure on the public services is allocated under a system of priorities.

Treasury Sanction

No proposal involving the expenditure of public funds is nowadays presented to the Cabinet until it has been examined both by the Treasury and any other department which may be concerned with the proposal. Indeed all proposals involving an increase in departmental expenditure on any new service require Treasury sanction.[1] Thus the financial implication of any policy which it is proposed to put into effect is ensured examination.

Estimates

The annual examination of the estimates by the Treasury also enables the Chancellor of the Exchequer to prepare the annual Budget statement in time for presentation to the House of Commons early in the new financial year.[2] An examination of the estimates can alone enable the Chancellor of the Exchequer and his advisers to determine whether or not additional taxation will have to be imposed, or again, whether the requirements of the ensuing year will enable him to remit some portion of the existing taxation.

[1] For Treasury control, see Sir Ivor Jennings, *Cabinet Government*, Chap. VII.
[2] Chap. 9, C.

Decline in Treasury Control

The decline in Treasury control which is due to the causes described has important results. The Treasury (or indeed the department concerned) is debarred from financial control over a new State service, once the measure initiating it has been placed upon the statute book. No alteration of policy is possible, except by the inelastic method of repealing or amending Acts, and a Government will seldom risk the unpopularity of a reversal of policy which would deprive the electors of an established service. The control exercised over the estimates by the House of Commons has long ceased to be more than formal. It is idle to maintain that there is any safeguard in the rule that there shall be no expenditure of public funds without the sanction of the House of Commons, so long as that House itself sets the pace by passing legislation which involves automatic increases in expenditure. Treasury control is thus ineffective in relation to those departments which are committed to fixed statutory charges.[1]

Revenue: Ordinary Revenue

The revenue of the Crown is divided into ordinary and extraordinary, the latter being derived mainly from taxation. The principal item of "ordinary" revenue is the income derived from Crown lands, which in the main have long since been surrendered to the public. The net rents and profits so derived are paid into the Consolidated Fund. The Crown is also, as part of its "ordinary" revenue, entitled to property found without any apparent owner. The most important illustration of this is the property of an intestate who dies without a spouse or blood-relations entitled to take under the Administration of Estates Act 1925 ss. 46 and 47, as amended by the Intestates' Estates Act 1952.

Extraordinary Revenue

The "extraordinary" revenue derived from taxation falls under several heads. The greater part of the sum raised annually by taxation is imposed by provisions in Finance Acts which do not require renewal, but stand until repealed or amended. The rate of income tax is, however, fixed each year.

[1] The functions of the Treasury in relation to war-time expenditure were substantially modified and control had to be relaxed, especially with regard to war service expenditure.

Indirect Taxation

The following are the most important items of indirect taxation, *i.e.* taxation which is, generally speaking, capable of being passed on to the consumer by the taxpayer.

Customs Duties

Customs duties are levied upon commodities imported into this country from other countries. Preferential rates are granted to products of the Commonwealth and the Colonies. With the abandonment of free trade in 1931, there was employed a novel and striking form of delegated legislation for controlling this mode of taxation; see now Import Duties Act 1958.[1]

The Customs and Excise Act 1952 contains a code of regulations and imposes penalties upon those who attempt to evade the duties. Dutiable goods may only be imported free of duty if they are deposited in a warehouse, the owner of which has entered into a bond with the Crown that the proper duties will be paid if, and when, the goods are released for sale at home. The provision of bonded warehouses is particularly useful for enabling goods intended for re-exportation to other countries to escape duty.

Excise Duties

Excise duties are imposed upon commodities produced for consumption in this country. The revenue officials have important powers of entry and search to check evasion of the tax. The term, excise duty, is not used strictly in the sense of a tax on commodities, but also covers a number of taxes in the form of licences to manufacture certain articles, *e.g.* beer and spirits; licences to carry on certain occupations, *e.g.* pawnbroker, money-lender, and retailer of beer, spirits, wine and tobacco; and licences to use certain articles, *e.g.* for keeping a dog, or driving a motor-car. Other duties under this heading are purchase tax levied on retail sales and the duty on entertainments.

Drawback

As an equivalent to the bonded warehouse in the case of imported goods, excise duties in the strict sense are generally subject to drawback, *i.e.* repayment of the duty, if the goods are exported to a foreign country. The exporter of beer is allowed a drawback on the excise duties paid on the manufacture. The object is to enable British

[1] P. 133, *ante*.

manufacturers to compete in foreign markets with foreigners who may not have had to pay duties on the same commodities. In the case of a customs duty on an article in the raw state, which is imported into this country for manufacture and then re-exported in the finished form, the manufacturer can claim repayment of the customs duties paid on importation. Tobacco to be manufactured into cigarettes for exportation is an example of this.

Direct Taxation

A direct tax may be broadly described as one which falls on the actual person who pays the tax.

Death Duties

Estate duty becomes payable to the Crown on the death of an individual leaving property the value of which exceeds £5,000. The duty is paid both upon property which the deceased enjoyed, and upon the interests to which others succeed on account of his death. It is payable by the personal representatives on all the property of the deceased, whether land, money or goods.

Stamp Duties

Stamp duties are levied upon certain legal instruments, such as instruments of transfer of land or stock and shares.

Income Tax and Surtax

The income tax is the direct tax which not only yields the largest sum of public revenue but affects directly the pay packet of the majority of workers in the country and all who derive their income from securities. By the Income Tax Act 1952 income is treated as falling under separate heads, called schedules, for the purpose of assessment to tax. In general income tax is levied on all income arising in the United Kingdom and on the income of residents in the United Kingdom wherever it arises.

There is a standard flat rate of income tax, but there are important allowances and deductions which have the effect of making income tax a graduated tax.

Surtax, an additional tax, is a graduated tax on the income of individuals above a certain figure. At present the tax is levied on the excess of unearned income over £2,500, or £4,000 for earned income, the rate rising with the amount of such excess.

Short-term capital gains arising from the acquisition and disposal of assets are treated as income; the tax is chargeable on gains taking place within 12 months after acquisition.

Capital Gains Tax

Capital gains on the disposal of assets after 6 April 1965 are chargeable to tax at the rate of 30 per cent. Assessment is on the total amounts of gains in each year, less allowable losses. The tax is levied on all forms of property, whether situated in the United Kingdom or elsewhere, other than sterling. The exemptions include gains on the disposal of the only or main residence of an individual. It is also leviable on the death of an individual on assets of which he was competent to dispose; the first £5,000 of gains deemed to arise from this notional disposal are exempt.

Corporation Tax

This tax has since 1965 replaced the income tax and profits tax for which companies were formerly liable. The principle is to separate the taxation of a company from that of its shareholders and involves a tax being levied twice over, once by corporation tax on the income of the company and again (by income tax) on the dividend paid to shareholders out of what remains after payment of corporation tax. The rate of the latter tax—at present 45 per cent—is fixed by Budget resolutions.

Selective Employment Tax

This is a tax levied weekly on employers for each of their employees since September 1966. It is collected through the National Insurance stamp. The purpose is two-fold, primarily to produce revenue by a new form of tax, not on all industry, but in the main on the service and non-manufacturing industries. But it is also intended to operate indirectly as a method of encouraging mobility of labour in the service industries. This is achieved by provisions for the refund of tax with a premium to the manufacturing industries. This tax is not dealt with directly by the Inland Revenue or the Customs. While collected by means of the insurance stamp, repayments are made by various Ministries depending on the nature of the employment concerned.

Administration of Income Tax

From a constitutional point of view something must be said about the administration of these taxes. The Commissioners of Inland Revenue are charged with the general management of the taxes and represent the interests of the Crown, *i.e.* the general body of taxpayers. The duties of the Commissioners in each district (the civil parish is the normal unit) are carried out by Inspectors, whose areas cover a number of adjoining districts. Inspectors are civil servants with an expert knowledge of tax law who are responsible for details concerning assessments and for dealing with claims and allowances. Also under the Commissioners of Inland Revenue are collectors of taxes. In each district there is a body, known as the General Commissioners (Commissioners of the General Purposes of the Income Tax) who are appointed by the Lord Chancellor; this body, which contains no official element, holds office independently of the Inland Revenue Commissioners, and is a tribunal interposed between the Crown and the individual taxpayer, from whose ranks its members are drawn. It is the duty of the General Commissioners to hear appeals by the taxpayer and the Revenue authorities on questions of law and fact. If a taxpayer so wishes, he may (and in the case of sur-tax must) appeal to the Special Commissioners rather than to the General Commissioners. From the General or Special Commissioners appeals lie on points of law only to the Chancery Division of the High Court, thence to the Court of Appeal and the House of Lords.[1]

[1] In 1970 the Income and Corporation Taxes Act and the Taxes Management Act have consolidated the law on the above taxes.

CHAPTER EIGHTEEN

THE POLICE

Local Police Authorities

ALTHOUGH the constable is an officer with powers long known to the common law and part of the special powers of the modern police officer are exercised by him as a constable, the professional police forces only date from the first half of the nineteenth century.[1]

The Metropolitan Police, whose jurisdiction extends over a fifteen-mile radius from Charing Cross, is the only police force in the United Kingdom which is under the direct control of the Home Secretary, who is the police authority. The executive head is the Commissioner of Police for the Metropolis, who is appointed by the Crown and is the disciplinary authority. The Commissioner makes appointments and has powers of suspension and dismissal. The City of London Police are an independent force, but the appointment of the Commissioner (Chief Officer) must be approved by the Home Secretary. The Court of Common Council is the police authority.

Elsewhere in England and Wales a police force is maintained by every county and county borough except where there is a combined area constituted by an amalgamation of forces. The local police authority for counties and county boroughs alike is a committee of the County or Borough Council which, in the case of counties is known as the Police Committee, and in the case of boroughs as the Watch Committee. In both cases the composition is the same; two-thirds of the members are elected members of the Council appointed by the Council, the remaining one-third are magistrates appointed in the case of the Police Committee by the Court of Quarter Sessions, and in the case of the Watch Committee by the magistrates for the borough from among their own number.[2] It is the duty of a police

[1] For a short account of the history of the police and parish constables, see Hart, *Introduction to the Law of Local Government and Administration* (Butterworth), 7th edn., Chap. 24. The control exercised by the Home Secretary is described in *The Home Office* volume of *The New Whitehall Series* (George Allen & Unwin).

[2] Although in the past county police authorities were composed as to one-half of county councillors and one-half of county magistrates, there are constitutional objections to making magistrates responsible for police administration. These are founded on the principle that the independent administration of justice is more difficult to preserve since the majority of the prosecutions brought before magistrates are initiated by the police.

authority to maintain an adequate and efficient police force for the area, and, subject to the approval of the Home Secretary, to appoint the chief constable and any deputy or assistant chief constables, and to determine the establishment of the force, to provide the requisite premises and to provide equipment. But a police force is under the direction and control of the chief constable or in his absence, his deputy, and not under the control of the police authority. The police authority is empowered to require the chief constable, the deputy chief constable and any assistant chief constable to retire in the interests of efficiency. The police authority must act with the approval of the Home Secretary who may himself take the initiative in requiring the police authority to retire their chief constable; he must be given an opportunity to make representations which the police authority must consider before they seek the approval of the Home Secretary to the retirement. Thus the police authority, and not the Home Secretary, is the disciplinary authority over each chief constable. Appointments and promotions to ranks below that of assistant chief constable are made by the chief constable. The police authority pays the salaries and wages of members of its force though the scale of payments is fixed on a national basis. The chief constable is the disciplinary authority over members of the force in the case both of county and borough forces.[1]

The effect of the provisions of the Police Act 1964 is that the police authority is responsible for providing an efficient force and supervising its use. The chief constable is responsible for using the force efficiently. The Home Secretary is responsible for ensuring that both the police authority and the chief constable are enabled to exercise their powers and in fact do so. There is nothing in the Act to suggest that, apart from the provisions for amalgamation which will be discussed below, the Home Secretary can deprive chief constables of their existing powers or diminish the status of police authorities. Rather the purpose of the legislation has been to redefine the respective functions of Home Secretary, police authority and chief constable in such a way that the first named may be answerable in Parliament for the efficient policing of the country rather than for the acts or omissions of a particular police force. Members of a police authority can be questioned on the discharge of the functions of the authority by members of county and county borough councils in the course of council proceedings.[2] But a police authority may be

[1] Formerly in boroughs disciplinary powers were exercised by the Watch Committee. See *Ridge* v. *Baldwin*, [1964] A.C. 40; K. & L. 529 discussed at pp. 641, 655–6, *post*, and also A. W. Bradley, *A Failure of Justice and Defect of Police* [1964] C.L.J. 83.

[2] Police Act 1964, s. 11; this is a new provision.

refused a report by its chief constable if the request for information relates to matters which ought not, in his view, to be disclosed in the public interest.[1]

Functions of the Home Secretary in relation to the Police

The central administrative control of the Home Secretary in relation to police forces outside the Metropolis was enacted in its present form by the Police Act 1964. Section 28 states in general terms that it is the duty of the Home Secretary to promote police efficiency by exercising his powers under the Act; he may therefore be questioned in Parliament with regard to the exercise or non-exercise of such powers. He has the ultimate power to require the resignation of a chief constable. He may require him to submit a report on any specific matter with regard to the policing of his area. A chief constable must also submit to the Home Secretary each year the annual report which he is required to render to his own police authority. The Home Secretary may set up a local inquiry under a person appointed by him into any matter connected with the policing of an area. By section 33 the Home Secretary is empowered to make regulations for the government, administration and conditions of service of the police forces, in particular with respect to rank, qualifications for appointment and promotion, probationary service, voluntary retirement, discipline, duties, pay and allowances. These regulations can only be brought into force after a draft has been submitted to the Police Advisory Board for England and Wales; the Home Secretary is required to take into consideration any representations made by that board. There is a similar board for Scotland. These Advisory Boards are constituted in such form as the Secretary of State may determine. Prior to 1964, regulations under the earlier Police Act 1919 could only be made after consultation with the Police Council, a body on which representatives of police authorities and all ranks of the police force sat. The Act of 1964 continues the Police Council as a statutory body to advise the Home Secretary for the consideration of questions relating to hours of duty, leave, pay and allowances, pensions, clothing and equipment.[2] In addition to these advisory bodies there is continued in existence by the Act the Police Federation for England and Wales and a separate Police Federation for Scotland. These Federations act through local and central representative bodies and are entirely independent of any body or persons outside the police service. Their object is to represent members of police forces in all matters affecting their welfare and efficiency other

[1] Police Act 1964, s. 12.
[2] Police Act 1969 extends the Council to include Northern Ireland.

than matters of discipline and promotion affecting individuals. There is a uniform system of police pensions throughout the country.[1] Any member of a police force who feels aggrieved by the decision of a local police authority in a disciplinary matter may appeal to the Home Secretary.[2] The right of appeal extends to questions of reduction in rank or rate of pay.

The Home Secretary has always exercised considerable control through the purse. Since 1856 a grant has been made out of the funds of the Exchequer towards the police expenses of local authorities, but the payment of this grant is, by statute, made conditional on the Home Secretary's certificate that the force is efficient in numbers and discipline. Inspectors of Constabulary have proved powerful instruments in maintaining efficiency. As the amount of the grant is one-half of the whole expenses, it is clear that no local authority can afford to forgo its certificate of efficiency. Both the Metropolitan and City of London Police are in receipt of similar grants, the balance of expenditure in the case of the former being contributed by the councils whose area is included in the Metropolitan Police District.

Amalgamation of Forces

The existence of a large number of independent police forces has often been criticised but the Royal Commission of 1962, with one dissentient member, came down in favour of retaining the system of local police forces. Provision was made in the resulting Act, the Police Act 1964, for the amalgamation of two or more police areas.[3] Such amalgamation can be proposed by the police authorities concerned or the Home Secretary may by order make such amalgamation scheme as he considers expedient if no scheme is submitted to him. The effect of an amalgamation scheme is to combine the areas affected for all police purposes. As a result of an active policy of amalgamation the number of forces had been reduced from 117 to 47 by the end of 1969. Under the Police Act of 1946 which itself achieved the amalgamation of non-county borough police forces with the county police forces concerned, provision was also made for both voluntary and compulsory amalgamations, but in the latter case no compulsion could be enforced upon a police authority having a population of over 100,000 to amalgamate with a larger authority without its consent. The idea of a national police force is repugnant to the English tradition of local government, and on

[1] Police Pensions Act 1948.
[2] Police Act 1964, s. 37.
[3] Police Act 1964, s. 21.

constitutional grounds there are objections to equipping the Executive with the equivalent of the continental gendarmerie. These objections did not, however, impress the Royal Commission on the Police,[1] which gave its conclusion that the police forces should not be brought under the direct central control of the Government mainly because they found the current system basically sound; it was also felt that advantages of local administration by lay persons familiar with the character and needs of the communities in which they lived were important. Not even in detective matters is there a national force, although for the purpose of unravelling complicated crimes the Criminal Investigation Department of the Metropolitan Police has a great advantage over local forces. The assistance of this department is available to the local forces, but it rests with the local force to decide whether or not assistance shall be invoked in any particular case which may arise in its area. A recent development has been the creation of regional crime squads for detection purposes.

Legal Status of a Police Officer

It is not easy to define the precise status of a police officer. Though appointed by a local authority and liable to dismissal by them, he is not in the legal sense their servant. On appointment a constable is sworn in before a justice of the peace. His oath requires him to serve the Sovereign as a constable. Though subject in some respect to local supervision and required to obey certain local police regulations, a police officer is as such a servant of the State or ministerial officer of the central power.[2] "The powers of a constable as a peace officer, whether conferred by statute or by common law, are exercised by him by virtue of his office and cannot be exercised on the responsibility of any person but himself . . . a constable, therefore, when acting as a peace officer, is not exercising a delegated authority, and the general law of agency has no application."[3] By section 48 of the Police Act 1964 liability for the wrongful acts of constables is placed upon the chief constable in respect of torts committed in the performance of their functions by constables under his direction and control in the same way as a master is liable in respect of torts committed by his servants in the course of their employment.[4] Prior to

[1] Cmnd. 1728 (1962), Chap. V. Dr. A. L. Goodhart in a Memorandum of Dissent, pp. 157–79, favoured the establishment of a national police force.
[2] *Fisher* v. *Oldham Corporation*, [1930] 2 K.B. 364.
[3] *Enever* v. *The King* (*Australia*) (1906), 3 C.L.R. 969, at p. 977.
[4] Any damages and costs awarded against a chief constable for vicarious liability are paid out of the Police Fund as is any sum required in connection with a settlement of such proceedings.

this Act neither a chief constable nor a police authority could be made liable in respect of a tortious act such as an unlawful arrest by a constable. A police officer has been held to be "a person holding office under Her Majesty" for the purpose of the Official Secrets Acts.[1] A local authority is not entitled to recover damages for injuries done to a police officer whereby the authority has lost his services and the officer has become entitled to a special disability pension payable by the authority.[2]

Complaints against the Police

In the nature of things the police are continuously brought into contact with individual members of the public. It follows that there must be machinery for investigating complaints by the public against the police. In an extreme case a policeman may have to face criminal proceedings for alleged assault on a person whom he has arrested or seeks to arrest. Civil liability usually takes the form of an action for damages for false imprisonment or malicious prosecution, though it is difficult to establish liability for the latter tort.

Apart from legal liability, when a member of the public makes a complaint against a member of the police force, the complaint must be investigated by the chief constable of the police area. He may for this purpose ask a chief constable of another police area to provide an officer to carry out the investigation, or he may be directed to do so by the Secretary of State. On receiving the report of such an investigation the chief constable must forward it to the Director of Public Prosecutions unless he is satisfied from the report that no criminal offence has been committed. It is the duty of each local police authority and of the Inspectors of Constabulary to keep themselves informed as to the manner in which complaints from members of the public against members of the force are dealt with by the chief constable.[3]

[1] *Lewis* v. *Cattle*, [1938] 2 K.B. 454; for criticism of this decision, see Sir Ivor Jennings in 2 M.L.R., 73

[2] *Receiver for Metropolitan Police District* v. *Croydon Corporation; Monmouthshire County Council* v. *Smith*, [1957] 2 Q.B. 154 approving *Attorney-General for New South Wales* v. *Perpetual Trustee Co. Ltd.*, [1955] A.C. 457, where it was held that a police constable is a holder of a public office and not a servant for whose loss of services a police authority can sue; and see *Commissioners of Inland Revenue* v. *Hambrook*, [1956] 2 Q.B. 641.

[3] Police Act 1964, s. 49; and s. 11 for questions at meetings of local councils represented on the authority. The Royal Commission of 1962, Cmnd. 1728, rejected such evidence as was given to it in favour of establishing an independent tribunal or an Ombudsman for the investigation of complaints against the police, but public opinion has since moved towards some kind of independent representation.

Special Constables

The authorities charged with the preservation of the peace have for long had power to appoint special constables to supplement the regular police force in an emergency. Nowadays this power is exercised by two or more justices of the peace. Able-bodied male residents between the ages of twenty-five and fifty-five may be enrolled, notice of appointment being given to the Home Secretary and the Lord-Lieutenant of the county. The Home Secretary may make regulations for the government, administration and conditions of service of special constables.[1]

[1] Police Act 1964, s. 34.

CHAPTER NINETEEN

ALLEGIANCE AND NATIONALITY; ALIENS; EXTRADITION; FOREIGN ENLISTMENT

A. Allegiance and Nationality

ALLEGIANCE may be natural or local. British subjects owe allegiance to the Queen at all times wherever they may be. The subjects of the Queen owe her allegiance and the allegiance follows the person of the subject. He is the Queen's liege wherever he may be, and he may violate his allegiance in a foreign country just as he may violate it within the realm.[1] The holders of certain public offices are required by statute to take the oath of allegiance, viz. Ministers of the Crown, certain high officers of State, members of both Houses of Parliament, judges and justices of the peace, the bishops and clergy of the Established Church of England and members of the armed forces who are serving on regular engagements.[2] Local allegiance is owed by all aliens within the realm and the Queen's protection.

> It was held in the celebrated treason case of the Second World War [3] that allegiance was owed by the holder of a British passport, which had been obtained on false statements, notwithstanding that he, being an American citizen, had gone to Germany and there committed treasonable acts in time of war. He had at no time, it would appear, contemplated putting himself while abroad under the protection of the Crown.[4]

Allegiance is probably owed by enemy civilians within the realm in time of war and possibly by prisoners of war interned within the realm. It is not owed before their capture by alien enemies coming to invade the realm.[5]

[1] *The King* v. *Casement*, [1917] 1 K.B. 98.

[2] National Servicemen did not take the oath; they signed a declaration regarding their obligations under the Official Secrets Acts 1911–39.

[3] *Joyce* v. *Director of Public Prosecutions*, [1946] A.C. 347.

[4] See 9 C.L.J. 330 and 10 C.L.J. 54 for articles sustaining and attacking this decision by Sir Hersch Lauterpacht and Professor Glanville Williams respectively.

[5] McNair, *Legal Effects of War*, 4th edn., Chaps. 2 and 3. The offence of treason is based on a breach of allegiance.

A resident alien's duty of allegiance does not cease when the Queen's protection is temporarily withdrawn, owing to the occupation of the British territory where he is residing by enemy forces in time of war.

In *De Jager* v. *Attorney-General of Natal*,[1] a resident alien was held guilty of treason, who, in such circumstances, joined an invading force, although that force was composed of nationals of his own country.

Protection

The extent of the Queen's duty to provide protection cannot be precisely defined. It is a duty which cannot be enforced by the courts so far as the provision of protection for British subjects in foreign parts is concerned. If special protection is given by the armed forces of the Crown, the subject can be required to pay for it by an action on an agreement to make payment.

In *China Navigation Company* v. *Attorney-General*[2] a shipping company registered in the United Kingdom but trading on the coast of China, sought protection from British forces at Hong Kong against piracy which took the form of robbery on board by native passengers who during the trip attacked the ship's officers and robbed the ship. After trying various devices the local Government supplied small military guards for each ship without charge. Later the shipowners were required to pay in full for the provision of these guards. In an action for a declaration it was claimed that the Crown had no authority to demand payment for providing protection against piracy.

The action failed because (i) there is no legal duty on the Crown to afford military protection to British subjects in foreign parts; (ii) the Crown, by virtue of its prerogative control over the armed forces, can enter into agreements for payment by a citizen for services rendered; (iii) such payment when made is covered by the system of appropriations in aid in the annual Appropriation Act, and therefore is not unauthorised taxation.

The only recognition of the nature of the duty of protection within the realm is to be found in the recognition by the courts that there is no obligation upon an individual to pay for ordinary police protection.

In *Glasbrook Bros.* v. *Glamorgan County Council*[3] an obligation to pay for special police protection to private property was enforced, though no such action would lie for ordinary services rendered by the police for the maintenance of public order.

[1] [1907] A.C. 326.
[2] [1932] 2 K.B. 197; K. & L. 146.
[3] [1925] A.C. 270.

British Nationality; Law before 1949

Prior to the operation of the British Nationality Act 1948, which came into force on January 1, 1949, in the United Kingdom and throughout the Colonies, the status of a natural born British subject who was born on or after 1915 was governed by the British Nationality and Status of Aliens Act 1914–43.[1] The Act recognised two principal criteria, place of birth and the nationality of the father as qualifications for nationality, *i.e.* membership as a citizen of the State. The status of British subjects born before 1915 was governed mainly by the common law which was based upon the place of birth (*jus soli*), and by the Naturalisation Act 1870.

The Act of 1914–43 was also enacted in statutes, which with some exceptions, especially as regards conditions of naturalisation, were identical, by the Parliaments of Canada, Australia, New Zealand and South Africa, the only Dominions with legislative competence in 1914 to enact separate nationality laws. Thus all British subjects had a common status, which rested on the basis of common allegiance to the Crown, and this was recognised by the legislation of different parts of the Commonwealth, as it later came to be called. The principle of a common code system was observed and alterations by any one of the five States could only in practice be made after consultation and agreement with the other four.

Even before the addition to the Commonwealth of India, Pakistan and Ceylon (to whose territories as well as to those of Southern Rhodesia and until 1948 of Burma the United Kingdom Act applied) the common code system was becoming unworkable in practice. Canada in 1946 passed a Citizenship Act which laid down conditions for the acquisition and loss of Canadian, as distinct from British, citizenship; it also enacted that all Canadian citizens were British subjects and that all persons who were British subjects by the law of any other part of the Commonwealth should be recognised as British subjects in Canada.

Act of 1948

These principles of separate citizenship for each State of the Commonwealth and mutual recognition of that qualification for the status of British subject or Commonwealth citizen—the terms have the same meaning in law—are accepted by the British Nationality Act 1948.[2] We are not here concerned with the current law of other

[1] It is convenient to refer to the Act of 1914 and the several amending Acts as a single statute.

[2] Cmd. 7326 (1948) gives a summary of the main changes which were subsequently enacted.

Commonwealth States or with the special position of a national of the Republic of Ireland who enjoys the status of a British subject within the United Kingdom and the Colonies.[1] The Act accordingly provided that after 1948 citizenship of the United Kingdom and Colonies should describe the qualification for British nationality of those nationals whose status was determined by the legislature of the United Kingdom Parliament, *i.e.* nationals of the United Kingdom, the Channel Islands, the Isle of Man and of all the Colonies, as distinct from the other States of the Commonwealth and of Rhodesia which had until 1965 legislative independence for this as for other purposes.

The Act repealed all the nationality provisions of the Act of 1914–43 and, unlike that Act, determined the status of all persons alive at the date of its coming into operation. But, except for some important changes with regard to married women, the qualifications for citizenship of the United Kingdom and Colonies closely resemble those laid down for the common status of British subjects by the previous Act.

Amendments and Additions

Since 1948 there have been a number of amendments and modifications of the principal Act. All of these have been made in British Nationality Acts or as part of the legislation granting independence to colonial territories or protected States. A feature of the latter is the provision for retention of United Kingdom nationality where a person does not take the nationality of the new independent State. Among the major amendments contained in British Nationality Acts are the provision of additional grounds for citizenship by registration [2] of persons who have always been stateless and satisfy certain conditions of parentage or place of birth.[3] The resumption and renunciation of citizenship are facilitated by an earlier Act of 1964.[4] Provision was made in 1965 for registration as British subjects of alien married women married to persons who are British subjects without citizenship or to citizens of the Republic of Ireland who were also British subjects in 1948.[5]

[1] British Nationality Act 1948, s. 3 (2); Ireland Act 1949, s. 2 (1).
[2] P. 249, *post*.
[3] British Nationality (No. 2) Act 1964.
[4] British Nationality Act 1964.
[5] British Nationality Act 1948, ss. 13 and 16, s. 2 and British Nationality Act 1965.

Qualifications for U.K. Citizenship

These qualifications are—

1. Birth in the United Kingdom or the Colonies, with exceptions in the case of children born (*a*) to non-citizen fathers who are in enjoyment of diplomatic immunity from suit and legal process; (*b*) to enemy alien fathers where the birth occurred in a place under occupation by the enemy (s. 4).

2. Descent. This qualification safeguards the citizenship of a person born abroad whose father is a citizen of the United Kingdom and Colonies at the time of the birth.

There are certain provisions which apply where the father himself acquired citizenship by descent; these limit citizenship to the child in those cases where

(*a*) the child is born or his father was born in a protectorate, protected state, mandated territory or trust territory or any place in a foreign country where by treaty, capitulation, grant, usage, sufferance, or other lawful means, Her Majesty then has or had jurisdiction over British subjects; or

(*b*) the child's birth having occurred in a place in a foreign country other than a place such as is mentioned in the last foregoing paragraph, the birth is registered at a United Kingdom consulate within one year of its occurrence, or, with the permission of the Secretary of State, later; or

(*c*) the child's father is, at the time of the birth, in Crown service under Her Majesty's Government in the United Kingdom; or

(*d*) the child is born in any country mentioned in sub-section (3) of section 1 of the Act in which a citizenship law has then taken effect and does not become a citizen thereof on birth (*i.e.* another State of the Commonwealth (s. 5)).

3. Registration.—A citizen of another State in the Commonwealth is entitled to be registered (without fee) as citizen of the United Kingdom and Colonies if he satisfies the Home Secretary that—

(i) he has been ordinarily resident in the United Kingdom for the five years[1] immediately preceding, or

(ii) he is in the service of the Crown under the Government of the United Kingdom, or

[1] Commonwealth Immigrants Act 1962, s. 12.

(iii) he is serving under an international organisation of which the United Kingdom is a member or in the employment of a society, company or body of persons established in the United Kingdom.

There is a discretion to refuse registration in the case of an applicant who has renounced or been deprived of citizenship and seeks re-admission. Registration under (iii) is not as of right, as it is apart from the above exception in the case of (i) and (ii). The Home Secretary may cause minors who are children of United Kingdom citizens to be registered upon the application of their parents or guardians; other minors may be registered at the discretion of the Home Secretary in special circumstances which are not defined (ss. 6–9).

Registration as a citizen of the United Kingdom and colonies can be claimed as of right by a person who has previously renounced such citizenship [1] for the purposes of acquiring or retaining citizenship of any Commonwealth country provided that the applicant has a specified connection with the United Kingdom, a colony or a protectorate.[2]

4. Naturalisation. Aliens and persons living under the protection of the Crown in protectorates or trust territories (British protected persons) may apply for a grant of citizenship by naturalisation if they have satisfied certain qualifications, which are in the case of an alien:—

(*a*) that he has either resided in the United Kingdom or been in Crown service under Her Majesty's Government in the United Kingdom, or partly the one and partly the other, throughout the period of twelve months immediately preceding the date of the application; and

(*b*) that during the seven years immediately preceding the said period of twelve months he has either resided in the United Kingdom or any colony, protectorate, or United Kingdom trust territory or been in Crown service, or partly the one and partly the other, for periods amounting in the aggregate to not less than four years; and

(*c*) that he is of good character; and

(*d*) that he has sufficient knowledge of the English language, and

(*e*) that he intends in the event of a certificate being granted to him—

[1] P. 256, *post*.

[2] British Nationality Act 1964.

(i) to reside in the United Kingdom or in any colony, protectorate or United Kingdom trust territory; or

(ii) to enter into or continue in Crown service under Her Majesty's Government in the United Kingdom, or service under an international organisation of which Her Majesty's Government in the United Kingdom is a member, or service in the employment of a society, company or body of persons established in the United Kingdom or established in any colony, protectorate or United Kingdom trust territory (s. 10 and 2nd Schedule).

A British protected person must satisfy the requirements as to character, linguistic ability and intention to reside or to serve in the Crown service, but he must have resided for five years prior to the application or be in the service of the Crown at the time of such application.

Citizenship may also be acquired by incorporation of territory in which event the Crown is empowered to specify by Order in Council the persons who shall be citizens of the United Kingdom and Colonies by reason of their connection with that territory (s. 11).

Women

The position of a married woman is the same as that of a single woman. Thus a woman who is a citizen of the United Kingdom and Colonies will not, as was the case before 1949, lose her citizenship by marrying an alien. Such a woman who was married before 1949 re-acquired her citizenship automatically (s. 14). A woman who is before marriage an alien, or a British protected person, is entitled after marriage to a citizen of the United Kingdom and Colonies to be registered as a citizen; she is required to take the oath of allegiance (s. 6 (1)). She can only be deprived subsequently of citizenship if the Home Secretary is satisfied that the registration was obtained by fraud, false representation or concealment of a material fact, a provision which applies to all who acquire citizenship by registration or naturalisation. A woman who before marriage is a citizen of another State in the Commonwealth is entitled to registration as a citizen of the United Kingdom and Colonies (see under Registration, *ante*).

A married woman is under no disability in the matter of acquiring or losing citizenship. An alien woman married to an alien husband can apply for naturalisation in her own right (s. 10). If a married woman who is a citizen of the United Kingdom and Colonies also possesses another citizenship, she will be free to renounce her citizenship of the United Kingdom by registering a declaration, as can any other citizen of the United Kingdom (s. 19).

The Home Secretary both in the case of applications for naturalisation and those for registration where he is given a statutory discretion has the right to refuse an application without giving any reasons. Nor can his refusal be called in question in any court of law, though he can, of course, be questioned in Parliament.

Commonwealth Citizenship

The nationality laws of the other States of the British Commonwealth are determined exclusively by their own Parliaments. The scheme of legislation which has been adopted by agreement is that each State shall define its own citizens and shall declare those citizens to be British subjects or Commonwealth citizens, at its option. Thus the legislation of some, but not all, States which have passed nationality statutes up to the present contains a common clause, the substantial effect of which is to ensure that all persons recognised as British subjects or Commonwealth citizens shall be so recognised throughout the Commonwealth; see *e.g.*, s. 1 of the British Nationality Act 1948. This has been extended to those States of the Commonwealth which have become independent since that date. The result is that citizens of the United Kingdom and Colonies only enjoy political and civil rights in other Commonwealth States if they are also citizens of the country concerned, or if that country has enacted in its own nationality law a provision similar to the above section of the United Kingdom Act. The Ceylon Citizenship Act 1948 does not contain the common clause. India did not pass its own enactment until 1955.[1] But citizens of other Commonwealth countries have in India the status of Commonwealth citizens, although that status is not given to Indian citizens by the Act. On the other hand, a citizen of Pakistan has the status of a Commonwealth citizen, but the Pakistan Citizenship Act 1951 does not contain the common clause. In the case of the Federation of Malaya (now Malaysia), where the bulk of the inhabitants before federation were British protected persons, the constitution [2] provided that a citizen of the Federation shall enjoy by virtue of that citizenship the status of a Commonwealth citizen in common with the citizens of other Commonwealth countries (art. 29). Rights may be conferred on the citizens of other Commonwealth countries on a basis of reciprocity (art. 155). In 1962 on the Union of South Africa leaving

[1] Citizenship Act 1955.
[2] Federation of Malaya Independence Order in Council 1957, S.I. No. 1533.

the Commonwealth and becoming a republic, a British subject whose title depended only on citizenship of the former Union of South Africa ceased to be a British subject; but temporary provision was made for such persons to register as United Kingdom citizens.[1]

Right of Entry

Until 1962 a citizen from any part of the Commonwealth was free to enter and to leave the United Kingdom without any restriction whatever. This right was sustained by long-established tradition. There was, however, no such right in other parts of the Commonwealth and at least forty territories, both independent States and colonial territories, had imposed some kind of restriction upon entry on citizens from other parts of the Commonwealth including the United Kingdom. The Commonwealth Immigrants Act 1962 enables an immigration officer to refuse admission to or to admit on conditions, *e.g.* of guaranteed employment, any citizen of the Commonwealth other than those who hold United Kingdom passports and their dependants. Admission may not be refused to such a person who can satisfy the immigration authorities that he is self-supporting or is going to take up employment which has been vouched for by the Department of Employment or where entry is for the purpose of a course of whole-time study. Dependants of immigrants are required since 1969 to be in possession of an entry certificate obtainable from the office of the United Kingdom High Commissioner in their own country.[2] There are still no restrictions on Commonwealth citizens leaving the United Kingdom. The occasion of this enactment was due to the arrival in large numbers of unskilled immigrants from, in particular, India and Pakistan, and, to some extent, the West Indies. The control of immigration provisions are subject to renewal by the annual Expiring Laws Continuance Act. The Act of 1962 also for the first time sanctioned the deportation from the United Kingdom of Commonwealth citizens who have been convicted of offences punishable with imprisonment and recommended by the court for deportation. Here again the power has no application to holders of United Kingdom passports.

Where a court recommends deportation under the Act an appeal to the court lies against the recommendation, but is quite distinct from an appeal against sentence.[3] Liability to deportation ceases after five years' continuous residence, which period may include up to six months' detention ordered by a court in the United

[1] South Africa Act 1962. s. 1 and 1st Schedule.
[2] Immigration Appeals Act 1969, s. 20.
[3] *The Queen* v. *Edgehill*, [1963] 1 Q.B. 593.

Kingdom having jurisdiction under the Act. Where the prosecution proposes to ask the Court to recommend deportation of a Commonwealth citizen, he must be given seven days' notice.

Commonwealth Immigrants Act 1968

The decision of the Government of Kenya to require in particular Indians who had not acquired local nationality in Kenya on or after independence to leave that State led to a marked exodus to the United Kingdom of such persons who had been guaranteed by the independence legislation the retention of their status of citizens of the United Kingd and Colonies and their entry as such citizens could not be restricted without legislation. The Act of 1968 is notable because it takes away from a non-resident citizen of the United Kingdom and Colonies the automatic right of entry into the United Kingdom, unless he, or at least one of his parents or grandparents, was born in the United Kingdom or is (or was) naturalised here, or he is a citizen of the United Kingdom by adoption or by registration under the British Nationality Acts 1948 to 1965. Entry of persons hereby excluded is by quota, administratively fixed at 1,500 per annum, for heads of households. It is difficult to see how admission can in practice be refused in cases where, for example, India has refused admission to its former nationals from Kenya.

Immigration Appeals Act 1969

In 1969 there was set up for the first time a system of appeals against decisions taken in the administration of immigration control under the Commonwealth Immigrants Act 1962 and the Aliens Restriction Acts 1914 and the Aliens Order 1953 made under the latter Act.[1] An appeal may lie against decisions of the immigration officers or the Home Secretary relating to:

(1) exclusion from the United Kingdom
(2) conditions imposed on admission
(3) deportation orders made by the Home Secretary
(4) directions for removal, *e.g.* in the case of the return of the immigrant in breach of a deportation order.[2]

Deportation orders may be made in respect of Commonwealth citizens who fail to comply with the conditions of their admission.[3] Appellants may be released on bail at any stage of the proceedings.

[1] S. 14. See p. 257, *post*. In the case of aliens the system required an Order in Council to bring it into force. Statutory Instrument. 1970 No. 118 (C.3.).
[2] S. 2–5.
[3] S. 16.

The appeal is in the first instance to adjudicators who are appointed by the Home Secretary; they are normally in a position to make on-the-spot decisions under (1) and (2). There is a further appeal to an Immigration Appeal Tribunal which is appointed by the Lord Chancellor. Leave either of the Tribunal or the adjudicator is normally required and the grounds must be either on a point of law arising out of the immigration rules or that the discretion should have been exercised differently by the immigration officer or the Home Secretary. If security considerations arise, the appeal goes to a tribunal drawn from a special panel, whose decision is subject to reversal by the Home Secretary. The category of Commonwealth citizens excluded under (1) consists mainly of those who had retained citizenship of the United Kingdom on the grant of independence to colonies, *e.g.* to Kenya.

Deprivation of Citizenship

It is only persons who have acquired the status of citizenship by registration or by naturalisation who can be deprived of citizenship of the United Kingdom and Colonies. Apart from the case of revocation of registration or of a certificate of naturalisation on the ground that it has been obtained by fraud (s. 20 (2)), a provision to which reference has been made in relation to alien women marrying citizens of the United Kingdom, the Home Secretary may revoke letters of naturalisation granted to aliens or British protected persons, but not the registration of citizens of other States in the Commonwealth, if he is satisfied that such a person—

(*a*) has shown himself by act or speech to be disloyal or disaffected towards Her Majesty; or

(*b*) has, during any war in which Her Majesty was engaged, unlawfully traded or communicated with an enemy or been engaged in or associated with any business that was to his knowledge carried on in such a manner as to assist an enemy in that war; or

(*c*) has within five years after becoming naturalised been sentenced in any country to imprisonment for a term of not less than twelve months (s. 20 (3)). Such persons, *i.e.* convicted persons, may not be deprived of citizenship if the result would be to make them stateless.[1]

The Home Secretary may only exercise his powers of deprivation if he is satisfied that it is not conducive to the public good that a naturalised citizen should continue to have that status. Provision is made for a judicial enquiry before the citizenship is revoked under s. 20 (2) or (3) and such enquiry may be granted in other cases.

[1] British Nationality (No. 2) Act 1964, s. 4.

Divesting of Citizenship

Nationality acquired by birth, as well as that acquired by naturalisation, may be divested. This was not so at common law. Acquisition of nationality of a foreign State does not, as it did under the Act of 1914, automatically cause loss of United Kingdom citizenship. Section 19 provides for renunciation by declaration in the prescribed manner.[1] The Home Secretary may withhold registration of the declaration if it is made during war by a person who is aiso a national of a foreign State. It was decided in *The King* v. *Lynch*[2] that a British subject who had taken the oath of allegiance to the enemy in the Boer War had not thereby lost his British nationality and that his attempt to become naturalised as an enemy subject was ineffective. He was accordingly convicted of treason.

There is no authority upon the effect of an attempt by a British subject to become naturalised to a non-enemy State in time of war.[3] But under s. 19 of the Act of 1948 the attempt, if made by a United Kingdom citizen in order to renounce his citizenship, can only succeed if the Home Secretary is willing to register the declaration. It is within the competence of the Sovereign to allow a subject to assume sovereignty over a foreign State.[4]

B. Aliens

Status of Aliens

An alien has full proprietary capacity, except that he may not own a British ship. He may not exercise the franchise, parliamentary or local. He may only be employed in the United Kingdom in a civil capacity under the Crown if a responsible Minister with the consent of the Treasury certifies his employment.[5] An alien has no right to be admitted into the Queen's realms and territories.[6] It is probable that the Crown may even in time of peace expel an alien under the prerogative.[7] The expulsion of aliens is now, however, regulated by statutory powers.

Admission, Supervision and Deportation

The admission and deportation of aliens is governed by the provisions of the Aliens Order 1953 made under the powers conferred

[1] The British Nationality Act 1964 enables a person to renounce his citizenship with a view to acquiring another nationality or citizenship.

[2] [1903] 1 K.B. 444.

[3] McNair, *Legal Effects of War* (4th edn.), p. 67.

[4] McNair, *International Law Opinions*, I, p. 21; Sir James Brooke and the State of Sarawak.

[5] Aliens' Employment Act 1955.

[6] *Musgrove* v. *Chung Teeong Toy*, [1891] A.C. 272.

[7] McNair, *Legal Effects of War*, p. 71.

by the Aliens Restriction Acts 1914 and 1919.[1] Articles 1 and 4 of the Order prevent leave being given to an alien to land in the United Kingdom, unless he complies with certain conditions, *e.g.* that he is in a position to support himself and his dependents, or that it is not undesirable on medical grounds that he should be permitted to land. A British protected person [2] is not an alien for the purposes of the Aliens Order; nor is a citizen of the Republic of Ireland, nor a member who is serving in the United Kingdom in the armed forces of any of the North Atlantic Treaty Powers.

The regulations fall under three heads:

1. *Admission.*

   The immigration officers have a general discretionary authority to grant or to refuse leave to land to any alien coming from outside the United Kingdom, but they must not grant leave to land to any alien who fails to fulfil the conditions laid down in the Aliens Order 1953. In the case of any alien seeking admission with a view to taking employment, leave to land cannot be granted, unless the alien is able to produce a permit issued to his prospective employer by the Department of Employment. An alien who is refused leave to land, or an extension of a time limit put upon his visit, has no right capable of being infringed in such a way as to entitle him to bring an action in the courts for assistance.[3]

2. *Supervision.*

   The registration and supervision of registered aliens is carried out by the police under Home Office instructions and is compulsory after three months' residence. The Acts permit of drastic supervision and restrictions in the event of war or a major emergency.

3. *Deportation.*

   The Home Secretary has power to order the deportation of any undesirable alien, if he considers it is conducive to the public good. He may consult an advisory committee in the case of proposed deportations which are based on any grounds other than landing in the United Kingdom without permission or failure to observe the conditions imposed on landing. The functions of the committee are exclusively advisory, and the

[1] The Act of 1914 applied only in time of war, imminent national danger or grave emergency. It was extended for one year in time of peace by the Act of 1919, which is itself renewed each year by an Expiring Laws Continuance Act.

[2] P. 249, *ante*.

[3] *Schmidt* v. *Home Secretary*, [1969] 2 Ch. 149. For appeals by aliens under the Immigration Appeals Act 1969, see p. 254, *ante*.

Home Secretary is not bound to consult the committee in every case where he proposes to make an order for deportation under the general discretionary power conferred by Article 20 (1) and (2) of the Aliens Order 1953. Where it is proposed to deport an alien who has been resident here for at least two years, and the proposal is not supported by the recommendation of a court there is a right to make representations to the Chief Metropolitan Magistrate.[1] This right was created under the prerogative by the Home Secretary to give effect to the European Convention on Establishment 1955 to which the United Kingdom is a party. It has now been made part of the statute law contained in the Immigration Appeals Act 1969. Of the first thirty-one cases of persons taking advantage of this right the order for deportation was cancelled in five cases. In the case of an alien convicted of a criminal offence, the power of deportation is usually exercised on a recommendation for the expulsion of any convicted alien which the court can make under the regulations. The High Court will restrain an excess of this power. Thus if the Home Secretary ordered the deportation of a British subject in the belief that he was an alien, the subject could have the issue of alienage or non-alienage determined in habeas corpus proceedings.[2] Since the power of deportation though founded on the prerogative is statutory, an action for false imprisonment of an alien may result from a wrong interpretation of the Aliens Order.[3] Similarly it seems the court could go behind an order for an alien's arrest, which though valid on its face, was a mere sham not made bonâ fide.[4] A deportation order cannot, however, be quashed by certiorari [5] on the ground that the Home Secretary held no enquiry.[6]

An alien physically within the realm can apply for habeas corpus. A deportation order is an executive act and there is no obligation on the Home Secretary to hear any representations before he makes the order. The distinction between deportation and extradition is not always strictly observed in practice. In fact only five per cent of the cases of expulsion of aliens are secured by the process of extradition.[7] The claim of the Home

[1] 557 H.C. Deb., *W.A.* 174–5; 595 H.C. Deb., col. 1349.

[2] *Eshugbayi Eleko* v. *Government of Nigeria*, [1931] A.C. 662, at p. 670.

[3] *Kuchenmeister* v. *Home Office*, [1958] 1 Q.B. 496.

[4] *The King* v. *Superintendent of Chiswick Police Station, ex parte Sacksteder*, [1918] 1 K.B. 578 and p. 259, note 1.

[5] P. 661, *post*.

[6] *Ex parte Venicoff*, [1920] 3 K.B. 72.

[7] Section C, pp. 260-3, *post*.

Secretary to determine the destination of a deportee who is expelled under the Aliens Order 1953 has been upheld.[1] In the case of an alien who is accused of, or has been convicted of, a crime in his own country, the power of expulsion can be exercised to achieve the same result as if the handing over was secured by extradition proceedings. Thus it is within the power of the Home Secretary to enlarge the class of offences in respect of which handing over can be granted by means of expulsion under the Aliens Order. This may be important since espionage is not an extraditable offence and therefore, for example, the United States of America could not seek extradition of one of its nationals accused of spying who was seeking refuge in the United Kingdom.

Alien Enemies

Alien enemies are inevitably in time of war subject to drastic restrictions imposed either under the prerogative, the Aliens Restriction Acts or Defence Regulations. Under the prerogative the Crown has the right to intern, expel or otherwise control an enemy alien at its discretion. But an enemy alien who has been permitted to remain in this country is within the Queen's protection and may sue in the Queen's courts. A person residing voluntarily on enemy territory, including territory occupied by the enemy,[2] or carrying on business in such territory is, on the other hand, debarred from suing in the United Kingdom, whether he be an enemy, a neutral or a British subject.[3] Such persons are enemies in the sense that they are on the other side of the line of war, and it is trade with enemies in this sense that is forbidden in time of war by the Trading with the Enemy Acts and also by common law.[4] Such persons can, however, be sued and, if judgment goes against them, they can appeal. The outbreak of war does not automatically bring about confiscation of enemy private property, but the Crown may before the conclusion of peace confiscate the property of an alien enemy (in the national sense) by the ancient procedure of inquisition of office.[5] It is customary to vest enemy private property in a custodian of enemy

[1] *The Queen* v. *Governor of Brixton Prison, ex parte Soblen*, [1963] 2 Q.B. 243; P. O'Higgins, *Disguised Extradition: The Soblen Case*, 27 M.L.R. 521.

[2] *Sovfracht (V.O.)* v. *N. V. Gebr. Van Udens Scheepvaarten Argentuur Maatschappij*, [1943] A.C. 203.

[3] *Porter* v. *Freudenberg*, [1915] 1 K.B. 857.

[4] Magna Carta. Cl. 41 provided that on the breaking out of war merchants of the hostile State who may be in England shall be attached without damage to their bodies or goods until it be known how our merchants are treated in such hostile State; and if ours be safe, the others shall be safe also.

[5] McNair, *op. cit.*, p. 130.

property and to provide for its disposition by peace treaty.[1] A cause of action which has accrued to any one who becomes an enemy on the outbreak of war is suspended, so long as a state of war exists.

C. Extradition [2]

Extradition relates to the surrender by one State to another of persons who are fugitives from justice. An alleged criminal when he removes himself to the territory of another State is protected by international law from seizure by the agents of the State on whose territory the crime was committed. The surrender from one State to another of such a person cannot therefore be demanded in the absence of a treaty. The delivery of the accused or convicted person is made on the request of the State seeking to secure the fugitive's person. It is possible for a person accused, or convicted in his absence, of a crime under the law of State A to be surrendered by State B, where he resides, as a fugitive criminal from State A without ever having been present in State A, and this is true even of a national of State B, if the relevant treaty provides for the extradition of nationals.

> In *The King* v. *Godfrey* [3] the court ordered the surrender of a British subject to the Swiss authorities on a charge under Swiss law of false pretences alleged to have been made in Switzerland by the partners of the accused to which he, a resident in England, was an accessory.

The need for extradition is recognised by practically all civilised States as a matter both of morality and expediency: of morality since mankind deprecates escape from the consequences of, at all events, serious crime; of expediency in that no State desires to become a haven of refuge for the underworld.

Extradition is controlled by two factors, namely (1) statute law defining the grounds of, and the procedure for, surrender of criminals and (2) treaties with foreign States. In order to secure the surrender, the crime must be within the particular treaty; it must be against the general law of the State which seeks extradition; and it must be a crime within the Extradition Acts 1870–1935.[4]

> Thus in *The Queen* v. *Wilson* [5] it was held that section 6 of the Extradition Act 1870, which provided that every fugitive criminal shall be liable to surrender, must be interpreted in light of the treaty

[1] See Distribution of German Enemy Property Act 1949 which provided for collection and distribution without a peace treaty.
[2] McNair, *International Law Opinions*, II, pp. 40–46.
[3] [1923] 1 K.B. 24.
[4] See Counterfeit Currency (Convention) Act 1935, s. 4.
[5] (1877), 3 Q.B.D. 42.

with Switzerland, which excluded at that time the surrender by Great Britain and Switzerland of their own nationals.

No proceedings can be taken unless an extradition treaty has been concluded with the foreign State which seeks the surrender of the fugitive, or into whose territory the fugitive has escaped or is sheltering from British justice. The Extradition Acts, which define extraditable offences and the procedure for surrender, require that the terms of a treaty be brought into force by means of an Order in Council. About fifty treaties have been concluded by the United Kingdom. In some cases there is no provision for the extradition of nationals of the contracting parties (though it is not essential that there should be reciprocity in this respect and British policy is to surrender a national without requiring reciprocity), *e.g.* an Italian who is wanted on a criminal charge in this country will not be extradited from Italy, if he has succeeded in escaping thither. This restriction does not, of course, affect any remedy which his own State may have against a national in respect of his crimes committed in the United Kingdom. There is one exception to the category of crimes in respect of which extradition proceedings may be brought under the treaties. No person accused of a purely political offence can be extradited. It is not, however, easy to define a purely political offence; [1] for such an offence may, or may not, involve violence; and if it is a crime of violence, it may be political on the ground of being incidental to a political disturbance, in which case extradition will not be ordered by the English courts, or committed merely to satisfy private vengeance, as with an isolated act of bomb-throwing by an anarchist. In the latter case the offender is not permitted to shield himself behind the exception. If the requisition for surrender has in fact been made with a view to a prosecution of a political character, although based on a non-political criminal charge, such as larceny or aggravated assault, the court must refuse the requisition.[2] The mere fact that an offence has become a political issue does not make it an offence of a political character. To constitute an offence of a political character the requesting State must be asking for surrender for reasons other than an enforcement of the criminal law in its ordinary aspect.[3] The idea behind a political offence is that the fugitive from justice should be in conflict with the State which has applied for his extradition on some issue connected with the political control or government of the country.

[1] *The Queen* v. *Castioni*, [1891] 1 Q.B. 149; *The Queen* v. *Meunier*, [1894] 2 Q.B. 415.

[2] *The Queen* v. *Governor of Brixton Prison, ex parte Kolczynski*, [1955] 1 Q.B. 540.

[3] *The Queen* v. *Governor of Brixton Prison, ex parte Schtraks*, [1964] A.C. 556.

Procedure

The process for securing the extradition of an offender who has escaped to this country is as follows: the diplomatic representative of the country desiring extradition of a fugitive offender makes a request to the Foreign Office for his arrest, sending at the same time evidence on which the charge is based, or, if the person has already been convicted in the country where he committed the crime, evidence of his conviction and sentence. The Foreign Office forwards the request to the Home Office, whereupon the Home Secretary, unless he considers the offence to be a political one, issues an order to the Chief Metropolitan Magistrate at Bow Street, who, in turn, issues his warrant for the criminal's arrest to the Metropolitan Police. This process may be curtailed, as the Extradition Acts provide for a warrant being issued on sworn information prior to the order for proceedings by the Home Secretary; but the order must be made later, if proceedings are continued. All cases have to be investigated before the Chief Magistrate or another of the Metropolitan Magistrates sitting at Bow Street. In the event of the magistrate deciding that the offender should be committed to prison to await his surrender, fifteen days must elapse, during which the offender may apply to the High Court for his release by means of a writ of habeas corpus. No court, even the House of Lords, can substitute its discretion for that of the Chief Magistrate. Though further evidence can be received to show that the Magistrate had no jurisdiction to make the order, it cannot be received to show that he exercised his discretion wrongly.[1] The surrender will not be ordered unless the offence alleged is one which substantially coincides with an indictable offence under English criminal law. It may also be refused on the following grounds:

(1) Insufficient evidence of identity.

(2) That the offence is not within the treaty.

(3) That the offence alleged is not against the law of the country requesting the surrender.

(4) That no *prima facie* case has been made out.

(5) That the offence is purely political, or that the surrender is sought for a political object.

Section 19 of the Extradition Act 1870 restricts the offences for which a surrendered person may be tried here to such crimes as may be proved by the facts on which the surrender is grounded.[2] For

[1] *Ex parte Schtraks, ante.*

[2] See *The King* v. *Corrigan* (1930), 47 T.L.R. 27.

example, a person surrendered by France on facts which supported a charge of arson could not after surrender be tried for forgery without being given an opportunity of first returning to France. Committal may not be refused on the grounds of oppression or the denial of natural justice if the examining magistrate has sufficient evidence of the alleged offence, but the Home Secretary has unfettered discretion to refuse surrender.[1] Nor can the court go behind a certificate of a foreign court which shows that the person whose extradition is sought had been convicted of an extraditable offence, for the court must assume that the foreign government will observe the conditions of its extradition treaty with the United Kingdom.[2]

Fugitive Offenders within the Commonwealth

Until 1966 the surrender of fugitives from justice to, or by, Commonwealth States and Colonies was governed by the Fugitive Offenders Act 1881. The procedure dispensed with diplomatic application in view of the constitutional status of overseas territories of the Crown at that date. Surrender could not be refused on account of the political character of the offence or on the ground that it was sought for a political object.[3] After consultation and agreement with other Commonwealth States, all of which had the power to enact their own legislation to vary the Act of 1881, the United Kingdom Parliament passed the Fugitive Offenders Act 1967 which brought the procedure more closely into line with that of the Extradition Act 1870.[4] The test now is that, where the charge relates to a relevant offence, the evidence would be sufficient to warrant the trial of the accused if the offence had been committed within the jurisdiction of the court. Similar legislation was proposed in Commonwealth legislatures. The Act of 1967 lists the twenty-eight offences under English criminal law for which applications for surrender can be made, recognises the principle of double criminality,[5] *i.e.* requires that the offence shall be punishable as a crime under the law of the applicant State, and prohibits surrender for a political offence (other than an offence against the life or person of the Queen) or one which carries

[1] *Atkinson* v. *United States Government*, (H.L.) [1969] 3 W.L.R. 1074.

[2] *Royal Government of Greece* v. *Governor of Brixton Prison*, (H.L.) [1969] 3 W.L.R. 1107.

[3] See *Zacharia* v. *Republic of Cyprus*, [1963] A.C. 634; *The Queen* v. *Governor of Brixton Prison, ex parte Enaharo*, [1963] 2 Q.B. 455, 674 H.C. Deb. cs. 1271 ff., 675 H.C. Deb. cs. 1287 ff. The Home Secretary has a statutory discretion to refuse surrender.

[4] Rhodesia and the few remaining Protectorates were excluded.

[5] *The Queen* v. *Governor of Brixton Prison, ex parte Gardner*, [1968] 2 Q.B. 399. Offence must under the 1967 Act be one under the law of England as well as that of the State seeking surrender.

the death penalty in the State seeking the surrender; that State may only prosecute an accused for the offence for which he has been handed over. Even if the offence charged is relevant in both countries, return of the accused may be refused if it is shown that the application has been made for the purpose of inflicting punishment on account of race, religion, nationality or political opinion or that the accused might be prejudiced at his trial by reason of the same considerations. All applications for surrender are made to the Home Secretary by the High Commissioner of the Commonwealth State seeking surrender. Hearings, as with extradition, are at the Chief Metropolitan Magistrate's Court and fifteen days must elapse before the Home Secretary acts on a recommendation for surrender to enable the accused to seek a writ of habeas corpus. There is a mandatory duty on the Home Secretary not to return an accused, if it would be unjust and oppressive to do so.

In the case of the Republic of Ireland the Extradition and Fugitive Offenders Acts do not apply. The handing over of persons in custody to the Republic rests upon legislation enacted during the Union, and in particular the Petty Sessions (Ireland) Act 1851. A procedure which is simpler than those for extradition or surrender to Commonwealth States has been sanctioned by the Backing of Warrants (Republic of Ireland) Act 1965.

D. Foreign Enlistment

To enable the Government of a neutral State to fulfil its obligations towards a belligerent State it is necessary for the former to control and sometimes to prohibit certain activities of its nationals. The Foreign Enlistment Act 1870 which applies to the Colonies and, until repealed or re-enacted locally, to the other States of the Commonwealth, prohibits (*a*) enlistment by a British subject in the military or naval service of any foreign State at war with a friendly State; (*b*) quitting by such person from Her Majesty's dominions for that purpose; (*c*) building, equipping or despatching a ship with intent or knowledge that it will be used in such military or naval service; (*d*) preparing or fitting out any naval or military expedition to proceed against the dominions of a friendly State. The last two prohibitions (*c*) and (*d*) apply to any person, subject or alien, within Her Majesty's dominions.

Breach of a blockade imposed by a foreign State and the carriage of contraband are normally [1] permitted by English law when the United Kingdom is neutral, though the Crown will not protect its nationals against the seizure by a belligerent of the property involved.

[1] See, however, Merchant Shipping (Carriage of Munitions to Spain) Act 1936.

CHAPTER TWENTY

FOREIGN AFFAIRS

A. Acts of State

Act of State, the wide sense

THOSE acts of the Crown which are done under the prerogative in the sphere of foreign affairs are known as acts of State.[1] Instances of acts of State are the declaration of war,[2] the making of peace, and the recognition of foreign Governments. The term, "act of State," means "an act of the Executive as a matter of policy performed in the course of its relations with another State, including its relations with the subjects of that State, unless they are temporarily within the allegiance of the Crown." [3] In *Nissan* v. *Attorney-General* [4] this definition, which had been accepted by the Court of Appeal, was considered in the House of Lords, where it was pointed out that what is a matter of policy is difficult to determine; the case decided that damage done to property while under requisition for military occupation in Cyprus after independence could be recovered and was not excused by a plea of act of State. In *Republic of Italy* v. *Hambros Bank Ltd. and another*,[5] the court refused to adjudicate on, or to take cognisance of a financial agreement between Italy and the United Kingdom. It gives rise neither to contractual rights nor claims in tort. The term "act of State" has been defined judicially as: "an exercise of sovereign power" which "cannot be challenged, controlled or interfered with by municipal courts. Its sanction is not that of law, but that of sovereign power, and, whatever it be, municipal courts must accept it, as it is, without question." [6] Such matters as

[1] P. 186, *ante*.

[2] But should the Crown come to any person not being a native of England, the nation is not obliged to engage in war for the defence of territories not belonging to the Crown of England without the consent of Parliament: Act of Settlement 1700.

[3] 'Act of State in English Law', by E. C. S. Wade, *British Year Book of International Law*, 1934, p. 98, and *Act of State as a Defence Against a British Subject*, by J. G. Collier, [1968] C.L.J. 102–130.

[4] [1970] A.C. 179.

[5] [1950] Ch. 315.

[6] *Per* Fletcher Moulton, L. J., in *Salaman* v. *Secretary of State for India*, [1906] 1 K.B. 613, at p. 639.

fall properly to be determined by the Crown as acts of State in this sense are not subject to the jurisdiction of the municipal courts, and rights alleged to be acquired thereunder, *semble* even by British subjects, cannot be enforced by such courts.[1] Acts resulting from a treaty of cession or by reason of annexation of territory fall into this class; such acts may confer a title to property on the Crown which must be accepted by municipal law.

In *West Rand Central Gold Mining Co.* v. *The King*[2] a British corporation failed to establish by petition of right the right to enforce against the Crown a claim for a wrong inflicted upon it by the Government of a State (the former South African Republic) which had been extinguished by acts upon the part of the Crown, namely, conquest and annexation. No interference with the rights of British subjects enforceable in British courts was thereby involved, and it lay within the discretion of the Crown to determine which, if any, of the liabilities of the extinguished State it was prepared to assume.

In *Nabob of the Carnatic* v. *East India Company*[3] there was dismissed a bill in equity founded upon treaties between the Nabob and the Company; the treaties were political and made between a foreign Power and subjects of the Crown acting as an independent State under charter and statutory powers; they were therefore not subject to the jurisdiction of the courts.

Effect of Acts of State on British Subjects

The Crown cannot justify in a British court an interference wherever taking place with the existing rights of British subjects by the plea of act of State, but an alleged right may be unenforceable because it is placed outside the jurisdiction of the municipal courts by the operation of such an act.[4] Thus the treaty-making power of the Crown does not dispense with the necessity for legislation where the creation of a treaty requires a modification of the existing rights of subjects.[5] On the other hand, acts which are within the undoubted power of the Crown may indirectly have an effect upon private rights. Thus the declaration of war will render it illegal to carry out existing contracts with alien enemies; the recognition of a foreign Government may affect the result of a lawsuit depending upon the validity or otherwise of a foreign decree confiscating property abroad;[6] the

[1] See *Rustomjee* v. *The Queen* (1876), 2 Q.B.D. 69, at p. 73; and *Civilian War Claimants' Association* v. *The King*, [1932] A.C. 14 (no right of subjects to sums payable to the State as reparations under the Treaty of Versailles, 1919.)

[2] [1905] 2 K.B. 391, at p. 409.

[3] (1792), 2 Ves. Jun. 56.

[4] *West Rand Central Gold Mining Co.* v. *The King.*

[5] Pp 276-9. *post.*

[6] Pp. 279-82. *post.*

recognition of the diplomatic status of a foreigner will render him immune from suit by a subject in a British court.

Act of State as Defence to Action in Tort

The plea, act of State, can be raised as a defence in a court of the United Kingdom to an act, otherwise tortious or criminal,[1] committed abroad by a servant of the Crown against a subject of a foreign State or his property, provided that the act was authorised or subsequently ratified by the Crown. The use of the term in such a case is in the nature of a special defence qualifying the rule of municipal law which normally prevents a wrongdoer setting up that his tortious act was done by command of the Crown.

This defence is illustrated by *Buron* v. *Denman.*[2]

> A naval commander stationed on the coast of Africa was ordered by the Governor of a British colony to secure the release of British subjects detained as slaves on foreign territory. He exceeded his instructions, since, in addition to releasing the slaves, he set fire to a barracoon belonging to a Spaniard who was trading in slaves at the place. The Spaniard brought an action in the English courts against the officer, but, the proceedings having been reported to the Home Government, the Crown adopted the act of the officer. The court held that the subsequent ratification by the Crown was equivalent to prior authorisation and that no action lay in respect of an act of State.

A prisoner of war cannot challenge his detention by a writ of habeas corpus because the function of the Crown when waging war, and, incidentally, capturing an enemy and holding him prisoner, is a prerogative function and cannot be challenged in the courts.[3]

When Defence not Available

Such a defence is not available against a British subject,[4] nor against an alien, the subject of a friendly State, who is resident in British territory. It is doubtful what the position would be if the Crown had formally withdrawn its protection from an alien owing to his treasonable acts.[5]

> Thus in *Walker* v. *Baird*[6] an action for trespass was brought against a naval captain who had seized the respondent's lobster factory under

[1] Such act would normally be subject to the prosecution of the offender in the courts of the foreign State where the act was committed.

[2] (1848), 2 Ex. 167.

[3] *The King* v. *Bottrill, ex parte Kuechenmeister*, [1947] K.B. 41.

[4] Stephen, *History of the Criminal Law*, Vol. II, 65; see *Nissan* v. *Attorney General*, [1970], A.C. 179.

[5] This point was raised but not decided in *Johnstone* v. *Pedlar*., p. 268, *post*.

[6] [1892] A.C. 491; K. & L. 169.

Admiralty orders with the object of enforcing the terms of a treaty with France. The lobster factory was situated on British territory. Held that the defence that the matters complained of were acts of State and so could not be enquired into by the courts was untenable and that legislation would have been required to legalise such action.

In *Johnstone* v. *Pedlar* [1] an American subject was arrested by the Dublin police (before the establishment of the Irish Free State) and subsequently sentenced to a term of imprisonment for illegal drilling. At the time of his arrest a considerable sum of money was found on his person. Having served his sentence, the prisoner sued the police for the return of his money. The police put in at the trial a certificate by the Chief Secretary for Ireland confirming the seizure of the money to the effect that the seizure was ratified on behalf of the Crown as an act of State. Held that the alien had a legal remedy for the recovery of the money, his status being as regards civil rights assimilated, with minor exceptions, to that of a subject.

In *Commercial and Estates Co. of Egypt* v. *Board of Trade* [2] the view was expressed *obiter* by Scrutton, L. J. that even against an alien, the subject of a friendly state, residing outside the realm, the defence of act of State is not available where his property has been seized within the realm.[3]

An act of State authorised by a foreign ruler may empower a British subject to seize British-owned goods on a British ship in foreign territorial waters.[4] It will not, however, be regarded by a British court as a justification of a wrongful act committed under the British flag outside the jurisdiction of the foreign ruler.[5]

Seizure and Destruction of Property in War

As recently as 1964 it was held by the House of Lords that where property has been destroyed by the Crown under its prerogative powers, as distinct from any statutory provision, to prevent it falling into the hands of an enemy, the subject is entitled to compensation.

In *Burmah Oil Company* v. *Lord Advocate* [6] extensive oil installations were destroyed in Burma during the Second World War not as part of actual hostilities but in order to prevent the installations falling into enemy hands in the event, which in fact happened shortly afterwards, of the territory being invaded by the Japanese enemy. The destruction was ordered by the commanding General not in the course of actual hostilities but as a form of economic warfare lest the installations should help the enemy cause if they were captured intact.

Before this case there was not a single instance in modern times of the taking or interfering with land without payment. The majority

[1] [1921] 2 A.C. 262; K. & L. 171.
[2] [1925] 1 K.B. 271, at p. 290.
[3] For requisition by the Crown within the realm under the prerogative in War, see page 190, *ante*.
[4] *Carr* v. *Fracis Times and Co.*, [1902] A.C. 176.
[5] *The Queen* v. *Lesley* (1860), Bell C.C. 220.
[6] [1965] A.C. 75.

of cases of seizure or destruction of private property have been governed by statutory provisions such as the Defence of the Realm Acts 1914–15 and the Emergency Powers Acts 1939–40. The decision seemed to accept the view that, apart at all events from damage done during the actual fighting, the exercise of the prerogative to the detriment of the subject attracts compensation just as there is a presumption in the interpretation of compulsory powers of acquisition conferred by statute that the acquisition must be accompanied by compensation. The War Damage Act 1965 reversed the House of Lords decision and removed the obligation to pay compensation in future under the prerogative power exercised in relation to the conduct of a war and resulting in damage to property.

Acts of State within the Commonwealth

The independent status of the several members of the Commonwealth raises a doubt whether the term, act of State, both in the wide sense of an act of policy on the part of the Executive and in the narrow sense of defence to an action in tort can nowadays be accepted by a municipal court if the plaintiff is a citizen of a Commonwealth State other than the United Kingdom and the injury of which he complains has been inflicted upon him outside the United Kingdom or colonial territory. For example, if under orders United Kingdom service aircraft dropped bombs on a foreign oil installation or on the high seas or in foreign territorial waters thereby injuring the person or property of a citizen of India who was not taking part in the local disturbances which led to the bombing, could the defence "act of State" be raised if the Indian sought redress in an English court for the injuries he received? It would seem that the answer to the question is to be found in the British Nationality Act 1948, s. 1, which recognises as British subjects or Commonwealth citizens the citizens of all countries to which the section applies. No one can doubt the independence of India as a State for the purpose of the conduct of its own foreign affairs; but its citizens by United Kingdom legislation enjoy the advantages of local citizenship, and therefore cannot be deprived by an English court of their right to redress on the plea of act of State, *i.e.* the consequences of military operations against hostile elements abroad. It would follow that if the injury were incurred in similar circumstances on the territory of any member State of the Commonwealth or of a colony, the defence, act of State, would not be available in an English court to the agent of the Government of the United Kingdom. In *Nissan* v. *Attorney-General* [1] the Lords left open the question whether, act of State,

[1] P. 265, *ante*.

could be pleaded for damage to property in hostilities as distinct from defence preparations when the property in question belongs to British residents overseas.

On the other hand, in the wide sense the term, act of State, is appropriate to describe, for example, the conclusion of a treaty between the Queen of the United Kingdom and the President of India, and there is nothing apart from conventional usage to prevent a duly authenticated treaty between the United Kingdom and the Republic of India being accepted in an English court as an act of State authenticated by the separate seals of the two countries.

B. State Immunity

The immunity of Heads of State and State property may be classified under three heads :

(*a*) Immunity of Heads of States.
(*b*) Diplomatic and consular immunity.
(*c*) Immunity in respect of public property of a foreign State.

The immunity is one from legal process.

In *Mighell* v. *Sultan of Johore* [1] the Sultan, while visiting this country, became engaged to a young woman to whom he disclosed his identity as being that of Mr. Albert Baker. The Sultan having failed to fulfil his promise of marriage, the lady attempted to serve a writ on him for breach of promise of marriage.

Held that as a ruler of an independent foreign State, Johore being so regarded for this purpose, the Sultan was immune from process, unless he submitted to the jurisdiction.

As a consequence of the independence of every sovereign authority a State will decline to exercise any of the territorial jurisdiction of its courts over the person of any sovereign or ambassador, or over the public property of any State dedicated to the public use, or over the property of any ambassador, even though the sovereign, ambassador or property be within its territory; *The Parlement Belge.*[2]

This statement was occasioned by the seizure, under process of the Admiralty Division (to secure redress for collision damage), of a packet steamer which had collided with a ship of a British subject. The vessel was the property of the King of the Belgians and carried mails for his Government, as well as private passengers and merchandise. It was held that immunity could be claimed.

The immunity may be waived by an unequivocal act of submission.[3] It is an immunity, not from liability, but from local

[1] [1894] 1 Q.B. 149.
[2] (1880), 5 P.D. 197.
[3] *Duff Development Co.* v. *Government of Kelantan*, [1924] A.C. 797.

jurisdiction. Accordingly when a foreign diplomatic agent on being sued for damages for negligent driving waives his immunity, upon instructions from his superior, and judgment is entered against him, his policy of motor-car insurance is enforceable by means of third party procedure against the insurance company, even though he could not have been sued except upon his own voluntary submission.[1] Even in face of a contractual agreement to submit to the jurisdiction, a State can claim immunity in an English court, but not if the undertaking to submit has been given to the court at the time when the other party has asked the court to exercise jurisdiction over the State in question: *Kahan* v. *Pakistan Federation*,[2] which left open the question whether Pakistan was a foreign sovereign State for this purpose.

(a) *Immunity of Head of State*

Heads of States consist of Monarchs and Presidents. A Monarch of a foreign State visiting this country with the knowledge of the Government is afforded certain honours and enjoys certain protection and immunities. In particular, he cannot be subjected to the criminal jurisdiction of the courts, nor compelled against his will to plead in a civil court. He may, of course, himself be a plaintiff. Under the so-called doctrine of extra-territoriality he is immune from all taxation and his residence is inviolable. The position of a President is less certain, but it may be assumed that, having regard to the increasing number of important States having this type of ruler, the practice does not differ substantially from that adopted in the case of visiting Monarchs.

(b) *Immunity of Diplomatic Representatives*

The immunity of diplomatic representatives is part and parcel of that enjoyed by the heads of the States which they represent, though some writers attribute it to the necessity of such persons being free from the local jurisdiction, in order the better to perform the duties they owe to the accrediting country. In English law the Diplomatic Privileges Act 1708, which remained on the Statute Book until it was replaced by the Diplomatic Privileges Act 1964, provided that:—

> all writs and processes that shall at any time hereafter be sued forth or prosecuted whereby the person of any ambassador or other publick minister of any foreign prince or state authorised and received as such by Her Majesty her heirs or successors, or the domestick or domestick servant of any such ambassador or other publick minister may be

[1] *Dickinson* v. *Del Solar*, [1930] 1 K.B. 376.
[2] [1951] 2 K.B. 1003.

arrested or imprisoned or his or their goods or chattels may be distrained or seized or attached shall be deemed and adjudged to be utterly null and void to all intents constructions and purposes whatever.

This Act was declaratory of the common law and international practice, and behind it lay the principle accepted by the courts in *The Parlement Belge* (*ante*). The person of a diplomatic envoy is inviolable and is protected by the criminal law, which makes interference with State envoys a misdemeanour. The protection is extended to their families, staffs, official residences, papers and mails. The immunity can be waived by the head of a diplomatic mission. For a diplomatic envoy is expected to conform to the law of the land, unless it is likely to interfere with the free conduct of his duties. He is liable to be recalled on representation made to his home Government by the Foreign Secretary.

Scope of Immunity

The principal consequences of the extraterritoriality granted to diplomatic agents, *i.e.* heads of missions or members of their diplomatic staffs, by the Diplomatic Privileges Act 1964 which made some changes in the previous municipal law in accordance with the Vienna Convention on Diplomatic Relations [1] are:—

(*a*) inviolability of the premises of the diplomatic mission which cannot be entered, except with consent of the head of the mission, by the agents of the United Kingdom government;

(*b*) exemption from national and local taxation for the premises of the mission;

(*c*) permission and protection for free communication by the mission for all official purposes both with the government and other missions of the sending State wherever situated. This privilege includes inviolability for official correspondence and the diplomatic bag;

(*d*) a diplomatic agent, *i.e.* the head of the mission or a member of his diplomatic staff, is not liable to any form of arrest or detention. His private residence enjoys the same protection as the premises of the mission, as do his papers and correspondence;

(*e*) a diplomatic agent has immunity from criminal jurisdiction and also from civil and administrative jurisdiction except in respect of real property privately held or civil actions relating to succession or in professional or commercial activity exercised outside his official functions. This immunity may be

[1] Cmnd. 1368 (1961).

waived by the diplomatic agent's State. If he initiates proceedings on his own behalf, he cannot invoke immunity in respect of any counterclaim;

(*f*) a diplomatic agent is also exempt from taxes and local rates other than indirect taxation incorporated in the price of goods and taxes due on real property privately held.

Members of the family of a diplomatic agent, provided they are not United Kingdom nationals, enjoy the same immunities as the agent, but administrative and technical staff have no immunity from civil jurisdiction with respect to acts performed outside the course of their duties. The domestic staff of the mission have no immunity from civil or criminal jurisdiction with respect to acts performed outside the course of their duties, but private servants of the head of a mission are exempted from income tax on their salaries.

The Diplomatic Privileges (Extension) Act 1941 extended diplomatic immunity to the representatives of allied Governments established in this country during the Second World War. The Diplomatic Privileges (Extension) Act 1944 enabled the Crown to concede further extensions to international organisations and their officers. This Act was amended in 1946 to give effect to a general convention on privileges and immunities of the United Nations, including its councils and other organs, and also to make provision for the immunities, privileges and facilities to be enjoyed by the International Court of Justice. A further amendment was made in 1950 consequent on the agreement embodied in the Statute of the Council of Europe to confer immunities upon members of Parliaments appointed to sit in the Consultative Assembly at Strasbourg. The Acts of 1944, 1946 and 1950 were replaced by the International Organisations (Immunities and Privileges) Act 1950, a consolidating statute. The Diplomatic Immunities (Commonwealth Countries and Republic of Ireland) Act 1952 conferred upon the High Commissioners of those countries and on their official staffs the same immunities as are enjoyed by the envoys of foreign States and their official staffs. In the case of citizens of the United Kingdom who are members of such staffs immunity can only be claimed for their official acts. The Diplomatic Privileges Act 1964 enables the withdrawal by Order in Council of personal diplomatic immunities when they are in excess of those granted to members of a United Kingdom diplomatic mission to the foreign State concerned. The Diplomatic Immunities (Conference with Commonwealth Countries and the Republic of Ireland) Act 1961 placed representatives of Commonwealth Governments and their staffs in the same position as representatives of foreign Governments when attending conferences in the United Kingdom, but limited the immunity to official acts in the case of members of staffs who are citizens of the United Kingdom and not also of the country represented. The Commonwealth Secretariat Act 1966 [1] conferred upon the Secretary-General and his staff the same immunities and privileges as are given to High Commissioners of Commonwealth States.

The International Headquarters and Defence Organisations Act 1964 was passed to enable the United Kingdom to ratify the protocol on the status of international military headquarters set up under the North Atlantic Treaty. It enables the Crown to designate any international headquarters or defence organisation set up for common defence and to confer on it legal capacity as a corporation and immunity from suit and legal process. The same Act extends the Visiting Forces Act 1952 to designated headquarters and organisations.[2]

Consular immunities are of less importance. The Consular Relations Act 1968 which gave effect to the Vienna Convention on Consular Relations, Art. 31, (scheduled to Act) gives inviolability for parts of consular premises used exclusively for work of the consular post.

(c) *Immunity in respect of Public Property of a Foreign State*

It was in connection with immunity of State property that *The Parlement Belge* (*ante*) was decided. The law relating to ships (other than men-of-war) which enjoy immunities in international law may be summarised as follows: [3]

(i) A British court of law will not exercise jurisdiction over a ship which is the property of a foreign State; nor can any maritime lien attach, even in suspense, to such a ship, so as to be enforceable against it, if and when it is transferred into private ownership.

(ii) Ships which are not the property of a foreign State, but are chartered or requisitioned by it or otherwise in its possession and control,[4] may not be arrested by process of the Admiralty Court while subject to such possession and control, nor will any action lie against the foreign State; . . . but when the governmental possession and control cease to operate and the ship is redelivered

[1] P. 455, *post*.
[2] Pp. 391-2, *post*,
[3] See Oppenheim, *op. cit.*, Vol. I, 8th edn., pp. 856–57.
[4] See *Government of the Republic of Spain* v. *S.S. Arantzazu Mendi*, [1939] A.C. 256.

to her owner, an action *in personam* will lie against him in respect of salvage services rendered to her while in governmental possession and control when he has derived a benefit from those services.

From the case of *The Porto Alexandre* [1]—a case of salvage—it appears that this immunity extends to the freight earned by such ships, and presumably to the cargo itself, if publicly owned. It is, however, not certain whether immunity attaches to all ships owned, chartered or requisitioned by States when engaged in trading, or only to ships so owned, chartered or requisitioned when "dedicated to public uses".

In *Campania Naviera Vascongado* v. *S.S. Cristina* [2] three members of the House of Lords indicated that if and when the question of the general immunity of foreign State property laid down by the Court of Appeal in *The Parlement Belge* (*ante*) and *The Porto Alexandre* (*ante*) came to the House of Lords it would be open to the House to take a more limited view of the scope of the immunity.

A sovereign State's user, direction or control of chattels cannot be the subject of proceedings in the courts here.

In *United States of America* v. *Dollfus Mieg et Cie, S.A.*,[3] an action for conversion of gold bars was stayed by the House of Lords because it violated the immediate right to possession of Governments who were bailors of the gold bars under a contract of bailment with the Bank of England.

But it is not enough for a foreign Government merely to assert a claim to property; the court must be satisfied that conflicting rights have to be decided in relation to that claim before staying the action.

In *Juan Ysmail & Co. Inc.* v. *Indonesian Government* [4] the claim to immunity was rejected on the ground that the title of the Government was manifestly defective.

The plea of immunity may also be raised in relation to a chose in action such as a debt.[5]

Importance of Immunity in respect of Property

The subject of immunity, while part of international law, is of constitutional importance, because the immunities enjoyed constitute a class of persons outside the ordinary law of the land. So long

[1] [1920] P. 30.
[2] [1938] A.C. 485.
[3] [1952] A.C. 582.
[4] [1955] A.C. 72.
[5] *Rahimtoola* v. *Nizam of Hyderabad and Others*, [1958] A.C. 379.

as the immunities were confined to the persons of sovereigns or other rulers and their representatives, they were comparatively unimportant. The same cannot be said of their extension to property. As Scrutton, L.J., said in *The Porto Alexandre* (*ante*):

> No one can shut his eyes . . . to the fact that many States are trading, or are about to trade, with ships belonging to themselves; and if these national ships wander about without liabilities, many trading affairs will become difficult; but it seems to me the remedy is not in these Courts. *The Parlement Belge* excludes remedies in these courts. But there are practical commercial remedies. If ships of the State find themselves on the mud because no one will salve them when the State refuses any legal remedy for salvage, their owners will be apt to change their views. If the owners of cargoes on national ships find that the ship runs away and leaves them to bear all the expenses of salvage, as has been done in this case, there may be found a difficulty in getting cargoes for national ships. These are matters to be dealt with by negotiations between Governments. . . .

The Brussels Convention of 1926 entered into by the United Kingdom and other maritime States embodied the general principle that ships and cargoes operated and owned by States for commercial purposes shall be subject in time of peace to ordinary maritime law. The convention has not yet been ratified by the United Kingdom or by the United States, both of whom still allow jurisdictional immunities to State-owned ships engaged in trade. Its ratification would involve legislation.

C. Treaties

Terminology [1]

No one but the Queen can conclude a treaty. The term, treaty, is used somewhat loosely of all international engagements in written form, but it must be remembered that such engagements are as capable of classification as documents in municipal law. Thus, just as it would be incorrect to describe the effects of a simple contract in writing and a conveyance as identical, so a commercial agreement with another State differs from a treaty of cession or from a law-making treaty. A more exact terminology of international agreements confines the term, treaty, to the more solemn agreements, such as treaties of peace, alliance, neutrality and arbitration. The term, convention, is used of multilateral law-making treaties, *e.g.* the Hague Conventions or the treaties concluded under the auspices of the League of Nations, such as the Slavery Convention 1926. Agreements declaratory of international law are sometimes styled

[1] See Lord McNair, *The Law of Treaties*, Part I, Chap. 1 (1961), Clarendon Press.

declarations, *e.g.* the Declaration of London 1909. A protocol denotes a treaty amending or supplemental to another treaty. The term, pact, has been made familiar by the Peace (Kellogg-Briand) Pact of Paris, 1928.

Constitutional Requirements

At first sight the treaty-making power appears to conflict with the constitutional principle that the Queen by prerogative cannot alter the law of the land, but the provisions of a treaty duly ratified do not by virtue of the treaty alone have the force of municipal law. The assent of Parliament must be obtained and the necessary legislation passed before a court of law can enforce the treaty, should it conflict with the existing law. Many treaties, however, such as treaties of guarantee, have nothing to do with the municipal law. In practice it must be remembered that treaties are concluded on the advice of Ministers, who will normally be in a position to command a majority in Parliament. Once a treaty has been made, Parliament can neither change nor reject it without in effect passing a vote of censure on the Government that made it. There is then no difficulty in obtaining from Parliament any consequential amendment of the law which the treaty may involve. International obligations in the nature of multilateral Conventions, intended to apply as municipal law, will normally be enacted by an Act of Parliament incorporating them. At the least Parliament will refrain from legislation which would conflict with such international obligations which are binding on the United Kingdom. Treaties involving the cession of territory were at one time thought to be exempt from this necessity of obtaining implementation by Parliament, just as are declarations of war. But nowadays treaties of cession are either made conditional on confirmation by Parliament (Anglo-Italian (East African Territories) Act 1925), or are subsequently submitted to Parliament for express approval (Anglo-Venezuelan Treaty (Island of Patos) Act 1942). It is easy to see that such treaties may sometimes involve an alteration in the substantive rights of subjects, particularly those who live in the ceded territory, in respect of their nationality. Moreover the assumption of part of the national debt appropriate to the ceded territory will normally involve a charge on the public funds of the State to which the territory is ceded, and this, in the case of the United Kingdom, requires parliamentary sanction. Treaties affecting belligerent rights are excepted from this requirement, as waging war comes under the prerogative. Thus the Hague Conventions which modify the rights of the Crown when engaged in maritime warfare and also the law administered in British Prize Courts, are recognised by the courts without legislation.

The question—When do British treaties involve legislation?—may be answered by the following summary: [1]

(1) Treaties which, for their execution and application in the United Kingdom, require some addition to, or alteration of, the existing law.[2] Thus a treaty which purported to confer immunity upon privately owned foreign merchant ships may deprive a British subject of his remedy and so constitute an alteration of his legal rights which can only be made enforceable by statute. The Geneva Conventions Act 1957 is a good example of the necessity for legislation to implement treaty provisions since it became necessary under the treaty obligation to create new offences and to provide for legal representation of persons brought up for trial for these new offences. The Queen will not be advised to ratify such treaties unless and until such legislation has been passed, or Parliament has given the necessary assurance that it will be passed. A treaty imposing upon the United Kingdom a liability to pay money, either directly or contingently, usually falls within this category, because, as a rule, money cannot be raised or expended without legislation.

(2) Treaties requiring for their application in the United Kingdom that new powers which it does not already possess shall be given to the Crown. Extradition treaties are in this category. Without statutory authority arrest by the Crown of a person accused of the commission of a crime in a foreign State with a view to his surrender can be challenged successfully by writ of habeas corpus.

(3) It is the practice, and probably by now may be regarded as a binding constitutional convention, that treaties involving the cession of territory require the approval of Parliament given by a statute.

Formalities of Treaty-making

The first step in negotiation of a treaty is the issue of a document known as a Full Power to one or more representatives, *e.g.* the Foreign Secretary, another Minister of the Crown or an Ambassador or other diplomat. The negotiating States submit their respective

[1] McNair, *op. cit.*, Part I, Chap. 3.

[2] This principle was declared in *The Parlement Belge* (1879), 4 P.D. 129, though on appeal the case was decided on a different ground. In *Walker* v. *Baird*, p. 267, *ante*, it was argued by the Crown that the Crown could interfere with private rights in order to compel its subjects to obey the provisions of a treaty having for its object the preservation of peace. The point was not decided.

Full Powers for verification. On the conclusion of the treaty the representatives, styled plenipotentiaries, sign and seal the formal document. The final stage is ratification, which means the sealing of the instrument of ratification by the Sovereign and the exchange or deposit of the treaty at an agreed place. Ratification is a requirement which normally depends upon express provision being made in the treaty; it is an act of the Executive in exercise of the royal prerogative and is not a parliamentary process. There is no general rule of international law that a treaty needs formal ratification, but it is not the practice of the United Kingdom Government to enter into a treaty unless they mean to ratify it in due course. Treaties requiring ratification by the Crown are usually laid before Parliament for twenty-one days before the instrument of ratification is submitted to the Sovereign,[1] but there is no legal requirement that the consent of Parliament is required before a treaty is either made or ratified by the Sovereign. A treaty *prima facie* operates from the date when it enters into force and this date, in the absence of contrary provision, is the date when the formalities of ratification have been completed. In the case of inter-governmental agreements, as distinct from treaties made between heads of States, ratification is not in practice required. Such agreements operate from the completion of exchange of deposit of signed copies.[2]

D. Declarations by the Executive relating to Foreign Affairs

There are certain matters, chiefly relating to foreign affairs, where the declaration of the Government is treated as a conclusive statement binding upon the courts. Such declarations may be described as acts of State. They relate to matters which it falls to the Crown to determine:

(*a*) Recognition of States or Governments.[3]
(*b*) Status of foreign States or Governments.[4]
(*c*) The question whether a person is entitled to diplomatic status.[5]
(*d*) The existence of a state of war.[6]
(*e*) The extent of British territory.[7]

[1] The so-called Ponsonby Rule which dates the practice from 1924.
[2] McNair, *op. cit.*, Part I, Chaps. 7 and 11.
[3] *A. M. Luther* v. *J. Sagor & Co., Ltd.* [1921] 3 K.B. 532.
[4] *The Dora*, [1919] P. 105; *Duff Development Co.* v. *Government of Kelantan*, [1924] A.C. 797.
[5] *Engelke* v. *Musmann*, [1928] A.C. 433.
[6] *Janson* v. *Driefontein Consolidated Mines*, [1902] A.C. 484; *The King* v. *Bottrill, ex parte Kuechenmeister*, [1947] K.B. 41.
[7] *The Fagernes*, [1927] P. 311.

Recognition

The question of the recognition or status of a foreign State is one for public international law, but the fact of recognition may have an important bearing on the result of litigation in English courts.[1] Once the court has decided that the law of a foreign State is to be applied in accordance with the English rules of private international law, recognition of that State determines what foreign law (the current law of the State so recognised) is to be applied.

In *Duff Development Co.* v. *Government of Kelantan* (*ante*), the House of Lords reaffirmed that it had

> for some time been the practice of the courts to take judicial notice of the sovereignty of a State and for that purpose (in any case of uncertainty) to seek information from a Secretary of State; and when such information is so obtained, the court does not permit it to be questioned by the parties.

For most purposes it is immaterial whether recognition is *de facto*, *i.e.* provisional and therefore liable to be withdrawn, or *de jure*. Legislative and other internal acts of a State which is recognised *de facto* are treated by the courts of the United Kingdom on the same footing as those of a State which has been recognised *de jure*.[2]

> In *Krajina* v. *Tass Agency*[3] it was held by the Court of Appeal that the certificate of the Soviet ambassador stating that the press agency was a department of the Soviet Government entitled the agency to assert the immunity normally attaching under international law to a department of a foreign State, *semble* even if the agency has a separate legal entity. Accordingly a writ for libel was set aside.

The sequel of this decision was the appointment of a departmental committee to inquire into the state of immunities under English law and to make recommendations having regard to the wide functions of a modern State. Since this country expects and usually receives reciprocity in the matter of State immunity, the questions of policy raised by the enquiry had wide repercussions.[4]

> In *A. M. Luther* v. *J. Sagor & Co., Ltd.* (*ante*), the recognition of the Soviet Government as a *de facto* government caused the Court of Appeal to find for the defendants, although it was expressly stated that the decision of the lower court in favour of the plaintiff was correct because at the time that it was given the Soviet Government

[1] Oppenheim, *International Law*, *op. cit.*, Vol. I, pp. 124–52, for the subject of Recognition of States as International Persons.

[2] But *cf. Haile Selassie* v. *Cable and Wireless Ltd.* (No. 2), [1939] Ch. 182—no entitlement by State succession in case of *de facto* rule by occupation of territory by another State.

[3] [1949] 2 All E.R. 274.

[4] The Report (Cmd. 8460, 1951) was, however, limited to diplomatic immunity.

had not been recognised by the British Government. The title of the defendants depended upon a confiscatory act by the Soviet Government in Russia operating on property then within Russian jurisdiction. Once the Soviet Government had been recognised, the validity of its decrees could not be impugned unless they were held to violate public policy, as understood in English law. Effect would be given to its legislative and executive acts retroactively as well as for the future; it would not be given unconditionally, *e.g.* if its meaning were called in question in evidence.[1]

Diplomatic Status

A statement made at the invitation of the court by the Attorney-General on the instruction of the Foreign Secretary as to the status of a person claiming immunity from process in the civil courts by reason of diplomatic privilege will be accepted as conclusive.[2] Such immunity is enjoyed by virtue of local municipal law which adopts the rules of international law, and it is for the court to determine whether such immunity shall be enjoyed by the person claiming it. But the fact of a person holding a position which would entitle him to diplomatic immunity is peculiarly within the knowledge of the Foreign Office, and the statement of that fact by or on behalf of the department is regarded by the courts as conclusive. There is no attempt in this case by the Foreign Office to interfere in the litigation; it merely furnishes a record of what had been done by virtue of prerogative powers in recognising the diplomatic status of one of the parties, apart altogether from the litigation in question.

Existence of War

By law the right to declare war and similarly to declare the return of peace belongs to the Crown as part of its prerogative. A declaration by the Executive, acting on behalf of the Crown, is conclusive to determine whether or not war exists,[3] and accordingly whether or not an alien is an "enemy alien." As we have seen,[4] any person who voluntarily resides or conducts business in any enemy State or enemy occupied territory is treated in law as an "enemy alien." Thus the recognition by the Crown of the existence of a state of war between the United Kingdom and a foreign power may by itself impose upon British residents in that country the disabilities attaching to enemy aliens.

[1] See *Bank of Ethiopia* v. *National Bank of Egypt and Liguori*, [1937] Ch. 513 and p. 53, *ante*, note 4.

[2] See *Engelke* v. *Musmann* (*ante*).

[3] *Janson* v. *Driefontein Mines* (*ante*); *The Hoop* (1799), 1 C. Rob. 196, *per* Lord Stowell, at p. 199.

[4] P. 259, *ante*.

Extent of British Territory

It is for the court to determine the extent of its territorial jurisdiction. But the court is bound to accept, through the Attorney-General, a statement made by a Minister as to whether the Crown claims that a place is within the limits of Her Majesty's jurisdiction.

In an action arising from a collision at sea in which one of the ships involved was Italian, the Court of Appeal accepted such a statement to the effect that the place where the collision had occurred was outside territorial waters over which the Crown claimed jurisdiction. This collision occurred in the Bristol Channel at a spot more than three miles from the nearest land; *The Fagernes*.[1]

Reprisals

More complicated is the acceptance by the courts of declarations by the Executive in regard to reprisals in time of war. By international law every belligerent must establish a prize court to determine claims in regard to captured ships and aircraft. Prize courts may be established by authority from the Queen or the Admiralty. In the United Kingdom the jurisdiction is by statute vested in the Admiralty Division of the High Court in London; in the past they have been set up in colonial territory on the authority of the Prize Courts Act 1894, and elsewhere on that of the Prize Act 1939, but in view of the attainment of independence by the colonial territories it is unlikely that this jurisdiction will again be exercised. Within the United Kingdom, as elsewhere, a prize court administers international law. A British prize court is bound by an Act of Parliament, but not by an Order in Council purporting to enlarge the rights of the Crown, though it will apply an Order in Council modifying those rights.[2] The Crown may by Order in Council recite facts showing that a case exists for reprisals (additional restrictions over and above those normally sanctioned by international law). A prize court will accept as conclusive the facts recited and will give due weight to an Order in Council as showing what in the opinion of the Executive is the only means of meeting an emergency, but this will not preclude the right of any party to contend, or the right of the court to hold that the reprisals taken are unlawful as entailing on neutrals an unreasonable degree of inconvenience.[3]

[1] [1927] P. 311.

[2] *The Zamora*, [1916] 2 A.C. 77. *Cf.* the right of the Crown to grant a licence to trade with the enemy: *The Hoop* (*ante*).

[3] *The Zamora* (*ante*).

CHAPTER TWENTY-ONE

PUBLIC BOARDS, INCLUDING NATIONALISED AGENCIES[1]

No account of the present-day machinery of government would be complete without some general consideration of

(1) the many statutory authorities with executive and regulatory functions of government which for various reasons are not directly under the control of a Minister answerable to Parliament for their administration;

(2) the public corporations which have been created since 1945 for the main public utility services (except water) and for the coal and iron and steel industries.

History

Independent organs of government have a long history. In the eighteenth century, when central control had been weakened through the curtailment of the powers of the Privy Council in the preceding century, there were innumerable bodies of commissioners created by statute, as often as not by private Acts, which enjoyed limited but autonomous powers for such purposes as police, education, paving, lighting and improvements of various kinds. They indulged freely in experiments and developments which were sometimes extra-legal in the sense that they lacked authorisation by Parliament. They were free from any effective administrative control by the Central Government; and the cumbersome control which could have been exercised through the courts by the prerogative writs was seldom invoked. These bodies were essentially local in character. It was not until after the Reform Act 1832 that there emerged a few notable experiments in autonomous administration covering the whole country. With the passing of the Reform Act ministerial responsibility, as it is understood to-day, began to take shape. Yet two years later, as a result of the Report of the Poor Law Commission, there was set up one of the most striking experiments in the administrative field without such responsibility. The Poor Law Commissioners, the Three Kings of Somerset House, enforced upon

[1] For this subject see *Nationalised Industries and Public Ownership*, W. A. Robson (George Allen & Unwin).

the local administration of poor law relief strict central control by means of orders and an inspectorate. No Minister answered for them in Parliament. This is not the place to discuss the history of this short-lived experiment, nor that of other examples taken from the nineteenth century, such as the General Board of Health or the Railway Commissioners. Non-departmental Boards formerly found favour in Scotland, and in greater variety in Ireland before 1920. In the early years of the present century the Insurance Commissions and the Road Board afford examples of this type of organisation in the United Kingdom. It is noticeable that the fate of most such bodies has in the past been that their functions eventually have been transferred to a government department.

Reasons for recent Developments

The years between the wars saw great activity in this field of governmental machinery, and since 1945 the public corporation has emerged as the chosen instrument for the public control of certain basic industries and public utilities. The constitutional consequences of entrusting functions to bodies which are not directly responsible to Parliament require examination, but in a field which is still experimental it is important to avoid dogmatic conclusions, as the changing pattern of these corporations shows. So far as it is possible to generalise, recent developments may be said to be due to several motives: (1) the decision to follow a policy of nationalising a basic industry; (2) the desire to keep a public service, and particularly one which is concerned with the administration of State benefits, as far removed from political influence as possible; (3) the recognition that civil service methods are not suitable for the conduct of an enterprise on a commercial basis. The independent authority is a compromise designed to avoid political fluctuations on the one hand and the rigours of bureaucratic control on the other. There are, however, some further reasons why experiments have been made in this field. Thus concentration, especially at high level, on a particular activity is easier to achieve in the case of an independent board concerned with the administration of a single functional activity than it can be in a government department dealing with several functions. Decisions at the top can be more quickly taken and are less liable to be changed by subsequent political fluctuations. Again, the device is a convenient means of securing uniform administration in a field which within the departmental machine is the responsibility of different Ministers in each part of the kingdom, as is the case with agriculture. A board too may be the means of preventing the overloading of the departmental organisation or, in the alternative, the increase in the already formidable number of departments and with it the number of ministerial posts to be filled by Members of Parliament. Fuller use may be made of expert knowledge in a particular field if the responsibility is concentrated in a small body of persons experienced in that field who are not under ministerial direction, at all events as regards day-to-day administration.

The Problem of Ministerial Control

But, whatever the motives for their creation or the advantages which may accrue in administrative convenience and efficiency, it is necessary for the constitutional lawyer to watch the growth of these experiments in relation to their cumulative effect on ministerial responsibility for national policy. There is little doubt that these agencies have their part to play in modern government, provided that each operates in a clearly defined field. But should they encroach upon matters of national policy which ought to be determined by Ministers directly responsible to Parliament? If the answer is No—and our tradition suggests that answer—then it is important to retain some form of direct control by Ministers over the policy-making activities of these agencies. This does not mean that for every act of day-to-day administration the Minister should be responsible, but that a general power of direction should be retained and that the board should not be irresponsible in the realms of policy and finance.

Considerations of Responsibility

Some considerations have to be taken into account in order to reconcile independent authority with ministerial responsibility, since it is undesirable to lay down rigid rules for the operation of institutions where flexibility and variety are essential if the practical aim for their establishment is to be achieved.

1. In general the public interest should be represented by a Minister who is responsible to Parliament for broad policy.

2. There should be as little interference as possible by the Minister with day-to-day administration.

3. The Minister should be required to approve general schemes and regulations and should have power to issue general directions on policy.

4. Where a board is financed from public funds, financial control is required in the form of approving capital expenditure and annual estimates. Even where a board is not dependent on public funds, such control is desirable, if its operations are conducted without

responsibility to the general public at whose cost as consumers charges are borne.

5. To compensate for the measure of independence from day-to-day ministerial control, appointments to boards and commissions, which are normally made by the Minister, should include persons of high standing who can exercise a detached and impartial judgment. They should not normally be confined to persons expert in the special work of the independent authority.

6. Mutual confidence between the Minister ultimately responsible and the members of the authority is required. This can be attained by staggering vacancies at fixed intervals, thus ensuring continuity of association between the authority and the Minister and his department.

7. There should be a means of resolving deadlocks between the Minister and the authority. Perhaps this can only be attained through a power of dismissal, though its exercise by the Minister save in the last resort would destroy the independence of the authority.

Types of Independent Authorities

This is not the place to attempt any classification of independent agencies. It may, however, help to an appreciation of the constitutional problem if some examples are given of the kind of function which has been entrusted to such bodies.[1]

In the first place there are a number of authorities which administer purely governmental services and make discretionary payment out of public funds, such as the former War Damage Commission which exercised a wide discretion with regard to payments out of public funds to owners of buildings destroyed or damaged by enemy action.

In a comparable category are the authorities, such as the British Council and the Arts Council of Great Britain which receive grants from public funds to expend at their discretion on cultural activities. Arguments which are valid for condemning the use of agencies not responsible to Parliament in a field susceptible of political controversy cannot be readily sustained against their use where questions of taste are paramount. So far as the British Broadcasting Corporation is an organ for entertainment and culture it belongs to this category. Unlike most other public corporations, the British Broadcasting Corporation was incorporated by royal charter which is limited in duration. It operates under licence from the Minister of Posts and

[1] For a full list see J. F. Garner, *Administrative Law*, 2nd edn., pp. 296–306.

Telecommunications, but no Minister is responsible for programmes or other matters of detailed organisation which remain the responsibility of the Corporation. On the other hand, it is a condition, if so requested by a government department, that the Corporation shall at its own expense broadcast any official announcement. Similarly the Minister may require the Corporation to refrain from sending any matter specified by written notice. As regards the external services, the Government may prescribe the languages and times for the transmission of programmes.[1]

Nationalised Industries

It is, however, with the third category of independent boards that the constitutional lawyer is most concerned. The production of coal, the railways and other related transport services, the production and distribution of electricity and gas, the overseas air-transport services and the production and distribution of iron and steel have all since the end of the Second World War been entrusted by Parliament to public corporations. Nor is this list exhaustive. Private ownership has disappeared and each corporation operates as a monopoly without the stimulus of competition (except in the case of air routes served by foreign air lines). The board of directors responsible to the shareholder who looks for financial results has been replaced by responsibility to Parliament, as representing the Exchequer, which contributes the capital and may have to bear the losses on working, and to the consumer public. There is no rigid pattern for the constitution of these corporations, but in all the Acts which have created these authorities there are to be found provisions which recognise that it is in the long run only through a Minister of the Crown that responsibility to Parliament can be adequately enforced.[2] The pattern which has emerged so far is that a Minister has the power to appoint and in certain conditions to dismiss members of the corporation itself; after consulting the corporation he can give general directions when the national interest so requires; his approval and that of the Treasury is required for financing capital expenditure; reorganisation schemes require his consent. But with day-to-day administration, including the appointment and dismissal of the higher executive officials, he is not concerned. Most of the corporations function through regional organisations and the very size of their undertakings demands some measure of decentralisation. The National Coal Board, the first of the nationalised corporations, retained both by law and by administrative practice a greater

[1] *Licence and Agreement*, Cmnd. 4095 (1969).
[2] *E.g.* Coal Industry Nationalisation Act 1946, ss. 2, 3, 4, 15, 26, 28, 42, 55, 59.

measure of central control than has been found expedient in the case of the corporations set up later. Centralised control makes ministerial direction easier; it may, on the other hand, clog the machine and increase the inevitably high costs of administration. Hence the tendency has been to increase the powers of the regional units at the expense of the central body. For example the Area Gas Boards are left relatively free from control by the Central Gas Council, whose members are, apart from the chairman and vice-chairman, all chairmen of the Area Boards, but in this case appointments to the Area Boards are made by the Minister.

Relationship to Parliament

The conduct of the independent corporations is entrusted to boards or commissions which are for many purposes autonomous. For example, they have complete powers to recruit their own staffs; they are responsible for operating their service or industry so as to balance income and expenditure, though not necessarily from year to year; and they are entirely responsible for the administration in their particular sphere of activity. There is no element of popular election. The boards and commissions are appointed by the Minister of the Crown whose functions are closest to those of the independent body, *e.g.* the Minister of Transport appoints members of the British Rail Board for terms of office laid down by statute and subject only to very general qualifications in the persons to be appointed. He has no power whatever over the staff who are engaged by a board, and accordingly the status of employees is not that of Crown servants and differs only from that of the employees of a large industrial undertaking, such as an oil or chemical company, in that the board is usually a monopoly undertaking and its staff may thus have no alternative employment of the same character in the event of dismissal.

There remains, however, the problem of responsibility of a board to Parliament. This arises because nationalisation, so-called, involves the transfer of ownership from shareholder to State, and in the absence of departmental administration of the newly acquired property, the State can only exert its authority through its elected representatives in Parliament. Here it is necessary to distinguish between the statutory functions of a board and those responsibilities which have been placed by the constituent Act fairly and squarely on the shoulders of a Minister. The earlier creations emphasised the centralisation of power in the board. Later creations inclined more and more to decentralisation in structure and function. It is clear that the more centralised the control the easier is ministerial direction.

General Directions

There is at all events sufficient responsibility placed upon Ministers to ensure that their knowledge of the working of a nationalised industry which is placed under their general direction is extensive. This means that there must be a certain duplication of staff in board and ministry alike. There is little evidence that powers of general direction have in fact been used. This is a matter upon which a Minister may be questioned in the House of Commons, and it is unlikely to escape attention in the annual reports which by statute must be presented to Parliament by each board. It is for the relevant Minister to take charge of any resulting proceedings such as a motion to take note of the contents of an annual report. One instance of the use of the ministerial power of direction attracted considerable criticism. Whether the matter was dealt with technically by way of a general direction or not is perhaps not clear, but in April 1952 the Minister of Transport intervened to stay an application by the then Transport Commission for an increase of fares on the railways. This intervention was justified by the wish of the Government to check the rising cost of living, but it had the effect of preventing the Transport Commission fulfilling its statutory obligation of "making ends meet." If it was the intention of Parliament that a power to give general directions in the national interest should be exercised only for purposes which are not the direct concern of the relevant board, it is difficult to see how the independence for day-to-day administration could long be maintained in face of general directions of this character which could only result in undermining the stability of the concern. Although the ministerial intervention in 1952 has not been the only cause, it contributed at the time to emphasising the insolvency of the railways. A proposal to give the sponsoring Minister power to issue a formal directive upon any specific subject if it is in the national interest so to do has found little favour with the Government.[1]

Minister's Ultimate Responsibility

Even if a Minister refrains from exercising his power to give general directions, the obligation of the board to obey a direction

[1] See Ministerial Control of the Nationalised Industries, Cmnd. 4027 (1969).

would seem to give him a strong bargaining point in any negotiations with a board placed under his supervision by Parliament. Doubtless many awkward situations have been met by compromises between Minister and board which have never been made public. In Parliament Ministers have avoided responsibility for day-to-day administration, but they have only achieved this by passing the enquirer on to the chairman of the relevant board. They have promised sympathetic consideration of questions which raise the general policy of the boards. It seems probable that in the long run a Minister could not avoid accepting responsibility for the general inefficiency of a board as illustrated by a variety of incidents in its day-to-day administration. It must be confessed that the relationship between Parliament and the so-called independent boards and commissions has not yet been satisfactorily settled. To the constitutional lawyer the question is—How can a public authority be controlled by Parliament except through a responsible Minister of the Crown?

Select Parliamentary Committees

From time to time attempts have been made to establish through the medium of a Select Committee a greater measure of parliamentary control. In the session 1954–55 a Committee was set up with terms of reference which included the duty of informing Parliament about the current policy and practice of some of the nationalised industries.[1] There were, however, excluded from the reference matters which had been decided by the Minister or which clearly involved his responsibility to Parliament. Excluded also were matters concerning wages and conditions of employment, matters which fell to be considered through formal statutory machinery and matters of day-to-day administration. In other words, the concern of Parliament was with matters which did not already clearly fall either on the Minister or the industry. The Committee reported in 1955 [2] that the terms of reference left them with insufficient scope, and they were accordingly discharged without rendering a further report. The Government had sought by the establishment of a Sessional Select Committee to set up a tradition of conduct which would result in the Committee being regarded by the nationalised undertakings not as an enemy or critic but as a confidant and a protection against public pressure, as well as a guardian of the public interest. Perhaps this was too much to expect of a body like a Select Committee, which is customarily composed of political opponents whose numerical representation corresponds closely to

[1] H.C. 332 (1952), and H.C. 235 (1953).

[2] H.C. 120 (1955).

that in the House of Commons itself, especially as the Government concerned had been in opposition hostile to the nationalisation legislation.

A further attempt to establish procedure by Select Committee was made at the end of 1956. The new Select Committee was appointed to examine the reports and accounts of the nationalised industries established by statute whose boards are appointed by Ministers and whose income is not wholly or mainly derived from parliamentary grants or Exchequer advances.[1] This step was a recognition that a Select Committee is the only practical means of creating a proper liaison between Parliament and the nationalised industries. Moreover, it was the traditional procedure of the House of Commons, and for it may be claimed the advantage that despite what has just been said about numerical representation Select Committees are in practice relatively free from party bias. Procedure by Select Committee, furthermore, is complementary to the other opportunities which Parliament has for discussion of this subject, such as motions on receipt of an annual report, motions on the adjournment, and questions. A Select Committee should enable continuous and sustained reporting to the House about these industries. The new Select Committee rendered its first report at the end of the first session by reporting on two Scottish Electricity Boards, as being the first to publish their annual reports and accounts after the Committee had been set up. This was followed by a factual investigation into the National Coal Board, which reviewed its policies and achievements as well as its relationship with the Ministry of Power and the Treasury. This latter was the first major enquiry about the workings of a large nationalised industry conducted by a Select Committee. The recommendations included one which would give the Minister of Power a greater financial control over investment. But it is clear from the two reports that the Select Committee was still feeling its way. In this connection it should be noted that, unlike the Public Accounts Committee, the Committee does not have the assistance of the Comptroller and Auditor-General. It may well be that the Committee's work could be made more effective by a special staff to perform functions equivalent to those of that officer.[2]

The first report also contained a memorandum on Treasury powers and the provision of finance for the nationalised industries.[3] The Committee commented on this that the Treasury's main concern is with the level of investment, both because of the national economic

[1] 561 H.C. Deb., cols. 590–656.
[2] H.C. 304 (1957); H.C. 187 (1958).
[3] H.C. 304 (1957), pp. 178–80.

issues involved and because of the fact that public money is at stake. "The review of expenditure planned some years ahead is especially important if there is any question of effecting economies." The Committee summarised the duties of the Treasury in relation to control over borrowing: under the various Acts most of the industry's borrowing is subject to Treasury approval as well as to the consent of the appropriate Minister. If an industry borrows from outside, it normally does so under Treasury guarantee. Investment programmes are reviewed annually, and thus, in conjunction with the appropriate department, the Treasury has an opportunity for influencing the policy of the nationalised board. When, as under the Finance Act 1956, the industries borrow from the Exchequer instead of by stock issues, there is even closer relationship with the Treasury. This report was only concerned with two Scottish Electricity Boards, neither of whom had any complaint to make of Treasury control. It was recognised that if a board was able to find its capital without external borrowing the influence of the Treasury would be diminished. Even so, the appropriate Minister would still have power to issue a general direction which might hamper the initiative of the board.[1]

The Committee's second Report examined the annual report and accounts of the National Coal Board for 1956 and provided more information on the workings of a nationalised industry than had previously been before the House.[2] Moreover, the Committee was able to discuss certain matters arising out of the relationship between the Board and the Minister, *e.g.* with regard to coal prices. A third report is critically informative on this relationship so far as concerns the Minister of Aviation and the two air corporations.[3] These corporations "tacitly allow powers to the Minister which the statutes do not." The report suggests that the many matters over which the Minister exercises his unofficial powers seem to constitute a degree of control far in excess of that contemplated by the statutes under which the air corporations were created. For example, there is no statutory power for the Minister to control orders for new aircraft, by far the largest item in the budget, or the opening of new routes. Yet the Minister's approval is in practice always sought before action is taken under these heads. In the Committee's view the exercise of unofficial powers by a Minister may lead to an undesirable diminution in the authority of a board. The recommendation is that "when a Minister wishes, on grounds of national interest, to override the commercial judgment of a

[1] H.C. 304 (1957), pp. 5–7.
[2] H.C. 187 (1958).
[3] H.C. 213 (1959).

chairman, he should do so by a directive which should be published."[1]

Other reports have followed and now form a valuable source of information.[2]

During the parliamentary session 1967–8 the Select Committee on the Nationalised Industries published two important reports. One recommended the enlargement of its terms of reference to include (*inter alia*) inquiry into the working of the Bank of England. The Government agreed to such an inquiry but restricted its scope to exclude the investigation of confidential government accounts.[3] The other report examined in great depth ministerial control over public corporations; the committee found weakness in the combination of two disparate and possibly conflicting responsibilities and obligations entrusted to ministers responsible for the corporations. The proposal made for a separate Ministry in the nationalised industries to bring together experience and controls throughout the public sector was rejected by the Government.[4] Possibly the enlargement later in the same year (1969) of the powers of the Minister of Technology may in due course achieve the object which the Select Committee had in mind.

Legal Status

To the lawyer other features are of interest. The principal powers and duties of the corporations are expressed by their constituent Acts in terms so general that it is doubtful whether they could be enforced by any legal process. So to a measure of political and financial irresponsibility must be added irresponsibility in law for non-feasance, though there remains the possibility of the courts restraining an *ultra vires* exercise of power.

> In *Tamlin* v. *Hannaford*[5] the Court of Appeal rejected the view that the British Transport Commission was the servant or agent of the Crown, notwithstanding that the Minister of Transport had statutory powers of control over the Commission which were greater than those possessed by any shareholder over a company incorporated under the Companies Act 1948.

It would seem that this decision governs the status of the other public corporations, unless they are expressly made to act by and on

[1] H.C. 213, para. 218.

[2] See article by a former chairman of the Committee in 40 *Public Administration*, pp. 1–15 (1962).

[3] H.C. 298 (1967–8).

[4] H.C. 371 (1967–8); for the reply of the Government, see Cmnd. 4027 (1969).

[5] [1950] 1 K.B. 18; K. & L. 25; *British Broadcasting Corporation* v. *Johns*, [1965] Ch. 32.

behalf of the Crown or are directly placed under the Ministers of the Crown, as in the case of the Regional Hospital Boards which are under the Minister of Health. In *Pfizer Corporation* v. *Minister of Health* [1] it was held that since a Hospital Board acts on behalf of the Minister the use of drugs is a government function under the National Health Service Act 1946 and therefore the Crown could make use of its rights under patent law for importing drugs. The courts have also had to consider, in the context of bequests to medical institutions, what is the meaning in law of the term, nationalisation, postulated as an event divesting gifts made to hospitals as private institutions. But these considerations are not very helpful in determining what special status in law a nationalised corporation has. In *Tamlin* v. *Hannaford* the Court of Appeal was attracted by the analogy of a limited liability company. Although the Court found that the Minister had been given by Parliament powers over the corporation at least as great as those possessed by the principal shareholder in a one-man private company, it held that the Transport Commission was not the agent of the Minister and in the eyes of the law it was its own master and answerable as fully as any other corporation. Thus it would seem that, since public corporations are mainly constituted on lines similar to the Transport Commission and have the same relationship with a Minister, they cannot be treated as enjoying any of the privileges and immunities of the Crown; that their servants are not civil servants; and that their property is not Crown property. Their liabilities at common law and by statute are the same as those of corporations which are not identified with organs of government.[2]

No doubt other questions will have to be answered besides that of the degree of ministerial control. One perhaps should be mentioned here—whether the public interest can be served if in addition to the Civil Service and the local government service there exists a third form of public service, what may be called the public corporation service. This at present, while too diversified to be called a separate service, enjoys greater freedom with regard to recruitment and conditions of service than the two older services.

Regulatory Boards

The fourth and last group is the most diversified. It is concerned with a variety of economic controls of enterprises, the ownership of

[1] [1965] A.C. 512.

[2] Both the Transport Commission and the Central Electricity Authority were successfully prosecuted; in both cases the proceedings were brought against divisional organs (Railway Executive and Yorkshire Electricity Board).

which remains in private hands. Of these the agricultural marketing boards have attracted most attention. These are organisations, of the guild type, set up for the internal regulation of production with a view to saving an industry from financial decline. They have been criticised on account of their price-fixing powers, since the consumer is unrepresented, and by reason of their disciplinary jurisdiction over the producers, whose membership is compulsory. During the war only the Milk Marketing Board remained in active operation after the establishment of the Ministry of Food but several other boards are now in operation. Other bodies are concerned more with planning and reorganisation, though they usually possess additional functions of an executive character. Finally under this heading come a number of licensing, registration and rate-fixing bodies, exercising powers of a quasi-judicial character, such as the Area Traffic Commissioners who license operators of public service vehicles and approve the routes for such vehicles. The Transport Tribunal, which in the railway sphere has replaced the Railway Rates Tribunal, is an expert body presided over by a lawyer, which was until 1968 concerned with fixing charges, a task which is neither wholly administrative nor judicial.

Boards under Ministers

There are many boards which, while separately constituted from the departments to which they are attached, are directly under a Minister of the Crown. The University Grants Committee, the Forestry Commission and the executive bodies of the National Health Service, the Regional Hospital Boards and the Regional Executives for general medical, dental and ophthalmic services are cases in point. All these are specialised agencies of government which for convenience of administration have been severed from the general departmental organisation. Their existence raises no special problem in relation to ministerial responsibility. It is, however, to be noted that the Regional Hospital Boards, and not the Minister, are by the National Health Service Act 1946, s. 13, made responsible for any liabilities, including tortious liability, in the exercise of their statutory functions on behalf of the Minister.

The University Grants Committee deserves special mention. It replaced in 1964 the former University Grants Committee which advised the Chancellor of the Exchequer with regard to the quinquennial grants to the universities. The present body, which consists of a salaried chairman, two vice-chairmen and some twenty other members all experienced in university education or administration, is responsible to the Secretary of State for Education and Science. Its existence is explained by the desire to maintain the independence of the universities notwithstanding that the greater part of their funds are derived from government grants. The Committee is an attempt to preserve independence for educational policy while recognising the part that the State must play in the provision of universities.

PART I: General Constitutional Law

THE JUDICIARY

The Machinery of Justice, 5th edn., by R. M. Jackson (Cambridge University Press).
The Criminal Prosecution in England, by Lord Devlin (Oxford University Press).
History of English Law, especially Vol. I, by Sir W. S. Holdsworth (Methuen), for reference.
Enforcing the Law, by R. M. Jackson (Macmillan).

CHAPTER TWENTY-TWO

THE COURTS

THIS chapter describes briefly the system of courts at the end of 1969. A new system of criminal courts was proposed by the Royal Commission on Assizes and Quarter Sessions which reported in September of that year. The recommendations have been accepted in principle by the Government, but legislation necessary to implement them will not be introduced before the Parliamentary Session 1970–1. A summary of the main proposals is given in the Appendix.[1] There is also under consideration in Parliament during the Session 1969–70 a Bill to create a Family Law Division of the High Court.

A. Criminal Courts

Justices of the Peace

A court of summary criminal jurisdiction consisting of two or more justices sitting in a petty sessional court-house forms a court of petty sessions (a magistrates' court). Magistrates are appointed as justices, *i.e.* members of the commission of the peace for each county of England and Wales and for such of the larger boroughs as have separate commissions. Appointments are made by the Crown on the recommendation of the Lord Chancellor who is advised

[1] Appendix D, p. 740, *post*.

in counties by a committee presided over by the Lord Lieutenant, and in boroughs by a separate advisory committee. Men and women are eligible for appointment. In practice the choice falls upon those who are regarded as the most suitable representatives of a class, a body or an interest; a knowledge of law is not a requirement. The duties are mainly judicial, but certain administrative functions survive as a residue of the "maid of all work" duties which county justices and, to a lesser extent, borough justices, performed before the days of modern elected local authorities; licensing the sale of liquor is the best known.

A course of training is now an obligation which has to be undertaken on appointment. Magistrates are not paid for their services, but they must undertake to attend at least eighteen court sessions annually; certain allowances may be claimed. The age of retirement is seventy.

In a few of the larger provincial towns stipendiary magistrates with legal qualifications are appointed at a salary on the recommendation of the Lord Chancellor after petition by the borough council. A stipendiary may sit alone and has the powers exercisable by two or more justices. In Inner London there are up to forty stipendiary metropolitan magistrates. Each is the sole judge in his court and has wider powers than a court of lay magistrates. Under a recent reorganisation lay magistrates have been appointed to share the petty sessional work of the London courts; they exercise the wider powers of a metropolitan stipendiary (subject to certain exceptions), provided that two or more hear the case.

Juvenile and Domestic Courts

Every bench of magistrates has a juvenile panel. At present the members are elected from among themselves by all the justices of the bench (*i.e.* the jurisdictional division of the commission). Special instruction in the law and procedure relating to children and young persons must be undertaken on appointment. The Lord Chancellor is empowered by the Children and Young Persons Act 1969 to provide for appointments to the panels and to make different provision for different areas. Sittings of a juvenile court are at different times from those of the ordinary courts (petty sessions) and preferably should be held in a different room.

The Act of 1969 introduced radical changes in the treatment of juveniles, some of which are to be brought into force by stages. The main theme of the legislation is that care and protection of the child take precedence over proceedings on a charge of an offence against the criminal law. When the Act is fully implemented, no charge will be brought against a child under the age of 14 (except for homicide). In the age group 14–17 the consent of an authorised person, *i.e.* police officer, Crown servant, children's officer of a local authority, is required; the authorised person is required to act on criteria to be laid down by the Home Secretary. Proceedings are restricted to cases where the child is in need of care and protection. Various forms of treatment are prescribed, but institutional custody must be in community homes. Approved schools and detention centres for juveniles are abolished.

Summary domestic proceedings for matrimonial causes (other than divorce), guardianship and affiliation orders are heard before a court of not more than three justices, one of whom should be a woman, and are separated from other business. As with juvenile courts the general public are excluded.

Justices' Clerks

Since the middle of the nineteenth century every bench of magistrates has had the assistance of a salaried clerk in the transaction of its judicial and administrative functions. The clerk advises the magistrates, since the vast majority of them are on appointment unacquainted with the law or legal procedure, on matters of court practice and points of law. He may not, however, himself adjudicate and therefore the magistrates must make up their own minds as to the guilt or innocence of an accused person rather than seek the advice of the clerk on that issue. Indeed the High Court, after a series of decisions which were critical of undue consultation of their clerk by magistrates, issued a directive in 1953 which limits consultation with the clerk to matters of law.[1] The clerk, who is nowadays normally a solicitor and in whole time employment, is appointed by the Magistrates' Courts Committee for the county or borough which has a separate commission of the peace. This Committee since 1953 has been given the responsibility for the administrative details of magistrates' courts as well as arranging for instruction to be given to newly appointed justices.

Summary Jurisdiction

Innumerable minor offences are tried by magistrates exercising summary jurisdiction in county and borough Petty Sessional Courts. A large number of indictable offences (such as thefts and other

[1] See *Practice Directions* issued by the Lord Chief Justice [1953] 2 All E.R. 1306.

offences under the Theft Act 1968), can also be tried summarily on the application of the prosecution, should the accused desire it and the magistrates consider it expedient. Conversely, where an offence triable summarily is punishable with more than three months' imprisonment, the accused may elect to be tried by a jury. The penalties which can be imposed by Petty Sessional Courts are imprisonment, normally with a maximum of six months, in which case a sentence must be suspended by the Court for a period of up to three years, unless the offender is charged with assault or threat of violence or illegal possession of weapons or indecent conduct with a child under sixteen or has already served a term of imprisonment or borstal training.[1] A first offender may not, however, be sentenced to imprisonment unless the court is of opinion that no other method of dealing with him is appropriate. The other methods include fine, placing on probation for not more than three years, a compensation order in the case of theft or damage to property, committal to a detention centre if between the ages of 17 and 21. In addition a conviction may be registered with an absolute or conditional discharge subject to the payment of costs. A person convicted summarily of an indictable offence may be committed in custody to Quarter Sessions if the magistrates are of opinion that greater punishment than they have power to inflict should be inflicted. A court of summary jurisdiction has no power to impose a period of Borstal treatment on an offender but may make recommendation in the case of young offenders between the ages of 15 and 21 for such a sentence to be passed by Quarter Sessions.

Preliminary Examination

Petty Sessional Courts also conduct preliminary inquiries into indictable offences to determine whether or not an accused person should be committed for trial.[2] The result of this is that every criminal prosecution is opened in a magistrates' court. Notwithstanding this it is important to realise that the preliminary inquiry is not a trial but simply an inquiry to determine whether the accused should or should not stand his trial on the facts disclosed by the prosecution. A coroner's court, which conducts inquiries (inquests) into the cause of violent or unnatural death or where the cause of death is unknown, may commit for trial on a charge of homicide.[3]

[1] Criminal Justice Act 1967, s. 39.
[2] A single justice may commit for trial: the procedure is described in Chap. 37.
[3] P. 355, *post*.

Appeals from Magistrates

From the justices sitting in Petty Sessions an appeal against a conviction lies to the justices of the whole county sitting in Quarter Sessions, or where a borough has its own Court of Quarter Sessions from Borough Petty Sessions to Borough Quarter Sessions sitting with the Recorder as sole judge. Such an appeal is a rehearing of the case. The prohibitive cost to the appellant of such appeals led to the passing of the Summary Jurisdiction (Appeals) Act 1933. This Act provided that in fixing the amount of recognisances to be entered into by appellants account shall be taken of their means and that such recognisances shall merely be conditioned to prosecute the appeal and not to pay costs, and further provided for the granting of legal aid to appellants. Means are also to be taken into account when a party is ordered to pay costs. From Quarter Sessions a further appeal lies on a point of law by means of a case stated at the request of the defendant or the prosecution for the opinion of the Queen's Bench Division of the High Court, or a case may be stated by the justices in Petty Sessions without any preliminary appeal to Quarter Sessions. Such appeals are heard by a Divisional Court of three judges of the Queen's Bench Division.

Suggested Reforms

The value of associating laymen with the administration of justice and the resulting economy to the State is obvious. The system, which was upheld by a large majority of the members of the Royal Commission which reported in 1948, is not without its critics.[1] Many benches of magistrates are efficient and fair, but there may be too great a readiness to accept police evidence, and to rely upon guidance from the professionally qualified clerk. Lay magistrates are perhaps too aware of local prejudices and personalities. It is true that the majority of persons elect to be tried summarily rather than to await trial at Quarter Sessions by a jury, but this can be attributed to the natural desire to avoid delay. Since the Justices of the Peace Act 1949 the practice has been developed of the appointment of whole-time clerks serving areas formed by grouping county divisions and the smaller boroughs into areas that can conveniently be served by a whole-time clerk.[2] The substitution of paid stipendiary magistrates for unpaid justices was rejected by the Royal Commission. It would involve great expense, in addition to losing the value

[1] Cmd. 7463 (1948).
[2] *Report of the Departmental Committee on Justices' Clerks*, 1944, Cmd. 6507 recommended this practice.

of the association of laymen with the administration of criminal law.[1]

Criminal Courts: Quarter Sessions

Charges for offences other than summary offences are triable on indictment (formal written accusation). Indictable crimes are tried with a jury at Quarter Sessions or Assizes or at the Central Criminal Court. Summary offences carrying a penalty of imprisonment for over three months may be similarly tried by a jury on the election of the defendant. Quarter Sessions has criminal jurisdiction over indictable offences, but certain offences are excluded, *i.e.* treason, murder, offences, other than burglary, which can be punished with life imprisonment and certain other offences which are of considerable gravity or likely to involve difficult questions of law, *e.g.* bigamy. Conversely, as has been seen some of the less serious indictable crimes may be tried summarily.[2] Quarter Sessions may transmit to Assizes any case which it considers should more properly be tried at Assizes owing to the gravity of the charge or the difficulty of the point of law involved.

The Chairman of a County Quarter Sessions must have special legal qualifications as defined in the Administration of Justice (Miscellaneous Provisions) Act 1938 (as amended by the Criminal Justice Administration Act 1962) which enlarged the jurisdiction of these courts provided that legally qualified chairmen or deputies preside. In practice most deputy chairmen also possess these special legal qualifications. Quarter Sessions are required to sit at least four times a year; they have power to adjourn at discretion or may be directed to do so by the Lord Chancellor. This requirement is intended to ensure that accused persons should be kept in custody for a minimum period before trial.

The Quarter Sessions of those boroughs which have their own Courts of Quarter Sessions are presided over by a Recorder, a practising barrister, as sole judge.[3] The Recorder is appointed by the Crown and is paid out of borough funds a salary prescribed by the Crown.

For Greater London there are five courts of Quarter Sessions, each with a whole-time chairman and one or more whole-time deputy

[1] For criticism of Magistrates' Courts and suggested reforms, see Jackson, *op. cit.*, pp. 178–99, and the Report of the Royal Commission. The Justices of the Peace Acts 1949 and 1968 removed some of the grounds of criticism.

[2] P. 299, *ante*.

[3] P. 360, *post*.

chairmen. For the office of deputy chairman of such a court in the London area a county court judge [1] from a Greater London district may be appointed.

Assizes

Criminal cases committed to Assizes are tried by juries before judges of the Queen's Bench Division travelling the seven circuits into which England and Wales are divided. These Courts of Assize are part of the High Court of Justice. The Judges trying criminal cases on circuit derive their authority from commissions of oyer and terminer and general gaol delivery. The former gives power to try all prisoners against whom an indictment may be preferred; the latter gives power to try all prisoners in gaol or who have been released on bail. These commissions are sometimes issued to Queen's Counsel and other Special Commissioners who are not judges of the High Court. Assizes are normally held three times a year in each county and in a few large towns which have their own Assizes. [2] In Manchester, Leeds and Liverpool the Assizes are held four times a year. At the Winter and Summer Assizes civil business is taken as well as criminal, but except in a few large towns the Autumn Assize is confined to criminal business. Judges taking civil business at Assizes derive their authority from commissions of assize and have the unlimited jurisdiction of the High Court, but the jurisdiction of the Chancery Division is scarcely ever exercised by the Assize Judges. Divorce, but not as a rule Probate or Admiralty, jurisdiction is exercised at Assizes and judges of the Probate, Divorce and Admiralty Division may go on circuit for that purpose.

Central and other Criminal Courts

The Central Criminal Court at the Old Bailey acts as the Court of Assize for criminal business for Greater London, and part of the Home Counties. The judges are the judges of the Queen's Bench Division, one of whom in rotation attends each of the monthly sessions of the Court, the Recorder of London, the Common Serjeant, the judges of the City of London Court and the judges authorised by Part II of the City of London (Courts) Act 1964. For some sessions as many as eight courts are required and for this purpose Commissioners are appointed as judges on the recommendation of the Lord Chancellor. In 1956 Crown Courts were created at Liverpool and Manchester and the Recorders of those cities became

[1] P. 306, *post*.
[2] The Administration of Justice Act 1970 confers a power on the Lord Chancellor to direct that Assizes be not held in certain towns where the business is small.

whole-time Judges of the Crown Courts. All but the most serious crimes are within the jurisdiction of these courts, only cases of exceptional gravity being reserved for the Assize Judges, as at the Old Bailey.[1] The Central Criminal Court has jurisdiction to try and determine indictable offences committed within Greater London. Sessions of the Central Criminal Court are held at least four times in every year and in practice the Court sits for eleven months of the year.

Criminal Jurisdiction of Queen's Bench Division

Certain offences of a special nature, *e.g.* crimes committed abroad by public officials, are tried in the Queen's Bench Division, unless the High Court (acting through the Queen's Bench Division) directs trial at the Central Criminal Court. Where owing to local prejudice it is impossible to secure a fair trial, the Queen's Bench Division may direct that a case be tried either at the Central Criminal Court or some other court of Assize or Quarter Sessions than the court which would otherwise have jurisdiction. The Queen's Bench Division may by order of certiorari [2] quash for an error of law the proceedings of Quarter Sessions or any inferior tribunal. Cases of grave importance are sometimes removed into the Queen's Bench Division in order to secure a trial at bar before three judges, as when Sir Roger Casement was tried for treason in 1916.[3] A trial may be ordered before three judges of the Queen's Bench Division sitting at the Central Criminal Court instead of a trial at bar.[4] The original, as opposed to the supervisory, jurisdiction of the Queen's Bench Divison, is rarely exercised; under the latter cases may be stated by a magistrates' court at the instance of the prosecution or the defence on a point of law.

Preliminary Inquiries; Grand and Petty Juries

With the exception of offences tried summarily at Petty Sessions criminal cases are tried by a jury unless the accused pleads guilty to the charge.[5] Such juries are known as petty juries and consist of twelve householders. Criminal proceedings in respect of indictable crimes (other than the considerable number of less serious indictable offences which can be tried on the application of the prosecution and by consent of the accused at Petty Sessions) begin with a preliminary

[1] Criminal Justice Administration Act 1956.

[2] Chap. 45.

[3] *The King* v. *Casement*, [1917] 1 K.B. 98.

[4] But William Joyce, the notorious traitor of the Second World War, was tried by a single judge in the Central Criminal Court.

[5] See Jackson, *op. cit.*, pp. 302-18, for a critical account of the jury system, and p. 480, *post*.

inquiry by magistrates, before whom an information is laid either by the police or a private prosecutor. It is as has been seen[1] the duty of the magistrates holding the preliminary inquiry to decide whether or not there is a case to go to trial and to decide whether to commit the accused to Assizes or Quarter Sessions where both have jurisdiction. Magistrates may not commit to Assizes a case triable at Quarter Sessions, unless they are of opinion that the case is unusually grave or difficult or that serious delay or inconvenience would result from committal to Quarter Sessions. There is also power to avoid delay by committal to the Assizes or Quarter Sessions of an adjoining county. Until 1933 committal for trial by a magistrate was followed by the presentation of a bill of indictment to a grand jury of not more than twenty-three nor less than twelve "good and loyal men" of the county—in practice justices of the peace and others of standing—selected by the Sheriff. The grand jury dated from the presentment of accused persons initiated by the Assizes of Clarendon (1166) and Northampton (1176). If the grand jury considered that there was a prima facie case to answer, they found a true bill and an indictment was presented to the petty (or trial) jury. Though regarded by some as a valuable constitutional safeguard, it was considered as an unnecessary waste of time and money that the careful investigation before magistrates should be followed by a further and necessarily less thorough inquiry by a grand jury. Grand juries were abolished in 1933. An indictment may now be presented to a petty jury either (*a*) where the prisoner has been committed for trial by a magistrate, or in the case of a murder or manslaughter by a coroner's court,[2] or (*b*) where a direction or consent of a judge of the High Court has been obtained, or (*c*) by order of the judge of any court in which the prisoner is suspected to have committed perjury.

Criminal Appeals

From both Quarter Sessions and Assizes an appeal lies against conviction or sentence for an indictable offence, but not against acquittal, to the Court of Appeal (Criminal Division). This Court has since 1966 taken the place of the Court of Criminal Appeal which was set up by the Criminal Appeal Act 1907[3] and consisted of the Lord Chief Justice and the puisne judges of the Queen's Bench Division. There was some criticism of the composition of the court, which usually sat with three judges, all of whom in their turn presided

[1] P. 300, *ante*.
[2] P. 355, *post*.
[3] The Criminal Appeal Act 1968 consolidates the statute law on this subject.

over criminal trials at Assizes and in some cases as chairmen of Quarter Sessions. Continuity of personnel in the court was thus not easy to achieve and only one judge of appellate rank (the Lord Chief Justice) was eligible to sit. The present arrangement ensures that two or three courts can be constituted with more constant membership. Those eligible are the Lord Chief Justice, the Lords Justice of Appeal (who up to 1966 had no criminal jurisdiction) and puisne judges of the Queen's Bench Division who sit at the request of the Lord Chief Justice and thus ensure current familiarity with criminal trials (in practice one puisne judge always sits). Appeal lies as of right on a question of law and by leave of the court, or of the trial judge, on a mixed question of law and fact or against sentence. Unlike its predecessor, the court has no power to increase sentences, which run from conviction, unless the court gives its reasons for ordering otherwise, *e.g.* that a sentence runs from dismissal of the appeal. There is a power in the court to admit evidence which has been excluded at the trial by force of circumstances, *e.g.* matters arising subsequent to the trial which could not reasonably have been given in evidence such as a later confession by another. An appeal may be allowed on the ground that the verdict was unsafe or unsatisfactory. A new trial may be ordered but solely on the ground of fresh evidence being available and the court being of opinion that a re-trial is required in the interest of justice.

An appeal lies to the House of Lords from the Court of Appeal with leave which may only be given if the court or the House of Lords considers that a point of law of general importance is involved.

B. Civil Courts

County Courts

County Courts, the chief lower courts for the trial of civil disputes, are presided over by judges appointed by the Queen on the advice of the Lord Chancellor. England and Wales are divided into fifty-four circuits; the maximum number of county court judges is ninety-seven.[1] The judge usually sits alone, but when fraud is alleged, the defendant may apply for trial by a jury of eight which may also be had for the trial of certain classes of action remitted from the High Court, *e.g* defamation. The qualification for appointment is at least seven years' standing as a barrister. An appeal lies to the Court of Appeal. County Court judges retire at seventy-two, with an extension to seventy-five at the discretion of the Lord Chancellor. County Court

[1] Administration of Justice Acts 1964, s. 5, and 1968, s. 1. County Court judges for a London district may also be appointed as deputy chairmen of one of the five London Quarter Sessions areas.

jurisdiction is local and limited. In general, only those cases can be tried in the County Court in which the amount involved does not exceed £750, but there are some exceptions to this rule. Where cases are brought in the High Court which could have been brought in the County Court, there are provisions penalising the plaintiff in costs.[1] Since 1968 the jurisdiction of designated County Courts has included undefended divorce petitions hitherto within the jurisdiction of the High Court only.

City of London Courts

The Court of Aldermen [2] appoints the Recorder of London who acts as a judge of both the Central Criminal Court and the Mayor's and City of London Court. The appointment of the Recorder must be approved by the Crown before he can exercise his judicial functions. The Mayor's and City of London Court is the County Court for the City. It is an amalgamation of two courts, the Mayor's Court with a jurisdiction unlimited as to amount and the City of London Court, a court for small cases. There sit as judges, in addition to the Recorder, the Common Serjeant and two judges of the City of London Court, one of whom is also a judge of the Central Criminal Court. Appeals lie to the Court of Appeal.

Borough Courts

Certain boroughs have ancient courts which exercise civil jurisdiction. Their jurisdiction is sometimes larger in regard to amount than that of the County Court. The most important are the Liverpool Court of Passage, the Salford Hundred Court and Bristol Tolzey Court. Appeals from these courts lie to the Court of Appeal.

Superior Civil Courts before 1875

Civil cases outside the jurisdiction of the County Courts are tried in the High Court of Justice, including the Assize Courts. There were, before 1875, several superior courts, each with its own special province, though between the three Common Law Courts there was much overlapping. The Common Law Courts were the Court of King's Bench, originally concerned with offences against the King's peace, the Court of Common Pleas for the trial of cases between subjects and the Court of Exchequer for the trial of matters touching the revenues of the Crown. Both the Court of King's Bench and the Court of Exchequer had invaded the original province of the Court of Common Pleas. There were also the Court of Chancery, exercising the equitable jurisdiction of the Chancellor, the Admiralty

[1] For account of County Court jurisdiction, see Jackson, *op. cit.*, pp. 29-36.
[2] Chap. 25, D.

Court, the Court of Probate and the Court of Divorce and Matrimonial Causes, and the Chancery Courts of the Counties Palatine of Lancaster and Durham. The Court of Appeal from the three Common Law Courts was the Court of Exchequer Chamber.[1] Chancery appeals immediately prior to the Judicature Act went to two Lords Justices in Chancery, sitting with or without the Lord Chancellor.

Judicature Act 1873

By the Judicature Act 1873 (now the Supreme Court of Judicature (Consolidation) Act 1925) all these courts (except the two Palatine Courts) and the Courts of Assize were amalgamated into the Supreme Court of Judicature, consisting of the Court of Appeal and the High Court of Justice. The Act was chiefly directed to the reorganisation of court machinery. So far as the substantive law was concerned it marked the fusion of law and equity. The High Court of Justice was divided into five Divisions: Queen's Bench; Common Pleas; Exchequer; Chancery; Probate, Divorce and Admiralty. These Divisions have now been reduced to three: Queen's Bench; Chancery; Probate, Divorce and Admiralty. The jurisdiction of the High Court is unlimited as to amount. Judges of the High Court are appointed by the Crown, on the recommendation of the Lord Chancellor. They must be barristers of at least ten years' standing. The retiring age is seventy-five.[2]

High Court Judges

The maximum number of puisne judges (judges of the High Court other than the Lord Chancellor, Lord Chief Justice and Master of the Rolls) is now seventy.[3] Unless the number falls below twenty-five, the Queen may not be advised to fill a vacancy unless the Lord Chancellor with the concurrence of the Treasury [4] advises that the state of business requires that the vacancy should be filled. A judge of the High Court is attached to such Division as the Lord Chancellor may direct, but not less than seventeen judges must be attached to the

[1] The judges of the two Common Law Courts other than the court from which the appeal came, *e.g.* Queen's Bench appeals came before the judges of the Common Pleas and Exchequer.

[2] The Judicial Pensions Act 1959, s. 2, provides that a Lord of Appeal and a judge of the Supreme Court will in future vacate office on attaining 75. A graduated pension scheme will enable him to retire at 70.

[3] Administration of Justice Act 1968, s. 1, which also gives power to increase the numbers by Order in Couhcil approved by both Houses of Parliament; this power extends to all categories of judges of the superior Court and the County Courts.

[4] The necessity of Treasury concurrence has been criticised as an infringement of the independence of the Judiciary.

Queen's Bench Division, not less than five to the Chancery Division, and not less than three to the Probate, Divorce and Admiralty Division. The Lord Chancellor may with the consent of the judge concerned transfer a judge from one Division to another, but no judge may be transferred from the Queen's Bench Division without the consent of the Lord Chief Justice, who presides over that Division, or from the Probate, Divorce and Admiralty Division without the consent of the President of that Division.

Queen's Bench Division

The Queen's Bench Division is concerned with every class of common law action, in addition to its criminal and appellate jurisdiction and its power to supervise inferior courts and judicial bodies by means of habeas corpus and the prerogative orders which will be discussed later.[1] It exercises the jurisdiction of the three former Common Law Divisions. It acts as the Assizes for London, so far as civil business is concerned, and many cases are tried in London in the Queen's Bench Division which might equally be tried on circuit at Assizes. It is for a Master, an officer of the court who deals with the preliminary stages of an action, or a District Registrar of the High Court who carries out the duties of Masters in certain provincial towns, to decide whether an action shall be tried in London or at Assizes. Cases in which many local witnesses are concerned are best tried in the county in which the dispute arose. Trials take place both before a judge and jury, and before a judge alone. There is a right to a jury in cases involving charges of fraud, unless there is involved a prolonged investigation of accounts or documents or a scientific or local investigation which cannot conveniently be made with a jury, and in cases of libel, slander, malicious prosecution, false imprisonment, seduction or breach of promise of marriage. In all other cases it is for the court in its discretion to decide whether trial shall be by a jury or by a judge alone.[2] A jury trial in civil cases is not nowadays often requested. The history of the jury links it with cases now tried in the Queen's Bench Division. Elsewhere it is sometimes used in contested probate and divorce cases. Even in actions for negligence where juries were formerly favoured, the majority of trials to-day are by a judge alone. In cases tried with a jury matters of law are for a judge, matters of fact are for the jury.[3] Until 1949 juries were either common or special. A special juror had a higher property qualification and either party could apply for a special jury in any civil case where trial by jury was appropriate.

[1] Chaps. 35 and 45.
[2] Administration of Justice (Miscellaneous Provisions) Act 1933, s. 6.
[3] For merits and defects of trial by jury, see Jackson, *op. cit.*, pp. 72–77.

The theory was that a more intelligent verdict could be obtained from a jury with higher qualifications; the objection which has prevailed was that political bias in one direction was more likely to influence such juries. Special juries were abolished by the Juries Act 1949; the term, common jury, has thus become obsolete, but a City of London special jury for the trial of commercial cases in the Queen's Bench Division can still be obtained.[1]

Chancery Division

The old Court of Chancery exercised the equitable jurisdiction of the King's Chancellor, delegated to him by the King in Council. This jurisdiction supplemented the common law by granting new remedies such as injunctions and specific performance and dealing also with matters, *e.g.* trusts, of which the common law courts took no cognisance. Equity, originally an elastic system for meeting hard cases, had developed an important body of law almost as fixed as the common law. As a result of the Judicature Act any judge of the High Court may sit in any Division, and any Division may give any remedies available, whether they are based on the common law or on equity. Each Division, however, has in practice its own particular business, and to the Chancery Division there are specifically assigned those matters formerly dealt with by the courts of equity. They include partnerships, mortgages, trusts, the specific performance of contracts and the administration of the estates of deceased persons. Company business also is administered by the Chancery Division. There are also assigned to this Division the revenue and bankruptcy jurisdictions of the High Court. The Lord Chancellor, who is President of the Supreme Court of Judicature, though still nominally president of this Division, has long ceased to sit. The Chancery Courts of Lancaster and Durham have a jurisdiction over Chancery suits which is limited as to area but unlimited as to amount. An appeal lies from them direct to the Court of Appeal.

Probate, Divorce and Admiralty Division

The business of the Probate, Divorce and Admiralty Division presided over by the President of that Division is apparent from its name. On the Admiralty side it exercises the jurisdiction of the old Court of Admiralty, and is concerned with maritime matters[2] and

[1] Juries Act 1949, ss. 18, 19, 20.

[2] Actions relating to the carriage of goods by sea are usually tried in the Queen's Bench Division in what is known as the Commercial Court, *i.e.* before a judge appointed to try commercial cases. The procedure is simple and speedier than that ordinarily employed in the Queen's Bench Division. A separate Commercial Court within that Division is authorised by the Administration of Justice Act 1970.

particularly collisions at sea.[1] On the probate side it takes the place of the Court of Probate, which in 1857 took over from the ecclesiastical courts the granting of probate of wills and letters of administration. On the divorce side it tries matrimonial causes, as successor to the Court for Divorce and Matrimonial Causes. Divorce jurisdiction in undefended cases has since 1968 also been given to selected local County Courts and all petitions originate there. Until 1857 the ecclesiastical courts could grant decrees of judicial separation, but could not dissolve marriages. The matrimonial business of those courts was transferred in that year to the newly constituted Court for Divorce and Matrimonial Causes, which was also given the new power of decreeing a dissolution of marriage. There is little in common between the three sides of this Division save that both probate and divorce business were originally exercised by the ecclesiastical courts, and that the law administered by all three sides of the Division is more influenced by Roman law than by either common law or equity. The combination of probate and divorce with admiralty is due, not to logic, but expediency. When the new High Court was formed, this Division was the residuary legatee of the old courts. A Divisional Court of two judges of this Division hears appeals from the justices in matrimonial matters under the Matrimonial Proceedings (Magistrates' Courts) Act 1960.[2]

Restrictive Practices Court

For the purpose of the judicial investigation of restrictive trading agreements including retail price maintenance there was established by the Restrictive Trade Practices Act 1956 a new superior court of record styled the Restrictive Practices Court. The Act also creates the office of Registrar of Restrictive Trading Agreements with whom restrictive agreements must be registered and whose duty it is to refer to the court any such agreements which under the Act are deemed to be contrary to the public interest. The Court consists of eight judges and not more than ten lay members, five of the judges being drawn from the High Court, two from the Court of Session, and one from the Supreme Court of Northern Ireland. One of these is the President of the Court. The jurisdiction of the Court is of special note because it is required to presume that a restriction is contrary to the public

[1] For jurisdiction in prize in time of war, see p. 282, *ante*.

[2] A Family Division of the High Court is established by the Administration of Justice Act 1970. Admiralty and Prize jurisdiction is transferred to the Queen's Bench Division for trial by puisne judges nominated for the purpose.

interest unless it is satisfied that one or more of the special circumstances set out in s. 21 of the Act should negative the presumption.[1]

Court of Appeal (Civil Division)

Except where it is limited by statute there is a right of appeal from any Division of the High Court and from the Restrictive Practices Court to the Court of Appeal. The judges of the Court of Appeal are the Lord Chancellor, the Lord Chief Justice, the Master of the Rolls, the President of the Probate, Divorce and Admiralty Division, the Lords of Appeal in Ordinary, if qualified to be Lords Justices,[2] ex-Lords Chancellors (all the above are ex-officio members of the Court), and up to thirteen Lords Justices of Appeal. All these judges are appointed by the Crown on the recommendation of the Prime Minister. There usually sit the Master of the Rolls and the Lords Justices. The Court sits in divisions up to four in number, each usually consisting of three judges. Additional judges may be drawn, when necessary, from the High Court. The Master of the Rolls presides over one division of the Court, a senior Lord Justice over the others, but the Lord Chancellor may appoint a Vice-President of the Court to preside in one division in the absence of an ex-officio member. The qualification of a member of the Court of Appeal is fifteen years' standing as a barrister or a judgeship of the High Court. Ordinary judges of the Court of Appeal may be required to sit as judges of the High Court.

House of Lords

From the Court of Appeal an appeal by leave of the Court or of the House of Lords lies to the House of Lords, the supreme tribunal of England and Wales, Scotland and Northern Ireland, in which is vested the ancient jurisdiction of the High Court of Parliament. The High Court may grant on the application of any party a certificate for appeal direct to the House of Lords on a point of law of general public importance relating to the construction of a statute or statutory instrument if it has been fully argued and considered in the judgment of the trial judge. Similarly when the trial judge is bound by a decision of either higher court, he may grant the certificate. Besides its normal appellate jurisdiction the House of Lords formerly had an active jurisdiction in criminal cases, as a court of first instance. It tried those impeached by the House of Commons and peers

[1] The Resale Prices Act 1964 increased the jurisdiction of the Court and added to its members and see Restrictive Trade Practices Act 1968.

[2] This excludes Scottish Lords of Appeal.

accused of treason or felony or misprision of either; the privilege of peers, which could not be waived by the accused, to be tried by their fellow peers was abolished in 1948. The sittings of the House of Lords for judicial business are ordinary sittings of the House, but in practice since *O'Connell's Case* [1] it has been a conventional rule that no lay peer shall take part in the exercise of appellate jurisdiction. In 1948 the House by motion authorised the hearing of appeals by the Appellate Committee. Although intended as a temporary measure, the Appellate Committee has continued in being. This expedient was devised when it became necessary to conduct judicial business away from the actual Chamber because building operations rendered the sittings inaudible. It has, however, resulted in changing the ancient practice which prevented the conduct of judicial business while the Chamber was being used for sittings of the House as a deliberative assembly. The Committee reports back to the House and thus enables judgment to be delivered by members of the Appellate Committee in the full Chamber. In that the practice might prevent the Lord Chancellor from presiding over the Committee when his presence was required on the Woolsack, this breach with tradition was regarded by some as an undesirable innovation. The judgments since 1963 are not delivered orally but handed down in print. Since 1966 the House has been less rigid in following its own decisions as binding precedents, particularly where a change of conditions seemed to justify a departure from precedent. This change of practice was made by the House of Lords sitting judicially; formerly the House was bound by its own decisions. It is arguable that the alteration required an Act of Parliament, but no such legislation has so far been mooted. The Law Lords are the Lord Chancellor, the eleven Lords of Appeal in Ordinary who are appointed by the Crown on the recommendation of the Prime Minister,[2] ex-Lord Chancellors and other peers who hold or have held high judicial office in a Superior Court in the United Kingdom or in the Judicial Committtee of the Privy Council.[3] The Lords of Appeal receive salaries and are under an obligation to sit; the other Lords serve voluntarily. A Lord of Appeal must have held high judicial office for two years or have been a practising barrister (or advocate in Scotland) of fifteen years' standing. The retiring age is 75. There is a convention, but no more than a convention, that ex-Lord Chancellors in receipt of pensions should serve when requested to do so by the Lord

[1] *O'Connell* v. *The Queen* (1844). 11 Cl. & Fin. 155.

[2] Appellate Jurisdiction Acts 1876–1947. Unless the number drops to six vacancies can only be filled if the state of business so requires.

[3] *E.g.* who have been Lords of Appeal, Judges of the Supreme Court or of the Court of Session in Scotland.

Chancellor. On the hearing of appeals there must be present three Law Lords. The House usually sits in divisions of five or three. Appeals may be heard when Parliament is prorogued. Before 1876 there were frequently only one or two peers with judicial experience, and the Lords frequently summoned the judges of the High Court[1] to advise them on questions of law, but since the creation in that year of the Lords of Appeal in Ordinary this practice has tended to fall into disuse. The judges were last summoned in a civil case in 1898 and in 1935 on the last occasion of the trial of a peer for felony.

Comparison with Judicial Committee of the Privy Council

It is interesting to compare the procedure of the House of Lords with that of the Judicial Committee of the Privy Council, the final court of appeal from the courts of such of the independent States of the Commonwealth as retain this jurisdiction and from those of the remaining colonial territories.[2] Since 1966 dissenting opinions may be given, as in the House of Lords. Formerly one speech only was delivered, expressing the opinion of the majority of the judges, should there be any difference of opinion. The House of Lords is moved that an appeal be allowed or dismissed and the order made is entered in the Journals of the House. The Judicial Committee humbly advises Her Majesty and the decision is formally embodied in a subsequent Order in Council. The House of Lords was before 1966 bound by its own decisions. The Judicial Committee is in theory and, to a modified degree, in practice free from precedent. In 1929 the Judicial Committee examined the validity of one of their own decisions given two years previously.[3]

Lay Peers and Barristers

A barrister who is a peer may practise before the House of Lords in appeals, when the House is a court in which there sit only peers with judicial qualifications, but he may not appear as counsel to argue before Committees of the House. He was unable to practise before the House when it was trying peers on criminal charges.[4]

Impeachment

The Commons may impeach any person before the Lords for any crime or political misdemeanour. Before the full development of ministerial responsibility impeachment was a useful weapon enabling the Commons to call to account Ministers appointed by and respon-

[1] P. 103, *ante*.

[2] Chap. 33.

[3] *Wigg and Cochrane* v. *Attorney-General of the Irish Free State*, [1927] A.C. 674; *Re Transferred Civil Servants' (Ireland) Compensation*, [1929] A.C. 242.

[4] *In re Lord Kinross*, [1905] A.C. 468.

sible to the Crown. There has, however, been no impeachment since 1805. The Commons now have direct control over Ministers and so do not need to employ the cumbrous weapon of impeachment. By the Act of Settlement 1700 a pardon from the Crown cannot be pleaded in bar of an impeachment, but it is nevertheless open to the Crown to pardon one who has been successfully impeached.

No Civil Jurisdiction in First Instance

It was at one time doubtful whether the House of Lords could try civil cases as a court of first instance. The exercise of such jurisdiction in the case of *Skinner* v. *East India Company*,[1] in the reign of Charles II, led to a prolonged dispute between Lords and Commons. Since that time no attempt has been made to exercise it. About the same time the case of *Shirley* v. *Fagg* [2] established the right of the Lords to hear appeals from the Chancery Court.

The Courts of Scotland: [3] *Civil Courts*

The Sheriff Court, roughly corresponding to the County Court in England, but with a wider jurisdiction which is not subject to any pecuniary limit, is the most important lower civil court in Scotland. The Sheriff, who is a lawyer usually in practice in the Court of Session, acts mainly as an appeal judge, the ordinary work being performed by several Sheriffs-Substitute. There is a further appeal to the Inner House of the Court of Session if the value of the cause exceeds £50. There is also a Justice of the Peace Civil Court for debts up to £5. Justices are appointed on the recommendation of the Secretary of State for Scotland.

Court of Session

The Court of Session has jurisdiction over the whole country. Originally emanating from the King's Council it assumed its present form in 1532 on the establishment of the College of Justice of which its judges, advocates and writers to the Signet are members. The judges are Senators of the College and number nineteen. Five (Lords Ordinary) sit as judges of First Instance (the Outer House). The remainder (Inner House) sit in two divisions presided over by the Lord President and the Lord Justice-Clerk respectively. From the Inner House an appeal lies to the House of Lords.

[1] (1666), 6 St. Tr. 710.
[2] (1675), 6 St. Tr. 1122.
[3] See D. M. Walker, *The Scottish Legal System*, 3rd edn., Chap. 5. (Green).

The High Court of Justiciary

The High Court of Justiciary was established as far back as 1672. It has appellate jurisdiction which dates from the Criminal Appeal (Scotland) Act 1926. As a court of first instance all the senators of the College of Justice, the judges of the court in civil matters, are judges in the Supreme Criminal Court. Unlike the Court of Session, the civil court, which sits only in Edinburgh, the Commissioners of Justiciary travel on circuit to try the graver crimes in the chief towns. Normally one judge sits with a jury. The High Court has exclusive jurisdiction in murder and certain other more serious crimes.

The Justiciary Court also hears appeals from conviction and sentence after trial on indictment, but unlike the Court of Appeal in England there is no further appeal to the House of Lords.

The Sheriff Court (Criminal)

The Sheriff Court has solemn jurisdiction to try serious crimes (other than those reserved for the High Court of Justiciary). The sheriff sits with a jury of fifteen but his powers of punishment are restricted to two years' imprisonment and therefore the Crown may prosecute in the higher court at its discretion.

The Sheriff Court is also a court of summary procedure. As in England a sentence of imprisonment is normally limited by statute to three months. There is an appeal by way of case stated to the High Court of Justiciary in much the same way as an appeal to the Divisional Court of the Queen's Bench in England. If a new statutory offence is created, it is implied that the sheriff will have power to try it rather than the other courts exercising summary jurisdiction.

Justices of the Peace Courts

Justices of the Peace have a much more limited jurisdiction than in England. The Justice of the Peace Courts have jurisdiction in counties; in the burghs there is a Burgh Police Court the judge of which is an elected local government representative. The only stipendiary magistrate are in Glasgow. The powers of punishment of these summary courts are normally limited to 60 days' imprisonment or a fine of £60. An appeal lies to the High Court of Justiciary on questions of law. By the Social Work (Scotland) Act 1968, (c. 49), juvenile courts were abolished and replaced by a system of children's panels for each local authority area.

Procedure for Committal

There is no public investigation by magistrates prior to committal for trial for serious crimes. A suspect after arrest must be brought before a magistrate (usually the sheriff) as soon as possible. Usually there is present at the hearing only the sheriff, the Procurator-Fiscal (the prosecutor), the accused and his law agent. No details of evidence may be published prior to the trial. As a result the examination is now usually a formality but the procedure has the advantage that the accused is brought by the police before a judicial officer at the earliest moment. Thereafter the procedure of committal is not dissimilar from that in England. There is a statutory limit on the period of detention pending trial of 110 days.

Prosecutions in Scotland

Private prosecutions are very rare for common law offences, *e.g.* homicide, theft. Nor can a private person prosecute for such an offence or a statutory offence punishable with imprisonment without the option of a fine except by leave of a public prosecutor, unless there is express statutory provision. Every criminal court has a public prosecutor who is in the High Court and by solemn procedure in the Sheriff Court the Lord Advocate, in the latter court for summary offences a Procurator-Fiscal.

CHAPTER TWENTY-THREE

THE JUDICIAL FUNCTION

The Queen as Judge

THE courts are the Queen's courts; "all jurisdictions of courts are either indirectly or immediately derived from the Crown. Their proceedings are generally in the King's name; they pass under his seal, and are executed by his office," but it is "impossible as well as improper that the King personally should carry into execution this great and extensive trust," [1] and further, as has been seen,[2] the British understanding of the separation of powers demands that the Judiciary should be independent of the Executive. It is enacted that the royal command shall not disturb or delay common justice, and that, although such commands are given, the judges are not therefore to cease to do right in any point.[3] Jurors must be duly empanelled and returned; excessive bail must not be imposed nor cruel and unusual punishments inflicted.[4] The early Kings delivered justice in their own courts. The delegation of this duty to judges was an early and inevitable result of the growth of the business of government and the development of a system of law requiring specialised knowledge. In 1607 James I claimed the right to determine judicially a dispute between the common law courts and the ecclesiastical courts. That the right of the King to administer justice himself no longer existed was decided by all the judges headed by Coke: *Prohibitions del Roy*: [5]

> The King in his own person cannot adjudge any case, either criminal, or treason, felony, etc., or betwixt party and party, concerning his inheritance, chattels or goods, etc., but this ought to be determined and adjudged in some court of justice according to the law and custom of England. God had endowed His Majesty with excellent science and great endowments of nature, but His Majesty was not learned in the laws of his realm of England, and causes which concern the life, or inheritance, or goods or fortunes of his subjects, are not to be decided by natural reason, but by artificial reason and judgment of law, which law is an art which requires long study and

[1] 1 Blackstone, *Commentaries*, Book I, Chap. VII.
[2] Chap. 3.
[3] Statute of Northampton 1328.
[4] Bill of Rights 1688.
[5] (1607), 12 Co. Rep. 63; K. & L. 108.

experience, before that a man can attain to the cognizance of it. The law is the golden met-wand and measure to try the causes of the subjects; and which protected His Majesty in safety and peace.

Of this case Dicey wrote: [1]

Nothing can be more pedantic, nothing more artificial, nothing more unhistorical, than the reasoning by which Coke induced or compelled James to forgo the attempt to withdraw cases from the courts for His Majesty's personal determination. But no achievement of sound argument or stroke of enlightened statesmanship ever established a rule more essential to the very existence of the constitution than the principle enforced by the obstinacy and the fallacies of the great Chief Justice.

The Creation of New Courts

A similar limitation of the prerogative is found in the rule that the Crown can no longer by the prerogative create courts to administer any system of law other than the common law. The common lawyers were the allies of Parliament in the struggle with the Stuarts, and the victory of Parliament meant the disappearance of the prerogative courts of the Star Chamber and the High Commission. Even the Court of Chancery barely escaped the destructive ardour of the Commonwealth. Thus the creation of a court of equity in a settled colony [2] would to-day require statutory authority either of the United Kingdom Parliament or the Colonial Legislature. Similarly no extraordinary tribunals can be established in this country without parliamentary sanction.

In the case of *In re Lord Bishop of Natal*,[3] where the Crown by letters patent had created a new Archbishopric with coercive jurisdiction over bishops and clergy, the Judicial Committee held that the Crown had no power to create a metropolitan see of Cape Town endowed with coercive authority and jurisdiction over a suffragan bishop.

" It is a settled constitutional principle or rule of law, that, although the Crown may by its prerogative establish courts to proceed according to the common law, yet it cannot create any new court to administer any other law."

The Executive and Criminal Proceedings

The vast majority of criminal prosecutions are instituted either by the police, a government department or a local authority, *e.g.* the revenue authorities for customs offences, a borough council for

[1] *Law of the Constitution*, 10th edn. p. 18.

[2] Chap. 31. Section 4 of the British Settlements Act 1887 provides for the conferment of jurisdiction by Order in Council on any court in any British possession in respect of matters arising in any British settlement as therein defined.

[3] (1864), 3 Moo. P.C. (N.S.) 115; K. & L. 113.

breaches of food regulations, but any person may initiate a prosecution whether or not he has been injured by the alleged crime. Certain prosecutions may, however, only be instituted with the consent of the Attorney-General, *e.g.* certain offences against the State, under the Official Secrets Acts or Public Order Act 1936 or offences where great harm might be occasioned by a vexatious charge, *e.g.* offences under the Punishment of Incest Act 1908, or for obscenity in dramatic or musical productions under the Theatres Act 1968.

Director of Public Prosecutions

The Director of Public Prosecutions—a barrister or solicitor—is appointed by the Home Secretary and works under the general supervision of the Attorney-General who makes regulations for the conduct of his office, with the approval of the Home Secretary and the Lord Chancellor. Although the title might suggest otherwise, the office is not that of a general prosecutor as in Scotland. The Director prosecutes in certain types of cases, where he is required by regulations to prosecute, *e.g.* all murder cases and in certain other grave crimes, when so directed by the Attorney-General, and also where it appears to the Director himself that he ought to take over a particular case because of its difficulty. He is required to prosecute for election offences under the Representation of the People Act 1949, Part III of which consolidates the Acts of 1883–95 relating to the prevention of corrupt and illegal election practices.

Political Crimes

The desirability or otherwise of a prosecution is never in ordinary circumstances brought before the Cabinet, but a political offence, such as sedition, may raise political issues, so as to cause the question of a prosecution to be considered by the Cabinet.[1] If the Attorney-General considers that the strict exercise of his duty to prosecute at his individual discretion would be against the public interest, it is his duty to consult the Cabinet.[2] But the responsibility for the decision to prosecute rests with the Attorney-General, free from any pressure by his colleagues. He should absolutely decline to receive orders from the Prime Minister or the Cabinet or any ministerial colleague that he should or should not prosecute. Formerly the Home Secretary could direct a prosecution; it is nowadays recognised that the Home Office is not a prosecuting authority.

[1] Jennings, *Cabinet Government*, pp. 235–7; 177 H.C. Deb. 581–704; 483 H.C. Deb. 683–90.

[2] Sir Patrick Hastings, Attorney-General, 177 H.C. Deb. 599.

Nolle Prosequi

The Attorney-General may at any time stop a criminal prosecution on indictment by the entry of a *nolle prosequi*, but normally when it is decided not to press a prosecution, no evidence is offered and acquittal follows as a matter of course. A *nolle prosequi* is not nowadays used to stop a vexatious prosecution. Its exercise is open to criticism by the Legislature, and any abuse can only be prevented by the ordinary principle of ministerial responsibility.[1] Otherwise a prosecutor can only withdraw a charge by leave of the court. The prosecution, normally the police, may sometimes refrain from bringing a person before the court on the ground that his assistance as an informer has alone made possible proceedings against a person whom the prosecution regards as a major offender.

The Prerogative of Pardon

It is possible to prevent criminal proceedings being brought by the exercise of the royal prerogative of pardon, but in practice this prerogative is only exercised by the Sovereign after conviction and sentence. The exercise of the prerogative is a responsibility of the Home Secretary and is used when there is some special reason why a sentence should not be carried out or why a conviction should be expunged. It is never used to stifle a prosecution at the outset. The Home Secretary acts on his individual responsibility in tendering his advice. Until 1908 English law provided no adequate means of reviewing judicially the judgment of a criminal court,[2] and accordingly the method of rectifying any injustice was by the grant of a pardon. Thus the Minister was forced into the position of a final court of appeal in criminal cases, without possessing any of the ordinary powers of a court of law, such as taking evidence on oath. The Criminal Appeal Act 1907 established the Court of Criminal Appeal—a similar court was established for Scotland in 1928—and thus the Home Secretary and the Secretary of State for Scotland are relieved of responsibilities which it was inconvenient that they should discharge. The prerogative of pardon is essentially an executive act and should not involve judicial issues. By section 7 of the Criminal Appeal Act 1968 the Secretary of State, whether or not there is an application by the convicted person, may (*a*) refer the whole

[1] *The Queen* v. *Allen* (1862), 1 B. & S. 850.

[2] By the Crown Cases Act 1848 the practice of the judges of holding informal meetings from time to time to discuss difficult questions arising at criminal trials was regularised by the institution of the Court for Crown Cases Reserved. This court had power to determine points of law reserved by the trial judge solely at his own discretion.

case to the Court of Appeal, and the case will then be heard and determined by the court, as in the case of an appeal by the person convicted, or (*b*) if he desires the assistance of the court on any point arising in the case, refer that point for their opinion thereon.[1] The prerogative of mercy was exercised on the Home Secretary's recommentation in cases of capital punishment, all of which by long-standing custom were reviewed.

Types of Pardon

Pardons under the prerogative are of three sorts:

(1) A free pardon rescinds both the sentence and the conviction.[2]

(2) A commutation, or conditional pardon, substitutes one form of punishment for another. A capital sentence was normally commuted to imprisonment for life, if the Home Secretary advised an exercise of the prerogative.[3]

(3) Remission reduces the amount of a sentence without changing its character, *e.g.* reduces a sentence of imprisonment from six months to two months, or remits part of a fine.

In addition to the above three modes of pardoning, there is a power to reprieve, *i.e.* respite, sentence. This postpones the carrying out of a sentence, and was largely resorted to in capital cases pending the formal grant of a commutation, or conditional pardon; the Secretary of State can signify the Queen's pleasure in this way by an order under her own hand, whereas the more formal modes, which formerly to have full legal effect had to be passed under the Great Seal, require a warrant under the Royal Sign Manual, countersigned by the Secretary of State.

Limitations on Prerogative of Pardon

The prerogative of pardon closely resembles the dispensing power. It can only be exercised subject to the following limitations:

(1) The offence must be of a public character, and the Crown has no power to remit judgment in suits between subject and subject.

(2) The pardon cannot be used as a licence to commit crimes. It can, however, be pleaded in bar of an indictment, or, after verdict, in arrest of judgment, except that under the Act of Settlement 1700 a pardon may not be pleaded in bar of an impeachment by the Commons in Parliament. Nor can the Queen pardon the unlawful

[1] For an example see *The Queen* v. *Podola*, [1960] 1 Q.B. 325.

[2] For specimen, see App. C, p. 738, *post*.

[3] See P. Brett, *Conditional Pardons and the Commutation of Death Sentences*, 20 M.L.R. 131, G. Marshall, *Parliament and the Prerogative of Mercy*, [1961] Public Law 8.

committal of any man to prison out of the realm.[1] By common law the commission of a public nuisance cannot be pardoned until the nuisance has been abated.

(3) A pardon only relieves from the penalty resulting from criminal proceedings, but not from the conviction, unless a free pardon is granted.

(4) It has been questioned whether there is any power to sanction a general reprieve for convicted persons. This doubt is based on the provision of the Bill of Rights 1688 which declared that the power of dispensing with the execution of laws by royal prerogative as exercised of late is illegal. It is unlikely that this issue will ever come before the courts, but it was on more than one occasion used in argument in Parliament against the granting of reprieves during the discussion of legislation proposing the abolition of the death penalty.

While the sentence is current, no motion will be accepted by the Speaker criticising in the House of Commons the Home Secretary by reason of his refusing to recommend a reprieve or pardon.

Bench and Bar

There are two main distinctions between the English judicial system and that of continental countries. In continental countries judgeship is a career. The young judge starts his career in one of the lowest courts and hopes to advance through judicial office and other posts under the Ministry of Justice to the highest courts. In England judges—both of inferior and superior courts—are appointed from practising members of the Bar. On the other hand the vast majority of justices of the peace who sit in the magistrates' courts are laymen. The judges have a tradition of independence and their affinities are with the Bar rather than the Executive and its servants. They are, too, less concerned with promotion. Few county court judges reach the High Court Bench. Promotion from the High Court to the Court of Appeal involves no increase in salary.

Lord Chancellor

The other main distinction is the absence of a Ministry of Justice. Appointments to the High Court Bench, to county court judgeships, to chairmanships of county quarter sessions, to recorderships of borough quarter sessions [2] and to the magistracy are made on the

[1] Habeas Corpus Act 1679.

[2] The Recorder of the City of London is appointed by the Court of Aldermen, and a few boroughs where Quarter Sessions have no criminal jurisdiction have the right to appoint their own recorder.

recommendation of the Lord Chancellor who has himself always had experience as a practising barrister. The Lord Chancellor is normally a member of the Cabinet, though in the Second World War he did not sit in the War Cabinet. He is also Speaker of the House of Lords,[1] and has the custody of the Great Seal. As the senior member of the judiciary he is entitled to preside over the two highest courts in the realm, the House of Lords and the Judicial Committee of the Privy Council, but the occasions on which two recent holders of the office have taken part in the hearing of appeals have been relatively few. The Lord Chancellor is responsible for the Land Registry and Public Trustee Office. The Public Record Office was placed under his direction by the Public Records Act 1958. There is an Advisory Council on Public Records of which the Master of the Rolls is chairman. Despite its judicial nature the office has remained political in that it is held by an eminent member of the Bench or Bar adhering to the party in office. A previous political career is not an indispensable qualification and four Chancellors have in the present century been appointed from the Bench or Bar without having been members of the House of Commons.[2] The administrative business of the Supreme Court and the appointment of court officials is partly in the hands of the Lord Chancellor and partly of the judges.[3] Rules of the Supreme Court are made by the Rules Committee consisting of the Lord Chancellor and other judges with two practising barristers and two practising solicitors. The secretariat is the Lord Chancellor's department. The Lord Chancellor appoints the County Court Rules Committee and may alter or disallow the rules made by it. He may appoint a similar committee for magistrates' courts. The Lord Chancellor too, as we have seen, appoints and removes lay magistrates. In the Lord Chancellor's Office there are departments for the County Courts and for Justices of the Peace. He may grant separate courts of quarter sessions to boroughs with a population of over 65,000 and upon his recommendation are appointed metropolitan and stipendiary magistrates. In the exercise of judicial patronage the Lord Chancellor acts on his personal responsibility and the doctrine of collective ministerial responsibility does not arise.

In 1958 the Lord Chancellor and the Secretary of State for Scotland appointed a standing Council on Tribunals. This is a statutory body established on the recommendation of the Franks Committee.[4]

[1] P. 123, *ante*.

[2] A full account of this office is given by Lord Schuster, for many years Clerk of the Crown, in 11 C.L.J. 175.

[3] Primarily the Presidents of the various Divisions of the Supreme Court.

[4] Tribunals and Inquiries Act, 1958, ss. 1, 2; pp. 702-3, *post*.

Law Reform Responsibilities

The Lord Chancellor has a general responsibility for law reform in England and Wales; in Scotland this falls to the Secretary of State. The Law Commission Act 1965 established Commissions for England and for Scotland to promote law reform and to keep under review all the law with which each is concerned, with a view to its systematic development, including codification. Members of the Law Commission in England are appointed by the Lord Chancellor for a term not exceeding five years. They must be qualified by holding judicial office (this is retained but release is given from judicial duties) or professional or academic experience of the law. Programmes prepared by the Commission, after approval by the Lord Chancellor, are laid before Parliament. Impressive lists of topics have been under consideration, but pressure on parliamentary time is a perpetual hindrance to the enactment of measures for the reform of civil law (contract, tort and property) which has little political appeal. The Commissions are required to consult with one another.

The Lord Chancellor is also assisted with advice from the Law Reform Committee to which he can refer specific topics of substantive or procedural law and by *ad hoc* committees where specialised qualifications of members can be concentrated.

Judicial duties of the Home Secretary

Other duties performed by a Minister of Justice elsewhere fall to the Home Secretary. The Home Secretary as the Minister responsible for law and order in 1959 appointed a Standing Committee for the Revision of the Criminal Law. This Committee, like the Law Reform Committee, consists of a small number of judges, practising barristers, solicitors and academic lawyers, but, unlike the Law Reform Committee, it is required by its terms of reference to accompany its recommentations by a draft Bill for their implementation. For this purpose a member of the staff of the Parliamentary Counsel to the Treasury works with the Committee. The administrative arrangements for metropolitan courts are under the control of the Home Office and the Home Secretary confirms appointments of clerks to justices which are made by magistrates' courts' committees. Magistrates' courts are independent judicial authorities and in the exercise of their judicial functions are subject to the Queen's Bench Division through the prerogative orders.[1] The Home Office, however,

[1] Chap. 45.

exercises the function of securing uniformity by means of advisory circulars in regard to such topics as the collection of fines, and sometimes containing advice in regard to the interpretation of statutes and regulations. The general administration of magistrates' courts is the responsibility of the Home Secretary. The Home Secretary is responsible for the probation system and the care of juvenile delinquents, and for the administration of prisons and Borstal institutions for the treatment of young offenders. He is also responsible for deciding whether a prisoner who has been certified as insane shall be discharged from the Broadmoor Institution, or other mental hospitals for criminals which are administered by the Ministry of Health. Approved schools to which persons under seventeen may be sent on conviction and remand homes are inspected by the Home Office.

Advocates of a Ministry of Justice argue that the present division of responsibility between the Lord Chancellor and Home Secretary is illogical and results in no one Minister being responsible for reform. On the other hand, to entrust all judicial appointments to a Minister of Justice might lead to obvious evils such as political appointments to the Bench and promotion by seniority rather than appointments based on merit. The current tendency is for the judicial patronage of the Lord Chancellor to be enlarged, *e.g.* by approving panels for chairmanship of administrative tribunals set up by departmental Ministers.[1]

The Judges and the Constitution

The primary function of the Judiciary is to determine disputes either between subjects or between subjects and the State. Judges must apply the law and are bound to follow the decisions of the Legislature as expressed in statutes. In interpreting statutes and applying decided cases they do, however, to a large extent make, as well as apply, law. In countries where there is a written constitution (*e.g.* United States) which cannot be overridden by the ordinary process of legislation, the Judiciary is in a special sense the guardian of the constitution and may declare a statute to be unconstitutional and invalid. In England the chief constitutional function of the Judiciary is to ensure that the administration conforms with the law. The supremacy of the will of the people as expressed by their representatives in Parliament rests upon the rule of law enforced by the courts.

[1] Tribunals and Inquiries Act 1958, s. 2 and 1st Schedule.

Judicial Independence

It is clearly desirable that judges should not only be independent of the Government, but also free from liability to vexatious actions for acts done in the exercise of their duty. It is better that private persons should suffer injuries than that judges should be influenced, to however slight a degree, in the dispensing of justice by fear of the consequences. These considerations apply to the judges of any country, but they apply with still greater force to the judges of a country in which individual rights and constitutional liberties depend upon the decisions of the ordinary courts and are not guaranteed by any formal constitution.

Employment of Judges for Extra-Judicial Purposes

In recent years there has been an increasing tendency to refer to investigation by a judge matters where political controversy has given rise to the need for an impartial opinion. Examples are to be found in the two investigations conducted by Lord Radcliffe in 1960 and 1962 into the working of the Security Services, and inquiries with a view to the resolution of industrial disputes such as the several conducted in the 1950s by the then Master of the Rolls, Lord Evershed. In a different context Lord Devlin, while still a Judge of the Supreme Court, presided over an inquiry into disturbances in Nyasaland (now Malawi).[1] The most controversial of these references to judges was the investigation conducted by Lord Denning at the invitation of the Prime Minister into the security aspects arising out of the resignation of a Minister of the Crown.[2] It is perhaps inevitable that such references should have led to allegations that the Government of the day was using the judiciary for its own ends. There is admittedly some danger lest political discussion should be stifled while an inquiry conducted by a judge is in progress. It is also inevitable that too frequent use of such references should lead to allegations, particularly on the part of the Opposition, that the Government is seeking to avoid its responsibilities by passing them over to the judiciary. It does not follow that an impartial investigation by a judge merits accusations that a Government is interfering with the independence of the judges. More questionable was the invitation in 1968 from the Leader of the Opposition to a judge of the Court of Session in Scotland to take part in an inquiry into possible changes in the constitutional provisions for the future government of

[1] Cmnd. 814 (1959).
[2] Cmnd. 2152 (1963), Lord Denning's Report.

that country. After some public controversy the judge withdraw his acceptance of the invitation which could be construed as breaching the tradition of judicial independence from involvement in political matters. Moreover it would have made available for the purposes of future policy of the Opposition the services of a high ranking whole-time judicial officer, even if he only served on the inquiry in his spare time.

Appointment and Dismissal of Judges

In the exercise of such powers as that of issuing the prerogative writ of habeas corpus [1] or in the trial of actions for false imprisonment and malicious prosecution the judges are in a position to control officers of the Government in the interest of the liberty of the subject. It is essential that they should be free from any fear of dismissal by the persons whom they may be asked by a litigant to control. Judges of the High Court and of the Court of Appeal, with the exception of the Lord Chancellor, are appointed by the Crown to hold their offices during good behaviour, subject to a power of removal by Her Majesty on an address presented to Her Majesty by both Houses of Parliament.[2] A similar provision applies to Lords of Appeal.[3] Judges' salaries are fixed and are charged and paid out of the Consolidated Fund.[4] The salary of the Lord Chancellor is such yearly sum as with the amount payable to him as Speaker of the House of Lords makes up the sum of £14,500 a year; the salary of the Lord Chief Justice is £12,500 a year; of Lords of Appeal, the Master of the Rolls and the President of the Probate, Divorce and Admiralty Division £11,250 a year; of Lords Justices of Appeal and Judges of the High Court £10,000 a year. The salaries of County Court judges and of the Chief Metropolitan Magistrate are £5,775 a year and of Metropolitan Magistrates, £5,300.[5] The Judges of the Crown Courts at Liverpool and Manchester receive £6,250. These salaries are also charged on the Consolidated Fund.

[1] Chap. 35.

[2] Supreme Court of Judicature Act 1925, s. 12. For similar repealed provision of the Act of Settlement, see p. 9, *ante*. Prior to the Act of Settlement judges were from 1625 to 1640 and after 1688 appointed during good behaviour and thus tenure of office was not at the King's pleasure.

[3] Appellate Jurisdiction Act 1876, s. 6. P. 313, *ante*.

[4] Supreme Court of Judicature Act 1925, ss. 13 and 15; Judges' Remuneration Act 1954.

[5] Judges' Remuneration Act 1965. All judicial salaries are pensionable, subject to qualifying periods of service before a maximum pension can be claimed as of right. Judicial Offices (Salaries) Act 1952; Judicial Offices (Salaries and Pensions) Act 1957 and Orders made under s. 1 (4); Judicial Pensions Act 1959. The Judges' Remuneration Act 1965 increased all salaries of Supreme Court Judges.

Procedure for Removal [1]

The Act of Settlement [2] provided that judges' commissions should be made during good behaviour "but upon the address of both Houses of Parliament it may be lawful to remove them". This wording suggests that Parliament intended to provide that, while a judge should hold office during good behaviour, Parliament itself should enjoy an unqualified power of removal. The equivalent provisions of the Supreme Court of Judicature Act 1925, substitute for "but" the words "subject to" a power of removal on an address presented to the Queen. It would seem that there was no intention to alter the effect of the Act of Settlement by this wording and therefore it is theoretically possible for a judge to be dismissed not only for misconduct but for any other reason which may induce both Houses of Parliament to pass the necessary address to the Sovereign. It is, however, extremely unlikely that Parliament will be willing to pass an address from any motive other than to remove from the bench a judge who had been guilty of misconduct. It was formerly the case that offices held during good behaviour could be determined by *scire facias*, criminal information or impeachment.[3] An address to the Crown for the removal of a judge must originate in the House of Commons. The procedure is judicial and the judge is entitled to be heard. There is only one instance of the removal of a judge being carried out by this method since it was introduced by the Act of Settlement, namely a judge in Ireland in 1830.[4] County Court judges may be removed by the Lord Chancellor for inability or misbehaviour. Magistrates may be removed from the commission of the peace by the Lord Chancellor, though in practice a magistrate is not removed unless his conduct becomes scandalous or he has been convicted for a criminal offence of some gravity or for persistent minor offences.

Judicial Salaries

The Act of Settlement provided that the salaries of the judges should be ascertained and established, though this principle was not

[1] For an historical sketch of this subject see Roberts-Wray, *Commonwealth and Colonial Law* (Stevens) at pp. 485–90.

[2] P. 9, *ante*.

[3] The processes of *scire facias* and criminal information were abolished in 1947: Crown Proceedings Act 1947, 1st Sched. but the Crown Office can still issue the writ for the cancellation of Crown grants and franchises; *Attorney General* v. *Colchester Corporation*, [1955] 2 All E.R. 124, at p. 127. For impeachment, see p. 314, *ante*.

[4] In 1924 a motion for the removal of a High Court judge was tabled in the House of Commons, but was subsequently withdrawn before being debated.

fully implemented until the Judicature Acts in the nineteenth century. It is perhaps unsatisfactory that, though an address by both Houses of Parliament is required to secure the removal of a judge, under the provisions of the Parliament Act 1911 the House of Commons alone might reduce a judge's salary by any amount.[1] Under the constitutions of the Commonwealth of Australia and of the Republic of Ireland judges' salaries may not be diminished during tenure of office.

Scotland

Judges of the Court of Session are appointed by the Crown and cannot be removed except on grounds of misconduct (*ad vitam aut culpam*).[2] There is no statutory provision for the removal of judges of the Court of Session, but sheriffs, sheriffs-substitute and stipendiary magistrates may be removed by the Secretary of State for Scotland on a report by the Lord President and the Lord Justice-Clerk. The retiring age is seventy five.

Judicial Immunity from Civil Actions [3]

It is a general proposition of the common law that no action will lie against a judge for any acts done or words spoken in his judicial capacity in a court of justice. "It is essential in all courts that the judges who are appointed to administer the law should be permitted to administer it under the protection of the law independently and freely, without favour and without fear. This provision of the law is not for the protection or benefit of a malicious or corrupt judge, but for the benefit of the public, whose interest it is that the judges shall be at liberty to exercise their functions with independence and without fear of consequences." [4] It can be argued from the authorities that the judge of a court of record is not liable for anything done or said in the exercise of his judicial functions, even if he exceeds his jurisdiction.

Scope of Immunity

In the case of acts done within the jurisdiction the immunity exists, however malicious, corrupt or oppressive be the acts or words complained of.[5] Immunity does not attach to a ministerial, as

[1] Judges' salaries were included in salary reductions effected by Order in Council made under the National Economy Act 1931; see Sir William Holdsworth in 48 L.Q.R. 25; E. C. S. Wade in *Law Times*, 2 and 9 April, 1932, and reply by Sir William Holdsworth, *Law Times*, 7 May, 1932.

[2] Claim of Right, 1689.

[3] For full discussion of this subject see D. Thompson, *Judicial Immunity and the Protection of Justices*, 21 M.L.R. 517.

[4] *Scott* v. *Stansfield* (1868), L.R. 3 Ex. 220, *per* Kelly, C.B., at p. 223.

[5] *Anderson* v. *Gorrie*, [1895] 1 Q.B. 668.

opposed to a judicial, act. Thus an action lies for a wrongful refusal to hear a case, but not for a wrong decision.[1] Moreover a judge is not liable where he exceeds his jurisdiction owing to a mistake of fact, unless he ought to have known the facts ousting his jurisdiction.[2] A similar immunity to that of judges attaches to the verdicts of juries,[3] and to words spoken by parties, counsel and witnesses in the course of judicial proceedings.

Inferior Courts

The same immunity exists in the case of inferior courts, *e.g.* county courts and magistrates' courts.

> In *Law* v. *Llewellyn*[4] the prosecutor on counsel's advice withdrew a summary charge of obtaining money by false pretences. The presiding magistrate, after the court had been informed that the charge was withdrawn, told the plaintiff that it was the opinion of the magistrates that the charge had been a gross attempt to blackmail and that it would have been well if the matter had come before the Public Prosecutor. "From what we have heard of this man" (the prosecutor) "he has been in the habit of trying to extort money from persons by illegal means and if he found himself in gaol for twelve months it would possibly do him a good deal of good." It was held that no action lies against a justice of the peace in respect of defamatory words spoken by him when exercising judicial functions or, in view of this case, while still in the court-room.

At common law a magistrate acting without jurisdiction was liable in trespass for all wrongful acts done pursuant to his order. When a magistrate was acting erroneously, although within his jurisdiction, no action lay against him unless malice was alleged and proved. But a magistrate who acted outside his jurisdiction had no protection. If he committed a tort, he could be sued. The Justices Protection Act 1848, s. 2, made it unnecessary for a plaintiff who sued in tort to allege that the act complained of was done maliciously and without reasonable or just cause; this requirement which was unnecessary at common law where liability was in trespass was required in cases of malicious prosecution. There is a proviso that no action will lie unless the conviction or order has first been set aside on appeal.[5] When a justice is sued in respect of his performance of administrative duties, it is necessary to prove that he acted

[1] *Ferguson* v. *Earl of Kinnoull* (1842), 9 Cl. & F. 251; K. & L. 425.
[2] *Calder* v. *Halkett* (1839), 3 Moo. P.C. 28.
[3] *Bushell's Case* (1670), 6 St. Tr. 999.
[4] [1906] 1 K.B. 487.
[5] *O'Connor* v. *Isaacs*, [1956] 2 Q.B. 288. See D. Thompson, *Judicial Immunity and Protection of Justices*, 21 M.L.R. 517 and L. A. Sheridan, *Protection of Justices*, 14 M.L.R. 267.

maliciously and without reasonable or probable cause.[1] The Crown Proceedings Act 1947, s. 2 (5), absolves the Crown from liability for the acts of any person discharging judicial duties or executing judicial process. The Administration of Justice Act 1964, ss. 26 and 27, provide for the indemnification out of public funds of justices and their clerks, recorders and clerks of the peace in respect of damages or costs payable in proceedings arising from acts done in the course of their duties. The absolute protection given to members of courts acting within their jurisdiction attaches also to the parties, their counsel and witnesses; it extends to members of tribunals which have the attributes of a court, *e.g.* a court-martial. Where a tribunal does not have the attributes of a court, its decisions and words spoken in the course of its proceedings are privileged only in the absence of malice, even though it is under a duty to act judicially, *e.g.* London County Council when sitting to grant music licences.[2]

Scotland

In Scotland a magistrate or justice of the peace will be liable in damages for acting without or in excess of jurisdiction provided that the conviction has been quashed and malice and want of reasonable and probable cause established.[3] The action must be brought within two months of the proceedings complained of.

Criminal Liability of Judges

The criminal law punishes corruption, neglect of duty or misconduct in the execution of judicial duties. The overriding importance of the protection of the liberty of the subject is shown by the fact that a High Court judge who unlawfully refuses to issue a writ of habeas corpus during vacation is liable to a fine of £500 to be paid to the person detained.

The Law Officers' Department

All government departments either have departmental solicitors or use the services of the Treasury Solicitor. The Home, and the Foreign, and Commonwealth Offices have legal advisers. The Law Officers of the Crown, the Attorney-General and Solicitor-General, represent the Crown in courts of justice, and act as legal advisers to the Government on more important matters. Both the Law Officers

[1] Justices Protection Act 1848, s. 1; *Everett* v. *Griffiths*, [1921] 1 A.C. 631, at p. 666. This Act probably does not apply to county justices in Quarter Sessions.

[2] *Royal Aquarium and Summer and Winter Garden Society Ltd.* v. *Parkinson*, [1892] 1 Q.B. 431.

[3] Summary Jurisdiction (Scotland) Act 1954, s. 75.

are invariably members of the House of Commons. They are assisted by Junior Counsel to the Treasury who are practising barristers and hold no political office. As representing the Crown, the Attorney-General and Solicitor-General take part in many judicial or quasi-judicial proceedings relating to the public interest, such as proceedings relating to the administration of charities and income tax. The appointments are political and are conferred on successful barristers who are supporters of the party in power. The Attorney-General has sometimes been a member of the Cabinet, but in view of his duties in connection with prosecutions [1] it is generally regarded as preferable that he should remain outside the Cabinet as the Government's chief legal adviser. In addition to the salaries of their offices the Law Officers formerly drew substantial sums in fees for Crown litigation, though private practice was prohibited. But the salaries are now fixed at £13,000 for the Attorney-General and £9,000 for the Solititor-General with no fees. Advancement to judicial or political office is more or less assured to the holders of either appointment, but the supposed claim of the Attorney-General to appointment as Lord Chief Justice would seem to have little foundation. Only twice since 1875 has the Attorney-General been appointed directly to the latter office. The Attorney-General is the head of the English Bar. The Dean of the Faculty of Advocates is head of the Scots Bar. The Lord Advocate and the Solicitor-General for Scotland are the Law Officers for Scotland. It has not always been possible to fill these offices from the ranks of sitting members of the House of Commons.

It is an established constitutional rule that the advice given to the Crown by the Law Officers must not be quoted. A Minister can be required to disclose to Parliament that he has consulted the Law Officers but he must accept responsibility without seeking to rely on their opinion.

Certain duties, *e.g.* consent to certain types of prosecutions, such as offences under the Official Secrets Acts 1911–1939, are by statute imposed upon the Attorney-General or the Lord Advocate. In the event of absence or illness or with special authority these duties may be carried out by the Solicitor-General or Solicitor-General for Scotland respectively.[2]

The Treasury Solicitor

The Department of the Treasury Solicitor is responsible for the legal work of those departments which have neither legal advisers nor

[1] P. 320, *ante*.

[2] Law Officers Act 1944.

solicitors to the department on their staff. In other cases it undertakes litigation only, leaving the other legal work to the department's own legal adviser. Generally speaking when a department becomes responsible for administering a statutory code, such as the National Insurance Acts 1946, it sets up its own legal department. The Department of the Treasury Solicitor is not a centralised legal advisers' office, but one which is responsible for a large residue of the legal work of government. The Treasury Solicitor holds office as Procurator-General and Treasury Solicitor. As Queen's Proctor he may intervene in divorce proceedings to prevent abuse of the processes of the court.

Legal Aid—Civil

The Legal Aid and Advice Act 1949 made provision for the financial assistance of litigants who cannot afford to bring their causes of action to the courts on account of the high cost of litigation. The purpose of the Act was to sustain the principle first set out in Magna Carta that justice should be denied to none. At first the aid was only made available in High Court actions with certain exceptions, notably for defamation. It was extended to the County Courts in 1956 and later to the provision of legal advice apart from litigation, actual or prospective. There are proposals for further extensions to proceedings before certain administrative tribunals and public inquiries.

Applications for legal aid are considered by local committees on which solicitors and barristers sit. Inflation has to some extent defeated the purpose of the system since legal aid is dependent on a means test which calls for frequent revision. The Legal Aid Act 1960, while preserving the requirement of contribution from applicants on an income scale, was intended to ease the pressure on modest incomes.

Alternative methods of assisting litigants have been canvassed, such as the inclusion of legal aid among the provisions covered by national insurance and the setting up of legal advice centres to cope with the vast area of legal problems where litigation is not likely to result. At present such advice is only obtainable from voluntary organisations, such as citizens' advice bureaux.

Legal Aid—Criminal

Legal aid for the defence in criminal cases was formerly given under the Poor Prisoners' Defence Act 1930. Despite some amendments in the Legal Aid and Advice Act 1949 the system did not follow the lines of aid in civil cases in that application had to be made to a court, normally a magistrates' court, and no contribution towards the cost of the defence to public funds was recoverable. By Part V of the Criminal Justice Act 1967 the system was retained, since it is considered to be impracticable, largely on account of the time factor, to refer applications for defence aid to an outside committee, but a court in making an order must consider what contribution towards the cost must be borne by the accused. For trivial offences an application will not usually be granted, nor where there is a plea of guilty in a straightforward case. In all other cases financial calculations have to be applied in order to determine the extent, if any, to which the accused shall make a contribution towards the costs.

For an indictable offence a defence certificate which entitles to free legal aid may be granted either by the committing justices or the judge of the trial court; in magistrates' courts for summary offences a certificate may be granted on the grounds of insufficient means if it is considered desirable to do so in the interests of justice.

Legal Aid—Scotland

Legal aid in civil proceedings in Scotland is governed by separate legislation, the principal Act being the Legal Aid and Solicitors (Scotland) Act 1949. In criminal proceedings the present statutory scheme derives from the Criminal Justice (Scotland) Act 1963.

Note.—No attempt has been made to give more than an outline of the judicial organisation. For a full account together with criticisms and suggestions for reform the student should read R. M. Jackson *The Machinery of Justice*, 5th edn. (Cambridge University Press) and, as regards magistrates' courts the *Report of the Royal Commission on Justices of the Peace*, 1946–48 (Cmd. 7463, 1948).

LOCAL GOVERNMENT

Principles of Local Government Law, by Sir Ivor Jennings, 4th edn., by J. A. G. Griffith (University of London Press).
An Introduction to the Law of Local Government and Administration, 8th edn., by W. O. Hart (Butterworth).
The Machinery of Local Government, 2nd edn., by R. M. Jackson (Macmillan).
The Development of Local Government, 3rd edn., by W. A. Robson (Allen & Unwin).
Principles of Local Government Law, 3rd edn., by C. A. Cross (Sweet & Maxwell).
The Ministry of Housing and Local Government, by Evelyn Sharp (Allen & Unwin).
Central Departments and Local Authorities, by J. A. G. Griffith (Allen & Unwin).

CHAPTER TWENTY-FOUR

GENERAL FEATURES

A. Development of Local Government

It is doubtful whether even the oldest of our central organs of government can be traced back to an earlier time than the reign of William the Conqueror, but the origin of our present counties and parishes can be found in the shires and hundreds, vills or townships of pre-Norman days. The achievement of the Norman and Plantagenet kings was to superimpose a strong system of central government upon existing local institutions. Modern times have caused the structure of local authorities to be completely recast, but the development of local government has always been influenced by strong local feelings inherited from previous days.[1]

Early Middle Ages

In the early Middle Ages each county or shire had its court or governmental assembly, presided over by the sheriff as the royal representative and composed of the freemen of the county. The county court performed general governmental as well as judicial functions. Within the county were hundred courts similarly composed and under the supervision of the sheriff. The manorial courts

[1] For the history of Local Government, see Hart, *op. cit.*, Part I, Chap. I.

of the feudal system were the courts of the smaller units, the vill and the township. Boroughs which obtained charters from the Crown possessed varying degrees of autonomy. The justices in eyre, royal judges with wide powers both administrative and judicial, controlled the local courts by means of periodic visitations. From the time of Henry II onwards royal justice began to cover the whole country through the circuits of justices of assize and general gaol-delivery. The local and manorial courts were superseded and with them the office of sheriff lost much of its former importance.

Justices of the Peace

From the fourteenth century the newly created justices of the peace acquired administrative as well as police powers. The parish, an ecclesiastical unit, also became the unit of local administration, just as in earlier times the feudal manor had given an organisation to the vills or townships. It was the parish which was liable for the repair of roads and later for the administration of the Elizabethan poor law. Justices exercised control over the parish and its officers. The justices themselves were controlled by the King's Council and the Court of Star Chamber, but this influence disappeared when the Long Parliament in 1640 curtailed the powers of the former body and abolished the latter.

Eighteenth Century

No attempt was made after the Revolution Settlement in 1689 to reimpose central administrative control. Outside the boroughs, where the borough corporations acting under their charter powers were virtually uncontrolled, general local administration was in the hands of the county justices sitting in Quarter Sessions. A measure of judicial control existed in the prerogative writs of mandamus, certiorari and prohibition issued from the Court of King's Bench.[1] With the older forms of local government becoming increasingly ill-equipped to deal with changing social conditions, this century saw the extensive development of the *ad hoc* authority—a separate body for a particular service as opposed to the general administrative authorities, the justices. By means of local Acts in particular, Parliament sanctioned the creation of many *ad hoc* authorities for different purposes, *e.g.* turnpike trustees or urban improvement commissioners.

Era of Reform

With the Report of the Royal Commission on the Poor Law in

[1] Chap. 45.

1834 there opened an era of local government reform. By the Poor Law Amendment Act 1834 there were established new *ad hoc* authorities (boards of guardians) to administer the reformed poor law; at the same time central control was imposed through the appointment of the Poor Law Commissioners, a body of three officials of the central government with no Minister responsible to Parliament for their activities.[1] Other reforms followed. The very diverse and often corrupt borough corporations were drastically reorganised by the Municipal Corporations Act 1835 and subjected to a common pattern through which corporate affairs were to be governed in the public interest by councils elected on a uniform franchise. This equipped the municipal corporations to receive the new powers of government which were increasingly conferred on them, especially by the Public Health Act 1875.

Elected multi-purpose Authorities

By the end of the nineteenth century the multi-purpose authority elected on a wide franchise was superseding the *ad hoc* authority as the main administrative agency in local government. Like the Act of 1835, the Municipal Corporations Act 1882 was concerned more with internal organisation and the administration of corporate property than with the conferment of powers of government. But the Local Government Act of 1888 completely transformed local government in the counties by creating elected councils and transferring to them nearly all the administrative powers of the county justices meeting in Quarter Sessions. It was this Act which conferred on many of the larger boroughs the status of "county borough", exempting them entirely from the jurisdiction of the new county councils. The Local Government Act 1894 made further provision for county areas outside the boroughs by converting into elected urban district councils the urban sanitary authorities which had been set up under various Public Health Acts; the Act also established elected rural district councils, to which were transferred the public health functions of the boards of guardians. As the lowest level of the new system, the Act established parish councils and parish meetings for civil parishes within rural districts.

Ad hoc authorities, however, continued to be established during the nineteenth century. Thus the Elementary Education Act 1870 provided for the creation of school boards with power to provide public elementary schools. But once the modern pattern of local authorities had been established, the Education Act 1902 wound up

[1] Their functions were in 1847 transferred to a Poor Law Board responsible to Parliament through its President, a Minister of the Crown.

the school boards, and many of the larger local authorities became education authorities. The principal remaining *ad hoc* authorities, the boards of guardians, were abolished by the Local Government Act 1929, which transferred poor law administration to the county and county borough councils. Although some *ad hoc* authorities survived, *e.g.* land drainage and fishery boards, the passing of the Local Government Act 1929 meant that most matters of local administration were now entrusted to one or other category of the elected multi-purpose authorities.

The Redistribution of Functions

There is, however, no finality in the distribution of functions between the various authorities. The central government encroaches upon local authorities, and larger authorities absorb the powers of smaller authorities. Certain matters once reasonably entrusted to local authorities come to require the application of a uniform national policy. Certain services of national significance cannot rightly remain a charge upon local areas. Thus relief of the unemployed became a national service with the setting-up of the Unemployment Assistance Board in 1934, and trunk roads were transferred in 1936 to the Minister of Transport. After 1945 there was a marked tendency to deprive local authorities, and particularly the smaller ones, of their powers in the interests of efficiency and uniform administration. Even where the central government does not wish to acquire powers, there is pressure for the transfer of services to the larger authorities and the creation of larger areas. After 1945 the county and county borough councils lost to the central government their hospital and public assistance services and local electricity and gas undertakings were transferred to nationalised boards. County councils acquired responsibility for (*inter alia*) town and country planning and fire services, the former at the expense of the district councils. The National Health Service added a range of *ad hoc* authorities under the direction and control of the Minister of Health and deprived local authorities of certain public health powers as well as of the hospital services. The pressure towards vesting services in larger authorities has been seen more recently in such diverse fields as the police and the public library service.[1]

The need for reform

This constant process of redistribution of functions may benefit individual services but it is not a means of reforming basic features of

[1] Police Act 1964; Public Libraries and Museums Act 1964.

the local government system. From the early 1950s onwards, weaknesses in the system became increasingly evident in the face of an expanding population, increased human mobility and the high standards set for modern services which require larger units of government able to support more specialised technical and professional work. Local government boundaries, always to some extent a compromise, too often did not meet the needs of particular services. Devices such as delegation from county council to district council, joint boards and joint committees [1] achieved a limited measure of flexibility but had their disadvantages. A basic difficulty was the wide diversity of resources, population and local needs among authorities with the same legal status. Thus in mid-1968, there were in England five administrative counties and one county borough with populations of over 1 million, and two counties and fourteen county boroughs with populations of under 75,000. Another difficulty was the division between town and country which was a feature of the late nineteenth-century legislation mentioned above. The expense of many modern services may be too heavy to be borne by rural areas on their own. Urban and rural areas are now realised to be inter-dependent: a person resident in one local area may work or spend his leisure in another area. Moreover, except for the regional organisation of some central departments, there was no level intermediate between local and central government at which the main strategic aims of town planning, communications, and social and economic development could be considered.[2] It was only in 1965 that regional advisory councils and executive boards were established for economic development and planning, and these operated essentially within the central government structure.

The Local Government Act 1958

Local government reform has proved an arduous and unrewarding task for successive governments. After several abortive steps towards revising local areas following the Second World War, the Local Government Act 1958 created special machinery for this purpose, namely separate Commissions for England and Wales. The English Commission was to review the boundaries of county councils and county boroughs, area by area throughout the country, from the viewpoint of the needs of effective and convenient local government. Only in five special review areas (the conurbations of Tyneside, West Yorkshire, South East Lancashire, Merseyside and the West

[1] P. 347, *post*.
[2] See J. P. Mackintosh, *The Devolution of Power* (Penguin).

Midlands) was the Commission not confined to considering the boundaries of counties and county boroughs but could also recommend a redistribution of functions as between county and district councils. In these areas it could propose what was called a "continuous county", *i.e.* a county within whose area there were no county boroughs, somewhat on the lines of the structure adopted for London by the London Government Act 1963.[1]

The Act of 1958 laid down a complicated procedure to be followed for local government reform. After consulting the local authorities and public bodies within a review area and taking other evidence, the Commission made a report to the Minister for Housing and Local Government, who had power to implement the recommendations if he so wished by making statutory instruments subject to parliamentary approval. Experience showed that the Commission's terms of reference were too narrow and the procedure too elaborate, involving as it did the likelihood of lengthy and costly public inquiries,[2] to achieve the radical reforms of the system that came to be considered necessary. By 1967 when the Commissions appointed under the 1958 Act were disbanded,[3] their work had led in England to the amalgamation of two pairs of small adjacent counties; the establishment of a pattern of five county boroughs in the West Midlands; and new county boroughs for Teesside, Solihull, Luton and Torbay as well as smaller boundary changes. In Wales, the Commission had in 1962 recommended a considerable reduction in the number of county councils and county boroughs.[4]

A Royal Commission on Local Government in England was appointed in 1966 under the chairmanship of Lord Redcliffe-Maud

> to consider the structure of local government in England, outside Greater London, in relation to its existing functions, and to make recommendations for authorities and for functions and their division, having regard to the size and character of areas in which these can be most effectively exercised and the need to sustain a viable system of local democracy.

In June 1969, the Commission reported its unanimous conviction that local government in England needed a new structure and that the local government map needed to be redrawn.[5] With a single dissentient the report proposed what was basically a single-tier system —58 all-purpose local authorities together with 3 metropolitan areas

[1] Pp. 362-4, *post*.
[2] See *Wednesbury Corporation* v. *Ministry of Housing*, [1966] 2 Q.B. 275.
[3] Local Government (Termination of Reviews) Act 1967.
[4] For the Government's proposed scheme, see Cmnd. 334 (1967).
[5] Cmnd. 4040 (1969).

round Birmingham, Liverpool and Manchester, in which a new two-tier system was proposed. These 61 areas should be grouped in 8 provinces, each with a provincial council elected by the new local authorities and responsible for settling the regional strategy and framework of planning within which the new local authorities would operate. Below the main operational authorities, it was proposed that "local councils" could be established on an optional basis, to represent local opinion, to express the identity of local communities, and to provide facilities for those communities. In proposing boundaries for the sixty-one new areas, the Commission took account of historical boundaries but did not regard them as conclusive.

B. Characteristics of Local Authorities

As will already have been realised, there is no hard-and-fast dividing line between the services administered by central and local government. Local authorities play an important part in certain major services (*e.g.* public health, highways, education, housing and police) but are excluded almost entirely from national services such as social security and the control of employment. Nonetheless local authorities have characteristics which distinguish them from departments of the central government and give to local administration a character different from that prevailing in an administrative structure drawn from the civil service and headed by a Minister responsible to Parliament.

Powers of Local Authorities

Local authorities, although representative bodies chosen by popular election, have not the autonomy of Parliament; indeed, they are dependent on Parliament for their powers. The powers of a local authority derive either expressly or by implication from statute and they are exercised subject to the rules of *ultra vires*. The application of these rules in disputed cases is a matter for the courts and no local authority can determine the extent of its own powers. But within the limits of its powers, and subject to the performance of statutory duties laid upon it, a local authority has a discretion in deciding how it is to administer the services for which it is responsible. In practice this discretion is subject to many forms of direct and indirect pressure from central government.

The detailed working of the *ultra vires* doctrine will be examined later.[1] The doctrine applies to local authorities for several reasons.

[1] Chap. 44, *post*.

Many local services involve interference with the citizen's common law rights, for which statutory authorisation is needed. Again, most local services involve public expenditure, and the courts have always been concerned to ensure that money raised from local taxation is spent only on lawful objects. In this respect a limited innovation was made in 1963, when, subject to a financial limit and other safeguards, local councils were authorised to incur expenditure for any purpose not covered by other statutory authority which in their opinion was in the interests of the inhabitants of their area.[1] Finally, most local authorities are statutory corporations, *i.e.* they are incorporated by virtue of statute and have legal capacity only in relation to the purposes for which they are incorporated.[2] In this respect local authorities resemble limited companies, except that the corporate purposes of a local authority can be changed only by legislation, whereas the Companies Act 1948 provides special machinery for amending the objects of a company.

These limitations on the corporate powers of a local authority mean, for example, that a contract entered into by an authority for a purpose beyond its powers is void and of no legal effect.[3] Formerly local authorities like other corporations could contract only under their common seal, an inconvenient formality which was often ignored. Contracts now bind a local authority regardless of formality, provided only that they would be valid if made in the same form between private persons, and that they are entered into by a person acting with express or implied authority.[4]

Party Politics

The membership of local authorities is decided through direct election of councillors, who must stand for election at three-yearly intervals; county and borough councils also include aldermen, in the proportion of one alderman to three councillors, who are elected by the body of councillors to serve for six-yearly periods. The political parties today play a large part both in the nomination of candidates and in organising electoral support. In councils where political rivalry is keen, party policy may largely govern the making of key decisions. Valuable political experience is to be gained in local government and the parties help to foster public interest in elections. Party control of a council also focuses responsibility for its policies on an organised group. But the influence of national party divisions

[1] Local Government (Financial Provisions) Act 1963, s. 6.

[2] Strictly borough corporations are common law corporations, but see p. 371, *post* for effect of statute.

[3] *Triggs* v. *Staines Urban District Council*, [1969] Ch. 10.

[4] Corporate Bodies' Contracts Act 1960.

at a local level may sometimes be excessive. Some councils are a local replica of the two-party system in the House of Commons, including the party whips; in others there is more scope for the independent member.

Members

Although reasonable remuneration may be paid to the mayor of a borough and the chairman of a county council, and an allowance for expenses may be made to the chairman of a district council, no payment is made to members of local authorities in return for their services. The Local Government Act 1948 permits reasonable travelling and subsistence allowances to be paid, and allowances may also be paid to cover loss of earnings and other expenses actually incurred on approved council business. But councillors essentially render only part-time, voluntary service. Their function is the direction of policy. It is for the salaried officers of the council to execute the policy of the council. In practice local government officers may be more closely controlled by the committees to which they are responsible than are civil servants by Ministers. Local authorities usually include a number of members of long experience, often serving as chairmen of the council's committees. The desire to ensure some continuity of service to and have a means of "co-opting" to the council those reluctant to contest an open election, may explain why the aldermanic system was extended from the boroughs to the county councils in 1888. But aldermanic elections have been used solely to strengthen and prolong the majority of the dominant party group on the council.

The Committee System

The administration by a single authority of the many diverse services entrusted to it is made possible only by the wide use of committees and subcommittees. Nearly every item of business is considered by a committee before it comes to the council; a typical council meeting is spent in considering reports and recommendations from the council's committees. All local authorities have a general power to appoint such committees as they think fit and, subject to special statutory provision in particular fields, they may delegate to the committees all the powers of the council save only the power to borrow money or to levy a rate.[1] The general rule is that at least two-thirds of the committee must be members of the council; the remainder may be co-opted. Some statutes make it obligatory for particular committees to be appointed and may regulate in detail

[1] Local Government Act 1933, s. 85.

their composition. Thus education authorities and planning authorities are required to appoint education and town planning committees, whose constitution is subject to detailed provision in the Education Act and the Town and Country Planning Act. County councils are required to appoint finance committees, whose membership is confined to members of the council. For each main activity of a council, there is a chief officer with professional or technical qualifications, and he is directly responsible to the appropriate committee, *e.g.* chief education officer to the education committee. The co-ordination of the committees with each other is primarily a matter for the clerk of the council, who may be a lawyer and as such also head of the council's legal department. In some councils all committee chairmen meet regularly as a co-ordinating committee; the powers of the finance committee also serve to co-ordinate the activities of the "spending" committees.

Meetings of the Council

The extent to which a council's powers are delegated to its committees, and not simply referred to them for consideration, depends largely on the frequency of the meetings of the whole council. All local authorities are required to meet at least four times each year. In practice many county councils do not meet more than five times a year and therefore greater use must be made of delegated powers; many borough councils have a monthly meeting and in this case committee decisions can more easily await confirmation from the council before they become binding.

Council meetings, and meetings of certain other public bodies, are required to be open to the public, except when the council resolves to exclude the public during consideration of a particular matter for which publicity would be prejudicial to the public interest.[1] Representatives of the press are entitled to be present while the public is there and reasonable facilities and information about the business of the meeting must be supplied to them. Press reports of proceedings, so long as they are fair and accurate, are protected by qualified privilege from liability for defamation.[2] Apart from education committees, the public and the press have no right to be present at meetings of committees, but because most matters discussed in committee are not re-discussed at the council meeting some local authorities allow press and public to attend committee meetings. One former method of excluding press and public from deliberations

[1] Public Bodies (Admission to Meetings) Act 1960; see also p. 522, *post*.
[2] P. 518, *post*.

of the whole council was the device of appointing a committee consisting of all members of the council, but since 1960 such a committee must be treated for this purpose as a meeting of the council.

Officers

The officers and other employees of local authorities are not Crown servants and in general each local authority as the employer has full powers of appointment and dismissal. Local authorities are empowered to appoint such officers as may be necessary and to pay them such reasonable remuneration as they may determine.[1] The appointment of certain chief officers is made obligatory by statute: a county borough council, for example, is required to appoint a town clerk, a treasurer, a surveyor, a medical officer of health, a public health inspector, a chief education officer and a children's officer. In general local authorities have complete discretion in deciding whom to appoint, but in some instances the approval of a central department is needed: *e.g.* the Secretary of State must be consulted when an education authority is appointing a chief education officer and he has a right to veto.[2] Subject to any particular statutory provisions, the relationship between officer and authority is governed by the general law of contract, unlike that between the Crown and its servants; thus when national conditions of service are negotiated between associations of local authorities and the employees' associations, and have been adopted by a local authority, these conditions can be enforced by contractual remedies, except where this would be contrary to statute. Most local government officers hold office at the pleasure of the employing council, subject only to a reasonable period of notice. But certain officers have special protection: thus a medical officer of health or a public health inspector can be dismissed only with the consent of the Secretary of State for the Social Services.

Under the principle laid down in *Mersey Docks and Harbour Board Trustees* v. *Gibbs*,[3] local authorities are vicariously liable for the torts of their servants. They did not share the Crown's former immunity in this respect. It was formerly the law that a police authority was not liable for wrongful acts of the police committed in the course of police duties, on the ground that a police constable, even if appointed and paid by the police authority, could not be regarded as a servant of the authority.[4] On analogous grounds a

[1] Local Government Act 1933, ss. 105–107.
[2] Education Act 1944, s. 88.
[3] (1866), L.R. 1 H.L. 93; K. & L. 381; p. 634, *post*.
[4] P. 242, *ante*, for present law.

local authority is not liable when its servant commits a tort while performing duties laid directly on him by central government.[1]

As a general rule, in carrying out their work, local government officers are subject to the control and direction of their council exercised through the appropriate committee. Although matters of policy or discretion may be delegated to committees, local authorities have no general power of delegation to individual officers.[2] Even a letter written by a chief officer in the course of his duties does not estop (*i.e.* bind) the local authority in the exercise of its statutory discretion.[3] In practice, the policies and decisions of a local authority are influenced very considerably by the advice and recommendations of the officers concerned. The individual officer is personally liable for any torts which he commits, and in exceptional circumstances he must exercise a personal discretion; thus a treasurer must disobey any instruction to make an illegal payment from the general rate fund on pain of rendering himself liable to refund the amount of the payment.[4]

Delegation Schemes

We saw earlier that one difficulty in allocating functions to local authorities is the wide differences in size and resources that may exist between authorities of the same class. One technique which assists in solving this problem is the delegation of functions from county councils to district councils. The Local Government Act 1958 provided that in certain circumstances a county council could be required to prepare delegation schemes for ministerial approval. The right to claim delegation for various health, welfare, education and town planning functions is now vested in borough or urban district councils with a population exceeding 60,000. The effect of a delegation scheme is that the county council retains overall financial and supervisory control but confers detailed responsibilities on the local district councils.

Joint Committees and Joint Boards

Where several neighbouring local authorities wish to co-operate in providing a joint service, a joint committee for the purpose may be created, members being appointed by each authority. Each authority may delegate to the committee the necessary powers, other

[1] P. 635, *post*.

[2] P. 644, *post*. But certain town planning decisions may now be delegated to officers: Town and Country Planning Act 1968, s. 64.

[3] *Southend-on-Sea Corporation* v. *Hodgson* (*Wickford*) *Ltd*., [1962] 1 Q.B. 416.

[4] *Attorney-General* v. *De Winton*, [1906] 2 Ch. 106.

than those of borrowing money and rating, but the parent authorities remain legally responsible and the joint committee does not have corporate personality. An alternative expedient, which does result in the creation of a new legal entity, is the joint board. Like the joint committee, this may be composed of members appointed by several local authorities but, unlike the joint committee, it is fully responsible for the service for which it has been created; if it relies on the rates for its income it must precept upon the local authorities in the area which it serves for the required amount.

C. Relationship with Central Government [1]

Although there are marked differences in organisation between central and local government, differentiation in function is not easy: many sectors of internal government call for action at both national and local levels. Take housing as an illustration. The proportion of public revenue of the central government which can be allotted to the subsidised scheme of public housing is determined by the Government. This in practice means that the Minister of Housing and Local Government has to agree the total with the Chancellor of the Exchequer each year. The requirements of each local housing authority are notified to the Minister who must then estimate how far the total sum at his disposal will meet the requirements of each council. In this way, although a housing authority can distribute over its area the number of new houses which the Minister sanctions each year, it cannot increase the maximum number which it is permitted to build. In the case of education the State scheme, as the law stands at present in the Education Act of 1944, can only be administered as a duty imposed upon the Secretary of State through the agency of the local education authorities. Apart from one or two highly specialised forms of school, the Secretary of State has no power, except on default by a local authority, to open or conduct a school. But so closely intermingled are the statutory duties of Minister and local authority that every important development requires ministerial sanction.

Another important factor in the relationship between central and local government is finance. However frequently local boundaries are revised, some local authorities will have greater resources than others, a situation accentuated by the limitations of the rating system as a method of taxation. The greater the proportion of a local

[1] See J. A. G. Griffith, *Central Departments and Local Authorities* (Allen and Unwin).

authority's income which comes from the national exchequer, the keener will be the interest of the central government in settling priorities and in ensuring an adequate level of services in all areas. Many controls which central government now exercises over local authorities were introduced in connection with the payment of grants from central funds.

The Ministry of Housing and Local Government

A principal characteristic of the nineteenth-century local government reforms was the conferment on a central body of at least some measure of supervision and control. After several short-lived experiments in the field of the poor law and public health, the Local Government Board was set up in 1871, its President being a member of the Government, primarily with poor law and public health functions. In 1919 the Ministry of Health was created and among other responsibilities succeeded to the functions of the Local Government Board. For over thirty years the Ministry was the government department most closely connected with local authorities, with public health, housing and many residual local government functions. The present Ministry of Housing and Local Government dates from 1951. In addition to housing, new towns, town planning and the control of water resources, the Minister is responsible for local government finance and boundary reform. Moreover, the Minister exercises a broad and undefined responsibility for the general health of local government. In 1969 the Ministry was placed under the co-ordination of a Secretary of State for Local Government and Regional Planning but there continued to be a Minister and a Ministry for Housing and Local Government.

Other Central Government Departments

The Minister of Housing and Local Government exercises no control over a number of important services within local government and his general powers stop short of responsibility for co-ordinating these. Thus the Ministry of Technology which was created in 1969 has powers over the location of industry, a matter which is closely related to local government, town planning and regional development policies.

The *Secretary of State for the Social Services* (formerly the Minister of Health), with a statutory responsibility for the general health of the community, is responsible through the Department of Health and Social Security for the National Health Service; this is mainly administered through an *ad hoc* structure and local authorities play but a small part in this. However the Department controls local authorities in what are known as the "local health services" (*e.g.* maternity and infant welfare, mental welfare, home nursing), in one or two services deriving from the Public Health Acts (*e.g.* control of infectious diseases) and in welfare schemes for the aged and disabled under the National Assistance Act 1948.

The task of the *Secretary of State for Education and Science* is to promote the education of the people and the progressive development of institutions devoted to that purpose. It is his duty to secure the effective execution by local authorities under his control and direction of the national policy for providing a varied and comprehensive educational service in every area of England and Wales. Thus the central department exercises direct control over a service which essentially depends upon a national rather than local policy, but which is administered by local authorities.

The *Minister of Transport* controls the exercise of the highway functions of local authorities, largely through grants given for the construction and upkeep of those roads for which they are responsible. He is himself the highway authority for trunk roads and special roads such as motorways and he may make use of the county councils as his agents in the carrying out of these functions. In 1969, the Ministry was brought under the co-ordination of the Secretary of State for Local Government and Regional Planning.

The *Home Secretary* has dealings with local authorities mainly through the police, civil defence, the fire service, and the probation and children's services; he also has the duty of confirming many local authority byelaws and of organising local government elections. Other Ministries with responsibilities for services partly administered within local government include the Ministry of Agriculture, Fisheries and Food (*e.g.* under food and drugs legislation) and the Board of Trade (local authority aerodromes).

Methods of Control

There is no universal right to appeal from a local authority to a government department, nor is every local decision automatically reviewed by the central government. But there is a great variety of methods by which both general and detailed central control may be exercised over local affairs. Some of these methods, *e.g.* the power of a Minister to hold public inquiries into certain decisions of local authorities, are of great importance within administrative law.[1]

The methods of control may be conveniently outlined under four heads, some of these being closely inter-related.

[1] Chap. 47, *post.*

(*a*) *Finance*. The accounts of most local authorities are audited by district auditors appointed by the Ministry of Housing and Local Government.[1] The sanction of a central department is needed before a local authority may exercise its borrowing powers, so that ministerial consent is needed before all major items of capital expenditure are incurred. The system of grants carries with it many opportunities of control, discussed in (*b*) and (*c*) below.

(*b*) *Policy*. In many services, *e.g.* town planning and education, the local authority is required to produce schemes or plans outlining the authority's policy over a stated period of years, and such plans are subject to ministerial approval. The volume of a local authority's activities in some fields (*e.g.* road improvement, school building, slum clearance) is dependent on the Government's allocation of resources, which in its turn is dependent on the Government's national economic policy. Certain decisions of a local authority, *e.g.* to initiate slum clearance or the compulsory purchase of land, are subject to confirmation by a Minister; if a landowner objects to such a scheme, or if he wishes to appeal to the Minister against a local planning decision, the Minister may appoint an official to hold a local public inquiry to hear the views of local authority and individuals. The publication of the Minister's decisions in such cases and of ministerial circulars containing advice to local authorities is a major influence on local policies

(*c*) *Standards and efficiency*. Ministerial participation in certain appointments made by local authorities is ensured by law: thus the Department of Education can ensure that a man with suitable qualifications and experience is appointed chief education officer.[2] In some services, *e.g.* education, there is regular inspection by inspectors acting on behalf of the Ministry and the payment of some specific grants, *e.g.* for the police, is conditional on satisfactory inspection. Under the Local Government Act 1966, s. 4, the Minister of Housing and Local Government may, subject to approval by the House of Commons, reduce the amount of the rate support grant otherwise payable [3] if he is satisfied that an authority has failed to achieve or maintain reasonable standards in the provision of any of its services, having regard to standards maintained by other local authorities. In many services, *e.g.* education and town planning, the Minister may assume the functions of a local authority if he considers that there has been default by the authority.

[1] P. 382, *post*.
[2] P. 346, *ante*.
[3] P. 379, *post*.

(*d*) *Legislation.*[1] As local authority powers and procedures are dependent on statute, the departments responsible for initiating legislation exercise general control over local government law. In many local services, the enabling Act confers on the Minister power to make detailed regulations which, as subordinate legislation, are binding on local authorities. Byelaws made by local authorities are subject to central confirmation, either from the Ministry of Housing and Local Government or from the Home Office. The Ministry of Housing has certain powers over the promotion by local authorities of private legislation. Under the provisional order procedure, statutory confirmation of a local authority's order depends on the co-operation of the Ministry concerned.

Conclusion

Despite these numerous and effective methods of central control, local administration and to a limited extent the initiation of policy remain functions of local authorities. Collectively, through the County Councils Association, the Association of Municipal Corporation, the Urban District Councils Association and the Rural District Councils Association, local authorities exercise considerable influence over general local government policy. The system depends at almost every turn on co-operation between local and central authorities; but in terms both of legal structure and practical operation, it remains important that the locally elected council is not a mere local branch of Whitehall.

[1] Chap. 26, B.

CHAPTER TWENTY-FIVE

LEGAL STRUCTURE AND GENERAL POWERS OF LOCAL AUTHORITIES

THE organisation of local government, despite the very substantial reduction in the total number of separate authorities achieved since the principle of the multi-purpose authority was accepted, is still complex. In mid-1968, taking account of reorganisation under the Local Government Act 1958 and the London Government Act 1963, there were in England, excluding Greater London, 45 county councils, 79 county borough councils, 227 non-county borough councils, 449 urban district councils, 410 rural district councils, and about 7,000 parish councils.

Within a county borough, the county borough council is the sole local authority and thus exercises all local government functions within the area, save only where joint authorities for specific purposes have been established; leaving aside these *ad hoc* bodies, this may be described as a single-tier system of local government. Outside the county boroughs, there is for most practical purposes a two-tier system, the county councils forming the upper tier, with a second tier comprising those boroughs which are not county boroughs (the non-county boroughs), the urban district councils and the rural district councils. Within the rural districts there is also a third tier in the parish councils and parish meetings, but these have minor functions. Within Greater London, a distinct two-tier structure exists under the London Government Act 1963, consisting of the Greater London Council and the Greater London Boroughs.

A. Organisation of Counties

Terminology

It is one of the most confusing features of local government that different institutions are called by the same name. The county affords an example. For parliamentary purposes, for local administration and taxation and for military organisation, the term " county " is used to describe areas which are not necessarily coterminous. The term is also used of the local civil court, the county court, though here the divisions make no pretension of corresponding with the county as depicted on the map of England. Again, the term is used to distinguish those boroughs which, by virtue of possessing a population of a certain size, are separated for administrative and parliamentary purposes from the area of the county in which they are situated. The county borough of Salford is in the county palatine of Lancaster, the county borough of Norwich in the county of Norfolk; yet for local government purposes these places are in effect quite separate from their respective counties.

Apart from the administrative services of the elected authorities, the organisation of the county comprises other offices.

The Lord-Lieutenant

Formerly a military representative of the King and, as such, commander of the local militia, yeomanry and volunteer forces, the Lord-Lieutenant is appointed by commission. Little remains of his official military duties except the power to recommend appointments to first commissions in the Territorial Army.[1] He may appoint not more than twenty Deputy-Lieutenants, subject to the Crown's power to decline approval. The Lord-Lieutenant is the head of the county commission of the peace, and *custos rotulorum* (keeper of the records). He recommends to the Lord Chancellor, with the assistance of an advisory committee, suitable persons in the county for appointment as justices of the peace, except in such county boroughs and boroughs as have a separate commission of the peace.

The Sheriff

The Sheriff is also a royal representative, who in former times played a far more important part in county affairs than to-day. As conservator of the Queen's Peace he had the duty to suppress riots, to repel invasion and pursue felony and could call on the *posse comitatus*[2] to assist him. He is still, however, the Crown's agent for the execution of processes of law. He summons juries, executes the judgments of the superior civil courts and, when the law permits capital punishment, is responsible for the carrying out of death sentences.[3] Sentences of criminal courts which involve detention are carried out by prison officials or the police, but the Sheriff remains responsible for carrying out any order unless the duty is imposed on someone else. Committals for contempt of court are carried out

[1] For position of Territorial Army, see p. 393, *post*.
[2] The county levy, now obsolete.
[3] Sheriffs Act 1887.

by the tipstaff, an officer of the court. The Sheriff executes judgments of civil courts through the bailiff, a Sheriff's officer. As a revenue official he collects certain Crown debts, such as fines imposed by higher courts and forfeited recognisances and bonds. He is the returning officer in the county parliamentary elections to whom writs for the election of members of Parliament are addressed. His duties as such are in practice performed by the clerk of the county council as acting returning officer. He is in attendance on the Judges of Assize. Some traces remain of the Sheriff's greater importance in former times. Selection is by the Crown from among three persons for each county nominated by a special court which meets annually on November 12. One of these names is subsequently "pricked" by the Queen at a special meeting of the Privy Council. This court is a kind of reproduction under a modern statute of the old Exchequer. Those entitled to sit are the Lord Chancellor, the Chancellor of the Exchequer, the Lord President of the Council, and other Privy Councillors, the Lord Chief Justice and the High Court judges. The qualification for the office of Sheriff is the holding of sufficient land within the county to answer for any damages that may be awarded against him for neglect of duty. Various persons are exempted from the office, such as members of Parliament and officers on the active list of the regular forces. The expenses of a Sheriff are such that in these days many qualified persons seek to be excused. No remuneration is payable, though the Sheriff is entitled to certain fines and a percentage of the Crown debts collected.[1]

The Under-Sheriff: The Deputy-Sheriff

The Sheriff must appoint an Under-Sheriff and a Deputy-Sheriff. In practice he performs none but the ceremonial duties of his office in person. His legal representative for local business is the Under-Sheriff, usually a solicitor whose firm practises in the county town. The Deputy-Sheriff is the Sheriff's London agent, who must have an office within one mile of Inner Temple Hall.

The Coroner [2]

The coroner was originally an officer of the Crown, below the rank of sheriff, with the function of safeguarding the Crown's

[1] The Criminal Justice Administration Act 1962 created the office of Sheriff of Hallamshire to enable an additional Assize Court for Yorkshire to sit at Sheffield. In 1969 the Royal Commission on Assizes and Quarter Sessions (Cmnd. 4153, para. 321) and the Committee on the Enforcement of Judgment Debts (Cmnd. 3909, paras. 658–67) proposed radical changes in the duties of the Sheriff relating to judicial administration.

[2] Coroners Acts 1887–1954.

interests in the administration of criminal justice. His duties are now to hold inquiries (in the form of inquests) into cases of sudden death and discovery of treasure trove.[1] Coroners must be barristers, solicitors or legally qualified medical practitioners of five years' standing. The coroner is appointed by the county council and his salary is paid from county funds. Larger counties appoint more than one coroner, the county being divided for this purpose into districts. The Coroners' Rules 1953 require inquests to be held in public and in general aim at restricting inquests to relevant matters without restraining the discretion of the coroner in the conduct of proceedings.

Justices of the Peace[2]

Justices of the peace for the county, as we have already seen, are appointed by the Crown, advised by the Lord Chancellor on the recommendation of the Lord-Lieutenant, who is assisted by an advisory committee. The county is divided into separate divisions for petty sessional purposes. Since the Local Government Acts of 1888 and 1894, only a few administrative powers remain vested in justices of the peace. They have, however, certain powers in connection with visiting prisons and the administration of the licensing law.

Clerk of the Peace

Formerly the clerk of the peace was also the clerk of the council of the administrative county, holding the latter more important office by virtue of tenure of the former. Appointments to the two offices are now made by separate bodies, the county council appointing its own clerk, quarter sessions its clerk of the peace. The two offices may still be, and usually are, held by the same person.[3] The clerk of the peace is an officer of the judicial county and acts as clerk of quarter sessions. The clerk of the county council is also the electoral registration officer of the parliamentary county, but not of the separate parliamentary boroughs within the county. Boroughs with separate courts of quarter sessions appoint their own clerks of the peace.

The County Council

The administrative county came into existence in 1888 when the

[1] Treasure trove, which consists of objects of gold or silver which have been hidden and of which the original owner cannot be traced, is the property of the Crown. The finder receives back the objects or their market value, provided he reports his discovery promptly to the Coroner of the district.

[2] Chap. 22.

[3] Local Government Act 1933, ss. 98, 101; Local Government (Clerks) Act 1931, ss. 1, 2, 4.

Local Government Act transferred administrative business from the justices of the peace sitting in quarter sessions to elected bodies. Generally, subject to the exclusion of the county boroughs from the administrative counties, the geographical county was taken as the area of the administrative county, although certain counties, such as Lincolnshire and Suffolk, were divided into parts, each with a separate council. For each administrative county there is an elected county council, which is a statutory corporation with a common seal. The council consists of chairman, aldermen and councillors, in the proportion of one alderman for every three councillors. A county council must hold four meetings in a year, including the statutory annual meeting. The chief executive officers [1] are the clerk, the county treasurer, the medical officer of health, the surveyor, the chief education officer, the children's officer, the chief fire officer, and other specialists and technical officials. The clerk of the council is usually a solicitor with special experience of local government.

Powers and Duties

The principal powers and duties of county councils relate to: child welfare; civil defence; education; fire service; health services under the National Health Service Act 1946; highways (including county bridges, all classified roads other than trunk roads for which the Minister of Transport is the highway authority, and all roads in rural districts); libraries; police [2]; town and country planning; and welfare services under the National Assistance Act 1948. There are also a wide variety of administrative and regulatory matters for which the county council is responsible, including the provision of small holdings, the licensing of cinemas and the implementation of food and drugs legislation.[3]

A county council has power to delegate many of its functions to the council of a county district and in certain circumstances may be required to do so.[4]

As the upper-tier authority, the county council has reserve powers in the fields of public health and housing, that may come into effect on the default of the district councils primarily responsible. A county council may subsidise particular activities of district councils, for example under the Rural Water Supplies and Sewerage Act 1944. Other "upper-tier" functions of the county council include the supervision of elections in parishes and rural districts, and the power

[1] See Local Government Act 1933, Part IV, for officers of local authorities.

[2] Pp. 238–44, *ante*.

[3] See Cross, *Local Government Law*, 3rd edn., Appendices I and IX.

[4] P. 347, *ante*.

to promote local legislation conferring powers on the district councils within the county.[1] Under the Local Government Act 1958, county councils were formerly under a duty to review the areas of county districts and to make proposals for reforming them as soon as the work of the Local Government Commission for an area had reached a point where it was practicable to deal with the detailed question of county district boundaries.[2] Notwithstanding such upper-tier powers Parliament has never entirely subordinated the district councils to the county council; a county council has no general power of approving a district council's decisions, and entire responsibility for some services is vested in the lower-tier authorities.

B. Organisation of Boroughs

Historically, the status of a borough was enjoyed by all those cities, towns and even villages, to whose inhabitants the Crown had been persuaded to grant a charter of incorporation. The contents of these charters varied widely, but would in general confer certain administrative, fiscal, trading and judicial privileges on the borough, exempting it for many purposes from the jurisdiction of the county justices, the sheriff and other county officials; the charter would also regulate the constitution of the corporation, the appointment of the corporation's officers, and the ownership of corporate property. Before the parliamentary reforms of the nineteenth century, borough status carried with it the right to send two members to the House of Commons. Today for each borough there is a municipal corporation, consisting in law of the mayor, aldermen and burgesses, or, in those boroughs which are also cities, of the mayor, aldermen and citizens. But this corporation is capable of acting only through the council of the borough, the composition of which was first given a common form by the Municipal Corporations Act 1835. The council now consists of the councillors, serving for three years, with one-third elected annually; the aldermen, in the proportion of one alderman for three councillors, elected by the councillors for six years, one-half retiring every third year; and the mayor, who need not be a councillor or alderman but must be qualified in the same way, elected annually by the councillors and the non-retiring aldermen.

Creation of Boroughs

Boroughs are still created by royal charter, but the issue of a charter of incorporation is subject to regulation by the Local

[1] P. 373, *post*.
[2] See now Local Government (Termination of Reviews) Act 1967.

Government Act 1933. An urban or rural district council which desires borough status must petition the Crown accordingly. The petition is considered by a committee of the Privy Council; notice of the petition must first be given to the county council concerned and to the Ministry of Housing and Local Government. The effect of the charter will be to extend to the borough the relevant provisions of the Local Government Act 1933; it will also prescribe the number of councillors and allocation of wards, and arrange for initial elections. A statutory scheme will also be prepared, providing for all adjustments to existing local authorities and services made necessary by the creation of the new borough.[1]

Powers and Duties

Although the constitution of every borough is governed by uniform provisions in the Local Government Act 1933, and although some general powers, like the power to make byelaws, are common to all borough councils, the functions of a borough council depend on whether it is a county or non-county borough. A county borough council exercises all local government functions within its area; a non-county borough council is a second-tier authority and its position may broadly be compared with that of an urban district council. Thus a non-county borough council has powers in relation to allotments, burial grounds, civic restaurants, coast protection, entertainments, highways (non-classified roads and, where the population is over 20,000, classified roads claimed from the county council), housing (slum clearance and the provision of new housing), libraries (subject under the Public Libraries and Museums Act 1964 to a population of 40,000 or being an existing library authority), markets, parks and recreation grounds, public health, weights and measures. Subject to satisfying the population limit, non-county borough councils share with urban district councils the right tc claim delegation of certain services primarily vested in the county councils. Borough councils have in some respects (*e.g.* the making of byelaws, the management of corporate land) wider powers than urban districts and are more likely to have acquired special powers by private legislation to provide trading, transport and other undertakings.

The status of a borough, with its mayor who has precedence within the borough's bounds, and its town clerk who is now the council's senior administrator and often its legal adviser, is jealously guarded by the minicipal corporations. It is not surprising that borough status has sometimes proved an obstacle to local government

[1] See Hart, *Law of Local Government*, 8th edn., pp. 69–73.

reform. The Local Government Act 1958 gave some protection to boroughs in the reform of areas and also created the status of "rural borough" for those boroughs which with too small a population by modern standards were absorbed into rural districts.

Cities

Some boroughs have the title of city, a status that makes no difference to the corporation's powers. Certain towns have at various times been called "cities" by royal charter or letters patent. Such towns are usually the cathedral towns of ecclesiastical dioceses or very large towns such as Leeds and Nottingham. There are also a few counties of cities, or counties of towns, formerly regarded as counties by themselves. At the present day these have separate sheriffs, and in some cases separate commissions of assize.

Commissions of the Peace

Most of the larger boroughs have a separate commission of the peace, justices being appointed by the Crown advised by the Lord Chancellor on the recommendation of the borough advisory committee. The majority of such boroughs have their own court of quarter sessions over which a recorder presides.[1] The grant of a separate commission of the peace enables the borough justices to act as a separate petty sessional division, and in practice county justices do not sit at borough petty sessions.[2] Borough justices have their own clerk and borough quarter sessions a clerk of the peace. A borough having a separate commission of the peace may apply to the Crown for the appointment of a stipendiary magistrate whose appointment is recommended by the Lord Chancellor.[3]

C. Organisation of Urban and Rural Districts

Urban and Rural District Councils

Within the administrative county, the second-tier of government comprises, in addition to the non-county boroughs, the urban and rural district councils. It has been mentioned already that the functions of the urban district council are broadly similar to those of a non-county borough. But the rural district council has ap-

[1] P. 302, *ante*.

[2] County justices probably have no jurisdiction where a borough possesses a separate court of quarter sessions, and cannot sit at borough petty sessions where the borough was exempt before the Municipal Corporations Act 1835.

[3] A stipendiary may also be appointed on application by the county council for the whole or any part of a county, or a joint county and borough area may be constituted for this purpose.

preciably fewer powers than either borough or urban district council. Thus in general rural district councils have no right to claim delegated powers from the county council, unlike boroughs and urban districts of over 60,000 in population. Both urban and rural district councils were in origin public health authorities, being established by the Local Government Act 1894 to replace a confusing variety of *ad hoc* sanitary bodies which sprang up during the nineteenth century. Their most important powers are today in public health and housing. District councils have also some highway functions and power to regulate buildings and streets, to provide water supplies and public parks. Many powers can be obtained by the adoption of Acts empowering the provision of public amenities or conferring increased regulatory powers. The Minister of Housing and Local Government has power by order to confer certain urban powers on rural district councils, either generally or on a named council. Both urban and rural district councils have the duty of levying and collecting rates and county councils address their demands for rates (precepts) to the district councils.

Both urban and rural district councils consist of a chairman, elected annually, and a fixed number of councillors elected for three years; the councillors retire either together or, as in the boroughs, at the rate of one-third each year. The chief officer of both urban and rural district councils is the clerk, who in the larger districts is likely to be a solicitor with experience like that of a town clerk or a county clerk. Every district council is required to appoint a clerk, a treasurer, a medical officer of health and a public health inspector, and an urban district council is also required to appoint a surveyor. Every district council is a body corporate, with a common seal.

Parish Councils

In rural districts there is a further unit, the parish council, elected by the local government electors of the civil parish, the boundaries of which are governed by the county councils and need bear no relation to the ecclesiastical parish. A parish council has a chairman and not more than twenty-one members, elected every three years at the same time as the rural district councillor for the parish is elected.[1] The parish council is entrusted with the management of parish property, the provision of amenities such as public seats and cycle parks, and some minor public health powers. More extensive powers may be obtained under adoptive Acts, *e.g.* the provision of street

[1] Local Government Elections Act 1956.

lighting, recreation grounds, and public baths and wash-houses, but the powers of a parish council to incur expenditure are subject to a relatively low maximum rate.[1]

Parish Meetings

In every rural parish there must be a parish meeting of local government electors each year and certain decisions of the parish council are subject to confirmation by this meeting. In smaller parishes there may not even be a parish council and in that case the parish meeting may exercise some powers of a parish council. The parish meeting is the only example of direct, as opposed to representative, government, to be found in England.

The parish council is a statutory corporation but its acts are signified by the signatures or seals of two members of the council. In parishes with no council, for the purposes of holding parish property and signifying the acts of the parish meeting there is a specially incorporated "representative body", which generally consists of the chairman of the meeting and the rural district councillor for the parish.

D. Local Government in Greater London

The vast resources and population of Greater London and its position as the national centre of government and commerce present great administrative problems, which formerly were accentuated by the fact that the physical spread of London was not accompanied by the redrawing of local government boundaries. The boundaries of the Metropolitan Board of Works, created in 1855, became those of the London County Council when the new county councils were created in 1888. These boundaries remained unchanged until the London Government Act 1963, by which time less than half the population of Greater London lived within the area of the London County Council. This Act completely reorganised the pattern of local government in Greater London and redrew the boundaries of the metropolitan area to correspond more closely with the physical facts. The new authorities set up by the Act were first elected in 1964 and became responsible for services on 1 April 1965.

City of London

The City of London stands apart. It was unaffected by the Municipal Corporation Acts and it shares with the Inns of Court

[1] Local Government Act 1933, s. 193; Parish Councils Act 1957. And see Cross, *op. cit.*, Appendix III.

the privilege of being a medieval corporation which has never undergone any reform from without. The City's constitution is unique and the City is still largely governed under its charters. Some local government functions are exercised by the City Corporation for its area of barely one square mile: public health, police, housing, open spaces and parks, libraries, markets and highways. Other local services, *e.g.* fire service, town planning and main drainage, are exercised in relation to the City's area by the Greater London Council, subject in the case of town planning control to a delegation scheme. The administrative structure of the City of London comprises three courts, whose composition is linked directly with the ancient City companies: the Court of Common Hall, the Court of Aldermen and the Court of Common Council. The latter body is the major governing body of the corporation and is named in statutes which vest local government powers in the City. It consists of the Lord Mayor, Aldermen and Councillors. The aldermen and councillors are elected at the wardmotes, the former for life, the latter annually, by the local government electors of the ward; formerly membership of a ward was confined to the liverymen of the city companies or guilds. There are less than 5,000 persons resident within the City and for the purpose of elections to the Greater London Council, the City forms a ward within the Greater London Borough of Westminster.

The London Government Act 1963

With effect from 1 April 1965, this Act abolished the London County Council, the Middlesex County Council, three county boroughs, 28 metropolitan borough councils, 39 non-county borough councils, 15 urban district councils and several *ad hoc* authorities. In their place were constituted the Greater London Council and thirty-two Greater London borough councils. The scheme is based on a two-tier structure which is significantly different both from the two-tier system outside Greater London, and from the former two-tier system within the area of the London County Council. The greater London boroughs are stronger in financial resources and population than the authorities they replaced and exercise much wider powers than the former metropolitan boroughs. The principle embodied in the 1963 Act, based on the recommendation of a Royal Commission,[1] was to confer as many functions as possible on the greater London boroughs, and to vest in the Greater London Council only certain vital powers which concerned the

[1] *Report of Royal Commission on Local Government in Greater London,* 1957–60, Cmnd. 1164.

whole area, in respect of traffic regulation, highways, town planning, housing, sewage disposal and some other regulatory and licensing functions. The greater London boroughs have important highways, traffic and planning functions and the Greater London Council may delegate powers to them; they are the primary authorities for housing, public health, personal health services, welfare and children's services, and they are also the rating authorities. For education, an *ad hoc* authority exists for the twelve inner boroughs, formerly the area of the London County Council; the twenty outer boroughs are themselves the local education authorities.

Certain local services for London continue to be provided by *ad hoc* authorities, *e.g.* the Metropolitan Police, the Metropolitan Water Board and the Port of London Authority. The Transport (London) Act 1969 established a new public corporation, the London Transport Executive, whose relationship with the Greater London Council is intended to be broadly similar to that which exists between the board of a nationalised industry and the central government.

The composition, constitution and general powers of the greater London authorities are governed by the Act of 1963 but are broadly comparable with those of local authorities outside the metropolis; thus a greater London borough council consists of a mayor, aldermen and councillors, the latter being elected every three years. Where the Act broke new ground was in the allocation of functions. between the Greater London Council and the borough councils.

Consequential changes in the structure of the criminal courts within Greater London were made by the Administration of Justice Act 1964.[1]

E. Scotland

The Scottish Office [2]

Local government in Scotland has had its own history but in recent years general legislation relating to local government in England and Wales has been applied in a modified form to Scotland. The Local Government (Scotland) Act 1947 is the counterpart for Scotland of the Local Government Act 1933, which applies only to England and Wales. For Scotland the place of the Ministry of Housing and Local Government is taken by the Secretary of State for Scotland, as the head of the Scottish Office; this Office is directly concerned with the Scottish local authorities through the Departments of Agriculture and Fisheries, the Education Department, the

[1] Pp. 298 and 302, *ante*.
[2] P. 214, *ante*.

Home and Health Department and the Development Department. The latter Department is responsible for the organisation and general health of local government, in addition to its responsibility for housing, town planning and transport.

Local Authorities

As with the English boroughs, the Scottish burghs are the oldest of the present local authorities, although in their elective form they are classed either as large or small, the small burghs having few important functions except housing. County councils were introduced in 1889 replacing the justices of the peace and the commissioners of supply. The Local Government (Scotland) Act 1929 abolished a number of *ad hoc* authorities in favour of the elected councils. Outside the areas of the burghs, there are district councils, but these have few important functions and correspond more to the English parish councils. There are also four counties of cities which have a position similar to that of the county borough in England.

The local government franchise is now the same as that in England.[1] Registration as an elector or residence are in general the qualifications for election to a council. Arrangements for elections are similar to those in England, with one-third of the town councillors retiring each year and the county councillors retiring together every third year.. One difference is that the members of the county council who represent the burghs are elected by the town councils and not directly by the electorate, and they do not have the right to participate fully in the county council's business. Although there is a different terminology for municipal offices (*e.g.* the provost of a burgh, the convener of a county council), the rules applicable to members of local authorities are similar to those in England; for example, a person who has a pecuniary interest in a contract with the council is disqualified from discussing or voting on any question relating thereto. Auditors are appointed by the Secretary of State to audit local authority accounts,[2] but they are not members of the Scottish Office and the power of surcharge is exercisable only by the Secretary of State, after receiving the auditor's report and, if requested, holding a local inquiry. As in England and Wales, the larger local authorities, and particularly the four counties of cities (Aberdeen, Dundee, Edinburgh and Glasgow) have acquired special powers under local legislation. The most commonly used procedure is that provided by the Private Legislation (Scotland) Act 1936, a procedure which is broadly similar to the provisional order procedure in England.[3]

[1] Chap. 26, *post.*
[2] P. 382, *post.*
[3] P. 376, *post.*

In Scotland, possibly to an even greater extent than in England, the present structure of local government displays extreme variation in population, needs and resources between local authorities; in many remoter areas of Scotland, the rating system is wholly inadequate to meet the expenses of local administration. Parallel with the work of the Royal Commission on Local Government in England 1966–9,[1] a Royal Commission under the chairmanship of Lord Wheatley examined the organisation of local government in Scotland. In 1969 it reported in favour of a radical reform of local government, recommending a new two-tier structure for Scotland of 7 regional councils and 37 district councils, to take the place of the 4 counties of cities, 33 county councils, 21 large burghs, 176 small burghs and 196 district councils.[2]

No attempt has been made in this chapter to describe in detail the powers and duties of the various local authorities in relation to the services executed by them. For a full account of local government in England and Wales, reference should be made to the works listed at p. 336 above. Local government in Scotland is described in J. D. B. Mitchell, *Constitutional Law*, (W. Green & Son) chap. 13.

[1] P. 341, *ante*.
[2] Cmnd. 4150 (1969).

CHAPTER TWENTY-SIX

LOCAL GOVERNMENT ELECTIONS, LEGISLATION AND FINANCE

A. Local Government Elections

Local Government Franchise

Prior to 1945 the local government franchise rested on the occupation of land or premises. The right to vote at a local government election was thus broadly coincident with liability to assessment for rating purposes. The Representation of the People Act 1945 extended to parliamentary electors as such the right to be registered and to vote as local government electors. The Act did not, however, assimilate the two franchises, since it preserved the previous local government franchise both in England and Wales and in Scotland for those owners and occupiers who did not qualify for the parliamentary franchise by reason of residence in the qualifying premises and for peers disqualified from voting at parliamentary elections. These qualifications were continued by the Representation of the People Act 1949 but the non-resident property qualification was abolished by the Representation of the People Act 1969. The main qualification for registration as a local government elector is now residence on the qualifying date within the area concerned. Only British subjects or citizens of the Republic of Ireland of full age who are not under any legal incapacity are entitled to be registered.

In addition, members of the forces wherever serving and civilian Crown servants employed outside the United Kingdom, and their wives residing with them, may also be registered, as if they were resident at the address at which they would be residing but for their service.[1] Electors in this class may vote by proxy.

The register comes into force each year on 16 February as a register of parliamentary and local government electors, those who are only qualified to vote at local government elections being marked to indicate that fact. The qualifying date for inclusion in the register is the preceding October 10.[2]

[1] P. 108, *ante*.
[2] Pp. 108–9, *ante*.

Qualifications for Membership

Whereas candidates for parliamentary elections may stand for any constituency, candidates at local elections have to satisfy a test of local connection. There are two alternative qualifications for election to membership of a local authority, in addition to that of being a British subject or citizen of the Republic of Ireland of full age:

(*i*) registration as a local government elector within the area of the local authority; or

(*ii*) residence within the area of the authority for the whole of the twelve months before the day on which the candidate is nominated for election.

A former qualification based on ownership of property within the area was abolished by the Representation of the People Act 1969, s. 15.

Where the successful candidate at an election does not fulfil one of these conditions, his election may be challenged by election petition and declared void.[1] Aldermen, who are elected by the councillors of county and borough councils, must either be councillors themselves or qualified to be elected; the office of councillor is vacated on election as an alderman. In the case of parish councils, the second qualification above is varied to residence within three miles of the parish boundaries since 25 March in the preceding year.

Disqualifications

The chief disqualifications from membership are:

(*i*) the holding of paid office or other place of profit in the gift or disposal of the council concerned or of any of its committees, other than that of mayor or chairman of the county council;[2]

(*ii*) bankruptcy, unless certified not to be attributable to the debtor's misconduct, or composition with creditors;

(*iii*) imprisonment for an offence for not less than three months without option of a fine within five years before election, or since election;

(*iv*) surcharge (consequent upon disallowance of expenditure) of more than £500 by a district auditor within the same periods;[3]

(*v*) conviction under enactments relating to corrupt or illegal practices at elections.[4]

Formerly a person was disqualified from membership of a county or borough council if he had directly or indirectly a share or interest

[1] E.g. *Re West Suffolk (East Ward) Election*, (1964) 108 Sol. Jo. 604.

[2] See *Lamb* v. *Jeffries*, [1956] 1 Q.B. 431, schoolmaster whose appointment subject to confirmation by borough council disqualified from council membership.

[3] P. 382, *post*.

[4] P. 110, *ante*.

in any contract with or employment by the council, a rule that completely excluded many business men and shareholders from local authority membership. In 1933 a different safeguard was introduced: if a member of a local authority has "any pecuniary interest, direct or indirect, in any contract or proposed contract or other matter", and is present at a council meeting or committee when the matter is being considered, he must disclose his interest and thereafter take no part in the discussion nor vote.[1] Many councils in their own standing orders require a member who cannot thus take part in a discussion to withdraw from the meeting until the decision is made. Certain interests which members may have as ratepayers, as members of the public, or as consumers of public utilities, are not affected, but a councillor who holds shares in a company which may contract with the council has an indirect pecuniary interest which must be disclosed; in the case of certain minority shareholdings with a nominal value of less than £500, ownership must be disclosed but voting and discussion are not affected. Disclosure has generally to be made of the interests of the councillor's spouse. The clerk of the council must keep a record of all interests disclosed. Breach of these rules does not in itself affect the validity of the council's decision[2], but is a criminal offence, subject to summary prosecution on the decision of the Director of Public Prosecutions, with a maximum penalty of £200. Although the Minister of Housing and Local Government has power to remove the ban on discussion and even that on voting if, *e.g.* so many members of the council are council tenants that the business of the council is impeded, the definition of "interest" has been interpreted stringently.[3] In 1964 Parliament provided that no pecuniary interest was to be relevant which was so remote or insignificant that it could not reasonably be regarded as likely to influence a member in considering the particular contract or other matter.[4] In 1967, the Minister granted a general dispensation to councillors who were tenants of council houses permitting them to speak and vote on matters of general housing policy.[5]

Just as members of local authorities are required to have some local attachment before being elected, so they are required to show a minimal interest in the affairs of the council after being elected: a member who fails throughout six consecutive months to attend any

[1] Local Government Act 1933, s. 76.

[2] But see *The King* v. *Hendon Rural District Council, ex parte Chorley*, [1933] 2 K.B. 696 for means of challenging council's decision, p. 650, *post*.

[3] *Brown* v. *Director of Public Prosecutions* [1956] 2 Q.B. 369; *Rands* v. *Oldroyd* [1959] 1 Q.B. 204.

[4] Local Government (Pecuniary Interests) Act 1964.

[5] Ministry of Housing and Local Government, circular No. 5/67.

meeting of the local authority, including committees, ceases to be a member of the authority unless his absence is due to a reason approved by the council.[1]

Conduct of Elections

The conduct of local elections is governed by the Representation of the People Act 1949 and related legislation. With certain modifications, *e.g.* a much lower limit for permitted expenses, local elections are conducted similarly to parliamentary elections. The ballot is secret, there are penalties for corrupt and illegal practices, and the results of elections can be challenged by way of petition to the High Court.

For the purposes of electoral areas, county councils are divided into single-member divisions; most boroughs are divided into wards each returning three members, one of whom retires each year. There may also be a ward division in the urban districts but in rural districts it is usual to have a single parish or group of smaller parishes returning one or more members. The division of a local authority's area into electoral areas is never within the absolute control of the authority itself. The alteration of electoral divisions in a county is a matter for the Home Secretary's decision, but the request for a review must come from the county council or a district council. The division of a borough into wards is initially provided by the borough's charter of incorporation; subsequent changes can be made only by Order in Council, following a petition from the borough council to the Queen in Council and an inquiry by the Home Secretary. Within urban and rural districts, electoral areas can be altered by order of the county council, subject to notifying the Home Secretary and the Ministry of Housing and Local Government and to considering representations received.

County council elections are held once every three years, all councillors retiring together, on a date in April fixed by the county council itself. Borough council elections are held each year on a date in May appointed for all boroughs by the Home Secretary. With urban and rural districts, although the Local Government Act 1933 envisages that one-third of the councillors shall retire annually, there is provision for the adoption of simultaneous retirement; in either event, elections are held on a date fixed by the county council after consultation with the district councils. Parish council elections are held triennially, on the same day as the rural district council election for the parishes concerned.[2]

[1] Local Government Act 1933, s. 63.
[2] Local Government Elections Act 1956.

B. Legislation affecting Local Authorities

A local authority is a body corporate, constituted by statute and endowed with statutory powers. County councils, urban and rural district councils, and parish councils are all statutory bodies deriving their general and particular powers from legislation. Municipal corporations are an exception to the general rule, in that having been created by royal charter issued under prerogative powers, they may be regarded as common law corporations and, as such, not subject to the same statutory limitations on their powers; for practical purposes however most powers exercised by boroughs are statutory and in particular, since the Municipal Corporations Act 1835, all municipal corporations have been subject to restrictions placed on their power to incur expenditure.[1]

Constituent Acts

General legislation relating to local authorities falls into two classes. The first class comprises what may be called the constituent Acts, those which relate to the constitution of authorities, their composition and manner of election, the position of members and officers, the power to appoint committees, enter into contracts and hold property, financial procedure, and so on. In this class, the Local Government Act 1933 is the most important; although it retained some of the historical distinctions between borough, county and district councils, it provided where possible a common code of general powers for all local authorities. This code has been modified and supplemented by such statutes as the Local Government Acts 1948 and 1958, the Local Government (Financial Provisions) Act 1963 and the Local Authorities (Land) Act 1963.

Acts relating to particular Services

The second class of local government legislation consists of those measures which enable a particular service to be carried on and for this purpose vest both powers and duties in a named class of local authority. Examples are the Education Act 1944, the Highways Act 1959 and the Town and Country Planning Act 1962. Although many of the powers conferred by these Acts are permissive, in the sense that the local authority is free to exercise them or not, the powers are none the less available to the authority if needed without any further formality or procedural step.

[1] Cf. *Attorney-General* v. *Leicester Corporation*, [1943] Ch. 86.

Adoptive Acts

An adoptive act also relates to a particular service, but directly it confers no powers on local authorities other than the power to take the steps prescribed in the Act for "adopting" the Act. If an authority wishes to adopt the Act, it must go through the stated procedure (*e.g.* special resolution of the council, followed by the approval of the Minister) and the scheme of powers in the Act thereupon becomes available. Once adopted, the authority must abide by the terms of the Act as it would those of any non-adoptive Act. The adoptive principle played a large part in the development of local government by consent during the last century. Today some powers are still adoptive.[1] But the modern equivalent of the adoptive procedure is the need to obtain consent from the Minister or the county council before certain powers are exercised.[2]

Private and Local Acts

The legislation discussed above is enacted by means of public general Acts. Local or private Acts are still important to local authorities in the acquisition of powers. In the eighteenth and nineteenth centuries they were the means by which local initiatives were expressed in law. Parliamentary procedures developed to safeguard private interests against excessive power being granted to new *ad hoc* authorities; this was essential for, by virtue of the supremacy of Parliament, the provisions of a local Act are as binding as those of a public general Act.[3] With the reforming general legislation of the period after 1832 the need for local legislation lessened. But today the demands on Parliament's legislative time are such that general legislation may have to wait for several years after the need for certain additional powers has become evident to local authorities and Government alike.[4] Thus, although the expense of legislation is high, larger local authorities may consider it worthwhile to promote their own Bills, either for acquiring a variety of general powers,[5] or for obtaining powers to carry through a single project which will involve large capital expenditure, the acquisition of land, the construc-

[1] *E.g.* see Public Health Acts Amendment Act 1890 and Public Health Act 1925.

[2] Compare the adoptive Public Libraries Acts 1892 and 1919 with the Public Libraries and Museums Act 1964.

[3] See *Lee* v. *Bude and Torrington Rly. Co.* (1871), L.R.6 C.P. 577; p. 47, *ante*.

[4] In 1956 it was recommended by a parliamentary committee that powers which had become common in local Acts should be extended to local authorities generally by Bills to be introduced by the Government at least every ten years: the Public Health Act 1961 was the first of these general measures.

[5] *E.g.* Walsall Corporation Act 1969.

tion of works and the exercise of additional control powers.[1] Private Bills may also be promoted in connection with the organisation and development of the public utilities; since the nationalisation of gas and electricity, the water supply industry is the major field for such legislation, but even here the Minister of Housing and Local Government has wide powers of attaining the same ends by statutory order.[2]

Procedure of Local Legislation

The parliamentary aspects of private Bill legislation have been described above.[3] All promoters of private legislation have to comply with the Standing Orders of each House of Parliament designed to prevent the abuse of Parliament's authority. All local authorities empowered to promote legislation (*i.e.* all except rural parishes) have in addition to comply with a procedure laid down in the Local Government Act 1933, intended to prevent a local authority recklessly embarking on the heavy costs of legislation. The Ministry of Housing and Local Government must consent to the council's resolution to promote a Bill; borough and urban district councils must also obtain the approval of a meeting of local government electors (town meeting) and, if requested, of a poll of all electors. Where a Bill is opposed, the proceedings in Parliament enable all affected interests and individuals to be heard in committee. Government departments are also able to comment on proposals which affect them. A further safeguard is provided in the House of Lords by the Lord Chairman of Committees, and in the House of Commons by the Chairman of Ways and Means, who consider in detail even unopposed Bills and may require a local authority's proposals to follow precedents in earlier legislation.

An example of the use to which private legislation can be put is the promotion by a county council of a Bill seeking to confer powers on the district councils within the county. The desirability of this practice was challenged in 1958, when the Kent County Council promoted a Bill of 442 clauses, of which 237 concerned only the district councils in Kent. A Joint Committee of Parliament on Private Bills to which the matter was referred found that it was of general convenience for a county council to promote legislation of this kind.[4]

One difficulty arises whenever, after many local authorities have

[1] *E.g.* Tamar Bridge Act 1957.
[2] Water Act 1945; Water Resources Act 1963.
[3] P. 150, *ante*.
[4] H.L. 176, H.C. 262 (1959).

acquired powers in a certain field, general legislation is passed relating to the same subject matter. To what extent does a local authority continue to enjoy its former special powers, which may not be subject to the same safeguards as the general legislation provides? Often it would be difficult or undesirable for the general Act to make a blanket repeal of all earlier local Act provisions; instead, the expedient is adopted of conferring on the appropriate Minister power by order to modify where necessary the private Acts concerned.[1] This is one of the exceptional situations where power is conferred on a Minister to alter an Act of Parliament by order.[2] It may be justified by the fact that many matters which formerly could be authorised only by private Act, such as the compulsory purchase of land, are now properly within the competence of a Minister.

Provisional Orders

In addition to the promotion of private or local Bills there are other ways open to local authorities, as well as to undertakings seeking statutory powers for the conduct of services, whereby statutory powers of local application can be obtained. The oldest of the methods, which dates from the mid-Victorian legislation relating to public health, is known as provisional order procedure. A provisional order is an order made by a Minister under authority conferred by an enabling Act on the application of a local authority or statutory undertaker where Parliament has sanctioned this course for a particular purpose. The order is provisional in the sense that it requires express confirmation by Parliament before it operates to confer the powers sought. This is given by a Provisional Order Confirmation Bill, which is a public Bill introduced by, or on behalf of, the Minister concerned. Opponents of the order may be heard at two stages. In the first place, if any objections are put forward by interested parties as a result of the advertisement of the application which is a necessary preliminary to its promotion, the making of the order by the Minister is preceded by a public inquiry. This is conducted by an official appointed by the Minister who is usually an officer with specialised knowledge of the matter at issue. Again, while the Confirmation Bill is pending in either House of Parliament, a petitioner can appear before the select committee to which the Bill is referred. The procedure thereafter follows the lines of that for private Bills. It has been used extensively under Acts relating to

[1] *E.g.*, Local Authorities (Land) Act 1963, s. 9; Local Government (Financial Provisions) Act 1963, s. 12.

[2] P. 606, *post*.

public health, water supplies and the extension of boundaries of local authorities. It is less expensive than the promotion of a private Bill, particularly when unopposed, and usually ensures that the promoter can learn the strength of the opposition he is likely to meet at an early stage. At the same time it preserves to Parliament the right, which is seldom exercised in practice, to reject or to amend the Confirmation Bill.

Ministerial Orders

When a provisional order is opposed, the provisional order procedure is almost as cumbrous as private legislation. The trend in this century has been to substitute for the provisional order the ministerial order, which comes into effect simply by ministerial action. This type of order is often made by a Minister to confirm a scheme put before him by a local authority after a local public inquiry at which the reasons for the scheme and objections to the scheme are publicly presented. Formerly the compulsory purchase of land could be authorised only by provisional order or by private legislation; today the Acquisition of Land (Authorisation Procedure) Act 1946 provides a uniform procedure by compulsory purchase order. Under this Act, the order takes effect as soon as the Minister's confirmation is announced and thereafter the order can be challenged in the High Court only on the ground of *ultra vires*.[1] From the point of view of opponents of the order, the defect of this procedure is that there is no opportunity of putting their case before a committee in Parliament if the Minister should overrule the objections presented at the public inquiry. This limitation seems even greater in a case where the proposal for the scheme is put forward, not by a local authority, but by the Minister himself, *e.g.* under the New Towns Act 1965. In such cases the Minister's confirmation may exceptionally be made subject to approval or rejection by Parliament.[2]

Special Parliamentary Procedure

Neither the provisional order nor the ministerial order is wholly desirable where both a measure of central control by Parliament is desirable on grounds of national policy and at the same time speedier action is required than is available for the passage of an opposed Provisional Order Confirmation Bill. In 1945 provision was made which, while preserving the right of interested parties to a public inquiry and to be heard before a parliamentary committee on objections to detail, affords an opportunity to any member of

[1] Pp. 667–9, *post*.
[2] New Towns Act 1965, s. 53; cf. p. 654, *post*.

Parliament to raise on the floor of the House any question of general policy that may be involved: the Statutory Orders (Special Procedure) Act 1945 applies to any future statutory powers for any authority to make or to confirm orders where the power is required to be subject to "special parliamentary procedure." [1]

Byelaws

Byelaws are an important means whereby a local authority exercises its regulative functions. No local authority has a residual power to make local laws affecting the public at large, but county councils and borough councils may make byelaws "for the good rule and government" of their areas and "for the prevention and suppression of nuisances".[2] There are also more specific powers to make byelaws conferred by such legislation as the Public Health Acts and the Water Act 1945.[3] The byelaw making power is restricted in various ways. The maximum penalty for breach of a byelaw is fixed in the enabling statute. Byelaws normally can come into force only after confirmation by the Ministry of Housing and Local Government or by the Home Office, as the case may be. In consequence of this central control, it is the practice to adopt, with or without modification, model sets of byelaws drawn up by the confirming department. Byelaws are subject to review in the courts: the courts may declare a byelaw invalid on the grounds of *ultra vires*, uncertainty, inconsistency with the general law,[4] and even unreasonableness, but a byelaw made by a public authority will not readily be condemned by a court on this ground.[5] In some fields the byelaw making power has given way to regulations made by the Minister: thus building standards are now regulated by ministerial regulations, no longer by byelaws.[6]

C. Local Government Finance

Sources of Revenue

There are four principal sources of revenue available to meet the needs of a local authority: (i) rates, (ii) contributions from the central government, (iii) loans, and (iv) fees, charges and income from trading undertakings and from estates.

[1] For details, including application to provisional order procedure under earlier Acts, see Hart, *op. cit.*, pp. 334–8.

[2] Local Government Act 1933, s. 249.

[3] See Cross, *Local Government Law*, Appendix VI.

[4] *Powell* v. *May*, [1946] K.B.330; *London Passenger Transport Board* v. *Sumner* (1935), 99 J.P. 387.

[5] *Kruse* v. *Johnson*, [1898] 2 Q.B. 91; K. & L. 48.

[6] Public Health Act 1961.

Rates [1]

Rates are a form of local taxation charged on the occupation of land and buildings. The amount varies with the annual value of the property. Some kinds of property, e.g. places of public worship, are exempted from rating altogether; property occupied by charitable or other voluntary organisations is subject to a reduction in the amount of rates paid. The inherent limitations of a tax based simply on the value of the land or building, without regard to the means of the occupier, have led to various expedients being devised to protect some types of property against excessive burdens; industrial property was subject to a proportion of de-rating between 1929 and 1963, and agricultural land is still exempt from rating. In 1963 new valuation lists came into force and several of these expedients disappeared, but temporary provision was made to protect the occupiers of certain dwelling-houses against too drastic an increase in their rate-burden. Since 1966, there has been permanent provision enabling ratepayers of low income to claim rate rebates in respect of private dwellings.[2] Although rates are in principle based on the occupation of property, rating authorities now have limited powers of rating the owners of unoccupied property.[3]

Rateable Value

A rate is assessed on the annual value of land or buildings, and statute prescribes in detail how this value may be calculated. The annual value represents the rent at which the property might reasonably be expected to be let from year to year, less the annual cost of repairs, insurance and other expenses. The law thus assumes the existence of a hypothetical tenant, and calculates what sum he would be prepared to pay for a lease on such terms. Special methods are provided for calculating the value of large undertakings, such as waterworks, harbours and mines. Special provision is also made for assessing the liability to pay rates, or sums in lieu of rates, of the nationalised transport, gas and electricity industries. Properties occupied for the purposes of the Crown are exempt from rating; in practice the Treasury makes a contribution in lieu of rates to the appropriate local authorities, based on a special valuation of Crown properties.

[1] The law of rating is now consolidated in the General Rate Act 1967.
[2] General Rate Act 1967, s. 49 and 9th Schedule.
[3] General Rate Act 1967, s. 17 and 1st Schedule.

Mode of Assessment

In 1948 the valuation of property for rating purposes was transferred from the local authorities themselves to the Commissioners of Inland Revenue. A valuation officer of the Inland Revenue Department prepares a valuation list, containing the individual values attributed to all properties in the rating area subject to rating. The list is published, and objections may be made to the valuation officer, who can himself revise the list after the period for objection has passed. Failing agreement, there is an appeal to the local valuation court, a special tribunal of three persons drawn from a local valuation panel, and thence to the Lands Tribunal,[1] or the case may by agreement be referred to arbitration. In principle, revaluation takes place every five years but proposals to alter the list may be made at any time by the owner or occupier affected or by the local valuation officer, and the rating authority also plays some part in the procedure of alteration.

Mode of Collection

The rating authorities are the borough, urban and rural district councils. County councils, parish councils and joint boards are not themselves rating authorities and precept on the rating authorities for the sums required. The rate is a uniform amount in the £ on the assessment of each rating unit (hereditament) of land and buildings. It is levied twice a year by the rating authority to meet the expenses of a fixed period, usually six months. The general rate is charged on all properties within the rating authority's area, but additional items of expenditure may in rural districts be charged on certain parishes only to meet the cost, *e.g.* of street lighting, incurred only for the benefit of those parishes. Similarly the county's expenses are either general, recoverable from the whole of the administrative county, or special, recoverable from certain districts only. The amount of the rate is fixed by relating the total sum needed to the total rateable value of the area. The demand note issued each half year to ratepayers follows a prescribed form, showing how the rate per pound is broken down among the different services financed from the rates. Payment of rates is enforceable only by summary proceedings in the magistrates' court for a distress warrant.[2]

Contributions from the Central Government

While local government remained simply a matter for local initiative, and the interests of the ratepayers dictated the services undertaken, the rates could be regarded as payment for benefits

[1] Pp. 699–700 *post*. And see *The Queen* v. *Paddington Valuation Officer*, p. 664, *post*.

[2] General Rate Act 1967, ss. 96–107.

received. The introduction of new services at the instance of the central government, the broader concept of a public service, the desire to maintain national standards, the disparity between the resources and needs of different local authorities and other shortcomings of the rating system, are all reasons why the central government should make grants to local authorities from the national exchequer. Government grants take two main forms:

(1) the specific grant in aid of a particular service, calculated as a fixed proportion of the costs of the service; the first grants of this kind were made to assist local authorities in administering the criminal law and the new police forces in 1835 and 1856 respectively; the Elementary Education Act 1870 also provided for grants towards the cost of elementary schools. This form of grant was accompanied by a measure of control over the receiving authorities, *e.g.* by inspection, Ministerial consents.

(2) the general grant to increase a local authority's overall income; the first grant of this kind was made in 1929, but since 1888 county authorities had been allowed to retain certain national taxes collected locally as a form of general grant. With a general grant, there is likely to be less detailed control of particular services.

The grant system has been recast several times.[1] In 1958, substantial amendments were made to local government finance with the aim of increasing the independence of local authorities in raising and spending money.[2] The present system, introduced in 1966,[3] marks a change of policy, in accepting the need for a progressive increase in the proportion of local expenditure borne from the Exchequer. The total amount of the rate support grant, which has replaced earlier general grants, is fixed by the Ministry of Housing with the consent of the Treasury, after consultation with local authority associations. It must take account of the current level of all revenue expenditure of local authorities (apart from housing), of any probable fluctuation in the demand for or cost of services and of the need to develop services. The total is then reduced by the amount of various specific grants paid by the Exchequer to local authorities and the balance is available for distribution. This comprises three elements (*a*) the resources element, paid to authorities whose rateable resources are below the national average; (*b*) the needs element, a general grant assessed for each council by a complex formula which takes account of such factors as population (including proportion of infants, school

[1] In particular, by Local Government Acts of 1888, 1929, 1948, 1958 and 1966.

[2] See Cmnd. 209, 1957, and Local Government Act 1958, Part I.

[3] Local Government Act 1966, Part I.

children and old people), road mileage and density of population; and (*c*) the domestic element, designed to shield the domestic ratepayer from the increasing burden of rates, and assessed on the basis of an amount in the pound which the Minister prescribes for deduction from the rate poundage levied on domestic property. When a "rate support grant order" embodying the results of these calculations is made by the Minister, it must be approved by the House of Commons before it comes into operation.[1]

The rate support grant is paid in aid of the revenues of a local authority generally, but some specific grants continue to be paid. These include police (50 per cent of net expenditure), highways (proportion varying according to class of road), housing (subsidy per dwelling, depending on the kind of house) and town planning (for the acquisition and development of land for various public purposes). Grants are also payable by the Home Secretary to local authorities undergoing special expenditure by reason of the presence of large numbers of Commonwealth immigrants and also to authorities in whose areas special social need exists.[2]

It is not easy to assess the extent to which the changes in the rating and grant systems made in 1958 and 1966 have increased local autonomy. Control of the level of local expenditure is now realised to be a major factor in controlling the economy. Moreover, the very high cost of education, local government's most expensive service, absorbs the greater part of the total grant. The residual control power of the central government to maintain standards of efficiency by withholding all or part of the general grant has already been mentioned;[3] the mere threat of exercising this power could force a local authority to meet the government's wishes, for more than half its income comes directly from the central government.

Loans and Other Revenue

Just as a trading company increases its capital by borrowing on the security of its assets to finance further developments, so a local authority, subject to strict statutory regulations, may raise loans for the purpose of financing its permitted activities. The security offered is that of the fund formed by the revenue under the authority's control and the land owned by it. The power to borrow may be

[1] For the year 1969–70, the total rate support grant for England and Wales was £1,528 million, being 56 per cent of the aggregate estimate of local revenue expenditure for that year: S.I. No. 1956 of 1968.

[2] Local Government Act 1966, s. 11; Local Government Grants (Social Need) Act 1969.

[3] P. 351, *ante*

conferred in three ways. A general power of borrowing for purposes which local authorities are empowered to carry out is given by the Local Government Act 1933. Its exercise is subject to the sanction of the Minister of Housing and Local Government, or, in the case of transport undertakings only, the Minister of Transport. In the second place, loans authorised by local Acts are raised by the larger urban authorities; in this way powers may be obtained over and above those conferred by the general law. Borrowing powers conferred by local Acts may be made exercisable without the sanction of the Minister, if the estimates are proved before the committee of Parliament which considers the Bill, but returns of the expenditure of the money so borrowed must be made to him. Thirdly, a provisional order may confer borrowing powers, in which case the previous consent of a government department is required, as well as parliamentary sanction. Local authorities can borrow from the Public Works Loan Commissioners, a body which was created in 1817 for the purpose of advancing money to municipal bodies, or from independent sources of finance, including the raising of a loan on the open market and the issuing of bonds. An important difference between borrowing by a local authority and the share capital of a limited company is that a local authority is required to repay the loan over a fixed period of years, subject generally to a maximum of 60 years. Subject to certain limits local authorities may set up capital funds to defray capital expenditure and may transfer to them limited amounts of rate-income. The larger local authorities may set up a consolidated loans fund, permitting them to average out the different rates of interest being paid.[1]

Other sources of revenue may be briefly noted: profits from public utility undertakings (chiefly confined to urban authorities), *e.g.* water and transport undertakings, markets, income from other corporate property and miscellaneous fees.

Financial Procedure

As with the central government and the House of Commons, local authorities observe a yearly financial cycle linked with the financial year which in local government begins on 1 April. The first stage is the preparation of estimates of income and expenditure by each spending committee for the coming year; these are then submitted to the council's finance committee which must consider the total effect of the estimates on the council's finances. When approved by the finance committee, the estimates are submitted to the whole council, with a recommendation from the finance committee as to the rate in

[1] Local Government Act 1958, s. 55.

the £ that should be levied, taking into account the government grants payable, the likely income from rents etc. The council then adopts the estimates and fixes the rate to be levied. All local authorities are required to set up a single fund through which in general all payments must pass; for district and borough councils this is known as the general rate fund, and for county councils the county fund. County and rural district councils have to maintain separate accounts distinguishing between general expenses, and special expenses borne only by some areas. Until 1958 there was stringent legal regulation of the making of payments by local authorities; thus in a borough, payments could only be made by the treasurer under the authority of the council, signed by three members and countersigned by the town clerk, with the possibility of challenge in the High Court by any person aggrieved. The present position is that local authorities are required to make safe and efficient arrangement for the receipt and issue of moneys, these arrangements to be carried out under the supervision of the treasurer.[1]

Audit

The authority's treasurer is responsible for the maintenance of proper accounts and for this purpose, as in every large undertaking, there will be a staff of qualified accountants exercising a continuing check on receipts and expenditure. All local authorities are subject to the further safeguard of external audit of each year's accounts, although the form of audit depends on the class of authority. The accounts of all county councils, district councils and Greater London authorities are subject to district audit, a public audit comparable with that carried out by the Comptroller and Auditor-General in relation to the accounts of government departments.[2] The district auditors are civil servants appointed by the Minister of Housing and Local Government, but in the performance of their duties they exercise an independent and quasi-judicial function. Any local government elector may object before the district auditor to items appearing in the accounts and the district auditor must disallow any payments which are not warranted in law. The amounts concerned must be surcharged upon the persons incurring the wrongful expenditure, whether elected members or officers of the authority. Even excessive expenditure on lawful objects may be surcharged.[3] There is a right of appeal against the district auditor's decision, either to the High Court or to the Minister.[4] A surcharge of over £500 disqualifies

[1] Local Government Act 1958, s. 58.
[2] P. 227, *ante*.
[3] See *Roberts* v. *Hopwood*, p. 645, *post*.
[4] P. 669, *post*.

the person surcharged from membership of the local authority concerned for five years. The district auditor cannot disallow any sum of expenditure which has been sanctioned in advance by the Minister; the need for this dispensing power may now be less in view of the general power of local authorities to incur expenditure for the benefit of the inhabitants of their area that was conferred in 1963.[1]

In the case of borough councils, the audit requirements are different. Certain accounts of all boroughs are subject to district audit (*e.g.* education, personal health services, child care and welfare services, and, so far as grants are paid, highways and housing). Apart from this, borough accounts may be audited by two elected borough auditors and a mayor's auditor, an ineffective system of audit dating from 1835; in practice most boroughs have changed either to district audit or to professional audit, as allowed by the Local Government Act 1933. Neither borough auditors nor professional auditors have powers of disallowance or surcharge.

District audit is not the only safeguard against unlawful expenditure by a local authority: it is possible to obtain an injunction restraining the authority from incurring the expenditure or a declaration that the expenditure is unlawful.[2] If such a remedy is sought, the prior consent of the Minister to the expenditure will be no justification.

[1] Local Government (Financial Provisions) Act 1963. s. 6. and p. 343, *ante*.
[2] See *Attorney-General* v. *Fulham Corporation*, p. 639, *post* and *Prescott* v. *Birmingham Corporation*, p. 620, *post*.

PART I: General Constitutional Law

THE ROYAL FORCES: MILITARY AND MARTIAL LAW

Manual of Military Law, especially Part II, Section I. (History of Military Law).
Law of the Constitution, 10th edn., by A. V. Dicey, Part II, Chaps. VIII and IX.

CHAPTER TWENTY-SEVEN

THE FORCES OF THE CROWN

THERE will now be considered the structure of central government in relation to defence, the composition and discipline of the armed forces, the nature of military law and the status of those who are subject to it. There will also be considered those special common law powers for the preservation of public order which may be exercised by the Executive and by military commanders in a time of major emergency. When an emergency arises or is foreseen, statutory powers are normally taken to enable the Executive to meet it, but the common law powers remain.[1] The common law imposes upon every citizen (and the soldier is no less a citizen because he is also a soldier) the duty to take all necessary steps to resist invasion and suppress insurrections. Those in command of troops are in the best position to deal with invasion or insurrection. In order to fulfil their duty it will be necessary for military commanders to interfere with the liberty of civilians. The imposition of the will of military commanders upon the civil population is often referred to—it is submitted unfortunately—as "martial law." It is convenient to discuss this topic in connection with the armed forces of the Crown.

A. Organisation for Defence

The responsibility for a unified defence policy rests upon the Secretary of State for Defence whose office has undergone several changes since the post of Minister of Defence was created and

[1] See 363 H.C. Deb., cols. 65 ff, and particularly the Attorney-General at col. 137.

occupied by Sir Winston Churchill in the Second World War;[1] the present structure, a unified Ministry for the three Services, which dates from 1964, absorbed the Admiralty, the War Office and the Air Ministry, together with their procurement responsibilities. Responsibility for the development and procurement of aircraft, guided weapons and electronics required by the Services rests with the Ministry of Technology. On the other hand, the Royal Navy, the Army and the Royal Air Force retained their separate entities. At the head of the Ministry is the Secretary of State for Defence; he is assisted by two Ministers of Defence who rank as Ministers of State; one is responsible for administration, the other for equipment. There are also three Parliamentary Under-Secretaries of State, one for each Service. The offices of First Lord of the Admiralty and of the Secretaries of State for War and for Air were abolished. In place of the Board of Admiralty,[2] the Army Council and the Air Council there are Boards of the Defence Council for each of the three Services.

The basic principles underlying the unification of defence organisation rest on the assumption that control of defence policy requires a greater knowledge of the background problems and currents of opinion within the Services than can be secured by separate departments responsible to separate Ministers. It is not enough for a Minister for Defence to control defence policy unless he is also responsible for the machinery for the administration of the three Services. In the old days each Service Department with separate military, scientific and administrative staffs proved unable to establish a line of authority or responsibility in defence matters. In practice the Secretary of State for Defence delegates much of his authority, since it is the object of the present organisation that the Services should preserve their separate identities in the interests of efficiency and morale despite their increasing interdependance. A unified Defence Ministry is also held to be essential if the defence budget is to strike a proper balance between the three Services.

It is not possible to discuss major questions of defence policy in purely military terms without reference to foreign and economic policy. Moreover, political relations with other members of the Commonwealth have an important bearing on policy, while the requirements of the Government's financial and economic policies affect the size, disposition and equipment of the Services. Thus the collective responsibility of Ministers for defence is now dealt with by

[1] See in particular *Central Organisation for Defence*, Cmnd. 476, 1958, and *Central Organisation for Defence*, Cmnd. 2097, 1963.

[2] For the assumption of the title of Lord High Admiral by the Queen, see p. 187, *ante*.

a Committee on Defence and Overseas Policy under the chairmanship of the Prime Minister. The Committee normally includes the Foreign and Commonwealth Secretary, the Chancellor of the Exchequer, the Home Secretary, and the Secretary of State for Defence.

In attendance on this Cabinet Committee are the Chief of the Defence Staff and the Chiefs of Staff of each of the three Services if the nature of the business so requires. Civilian officials such as the Permanent Under-Secretary of State or the Chief Scientific Adviser may also attend as required. The Committee is supported by a Committee of senior officials. On appropriate occasions the Chief of the Defence Staff and the Chiefs of Staff, as in the past, are invited to attend meetings of the full Cabinet. They have a right of access to the Prime Minister.

All statutory powers for the defence of the realm which formerly were vested in the Service Ministries are now vested in the Secretary of State for Defence. There is a Defence Council consisting of the Secretary of State, the two Ministers of Defence, the three Parliamentary Under-Secretaries of State (one for each Service) the Chief of the Defence Staff, the three Chiefs of Staff, the Chief Adviser (Personnel and Logistics), the Chief Adviser (Projects and Research) and the Permanent Under-Secretary of State. This is the Council which deals mainly with major defence policy. Actual management of the Services is delegated to separate Boards for Navy, Army and Air Force.

The Chiefs of Staff Committee [1] remains in its previous form with collective responsibility to the Government for professional advice on strategy and military operations and on the military implications of defence policy. Since the Chiefs of Staff are the professional heads of their own Services, there may be a divergence of view. When this arises, the Chief of the Defence Staff is empowered to submit the alternatives, when they have been discussed and defined, to the Secretary of State for a decision or, if necessary, for reference to Cabinet level.[2]

By the Act of Settlement 1700, s. 3, civil and military offices of trust may not be held by non-nationals. Section 16 (1) of the Armed Forces Act 1966 empowers the Crown by regulation to vest command of any of the Armed Forces of the United Kingdom in persons who are members of forces outside the Commonwealth ("Her dominions").

[1] P. 206, *ante*.

[2] For organisation of the Defence Staff and the Scientific Staff see *Central Organisation for Defence*, Cmnd. 2097, 1963 and the Defence (Transfer of Functions) Act 1964.

B. Composition and Discipline of the Army

Feudal Levy

In early times there were two distinct national forces, the Feudal Levy and the National (or Militia) Levy.[1] The Feudal Levy had, since in the twelfth century actual service was commuted for a money payment (scutage), ceased to be of importance, though the payment of scutage constituted a burdensome incident of land tenure until it was remitted in 1385.

National Levy

The National Levy was a defensive force, organised by counties, with no liability, save in case of invasion, to serve outside the county. The force, which had its origin in pre-Norman days, was revived and reorganised after the Conquest, and at its head the Sheriff was replaced by the official now known as the Lord-Lieutenant. There was a general liability to military service in this force, though the actual forces of the Crown for war came to be raised by commissions of array, whereby each county supplied a compulsory quota for the King's Army. Strictly speaking, forces so raised could not, apart from invasion, be compelled to serve outside their own counties.

Standing Army

These commissions were a frequent ground of complaint in the time of the first three Edwards; by them and by other means the Crown strove to acquire a third force (a standing army), which could be employed, as the need for a permanent force began to be recognised, irrespective of the limitations as to time and place which attached to the Feudal and National Levies. The King provided himself with such an army either by voluntary enrolment, by impressment, or by contract, if he could afford to pay for it, or if Parliament granted him the necessary funds. How far such a force had a lawful basis in time of peace is doubtful. The Petition of Right 1628, moreover, furnished a difficulty in maintaining army discipline, because no departure from the ordinary law was henceforth permissible, except on actual service. Commissions of martial law (the law of the Constable and Marshal) were thereby expressly declared illegal, though they were probably illegal apart from this declaration.

[1] See *China Navigation Co.* v. *Attorney-General*, [1932] 2 K.B. 197, at pp. 225ff.

The Militia

The National Levy, by this time known as the Militia, was reorganised after the Restoration by the Militia Act 1661. This Act declared that:

> the sole supreme government, command and disposition of the Militia and of all forces by sea and land is, and by the laws of England ever was, the undoubted right of the Crown.

The King was not, however, henceforth permitted to keep a standing army beyond "guards and garrisons" of unspecified numbers. On this footing, with constant disputes between King and Parliament, the matter continued until the Revolution of 1688. The Bill of Rights provided that:

> The raising or keeping of a standing army within the Kingdom in time of peace, unless it be with consent of Parliament, is against law.

This provision was due not so much to objection to military service as to the realisation that the army might be dangerous to the liberty of the subject in the hands of an unwise ruler.

Mutiny Acts

Thus in the absence of enabling legislation a standing army within the realm in peace time was (1) unlawful; (2) its discipline could not be enforced by rules differing from the ordinary law; and (3) the supplies necessary for its maintenance were lacking, since the King had no private revenue to meet the expenditure. There was no doubt that a permanent army was required for national security and, even though an army could be raised in an emergency under the royal prerogative, it could not be maintained without the grant of supplies by Parliament. For a long while the first two legal objections were overcome by a succession of Mutiny Acts, the first of which was passed some time previous to the Bill of Rights in 1688. These Acts served the double purpose of legalising for a fixed period, which became in practice for one year only, the keeping of permanent land forces by the Crown and of providing a code of rules for enforcing discipline in their ranks. From 1713 to 1879 there was no break in these Acts.

Army Act 1881 and the Army and Air Force (Annual) Act

In 1879 military law was codified in a single enactment, subsequently replaced by the Army Act 1881. The code was until 1955 continued in force from year to year by an annual Act, known formerly as the Army (Annual) Act and after 1917 as the Army and Air Force (Annual) Act. The preamble to this annual Act expressly fixed the maximum numbers of the land forces and thus waived the prohibition contained in the Bill of Rights. A separate Air Force was constituted in 1917 by the Air Force (Constitution) Act of that year. The Army Act 1881 with modifications governed the discipline of the Air Force.

Army Act, Air Force Act, 1955 [1]

In 1955, following a series of reports of departmental committees and four reports[2] from a Select Committee of the House of Commons, which sat for three successive sessions and redrafted separate Bills to replace for the Army and for the Air Force the existing Acts, there were enacted the Army Act 1955 and the Air Force Act 1955. Not only were certain changes made in those Parts of the Acts which deal with disciplinary offences (some of these were called for by the presence of a high proportion of young national servicemen in the forces), but there was a departure from the old practice of requiring an Annual Act to continue the present legislation in force for another year. This practice ensured that each year amendments could be considered to the law relating to the Army; but lawyers also regarded the Annual Act as necessary to meet the prohibition against a standing Army in the Bill of Rights. The official view, however, is that the prohibition is lifted by the annual Appropriation Act which sanctions the votes for Army and Air Force pay and therefore by implication allows the forces who are in receipt of such pay to be maintained. The new Acts make two other changes; they extend a modified application of the disciplinary code to nine separate categories of civilians, including families of servicemen who are outside the United Kingdom, when not on active service; and the Army Act applies to the Royal Marines, though this force is at times also subject to the Naval Discipline Acts, *i.e.* when carried on the books of one of Her Majesty's Ships.

Terms of Service: (a) Other Ranks

So far as the rank and file are concerned, members of all the forces are recruited by voluntary enlistment [3] for varying fixed periods of service, with liability to serve anywhere within or without the realm. Enlistment, which requires attestation before a recruiting officer, is in the nature of a contract between the soldier and the Crown.

[1] Chap. 28.
[2] H.C. 244 (1952), 331 (1952), 289 (1953), 223 (1954).
[3] For compulsory service below and see pp. 394–5, *post*.

The Crown cannot vary the terms of enlistment without the soldier's consent, but like any other servant of the Crown a soldier is employed at the pleasure of the Crown; a member of the armed forces cannot sue for service pay or pension.[1]

(*b*) *Officers*

Officers, in all branches of the forces, are appointed by the Queen's commission. They cannot resign or retire without leave, though they are usually in peace time permitted to retire at their own request.[2] They, too, are liable to be discharged at the pleasure of the Crown.

National Service

The National Service Act 1948, as amended in 1950, fixed the period of whole-time service at twenty-four months, to be followed by three and a half years' service in one of the reserve forces. It required compulsory service with one of the armed forces for all males between the ages of eighteen and twenty-six,[3] though those engaged in a few important occupations of national importance in time of war were not called up. National service was terminated by Order in Council in 1960, though a limited category of national servicemen was retained under the Army Reserve Act 1962 for short periods which have since expired.

All ranks of the Regular Army, whilst actively employed, are subject to military law. This liability applies to the soldier whether he is serving at home or overseas.

Military Forces of the British Commonwealth

Each of the other Member States of the British Commonwealth has its own military and air forces, and they may be classified as regular forces. Their permanent organisation is, in most cases, on a skeleton footing, providing for expansion in time of war or other emergency. Except in the Republics they are part of the forces of the Crown, but their organisation, discipline and employment are exclusively under the control of their respective Governments. All legislation affecting them is enacted by their own Parliaments. There are also forces raised in certain colonies.

Visiting Forces

The Visiting Forces (British Commonwealth) Act 1933 empowered the military and naval authorities of a Dominion to exercise

[1] *Leaman* v. *The King*, [1920] 3 K.B. 663. Chap. 46.

[2] *The Queen* v. *Cuming, ex parte Hall* (1887), 19 Q.B.D. 13.

[3] The age was extended to thirty-six in the case of British subjects resident abroad.

in the United Kingdom all the powers conferred by their own law in relation to the discipline and internal administration of a Dominion force visiting the country. The Act contained provisions enabling the authorities of this country to arrange for the arrest of alleged offenders at the request of the commander of a visiting force and to hand over deserters. During the Second World War similar rights were conferred by the Allied Forces Act 1940 in respect of forces of allied States stationed in this country. The jurisdiction conferred by these Acts did not exclude the jurisdiction of the courts of this country in respect of offences committed by members of a visiting force, but by the United States of America (Visiting Forces) Act 1942 exclusive jurisdiction was given to the American authorities in respect of criminal offences committed in this country by members of visiting American forces. This was a striking constitutional innovation made on grounds of political expediency. By the Allied Powers (Maritime Courts) Act 1941 provision was made for the establishment during the war in the United Kingdom of maritime courts of allied States with jurisdiction over their merchant seamen; here the jurisdiction was not exclusive of that of our courts.

Visiting Forces Act 1952

In June 1951 agreement was reached by the States which are parties to the North Atlantic Treaty on the legal status of the armed forces of one of the parties when stationed in the territory of another.[1] The United Kingdom and Canada are the only Commonwealth States who are parties to this treaty. It thus became necessary to introduce in the United Kingdom Parliament, as in the Canadian Parliament, the necessary legislation to bring the agreement into force as part of the law of the United Kingdom. At the same time the Government of the United Kingdom agreed with all the Commonwealth Governments to amend the existing law relating to Commonwealth Visiting Forces so as to bring it into line with the Agreement. Accordingly, the Visiting Forces Act 1952, which repealed the Allied Forces Act and the United States of America (Visiting Forces) Act and the relevant part of the Visiting Forces (British Commonwealth) Act, now provides a comprehensive statement of the law applicable to Visiting Forces both from all the States which are parties to the North Atlantic Treaty and from the principal States of the Commonwealth; the Act can be extended to other countries by Order in Council. It has been extended by agreement to cover the United Nations forces in Japan. As a result of this repeal the service courts

[1] Cmd. 8279 (1951).

of the United States no longer have an exclusive criminal jurisdiction over their armed forces while in the United Kingdom.

The principal provisions of the Act of 1952 may be summarised as follows:—[1]

(1) The service courts and authorities of Visiting Forces may exercise in the United Kingdom all the jurisdiction which is given to them by the law of their own country over all persons (including members of a civilian component) who may be subject to the law of that country governing their armed forces; the death penalty may not, however, be carried out in the United Kingdom unless under United Kingdom law the sentence of death could have been passed in similar cases.

(2) This jurisdiction is not exclusive of that of the criminal courts in the United Kingdom, but a member of a Visiting Force will not be liable to be tried for a criminal offence by a United Kingdom court if—

(*a*) the alleged offence arises out of and in the course of duty; or
(*b*) the alleged offence is one against the person of a member of the same or another Visiting Force; or
(*c*) the alleged offence is committed against the property of the Visiting Force or of a member thereof.

"An offence against the person" includes murder, manslaughter and all the more serious offences involving personal injury under the criminal law of England and of Scotland. It is only in the above cases that the jurisdiction of the criminal courts of the United Kingdom is excluded, unless the appropriate authority of the Visiting Force waives the jurisdiction. Thus a visiting soldier or airman will be tried for an offence against the Road Traffic Acts in the ordinary magistrates' courts or by a judge and jury.

(3) A member of a Visiting Force who has been tried by his own service court cannot be put on trial in a United Kingdom court for the same offence.

(4) From civil liability there is no immunity apart from the immunity afforded to a foreign State or its property by United Kingdom law.[2] Provision is however made for the satisfaction of civil claims in tort, but not in contract, by the Secretary of State for Defence, whether or not the immunity can be claimed. In the event of the Minister declining to admit the claim the claimant is entitled to sue the member of the Visiting Force in the ordinary way. This provision applies where the defendant commits the tort while on duty or off duty; in the latter case any compensation paid on behalf of the Visiting Force is made without accepting liability.

The above provisions are in operation as the law of the United Kingdom irrespective of the provision of reciprocal facilities by the other countries to whose armed forces they apply in the United Kingdom.

[1] These provisions came into operation in 1954.
[2] Pp. 270–6, *ante*.

Reserve Forces

The bulk of the Reserve Forces in the Regular Army, as in the Navy and Royal Air Force, are drawn from regular officers on the retired list who are liable to recall and other ranks whose regular service has expired but who enlisted on terms which make them available for a period of years for service in case of national danger. In addition to the regular reserve there is, for the army, a volunteer reserve force now known as the Territorial and Army Volunteer Reserve which deserves separate mention.

The Territorial and Army Volunteer Reserve (formerly the Territorial Army)

Since 1907 until the past decade under reforms linked with the name of Lord Haldane as Secretary of State for War, the Territorial Army—the part-time citizen force which absorbed and revitalised the former volunteers and yeomanry—provided a home defence army which could be put on an active service footing for service at home or overseas after the Army Reserve had been called out, as in both World Wars in 1914 and 1939. Recruitment and administration was on a county basis.[1] In 1967 the Territorial Army was substantially reorganised. The Reserve Forces Act 1966 (which made new provision as to the circumstances in which all the reserve forces might be called out) re-named it as the Territorial and Army Volunteer Reserve (the T. and A.V.R.), and an Order of the Queen, made under the Auxiliary Forces Act, provided for it to be constituted into specified units divided into three categories known as T. and A.V.R. I, II and III. The first two categories were given a general function of reinforcement and support (particularly of the Regular Army) in military operations overseas, while the third (T. and A.V.R. III) was given the rôle of a force for home service. In 1969 the Government decided to put this force on a care and maintenance basis and so its former rôle as a national army ceased. The units of T. and A.V.R. III were disbanded and the separate categories of the T. and A.V.R. were abolished. Small cadres (having names similar to those of the former T. and A.V.R. III), each of eight officers and non-commissioned officers, were however retained as part of the volunteer reserve and thus reorganised. In the result, the main function of that reserve is to reinforce the Regular Army in the event of war. Home defence by a volunteer reserve land force is thus ruled out as immediately practicable in wartime.

[1] See the Auxiliary Forces Act 1953 (Air Force Auxiliary units were similarly raised and administered).

Ulster Defence Regiment

In consequence of the Report of the Advisory Committee set up in 1969 under Lord Hunt to advise on the police in Northern Ireland (Cmd. 535) the Government has provided for the establishment of a new part-time military force (in effect, in replacement of the Ulster Special Constabulary) called the Ulster Defence Regiment. Provision for this Regiment is made by the Ulster Defence Regiment Act 1969 which establishes the force as part of the armed forces of the Crown and for the control of its size by Parliament. It is a disciplined force, under the command of the General Officer Commanding, Northern Ireland, and liable to be called out, when needed, for emergency service in Northern Ireland in defence of life or property there against armed attack or sabotage.

War-time Legislation and Compulsory Service

In 1939 for the second time in twenty-five years the United Kingdom was forced to adopt a system of compulsory service. Conscription had long been regarded as an evil which should not befall a British subject in time of peace, though historically its abhorrence is based on the fear lest the King should be possessed of too powerful a weapon with which to coerce the people. On the outbreak of war the various reserve and auxiliary forces were absorbed into the regular forces and the statutory provisions relating to length of service, liability to serve overseas and terms of enlistment were all superseded by the introduction of compulsory military service. Earlier, in May 1939 there had been passed the Military Training Act 1939 which provided for the compulsory military training and enlistment as militiamen of male British subjects ordinarily resident in Great Britain between the ages of twenty and twenty-one. That Act too was superseded by the introduction of compulsory service for all males of military age after the outbreak of war. The Reserve and Auxiliary Forces Act 1939 also passed in May of that year, provided for calling out for service by Order in Council the members of any of the reserve or auxiliary forces, and under it the Naval Reserve, Army Reserve and Air Force Reserve were called out and the Territorial Army and Auxiliary Air Force were embodied. The Armed Forces (Conditions of Service) Act 1939 permitted enlistment in the regular forces for the duration of "the present emergency," transfer to any corps without consent, the ordering abroad of any embodied part of the Territorial Army and of any part of the Auxiliary Air Force. The Military and Air Forces (Prolongation of Service) Act 1939 provided that no member of the regular, reserve or auxiliary forces should be entitled to be discharged until the end of the emergency. The National Service (Armed Forces) Act 1939 introduced liability to compulsory military service for all males—subject to certain total or conditional exemptions for, in particular, conscientious objectors and regular ministers of any religious denomination—between the ages of eighteen and forty-one. The Act contained provisions for reinstatement in civil employment. The National Service Act 1941 extended the liability to compulsory whole-time service to service in the Civil Defence Forces. Later in the same year the National Service (No. 2) Act 1941 raised the age of liability to compulsory service in the forces to fifty-one and rendered women so liable as well as men. Women could be called up to serve in the Women's Royal Naval Service, the Auxiliary Territorial Service and the Women's Auxiliary Air Force. A woman could not, however, be required to use a lethal weapon without her written consent. This Act declared all persons of either sex to be liable to national service, whether under the Crown or not, and whether in the armed forces of the Crown, in civil defence, in industry, or otherwise. Liability to whole-time service in the forces remained restricted to those between the ages of eighteen and fifty-one, but any person might by Defence Regulations be directed to part-time service in the armed forces or civil defence forces or to whole or part-time service in other forms of national service. The Emergency Powers (Defence) Act 1940 had made provision for Defence Regulations to compel persons to place themselves, their services and their property at the disposal of His Majesty, and these Regulations were made under the authority of this Act which was intended to rally the nation to resist invasion. The Civil Defence Forces were the Police War Reserve, the Civil Defence Reserve, the National Fire Service, and the Kent County Civil Defence Mobile Reserves. The range of civil defence services was, however, wider and embraced service under the local authorities as air-raid wardens, rescue workers, ambulance drivers, mainly as part-time workers with a nucleus of whole-time salaried officers. The Allied Powers (War Service) Act 1942 provided that the National Service Acts 1939 to 1941 might apply to the nationals of allied States who were not serving in their own forces. Thus was rapidly built up by a series of elaborate statutory provisions, partly Acts of Parliament, partly Defence Regulations and orders and directions issued thereunder, the concept of national service for total war. Compulsory military service for men was continued throughout the war and until the operation of the National Service Act 1948 was brought to an end by Order in Council in 1960.

The exemptions in favour of conscientious objectors and certain other classes were continued and there were provisions against persons being penalised as regards employment prior to as well as after service.

C. Composition and Discipline of the Royal Marines, Navy and R.A.F.

Royal Marines

The Royal Marines, formerly a force of infantry and artillery, form part of the regular forces and are liable for general service on board ship and on shore. Their present role is that of furnishing commando units. Although this force is raised and maintained for naval service, its discipline and regulation is provided for by the Army Act. When on board one of Her Majesty's ships a marine also comes under the Naval Discipline Acts. There is a Royal Marines Reserve.

The Royal Navy

The Navy is the senior branch of the forces, but its constitutional interest is less. Unlike the Army, the Navy did not in former times come under the suspicion of Parliament. There is no reason to suppose that naval service was regarded as less burdensome than service in the Army, or that naval discipline could be enforced without interfering with the common law rights of the sailor as citizen. But the Navy had never been used by the King to coerce Parliament and so was not included in the prohibition in the Bill of Rights against a standing armed force. It has remained a prerogative force maintained on a permanent footing. So much is this so that the recruitment of the Navy by impressment has never been declared illegal, though the press-gang has, of course, long fallen into disuse. Enlistment is governed by the Armed Forces Act 1966, Sections 2–11, and discipline by the Naval Discipline Act 1957. Both enactments are permanent and do not come under review by Parliament for renewal. Conditions of service and regulations for discipline resemble those applicable to the Army and Air Force and they do not call for separate discussion.[1] Despite its prerogative basis, the Navy comes under the control of Parliament, since its estimates are presented annually, as are those of the other services, to Parliament and the consequential votes afford full opportunity for discussion of naval administration and expenditure, which on account of constructional requirements is often controversial.

[1] A civilian on board a naval vessel may be tried by naval court-martial for seducing from their duty or allegiance members of the navy: Naval Discipline Act 1957, s. 94.

Naval Reserve

The Royal Naval Reserve is recruited from members of the merchant navy and from volunteers. A division of the Naval Reserve is known as the Royal Fleet Reserve, in which men may be required to serve as part of their engagement in naval service or in which they may voluntarily enter at the end of their engagement.

Commonwealth States and Colonies

Naval forces, under the control of their own Parliaments and Governments for all purposes, including discipline,[1] except when serving with the Royal Navy,[2] are maintained by Canada, Australia, and New Zealand. India possesses, as does Pakistan, a comparatively small force largely for the purpose of replacing the Royal Indian Marine. Other States maintain small coastal forces. The Colonial Naval Defence Acts 1931 and 1949 authorised the maintenance and use of warships outside a colony by a naval force raised for its own defence; all the major colonial territories have now become independent.

Royal Air Force

The Royal Air Force was constituted in 1917 as a force separate from both the Army and the Navy. The naval arm was transferred back to the Royal Navy before the Second World War as the Fleet Air Arm. and is now part of the Executive branch of the Navy. The Air Force does not call for separate notice from the point of view of constitutional law, as its position closely resembles that of the Army.

D. Women's Forces

Women in the Post-War Armed Forces

The women's land, air and naval forces raised during the Second World War were not disbanded and have since become part of the regular and reserve forces under the titles of Women's Royal Army Corps, Women's Royal Air Force and Women's Royal Naval Service. The Army and Air Force (Women's Service) Act 1948 gave power to raise and maintain the land and air forces, to grant commissions to women officers and to make the necessary adaptations of the Army Act and the Air Force Act to bring women under

[1] See Naval Discipline Act, 1957, ss. 114 and 135.
[2] See Colonial (Naval Defence) Act 1931.

military law. The naval service does not come under the Naval Discipline Act, but maintains its discipline by expulsion and submission voluntarily to its code of service conduct. The National Service Act 1948 excluded women from any form of compulsory service. Women's units are serving as regular arms of all three Services as well as in the Territorial and Army Volunteer Reserve and Air Force Reserve.

CHAPTER TWENTY-EIGHT

MILITARY LAW AND COURTS-MARTIAL

A. Military Law

Nature of Military Law

MILITARY LAW for the Army is contained in the Army Act 1955 and the Acts relating to the auxiliary and reserve forces. A similar system is applied to the Royal Air Force by the Air Force Act 1955. These Acts, which replace with important amendments the Army Act 1881 and its application since 1917 to the Royal Air Force, are supplemented by rules of procedure made under the 1955 Acts, by Queen's Regulations and other regulations issued under the prerogative, by Royal Warrant, *e.g.* as to pay and promotion, and by Army Orders. Thus while the basic disciplinary code is statutory, other matters are dealt with by prerogative instruments. The Acts were limited in duration to twelve months, but for a period of five years, they could be continued in force from year to year without amendment by resolutions passed by both Houses of Parliament. No legislation was thus required until the end of five years from the coming into force of the Acts of 1955.

The Army and Air Force Act 1961 continued until the end of 1962 the two Acts of 1955. Provision was made thereafter for each Act to be continued for twelve months at a time by Order in Council approved by resolution of each House of Parliament until the end of 1966. The disadvantage of this method is that amendments to the Acts are not possible without a new statute. Such a statute was passed in 1966, the Armed Forces Act, which contained amendments to the two Acts of 1955 and to the Naval Discipline Act 1957. The Acts of 1955 still require annual renewal by Order in Council and are due to expire at the end of 1971.

An army cannot be disciplined by the ordinary law applicable to civilians. Any association of individuals organised for the achievement of a particular object is bound to lay down certain rules by which the members agree to be bound on joining. In the case of a "members" club these rules are purely contractual and in no way conflict with the ordinary law of the land, to which all the members remain subject. In the case of the learned professions, particularly the law and medicine, the special rules are to some extent impressed with the authority of the State, being enforceable in some cases by statutory courts of discipline. With the armed forces of the Crown the sanction of Parliament is required for the more stringent provisions which are essential for preserving military discipline. The courts through the prerogative orders of certiorari and prohibition or by writ of habeas corpus are able to supervise, so far as excess of jurisdiction is concerned, the military tribunals (courts-martial) which are established by the Army Act for adjudication upon offences against military law. There is also power to make rules of procedure for the administration of military law. These rules must not conflict with the Army Act and must be laid before Parliament. They are an important safeguard ensuring the conduct of a trial by court-martial on the lines of a criminal trial in a civil court, but there is no jury.

Offences under Army Act

The offences created by the Army Act include mutiny, desertion, absence without leave, fraudulent enlistment, and two offences which well illustrate the difference between military law and ordinary law. Section 64 of the Act provides that an officer who behaves in a scandalous manner unbecoming the character of an officer and a gentleman shall, on conviction by court-martial, be cashiered. Section 69 provides that any person who is guilty of any act, conduct, disorder or neglect to the prejudice of good order and military discipline shall be liable to be sentenced to two years' imprisonment. Section 64 is rarely used as it lays down a minimum punishment, but section 69 is often used. This section gives a wide discretion to a court-martial to treat any conduct as a criminal offence, and it has been urged that military offences should be framed with greater particularity. For the military offence of mutiny there are two categories. It is only when the offence involves violence or refusal of service in operations against the enemy that the death penalty is retained. With minor exceptions punishments for which officers and other ranks are liable for offences under the Act are similar, but where an officer is sentenced by court-martial to imprisonment he must also be sentenced to be cashiered, but other ranks are not necessarily discharged in consequence of a sentence of imprisonment.[1]

[1] Ss. 71, 72.

Administration of Military Law

The administration of military law by courts-martial composed of serving officers is supervised by the Judge Advocate General of the Forces, whose functions until 1948 combined those of prosecutor, judge and appellate tribunal as well as legal adviser to the Secretaries of State for War and for Air. The functions relating to prosecutions have been transferred to the separate departments of the Army and Air Force Legal Services, each under a Director, who is independent of the Judge Advocate General. In practice the separation had been secured before 1948, but the principle of combining these functions with a judicial office was clearly inappropriate.

The Judge Advocate General, who is appointed by the Crown on the recommendation of the Lord Chancellor to whom he is responsible, is thus now a judicial officer. He provides a judge advocate at all trials by general court-martial held in the United Kingdom and at the more serious cases tried by district court-martial as well as for important trials abroad by general or field general court-martial. The judge advocate attends the court in an advisory capacity. The review of the proceedings of all courts-martial with a view to seeing whether they have been regular and legal is undertaken by the department of the Judge Advocate. Legal advice may be tendered on confirmation or review or on petition. The Judge Advocate General has deputies and staffs with the major commands abroad as well as at home.

Military Courts

The Army Act regulates the constitution and proceedings of courts-martial for the enforcement of military law. Their jurisdiction is exclusively over persons subject to military law. They are convened by high military officers. The convening order details the officers who are to serve on the court, and, if qualified by length of service, all officers are liable to serve. There is a similarity between the constitutional procedure of civil and military courts. The lowest military court, apart from the summary and investigating powers of company and battery commanders, is the commanding officer, normally a lieutenant-colonel commanding a battalion or regiment. Non-commissioned officers and soldiers charged with military offences are brought before him on remand by the company commander, and his duty corresponds with that of a court of summary jurisdiction. After hearing the evidence he can either dismiss the charge or, if it is a minor charge against a soldier, he may deal with it summarily (his power of punishment is limited to twenty-eight days' detention) or order a summary of the evidence to be taken with a view to determining whether or not to send the accused for trial by court-martial. The accused has the right to trial by court-martial if the commanding officer proposes to order detention or forfeiture of pay. There is also a summary procedure for disposing of less serious charges against officers and warrant officers. A commanding officer can in the appropriate cases refer the charge for adjudication by a superior authority, *i.e.* an officer having power to convene courts-martial.[1]

Courts-Martial[2]

Should the commanding officer be of the opinion that a case cannot properly be dealt with summarily, he should send the offender for trial by court-martial. There are three forms of court-martial.[3]

A General Court-Martial, which must consist of at least five officers, can try any offence under the Army Act or Air Force Act, whether committed by an officer or a member of the rank and file.

A District Court-Martial cannot try an officer or award the punishment of death or more than two years' imprisonment; otherwise any offence under the Acts is within its jurisdiction. The court is constituted by at least three officers. These two courts correspond approximately with Assize Courts and Quarter Sessions.

A Field General Court-Martial is for the trial of offences committed on active service, where a general or district court-martial cannot be convened without serious detriment to the public service.

A trial by court-martial is very much like a trial in an ordinary criminal court. If the offender so desires, a convening officer may appoint an officer to defend. A judge advocate may be (and in the case of a general court-martial must be) appointed to advise the court as to law and to summarise the facts, but he does not, as formerly, retire with the court when it is considering its findings. The same rules of evidence and presumption of innocence apply (as also before a commanding officer) as in a criminal court. Findings must be pronounced in open court at once and sentences announced as

[1] Army Act 1955, ss. 78 and 79.

[2] For a short history of the Court-Martial System and the Office of Judge Advocate General, see the *Report of Army and Air Force Courts-Martial Committee*, 1946, Cmd. 7608 (1949).

[3] The tribunals, also called courts-martial, for the trial by officers of members of the Royal Navy and of other persons subject to the Naval Discipline Act 1957, do not call for separate treatment.

soon as determined. The main differences between a trial by court-martial and trial by a criminal court are:

(*a*) The court may arrive at its finding or sentence by a simple majority, whereas a jury must be unanimous or agreed by 10–2.[1]

(*b*) Members of the court fix the sentence subject to confirmation, whereas a jury has nothing to do with sentence.

Review of Sentences

A person sentenced by a court-martial may complain by petition of a reviewing authority. Independently of petitions the proceedings to all courts-martial are reviewed in the office of the Judge Advocate General in order to detect any miscarriage of justice. Sentences must be confirmed by a competent higher military authority and may be modified by that authority. There is no power to increase the sentence awarded by the court.

Courts-Martial Appeal Court

The Courts-Martial (Appeals) Act 1951 established a Courts-Martial Appeal Court. The Court and its jurisdiction are now governed by the Courts-Martial (Appeals) Act 1968—a consolidating statute—the Act also covers appeals to the House of Lords. The judges are the Lord Chief Justice and the puisne judges of the High Court (in practice the judges of the Queen's Bench Division) and the corresponding judges for Scotland and Northern Ireland, who may be nominated for the purpose, together with such other persons of legal experience as the Lord Chancellor may appoint. Like the Court of Appeal for England the Courts-Martial Appeal Court is constituted by an uneven number of judges, not less than three sitting; it may sit in divisions and may sit within or without the United Kingdom as the Lord Chief Justice may direct. It normally sits in London. Although the Court operates on similar lines to the Court of Appeal [2] leave to appeal can only be granted by the court itself and must be obtained even for an appeal on a question of law. But before application for leave can be made, a convicted person must await confirmation of the sentence by the convening authority and, unless he is under sentence of death, must petition the Defence Council for the quashing of his conviction and await the decision of that authority refusing the petition. An appeal lies by leave to the House of Lords on a point of law of public importance. Thus when a civil offence is tried by court-martial and the consent of the Director of Public

[1] Criminal Justice Act 1967, s. 13.

[2] P. 305, *ante*; there is no appeal against sentence only.

Prosecutions is necessary for prosecution in a civil court, the House of Lords has held that such consent is also required before trial by court-martial under the Naval Discipline Act 1957; *Secretary of State for Defence* v. *Warn*.[1]

Civil Courts in relation to Courts-Martial

Courts-martial are limited to the powers conferred on them by statute. For an unlawful act done by such a court or by a military officer exercising his summary powers under the Army Act, the person injured has his remedy in the High Court. An excess of jurisdiction may be questioned by application to the Divisional Court of the Queen's Bench Division for the writ of habeas corpus or an order of certiorari or prohibition. There is no doubt that certiorari lies, at the discretion of the High Court, to control the limits of jurisdiction of a court-martial, just as it lies to control all inferior courts which are shown to have exceeded their jurisdiction. Civil tribunals may also be controlled when there is an abuse which may vitiate an otherwise lawful exercise of jurisdiction, as when the tribunal is shown to have acted maliciously or from corrupt motives. But the courts have shown a marked disinclination to interfere with the decisions of a court-martial or military court of enquiry, or even with the exercise by a commanding officer of his summary powers under the Army Act and the equivalent statutes, if the objection is based on malice or lack of reasonable and probable cause. The argument is that matters falling within the scope of military discipline should be subject to review only by higher military authority. In *Heddon* v. *Evans* [2] the court made a distinction between liability for an act done in excess of, or without jurisdiction, by the military tribunal, which amounts to an assault, false imprisonment or other common law wrong, and one which, though within jurisdiction and in the course of military discipline, is alleged to have been done maliciously and without reasonable and probable cause. Only in the former case would the courts entertain proceedings against military officers. The distinction appears to lie in the fact that only when there is an excess of jurisdiction is any common law right of the complainant infringed. But this distinction, if upheld, would deprive a soldier of a civil remedy if the prosecution at the court-martial was malicious.

It is still open to the House of Lords to review the whole issue of the powers of the civil courts over the exercise of disciplinary powers in the armed services and in particular to decide whether the dis-

[1] [1970] A.C. 394. [2] (1919), 35 T.L.R. 642.

missal of an officer or man from the service could give rise to civil liability.[1] This reluctance of the court to intervene in matters properly falling within the sphere of military affairs was also illustrated in an action for libel brought by a subordinate officer against his commanding officer. The action was based on letters written by the latter to the Adjutant-General in the course of military duty. The plaintiff's remedy lay through military channels as provided nowadays by Queen's Regulations.[2] But if the military court has exceeded its jurisdiction by applying military law to persons not subject to that law,[3] or, in the case of persons so subject, misapplying military law by punishing without regular trial or inflicting a punishment in excess of its jurisdiction, the writ of habeas corpus or certiorari order afford means of reviewing the case, and the officers concerned may be liable to an action for damages or criminal proceedings for assault, manslaughter or even murder.

In *The King* v. *Governor of Wormwood Scrubs and the Secretary of State for War, ex parte Boydell*,[4] a writ of habeas corpus was granted on the application of an officer, who had been arrested at his home a year after his release from the Army, tried and sentenced by court-martial in Germany for an offence committed while serving there and imprisoned in an English gaol to serve his sentence. Section 158 (1) of the Army Act 1881 (which was amended in consequence of the case) [5] excluded liability to trial by court-martial of such a person at so long a period after he had ceased to be subject to military law.

B. Status of Members of the Forces

Venue for Trial of Offences

A person subject to the Army Act does not cease to be subject to the ordinary law and may be tried by any competent civil court for offences against the criminal law. The position of a member of the Royal Navy or Royal Air Force is similar. Except so far as the statutes creating military law provide, a soldier enjoys all the rights of the ordinary citizen and his obligations as a soldier imposed by the Army Act and Queen's Regulations are in addition to his duties as a citizen. In practice most criminal offences committed by members of the Army and Royal Air Force are dealt with in peace time by the civil courts, but an offence against the ordinary law committed by a person subject to military law is, at the discretion of the

[1] *Fraser* v. *Balfour* (1918), 87 L.J.K.B. 1116; *Richards* v. *Naum*, [1967] 1 Q.B. 620.
[2] *Dawkins* v. *Paulet* (1869), L.R. 5 Q.B.D. 94; K. & L. 182.
[3] *Wolfe Tone's Case* (1798), 27 St. Tr. 614.
[4] [1948] 2 K.B. 193.
[5] See now Army Act 1955, ss. 131, 132.

competent military authorities, triable by court-martial, with the exception of certain serious felonies, such as murder, which must, if committed in the United Kingdom, be tried by the competent civil court (the Assizes or the Central Criminal Court).

Privileges

A person subject to military law enjoys the benefit of certain privileges and exemptions from the ordinary civil law and its processes. He is entitled to vote at parliamentary and local elections by post or if necessary, by appointing a proxy.[1] When on active service he can make a will in nuncupatory form without complying with the formalities of the Wills Act 1837, and even if he be a minor.

Dual Liability

When a person subject to military law has been tried for an offence by court-martial or has been dealt with summarily by his commanding officer, a civil court is debarred from trying him subsequently for an offence which is substantially the same as that offence.[2] Apart from this there is no restriction on a civil court trying a member of the armed forces for an offence under the criminal law. A person acquitted or convicted by a civil court in the United Kingdom or elsewhere is not liable to be tried by court-martial in respect of the same offence. Persons who have been released from the Army or the Royal Air Force may be tried by court-martial with the consent of the Attorney-General in respect of an offence committed outside the United Kingdom if the offence is one which would, when committed in England, be punishable under English law.[3] Offences committed by such persons in the United Kingdom are only triable by court-martial if the trial begins within three months of the release; but for the offences of mutiny, desertion and fraudulent enlistment there is no such time limit.

Conflict of Duty

It is sometimes alleged that obedience to military law may conflict with a soldier's duty as a citizen. Military law is, however, part of the law of the land and obedience to it cannot be unlawful. A soldier is only required to obey orders which are lawful,[4] and an order which is contrary to the common law is not a lawful order.

[1] P. 120, *ante*.
[2] Armed Forces Act 1966, s. 25.
[3] Army Act 1955, s. 132
[4] Army Act 1955, s. 34.

If an order involves a breach of the law, a soldier is not only under no obligation to carry it out, but is under an obligation not to carry it out. It may truly be said that this places the soldier in an awkward position. He has not time to weigh up the merits of an order; his training makes compliance instinctive. None the less unlawful injury inflicted as the result of compliance renders him liable to civil or criminal proceedings. The defence of obedience to the orders of a superior is not accepted by the civil courts. On the other hand, if a soldier disobeys an order on the ground that it is unlawful, a court-martial may hold that it was lawful. In practice, however, a tribunal, whether court-martial or a judge and jury, should take all the circumstances into consideration and it is probably better to leave the soldier in a position of difficulty than to place him outside the ordinary law. If a prosecution results from obedience to an order, there is some authority for saying that, if the order was not necessarily or manifestly illegal, the soldier who obeys it cannot be made criminally liable. In *Keighley* v. *Bell* [1] this opinion was expressed *obiter* by Willes, J., and it has been followed by a special tribunal in South Africa [2] which acquitted of murder a soldier who had shot a civilian in time of war in obedience to an unlawful order given to him by his officer. It would seem that for the defence to succeed the mistaken belief in the legality of the order must be reasonable.

In connection with the violation of the recognised rules of warfare by an enemy (war crimes) the defence of superior orders had for many years been recognised by the Manual of Military Law, which contains the official view on the laws and usages of war—matters of public international law. In 1944 the Manual was amended and it is no longer stated as a defence for a person accused of a war crime to plead that the orders of a superior confer upon him any immunity from punishment by the military courts of the injured belligerent State. The defence may put the plea in mitigation of punishment, but in no circumstances can the plea deprive the act of its character as a war crime. This change in the official view may be regarded as a necessary corollary to the rule of English criminal law that members of the armed forces are only bound to obey lawful orders. But it is to be noticed that the defence that an unlawful superior order which was not necessarily or manifestly illegal could be pleaded was not laid down in the Articles of the Nuremberg Charter of 1945 under which the International Military Court tried persons accused of major war crimes.

[1] (1866), 4 F. and F. 763, at p. 790.

[2] *The Queen* v. *Smith* (1900), 17 Cape of Good Hope Supreme Court Report, 561; K. & L. 188; see also Kenny, *op. cit.*, p. 62.

CHAPTER TWENTY-NINE

MARTIAL LAW

Meaning of Martial Law

THE term, martial law, means in international law the powers exercised by a military commander in occupation of foreign territory. The term, martial law, is also used to describe the action of the military when, in order to deal with an emergency amounting to a state of war, they impose restrictions and regulations upon civilians in their own country. It is this meaning of martial law that will be discussed in this Chapter. That the military may in a time of major emergency exercise such abnormal powers is recognised by common law.[1] The term, martial law, is, however, misleading. The powers of the military are different only in degree and not in kind from those of the ordinary citizen. Moreover they are part of the ordinary law of the land. Every citizen (and a soldier is a citizen) is under a duty to assist in the suppression of riotous assemblies and insurrections and in repelling invaders. The task of dispersing riotous assemblies in time of peace is best directed by the local civil authorities who have knowledge of local conditions. Normally an officer in command of troops will act only if called upon to do so by a magistrate. None the less he must exercise his own judgment whether to use force and, if so, how much force to use. The instructions of the civil authority will, however, rightly influence his judgment and will normally be followed.[2] In time of invasion or insurrection on a wide scale a reverse state of affairs arises. Both citizen and soldier have the same duty, but the military are in a state of war the best judges of the steps that should be taken. They are then entitled to give directions to and impose restrictions upon civilians in order to fulfil their duty to repel invaders or suppress rebels. This duty is a duty not only of the citizen but of the Executive. In time of war the Executive would normally act through military commanders. The duty is that of the Crown and its servants and of all citizens.

[1] *Marais* v. *General Officer Commanding*, [1902] A.C. 109.

[2] See Evidence of Lord Haldane, then Secretary of State for War, before a Select Committee on Employment of Military in Cases of Disturbance (H.C. 236 (1908)); *Manual of Military Law*, Part II, Section V.

Interference with Civilians

When the Government desires extraordinary powers for the military, emergency statutes are passed by Parliament, *e.g.* the Defence of the Realm Acts 1914–15 and the Emergency Powers Act 1939. Power may be taken to declare what is indistinguishable from a state of martial law at common law. For at common law there exist, apart from statute, powers to repel force by force and to take all necessary steps to preserve order. In the exercise of such powers the military may find it necessary to interfere with the actions, and even with the life and liberty of civilians. The relationship between the military and civilians known as a state of martial law has not arisen in this country since the Civil War of the seventeenth century. A state of martial law has, however, existed during the present century in South Africa, Southern Ireland, Palestine and parts of India while these territories were under British rule. The degree to which the military may interfere with civilians will vary with the circumstances. The test is whether the interference is necessary in order to perform the duty of repelling force and restoring order. The military authorities would be justified in ordering civilians to quit their homes, to obey a curfew order, to dig trenches or to render services, provided such orders were necessary for the defence of the country. If a civilian refuses to comply with such an order, the military are justified in enforcing obedience.

Military Tribunals

In order to establish whether breaches of duty have been committed, the military may find it necessary to set up military tribunals to try civilians. Prompt punishment may be necessary as an example to others. In exceptional circumstances offenders may be condemned to death. It would on occasion be justifiable to shoot an offender without any trial at all, *e.g.* an officer in charge of troops might justifiably order his men to shoot anyone about to cut a cable with intent to assist the enemy. In every case the action taken must be judged by the test of necessity. Sometimes it would not be justifiable even to bring an offender before a military tribunal. It might be sufficient to detain him in custody until he could be brought before a civil court. The tribunals established by the military are not judicial bodies and must be distinguished from courts-martial set up to try persons subject to military law for offences under the Army or the Air Force Acts 1955.[1] They are merely bodies set up to advise the military commander as to the

[1] P. 402, *ante*. In time of emergency additional statutory powers may be conferred upon courts-martial; see pp. 413–15, *post*.

action he should take in carrying out his duties.[1] It is, however, in regard to the establishment of these military tribunals that the most difficult problems regarding a so-called state of martial law arise. Before the establishment of military tribunals there will usually be a proclamation of a state of martial law, but it is not the proclamation which makes martial law, but the events which have created the emergency. Subjects have the right to question any act of the Executive or military in the courts which must decide whether or not a state of martial law exists. A proclamation may be evidence of such a state being already in existence, but it cannot change existing conditions from a peace-time footing to one of war within the realm. The prerogative of declaring war does not enable the Crown to declare war on the people. But the Executive has a common law duty, which it shares with every subject and with the military to assist in the maintenance of order. If it is compelled in the exercise of this duty to hand over control to the military forces, it acts at its own risk as regards legal responsibility, and there is a state of martial law, which is not law in the sense of a code of rules, but a condition of affairs.

When does an Emergency amount to Martial Law?

There can be no precise test to determine the state of emergency in which martial law exists. Clearly in any true emergency the authorities may have to act without regard to their strict legal powers, since peril to the public safety cannot always be suppressed by prosecuting under the criminal law or applying for an injunction in the civil courts. If the civil courts have on account of hostilities ceased to sit for the time being, the maintenance of order passes from the civil power to the military. The military can, it may be safely asserted, then take control. What is necessary in such a situation is primarily a matter of discretion for the commander-in-chief and his advisers. Even so, when the courts are again able to sit, the acts of the military may be shown to be illegal as having been in excess of what was necessary, unless confirmed or excused by an Act of Indemnity. Much has been written as to whether the test in such cases would be strict necessity or *bona fide* belief in the necessity of the action, and as to whether it would be for the defendant to show that the test had been complied with or for the complainant to show that it had not been complied with. There is no authority which makes it possible to answer these questions. Supposing that the courts have not ceased entirely to operate, as where the insurrection is confined to part of the country, military government may none the

[1] *Re Clifford and O'Sullivan*, [1921] 2 A.C. 570. P. 412, *post*.

less be necessary. Martial law is thus a state of fact not to be decided by the simple test: Were the civil courts sitting at the time? The test would seem to be: Is the insurrection of such a kind that military rule is justified? It falls to the civil courts alone to determine this difficult question.

Control of Military by Civil Courts

This leads to a further problem. In so far as the civil courts may be sitting, what control, if any, have they over the acts of the military? In *Marais* v. *General Officer Commanding*,[1] the Privy Council held that such acts are not at the time justiciable by the ordinary courts sitting in a martial law area where "war is still raging." The courts will determine for themselves whether or not war exists.[2] Once a state of war is recognised by the courts, and such recognition in the nature of things must be *ex post facto*, the Executive, with the aid of its military forces, may conduct warlike operations with impunity. They may deal with the inhabitants of a martial law area on the same footing as with the population of hostile invaded territory in time of war, subject only, it may be presumed, to such rules of warfare as international law prescribes. It is difficult to say how far the military authorities could be called to account in the civil courts after hostilities, because an Act of Indemnity in the ordinary course would be passed by Parliament to protect them from legal proceedings.[3] Presumably such an Act would not indemnify them for acts done otherwise than in the course of *bona fide* operations for the suppression of the insurrection.[4] But in the absence of such an enactment, it would seem that the acts of the military during war or rebellion could be challenged in the courts, though the action would not be tried so long as a state of hostilities continued.[5]

Cases from Ireland

The *Marais Case* was followed by the Irish courts in 1920–21. At that time the Restoration of Order in Ireland Act 1920 was in force. That Act gave exceptional powers to the Executive, and the military were employed to execute those powers. In *The King* v. *Allen* [6] the King's Bench Division of Ireland accepted the statement

[1] [1902] A.C. 109; K. & L. 242.

[2] *The King* v. *Strickland* (*Garde*), [1921] 2 I.R. 317, at p. 329.

[3] See *Tilonko* v. *Attorney-General of Natal*, [1907] A.C. 93, for an unsuccessful petition for leave to appeal from a judgment of a military court, the sentences of which had been subsequently declared lawful by the legislature of the Colony.

[4] *Wright* v. *Fitzgerald* (1798), 27 St. Tr. 765. See, however, P. O'Higgins in 25 M.L.R. 413 where it is shown that there have been other cases brought against military authorities after rebellion which qualify this authority.

[5] *Higgins* v. *Willis*, [1921] 2 I.R. 386.

[6] [1921] 2 I.R. 241; K. & L. 246.

of the military authority that the statutory powers were insufficient and declined to interfere with a sentence passed by a military tribunal, which was not a statutory court-martial, sitting in an area where the rebellion was raging. In one case the statutory powers were exceeded and the prisoner was released as the result of habeas corpus proceedings; *Egan* v. *Macready*.[1] The decision of the Irish Chancery Division in this case is difficult to reconcile with *The King* v. *Allen* and has been criticised on the ground that the exceptional statutory powers were not, like the statutory powers in the *De Keyser Case*,[2] exclusive of the common law powers, and that the common law gives the Executive the right to conduct operations without interference from the courts, if a state of war is raging. The better opinion is that inadequacy of statutory powers does not disable the military from taking whatever steps are deemed necessary in good faith to restore order.[3]

Prohibition

There is only one decision on martial law which can be regarded as binding on an English court. The House of Lords in *Re Clifford and O'Sullivan* (*ante*), (a case from Ireland before the establishment of the Irish Free State), discussed an application for a writ of prohibition to stay proceedings of a military tribunal set up after a proclamation of martial law. The decision turned upon the technical scope of the writ, which is only available against persons or bodies in the nature of inferior courts exercising a jurisdiction. It was held that the military tribunal in question was not such a body, but only an advisory committee of officers to assist the commander-in-chief, against which the writ could not lie. The House of Lords expressly refrained from discussing the merits of an application under a writ of habeas corpus or other process than prohibition.

Conclusion

Thus the law, if it be correctly stated above, affords little protection to persons in a martial law area, at all events to those who have been convicted of capital offences under the military regime. If the courts are not sitting, they have no remedy. If the courts are in session, an order of prohibition, according to the decision in *Re Clifford and O'Sullivan* (*ante*) will not be granted, while the writ of habeas corpus is probably only available if the courts hold that war was not raging at the time of the commission of the offence (*The King* v. *Allen*, *ante*). On the other hand, it must be noted that

[1] [1921] 1 I.R. 265.
[2] P. 191, *ante*.
[3] P. 408, *ante*.

neither *Marais'* nor *Allen's Cases* are binding on the English courts, which are, therefore, competent to say, should occasion arise, that even during a state of war the acts of the military are subject to the writ of habeas corpus.

The United Kingdom: First World War

Although the military obtained, under the Defence of the Realm Acts 1914–15 a large measure of control in Great Britain and in Ireland, it cannot be claimed, apart from the Irish disturbances, that at any time between 1914 and 1918 a state of war was raging, despite hostilities by way of occasional enemy air-raids and bombardments from the sea. The control exercised during that period over the civilian population was strictly legal, while the courts were exercising, under certain statutory restrictions, their full functions. By the first of the Defence of the Realm Acts passed in 1914 trial by court-martial was authorised for the enforcement of regulations forbidding the sending of information to the enemy or for securing the means of communication, such as the railways and docks. Later there were added to the offences triable by court-martial rumourmongering and offences against the Defence Regulations committed in areas where troops were being trained or concentrated. The Defence of the Realm (Amendment) Act 1915 drastically curtailed the jurisdiction of courts-martial to try offences against the Regulations (except in case of invasion) and restored to British subjects the right to be tried by a jury in a civil court for those offences which had hitherto been punishable by courts-martial. Both civil and military authorities exceeded their legal powers from time to time, and there were many cases of the courts intervening at the instance of persons aggrieved. It is of interest to reproduce here the main operative section of the Indemnity Act 1920 which, subject to certain provisos, expressly restricted the indemnity afforded to the authorities to acts done in good faith and in the public interest.

Indemnity Act 1920, s. 1 (1)

> No action or other legal proceeding whatsoever, whether civil or criminal, shall be instituted in any court of law for or on account of or in respect of any act, matter or thing done, whether within or without His Majesty's dominions, during the war before the passing of this Act, if done in good faith, and done or purported to be done in the execution of his duty or for the defence of the realm or the public safety, or for the enforcement of discipline, or otherwise in the public interest, by a person holding office under or employed in the service of the Crown in any capacity, whether naval, military, air force, or civil, or by any other person acting under the authority of

a person so holding office or so employed; and, if any such proceeding has been instituted whether before or after the passing of this Act, it shall be discharged and made void. . . .

Second World War

In 1939 Parliament was not asked to supersede the jurisdiction of the ordinary courts by conferring on courts-martial the power to try persons not subject to military law. When in 1940 it became necessary to modernise the law of treason by creating the equivalent offence of treachery, the bar on trial by courts-martial was lifted, but only in respect of enemy aliens on the specific direction of the Attorney-General.[1] Trial by court-martial must be distinguished from trial by special civil courts. The Emergency Powers (Defence) (No. 2) Act 1940 which was passed under the imminent threat of invasion, made it possible to substitute for a central system of administration of the criminal law a system of special war zone courts. These courts were only to exercise jurisdiction if the military situation was such, on account of actual or immediately apprehended military action, that criminal justice must be more speedily administered than it could be by the ordinary courts.[2] It was a condition precedent to the exercise of jurisdiction that the Minister of Home Security should first declare a particular area to be a war zone. The constitution of the war zone courts was essentially that of civil courts of record. They were never required to sit. These provisions only governed the procedure to be followed by the civil courts in the event of invasion. They did not in any way affect the common law powers of the military, but the fact that they were enacted on the eve of invasion shows the utter abhorrence of our people to any form of martial law, whatever be the academic doctrine with regard to the powers of the military to impose their will on civilians.

Contrast between First and Second World War

In 1914 the range of offences triable by court-martial at first grew in number, but within seven months of the outbreak of war the right to trial by jury in a civil court had been restored to British subjects. In 1939 it was not intended to deprive the ordinary courts of jurisdiction, but the threat of invasion in the next year necessitated provision to guard against a breakdown in the ordinary administration

[1] Treachery Act 1940, since repealed.

[2] The Administration of Justice (Emergency Provisions) Act 1939 had made elastic provisions for the sittings of the ordinary courts so that the Lord Chancellor could adapt the whole judicial system to the requirements of unforeseen crises. See Sir Cecil Carr, *Concerning English Administrative Law*, p. 81.

of justice, and a solution was found which stopped short of substituting courts-martial for the ordinary courts. Thus within a few months of the outbreak of both wars trial in the ordinary courts was safeguarded except in the event of invasion. In 1915 courts-martial were to replace the civil courts in that event. In 1940 special civil courts were substituted, except that enemy aliens could for the most grave of all war-time offences be tried by court-martial.

PART I: General Constitutional Law

THE BRITISH COMMONWEALTH

Constitutional Laws of the Commonwealth, Vol. I, Chaps. I–III, by Sir Ivor Jennings (Clarendon Press).
Halsbury, *Laws of England*, 3rd edn., Vol. 5, Title *Commonwealth and Dependencies*, ed. S. A. de Smith and Olive M. Stone (Butterworths).
Constitutional and Administrative Law, 4th edn., by O. Hood Phillips (Sweet & Maxwell).
The Constitutional Structure of the Commonwealth, by K. C. Wheare (Clarendon Press).
Parliamentary Sovereignty and the Commonwealth, by G. Marshall (Clarendon Press).
The New Commonwealth and its Constitutions, by S. A. de Smith (Stevens).
Commonwealth and Colonial Law, by Sir Kenneth Roberts-Wray (Stevens).

CHAPTER THIRTY

THE UNITED KINGDOM, CHANNEL ISLANDS AND ISLE OF MAN

ENGLAND and Wales, Scotland and Northern Ireland form the United Kingdom of Great Britain and Northern Ireland. Though England and Wales and Scotland possess a common legislature,[1] and are united for most purposes of central government,[2] Scotland has her own system of law and her own courts,[3] and her own established Church.[4] The Parliament of the United Kingdom has functions in relation to colonial territories overseas, and, as such, exercises legislative supremacy over the few remaining Colonies and still has a special relationship with Canada on a few subjects of constitutional amendment.[5]

Northern Ireland[6]

Northern Ireland possesses her own Executive, a Governor and Cabinet, and a Legislature of two Houses, the Senate and House

[1] Chap. 7.
[2] Chap. 15.
[3] Chap. 22.
[4] Chap. 34.
[5] British North America (No. 2) Act 1949, s. 1.
[6] H. Calvert, *Constitutional Law in Northern Ireland* (Stevens and N.I.L.Q.), is a detailed study of regional government.

of Commons. It was originally intended that Ireland should be given a wide measure of Home Rule, while remaining part of the United Kingdom. Though abandoned as far as Southern Ireland was concerned, the constitution enacted with this intention by the Government of Ireland Act 1920 came into force in Northern Ireland. Northern Ireland has retained representation in the United Kingdom Parliament and is subject to its legislative supremacy. Certain subjects, *e.g.* laws in respect of the Crown, treaties and foreign relations generally, defence, foreign trade and coinage are reserved for the United Kingdom Government and Parliament. There is a Supreme Court consisting of the High Court and Court of Appeal; from the latter appeal lies to the House of Lords. Constitutional issues may be referred for determination to the Judicial Committee of the Privy Council.[1] In the event of a deadlock between the Senate and the House of Commons the Governor may, if a Bill is passed by the House of Commons in two successive sessions and is not agreed to by the Senate, convene a joint sitting of the two Houses. Any Bill passed by a majority at such a joint sitting becomes law. In the case of a financial Bill a joint sitting may be convened in the same session that the Bill is rejected.

The relationship thus established between the United Kingdom and Northern Ireland is not unlike a federal one with the important difference that the Parliament of the United Kingdom can legislate in amplification or in derogation of the powers of the Parliament of Northern Ireland. The Northern Ireland (Miscellaneous Provisions) Act 1932 removed some of the causes of friction to which this relationship had given rise by giving the Parliament of Northern Ireland some additional powers, *e.g.* to enable the repeal and re-enactment of imperial legislation for purposes of consolidation. The Ireland Act 1949, which recognised that the Republic of Ireland ceased to be part of Her Majesty's dominions, affirmed that Northern Ireland remained part of the United Kingdom and that its status would not be altered without the consent of the Parliament of Northern Ireland.

In 1969 civil disorder erupted in Northern Ireland; this necessitated the employment of troops of the Regular Army at the request of the Government in Belfast. A sequel was the reorganisation of the Royal Ulster Constabulary; this required legislation by the local Parliament. Other legislation by the Parliament at Westminster sanctioned assistance from the police forces of Great Britain and the establishment of a part-time volunteer regiment of the British Army for the

[1] Government of Ireland Act 1920, s. 51.

defence of Northern Ireland.[1] These measures were from a constitutional point of view within the provisions of the Government of Ireland Act 1920. The political situation was handled by the Home Secretary as the responsible Minister in the United Kingdom Government and emphasis was put upon the preservation of the rights of the Northern Ireland Government as conferred by the Act of 1920. The future may show that only by amendment of that Act can order be restored and maintained.

Channel Islands

The Channel Islands, like the Isle of Man, are included among the British Isles, but do not form part of the United Kingdom. Their citizens are entitled to be known as "of the United Kingdom, Islands and Colonies." [2] The laws of the Channel Islands are based on the ancient customs of the Duchy of Normandy, of which they formed part until 1204; this particularly applies to land law, inheritance and judicial procedure. The sovereignty of Her Majesty is to the present day only admitted in her right as successor to the Dukes of Normandy. These islands have never been colonies and enjoy a full measure of autonomy for most purposes, including taxation. The Channel Islands are subject to the legislative supremacy of the United Kingdom Parliament, which is exercised for them in relation to such subjects as nationality and defence. In practice the views of the Insular Authorities are usually sought before legislation affecting the Islands is laid before Parliament. Some details of the constitution of Jersey and Guernsey are of interest. Apart from their antiquity these constitutions were the only precedents for the government of overseas territories when colonial expansion raised the question how the new territories should be governed. Early examples of colonial constitutions did not seek to separate the legislative from the executive function. To this day it is committees of the legislature to whom are entrusted the tasks of executive government in the Channel Islands.

Jersey

The Sovereign is represented by Her Lieutenant-Governor and Commander-in-Chief who acts as the channel of communication between the Government of the United Kingdom and the Insular Government. He is entitled to sit but not to vote in the Assembly of the States (the legislative assembly) and also to a seat in the Royal

[1] Police Act 1969; Ulster Defence Regiment Act 1969.

[2] **British Nationality Act 1948, s. 33 (2).**

Court. The chief judicial and executive officer is the Bailiff who, like the Lieutenant-Governor, is appointed by the Crown. He is President both of the States and of the Royal Court. Any of his functions may be discharged by the Deputy Bailiff. The Assembly of the States consists of twelvc Senators elected for the whole island for a term of nine years, four retiring every third year; twelve Constables, one for each parish, elected triennially; twenty-eight Deputies, similarly elected but in different constituencies. Legislation takes the form of (i) permanent Laws passed by the States and sanctioned by Order in Council which is registered thereafter in the Royal Court; (ii) Regulations, and (iii) Orders made by Committees of the States. The Judiciary consists of the Royal Court, constituted by the Bailiff and twelve Jurats. The latter used to be elected by popular franchise, but since 1948 the election has been conducted by an Electoral College, a body composed of the Jurats, members of the States and legal practitioners of seven years' standing. The Court has full civil and criminal jurisdiction. In criminal trials the jury numbers twenty-four and nine dissentients acquit.

Guernsey

The Bailiwick of Guernsey includes the islands of Guernsey, Alderney, Sark, Herm and Jethou. The Sovereign's representative, as in Jersey, is the Lieutenant-Governor. Similarly the Bailiff is the civil head of the administration as well as President of the States of Deliberation (the legislature) and the Royal Court (the judiciary). The legislature consists of twelve Conseillers elected by an Electoral College for six years, thirty-three Deputies, elected triennially on a parochial basis by adult suffrage, ten Douzaine representatives, one elected by each of the ten parishes annually. Legislation originates in the States either as a Law or an Ordinance. A Law is passed by the States on the proposal of one of its Committees and requires the sanction of an Order in Council duly registered in the Royal Court. An Ordinance comes into operation as soon as it is passed by the States but may not be used to impose taxation or to alter a Law or the common law. Ordinances are also used to implement Laws. The States of Guernsey legislate for the adjoining islands, subject in the case of Alderney to the consent of the local States, and in Sark to that of the Chief Pleas (the island legislatures).

The States of Deliberation, working through various Committees, exercise the executive power. The Judiciary consists of the Bailiff (President) and twelve Jurats, elected by an Electoral College (the States of Election, a body similar in composition to the States of

Deliberation, together with the existing Jurats and ten Rectors). The Court sits in two Divisions (the full court and the ordinary court). Jurisdiction in civil suits is exercised in the ordinary court. Indictable offences are dealt with in the full court.

Channel Islands Courts of Appeal

There are separate Channel Islands Courts of Appeal for Jersey and Guernsey with both civil and criminal jurisdiction. The judges are the Bailiffs of Jersey and Guernsey and their deputies together with such persons as may be appointed by the Queen from those who are qualified by having held judicial office in the Commonwealth or as senior practitioners at the Bar in any part of the United Kingdom, the Isle of Man, Jersey or Guernsey as the case may be. The Bailiff of Jersey is sworn in for the purpose of hearing appeals from Guernsey Royal Court, and similarly the Bailiff of Guernsey for Jersey appeals. From a decision of the Courts of Appeal in civil matters appeal lies to the Judicial Committee of the Privy Council by leave either of the Court or the Judicial Committee, where the value of the matter in dispute is over £500.

The Privy Council

There is a Committee of the Privy Council for Channel Islands matters. As has been seen in the case of Jersey and Guernsey, the most formal type of island legislation requires to be sanctioned by Order in Council. It has always been doubtful how far such Orders which have to be registered in the Royal Courts of the Islands are effectual until so registered. The Royal Courts may request reconsideration by the Privy Council Committee of an Order in Council but can in the last resort be compelled to register it.[1]

Isle of Man [2]

The Isle of Man, an ancient kingdom, was, until 1266, feudatory to the Kings of Norway: traces of this Norse heritage survive in Manx law and government. From the reign of Edward I sovereignty over the Island was disputed between Scotland and England; eventually, in the reign of Henry IV, the English claim prevailed, and in 1405 the Island was granted to the Stanley family, Earls of Derby, by Letters Patent with the title of King (later Lord) of Man. In 1736 the Lordship passed to the Dukes of Atholl. The Atholl rights in

[1] Halsbury, *Laws of England*, 3rd edn., Vol. 5, p. 638.

[2] See the *Report of the Commission on the Isle of Man Constitution* (1959) and the *Report of the Joint Working Party on the Constitutional Relationship between the Isle of Man and the United Kingdom* (1969).

the Island were bought out by the Crown by statutes of 1765 and 1825, and since then the Manx people have prided themselves on their direct connection with the Sovereign as Lord of Man.

The United Kingdom Parliament can legislate for the Isle of Man, either directly or by extending Acts of Parliament by Order in Council: in practice this power is confined to matters relating either to defence or to international affairs (*e.g.* copyright, merchant shipping and civil aviation).

The Manx legislature is known as Tynwald and consists of the Sovereign as Lord of Man (represented by the Lieutenant-Governor), the Legislative Council and the House of Keys. The Council consists of the Lieutenant-Governor and ten official and nominated members. The House of Keys has twenty-four members, popularly elected for five years. Legislation is usually passed by both chambers sitting separately, although since 1961 the Council has had no blocking power. Acts of Tynwald, which require the Royal Assent by Order in Council, cover all domestic matters: in particular, by the Isle of Man Act 1958, the Manx legislature can regulate the Island's finances, customs and harbours.

Executive power is divided between the Lieutenant-Governor and Tynwald. The former is the channel of communication with the United Kingdom Government and is responsible for public order and good government, with ultimate financial control. Tynwald Court, consisting of the Council and Keys sitting together, has general administrative and financial responsibility for the public services, with control delegated to Boards of Tynwald. The Lieutenant-Governor is advised by an Executive Council elected by Tynwald.

The Isle of Man has its own courts. There are two High Court judges known as Deemsters, one of whom presides also over the criminal Court of General Gaol Delivery. The appeal court, known as the Staff of Government, is presided over by a Deemster and the Judge of Appeal, an English barrister appointed by the Crown. An ultimate appeal lies to the Judicial Committee of the Privy Council.

CHAPTER THIRTY-ONE

THE COLONIES

DURING the first half of the twentieth century the Commonwealth overseas, as the British Empire came to be called, could be divided into two clearly distinguishable groups. Together with the United Kingdom as free and equal members of the British Commonwealth of Nations were Canada, Australia, New Zealand and South Africa, and after the Second World War India, Pakistan and Ceylon were added. The colonial territories, on the other hand, consisted of a large number of communities, all of which were subject to the legislative supremacy of the Parliament of the United Kingdom, seldom though it was exercised in practice, and to the right of the Crown to disallow the enactments of the local legislatures which had been set up in all the larger communities. This right was exercised on the advice of the Secretary of State for the Colonies, and therefore all the territories came under the ultimate rule of Westminster and Whitehall. It was, however, the generally accepted policy that the ultimate goal for all viable communities was self-government. To this end many of the more important colonial territories advanced rapidly to a status of virtually complete internal independence. This was brought about by the introduction of constitutions framed by the Secretary of State for the Colonies which granted a full or partial measure of ministerial responsibility to the local executive councils. This responsibility was normally attained at no long interval after the introduction of elected (as opposed to nominated) legislatures. In other words, once representative government had been reached the grant of ministerial responsibility inevitably followed and the colony could claim to become independent of the United Kingdom.

The second half of the century has seen the attainment of independence by the greater part of the former colonial territories both in Africa and Asia as well as by the larger islands of the British West Indies. For the smaller islands a system of association with full internal independence was set up by the West Indies Act 1967. It follows, therefore, that the Government and Parliament of the United Kingdom have ceased to be bound by legal links with the other Commonwealth States, though in a few cases the new State has chosen to retain a judicial link by preserving the former right of appeal from its courts to the Judicial Committee of the Privy Council.

Once a colony has acquired independence from the United Kingdom it is free to choose whether or not to apply for membership of the Commonwealth. It is for all the existing Commonwealth States to decide whether or not the application for membership should be accepted. In practice, however, whenever it has been the wish of a former colony to remain in the Commonwealth, the application has been granted.

That the Commonwealth link cannot be described in terms of law is shown by the recognition which dates from the Declaration of London, 1949, that the adoption of a constitution as a sovereign independent republic is not incompatible with membership.[1] Under colonial rule common allegiance to the Crown was the legal link. This is necessarily replaced when the constitution provides that a President shall be head of State, but, as has been seen,[2] each monarchical State is free to define its nationality laws and the scope of allegiance to the Queen.

What follows will explain how membership of the Commonwealth has evolved out of colonial rule. In this connection, although India and Pakistan were never colonial territories so far as they formed part of the old Indian Empire, (as distinct from the Indian Native States) they were ruled through a separate Secretary of State who, like the Colonial Secretary, was responsible as a member of the Cabinet to the United Kingdom Parliament. Some knowledge of the constitutional status of a colony is essential to understand the part played by the United Kingdom Parliament in this process of evolution to independence. In addition to colonies proper there were territories known as the Protectorates and Trust Territories which were governed in much the same way as colonial territory under the authority of the Prerogative as extended by the Foreign Jurisdiction Acts 1890 and 1913.[3]

When the inhabitants of colonial territories cease on independence to share a common citizenship with those of the United Kingdom, they have, at all events in the first instance, almost without exception, chosen a form of government which follows the model of cabinet government on the United Kingdom lines. In some of the larger territories independence has been accompanied by the adoption of a federal constitution. Federation presupposes a desire for some form of union among independent States which nevertheless wish to

[1] Pp. 459–60, *post*.
[2] Chap. 19.
[3] The government of these territories was described briefly in Seventh Edition, pp. 426–30.

preserve their identity and some measure of independence. In the case of Canada the strong bi-racial element (English and French) was responsible for the federal constitution. In the case of Nigeria and other African territories, there is the complication of tribal interests and a federal constitution has been adopted in the hope of preserving some measure of local independence. The protection of the rights of minorities can also be safeguarded by the inclusion of a Bill of Rights as part of a constitution whether federal or unilateral. This led Canada in 1960 to enact a Bill of Rights which, however, was not enacted as an amendment to the constitution which is contained in the British North America Acts 1867–1949. Starting with the Nigerian Constitution in 1960, practically every new member of the Commonwealth has included in its constitution guarantees of liberty which bear a closer resemblance to the American Constitution than to the English Bill of Rights of 1688.

The Colonial System [1]

Variety and individuality were the features of the British colonial system. Colonial constitutions were not of a standard pattern. Variety extended to the franchise and to methods of election to legislative councils where these existed. Colonial constitutions were, and still are mainly enacted (1) by letters patent issued by the Queen in Council constituting the office of Governor and providing for the government of the colony (including, if necessary by separate letters patent, provision for a legislative council) and (2) by formal instructions to the Governor issued by the Queen under the royal sign manual. The appointment of a Governor is by commission under the royal sign manual countersigned by the Secretary of State for the Colonies.[2]

It is competent for the Parliament of the United Kingdom to enact or amend [3] a colonial constitution. In the past this was done to give settlers from Great Britain and Ireland representative legislatures or to give legal force to a constitution Bill promoted by a colonial legislature before the enactment of the Colonial Laws Validity Act 1865 [4]; see, for example, the Victoria Constitution Act 1855. Even where statutory authority has been required, as with

[1] Though much of what follows has now become of historical interest only, it has been retained since a few colonies still remain under the United Kingdom.

[2] See *The Making of a Colonial Constitution*, by O. Hood-Phillips, 71 L.Q.R. 51, for an interesting account of the negotiations and stages in the enactment of a new colonial constitution.

[3] Southern Rhodesia Act 1965 is an example, though, as it was enacted after the unilateral declaration of independence by the local government, it has never been enforced in Rhodesia.

[4] Pp. 435–7, *post*.

legislative councils constituted under the British Settlements Act 1887 or in the case of protectorates, the Foreign Jurisdiction Act 1890 or by separate Act, such as the Bahama Islands (Constitution) Act 1963, Parliament has authorised the Crown to grant a constitution or constitutional amendment by Order in Council. As will be seen when the Statute of Westminster is considered [1] it has been necessary for the Parliament of the United Kingdom to pass an independence Act renouncing its constitutional connection with a new State which is then free to enact its own constitution.

Distinction between Settled Colonies and those acquired by Conquest or Cession

When settlers annexed for the Crown territory which had no civilised system of law, the law of the colony was the common law of England and, in so far as it was applicable, the statute law existing at the time of the settlement. The Crown could grant institutions, but could not take away rights; it had no powers of legislation; nor could it impose a tax. It followed that in such colonies changes in the constitution, like all changes of law, could only be effected by Act of the United Kingdom Parliament. But in 1887 general powers to alter the constitutions of settled colonies were granted to the Crown (acting by delegation if desired) by the British Settlements Act.[2] The Act applied to any settled colonies which were not at that time within the jurisdiction of a colonial legislature, *e.g.* the Falkland Islands, the Gold Coast. Thus for constitutional purposes henceforth there was no difference between such colonies and those which had been acquired by conquest or cession. For in the latter case it always had been, and still is, competent for the Crown to legislate by prerogative. But in colonies so acquired there was no automatic application of English law, the law in force at the time of the conquest or cession remaining in force until altered. Illustrations of this are to be found to-day in Ceylon, where the basic law is Roman-Dutch, and in Quebec where the pre-Napoleonic French law still provides elements in the law of the Province.[3]

Rule in Campbell *v.* Hall

So far as the form of government was concerned it rested with the Crown to grant or withhold a constitution as a matter of prerogative right in the case of territory which had been ceded to it or conquered. But once a grant of a representative legislature was made to such

[1] Chap. 32.

[2] British Settlements Act 1945 removed the requirement that delegation must be to three or more persons.

[3] The law of the Republic of South Africa is also based on Roman-Dutch law.

a colony, the power to legislate or to raise taxes by prerogative was abandoned, so long as the legislature continued in existence. This was laid down in the case of *Campbell* v. *Hall* in 1774 in relation to the Island of Granada. But there may be expressly reserved by the instrument creating the legislature, or by a subsequent Act of the Parliament of the United Kingdom, a power of concurrent legislation by prerogative.[1] The definition of representative legislature given by section 5 of the Colonial Laws Validity Act 1865 [2] is limited to that Act. When *Campbell* v. *Hall* was decided such a legislature meant any assembly of the inhabitants summoned by the Crown. In the days of the old Colonial Empire, which came to an end with the revolt of the North American Colonies, elected majorities sat in most legislative councils along with the Governor and his Executive Council, but with the advent of colonies with an overwhelming preponderance of native inhabitants the acquisition of a representative legislature only came as a stage in the process of acquiring self-governing powers. In practice in most letters patent creating colonial constitutions with representative legislatures power was expressly reserved to revoke the grant. Where the Crown, as in Ceylon, originally a conquered and ceded colony, had reserved the power to revoke, alter or amend the constitution, the power could be exercised retrospectively and this is still the position today in the case of any remaining such colonies in this category.

In *Abeyesekera* v. *Jayatilake* [3] the respondent had rendered himself liable to penalties for sitting and voting in the Ceylon Legislative Council by reason of disqualification under an Order in Council of 1923; it was held that a later Order of 1928 had retrospectively removed the disqualification.

Where power to legislate was not reserved, an Act of the Imperial Parliament was necessary to authorise constitutional amendment by Order in Council.[4] Many colonies which in early colonial days

[1] *Campbell* v. *Hall* (1774), Lofft 655; C.L.C. 59; as interpreted in *Sammut* v. *Strickland*, [1938] A.C. 678, which raised the question of the validity of an executive ordinance imposing customs duties, especially at p. 704, which makes it clear that the continued existence of the legislature is requisite. If the legislature is surrendered, the prerogative is revived. Roberts-Wray, *op. cit.* pp. 158–62 forcefully challenges the view that the case extended to constitutional powers being lost by the Crown.

[2] P. 437, *post*.

[3] [1932] A.C. 260.

[4] There is no justification for the suggestion made in *North Charterland Exploration Co.* v. *The King*, [1931] 1 Ch. 169, that the rule in *Campbell* v. *Hall* has no effect since the passing of the Foreign Jurisdiction Acts 1890–1913. These Acts, which regulate the exercise by the Crown of jurisdiction in foreign territory, have no application to British territory, and the rule is still of authority; see *Abeyesekera* v. *Jayatilake*.

received grants of representative legislatures subsequently surrendered their constitutions and received in exchange constitutions which reserved the right of the Crown to legislate by Order in Council. Thus to the greater number of colonies the rule in *Campbell* v. *Hall* had latterly no application. The intervention of Parliament was not required to make changes in the constitution. These could be effected by Order in Council or Letters Patent on the advice of the Secretary of State for the Colonies after consultation with the Governor.

Annexation

Where annexation was the result of a treaty of cession with a native ruler, the treaty might contain provisions preserving or modifying private or community rights.[1] The annexation of territory was, however, an act of State [2] and an obligation undertaken upon annexation to protect private property, though in accordance with international law, was not enforceable by a municipal tribunal, unless the terms of the treaty of cession had been made part of municipal law.[3] An act of State must be accepted as effective,[4] and no special formality was required for annexation.[5]

Powers of Colonial Legislatures

The great legal landmark in colonial constitutional law, the Colonial Laws Validity Act 1865, will be discussed in the next chapter as part of the evolution to self-government and Commonwealth status. Here it is sufficient to remark that it made colonial legislatures supreme in their own spheres and therefore able to change the common law of England or whatever system prevailed in the colony; but so long as they remained subject to the Parliament at Westminster, they could not change statute law contained in such Acts of Parliament as applied to the colonies, *e.g.* the British Nationality Act 1948.

Governors [6]

The Governor of a colony is both in form and in fact the executive.

[1] *Amodu Tijani* v. *Secretary, Southern Nigeria*, [1921] 2 A.C. 399.

[2] Chap. 20, A.

[3] *Cook* v. *Sprigg*, [1899] A.C. 572; *Hoani Te Heuheu Tukino* v. *Aotea District Maori Land Board*, [1941] A.C. 308; *Secretary of State for India* v. *Sardar Rustam Khan*, [1941] A.C. 356.

[4] *Salaman* v. *Secretary of State for India*, [1906] 1 K.B. 613.

[5] *In re Southern Rhodesia*, [1919] A.C. 211, at p. 238.

[6] This paragraph and all that follow down to p. 431 give an account of colonial rule as it applied in many territories which have become independent States since 1948.

There are still a few dependencies which are thus subject to the direct rule of the Governor. In most cases he is assisted by an executive council which he must consult, though he is only required to follow its advice so far as responsibility for certain subjects is under the constitution entrusted to members chosen from the legislative council to act as Ministers. Such councils consist of a single chamber of elected members who sit with the chief officers of the Colony and some unofficial members appointed by the Government. Councils are thus semi-representative, but the Governor cannot be held responsible to the legislature and therefore cabinet government with the executive responsible to the legislature does not prevail. That stage of constitutional development is only reached when the Governor receives instructions which require him to select his executive council from members of the legislative council who can command a majority in that body. Then self-government is attained, though it may be applied with reservations as to special topics, such as defence and foreign affairs. The Governor is appointed by the Crown, represents the Crown, and is responsible to the Crown. He must obey any instructions that he receives from the Secretary of State for the Colonies through the Colonial Office. The chief officer under the Governor of a colony which has not attained to responsible government is the Chief Secretary. A Governor is appointed to hold office during Her Majesty's pleasure, but does not normally hold office for more than six years. He derives his authority from his commission. He does not by virtue of his office enjoy the full immunities or prerogatives of the Queen, but only such as are expressly or impliedly conferred upon him by statute or by his commission.[1] The commission does not enumerate specific powers, but refers to the letters patent constituting the office of Governor and providing for the government of the colony and to the instructions to the Governor of the colony. These two documents form the constitution of a colony. The former lays down the constitutional framework, *e.g.* it provides for the establishment of an executive council. The latter sets out the Governor's duties, *e.g.* it provides for the Governor's obligation to consult his executive council. On attainment of independence the Governor is usually appointed temporarily as Governor-General to represent the Queen if the new State adopts a monarchical form of government. After a short interval he is usually replaced by a leading political figure in the territory. If a republican form of government is adopted the

[1] This applies also, as does the method of appointment, to a Governor-General of a Commonwealth State; see, however, p. 453, *post*.

Governor is replaced by a President who, like a Governor-General, acts on the advice of his responsible Ministers.[1]

The Official Element

The official element in the legislative council is composed of those who sit by virtue of their office in the colonial executive. In addition to the Governor who presides, members of the executive council such as the Chief Secretary, the Attorney-General, the Financial Secretary, the Director of Medical Services, the Secretary for Native Affairs will sit along with other directors of departments who are not members of the executive council. Thus there is assured a body of homogeneous opinion which affords the executive council support from the legislature.

In the past it was possible to make the generalisation that the official majority was the very kernel and essence of Crown colony government.[2] It is still the characteristic institution in the smaller or less developed territories which remain colonies. Since the consent to legislation and to the annual estimates is assured where the official element forms a majority, it may well be asked whether a legislative council is really legislative in its function as the capacity of unofficial members is advisory only. But it does secure a full and public discussion of legislative proposals, even if it fails to create effective political authority in the unofficial element, whether nominated or elected. Moreover it affords a platform for the discussion of grievances arising from the administrative services in just the same way as the Opposition in the House of Commons can ventilate such grievances on Supply Days.[3]

Courts in the Colonies

In every colonial territory there is a court of unlimited jurisdiction established by Order in Council or local statute. The judges are appointed by the Governor, on the instructions of the Queen which are given through the Secretary of State for the Colonies, as the responsible Minister. They hold office at the pleasure of the Crown, but it has been the practice since 1870 that the dismissal of a colonial judge of a superior court should be subject to a reference to the

[1] In some cases the offices of President and Prime Minister have been combined.

[2] Sir Anton Bertram, *The Colonial Service* (Cambridge University Press), p. 168; Wight, *The Development of the Legislative Council* (1606–1945), (Faber), pp. 73, 100–01.

[3] Chap. 9.

Judicial Committee of the Privy Council.[1] This system is different from the safeguards given to the higher judiciary in England by the Act of Settlement and copied by the older Dominions. It recognises, moreover, that a legislative assembly is not necessarily the most appropriate body to pass judgment on judicial conduct. The chief court in each colony is styled the Supreme Court.

Appeals lie from the highest court in any colony [2] to the Judicial Committee of the Privy Council.[3] A writ of habeas corpus may not issue out of England to any colony which has a court with authority to issue the writ, but where there is no such court in a colony, an English court will grant the writ.[4]

Below the level of the Supreme Court (the Chief Justice and puisne judges) which enjoys independence in all its relations with the executive, there is a variety of judicial institutions adapted to local conditions. The place of the lay justice of the peace in England is taken by the district magistrate who exercises summary powers as well as investigating in the first instance more serious cases before trial. Often he has limited jurisdiction in civil cases. In the smallest colony it may suffice to have a Chief Justice and a single magistrate. Elsewhere there may be an intermediate judiciary working on a centralised system. The jury system in criminal cases prevails in some colonies; in others the trial is by a judge with two or more assessors.

[1] See Note in [1954] C.L.J. 2–7; and *Terrell* v. *Secretary of State for the Colonies*, [1953] 2 Q.B. 482. The procedure for reference is set out in Colonial Regulations which have, however, no binding force in law.

[2] Where colonies are grouped for the purpose of appeals, there is sometimes a right of appeal to the Privy Council from the appellate court only; sometimes both from the appellate court and also direct from the colonial Supreme Courts

[3] Chap. 33.

[4] Habeas Corpus Act 1862; *cf. Sprigg* v. *Sigcau*, [1897] A.C. 238, see pp. 491 ff., *post*.

CHAPTER THIRTY-TWO

COMMONWEALTH CONSTITUTIONAL RELATIONS

A. Introductory

So numerous have been the changes with the grant of independence to colonial and other subject territories in the past few years, and their subsequent admission to the Commonwealth, that it is no longer possible in a book on constitutional law of the United Kingdom to examine one by one the constitutions of these new States. Since, however, the historical evolution of the Commonwealth could not have taken the form it has but for the enactment in 1865 of the Colonial Laws Validity Act and in 1931 of the Statute of Westminster, it is still necessary to examine the historical background of these statutes and what they achieved before discussing the present position of the Commonwealth. In 1931 five territories other than the United Kingdom had full self-governing status. Of these the Dominion of Canada, the Commonwealth of Australia and New Zealand remain in the Commonwealth. There will be full discussion of the Colonial Laws Validity Act and Statute of Westminster. For study of any particular constitution there are several text-books available for the larger States in addition to Sir Kenneth Roberts-Wray's *Commonwealth and Colonial Law* which covers the whole of the independent and dependent States.

Membership of the Commonwealth

Before considering the relationship of Commonwealth States with the United Kingdom it may be helpful to summarise what is involved in membership of the Commonwealth. Independence and membership of the Commonwealth are not the same. Independence has been granted when the Government of the United Kingdom has decided that the time has come for action. This decision is reached in agreement with the territory concerned. This has been true not only of the attainment of independent status by

West and East African colonial territories in the recent past, but really dates back to the acceptance of the Durham Report of 1839. To admit a new member to the Commonwealth requires the agreement of all existing members. Up to date no application has been rejected. This may possibly be a consequence of the decision to grant independence resting with the United Kingdom. If it was known beforehand that other members might decline to admit a new candidate for membership, the United Kingdom might well have retarded the constitutional advancement of the territory until a more favourable occasion for admission to the Commonwealth arose. It is possible for a newly created independent State to apply for membership of the United Nations irrespective of its desire to remain in the Commonwealth, as in the case of Burma in 1946.

Since there is no doubt that independence normally carries with it the opportunity to acquire membership of the Commonwealth, it is convenient to examine what that membership involves. Lord Jowitt as Lord Chancellor [1] spoke of the great benefit of "joint consultation, alike in matters civil and military, the sharing of opinion and the resulting solution of common difficulties". Another authority whose professional life was spent as legal adviser to the Colonial and Commonwealth Relations Offices has summarised some primary principles which form the background of the co-operation which membership involves.[2] In the first place the older members of the Commonwealth in the past have been united by a common allegiance to the Crown; new members of the Commonwealth for the most part, at all events at first, recognise the Sovereign and owe her allegiance under their local nationality laws. But most of these while remaining members of the Commonwealth sooner or later declare republican status but continue to recognise the Sovereign "as the symbol of the free association of the member nations and as such the Head of the Commonwealth". The second principle which has already been discussed is that admission depends on the decision of existing members which has always been unanimous. In the third place there is something like a constitutional convention that one member will not intervene in or even comment upon the domestic affairs of any member, and that action by one which may affect another requires prior consultation or at least information. By way of comment, it may be suggested that this convention is not universally observed; for example, it would be unlikely that India and Pakistan in view of their continuing differences over Kashmir could

[1] 159 H.L. Deb. Cols.1092–3.

[2] Sir Kenneth Roberts-Wray, *Changing Law in Developing Countries,* Editor, J. N. D. Anderson, pp. 52–6.

observe such a convention. Representation of one member State is secured by accrediting a High Commissioner with ambassadorial status and the enjoyment of diplomatic immunity for himself and his staff in each of the other member States. Nevertheless, the element of specific obligation is generally absent and there are few, if any, topics on which there can be said to be a definite Commonwealth doctrine or policy.[1] As regards the machinery for securing such consultation and exchange of information as may be derived from the fact of membership of the Commonwealth, there are a number of organs upon which all members of the Commonwealth are entitled to be represented. A Commonwealth Secretariat for the dissemination of factual information to all members was established in 1965. It has no executive functions.[2] In the field of finance and economics a Commonwealth Economic Consultative Council forms the meeting place at regular intervals of Ministers of Finance. In the United Kingdom it is possible for other States of the Commonwealth to seek loans which secure trustee status on the London market. Commonwealth preference rests upon bilateral agreements. There is a somewhat loose organisation known as the Commonwealth Education Liaison Committee for improving educational co-operation. The subject of communications on external affairs between other members and the United Kingdom Government is dealt with later in this chapter.[3] In the field of defence, apart from common membership of such organisations as N.A.T.O. of which there are two Commonwealth members, there are opportunities for combined exercises, exchange of military missions and common systems of training and equipment. For most people it is only the periodic meetings of Prime Ministers of the Commonwealth which attract attention.[4]

Equality of Status

Members of the Commonwealth are " equal in status, in no way subordinate one to another in any aspect of their domestic or external affairs, though united by common allegiance to the Crown and freely associated as members of the British Commonwealth of Nations." [5] These words which the Imperial Conference of 1926 accepted from a committee over which Lord Balfour presided are, so far as they postulated common allegiance, no longer apt to describe the status even of the older members. By substituting for a

[1] See Roberts-Wray, *op. cit.*, p. 54.
[2] P. 455, *post*.
[3] P. 456, *post*.
[4] Pp. 454 ff., *post*, for further discussion.
[5] Imperial Conference, *Summary of Proceedings*, Cmd. 2768, 1926.

common nationality law enactments of varying content to determine local citizenship which, as we have seen,[1] is accepted as the qualification as Commonwealth citizen (a term of law alternative to British subject), nationality depends upon a different law in each State.

We will first discuss the meaning which was given to dominion status. For, although the advent of the independent Commonwealth States in Asia and in Africa has resulted in the substitution of the term, Commonwealth status, the former term was in universal use in the critical deliberations between the World Wars which resulted in the 1926 formula and the subsequent enactment in 1931 of the Statute of Westminster. In what follows we are primarily concerned with the older member States of the Commonwealth rather than the States in Asia and Africa where independence has been attained by native Governments. It should be remembered that there was no precedent for the evolution of a colony into an autonomous State which nevertheless retained common allegiance to the head of the colonial power to which it was formerly in subjection. This explains why the attainment of independence has been by a process of trial and error in which conventions have been all the time ahead of the rules of constitutional law. Thus when the Imperial Conference (a term now obsolete to describe the periodic meetings of Commonwealth Prime Ministers) in 1926 affirmed that equality of status was the root principle governing the relations of members with one another, it was careful to state: "But the principles of equality and similarity appropriate to status do not universally extend to function. Here we require something more than immutable dogmas."[2] Whatever may be thought about equality of function, it is no longer possible to argue that equality in law has not been attained by each State of the Commonwealth. Indeed it is expressly stated in the later Acts granting independence that the jurisdiction of the United Kingdom Government and Parliament have ceased. But at the earlier date the supremacy of the Parliament of the United Kingdom survived and was actively in operation in a few spheres of law, such as nationality, merchant shipping and the royal title. Constitutional amendments have been made independently within the State affected. But Canada on account of dominion-provincial relationships hesitating long before seeking to acquire full constitution-making powers which no longer require to be enacted at Westminster. British North American Bills can be sent

[1] Chap. 19.

[2] *Imperial Conference, Summary of Proceedings*, 1926, Cmd. 2768.

across the Atlantic with the knowledge that not a comma of the Canadian draftsman's work will be changed.

Responsible Government

All the States have, like the United Kingdom, responsible government, that is, government by an executive which is responsible to, and must normally command a majority in an elected legislature, which alone can impose taxes and without whose authority laws cannot be made. The grant of representative institutions and the establishment of an independent judiciary in a colony have usually been stages on the road to responsible government. An irresponsible executive cannot for long work in harmony with an elected legislature. Those colonies that attained representative institutions have advanced to responsible government. Not all have retained it. As a result of *coups d'état* in the case of Pakistan and several African States, an autocratic régime has replaced Cabinet government on the Westminster model, usually with the promise to return to a constitutional régime and a general election. Responsible government in the Dominions was inspired by the Durham Report of 1839. Instructions were first sent to the Governor of Nova Scotia and to Lord Elgin in Canada in 1848 that they should act on the advice of Ministers acceptable to the representative legislatures. There followed the grant of responsible government to Newfoundland, the other colonies of British North America and the Australian and South African colonies. In each case a relaxation of imperial control followed the grant of responsible government, although, just as responsible government was granted without being expressly embodied in the several constitutions, so the formal legal supremacy of the Imperial Parliament was not limited until the Statute of Westminster 1931; but for long all these have exercised complete internal sovereignty and have been free from all control by the Parliament and Government of the United Kingdom.

Colonial Laws Validity Act 1865

The first great legal landmark after the granting of responsible government was the passing of the Colonial Laws Validity Act 1865. The courts of South Australia, in a series of judgments delivered by Mr. Justice Boothby in the middle of the nineteenth century, cast doubts upon the validity of colonial legislation that conflicted with English law. This application of a doubtful common law rule that legislation by a colonial legislature was void if repugnant to the law of England, whether common law or statute law, would have stultified the recent grants of responsible government by disabling the legislature over a wide field of legislation. Accordingly the Act was passed in order to make it plain that within its own sphere a colonial legislature was sovereign and was subordinate only to the Imperial Parliament. By this Act, "An Act to remove doubts as to the validity of colonial laws," a legislature is defined as the authority, other than the Imperial Parliament or the Queen in Council, competent to make laws for the colony and a representative legislature is defined as a legislature comprising a legislative body of which one-half are elected by the inhabitants of the colony. The provisions of the Act relate only to colonies possessing legislatures. It was enacted—

(*a*) that colonial laws which are in any respect repugnant to an Act of the Imperial Parliament extending to such colony shall be read subject to such Act and to the extent of such repugnancy shall be void and inoperative;
(*b*) that no colonial law shall be void by reason only of repugnancy to the law of England, *i.e.* the common law as opposed to statute law applicable to the colony;
(*c*) that no colonial law shall be void by reason of any instructions given to the Governor other than the formal letters patent which authorise the Governor to assent to Bills;
(*d*) that every colonial legislature shall have power to establish courts of judicature and every colonial representative legislature shall have power to make laws respecting the constitution, powers and procedure of its own body, provided that such laws are passed in such manner and form as may from time to time be required by any Act of Parliament, letters patent, Order in Council, or colonial law for the time being in force in the said colony.

Thus, while the supremacy of the United Kingdom Parliament remained unchallenged, henceforth a colonial legislature could depart from the rules of the common law without fear of challenge in the courts. Nor could a Governor be ordered to revoke his assent to a particular enactment, but must rely upon the provisions as to veto or reservation contained in the constitution of his colony. The provision enabling colonial legislatures to establish courts of justice was essential for the extension to the colony of the independence of the judiciary, a matter which was treated by the United Kingdom Government as a condition precedent to the grant of responsible government.

Powers of Constitutional Amendment

The final provision may be illustrated by the following case:

The Privy Council, affirming a decision of the High Court of Australia, held invalid a Bill to abolish the Legislative Council of New South Wales which was not passed in accordance with a colonial Act requiring the approval of the electorate to be given to such a measure.[1] The Colonial Laws Validity Act 1865 required that a law respecting the constitution should be passed in the manner and form provided by existing legislation. The Privy Council rejected the argument that the colonial Act requiring the approval of the electorate was invalid as fettering the freedom of a future legislature, but was not called upon to decide whether the Supreme Court of New South Wales had been right in granting an injunction to restrain the officers of the legislature from presenting the Bill for assent.

Imperial Conferences

During the latter half of the nineteenth century the Dominions attained nationhood rapidly. Since 1887 there had been periodic conferences for the purpose of consultation between the Governments of the Commonwealth. They were conferences of Governments, meeting under the chairmanship of the Prime Minister of the United Kingdom, not of delegates with power to commit their respective Parliaments. These conferences were first named Imperial Conferences in 1907, when the term, Dominion, was introduced in the sense of being contrasted with the term, colony. At the Imperial Conference of 1926 it was realised that political reality had outgrown legal status. The Dominions had obtained, as a result of the Imperial Conference, 1923, the right to make separate treaties with foreign powers in the name of the Crown without the participation of the Imperial Government or Parliament, except that a United Kingdom Secretary of State had to take part in the affixing of the Great Seal to the formal instruments for the grant of full powers and of ratification.[2] The right of separate diplomatic representation had been conceded. The Dominions had complete internal freedom from interference; they were (with the exception of Newfoundland) separate members of the League of Nations; and they had taken their place as equals at the Congress of Versailles held at the close of the First World War, in which they had participated. A conference mainly of experts which reported to the Imperial Conference, 1930, was called to consider how far legal powers should be changed

[1] *Attorney-General for New South Wales* v. *Trethowan*, [1932] A.C. 526; C.L.C. 78; and see pp. 50–1, *ante*.

[2] Pp. 456–7, *post*, for present practice.

and brought into line with existing facts.[1] The last formal Imperial Conference met in 1937. During the Second World War the Dominions were represented at periodic meetings of the War Cabinet by visiting Ministers or their High Commissioners, but it was not until 1944 that a meeting of Prime Ministers took place in London. Since that date meetings have been held at intervals for the discussion of common political problems.[2]

B. The Statute of Westminster 1931

Limitations upon Dominion Autonomy

There were before the passing of the Statute of Westminster 1931 the following limitations upon the legislative autonomy of the Dominions which were considered and reported upon by the Conference on the Operation of Dominion Legislation and Merchant Shipping Legislation 1929. It is important to remember that the Statute of Westminster was concerned only with legislative powers. Changes in, for example, the exercise of functions and the status of Governors-General, were made by executive action following declarations of policy made at Imperial Conferences.

Disallowance

(*a*) There still existed the power of disallowance, but this power had become obsolete. It had not been exercised in relation to Australian legislation since 1862 or Canadian legislation since 1873, and never in relation to New Zealand. But admission to the list of trustee securities in the United Kingdom was, under the Colonial Stock Act 1900, given to dominion securities provided that the Dominion concerned consented to the disallowance of any legislation affecting such admitted stocks. The Conference for this reason did not recommend the abolition by imperial legislation of the power of disallowance, but suggested that it should be left to the Dominions either to abolish the power by constitutional amendment, or, where an imperial Act is required for such amendment, as in the case of Canada, to request the passing of such Act. The Dominions concerned have taken no steps. By the Colonial Stock Act 1934 there may be substituted an undertaking by a Commonwealth Government that legislation affecting the existing rights of stockholders shall

[1] *Report of the Conference on the Operation of Dominion Legislation and Merchant Shipping Legislation*, 1929, Cmd. 3479.

[2] For post-war consultation p. 454, *post*.

not be submitted for the royal assent except by agreement with the Government of the United Kingdom. This safeguards the rights of investors in lieu of the protection afforded by the power of disallowance.

Reservation

(*b*) There still existed the Governor-General's discretionary power to reserve Bills which had only been exercised on one or two occasions in the twentieth century, and also constitutional provisions requiring the reservation of Bills dealing with particular subjects and provisions requiring reservation in certain imperial statutes, *e.g.* the Merchant Shipping Acts.[1] The Imperial Conference of 1926 [2] had placed it upon record that it was recognised that it is the right of the Government of each Dominion to advise the Crown in all matters relating to its own affairs, and that consequently it would not be constitutional for the Government of the United Kingdom to advise the King upon any matter relating to a Dominion against the views of the Government of that Dominion. It was, therefore, recommended that, as in the case of disallowance, it should be left to each Dominion to take such steps as it should desire to abolish both discretionary and compulsory reservation. In regard to South Africa the Status of the Union Act 1934 abolished discretionary reservation. Compulsory reservation was retained in respect of Bills limiting the right to request special leave to appeal to the Privy Council.[3]

Repugnancy

(*c*) Under the provisions of the Colonial Laws Validity Act 1865 [4] dominion legislation would be held void if repugnant to an Act of the Imperial Parliament applying to such Dominion.[5] The Conference recommended that this Act should cease to apply to the Dominions which would thus secure the power to amend any such Acts. Examples of such Acts were Acts of the Imperial Parliament relating to fugitive offenders, extradition, foreign enlistment, *e.g.* Extradition Act 1870 and Fugitive Offenders Act 1881.

Extra-Territorial Legislation

(*d*) The Dominions had no general power to pass legislation taking effect outside their own territories, *e.g.* to punish crimes

[1] See *Report of Conference on the Operation of Dominion Legislation*, p. 13.
[2] *Summary of Proceedings*, p. 17.
[3] Such appeals were abolished in 1950.
[4] P. 436, *ante*.
[5] *Nadan* v. *The King*, [1926] A.C. 482; C.L.C. 113.

committed abroad.[1] The extent of this limitation was difficult to define,[2] but it was of grave inconvenience in relation not only to criminal law, but, *e.g.* to the control of dominion forces abroad. The Conference recommended the abolition of this limitation. A Dominion and probably also a Colony could—apart from the Statute of Westminster—pass legislation having extra-territorial operation where such is necessary to give effect to enactments which are within the competence of the Dominion as being for the peace, order and good government of the Dominion: *Croft* v. *Dunphy*,[3] though it has been doubted whether the authority of this case extended beyond customs law. It has been suggested—and the point is still of importance to the Australian States and Canadian Provinces since the abolition of the limitation by the Statute does not operate there—that the test is whether the law in question does not, in some aspects and relations, bear upon the peace, order and good government of the territory either generally or in respect to specific subjects.[4]

Power of Imperial Parliament to legislate for Dominions

(*e*) The Imperial Parliament still had legal power to legislate for the Dominions. In fact, this power was by constitutional usage only exercised at the request and with the consent of the Dominions, and the Conference recommended that the constitutional convention should receive legislative recognition.

Limitations upon Constitutional Amendment

(*f*) The Constitution of Canada could, as we have seen, only be amended by an Act of the Imperial Parliament, and an Act of the Imperial Parliament was also necessary for the amendment of sections 1 to 8 of the Commonwealth of Australia Constitution Act 1900. Any enlargement of the powers of Canada or Australia in this respect would have affected both the Provinces and States as well as the Dominion and Commonwealth, and the Conference made no positive recommendations upon this matter.

The Statute of Westminster 1931

The recommendations of the Conference were with minor modifications adopted by the Imperial Conference of 1930,[5] and they

[1] *In re Criminal Code Bigamy Sections, Canada* (1897), 27 S.C.R. 461.
[2] See C.L.C. 53–4.
[3] [1933] A.C. 156; C.L.C. 106.
[4] *Trustee Executors and Agency Co. Ltd.* v. *Federal Commissioner of Taxation* (1933), 49 C.L.R. 220; C.L.C. 109.
[5] *Summary of Proceedings*, pp. 17–21, 1930, Cmd. 3717.

were given legal effect by the passing of the Statute of Westminster 1931 by the Imperial Parliament on December 11, 1931.

Preamble; Succession

The preamble to the Statute affirms the free association of the members of the British Commonwealth of Nations united by a common allegiance to the Crown, and records that it would be in accord with the established constitutional position that any alteration in the law touching the succession to the throne or the royal style and titles should hereafter require the assent as well of the Parliaments of all the Dominions as of the Parliament of the United Kingdom.[1] The preamble further sets out, in addition to a similar provision made in section 4 of the Statute itself, that it is in accord with the established constitutional position that no law hereafter made by the Parliament of the United Kingdom shall extend to any of the Dominions otherwise than at the request and with the consent of that Dominion. Section 4 requires an express declaration in the Imperial Act that the Dominion has requested and consented to the enactment thereof. On the abdication of Edward VIII in 1936 the request and consent of Canada were recited in the preamble to His Majesty's Declaration of Abdication Act 1936 passed on December 11, 1936; the assent of the Dominion Parliament was signified when Parliament re-assembled early in 1937 by the passing of an Act of Assent. Australia had not at that date adopted the Statute of Westminster, so convention only, not strict law, had to be considered. A resolution of the Commonwealth Parliament was passed on the same day and before the Imperial Act was passed. The assent of the Commonwealth of Australia and of New Zealand and South Africa, which was at that date a Dominion in the Commonwealth, was referred to in the Imperial Act. The Government of New Zealand requested the passing of the Imperial Act and the assent of the New Zealand Parliament was subsequently given. The South African Government took the view that the throne was vacated by Edward VIII immediately he signed the Instrument of Abdication on December 10, and therefore George VI was King in South Africa before the passing of the United Kingdom Abdication Act on December 11. The Status of the Union Act 1934 provided (section 5) that the heirs and successors of the Crown mean His Majesty's heirs and successors in the sovereignty of the United Kingdom as determined by the laws relating to the succession of the Crown of the United Kingdom. By His Majesty King Edward the

[1] Pp. 171–3, *ante*.

Eighth's Abdication Act 1937 the Union Parliament recorded its assent to the alterations in the law touching the succession to the throne and reaffirmed that George VI had been King since December 10, 1936.[1] The Irish Free State by the Executive Authority (External Relations) Act 1936 passed on December 12, provided that King Edward's abdication should take effect immediately upon the passing of the Act. The Irish Free State had thus, like South Africa, for the space of part at least of one day, a different sovereign from the rest of the British Commonwealth.

In the operative part of the Statute of Westminster it was enacted:

Colonial Laws Validity Act 1865: Statute of Westminster 1931, s. 2

(*a*) That the Colonial Laws Validity Act 1865 should cease to apply to the Dominions or to the Provinces of Canada; that the Dominions and the Provinces of Canada should have power to repeal or amend Acts of the Imperial Parliament in so far as they form part of the law of that Dominion; and that no law of either a Dominion or a Province of Canada should be void on the ground of repugnancy to an Act of the Imperial Parliament or to the law of England.

Canada by statute gave extra-territorial operation to all statutes passed before December 11, 1931, which by their terms or by necessary implication were intended to have such operation. It was argued [2] that section 2 of the Statute of Westminster did not enable a Dominion to exercise powers, *e.g.* of constitutional amendment, which it could not exercise under the original Act which enacted its powers. It was suggested that section 2 merely removed the restriction of repugnancy to an Act of the Imperial Parliament and did not enlarge the ambit of the powers of a Dominion Parliament. The Privy Council, however, held [3] that by section 2 a Dominion Parliament was given full legislative powers, save in so far as such powers were restricted by subsequent sections of the Statute of Westminster itself. The Statute can be amended by a Dominion Parliament so far as it is part of its own statute law.

Royal Prerogative

It was argued that in the absence of express words the Statute

[1] For a very full study of this complicated subject, see *The Abdication Legislation in the United Kingdom and in the Dominions*, by K. H. Bailey, Politica, Vol. III, pp. 1–26, 97–117.

[2] K. C. Wheare, *The Statute of Westminster and Dominion Status*, 5th edn., at pp. 180 ff.

[3] *Moore* v. *Attorney-General of Irish Free State*, [1935] A.C. 484; C.L.C. 151.

of Westminster did not enable a Dominion to legislate so as to affect the royal prerogative. Though the decision was based also on other grounds, the Privy Council held that a Dominion may now legislate so as to affect the prerogative in regard to the Dominion.[1] In *Attorney-General for Ontario* v. *Attorney-General for Canada* [2] it was held on a reference to the Judicial Committee that it would be *intra vires* the Parliament of the Dominion to enact legislation to abolish all appeals from all Canadian Courts, Dominion and Provincial, civil and criminal, to the Privy Council, including special leave to appeal granted under the prerogative. The Bill to enact this was not proceeded with at the time, but the Supreme Court Act 1949 (R.S.C.), abolished all such appeals.

Extra-Territorial Legislation: Statute of Westminster, 1931, s. 3

(*b*) That the Dominion Parliaments shall have full power to make laws having extra-territorial operation.[3]

There still remains a difficulty in that no such power is given to the Provinces of Canada or States of Australia, although criminal law is in general within the powers of the States and accordingly there is difficulty in providing for the punishment of offenders who have committed offences outside a State's jurisdiction.[4]

Legislation by the Imperial Parliament: Statute of Westminster 1931 s. 4

(*c*) That no Act of Parliament of the United Kingdom passed after the commencement of the Statute of Westminster shall extend to a Dominion as part of the law of that Dominion, unless it is expressly declared that that Dominion has requested and consented to the enactment thereof.

It is not clear how far the word, Dominion, should here be interpreted territorially, *i.e.* whether the Imperial Parliament could no longer pass legislation for the Provinces of Canada on matters within the provincial sphere. It is probable that the power no longer exists, and it is noticeable that it is expressly stated in the Statute that the power of the Imperial Parliament to legislate for the States of Australia remains (section 9), and that

[1] *British Coal Corporation* v. *The King*, [1935] A.C. 500, at p. 518; C.L.C. 160.

[2] [1947] A.C. 127; C.L.C. 170.

[3] In *Croft* v. *Dunphy*, *ante*, the Judicial Committee refused to decide whether this provision was retrospective. See C.L.C., pp. 51–2, for a discussion of the restriction on such legislation, a question which is still important to the Colonies.

[4] Cf. *Macleod* v. *Attorney-General of New South Wales*, [1891] A.C. 455; C.L.C. 99.

the exercise of such power shall not require the concurrence of the Commonwealth where before the Statute such consent would not have been required by constitutional practice. It is expressly provided by section 9 (3) of the Statute that in regard to the Commonwealth of Australia the request and consent referred to in section 4 shall mean the request and consent of both the Parliament and Government of the Commonwealth.[1] Lord Sankey, L.C., stated in *British Coal Corporation* v. *The King*, *ante*, "it is doubtless true that the power of the Imperial Parliament to pass on its own initiative any legislation that it thought fit extending to Canada remains unimpaired. Indeed, the Imperial Parliament could, as a matter of abstract law, repeal or disregard section 4 of the Statute. But that is theory and has no relation to realities." A contrary view was expressed by an eminent Australian constitutional lawyer who has said of section 4 that it "is a restriction upon British parliamentary supremacy of the law." [2] The same view has been expressed by the Supreme Court of South Africa—"freedom once conferred cannot be revoked." [3]

Post-1931 Independence

It has been seen that after the Statute of Westminster the aspects of inequality between the United Kingdom and overseas territories which were removable only by legislation at Westminster had ceased to be important except in the case of those territories which were still colonies. It is true that there were a few Acts which still applied to all parts of Her Majesty's realms, but these were capable of repeal by the Parliaments of those Dominions which had adopted the relevant sections of the Statute of Westminster. By far the most important of these statutes were those containing the Canadian, Australian and New Zealand Constitutions. Even after 1931 much of the Canadian Constitution and some parts of those of Australia and New Zealand could only be amended by the United Kingdom

[1] *E.g.* Christmas Island Act 1958 which placed the island under the authority of the Commonwealth of Australia at the request of the Parliament and Government thereof. This is one of the very few examples of the United Kingdom Parliament legislating under s. 4.

[2] *The Law and the Constitution*, 51 L.Q.R. 611, by Mr. Justice Dixon; see H. V. Evatt, *The King and His Dominion Governors* (Clarendon Press), Appendix.

[3] *Ndlwana* v. *Hofmeyr*, [1937] A.D. 229, at p. 237; although this decision was overruled by *Harris* v. *Minister of the Interior*, [1952] (2) S.A. 428 A.D., the sovereignty of the Union Parliament was expressly confirmed. For a critical discussion of the constitutional issues involved in the latter case, see *Legislature and Judiciary*, by D. V. Cowen, 15 M.L.R. 282, 16 M.L.R. 273; and see generally *Parliamentary Sovereignty and the Commonwealth*, by G. Marshall, esp. Chap. XI.

Parliament. Here the long standing convention that the necessary legislation would be passed at Westminster on the request of the Dominion concerned removed any possibility of friction. Other topics which rested on United Kingdom legislation included nationality and the rules governing the extradition of criminal fugitives within the Commonwealth. The definition of Commonwealth nationality has now been enacted separately by each State, and in the process what was left of common allegiance to the Crown had disappeared even before the advent of republican States with a President as Head of State whose continued membership of the Commonwealth was recognised by the Declaration of London in 1949.

Since the Statute of Westminster only removed inequality in the sphere of legislation, the question necessarily arose in the case of those colonies and other territories which attained independence after 1931, whether it was sufficient to reproduce in the Independence Acts which were enacted at Westminster only the relevant provisions of the 1931 Statute, leaving the remaining aspect of independence to depend upon the convention of non-interference. In practice the various Independence Acts provided categorically that from the date of independence all responsibility of the United Kingdom Government for the government of the newly independent country should cease, and that no further United Kingdom Act should extend to it as part of its laws. Here, despite the powers of the United Kingdom Parliament under English law, was the clearest indication that both Government and Parliament of the United Kingdom had abandoned all powers, notwithstanding the claim to sovereignty of the Parliament of the United Kingdom.[1] Here it may be remarked that even Dicey accepted the view that the sovereignty of Parliament did not prevent a curtailment of the area over which those powers could be exercised.[2] The purpose of the provisions was that, since the Statute of Westminster did not confer independence except in the legislative sphere, the Independence Acts covered the whole ground, except curiously the field of judicial independence which in each case was left to the constitution of the new member of the Commonwealth concerned. This no doubt was deliberate, due partly to the ambiguous method adopted by the Act of Settlement in the case of the United Kingdom, but mainly because political independence was never granted until provision had been made for securing the independence of the local High Courts.

[1] See the Independence Acts passed between 1960 and 1969 for newly independent territories in Africa and the Caribbean.

[2] Dicey, *Law of the Constitution*, 10th edn., p. 68.

C. The Present Position of the Commonwealth

Constitutions modelled on Westminster

Professor de Smith has stated that the Westminster model is a term which will never appear in a legal dictionary. "In its widest sense it may be said to comprise all the main features of the British Constitution."[1] The Westminster model, if not copied, is certainly recognisable in most of the new Commonwealth constitutions at the time of the grant of independence. But the very fact that each of these constitutions is written has produced features which are foreign to Westminster. The limitation of parliamentary sovereignty, guarantees of fundamental human rights and judicial review of the constitution itself are among matters for which provision is normally made. It is therefore clearly not enough simply to reduce parliamentary sovereignty and judicial independence to formal provisions in the constitution and leave the rest of the reproduction of the parliamentary system of government to the working of conventions. It is not surprising, then, to find a great deal of variety in the way in which the Westminster model is reproduced overseas. In colonial days the Governor was the direct representative of the Sovereign. It was by the Sovereign's orders under the prerogative that the Governor as effective head of the executive was converted into the equivalent of a constitutional monarch when independence was attained in the Canadian and Australian States. The process is necessarily more peremptory when the Governor of a colony is replaced overnight by the President-Prime Minister of a newly independent territory as has happened in recent years in an African State. On the whole it may be claimed that there are advantages to be obtained from enacting constitutional conventions for a new State, provided that the enactment is in sufficiently general terms to leave the executive government free from subsequent challenge in the courts. In other words, the efficacy of conventions depends upon political considerations rather than judicial interpretation. There is often something to be said for the old practice which has been followed in one or two cases, *e.g.* Ceylon, of incorporating, without explicitly detailing them, the corresponding United Kingdom conventions as far as may be relevant to the new constitution. Experience has already shown that Westminster conventions relating to such matters as the dissolution of Parliament and the dismissal of a Prime Minister cannot readily be reduced to workable legislative form.

[1] *The New Commonwealth and its Constitutions*, p. 77.

Protection of Minorities

One of the essential safeguards for the working of the Westminster model is the recognition of the rights of minorities. Responsible parliamentary government may not involve all the checks and balances which the United States constitution is designed to secure, but it does demand that there should be some formal recognition of the need to protect the rights of minorities. This is why there is invariably found in a written constitution, the safeguards to prevent important provisions from being altered except by a special procedure which requires more than a bare majority in the legislature to enact a constitutional change. To secure this the courts are normally given jurisdiction to review a measure and hold it void if it offends the relevant provisions of the constitution. The practice of entrenched constitutional provisions in Commonwealth countries dates back as far as the British North America Act 1867. Another safeguard against the abuse of majority power is to give full recognition to the office of leader of the Opposition. This has indeed been done in the case of the United Kingdom by the provision of a salary. But in the case of emerging African States it is normally the fate of the Opposition, at all events in the earlier years, to be overridden even to the extent of excluding them from the legislature and keeping them in compulsory confinement. This suppression of formal opposition which is easy enough where no organised parties have as yet come into being, is a sign that parliamentary government is not capable of working in the political situation which prevails in a newly independent State. Indeed there may be no basis for an opposition party at the initial stage. Pressure for independence will naturally come from the vast majority of the politically minded element which at first provides the new government. A potential opposition, *e.g.* on a tribal basis, is unlikely therefore to assert itself in the earliest stage of political development in the new State.

Bills of Rights

It was stated at the beginning of this book that the practice of guaranteeing constitutional rights has become an accepted feature of Commonwealth constitutions.[1] It has generally been the case that the leaders of the native population whose political activities have hastened the day of independence represent the more advanced elements in the territory. The universal acclaim which the grant of independence receives may conceal the existence of minority interests whose views are unlikely ever to prevail through the ballot box

[1] P. 2, *ante*.

sufficiently to secure for them the control of government. It is for this reason above others that constitutional Bills of Right have become a feature of Commonwealth constitutions, notwithstanding the preference among English public lawyers for avoiding constitutional guarantees by this method. Of the older members of the Commonwealth only Canada has felt the need for a Bill of Rights.

One of the reasons why the plea for fundamental rights in Commonwealth constitutions succeeded lay in the fact that the United Kingdom Government had ratified in 1951 the European Convention on Human Rights which imposed legal obligations on the parties to it to ensure that their laws are in conformity.[1] The first of the African Commonwealth constitutions to include a Bill of Rights was that of Nigeria in 1960, and there are many points of similarity between that constitution and the European Convention. Both place the emphasis on individual liberal freedoms which in England are protected by the common law, as Dicey explains in his analysis of the rule of law.[2]

Dominion of Canada

In 1960 the Dominion Parliament enacted a Bill of Rights [3] for the purpose of recognising and protecting human rights and fundamental freedoms. The operative section recognises and declares the absence of discrimination by reason of race, national origin, religion or sex and restates the six fundamental freedoms of personal liberty, equality before the law, freedom of religion, of speech, of assembly and association and of the Press. The statute applies as a matter of construction the provisions of the section to every law of Canada unless expressly declared to operate notwithstanding the Bill of Rights. This rule of construction has in particular to be applied to prevent a law of Canada being construed to authorise illegal detention, to impose cruel and unusual punishments, to deprive an arrested person of his usual rights to be told the reason for his arrest, to have legal representation or to seek the remedy of habeas corpus. Other matters to which the rule of construction applies are protection against incrimination, deprivation of a fair hearing and deprivation of the presumption of innocence until proof of guilt after a public hearing by an impartial tribunal.

It is the duty of the Minister of Justice to examine all proposed legislation in draft form in order to ascertain whether any proposed

[1] P. 481, *post*, for acceptance of the right of an individual to petition the European Commission.

[2] Dicey, *op. cit.*, chapter 5, esp. pp. 180–93

[3] An Act for the Recognition and Protection of Human Rights and Fundamental Freedoms 1960 R.S.C. c. 44.

provision is inconsistent with the Bill of Rights. Such inconsistency must be reported forthwith to the Dominion House of Commons.

But Canada did not feel it necessary to incorporate the Bill as part of her constitution and therefore it can be amended or repealed by the Federal Parliament by ordinary process. The fact that the rights and freedoms are stated in the Bill of Rights in broad terms makes it difficult for a court to interpret alleged infringements.

Judicial Appointments

A common device which serves to remove judicial patronage from the hands of the executive is the establishment of a Judicial Service Commission which after independence is entrusted by the constitution to give binding advice on the appointment of superior judges other than the Chief Justice since the latter is usually chairman of the Commission. In the case of federal constitutions, it is in the interests of the member States, which themselves may have Judicial Service Commissions, that they should be represented on the Federal Commission. In view of the long established tradition of a Civil Service Commission in the United Kingdom, it is a matter for comment that so little has been heard of the device of the Judicial Service Commission for appointments to the English and Scottish judiciary. The establishment of Public Service Commissions and also of Electoral Commissions for the purpose of securing equality of representation in constituencies are common features of the new Commonwealth constitutions.

Security of Judicial Tenure

In colonial territories the majority of Supreme Court judges were dismissible at the pleasure of the Crown. In practice these judges were independent of the executive and would not be removed unless the matter had first been referred to the Judicial Committee of the Privy Council. Judicial independence has always been a condition precedent to the grant of independence, but it is not easy to reproduce in a modern constitution the provisions of the Act of Settlement which remain the basis of judicial independence in the United Kingdom. Accordingly a new procedure was evolved by the lawyers of the former Colonial and Commonwealth Relations Offices whereby a judge is entitled to have the question of his removal determined by a judicial body instead of by the legislature, as in the case of the United Kingdom. Such body might be a tribunal of judges from other States, or the Judicial Committee.

Federalism in the Commonwealth

The main features of the federal constitutions of Canada and Australia have remained intact. Like all such constitutions they were intended by the member States which formed them to retain decentralised government and administration. It is too early to draw any conclusions from the examples of federation in the new Commonwealth States. It may be noted that in two cases, the Central African Federation and the Federation of the West Indies, the experiment had to be abandoned. On economic grounds there was much to be said for the new East African States federating at an early stage in their independent history, but neither this Federation, nor the federation of African States in general to form a United States of Africa, seems likely of early achievement. But a list which includes Canada, Australia, India, Malaysia, Nigeria, Pakistan and Kenya, constitutes a sufficiently formidable addition to the United States, the Soviet Union, Brazil and Switzerland to call for some comment as a constitutional device developed within the Commonwealth. Professor de Smith has commented that the most obvious feature of the new Commonwealth federations is the dominance of central authority as revealed by the amplitude of federal legislative and executive powers and the financial supremacy of the central government.[1] It would seem inevitable that, unless the union is achieved voluntarily by States already independent, the political progress of a new State must depend on the dominance of central authority. This has been seen in the difficulty of reproducing the position of an official Opposition in the new legislatures. If there is one reason above others for launching a new State with a federal form of government, it must lie in the need for recognising regional differences. The history of Nigeria since 1960 shows that despite the influence of the courts in interpreting the law of the new constitution, the protection of the regions from the federal government has not been effective, notwithstanding the wealth of detail written into the Nigerian constitution. If the older federal constitutions may properly be criticised as leaving too many gaps, the extreme complexity of the new federal constitutions results in such prolixity as to endanger their effectiveness in the hands of those called upon to work them. Happily the student of the United Kingdom constitution is spared this task. Nevertheless it is important even for a lawyer in the United Kingdom to realise how great the contributions to this type of constitution the Parliament at Westminster and the former Colonial Office have made.

[1] *Op. cit.* p. 268.

Legislative Autonomy

Inasmuch as the status of the Commonwealth is without precedent, it is difficult to describe it accurately. While it is possible to argue that the legal supremacy of the Parliament of the United Kingdom has not been abolished in relation to other members of the Commonwealth, it remains only to be exercised at their request and with their consent so far as they are parties to the Statute of Westminster or subsequent legislation on similar lines.[1] In the case of some of the newer States, the Statute of Westminster formula has not been employed in United Kingdom legislation; in its place it is indicated categorically that no Act of the United Kingdom Parliament passed after the date for independence shall extend to the new State, and further that the Government of the United Kingdom shall have no responsibility for future government.[2]

The Crown

Even in those States which accept the Queen as their sovereign little is left of the formal unity of the Commonwealth in which the Crown played the predominant part. Common allegiance to the Crown has ceased to be the one legal link which joins members of the Commonwealth. The position of the Crown involves difficulties that can only be solved by co-operation and adjustment. It is agreed that the Crown will only be advised upon matters relating to a Commonwealth State overseas by the Ministers of that State. It might be that the Ministers of one State would advise a course of action hostile to another State. It is no answer to this difficulty to say that the powers of the Crown will only be exercised by the Governor-General, and that the Queen herself will not receive conflicting advice. The prerogatives of declaring war and making peace have not been delegated to Governors-General.[3] There are occasions where the interests of two Commonwealth States might be vitally concerned, where the assent of the Crown would be necessary, and where conflicting advice might be given. These are not problems that lawyers can solve. So far as the newer members of the Commonwealth have chosen a presidential rather than a monarchical form of government the Crown has no legal or constitutional functions, though as a matter of courtesy the Queen may be recognised as Head of the Commonwealth.

The present position seems to be that in those States which still

[1] See *e.g.* Christmas Island Act 1958 which enabled the Queen to place the Island under the Commonwealth of Australia.

[2] *E.g.* Nigeria Independence Act 1960, s. 1.

[3] In Canada full prerogative powers were delegated in 1937; (see p. 453, *post.*)

acknowledge the Crown as their Sovereign, the Queen rules over a separate Kingdom which has acquired that status of its own right. Even if the United Kingdom adopted a republican form of government, the Queen would still be Queen of Australia. Thus to all intents and purposes the old doctrine of the indivisibility of the Crown has been replaced by the Sovereign of the individual State. Each State conducts its *inter se* relations under public international law rather than under any constitutional law common to the whole Commonwealth. There is, however, an understanding that the jurisdiction of the United Nations does not extend to disputes and differences between members of the Commonwealth. Even this has been subject to exceptions, as, for example, in the recent endeavours to settle the long-standing dispute over Kashmir between India and Pakistan. To this it is perhaps necessary to add a qualification in the case of the federal constitutions of Canada and Australia. Such a constitution "in its very nature presupposes the separate and independent existence of the King as representing the community in each State." In this constitution there are separate political entities but the same King.[1]

Governors-General

In the monarchical as distinct from the presidential States ordinary difficulties can be avoided by the fact that the powers of the Crown are exercised by the Governors-General, who no longer in any way represent the Government of the United Kingdom. The appointment of a Governor-General is made on the advice of the Government concerned. This change of practice first received recognition in the formal instruments when the Governor-General of Canada was appointed in 1931. Citizens of the State concerned are usually chosen in every member State except New Zealand.

Exercise of Prerogative of Dissolution

It was for a long time debated how far a Governor-General could constitutionally reject the advice of his Ministers. In 1926 Lord Byng refused a dissolution to the Prime Minister of Canada, and then granted one to his successor. The refusal took place during the progress of a motion of censure on the Government and followed closely a previous dissolution, as a result of which the Government had failed to obtain a clear majority. The new Prime Minister was unable to avoid defeat in the Commons. This action aroused acute controversy, and as a result the position of a Governor-General was defined by the Imperial Conference of 1926. It was laid down "that

[1] See D. P. O'Connell, *The Crown in the British Commonwealth*, 6 I.C.L.Q. 103.

it was an essential consequence of the equality of status existing among the members of the British Commonwealth that the Governor-General of a Dominion is the representative of the Crown, holding in all respects the same position in relation to the administration of public affairs in the Dominion as is held by His Majesty the King in Great Britain, and that he is not the representative or agent of His Majesty's Government in Great Britain." [1] The conventions, however, which regulate the constitutional duty of the Sovereign in relation to such questions as the granting of a dissolution are not entirely clear.[2] No step has ever been taken to free a Governor-General from the legal liabilities of a colonial Governor; in practice no question is likely to arise, as any liabilities would be those of the responsible Minister (apart from personal affairs).[3] The legal status of a President is determined by the local constitution, *e.g.* that of India, but questions of liability, if any, will still fall on a responsible Minister.

Delegation of Prerogative

It has been seen that the vital external prerogatives of declaring war and making peace and of accrediting diplomatic representatives have not been delegated to the Governor-General. Specific delegation from the Crown is required for each case. The Governor-General of Australia in 1941 declared war against Japan under a power specially assigned to him by the King on the exclusive advice of his Australian Ministers.[4] It may be assumed that since the Statute of Westminster 1931 there are implicit in the office of Governor-General all such prerogatives as are necessary for the government of the State concerned, while it must be left to convention to determine what prerogatives the Queen will still exercise in person, such as opening a session of Parliament and conferring honours when present in person during a visit. In the case of Canada, however, letters patent issued in 1937 gave the Governor-General authority to exercise on the advice of Canadian Ministers all the royal powers and prerogatives in respect of Canada. This made the exercise of all prerogative acts possible without reference to the Sovereign; previously the authority to enter into treaties and to appoint ambassadors to represent Canada had not been vested in the Governor-General. In the republican States the prerogatives of the Crown are replaced by the powers of the President and the

[1] *Summary of Proceedings*, 1926, Cmd. 2768, p. 7.

[2] H. V. Evatt, *op. cit.*

[3] See *The Imperial Conferences, 1926–30, and the Statute of Westminster*, by Professor W. P. M. Kennedy, 48 L.Q.R. 191 at pp. 198–201.

[4] P. 458, *post*.

constitution determines when, if ever, the President may act at his own discretion, as for example the President of India in concluding a treaty.

Communications with the United Kingdom

The Secretary of State for Foreign and Commonwealth Affairs is the member of the United Kingdom Cabinet who is responsible for inter-Commonwealth relations. In the nature of things much business with which the Office deals is unknown to the other Governments of the Commonwealth unless and until it is communicated to them. The normal channel is the Secretary of State and through his office there is a constant interchange of information between the Governments of the Commonwealth, but this does not exclude direct communications between the Prime Ministers or Finance Ministers on important occasions.

Not only is it important to hold periodic conferences of Ministers, but provision must be made for regular representation of each Government at other capital cities in the Commonwealth. The representation is by High Commissioners who are members of the Diplomatic Service and equal in rank and status to Ambassadors representing foreign States. For a time, in 1932 and 1933, Mr. S. M. Bruce, a former Prime Minister of the Commonwealth of Australia, combined membership of the Commonwealth Cabinet with the task of representing the Commonwealth in London, thus giving the Australian Cabinet the opportunity of direct audience whenever desired with the King through one of its members.[1]

Changes since 1939

Formerly Imperial Conferences were held periodically and representatives of the Dominions attended the Committee of Imperial Defence.[2] During the Second World War the Prime Minister of the United Kingdom was in direct communication with the other Commonwealth Prime Ministers. There was also a daily stream of telegrams through the Dominions Office (as it then was named). Daily meetings of High Commissioners in London were presided over by the Secretary of State for Dominion Affairs and attended by a representative of the Foreign Office. Dominion Prime Ministers and other Ministers visited London from time to time, and Mr. Churchill visited Canada. On the occasion of his second visit in 1943 there was held a joint meeting of the Canadian War Cabinet Committee and the British War Cabinet. The Australian High Commis-

[1] In 1950 the Commonwealth Minister of Defence was resident in London.
[2] P. 201, *ante*, and p. 438, *ante*.

sioner in London was given the right to attend meetings of the United Kingdom War Cabinet whenever matters of direct and immediate concern to Australia were under consideration. In 1944 there was held in London a meeting of Prime Ministers attended by the Prime Ministers of the United Kingdom, Canada, Australia, New Zealand, South Africa and Southern Rhodesia and representatives of India. To meet the special needs of the Pacific there were set up Pacific War Councils in both Washington and London. Canada, Australia and New Zealand were represented on both bodies. Subsequent meetings of Prime Ministers have taken place at intervals of one to three years. Such meetings are much less formal than were the Imperial Conferences and, in particular, brief and uninformative communiques have replaced the detailed reports which in the years between the wars contained much of interest on the constitutional developments of the period. On the other hand the new methods are much more flexible and, with constitutional issues largely settled, the volume of exchange of information has greatly increased as the political problems have increased in number and complexity.

Recent Commonwealth Conferences have reflected doubts whether the Commonwealth as an entity has any further rôle to play even in the political field. So long as the United Kingdom occupied a special position as one of the Great Powers there was much which could be discussed with other governments of the Commonwealth at meetings of Prime Ministers. Today that special position only survives in the permanent membership of the United Kingdom in the Security Council of the United Nations. Moreover the less attractive traits of some of the new States—authoritarian executives, controlled legislatures, insecure civil liberties—even if their origin can be traced to former colonial rule, restrict the contributions which their representatives can make in an assembly of political heads of State. No common system of public law is likely to develop; nor is this the purpose of these conferences. There is some danger of the occasion being used to attack the United Kingdom, as witness the conferences which followed the unilateral declaration of independence by Rhodesia.

Yet there is reluctance, even from unexpected quarters where republican forms of government have superseded the monarchical, to abandon this form of association. As late as 1965 the Prime Ministers meeting in London agreed to establish a Commonwealth Secretariat and this decision was implemented by the United Kingdom Parliament passing the Commonwealth Secretariat Act 1966. The Secretariat is headed by a Secretary-General, a Canadian being the first holder of the office. The headquarters are at Marlborough

House in London; this former royal residence had for some years been used as a meeting place for statesmen and other public visitors from the Commonwealth. The Secretariat has no executive functions; it distributes factual information on international questions of common concern and in the economic field enables data relating to development projects to be shared. The servicing of Commonwealth conferences is its responsibility and in the person of the Secretary-General there is provided an official to act as secretary for each meeting. This secures some continuity in the arrangements in particular for meetings of the Prime Ministers. Finance is provided on a contributory basis, the United Kingdom bearing 30 per cent of the cost.[1]

Foreign Affairs

As was stated by the Imperial Conference of 1926 equality of status does not necessarily involve equality of function. All the member States have the right to separate diplomatic and consular representation in foreign countries. But a State may request the United Kingdom representative to act on its behalf where it has not appointed its own representative. Whilst most States maintain their own defence forces, the older States have in the past looked to the United Kingdom for ultimate defence against aggression. The Canadian Navy with its air arm was, however, increased during the Second World War so as to enable it to play a vital and substantial part in the Battle of the Atlantic as a separate fleet, and the Australian Navy played a vital part on the Pacific. It is perhaps not without significance that it was to the United Kingdom rather than to any other Commonwealth or foreign State that some of the newer African States turned in the first instance for military assistance against internal subversion in 1964. The Queen's Ministers, say in Australia, may advise the Crown to exercise the prerogative power of treaty making, and thus the Commonwealth of Australia may make a treaty without the consent of the United Kingdom Government. Where a treaty is made in the name of the Crown to which several Commonwealth States are parties,[2] a United Kingdom plenipotentiary signs on behalf of Great Britain and Northern Ireland and all territories overseas which are not separate members of the United Nations; separate plenipotentiaries sign for each of the other member States. A treaty to which a Member of the Commonwealth is a party is signed by the plenipotentiaries in the name of the Queen or presidential head of State and ratified at the instance of the Member

[1] See Sir David Keir, *Constitutional History of Modern Britain*, 8th edn., pp. 541–69 for a short historical treatment of the end of the British Empire.
[2] Chap. 20.

concerned.[1] There is great variety as to actual forms of treaty making. The procedure may involve the issuing of formal powers under the Great Seal of the Realm and therefore the concurrence of a Minister of a United Kingdom Government, but it would be unconstitutional for such Minister to give advice contrary to that of the Member concerned. Canada has its own Great Seal, thus obviating the formal intervention of a United Kingdom Minister. In India the President may negotiate treaties, but they require the subsequent approval of the Federal Parliament.

The Commonwealth in International Law

Declarations and changes of practice within the Commonwealth do not in themselves alter international law, and cannot in themselves bind foreign States. The position in international law is still not entirely clear. Each member State has a separate membership of the United Nations and the older Dominions were members of the League of Nations. On giving separate adherence to the International Court of Justice many have excluded inter-Commonwealth disputes. These factors go a long way towards establishing the recognition of the independent status of members by foreign States. But the conception of the Commonwealth as an entity recognised in international law has not been in issue. As between the members of the Commonwealth it is recognised that a State is not bound by a treaty made in the name of the Crown to which it has not assented and which it has not ratified. Similarly no State would be regarded as under any obligation to assist in a war declared without its consent. These are matters, not of international law, but of Commonwealth relations. The Crown, however, is the formal head of the Commonwealth, though in the case of the Presidential States the Queen is accepted only as the symbol of free association between independent States and allegiance is not owed to her.

Declaration of War

The question whether the Crown can be both at war and at peace has not yet been answered by any formal pronouncement. The position of Southern Ireland (then the Irish Free State) during the Second World War may be regarded as a precedent, but by that date the link with the Crown had already been severed and the State remained neutral throughout the war. It was, however, the fact that on the outbreak of war formal declarations of war were made on different dates by members of the Commonwealth. Canada

[1] Imperial Conferences, 1926 and 1930, *Summaries of Proceedings*, Cmd. 2768 and 3717.

did not formally declare war on Germany until seven days after the United Kingdom. On September 10 1939 a separate formal declaration of war on Germany was made by the King on the advice of his Canadian Ministers following the acceptance by the Canadian Parliament of an address from the Throne. On September 3 Australian Ministers met in Melbourne and the Cabinet approved a notification that a state of war existed with Germany. A different procedure was followed by Australia in 1941 in declaring war against Japan. War was declared by the Governor-General under powers specially assigned to him by the King acting on the exclusive advice of the Australian Government. On September 6 1939 the Governor-General of South Africa issued a proclamation notifying a state of war with Germany. It is thus difficult to contend that a declaration of war by the Government of the United Kingdom would bind the other members of the Commonwealth without their Governments making separate declarations. Such declarations, being by the Crown, could not in any case bind any of the States with presidential constitutions.

Secession

A Member of the Commonwealth can make a declaration of independence which for international validity requires a treaty or some form of recognition. When Burma was granted independence by the decision of the United Kingdom Government in 1947, she elected not to remain within the Commonwealth and section 1 of the Burma Independence Act 1947 gave effect to this choice. Burma's relationship with the members of the Commonwealth is therefore limited to treaty obligations. In the case of Ireland's decision in 1949 to sever all ties with the United Kingdom which she effected by statute in her Parliament, the new status was expressly recognised by the subsequent enactment of the Ireland Act 1949 by the Parliament of the United Kingdom. In a more limited sphere the question of the right of Western Australia to secede from the Commonwealth of Australia and resume its position as a unitary Dominion was considered in 1934. As the law stands, this secession could only be effected by an Act of the Parliament of the United Kingdom, even since the Commonwealth has adopted the Statute of Westminster. That Parliament took the view that such a matter could only be considered on the initiative of the Commonwealth. In effect the State was told that its constitutional rights were as a matter of constitutional practice limited by the federal system.

When the Union of South Africa left the Commonwealth and adopted the status of an independent republic it withdrew its application for continued membership in 1961. The legislation passed by the United Kingdom Parliament amended the British Nationality Act 1948 to omit South Africa, but continued the operation of certain enactments to give effect to the enjoyment by the new Republic of existing tariff preferences.[1]

Rhodesia

Since constitutional law cannot prevent revolutions, the problems created by the declaration in 1965 of independence by the then lawful Government of Rhodesia have not been discussed. The reason why the declaration and the subsequent secession from the Commonwealth are legally irrelevant lies in the fact that Rhodesia has never ceased to be a colony of the United Kingdom, though it has been allowed self-government in practice since 1923. Independence could therefore only be granted in law by the action of the Government of the United Kingdom. That consent having been withheld, only a revolution (happily without bloodshed) could give the desired result. The constitution in force in November 1965 derived from the Southern Rhodesia (Constitution) Act 1961 of the United Kingdom Parliament. The new constitution annexed to the declaration by the Rhodesian Ministers who were later dismissed by the Crown, though it followed the lines of the 1961 Constitution, was made without legal authority; in particular it gave Rhodesia autonomous legislative powers on the Statute of Westminster model. Only an Act of the United Kingdom Government could achieve this result for the colony.[2]

The Declaration of London, 1949

The following is the text of a communique issued at the conclusion of a meeting of the Prime Ministers of the Commonwealth in April, 1949.

> The Governments of the United Kingdom, Canada, Australia, New Zealand, South Africa, India, Pakistan and Ceylon, whose countries are united as Members of the British Commonwealth of Nations and owe a common allegiance to the Crown which is also a symbol of their free association, have considered the impending constitutional changes in India.
>
> The Government of India have informed the other Governments of the Commonwealth of the intention of the Indian people that under the new constitution which is about to be adopted India shall become a sovereign independent republic. The Government of India have, however, declared and affirmed India's desire to continue her

[1] South Africa Act 1962.
[2] Page 51, *ante*.

> full membership of the Commonwealth of Nations and her acceptance of the King as the symbol of the free association of its independent member nations and as such the Head of the Commonwealth.
>
> The Governments of the other countries of the Commonwealth, the basis of whose membership of the Commonwealth is not hereby changed, accept and recognise India's continuing membership in accordance with the terms of this declaration.
>
> Accordingly the United Kingdom, Canada, Australia, New Zealand, South Africa, India, Pakistan and Ceylon hereby declare that they remain united as free and equal members of the Commonwealth of Nations, freely co-operating in the pursuit of peace, liberty, and progress.

The lawyer will note that, since India ceased to owe allegiance to the Crown on becoming a republic, King George VI did not become the Head of the new State and ceased to be represented by a Governor-General appointed by himself. He thus had no constitutional functions to perform in the Republic which acclaimed him as the symbol of its membership of the Commonwealth. But the document shows that there was a unanimous wish that India should remain a full member.

A similar communique was issued in February 1955 in relation to the declared intention of Pakistan to become a republic within the Commonwealth. The occasion was another meeting of the Prime Ministers of the Commonwealth. There has so far been no difference in the recognition of republican status within the Commonwealth on the part of the other member States, a number of which are now republics. It is to be observed that on occasions some of the newer African States have severed diplomatic relations with the United Kingdom without repudiating their membership of the Commonwealth.

CHAPTER THIRTY-THREE

THE JUDICIAL COMMITTEE OF THE PRIVY COUNCIL

Jurisdiction

THE Judicial Committee of the Privy Council exercises in respect of appeals from the courts of colonies and also from the courts set up by the Crown in protectorates and trust territories [1] the ancient jurisdiction of the King in Council which has been confirmed by statute [2] to hear appeals from the Overseas Dependencies. In respect of appeals from the courts of States of the Commonwealth this jurisdiction of the Judicial Committee has been abolished or limited according to the wish of the particular member State concerned.[3] The Judicial Committee is also the final Court of Appeal from the Channel Islands and the Isle of Man, and from Prize Courts in the United Kingdom and Colonies. An appeal lies to the Committee against a decision by the Disciplinary Committee of the General Medical or Dental Council to strike a practitioner off the register.[4] Its former appellate jurisdiction in ecclesiastical causes was abolished, except in faculty cases from the consistory courts, by the Ecclesiastical Jurisdiction Measure 1963.[5] In addition to its appellate jurisdiction the Judicial Committee has jurisdiction also confirmed by statute [6] to determine by its advice references made to it by the Crown. The Committee has no power to place any limit as to the matters which may be so referred; they may be matters of original jurisdiction, as in the dispute between the Dominion of Canada and Newfoundland as to the Labrador territory.[7] The Committee also hears references under certain statutes, *e.g.* with relation to the review of ecclesiastical benefices under the Union of Benefices Measures 1923–36.

Basis of Appellate Jurisdiction

The appellate jurisdiction of the Privy Council is based on "the

[1] *Jerusalem and Jaffa District Governor* v. *Suleiman Murra*, [1926] A.C. 321; C.L.C. 32.

[2] Judicial Committee Acts, 1833 and 1844.

[3] P. 466, *post*.

[4] Medical Act 1956, s. 36 (3); Dentists Act 1957, s. 29.

[5] Pp. 474–7, *post*.

[6] Judicial Committee Act 1833, s. 4.

[7] *In re Labrador Boundary* (1927), 34 T.L.R. 289.

inherent prerogative right, and on all proper occasions, the duty of the King in Council to exercise an appellate jurisdiction, with a view not only to ensure, as far as may be, the due administration of justice in the individual case, but also to preserve the due course of procedure generally." An appeal may be entertained in any matter, whether civil or criminal, by whichever party to the proceedings the appeal is brought, unless the right has been expressly renounced.[1] The ancient jurisdiction of the King in Council to hear appeals from overseas, which was in practice exercised by the legal members of the Council, was made statutory by the Judicial Committee Act 1833 (as amended by the Judicial Committee Act 1844 and subsequent Acts) which set up a Judicial Committee to hear appeals either under the Act itself or under the customary jurisdiction of the Privy Council. The Judicial Committee does not in theory deliver judgment. It advises the Sovereign who acts on its report and issues an Order in Council to give effect thereto. Until 1966 a single opinion was given, but dissenting opinions are now permissible.[2] They may be delivered in open court with reasons given. The constitutional nature of the Committee's functions was well described by Viscount Haldane at the time of the hearing of the first appeals to the Judicial Committee from the Irish Free State:—[3]

> We are not Ministers in any sense; we are a Committee of Privy Councillors who are acting in the capacity of judges, but the peculiarity of the situation is this: it is a long-standing constitutional anomaly that we are really a Committee of the Privy Council giving advice to His Majesty, but in a judicial spirit. We have nothing to do with policies, or party considerations; we are really judges, but in form and in name we are the Committee of the Privy Council. The Sovereign gives the judgment himself, and always acts upon the report which we make. Our report is made public before it is sent up to the Sovereign in Council. It is delivered here in a printed form. It is a report as to what is proper to be done on the principles of justice; and it is acted on by the Sovereign in full Privy Council; so that you see, in substance, what takes place is a strictly judicial proceeding.

The Judicial Committee is not "an English body in any exclusive sense." There sit among its members Privy Councillors from the other member States of the Commonwealth. It has in the past been described as an "Imperial Court which represents the Empire and not any particular part of it."[4]

[1] *The Queen* v. *Bertrand* (1867), L.R. 1 P.C. 520; *Attorney-General of Ceylon* v. *Perera*, [1953] A.C. 200, where an order for a new trial made by the Court of Criminal Appeal in Ceylon was set aside and the conviction restored.

[2] Judicial Committee (Dissenting Opinion) Order 1966 (S.I. 1966, No. 1100).

[3] *Hull* v. *M'Kenna and Others*, [1926] I.R. 402.

[4] *Hull* v. *M'Kenna*, *ante*.

Composition of Committee

The Judicial Committee is composed of the Lord Chancellor, the Lord President of the Council, and former Lords President and such members of the Privy Council as hold or have held high judicial office (including the eleven Lords of Appeal in Ordinary [1]); judges or ex-judges of the superior Courts of the Commonwealth States (or of any Colony that may be determined by Order in Council) who are Privy Councillors.[2] The present membership includes judges from Australia, New Zealand, and Trinidad and Tobago. The Queen may also appoint two other Privy Councillors with no restrictions as to their qualifications. Any judge of a Superior Court of a Commonwealth State (or of any Colony that may be determined by Order in Council) from which an appeal is being heard may be summoned to sit as an assessor. Appeals are heard by three or more members; usually five constitute the Board, as sittings are called.

Right of Appeal in Civil Cases

Appeals are either without the special leave of the Privy Council or with special leave. Appeals without special leave are regulated by Order in Council or local Acts or in some cases by an Act of the United Kingdom Parliament. Under such Orders or Acts the right to appeal is regulated according to the amount at stake in the suit, and in addition the local court may give leave to appeal in other cases. Where appeals lie as of right, application must first be made to the court from which the appeal comes for a decision whether there is a right under the statutory provisions applicable. The Judicial Committee will itself interpret local legislation regulating the right of appeal.[3] The Judicial Committee may always give special leave to appeal where any point of importance is involved, except when prevented from so doing by Act of Parliament or a statute made under the authority of such an Act.

Criminal Appeals

Appeals are not allowed in criminal matters, unless there has been a disregard of the forms of legal process, or as the result of some violation of the principles of natural justice, or otherwise, substantial and grave injustice has been done.[4] In *Knowles* v. *The King* [5] an

[1] Chap. 22.
[2] The former limitation of this class of members to seven was repealed by the Administration of Justice Act 1928, s. 13.
[3] *Davis* v. *Shaughnessy*, [1932] A.C. 106.
[4] *In re Dillett*(1887), 12 App. Cas. 459.
[5] [1930] A.C. 366.

appeal was allowed from the decision of a judge in Ashanti, who, sitting without a jury, convicted and sentenced a man to death for murder without considering the possibility of manslaughter. In *Ras Behari Lal* v. *The King Emperor* [1] the appeal succeeded on disclosure that a member of the jury did not understand the language in which the trial was conducted.[2] In *Mahlikilile Dhalamini* v. *The King* [3] an appeal succeeded where there had been a failure to hold in public the whole of the proceedings in a murder trial.

Commonwealth Appeals

While the Privy Council retains, unless and until modified or abolished by or at the wish of the member State concerned, the right to grant special leave to appeal from courts of other States in the Commonwealth, it has long been recognised that in deciding whether or not to grant special leave regard should be paid primarily to the wishes of the State concerned.[4] Until the passing of the Statute of Westminster the appeal by special leave could only be abolished by an Act of the Parliament at Westminster. In *Nadan* v. *The King* [5] the Judicial Committee held invalid a section of a Canadian statute [6] abolishing appeals to the Privy Council in criminal cases. The section was repugnant to the provisions of the Judicial Committee Acts of 1833 and 1844 and was therefore void under the Colonial Laws Validity Act 1865.[7] Furthermore the section could only be effective if construed as having extra-territorial operation, whereas according to the law at that time a Dominion Statute could not in general have extra-territorial operation.[8] A similar section was enacted in 1933 and challenged before the Privy Council; *British Coal Corporation* v. *The King*.[9] It was argued that, though under section 2 of the Statute of Westminster Canada could enact legislation repugnant to the terms of the Judicial Committee Acts of 1833 and 1844, yet the power of the Crown to grant special leave to appeal to the Privy Council was an essential part of the royal prerogative which could only be restricted under the express authority of an Act of the Imperial Parliament. The argument was rejected. By section 91 of the British North America Act 1867 the Dominion Parliament had power to

[1] (1933), 102 L.J. (P.C.) 144.

[2] *Cf. King* v. *Thomas*, [1933] 2 K.B. 489.

[3] [1942] A.C. 583.

[4] "It becomes with the Dominions more and more or less and less as they please "—Viscount Haldane in *Hull* v. *M'Kenna, supra*.

[5] [1926] A.C. 482; C.L.C. 113.

[6] Criminal Code Amendment Act 1933 (R.S.C.).

[7] P. 436, *ante*.

[8] P. 443, *ante*.

[9] [1935] A.C. 500; C.L.C. 160.

make laws for the peace, order and good government of Canada in relation to (*inter alia*) criminal law including criminal procedure. The appeal by special leave was but one element in the general system of appeals in the Dominion. By necessary intendment section 91 of the British North America Act gave to the Dominion of Canada power to prohibit in cases within its jurisdiction the appeal to the King in Council.

Despite certain wide statements as to Canadian sovereignty the decision in the *British Coal Corporation* case applied only to criminal appeals. It was still doubtful whether special leave to appeal in civil cases could be restricted by a Dominion Act. The chief function of the Privy Council in regard to Canadian appeals had been for many years the determination of disputes between the Dominion and the Provinces as to their respective powers under the federal constitution established by the British North America Act 1867. The view was widely held in Canada that the Privy Council had been unduly restrictive in its construction of Dominion powers. By Bill 9 introduced into the Canadian Parliament in 1939 it was provided that the Supreme Court of Canada should exercise final and exclusive ultimate appellate civil and criminal jurisdiction within and for Canada. Appeals by special leave in civil and criminal cases would be abolished. The Bill applied to both Dominion and Provincial courts. On a reference by the Governor-General in Council the Supreme Court of Canada upheld the validity of the Bill.[1] The Judicial Committee upheld the view of the Supreme Court of Canada in the case of *Attorney-General for Ontario* v. *Attorney-General for Canada*.[2] Section 101 of the British North America Act 1867 authorised the Dominion Parliament to establish a general court of appeal for Canada. The section vested in the Dominion Parliament plenary authority to legislate in regard to appellate jurisdiction. This authority was qualified only by that which lay outside the Act, namely the sovereign power of the Imperial Parliament. Since the passing of the Statute of Westminster the authority stood unqualified and absolute. Viewing the matter from a wider point of view it is not consistent with the political conception which is embodied in the Commonwealth of Nations that one member of the Commonwealth should be precluded from setting up a supreme court of appeal having a jurisdiction both ultimate and exclusive of any other member.[3] It is now clear beyond doubt that any State may abolish the right of appeal to the Privy Council.

[1] [1940] S.C.R. (Can.) 49.
[2] [1947] A.C. 127; C.L.C. 170.
[3] *Per* Lord Jowitt, L.C., [1947] A.C., at p. 153.

Present Jurisdiction

The jurisdiction of the Judicial Committee to hear appeals from overseas territories still subsists in the State jurisdiction of the Commonwealth of Australia,[1] in New Zealand, Ceylon,[2] Sierra Leone, Jamaica, Trinidad and Tobago and Malaysia; in the latter case jurisdiction may be conferrred by Order in Council to give effect to any arrangements made between the Queen and the Head of the Federation which is an independent monarchy.[3] The right of appeal in criminal cases was abolished in the Dominion of Canada in 1933 and in civil matters in 1949 by legislation enacted locally. Appeals had been abolished in the case of South Africa and Ireland in 1933 (before either had left the Commonwealth) by India in 1949 and Pakistan in 1950 and in 1968 from the High Court of Australia where the right had been restricted by the Constitution of 1900. The republican members of the Commonwealth, in Africa, *e.g.* Ghana, Nigeria and Uganda have all abolished the right of appeal, though appeals pending at the time of independence were retained. Appeals to the Privy Council from Cyprus were abolished by the Cyprus Act 1960 on Cyprus becoming independent.

In the case of Ceylon the Judicial Committee were called upon in 1963 to examine whether on Ceylon ceasing to be a colony the prerogative to hear criminal appeals ceased.[4] The Constitution was enacted by an Order in Council. The Ceylon Independence Act 1947 gave full independence from the Parliament and Government of the United Kingdom; but the structure of the courts and the system of appeals existing at the date of independence were not affected by the constitutional instruments which confirmed their status. Accordingly the Judicial Committee retained power to make an Order giving effect to its judgments. In reaching this decision the Judicial Committee relied on *Hull* v. *M'Kenna.*[5]

Future Jurisdiction

The British Commonwealth has now reached the stage at which the link through the provision of appeals to the Judicial Committee sitting in London has worn thin. Whatever jurisdiction may remain, it will no longer fall to the Committee to act as the final interpreter of federal constitutions, in which task it has been the counterpart of

[1] Commonwealth of Australia Act 1900 s. 74.

[2] Subject to local legislation after *Ibralebbe's* case, *post*.

[3] Federation of Malaya Independence Act 1957 s. 3. S.I. 1958 No. 426 extended by Malaysia Act 1963 s. 5.

[4] *Ibralebbe* v. *The Queen* [1964] A.C. 900.

[5] P. 462, *ante*.

the Supreme Court of the United States, in exercising jurisdiction on appeal from the Supreme Court of Canada and up to a point from Australian and Indian courts. The results have been on occasions freely criticised, especially on account of the composition of the Committee on which judges of the United Kingdom unversed in the complexities of federal organisation have normally been the main, if not the exclusive, element. Yet there can be little doubt that the Committee has made great contributions towards moulding the constitutions of the older member States of the Commonwealth remote from the local political background.

Wherever the common law has been planted, outside the United States, the Judicial Committee has been the unifying agency; it has enjoyed prestige in this respect from the knowledge that most of its members are engaged in the judicial work of the House of Lords. It is apparent that far greater diversity would have developed in the common law countries without its guidance. The amount of uniformity in legal principles which was introduced by the appellate jurisdiction of the Council in the seventeenth and eighteenth centuries helped to root those principles so firmly across the Atlantic in the first British Empire that they survived the War of Independence.[1] In criminal cases the Judicial Committee has been the means of avoiding grave miscarriages of justice in colonial territories, even in recent years. Much of its jurisdiction has been outside the common law in hearing appeals from countries where Hindu or Mohammedan or Roman-Dutch law is in force. For the future its jurisdiction will mainly be restricted to appeals from the Australian States, New Zealand, Ceylon and the few colonial territories. If so, its history can now be written. The task may well be entrusted to lawyers who have travelled from Canada, from Australia and from India to plead before it.

[1] H.E.L., Vol. X, 101.

CHAPTER THIRTY-FOUR

CHURCH AND STATE

Canon Law, by the Rev. E. Garth Moore (Oxford University Press).
Establishment in England, by Sir L. T. Dibdin (Macmillan).
Church and State in England, by Dr. Cyril Garbett (Hodder & Stoughton).

A. Religious Bodies

Religious Freedom

THERE are no restrictions upon freedom of worship and with but few exceptions there are to-day no disabilities attached to membership of any particular religious community. The Church of England, however, has a special status as an established church and its consequent connection with the State will require examination. Under the provisions of the Act of Settlement the Sovereign must join in communion with the Church of England, and Roman Catholics and those who marry Roman Catholics are expressly excluded from the Throne. It is probable that a Roman Catholic may not hold the office of Lord Chancellor or High Commissioner of the Church of Scotland.[1]

Effects of Recognition

The recognition by the State of religious bodies necessarily involves relationship between these bodies and the State. The position of the Church of England as an established church is special and requires separate treatment, but all other religious bodies in England can be regarded as being upon the same footing as far as their relations with the State are concerned. The Roman Catholic Church, though an international organisation, is to the constitutional lawyer in this country a non-conformist religious body distinguished from other non-conformist bodies only because Roman Catholics remain under certain statutory disabilities. Religious bodies may hold property in relation to which the courts administer the ordinary law of charitable trusts. The courts, too, may be required to enforce and pronounce upon the validity of the rules by which religious communities are governed. Members of a religious

[1] See speech of Viscount Simon, L.C.: 127 H.L. Deb., col. 463.

body may bind themselves to observe rules, and tribunals may be created to enforce such laws. Such tribunals, like other domestic tribunals, may be restrained by the courts from violating their own rules or the rules of natural justice. It may be necessary for the courts to determine as a question of fact the nature of the doctrines of a religious community. Thus, in the famous case of *Free Church of Scotland* v. *Lord Overtoun*,[1] the House of Lords held that a majority of the members of a religious community might not, without committing a breach of trust disentitling them to hold the property of their community, change the doctrines on which the identity of the community was based.

Church of Scotland

The Established Church of Scotland is a Presbyterian Church with only a limited connection with the State. Its preservation was an essential term of the Act of Union between England and Scotland. Church Government in Scotland is based upon the presbytery, or assembly of ministers of a district and of representative laymen, called elders. The supreme legislative and judicial body of the Scottish Church is the General Assembly. Though presided over by the Moderator—an officer of the Church—there is present at its meetings the High Commissioner, appointed by the Crown, who takes no part in discussions, but represents the connection between Church and State.

Welsh Church

In Northern Ireland and Wales there are now no established churches, but the Church in Wales retains in relation to marriage laws the privileges of the Established Church in England.

B. The Church of England

The Establishment and Patronage

As the result of the Reformation Settlement of the sixteenth century the Church of England became a separate national church independent of the Pope. As an established church its acts and decrees are given legal sanction. The Sovereign is the Supreme Governor of the realm in all spiritual and ecclesiastical causes as well as temporal.[2] The Royal Supremacy is exercised on the advice of Ministers who are responsible to Parliament and has been subject since 1689 to parliamentary control. The Church has special privileges in relation to, *e.g.* marriage laws, the Coronation, and since

[1] [1904] A.C. 515.

[2] Act of Supremacy 1558.

1921 legislation. Its laws are enforced by its own ecclesiastical courts. Its chief officers, the archbishops and bishops, who to the number of twenty-six sit in the House of Lords as spiritual peers,[1] are appointed by the Crown, on the recommendation of the Prime Minister who is understood to consult the Archbishop of Canterbury. The Crown sends to the Dean and Chapter a *congé d'élire* with letters missive containing the name of the person who is to be elected as bishop. This permission to elect is a form only. If the election were not made, the Crown would appoint by letters patent.

Church Organisation

The Church of England is divided into two provinces, the province of Canterbury and the province of York. Each province is governed by an archbishop. The Archbishop of Canterbury is not only the ruler of his own diocese and province, but is also Primate of All England and the President of the Church Assembly. Each province is divided into dioceses governed by bishops. Dioceses are divided into archdeaconries, and archdeaconries into rural deaneries. A rural deanery is composed of parishes, each with its church and parish priest. Ecclesiastical parishes do not necessarily coincide with civil parishes.[2] Parishioners, *i.e.* all who reside in a parish, have, as such, rights in relation to their parish church, *e.g.* to receive the ministrations of the clergy.

The Church may legislate for itself, but its legislation requires the consent of the State. Its forms of worship cannot be altered without the consent of Parliament.

Convocations

The ancient legislative assemblies of the Church are the Convocations of the two provinces of Canterbury and York. In each Convocation the bishops of the province form the Upper House, and the elected representatives of the clergy form the Lower House. The convocations can meet only when summoned by the Crown whose power to summon and dissolve them can, since 1965, be exercised independently of the similar powers relating to Parliament. Legislation relates only to worship, doctrine and liturgical matters and takes the form of canons, which are of no effect without the royal assent. A convocation is dissolved after five years. Unless they subsequently receive the authorisation of Parliament or merely declare ancient custom, such canons bind only the clergy and laymen holding ecclesiastical office, *e.g.* church-wardens.

[1] Chap. 7. [2] Chap. 25, C.

National Assembly of the Church of England

The difficulty of obtaining proper discussion in Parliament of proposals for legislation affecting the Church and the pressure of ordinary business upon parliamentary time led in 1919 to the passing of the Church of England Assembly (Powers) Act and the setting up of a new legislative assembly for the Church under the name of the National Assembly of the Church of England. The Assembly comprises three Houses. The House of Bishops and the House of Clergy consist respectively of the members for the time being of the Upper and Lower Houses of the Convocations of Canterbury and York. The House of Laity consists of representatives elected by a system of indirect representation, the foundation of which is the parochial church council elected by parishioners on the electoral roll of each parish at the annual parochial church meeting.[1] The House may co-opt not more than ten additional members. The Assembly may pass measures to be submitted by its Legislative Committee to the Ecclesiastical Committee of Parliament, which consists of fifteen members of the House of Lords and fifteen members of the House of Commons, nominated at the beginning of each Parliament by the Lord Chancellor and the Speaker. The Ecclesiastical Committee reports to Parliament upon the expediency of measures submitted to it, especially with relation to the constitutional rights of Her Majesty's subjects. Before reporting to Parliament the Ecclesiastical Committee submits its report to the Legislative Committee of the Church Assembly and does not present the report to Parliament, unless the Legislative Committee desires it. If the report is not presented, the measure is dropped. The report and the proposed measure are laid before both Houses of Parliament, and, upon the passing by both Houses of simple resolutions to that effect, the measure is presented for the royal assent. There is no power to amend a measure. On the receipt of such assent a measure has all the force and effect of an Act of Parliament and is published in the annual volume of the statutes. This procedure preserves the control of the State, while enabling the Church to prepare its own measures with full deliberation. The formation of the Church Assembly gave to the laity for the first time an official voice in the counsels of the Church. The National Assembly is a deliberative, and not a judicial, body, and prohibition does not lie to it from the High Court.[2] The power of

[1] Any member of the Church of England is entitled to be placed on the electoral roll. Those elected must be communicants.

[2] *The King* v. *The Legislative Committee of the Church Assembly, ex parte Haynes-Smith,* [1928] 1 K.B. 411. P. 660, *post.*

Parliament to legislate for the Church in the ordinary way remains unfettered, but in practice has not, since 1921, been exercised. The procedure which regulates the relationship between Parliament and the Church Assembly may form a model to be followed, should parliamentary powers ever be devolved on regional legislatures for, *e.g.* Scotland and Wales.

Synodical Government Measure 1969

The provisions of this measure make substantial changes in the constitutional position of Convocation and in the relations between Convocation and the National Assembly. They will operate from a day to be appointed by the Archbishops of Canterbury and York.[1] The General Synod, which is the new title for the National Assembly, is constituted by joining the Convocations of Canterbury and York into a single House of Bishops and a single House of Clergy together with the House of Laity of 250 elected members. Synods, consisting of two houses, clergy and laity, are also established at diocesan and deanery (of parishes) level. The power of the General Synod to legislate is by canon; proposals touching doctrinal formulae, services, ceremonies or the administration of the sacraments are referred to the House of Bishops and then submitted in such form as that House may propose. The two Convocations may continue to meet separately for this and certain other purposes. Measures of General Synod for permanent changes in baptism, holy communion, the ordinal and schemes for constitutional union or substantial changes in the relationship of the Church of England and another Christian body are not to be approved finally by General Synod, unless at a stage to be determined by the two Archbishops the Measure, scheme or substance of the proposals has been approved by a majority of dioceses in Diocesan Synods. There is a legislative committee of General Synod for the purpose of presenting Measures to have the force of Acts of Parliament as under the Church of England Assembly (Powers) Act 1919.

Church and State

Many churchmen consider that the House of Commons, comprising not only many non-churchmen, but even professed non-Christians, is not a fit body to legislate for the spiritual needs of the Church of England. The forms of worship of the Church of England, though not a result of parliamentary authorship, are sanctioned by parliamentary authorisation, and without such authorisation cannot

[1] November, 1970.

be changed. The Prayer Book of the Church was given statutory force by the Act of Uniformity of 1558, and subsequent changes were authorised by Parliament in 1662 and again in 1872. The need of the sanction of King and Parliament for an alteration to the services of the Church is an essential part of the Royal Supremacy and the Establishment as regulated by the Elizabethan settlement. The dissatisfaction felt with the existing position is due to the change in conditions since the sixteenth century. In Elizabethan England there was no antithesis between Church and State. Every member of the State was a member of the Church. A conflict between Church and State meant only a conflict between the laity of the Church and Clergy. "The amalgamation of Church and State had been brought about less by the Act of Supremacy than by the admission of the laity to the churchman's privileges and of the clergy to the layman's."[1] It was expected by many that the creation of the National Assembly would avert any conflict between the Church and the State; that the House of Commons would not resist the demands of a body representing the lay as well as the clerical element in the Church of England; that spiritual freedom could thus be obtained without the need of disestablishment. These expectations were not fulfilled when there was rejected in 1927, and again in 1928, a revised Prayer Book which had been carried by a large majority in both Convocations and in the National Assembly.[2] This rejection led to a movement for the disestablishment of the Church of England. A large body in the Church insists upon the need of complete freedom to legislate upon spiritual matters, while the fear of "Romish" tendencies in a section of the Church, combined with the ancient non-conformist hostility to Church privileges, makes it unlikely that Parliament would consent to the maintenance of the privileges of the Establishment, together with the abandonment of State control.

Ecclesiastical Jurisdiction

The result of the Church of England being established means that ecclesiastical law is part of the law of the land and therefore separate classification is merely for convenience of treatment. In the technical sense ecclesiastical law is law administered in ecclesiastical courts as distinct from temporal courts. Much of the law relating to the Church of England is a matter for the temporal courts. The law administered by ecclesiastical courts to the exclusion of the temporal courts relates to matters of doctrine, ritual or ceremonial, the discipline of the clergy, the granting of faculties and

[1] A. F. Pollard, *Political History of England*, Vol. VI, Chap. XI (Longmans).
[2] See now the Prayer Book (Alternative and other Services) Measure 1965.

marriage licences, whereas the temporal courts adjudicate on matters concerning advowsons, Church property and burial rights. The ecclesiastical courts have no power to award damages nor to imprison. The penalties which can be imposed are deprivation, disqualification from office, inhibition, suspension and deposition from holy orders which can follow a sentence of deprivation or disqualification from holding preferment. The law of the Church consists of (*a*) statute law, *i.e.* Acts of Parliament and, since 1921, Measures of the National Assembly, (*b*) such canons and ancient customs as were in force in England before the Reformation and have been continuously acted upon since, and are not in conflict with the laws of the land, and (*c*) post-Reformation canons which have received the royal assent. As regards statute law, from the time of Elizabeth I to the creation of the National Assembly numerous statutes have regulated Church affairs, *e.g.* Acts disestablishing the Church of Ireland (1869) and the Church of England in Wales (1914), Acts founding new dioceses, authorising the creation of new parishes, establishing the Ecclesiastical Commissioners to administer church property and providing for clerical discipline. Such matters are now dealt with by Ecclesiastical Measures in the National Assembly.

The Ecclesiastical Courts

The Ecclesiastical Courts constitute a graduated hierarchy. They formerly consisted of the Court of the Archdeacon, the Consistory Court of the Bishop of each Diocese and the Provincial Court of the Archbishop of each of the two Provinces. The Court of the Archdeacon was abolished by the Ecclesiastical Jurisdiction Measure 1963, but it had long been in practice obsolete, though the Archdeacon still exercises jurisdiction in his annual visitation. The Measure created a new Court of Ecclesiastical Causes Reserved for dealing with matters of doctrine, ritual or ceremonial. The Consistory Court is retained as a court of first instance for all faculty cases and for the trial of clergy below the rank of bishop accused of moral offences. These courts are courts in the full sense, co-ordinate with the courts of common law, but administering a different system of law. An order for certiorari does not lie from the Queen's Bench Division to review their decisions.[1] Prohibition lies to the ecclesiastical courts from the Queen's Bench Division when they act without jurisdiction or contrary to the rules of justice.[2] The judge

[1] *The King* v. *Chancellor of St. Edmundsbury and Ipswich Diocese, ex parte White*, [1948] 1 K.B. 195.

[2] *The King* v. *North, ex parte Oakey,* [1927] 1 K.B. 491.

of the Consistory Court is called the chancellor of the diocese. He is appointed by the bishop from whom he derives his authority. He must be a barrister of at least seven years standing (unless he has held high judicial office) and he must be a communicant. He holds office without limit as to tenure but he may be removed by the bishop if the Upper House of Convocation [1] of the Province so resolves. The Measure of 1963 repealed the Clergy Discipline Act 1892 which dealt with moral offences committed by the clergy and provided for an appeal either to the Provincial Court or to the Judicial Committee of the Privy Council. The Measure also repealed the Public Worship Regulation Act 1874 which dealt with ritual offences. Under that Act the ritualistic clergyman could be tried by the Provincial Court and there was an appeal to the Judicial Committee. The severity of the procedure was such that in the early years a small group of clergymen suffered imprisonment, but in the present century the Act has fallen into disuse.

The Court of Ecclesiastical Causes Reserved

Under the 1963 Measure matters of doctrine, ritual and ceremonial are dealt with by the new Court of Ecclesiastical Causes Reserved. Since the matters before the court are not the concern of a single diocese but of the whole church the court operates throughout England. It is composed of five judges appointed by the Crown, two of them being persons who hold or have held high judicial office and are communicants, and three of them diocesan bishops. There is an appeal to a new appellate tribunal, a Commission of Review, which will be appointed by the Crown on the petition of the appellant on each occasion and will consist of three Lords of Appeal who are communicants and two bishops with seats in the House of Lords. But before the court exercises jurisdiction a complaint against a priest or deacon may be vetoed by his bishop and one against a bishop by his Archbishop. Moreover, before the case reaches the court, there is a preliminary enquiry by a Committee to decide whether there is a case for the accused to answer on trial. A Committee of Inquiry in the case of a priest or deacon consists of the diocesan bishop, two members of the Lower House of Convocation of the Province and two Diocesan Chancellors. There are other provisions where the accused is a bishop. If the Committee allows a case to go forward, the Upper House of Convocation appoints a complainant against the accused in the Court of Ecclesiastical Causes Reserved where the procedure resembles that of an assize court exercising criminal jurisdiction but without a jury. The verdict can

[1] P. 470, *ante*.

be by a majority of the court which sits with advisers chosen from panels of theologians or liturgiologists. Advisers similarly sit on an appeal with the Commission of Review. The previous jurisdiction of the Judicial Committee of the Privy Council is abolished and neither the Court nor the Commission of Review is bound by any decision of the Judicial Committee in relation to doctrine, ritual or ceremonial.

The Consistory Court

The jurisdiction of the Consistory Court of each diocese can only be invoked in the case of a priest or deacon who is accused of an offence not involving matters of doctrine, ritual or ceremonial after the bishop has given the complainant and the accused an opportunity of seeing him. The bishop may decide that no further step be taken. If the case is to go forward, the bishop refers it in the first instance to an examiner with legal qualifications who is a communicant. It is his duty to decide whether there is a case to answer. If he decides that there is, the case is in effect committed for trial before the chancellor who is required to appoint a deputy with appropriate experience if he himself is inexperienced in criminal law. The "jury" consists of four assessors, two in orders and two laymen. The judge is required to sum up in open court to the assessors who are the sole judges of fact; their verdict must be unanimous. Thus the procedure followed resembles that of a criminal trial for an indictable offence. Under the now repealed Clergy Discipline Act 1892 the chancellor was the sole judge of fact as well as of law.[1]

If the chancellor certifies that the case involves a question of doctrine, ritual or ceremonial, appeal will now lie to the Court of Ecclesiastical Causes Reserved and thence to a Commission of Review. In all faculty cases the appeal as hitherto goes first to the Provincial Court and thence to the Judicial Committee of the Privy Council. This is the only remaining jurisdiction which the Judicial Committee exercises. For many years dissatisfaction had been expressed with the Judicial Committee as a final court of appeal for the church. In the Judicial Committee the voice of the church was only represented by the advice of episcopal assessors and could be disregarded by the lay tribunal.

Provincial Courts

An appeal lies from the Consistory Court to the Court of each Province (Canterbury and York). The judge of the Provincial Court

[1] The first case was heard in the Consistory Court of the Gloucester diocese in 1969.

of Canterbury is the Dean of the Arches and of the Province of York the Auditor of the Chancery Court. The judge sits with four other judges, two being clergymen appointed by the Lower House of Convocation and two laymen appointed by the Chairman of the House of Laity after consulting the Lord Chancellor as to their judicial qualifications. There is no further appeal.

The Clergy

The clergy, like members of the armed forces, are subject not only to special laws, but also to the ordinary laws of the land. They have certain privileges (*e.g.* exemption from jury service and compulsory national service) and also certain disabilities. The most important legal disability is that no clergyman of the Established Church of England, the Church of Ireland, or the Church of Scotland can be elected to the House of Commons.[1] It has been seen that the clergy are still summoned to Parliament by the *praemunientes* clause.[2]

Property

The Church of England is not a corporate body, and church property is the property of various corporations, sole and aggregate, which exist within the Church, *e.g.* the dean and chapter of a cathedral or the rector or vicar of a parish. There must be specially mentioned the ancient liability on all landowners to pay tithe for the benefit of the Church, mainly for the support of the parochial clergy. Tithe, originally a tenth of the fruits of the land, was commuted in 1836 for a charge upon land varying with the price of corn. The Tithe Act 1925 stabilised tithe rent charges and provided for their payment in trust for tithe owners to Queen Anne's Bounty, a corporation originally set up to administer property restored to the Church in the reign of Queen Anne. By the Tithe Act 1936 tithe rent charges were extinguished. Tithe owners received stock in lieu of tithe rent charges, and land subject to a tithe rent charge was made subject to the payment of a redemption annuity for a period of sixty years.

Church Commissioners

The largest holders of Church property were formerly the Ecclesiastical Commissioners. In the reign of William IV there was a redistribution and fixing of the incomes of many bishops and cathedral chapters. The surplus income was handed over to the Ecclesiastical Commissioners, a corporation appointed by Act of Parliament, to be administered for the general benefit of the Church. In 1948 the

[1] P. 110, *ante*. Priests of the Roman Catholic Church are also disqualified by law.

[2] P. 102, *ante*.

Commissioners and those for Queen Anne's Bounty were merged in a single body, the Church Commissioners for England, by the Church Commissioners Measure 1947. The properties of the Commission are administered by an Estates and Finance Committee consisting of three Church Estates Commissioners, of whom two are appointed by the Crown, and not more than four of the Church Commissioners. The second Church Estates Commissioner is usually a member of Parliament who, though not a Minister of the Crown, replies to parliamentary questions on the Commission's affairs.

Advowsons

An advowson is the right to present a clergyman to a benefice. Advowsons are a species of property. The right to present can since 1931 only be exercised after consultation with the parochial church council. In the event of disagreement between a patron and a church council the patron may only present if he obtains the approval of the bishop of the diocese. If the bishop refuses to approve the patron's nominee, the patron may submit the bishop's decision to the archbishop of the province for review. Advowsons may be transferred, but may not be sold or transferred for valuable consideration separately from the land to which they are appendant after two vacancies have occurred subsequent to July 14, 1924.[1] Advowsons are held by laymen as well as by bishops, chapters, clerical trusts, and colleges in the older universities. Many benefices are in the patronage of the Crown, which is not bound by the provisions set out above in regard to consultation with parochial church councils.

[1] Benefices Act 1898 (Amendment) Measure 1923.

PART II: The Citizen and the State

The law of England (and Wales) only is discussed in this Part, except where Scots law is expressly mentioned.

Law of the Constitution, 10th edn., by A. V. Dicey, Part II (The Rule of Law), Chaps. V, VI and VII (Macmillan).
History of English Law, by Sir W. S. Holdsworth, Vol. X, pp. 644–713 (Methuen).
Freedom under the Law, by Sir Alfred Denning, Chaps. I and II (Stevens).
The Problem of Power, by Lord Radcliffe (Reith Lectures).
The Criminal Prosecution in England, by Lord Devlin (Oxford University Press).
Freedom, the Individual and the Law, 2nd edn., by H. Street (Penguin).
Keeping the Peace, by D. G. T. Williams (Hutchinson).

CHAPTER THIRTY-FIVE

FREEDOM OF PERSON AND PROPERTY

A. Personal Freedom

No Constitutional Guarantees

WE have already seen [1] that under the constitution there are no formal guarantees of liberty apart from the declarations of rights contained in the ancient charters and the restrictions on the arbitrary power of the Crown imposed by the Revolution Settlement of 1688. The citizen may go where he pleases and do or say what he pleases, provided that he does not commit an offence against the criminal law or infringe the rights of others. If his legal rights are infringed by others, *e.g.* by trespassing upon his property or defaming his reputation, he may protect himself by the remedies provided by the law. It is in the law of crimes and of tort and contract, part of the ordinary law of the land, and not in any fundamental constitutional law, that the citizen finds protection for his political liberty, whether it is infringed by officials or by fellow-citizens. In times of emergency the Executive is accorded special powers by Parliament, but there are no formal guarantees—such as are to be found in a constitutional code formally enacted—which have to be suspended. It follows that a text-book on constitutional law can only deal in bare outline with the law relating to the fundamental freedoms, such

[1] P. 6, and p. 65, *ante*.

as freedom of the person, free speech, free elections. For detail the student must turn to text-books covering the branch of the law concerned. Freedom of speech means that a man may say whatever will not expose him to a prosecution for incitement to violence or a civil action for defamation. To know what utterances will so expose him the citizen must familiarise himself with the intricacies of the law of defamation. The enjoyment of property is conditioned by the common law principle that one must use one's property in such a way as not to inflict injuries upon one's neighbour. The advent of the welfare State has brought other features into the legal relationship between citizens and government. The various social services have each created their legal and administrative problems; for example, disputed claims on the national insurance funds, liability to patients of hospitals and of medical practitioners in the health service, restrictions designed to ensure the better use of land and a higher standard of production on the farms. The liabilities in contract and tort of public authorities and the means of reconciling private rights with the public interest by litigation will be referred to in later chapters. But it is necessary to emphasise that there is a wide field for discussion of the part played by the State in economic and industrial relations as well as for discussion of the striking movement away from contract to status which has resulted from the standardisation, although not necessarily directly imposed by the State, of so many aspects of current conditions of living.

Trial by Jury

The right to trial by jury, which is the right of everyone accused of an indictable offence, may be regarded as a substitute for a formal constitutional guarantee that no person can be deprived of his liberty unless the prosecution has satisfied a jury of his fellow citizens of his guilt. Although the jury system has come under much criticism and no one would claim that the institution is infallible, it is nevertheless an important safeguard against arbitrary imprisonment at the instance of the executive, including the police. An important change was made in 1967 by the introduction of majority verdicts.[1] As a forum for the determination of civil liability the jury has ceased to be of much practical importance except in cases of defamation and wrongful arrest. It is not without significance that the right to a jury in actions for false imprisonment ranks it with the absolute right to such trial in prosecutions for indictable offences.[2]

[1] Criminal Justice Act 1967, s. 13.

[2] R. M. Jackson, *Machinery of Justice*, 5th edn., pp. 302–18, for a critical account of juries.

International Aspect

There is an international aspect of civil liberty since the United Kingdom has ratified the European Convention for the Protection of Human Rights and Fundamental Freedoms. Article 5 provides that everyone has the right to liberty and security of person; that no one shall be deprived of his liberty save in specified cases, such as after conviction by a competent court; and that everyone deprived of his liberty by arrest or detention shall be entitled to take proceedings by which the lawfulness of the arrest shall be decided. Provision is made for the legality of measures conflicting with these obligations in time of war or other emergency which threatens the life of the nation. When a leading political figure was deported from Cyprus to the Seychelles, the legality of his arrest and detention could not be successfully challenged either in Cyprus, where emergency regulations were in force, or in the Seychelles, where special legislation operated. There was some doubt whether the deportation was not in breach of the Convention and therefore a matter which would come before the European Court of Human Rights by petition addressed to the European Commission which first examines complaints. This situation whereby an individual seeks to protect his rights in an extra-national court when he has no remedy in the courts of his own country is a sufficient commentary on the importance which is attached to the right to liberty in the Western World. The United Kingdom in 1966 accepted the jurisdiction of the Court whereby private citizens can seek redress against their own government by petition to the Commission.

Justification for Imprisonment

A British subject cannot claim his freedom to be guaranteed but he can, nevertheless, protect himself by proceedings in the civil and criminal courts against those who interfere with his liberty. A privilege is of little use unless it is protected and enforced. Under English law interference with freedom, *i.e.* physical coercion and restraint, can only be justified on certain grounds. If none of these be present, the person detained has a prima facie cause of action for damages for false imprisonment against his gaoler, or he may be in a position to prosecute him for assault. The principal grounds for lawful detention are:

(1) Arrest and detention pending trial on a criminal charge.

(2) Sentence of imprisonment or detention imposed after due trial

by a court, *e.g.* in a Borstal Institution after conviction on a criminal charge, or committal to an approved school.[1]

(3) Imprisonment for civil debt [2] and for contempt of court, including imprisonment for contempt of either House of Parliament.

(4) Detention under the law relating to mental treatment under the Mental Health Act 1959 or detention of a child in need of care or protection under the Children and Young Persons Acts 1933 to 1963.

(5) The exercise of parental authority over an infant. A husband has no such authority over his wife.[3]

Arrest with Warrant

The extent of the power of arrest and the kindred power of search has been discussed in many leading cases of constitutional importance. An arrest may lawfully be effected by a police officer who acts on a written warrant for arrest granted by a justice of the peace or other judicial authority who is empowered to issue warrants after application (a written information) substantiated on oath outlining the alleged offence. The warrant must indicate specifically the person whose arrest is to be effected. There is no power to issue a general warrant to search for and to arrest an unnamed person.

Arrest without Warrant

More complicated is the extent of the power and duty of police officers and private persons to arrest without warrant where they suspect that a crime has been committed or to prevent the commission of a crime. The Executive has no power to interfere, through the police or otherwise, with the personal freedom of the subject by means of arbitrary arrest; for the plea of an act of State is no defence to an action brought by a subject in defence of his private rights.[4] There are, however, numerous occasions where arrest without warrant is justified either by common law or statute.[5]

[1] Community homes will replace approved schools which are to be superseded by the provisions of the Children and Young Persons Act 1969 when local authorities have made the necessary changes.

[2] Since the Debtors Act 1869 imprisonment for debt has been confined to the case of persons of proved capacity to pay who decline to obey the order of the court to satisfy a judgment debt or other order of a court for payment. The Administration of Justice Act 1970 abolishes the imprisonment of defaulting debtors (with certain exceptions *e.g.* maintenance, taxes). Power to attach wages is substituted, and includes the excepted debts.

[3] *The Queen* v. *Jackson*, [1891] 1 Q.B. 671.

[4] *Leach* v. *Money* (1765) 19 St. Tr. 1002; *Entick* v. *Carrington* (1765), 19 St. Tr. 1030; K. & L. 174; p. 486, *post*.

[5] Kenny, *Outlines of Criminal Law*, 19th edn., pp. 576–81.

The powers of a police officer are somewhat wider than those of a private citizen. Any person may arrest without a warrant anyone who is, or whom he with reasonable cause suspects to be, in the act of committing or attempting to commit an arrestable offence. Such an offence is one for which the sentence is fixed by law, *i.e.* for life in the case of murder, or may carry imprisonment for a maximum of five years or longer period. If such an offence has been actually committed, the arrest may be by any person who has reasonable cause to suspect anyone to be guilty of the offence (or anyone who is guilty of it). A police constable has the additional power to arrest without a warrant; this is exercisable on suspicion with reasonable cause that an arrestable offence has been committed; he may then arrest anyone whom with reasonable cause he suspects to be guilty of that offence.[1] A constable may also arrest without warrant anyone whom he suspects with reasonable cause to be about to commit an arrestable offence. All these powers are conferred by the Criminal Law Act 1967, s. 2, and result from the abolition of the former differences arising from the division of offences into felonies and misdemeanours. All offences are now treated as misdemeanours (treason remains separate). For certain offences both at common law, *e.g.* where a breach of the peace is caused, and by statute, power to arrest without a warrant is given to the police and this power remains in force. Entry (if need be by force) and search of premises are permitted to the police when seeking to arrest without a warrant for any arrestable offence. A person may use such force as is reasonable in the circumstances in the prevention of crime, or in effecting or assisting in the lawful arrest of offenders, actual or suspected, or of persons unlawfully at large, *i.e.* escapers from goal.[2] An illegal arrest without a warrant for a petty offence cannot be subsequently justified on the grounds that there was a reasonable suspicion that the person arrested had in fact committed an arrestable offence. A person on being arrested without a warrant is entitled to be told then and there on what grounds he has been detained unless he is caught in the actual commission of an offence, such as burglary.[3] Any passer-by may be called upon to assist a constable who has seen a breach of the peace committed by more than one person or who has been assaulted or obstructed in making an arrest and has had reasonable necessity for calling upon others to assist him. To refuse assistance in such

[1] In this case a private citizen has no power to arrest if the offence has not been committed by anyone; *Walters* v. *W. H. Smith and Son Ltd.*, [1914] 1 K.B. 595.

[2] Criminal Law Act 1967, s. 3, replacing the dubious and unclear rules at common law.

[3] *Christie* v. *Leachinsky*, [1947] A.C. 573; K. & L. 320.

circumstances is an offence.[1] It has been held that a police officer may enter private premises to prevent a breach of the peace, and *per* Hewart, C.J., to prevent the commission of any offence that he reasonably believes is imminent or is likely to be committed.

In *Thomas* v. *Sawkins*,[2] police officers successfully maintained their right to be present, though not invited by the organisers, at a meeting held on private premises which the general public had been invited by advertisement to attend.

Numerous statutory provisions authorise a police officer to arrest without a warrant in particular cases.[3] For example, when a breath test under the Road Safety Act 1967, s. 2, indicates that the blood of a car driver contains alcohol in excess of the statutory limit, or when a driver refuses to take the test. See also Highways Act 1959, s. 121 (2), wilful obstruction of highway; Dangerous Drugs Act 1967, s. 6 (1), search of person on suspicion; Road Safety Act 1967, s. 30, arrest by uniformed constable of suspected disqualified driver. There are at least eighty such powers.

Questioning of Suspected Persons

In 1912 the judges of the King's Bench Division drew up certain rules to govern the taking of statements from persons who may subsequently be put on trial after questioning conducted by the police. The rules, which are known as the Judges' Rules, have not the force of law, but statements obtained contrary to the rules may, and normally will, be rejected by the judge at the trial. These Rules were amended in 1964. The constitutional importance of the rules lies in the protection which they afford against a confession being made by an accused person under duress or without being aware that any statement he may make after being taken into custody can be used in evidence against him, as well as in his favour, at his trial. These rules are not the least important of the safeguards contained in the rules of evidence relating to criminal cases which secure a fair trial and thus they are an important part of the protection afforded to the citizen against an abuse of power by the police. The rules in their recently revised form require that a caution shall be administered to any person who is being questioned by the police whenever there is evidence which would afford reasonable grounds for suspecting that the person has committed an offence. Once a person

[1] *The Queen* v. *Brown* (1841), Car. & M. 314; K. & L. 220.

[2] [1935] 2 K.B. 249. For discussion of this case, see *Thomas* v. *Sawkins: A Constitutional Innovation*, by A. L. Goodhart, 6 C.L.J. 22; pp. 559–61, *post*.

[3] Kenny, *op. cit.*, pp. 561–66. The complicated state of the common law was clarified by the House of Lords in *Christie* v. *Leachinsky* (*ante*).

has been charged or told that he may be prosecuted for an offence, he must again be cautioned.[1]

In the Introduction to the 1964 edition of the rules the Judges emphasise that the rules are not to affect certain principles:

(*a*) that the citizen is under a duty to help a police officer to discover and apprehend offenders;

(*b*) that a police officer otherwise than by arrest cannot compel any person against his will to come to or remain in any police station;

(*c*) that every person at any stage of an investigation should be able to communicate and consult privately with a solicitor; and

(*d*) generally, that a person should be charged with an offence as soon as there is enough evidence to prefer the charge, and that no evidence should be admitted against him unless it is voluntary in the sense that it has not been obtained from him by fear of prejudice or hope of advantage exercised or held out by a person in authority or by oppression.

The rules have been criticised as hampering police inquiries. The frequent repetition of the traditional caution at every stage of an investigation seems unnecessary and misconceived. Their complexity must confuse even the more sophisticated members of the police.[2]

General Warrant Cases

The principle that a plea of the public interest does not justify a wrongful act was established by the eighteenth-century cases known as the *General Warrant Cases*. The practice of issuing general warrants to arrest unspecified persons and to search property is said to have originated with the Court of Star Chamber. It is obviously a powerful weapon to assist an embarrassed Executive to obtain material upon which to formulate charges against persons suspected of hostility towards the Government. At a later stage the practice was authorised by the Licensing Act 1662 for use by a Secretary of State to prevent publication of unlicensed material, and such warrants continued after the lapse of that Act in 1695. The *General Warrant Cases* arose out of the attempt of George III's Government to stifle the political activities of John Wilkes and others and publications such as the *North Briton*. Even at a later date the severity of the law against seditious publications was maintained largely by

[1] For the text of the Judges' Rules. see [1964] 1 All E.R. 237.

[2] See *Rice* v. *Connolly*, [1966] 2 Q.B. 414, for the problem of police handling of suspected persons who decline to co-operate in answering questions. A suspect has a right to preserve silence under police questioning.

executive action, but the cases decided once and for all the illegality of general warrants and thus deprived the Executive of a formidable instrument of oppression.

Of these three cases *Leach* v. *Money*[1] decided that a general warrant to arrest unnamed persons (the printers and publishers of the *North Briton*), against whom a charge had not yet been formulated, was illegal; *Wilkes* v. *Wood*,[2] that the papers of an unnamed person could not be seized on a warrant of this description; *Entick* v. *Carrington*,[3] that there was no inherent power in the Secretary of State as a Privy Councillor[4] to order an arrest except in cases of treason, and that a general warrant as to the papers of a named person was illegal. The warrant had specified the name of the person against whom it was directed but as regards the papers it was a general search warrant giving authority to the messengers to take all Entick's books and papers.

The sequel to these cases was a successful action against Lord Halifax as the Secretary of State who had issued the warrants. A modern decision has, however, seriously diminished the protection afforded by *Entick* v. *Carrington* in cases where the police have effected the lawful arrest of one man, but are in search of evidence of the commission by a different person of another offence. The police have a right by common law to search the person of anyone who is arrested on a warrant and in practice the search extends to anything in the possession and control of arrested persons which may be relevant to the charge brought against them. It is also customary to search all persons taken into custody on a serious charge, whether arrested on a warrant or not. In *Elias* v. *Pasmore*,[5] it was held that upon the arrest by lawful process of an accused person the police can search the premises where the prisoner is arrested and seize material which is relevant to the prosecution for *any* crime committed by *any* person, not merely by the prisoner himself.[6] The seizure of the contents of premises entered on a warrant so far as any of the contents are believed upon reasonable grounds to be stolen goods which would form material evidence on a criminal charge of theft or receiving is lawful.[7]

Passports may not be taken and retained after a request for their

[1] (1765), 19 St. Tr. 1002.
[2] (1763), 19 St. Tr. 1153.
[3] (1765), 19 St. Tr. 1030; K. & L. 312.
[4] All Privy Councillors are by custom Justices of the Peace and can therefore commit for any indictable offence.
[5] [1934] 2 K.B. 164, and Chap. 36.
[6] See *Police Search.* by E. C. S. Wade, 50 L.Q.R. 354.
[7] *Chic Fashions* (*West Wales*) *Ltd.* v. *Jones*, [1968] 2 Q.B. 299.

return by the holders, simply in order to assist pending police inquiries. Unless there are grounds for arresting the holders, they shoud be allowed to leave the country, even where a case of murder may be involved.[1]

Search Warrants

There are a number of cases where search warrants may lawfully be issued under the authority of a statute. Such cases in effect form exceptions to the rule that general warrants are illegal. The oldest and, indeed, one which was admitted in *Entick* v. *Carrington* (*ante*) to exist at common law, permits the issue of a warrant for the search of premises which are suspected of being made a receptacle for goods where there is a reasonable suspicion of a theft.[2] The more important from the constitutional point of view are those conferred by the Official Secrets Act 1911, s. 9; and the Incitement to Disaffection Act 1934, s. 2 (2); the former provision reads as follows:

> (1) If a justice of the peace is satisfied by information on oath that there is reasonable ground for suspecting that an offence under this Act has been, or is about to be committed, he may grant a search warrant authorising any constable named therein to enter at any time any premises or place named in the warrant, if necessary, by force, and to search the premises or place and every person found therein and to seize . . . anything which is evidence of an offence under this Act having been or being about to be committed. . . .
>
> (2) Where it appears to a superintendent of police that the case is one of great emergency and that in the interests of the State immediate action is necessary, he may by a written order . . . give to any constable the like authority. . . .

Normally application for a warrant, whether for an arrest or a search, is made to a magistrate in private; it must be made under oath and the magistrate should be satisfied that there are reasonable grounds to support it.

In the Incitement to Disaffection Act 1934 [3] a High Court Judge is substituted for a justice of the peace, and elaborate restrictions are imposed upon the right to search (s. 2 (2)–(4)).

Under the authority of a large number of statutes search warrants related to an alleged offence may be issued, *e.g.* for explosive substances intended to be used for felonious purposes; for unlicensed firearms; for forged documents and instruments of forgery; for counterfeit coins and coinage tools; for goods which infringe the

[1] *Ghani* v. *Jones*, a decision of the Court of Appeal, [1969] 3 W.L.R.1 158.

[2] *Jones* v. *German*, [1896] 2 Q.B. 418; extended to goods obtained by other fraudulent practices by the Theft Act 1968, s. 26.

[3] P. 528, *post*.

provisions of the Trade Descriptions Act 1968, s. 28 (3) which authorises a warrant to weights and measures inspectors. Search for a woman or girl detained for immoral purposes, or for ill-treated or neglected children, may also be authorised by warrant. In certain special cases any constable may be authorised in writing by a chief police officer without a justice's warrant to search premises for stolen property.[1] Sometimes a warrant is dependent on a belief that a breach of the law has occurred; in other cases the warrant may be issued by a justice on complaint that there is reason to suspect an offence. In the former category come offences under the Licensing Act 1964, relating to clubs, the holding of parties for gain on premises where intoxicants are supplied or consumed outside permitted hours, and the sale of intoxicants by retail on unlicensed premises. Examples of the latter type may be found in the Betting, Gaming and Lotteries Act 1963, s. 7 (use of a house for unlawful gaming), under the Dangerous Drugs Acts 1965 and 1967 (suspicion of drugs being in possession) and the Children and Young Persons (Harmful Publications) Act 1955 (suspicion of possession of works to which the Act applies). In the case of obscene articles before the Obscene Publications Act 1959 it was necessary to swear to a belief that obscene articles were kept on the premises and that there had been a sale.[2] Under s. 3 of the 1959 Act, it is only necessary to satisfy a justice by information on oath that there is reasonable ground for suspecting that obscene articles are kept for publication for gain on the premises. There is no longer any need to prove a sale of the offending articles but the information may only be laid by the Director of Public Prosecutions or by the police.[3]

Civil Detention

Compulsory admission to hospital in the case of mental patients formerly required judicial authority in addition to medical advice. Under the Mental Health Act 1959, Part IV, compulsory admission for observation or for treatment is founded on the written recommendations of two medical practitioners, one of whom only must have had special experience in the diagnosis or treatment of mental disorders; judicial sanction, a power which was formerly given to justices of the peace, is no longer required. But courts of criminal jurisdiction have the power to make orders for compulsory detention of persons suffering from mental disorder who come before them.

[1] Theft Act 1968, s. 26 (1).
[2] Obscene Publications Act 1857, s. 1.
[3] Criminal Justice Act 1967, s. 25. P. 572, *post*.

In certain circumstances hospital admission can be ordered without recording a conviction.

The provisions of Part IV of the Mental Health Act thus enable a patient to be deprived of his liberty simply on medical recommendations without the normal safeguard of an order of a court, judge or magistrate. This innovation is doubtless justifiable in the interests of equating the treatment of mental illness to that of other diseases. But this is the only instance known to English law, apart from the powers of parents over their children, where liberty can be taken away without judicial sanction. Provision is, however, made for appeals to mental health review tribunals, one for each area for which a regional hospital board is constituted. The members of the tribunal are appointed by the Lord Chancellor, who must appoint a member with legal qualifications to be chairman.

Remedies for Infringement of Freedom

For interference with freedom of the person on any grounds other than those permitted by law, the subject has four types of remedy, if the first may properly be called a remedy at all. These are: self-defence, a prosecution for assault, an action in respect of wrongful arrest, and the prerogative writ of habeas corpus. The remedies are available equally against an official or a private citizen.

Self-Defence

Although the law is by no means clear, some right of self-defence is recognised. If a charge which does not justify arrest without a warrant has been expressly made, the person charged is entitled to resist arrest whether by a police officer or a private citizen, but the right to resist is limited by the duty to submit to arrest by a police officer, even though the reason for arrest is not at once given. Resistance to an arrest which is made on insufficient grounds is justifiable if the officer conceals some other ground for arrest which he later brings forward in justification of having made the arrest. But if a police officer arrests without a warrant a person without notifying the charge and the person arrested knows that he is a police officer, resistance which causes the death of the officer cannot be justified, and the person resisting, even though innocent of the offence for which he has been arrested, may be guilty of murder.[1] It is inexpedient to resort to self-defence to resist arrest by a police officer, because,

[1] *Christie* v. *Leachinsky, ante, per* Lord du Parcq, at p. 601, citing *The King* v. *Woolmer* (1832), 1 Mood. 334.

if the resistance cannot be justified on this ground, the consequential assault of the officer is aggravated by reason of his being a policeman, but if it can be justified, such resistance may excuse the use of reasonable force against the police.[1] Self-defence does not appear to mean that the use of any amount of necessary force is lawful. The amount of force used must not merely be necessary for the protection of liberty, which includes freedom from interference both for one's person and property, but also proportionate to the harm it is intended to avert. For example, if a person, walking along the coast alone, is compelled to turn aside from his path by the aggression of three men who accost him, he is not at liberty to shoot them dead, merely because they threaten to assault him if he does not turn back. But if the same person is surrounded by the trio on the top of Beachy Head and they gradually force him to the cliff's edge, thereby imperilling his life, it is both necessary for the protection of his person and also proportionate to the harm which he desires to avert from himself, namely death, that he should shoot his aggressors. When self-defence is pleaded, *e.g.* on a charge of assault, it is the duty of the prosecution to prove that the acts were not legitimate acts of self-defence.[2] There is some authority for saying that a man who is set upon in his own house may shoot to kill anyone who seeks forcibly to evict him, because he cannot reasonably be expected to retreat further.

> In *The King* v. *Hussey*[3] a conviction for unlawful wounding was quashed, the circumstances being that the tenant shot his landlord through the keyhole, while the latter and some friends were seeking forcibly to evict him.

There is a general liberty, even as between strangers, to restore the peace by rescuing a person attacked and to do what is necessary and reasonable for the purposes of the rescue.[4]

Action in respect of Wrongful Arrest and Prosecution for Assault

A civil action for damages lies for assault or false imprisonment; further, an action for malicious prosecution may be maintained by any person who is prosecuted for an offence in the criminal courts maliciously and without reasonable and probable cause. These remedies may be used against anyone, including public officials,

[1] *The Queen* v. *Waterfield & Lynn*, [1964] 1 Q.B. 164.
[2] *The Queen* v. *Julien*, [1969] 1 W.L.R. 839.
[3] (1925), 41 T.L.R. 205.
[4] *The Queen* v. *Duffy*, [1967] 1 Q.B. 65—a case of one sister separating an assailant from another sister.

police officers and superintendents of mental hospitals. In addition, criminal proceedings may be brought for assault, and it is in the criminal law that the greater safeguard of the subject is provided against his fellow-citizen's interference with personal liberty.[1]

Prerogative Writ of Habeas Corpus

It is not sufficient that the subject should be able to defend himself or pursue his remedy under the ordinary law in the courts. For he may be detained by order of the State, or, for that matter, by an individual, and so not to be in a position to institute legal proceedings. Accordingly the law of England provides in the writ of habeas corpus a process by which a person who is confined without legal justification may secure release from his confinement.[2] The wrongdoer is not thereby punished, but the person imprisoned procures his release and is then at liberty to pursue his remedies against the wrongdoer in the ordinary way. The writ of habeas corpus is with one exception available to all persons within the Queen's protection, including any alien enemies who may be permitted to be at large in time of war. It is not, however, available to an enemy who is a prisoner of war nor to an interned enemy alien, nor can a notice of intended internment be challenged by application for the writ.[3] The following passage from Blackstone describes the nature of the process, namely, the prerogative writ of habeas corpus:

> The great and efficacious writ, in all manner of illegal confinement, is that of *habeas corpus ad subjiciendum*, directed to the person detaining another, and commanding him to produce the body of the prisoner, with the day and cause of his caption and detention, *ad faciendum, subjiciendum et recipiendum*, to do, submit to and receive whatsoever the judge or court awarding such writ shall consider in that behalf. This is a high prerogative writ, and therefore by the common law issuing out of the Court of King's Bench not only in term time, but also during the vacation by a *fiat* from the chief justice or any other of the judges and running into all parts of the King's dominions; for the

[1] Certain prosecutions require the consent of the Attorney-General (*e.g.* prosecutions under the Official Secrets Acts), but in general any person may initiate a prosecution for any criminal offence. Prosecutors are, however, normally the police or departments of central or local government.

[2] For the equivalent of the process in Scotland see p. 499, *post*, and the Criminal Procedure (Scotland) Act 1887, s. 43, superseding the Act of 1701 "for preventing wrongous imprisonment and against order and delays in trials" which now only applies to persons in prison on a charge of treason.

[3] *The King* v. *Vine Street Police Superintendent, ex parte Liebmann*, [1916] 1 K.B. 268; Lord McNair (*Legal Effects of War*, 4th edn., p. 98) has little doubt that the reason is to be found in the prerogative of the Crown to wage war and incidentally to capture enemy persons and hold them in captivity; p. 267, *ante*.

King is at all times entitled to have an account, why the liberty of any of his subjects is restrained, wherever that restraint may be inflicted.[1]

Again, Broom says: [2]

> This great constitutional remedy rests upon the common law declared by Magna Carta and the statutes which affirm it, rests, likewise, on specific enactments ensuring its efficiency, extending its applicability, and rendering more firm and durable the liberties of the people . . . and the right to claim it cannot be suspended, even for one hour, by any means short of an Act of Parliament.

Procedure

The writ of habeas corpus is obtainable by any person on behalf of the prisoner if access to the prisoner is denied so that no instructions can be received from him.[3] This is an important safeguard, though in practice every facility is granted to a person in prison to make application for the writ if he so wishes. The procedure is as follows: [4]

Application is made *ex parte* supported by an affidavit to the Divisional Court or in vacation or in a case concerning the custody of an infant to the Judge in Chambers. If *prima facie* grounds are shown, the Court or Judge ordinarily directs that notice of motion be given or a summons issued. Argument on the merits of the application then takes place on the day named. If the Court decides that the writ should issue, it orders the release of the prisoner or the handing over of the infant to the applicant, and this order is sufficient warrant for the release. Under this practice there is no need to produce the prisoner in court at the hearing and no return to the writ is actually made. The Court or Judge has power on the *ex parte* application to order the issue of the writ forthwith; this power it uses in exceptional cases, particularly where there is danger of the person detained being taken outside the jurisdiction; where this is ordered, argument as to the legality of the detention takes place on the return to the writ.[5]

This procedure may be illustrated by the following documents which were cited by Lord Finlay in *Secretary of State for Home Affairs* v. *O'Brien*.[6]

[1] 3 Bl., *Commentaries*, 131.
[2] See *Constitutional Law*, 2nd edn., p. 223, cited by Lord Shaw of Dunfermline in *The King* v. *Halliday, ex parte Zadig*, [1917] A.C. 260, at p. 296.
[3] *Ex parte Child* (1854), 15 C.B. 238.
[4] R.S.C. Order 54, rules 1–10.
[5] This was the ordinary procedure at an earlier date.
[6] [1923] A.C. 603.

IN THE COURT OF APPEAL [1]

ON APPEAL FROM THE HIGH COURT OF JUSTICE
KING'S BENCH DIVISION

Friday the 13th day of April 1923.

ENGLAND.—Upon reading the affidavit of Art O'Brien and the several exhibits therein referred to it is ordered that Monday the 23rd day of April instant be given to His Majesty's Secretary of State for Home Affairs to show cause why a writ of habeas corpus should not issue directed to him to have the body of Art O'Brien immediately before this Court at the Royal Courts of Justice London to undergo and receive all and singular such matters and things as this Court shall then and there consider of concerning him in this behalf.

Upon notice of this order to be given to His Majesty's Secretary of State for Home Affairs in the meantime.

IN THE COURT OF APPEAL

ON APPEAL FROM THE HIGH COURT OF JUSTICE
KING'S BENCH DIVISION (ENGLAND)

Wednesday the 9th day of May 1923.

Upon reading the affidavit of the Right Honourable William Clive Bridgeman and upon hearing Mr. Attorney-General of Counsel for His Majesty's Secretary of State for Home Affairs and Mr. Hastings of Counsel for Art O'Brien it is ordered that a writ of habeas corpus do issue directed to His Majesty's Secretary of State for Home Affairs commanding him to have the body of Art O'Brien immediately before this Court at the Royal Courts of Justice London to undergo and receive all and singular such matters and things as this Court shall then and there consider of concerning him in this behalf. And it is ordered that the said Secretary of State for Home Affairs be allowed until the 16th day of May instant within which to make his return to the said writ.

With liberty to apply,
BY THE COURT.

Efficacy of Writ against the Executive

The case from which the above documents are taken illustrates the efficacy of the writ to put an end to unlawful detention at the hands of the Executive and to free the prisoner to pursue his ordinary

[1] The Divisional Court refused the writ; hence the appeal, which was not treated as being in a criminal cause or matter (see p. 495, *post*).

remedies in the courts against those responsible for his imprisonment. The order for O'Brien's detention was made by the Home Secretary, a member of the United Kingdom Government, and authorised arrest in England, deportation to the newly-established Irish Free State and handing over to the Government there, over which the United Kingdom Government had no control. Thus the order made in England was plainly illegal. Moreover the House of Lords recognised that the Home Secretary could not give effect to the order to produce O'Brien in the High Court in London without the assistance of the Government of the Free State, which in this case was given.[1] Thus the writ affords a guarantee for questioning the legality of detention which is effective only so long as the prisoner is not sent out of the country; against this event the Habeas Corpus Act 1679 (*post*), provides severe penalties.

Applications for Writ

On a criminal application for habeas corpus an order for the release of the prisoner can only be refused by a Divisional Court of the Queen's Bench Division, whether the application is made, as is normal, in the first instance to that court or to a single judge, who can, *e.g.* in vacation, grant the writ. If a single judge refuses the writ, the applicant can apply to the Divisional Court. Although there were some doubts on the point, there was until shortly before the Administration of Justice Act 1960 a right to apply in term time from one judge to another or from one Divisional Court to another differently constituted. Under the present law a second application, whether in a criminal or civil case, can only be made if fresh evidence can be adduced in support.[2]

It has always been possible in a civil case for an applicant to appeal from the Divisional Court to the Court of Appeal and thence, subject to the ordinary rules as to leave, to the House of Lords. But until 1960 in a criminal case the decision of the Divisional Court was final, since the Court of Appeal had never had any criminal jurisdiction and the Court of Criminal Appeal could hear only appeals against

[1] *Cf. Zabrovsky* v. *G.O.C., Palestine*, [1947] A.C. 246, where the applicant was detained outside the jurisdiction of the Government of Palestine which had ordered the arrest, but under orders which were lawful both in Palestine, so far as deportation and exclusion were concerned and as to detention in Eritrea, the place of imprisonment.

[2] For the earlier law see *Eshugbayi Eleko* v. *Government of Nigeria* [1928] A.C. 459, which was not followed in *Re Hastings* No. 2, [1959] 1 K.B. 358 and No. 3, [1959] Ch. 368. No such application can be made to the Lord Chancellor, s. 14 (2); *In re Kray* [1965] Ch. 736.

conviction or sentence. The Act of 1960 [1] provides in both civil and criminal causes that a right of appeal is available both to the applicant for a writ of habeas corpus and to the respondent. The appeal in criminal cases is governed by the provisions of section 1 of the Act which gives a right of appeal in a criminal cause or matter from a Divisional Court to the House of Lords. It is not necessary in habeas corpus appeals as in other cases to establish that a point of law of general public importance is involved. Thus there was created an unrestricted right of appeal in an application for habeas corpus in a criminal case subject only to the House of Lords giving leave for the appeal to be brought. On the other hand the Act provides for the first time that an order for the release of a prisoner can be upset on an appeal and therefore a successful applicant may be liable to be detained afresh or alternatively released on bail instead of unconditionally. But the court in granting leave to appeal may refuse to order the applicant's continued detention: in that event he will not be liable again to be detained as a result of an adverse decision of the House of Lords.[2] In a civil case release on the issue of the writ is unconditional.

Until the Act of 1960, if any court had ordered the release of the applicant from custody after hearing the merits of the case, there was no appeal from the order of that court available to the person who was ordered to obey the writ by discharging the prisoner, and this was so whether the person detained in custody had actually been released under the order or was still detained.[3] An appeal by the respondent is available in those cases where habeas corpus proceedings are employed as a means of determining which of two or more persons has the right to the custody of a child.[4] Disobedience to the writ is punishable by fine or imprisonment for contempt of court, and the offender may be exposed to heavy penalties recoverable by the person injured. Not only is the writ used against governors of prisons to prevent a prisoner being detained in custody without trial, but by this means a wife may question the legality of her husband's detention of herself, or parents may establish that a child is detained in an institution, such as an orphanage or rescue home, contrary to their wishes.[5]

[1] S. 15.

[2] S. 15 (4), s. 5.

[3] *Cox* v. *Hakes* (1890), 15 App. Cas. 506; *Secretary of State* v. *O'Brien* (*ante*). A release from detention on the ground that the prerequisites of lawful detention under Defence Regulations had not been complied with was no bar to a subsequent valid order for detention: *The King* v. *Home Secretary, ex parte Budd*, [1942] 2 K.B. 14.

[4] *Barnardo* v. *McHugh*, [1891] A.C. 388.

[5] *Barnardo* v. *Ford*, [1892] A.C. 326.

History of Writ of Habeas Corpus [1]

In origin the writ of habeas corpus enabled a court to bring before itself persons whose presence was necessary for some pending legal proceeding. The writ could be used for many purposes; for example to assert jurisdiction against a rival court and to release persons imprisoned by order of such a court in excess of the jurisdiction. Thus it came to be a writ by which persons unlawfully imprisoned could get released. Constitutional statesmen of the seventeenth century saw in this writ and particularly in the variety known as habeas corpus *ad subjiciendum* an instrument to check arbitrary arrest and made it more efficient. The writ was to issue out of the King's Bench or Common Pleas. Further in 1628 the Petition of Right declared that the decision in *Darnel's Case* [2] was not the law and that the King could not imprison *per speciale mandatum* without showing cause. In 1640 the Habeas Corpus Act, sometimes cited as the Star Chamber Abolition Act,[3] imposed the same requirement on commitments by the Council or any conciliar court.

The Act of 1679 made the writ of habeas corpus *ad subjiciendum* effective for protecting the liberty of the subject by providing for speedy enquiry into the legality of imprisonment on a criminal charge and for speedy trial of a person remanded in custody on such a charge.[4] The provisions of the Act may be summarised as follows:

The writ must issue from the Lord Chancellor [5] or any of the judges of the superior courts in term or in vacation, unless the prisoner is committed on conviction for a crime or by some legal process.

The term is to be specified within which the return of the writ must be made and within which the court must adjudicate upon the writ (ss. 2 and 3).

There can be no re-committal for the same offence of a person who has secured his release by the writ (s. 6).

Provision is made in cases of treason for speedy trial or release on bail (s. 7).

Evasion by transfer of a prisoner to another gaol or to a place outside the jurisdiction of the court, *i.e.* to Scotland, Ireland or abroad, is prohibited (s. 11).

The Act, however, did nothing to check the evil of a judge or magistrate requiring excessive bail as a condition of release. The Bill of Rights ten years later merely declared that "excessive bail ought

[1] H.E.L., I, 227–8; IX, 108–25.
[2] P. 183, *ante*.
[3] 16 Car. I. c. 10, s. 8.
[4] H.E.L., IX, pp. 112–25.
[5] See note 2 on p. 494, *ante*.

not to be required." [1] Nor had the court power to examine the truth of any return made by the gaoler. There is no reported case of habeas corpus being granted on the ground of excessive bail being required, although there have been cases where the Divisional Court has remitted a case with an instruction to admit to bail,[2] nor has the High Court any inherent jurisdiction to reduce the amount of bail fixed by magistrates in the exercise of their statutory powers.[3]

Acts of 1816 and 1862

The Act of 1679 only applied to detention on a criminal charge. Later the writ became commonly used, but without the benefit of the provisions of this Act, to secure relief from imprisonment by private persons or on other than criminal charges, such as imprisonment for military service. The Habeas Corpus Act 1816 provided that the Act of 1679 should apply to persons deprived of their liberty otherwise than by reason of a charge of crime, unless they were imprisoned for debt or on a process in a civil suit; these forms of imprisonment were not modified until 1869 [4] and therefore the writ of habeas corpus was not available to the many persons who at that time suffered imprisonment for debt. The Act of 1816 also provided that in the civil cases to which it applied a judge should have power to enquire into the truth of a return.[5] This provision was not applied to criminal cases by the Act, but the strict rule of incontrovertibility has been relaxed by the judges.[6] Where the Executive is claiming the power to detain, the onus is on it to negative the challenge of the applicant for the writ.[7] The Habeas Corpus Act 1862 precluded the writ from issuing from the High Court to any colony or other overseas territory in which there is a court with authority to grant and issue the writ and with power to ensure its execution. So to-day the writ cannot be issued by the High Court to any member State in the Commonwealth or to any colonial territories where the local high court is competent. The writ will, however, extend to territories which, like protectorates, can be said to be under the subjection of

[1] P. 8, *ante*, and p. 498, *post*.
[2] *The Queen* v. *Manning* (1888) 5 T.L.R. 139.
[3] *Ex parte Speculand* [1946] K.B., 48; *ex parte Thomas* [1956] Criminal Law Review 119.
[4] Debtors Act 1869.
[5] *The Queen* v. *Board of Control*, *ex parte Rutty*, [1956] 2 Q.B. 109.
[6] H.E.L., IX, pp. 119–22; Church, *Writ of Habeas Corpus*, pp. 212–13—an American work published in 1884.
[7] *The Queen* v. *Governor of Brixton Prison*, *ex parte Ahsan* [1969] 2 Q.B. 222.

the Crown, although not British territories, provided that the internal government is in legal effect indistinguishable from a British colony.[1]

Double Purpose of Writ

The writ of habeas corpus protects the citizen in two ways from an arbitrary Executive. If the cause of detention shown to the court is insufficient, the prisoner must be discharged forthwith; but even if the cause is sufficient, by means of the writ the prisoner can secure a speedy trial and so prevent the Executive from detaining him for as long as is considered expedient. A prisoner must be released on bail, if he is not indicted at the next Assizes after his committal, unless the witnesses for the Crown cannot appear. If he is not indicted and tried at the next subsequent Assizes, he must be discharged from custody.[2] The Assizes Relief Act 1889 ensured the speedy trial of all persons committed to Quarter Sessions. Curiously there was no similar provision in respect of misdemeanants committed to Assizes. Accordingly it is uncertain today how far the above is a correct statement of the law, since the provisions of the Habeas Corpus Act only applied to treason and felony. By the Criminal Law Act 1967 which abolished the distinction between felony and misdemeanour the law and practice relating to all offences is that relating to misdemeanours.

Bail

Bail may be granted either by justices or by the High Court; in the latter case the application is made to a Judge of the Queen's Bench Division sitting in chambers. Before a person is committed for trial, the justices conducting the preliminary investigations have discretion as to bail in case of both alleged felony and misdemeanour, and the High Court will be slow to interfere with this discretion. Justices who refuse bail must inform the accused upon committal for trial, other than for treason or murder, of his right to apply to the Queen's Bench Division.[3] The High Court has discretion to refuse bail in all cases.[4] The High Court may grant bail to a person who has given notice of appeal to Quarter Sessions from a conviction or sentence by a court of summary jurisdiction, as can the summary court. Bail may also be granted where application has been

[1] *In re Mwenya*, [1960] 1 Q.B. 241.

[2] But see *The Queen* v. *Campbell*, [1959] 2 All E.R. 557, where the efficacy of this to-day is doubted.

[3] For restrictions on refusal of bail and special conditions which may be imposed, see Criminal Justice Act 1967, ss. 18, 19 and 21.

[4] *The King* v. *Phillips* (1922), 38 T.L.R. 897.

made for a case to be stated for the opinion of the High Court on a point of law or for review by an order of certiorari.[1] Bail may also be granted to a person who has been convicted summarily of an indictable offence and has been sent to Quarter Sessions for sentence by reason of his previous character.

Dicey: Views on Habeas Corpus

The net result of the habeas corpus procedure is that " while the Habeas Corpus Act is in force, no person committed to prison on a charge of crime can be kept long in confinement, for he has the legal means of insisting upon either being let out upon bail, or else of being brought to speedy trial." [2]

Safeguards in Scotland

The writ of habeas corpus has no counterpart in Scots Law, but there is statutory provision to ensure the speedy trial of a person who is held in custody on a criminal charge. This is based on the Scottish Act of 1701 for preventing wrongful imprisonment and against undue delay in trials. Scotland had been greatly exercised over the excesses of the later Stuarts. It had no Magna Carta and no habeas corpus. The Act of 1701 provided that a person "incarcerated" could run his letters, the effect being to charge all concerned, both prosecutor and courts of law, that tried he must be within 60 days and if not so tried he must be set free.[3] The Act was temporarily suspended by the United Kingdom Parliament in relation to treason cases in 1794–95. Nowadays the Criminal Procedure Act 1887, s. 17 gives to a person arrested on any criminal charge the right to have access to a lawyer and to obtain a delay of 48 hours in his examination before the magistrate (Sheriff-substitute) to allow of the attendance of the lawyer. The same Act provides that a person who has been committed for trial must receive an indictment within 60 days of commitment; or, if he has been in prison for 80 days, he must be brought to trial and the trial concluded within 110 days in all from the date of commitment, unless the delay is due to the illness of the accused or some other sufficient cause for which the prosecution is not responsible.

[1] Criminal Justice Act 1948, s. 37, which extends the powers of the High Court and of Quarter Sessions.

[2] Dicey, *op. cit.*, p. 218; for suspension of Act, see p. 719, *post*.

[3] Lord Shaw of Dunfermline in *The King* v. *Halliday*, [1917] A.C. 260, at p. 297 and p. 301.

B. Racial Discrimination

A subject which has until recently not called for discussion in a book on constitutional law is racial discrimination. A place has always been found for control over the admission and residence of aliens and lately the admission of Commonwealth immigrants has been restricted by legislation.[1] How to integrate into society those who settle here is principally a social rather than a legal problem, but Parliament by enacting the Race Relations Acts 1965 and 1968 has attempted to control discriminatory acts which offend against the notion of equality of treatment for all the Queen's subjects resident in the United Kingdom. The legislation relies on conciliation enforceable in the last resort by civil process and only resorts to the sanctions of the criminal law to suppress incitement to hatred.

The occasion for State intervention was the realisation that growing numbers of coloured immigrants who were established as residents in the United Kingdom had generated inter-racial friction. From the West Indies came unskilled workers and their families to escape from unemployment at home. They found work in the transport services of London and other centres of population without difficulty and indeed proved such a valuable addition to the supply of labour that agencies actively recruited them from their island homes. For similar reasons nationals of India and Pakistan in particular were attracted by the higher standard of living in the West and came to form a considerable fraction of the labour employed in certain unskilled or semi-skilled industrial occupations, particularly in the Midlands. Frictions developed and integration with the local white population was conspicuously lacking. The acute shortage of houses resulted in overcrowding and squalor, nor were such public services as education in a position to absorb the new population, a great part of which spoke only their own language. The immigrants retained their native modes of living, religion and culture which were little understood and thus resented by their near neighbours. It was realised that racial differences were unlikely to be lessened by relying on the criminal law to punish action prejudicial to integration and that conciliation machinery was the most hopeful approach to the problem. It was, however, necessary to create a new criminal offence of incitement to racial hatred to restrict the activities of those who advocated hatred by threats, abuse or insult. Accordingly Section 6 of the Race Relations Act 1965 made it a criminal offence punishable summarily or on indictment, to incite to hatred by written or spoken

[1] Chap. 19, *ante*.

word in public against any section of the public in Great Britain distinguished by colour, race or ethnic or national origins. Prosecutions in England and Wales require the consent of the Attorney-General. Relatively few cases have been brought to trial.

The conciliation machinery was the main achievement of the Act even though it operated in a restricted field, that of discrimination against access to places of public resort, including eating houses, places of entertainment and public transport. This field was extended by the Race Relations Act 1968 to cover employment, housing, trade union membership and the provision of goods, facilities and services.[1] The machinery for dealing with complaints is as follows: the Race Relations Board, of up to twelve members appointed by the Home Secretary, is required to establish local conciliation committees to deal with complaints of discrimination within the spheres covered by the two statutes. Failure to reach a settlement must be reported to the Board; this body may in turn report to the Attorney-General (in Scotland to the Lord Advocate). The Board may institute civil proceedings in a county court for an order prohibiting *e.g.* denial of access to a place of entertainment to coloured patrons. The judge sits with two assessors; selected county courts alone are given this special jurisdiction. The court may grant an injunction to prevent further discrimination or award damages arising specially from the unlawful act and for loss of opportunity.

The Act of 1968 established a Community Relations Commission —an advisory body appointed by the Secretary of State—to encourage and assist in the establishment of harmonious community relations, to provide courses and to promote conferences for this purpose. The legislation applies to the public services both of the central and local government, including the police. The House of Commons set up a Select Committee on Race Relations in the session 1968–9.

C. Enjoyment of Property Rights

Public Control of Land

The right freely to enjoy property is conditioned by the obligations which the law imposes upon the owner or occupier. The common law recognises obligations to neighbours and others and these have been supplemented by statutory duties relating to the use of land and other forms of property. In the twentieth century, the relationship between the individual owner of land and buildings and the State has

[1] There are a number of detailed exceptions to unlawful conduct arising from discrimination by refusal by the occupier of accommodation in small houses and refusal of employment by an employer of less than ten persons.

been radically changed, without, however, altering the obligations which occupation of land imposes towards neighbouring owners. Although the content of proprietary rights has been modified by statute, the common law with regard to nuisance, negligence and trespass, so far as it concerns land, has been little changed, and private control over the use of land may still be exercised through restrictive covenants. The universal system of planning control contained in the Town and Country Planning Acts means that before an owner can develop his land, *e.g.* erect new buildings on it, or change the use of existing buildings from flats to offices, he needs planning permission from the local planning authority. From the local authority's decision there is a right of appeal to the Minister, but at both levels the decision is based on considerations of planning policy and no owner can rely on the principle that he should be free to do what he likes with his own land. Moreover, where planning permission is refused there is no general right to compensation, although limited compensation is payable in certain situations.[1]

Compulsory Purchase; Powers and Procedure

A further necessity of modern society has been the sanctioning by Parliament, subject to compensation, of the compulsory acquisition of land for stated public purposes. Even an individual who claims nothing more than the freedom to continue using his land in the way in which it has always been used may be compelled to transfer his ownership to a government department or local authority. Most public authorities have powers of compulsory purchase of land for their statutory functions and, even where general powers of this kind are not relied on, an authority may promote a private Bill in Parliament for the acquisition of specified land. In some instances, powers of acquisition are available to commercial undertakings; thus by the Pipe-lines Act 1962 an oil company may be authorised to acquire land compulsorily for the construction of a pipe-line. Public authorities enjoy wide powers of compulsory purchase of land under town planning legislation. Thus one cannot today discuss freedom of enjoyment of property without taking account of the possibility of compulsory purchase, the system of town planning control, as well as other social legislation affecting land, such as the Housing Acts and the Public Health Acts.

Property may be compulsorily acquired for public purposes where a statute so authorises. Without statutory authority the central government has no power to acquire land except by agreement with

[1] See Town and Country Planning Act 1962, Parts VI and VII, s. 43.

the owner, while a local authority requires statutory authority even for acquisition by agreement. Public corporations like the Transport Boards also require powers of compulsory purchase. These powers may be given either by an Act of Parliament authorising the acquisition of specific property for a specific purpose or by orders made under an Act conferring general powers to be exercised for purposes and under conditions laid down in the Act. In the latter case land can be acquired by a public utility undertaking (such as a waterworks company) or by a local authority on an order made by a Minister. The authority of a central department is required in all such cases.

Formerly compulsory purchase was authorised by private legislation or by the provisional order procedure.[1] Today the standard procedure is by compulsory purchase order confirmed by the Minister under the Acquisition of Land (Authorisation Procedure) Act 1946. Parliamentary approval is needed only when special classes of land, *e.g.* common land, National Trust property, are affected. To discover to what extent the right of ownership is protected one must look at the details of the authorisation procedure; the constitutional importance of this procedure in mediating between the individual's rights and the public interest is illustrated later in Part III, Administrative Law. Although the courts can help to ensure that a fair procedure is observed, the decision whether particular land should be acquired compulsorily is essentially a government decision for which there is political responsibility to Parliament. Once acquisition has been authorised, the machinery for taking over the land is provided by other statutes,[2] which are generally applied to every Act which authorises the compulsory purchase of land.

Compensation

Where a statute authorises the compulsory acquisition of property, it is the invariable practice to provide for the payment of compensation. It is an established rule of construction that express words are required to authorise the taking of property without payment.[3] It is important that the statute should provide not only rules for assessing compensation but also machinery for securing an impartial

[1] See Chap. 26 B.

[2] See now Compulsory Purchase Act 1965; also Land Commission Act 1967, ss. 7–11 and Town and Country Planning Act 1968, s. 30.

[3] *Newcastle Breweries* v. *The King* [1920] 1 K.B. 854. The decision, though not the principle mentioned, was disapproved in *Hudson Bay Co.* v. *Maclay* (1920), 36 T.L.R. 469, at p. 478, and *Robinson* v. *The King*, [1921] 3 K.B. 183, at p. 197. The question of what constitutes the taking of property for this purpose was considered in *France Fenwick and Co.* v. *The King*, [1927] 1 K.B. 458; see also, in relation to town planning control, *Belfast Corporation* v. *O.D. Cars Ltd.*, [1960] A.C. 490.

assessment of compensation in accordance with the rules. The amount of compensation should not be left to the discretion of the acquiring authority, nor should an owner be able to require payment of an exorbitant sum. At one time the Land Clauses Acts provided for the independent adjudication of compensation but without any rules for assessment, with the result that awards of compensation heavily favoured the owner by the inclusion of an almost punitive element as if for damages in trespass. Since 1919 acquisition by public authorities has been subject to detailed rules of compensation, the basic rule being that compensation should be the amount which the land might be expected to realise if sold in the open market by a willing seller.[1] This rule envisages a free market in land, but the advent of strict planning control after the Second World War meant that the value of land, particularly where it was undeveloped, might depend almost entirely on the decisions of the local planning authority and the Minister in granting or refusing permission for development. The Town and Country Planning Act 1947 attempted a lasting solution of this problem by which, in effect, the State acquired once and for all the development value of all land in return for statutory compensation, leaving the owner simply with the value of the land for its existing use. As part of this general solution, on the compulsory purchase of land the owner was compensated only for the existing use value of the land. Although there were good reasons for the introduction of the scheme, in practice it proved difficult to operate and unpopular in that owners who were forced to sell to a public authority might receive appreciably less than on a sale by agreement to another private owner; this discrepancy led to discontent not only with the rules of compensation but also with the powers and procedures of compulsory acquisition.[2] In 1959, there was a return to the basis of open market value, including the element of development value, but subject to complex rules for taking account of town planning control.[3] The general rules of compensation may be modified by statute for special purposes; thus the owner of a dwelling-house which is condemned as unfit for human habitation may receive only the site value of his property and nothing in respect of the house itself.[4] Where the owner and the acquiring authority cannot agree as to the amount of compensation payable, the dispute is referred to the Lands Tribunal, which in effect is a specialised court

[1] See now Land Compensation Act 1961, s. 5.
[2] Report of the Franks Committee on Administrative Tribunals and Enquiries 1957, Cmnd. 218, p. 61.
[3] Land Compensation Act 1961, Parts II–IV.
[4] Land Compensation Act 1961, s. 10 and Second Schedule.

for the valuation of land.[1] In operation it is independent of ministerial pressure, and is subject only to the statutory rules of compensation and to the right of appeal on a point of law from its decisions to the Court of Appeal.

Defence

Under the prerogative there is power to deprive the subject of possession of his property for the defence of the realm in time of national danger.[2] The various precedents extending back to the seventeenth century point to a usage of payment but did this impose an obligation upon the Crown to pay compensation? In *Burmah Oil Company, Ltd.* v. *Lord Advocate*,[3] the House of Lords by a bare majority held that if, in the exercise by the Crown of the royal prerogative in relation to war, a subject was deprived of property for the benefit of the State, the subject was entitled to compensation at the public expense, except where damage was done to the subject's property in the actual course of battle. But this decision was retrospectively overruled by the War Damage Act 1965, which abolished the owner's right to compensation for property damaged or destroyed on the authority of the Crown during a war in which the Crown was engaged.

There are permanent Acts which govern the acquisition or requisition [4] of land for defence purposes (Defence Acts 1842 to 1873 and the Land Powers (Defence) Act 1958) and under these Acts compensation is payable. During both the First and Second World Wars additional powers were taken. The Defence of the Realm Act 1914 provided for the suspension by regulation of any restrictions on the acquisition of land contained in the Defence Acts, though the Crown was not thereby relieved of the obligation to pay compensation: and an owner of requisitioned property was not bound to accept a rent assessed on an *ex gratia* basis by a non-statutory tribunal.[5]

During the Second World War, extensive powers of acquiring, requisitioning and controlling private property, including land, were made available to the Crown by the Emergency Powers (Defence) Acts.[6] The assessment of compensation for the use of land and the acquisition of other property was regulated by the Compensation

[1] P. 699 *post*.

[2] *Attorney-General* v. *De Keyser's Royal Hotel Ltd.*, [1920] A. C. 508; K. & L. 118; pp. 191–2, *ante*.

[3] [1965] A.C. 75; p. 268, *ante*. See now War Damage Act 1965.

[4] Requisition, as opposed to acquisition, implies temporary occupation.

[5] *De Keyser's Hotel Case*, *ante*.

[6] P. 721–3, *post*.

(Defence) Act 1939.[1] This Act established two specialised tribunals—a General Claims Tribunal and a Shipping Claims Tribunal. Both tribunals could be compelled by the High Court to state a special case for the opinion of the court on a point of law.

General Restrictions on Use of Property and Freedom of Contract

The law does not allow a private owner unlimited and unlicensed use of his property. At one time, the main restrictions on the owner's use of his property were provided by rules of the common law, many of which still apply. Thus, the owner or occupier may not use his land so as to constitute a nuisance either to the public at large or to his neighbour in particular. Both as to land and other forms of property there are today very many restrictions on use or disposition, imposed by such statutes as the Public Health Act 1936, the Coal Industry Nationalisation Act 1946, and the Town and Country Planning Act 1962. The relationship of landlord and tenant is for the most part controlled by statutes which restrict freedom of contract with the object of protecting the tenant who has been granted a wide variety of rights unknown at common law.[2] Freedom of contract in other spheres is often restricted; thus employers must contribute for the benefit of their employees to the national insurance scheme and also to the insurance of their employees against industrial injuries received in the course of employment.

The catalogue of restrictions which are now a permanent part of the welfare State must not lead to the inference that similar restraints exist in the sphere of political, as compared with economic, liberty. Freedom of the person from arrest and freedom of speech in all its aspects could be restricted in the same way as freedom of contract and economic activity have been restricted, namely by Parliament. But the climate of political opinion is the constitutional safeguard against an abuse of the legal power of Parliament. That the legal power exists is illustrated by the account of emergency powers given in Chapter 48.

[1] This Act gave rise to a good example of administrative quasi-legislation (p. 617, *post*). The Act excluded fair wear and tear from the Crown's liability to make good damage done. The Treasury ruled that fair wear and tear might be taken into account. It may be suggested that the proper course would have been to amend the Act by deleting the exclusion. As it was, the subject had no right enforceable by law to claim for fair wear and tear.

[2] See *e.g.* Leasehold Reform Act 1967.

CHAPTER THIRTY-SIX

LIBERTY OF DISCUSSION

Secret Ballot

"WITHOUT free elections the people cannot make a choice of policies. Without freedom of speech the appeal to reason which is the basis of democracy cannot be made. Without freedom of association electors and elected representatives cannot band themselves into parties for the formulation of common policies and the attainment of common ends." [1]

In this chapter, then, consideration will be given first to the Representation of the People Act 1949, which contains the law under which free and secret elections for Parliament and for local government authorities are guaranteed. As early as the thirteenth century it was provided by the Statute of Westminster I 1275, that there should be no interference with free elections by force of arms, malice or menaces. It was not, however, until the disappearance of the hustings that secrecy of elections was achieved. It was the Ballot Act 1872 which became the keystone of electoral law. Although there has been some change in the language of the enactment, that part of the Representation of the People Act 1949 which secures secrecy of elections reproduces in substance the provisions of the earlier Act, the principles of which may be regarded as sacrosanct. Modern facilities of communication have made it possible to extend the right to vote by post or by proxy to members of the Forces and certain other classes of voters temporarily away from home. This has necessitated a slight modification to the absolute guarantee of the secrecy of the ballot; otherwise the provisions of the Ballot Act 1872 have stood the test of time and so have remained unaltered.

Corrupt and Illegal Practices; Prevention

It was not, however, enough simply to secure secrecy in the polling booth. Accordingly a series of Corrupt and Illegal Practices Prevention Acts, which have been re-enacted in Parts II and III of the Representation of the People Act 1949, imposed penalties on those who attempt to influence elections by bribery, treating, intimidation, excessive expenditure and other practices which might tend to

[1] Sir Ivor Jennings, *Cabinet Government*, p. 14.

influence the voters' freedom of choice. So strict are these provisions that even in these days of the universal use of motor transport a free ride to the polling booth could only be given to voters in a strictly limited number of private cars expressly registered for the occasion until the Representation of the People (Amendment) Act 1958 removed the restriction. In recent years the penal provisions of the Representation of the People Act have seldom been invoked. For this there are several reasons. In 1872 the number of electors in each constituency amounted at most to a few thousand and in some cases a few hundred; to-day the quota of electors for each constituency is in the region of 60,000. Electors in such numbers could hardly be bribed or intimidated even by the richest of candidates. But no doubt the main reason for the obsolescence of the law dealing with corrupt and illegal practices is due to the better education of the public who look now to television and sound broadcasting for their political education rather than to gifts of money and beer distributed freely during an electoral campaign. It is, however, necessary to emphasise that the law relating to the conduct of an election, some account of which has been given in Chap. 7, is strictly enforced and in such matters as the return of authorised expenditure in connection with the campaign a candidate or his agent may easily find that he has been guilty of an illegal, if not a corrupt, practice. In the case of a parliamentary election where a candidate has secured election and he or his election agent has committed or acquiesced in corrupt or illegal practices, the former may be unseated on petition. An election petition is heard by two nominated judges of the Queen's Bench Division in the county or county borough where the constituency is situated.[1]

Freedom of Association

The conclusion reached by Professor A. V. Dicey was that "freedom of discussion is, then, in England little else than the right to say anything which a jury consisting of twelve shopkeepers think it expedient should be said or written." [2] Here liberty of discussion was being considered in relation to the law of defamation, including sedition, and of obscenity and blasphemy. But the law of libel, important though it has been in the past, to-day plays a negative role in securing freedom of political discussion. Far more important as a positive factor is the law which has secured freedom

[1] Details of the law relating to parliamentary and local government elections may be found in Parker, *Election Agent and Returning Officer*, (Charles Knight & Co.) and see p. 163, *ante*.

[2] *The Law of the Constitution*, 10th edn., p. 246.

of association for political purposes to all sections of the community. It is curious that books on constitutional law have been content to pass over this topic with perhaps a passing reference to trade unions. Freedom of association for political as well as for other purposes does, however, rest upon the common law as well as on the relatively modern statutes which deal with the organisation of labour, *e.g.* the use of funds for political purposes by a trade union.[1]

Trade Unions

Without entering into a detailed account of the law relating to the combination of persons, which takes one into the complex structure of case law relating to conspiracy, it is possible to say that the status of trade unions and similar industrial associations evolved during the nineteenth century. No longer was agitation by workmen for improving the conditions of employment a criminal conspiracy but the recognition of the trade union was hampered by the reluctance of the common law to give recognition to any organisation, the object of which was in restraint of trade. When recognition by Parliament came to the trade unions in 1871, it fell short of equating their status to that of trading and other corporations. In particular the Trade Union Act of that year, while giving legal entity to a union, forbade the direct enforcement by action of agreements between a union and its members, *e.g.* in relation to benefits or between one union and another. This state of affairs has never been formally altered, though procedural devices have enabled members to assert their rights against their unions in the High Court. This peculiar legal position did not, however, protect the unions from liability in tort until Parliament expressly conferred this immunity by the Trade Disputes Act 1906.[2] Parliament again intervened in 1913 when it reversed the decision of the House of Lords in *Osborne* v. *Amalgamated Society of Railway Servants*,[3] which had extended the rule of *ultra vires* to the activities of a trade union in the political field, notwithstanding that they were denied the legal status of incorporation, which attracts the rule, even after the Act of 1871. This Act made lawful the application of the funds of a trade union for political objects, but allowed a member to claim exemption from contributing to the political funds without suffering any exclusion from benefits or other disability (s. 3). Today the importance of the influence of trade unions in the political world needs no emphasis.

[1] Trade Union Act 1913, s. 3.
[2] Pp. 71–2, *ante*.
[3] [1910] A.C. 87.

It is curious that there is no particular pressure brought to bear upon Parliament to give full recognition as corporate bodies to these important organs in the State.[1] One difficulty of granting full legal personality is that such a step would destroy the case upon which rested the claim for immunity from tortious liability which was granted by the Trade Disputes Act 1906. In any discussion of the right to associate freely for political purposes it must be borne in mind that as the law stands at present no action in tort, including, of course, defamation, can be brought against a trade union, or the members acting on behalf of the union, as distinct from a member in his individual capacity, whether or not the act complained of was done in contemplation of an industrial dispute.

Settlement of Disputes

Freedom of association in the industrial field has borne fruit in the elaborate structure of wage agreements and the methods for their enforcement which are such a prominent feature of industrial law. As such agreements seldom come before the ordinary courts their jurisprudence has become a highly specialised topic. For these reasons it would be out of place to develop the subject further in a book on constitutional law. This is not to say that trade unions are not political institutions of the highest importance in the modern State. There is nowadays a danger lest industrial disputes should threaten the economy of the State and, therefore, a Government, irrespective of its political colour, will on occasions consult the Trade Union Congress as readily as the Confederation of British Industries. Nevertheless it is the practice not to intervene in a trade dispute until the internal machinery which each main industry possesses for the settlement of difficulties with its employees has failed to produce a solution. It is notable that when under the Defence Regulations of the Second World War many strikes which were technically illegal took place, prosecutions were rare and seldom successful. So it is neither to the civil nor to the criminal courts that one can look for the solution of industrial disputes as to wages or other conditions of employment.

Public Demonstrations

The other aspect of freedom of association as distinct from individual freedom of expression relates to the dissemination of political views in public meeting or procession or other form of demonstration. Here there is a considerable volume of law, both common law

[1] But see the Industrial Relations Bill, 1970.

and statute, which deals with the question of when and where is it lawful to exercise the so-called right of free speech. Apart from this body of law there is one general statutory restriction of constitutional interest. Arising out of the activities of Fascists and Communists, Parliament in 1936 enacted the Public Order Act. The principal object of the Act was to suppress political organisations which were attempting to usurp the functions of the Government for the maintenance of order. Accordingly the Act makes it an offence to take part in the control or management of any association of persons which is organised or trained and equipped with a view to usurping the powers of the Police or the Armed Forces of the Crown. Similarly, it is an offence to take part in such an association if its purpose is to use or display physical force for promoting any political object. It is sufficient to constitute such an offence if the association by its members acts in such a way as to cause reasonable apprehension that it exists for promoting political objects by force. To the same end the Act forbids the wearing without police permission in any public place or at a public meeting of uniform which signifies association with a political organisation or with the promotion of a political object. Other provisions of the Act relate specifically to public meetings and processions. There is no doubt that the Public Order Act succeeded in driving underground the Fascist movement. Nevertheless three years later at the outbreak of war an emergency regulation was required to authorise the detention on suspicion of *inter alia* members of the British Union of Fascists. In 1962 there was a prosecution arising out of fascist activities in Trafalgar Square.[1]

In 1953 the Prevention of Crime Act made it an offence to be in possession in a public place of an offensive weapon without lawful authority or reasonable excuse. The onus is on the defence to explain the possession of such weapons by the accused. The Prevention of Crime Act was enacted with no political object in view. It did, however, prove a useful instrument for bringing to justice members of gangs who seek to exploit local prejudice against the coloured population, a political problem which has developed in this country and has since been the cause of legislation against racial discrimination.[2]

[1] The Trafalgar Square Act 1844 gives care, control, management and regulation of the Square to the Minister of Public Building and Works who can thus prohibit meetings there. This is the only example of a ministerial power to prohibit a public meeting in advance, and see *The Queen* v. *Cunninghame Graham and Burns* (1888), 16 Cox C.C. 420.

[2] P. 547, *post*, for application of Public Order Act to display of written material inciting racial hatred.

The Law relating to Liberty of Discussion

From these general observations on the problem of the control of expression of opinion we can turn to a discussion of the topic on the orthodox lines. Liberty of discussion takes precedence over freedom of meeting for two reasons. (1) The place where speeches are made is normally irrelevant so far as the speaker is concerned if he confines himself to utterances which are in law unobjectionable. (2) Political education nowadays is more and more dependent upon television and sound broadcasting with the result that the public meeting has become a less important political instrument. Accordingly the opportunities for creating disorder in such meetings has declined, though demonstrations, largely in the form of proceedings protesting against aspects of government policy including that of Foreign States, have created a formidable police problem in maintaining order in the streets of the metropolis and other big towns, as well as some universities.

Law of Defamation

That the law of defamation is still a considerable brake upon political discussion cannot be denied. Actions for libel are among the remaining actions where either party can ask for trial by jury. It is the jury, therefore, which determines the liability of an organ of the Press, and equally that of a private individual, by reference to the ordinary law. It is the jury also which awards damages to a successful plaintiff. No ready rule exists for the assessment in terms of money of damage to the reputation. With newspapers competing publicly in the race for circulation records it is easy for a jury to take a generous view of the capacity of the proprietors to pay. The libel, on the newspapers' own showing, must reach hundreds of thousands of readers. Not even the paper with the highest circulation can afford often to face a libel action. The result is that for every case fought out in court a very large number are settled before trial. Even with the changes enacted by the Defamation Act 1952, which was designed to reduce the measure of liability for unintentional defamation, the substantive law is relatively severe as compared with that of other countries. Accordingly, although it is true to say that there is no special Press law in this country and the liability of an organ of the Press is determined by reference to the ordinary law, that law, if it is invoked to stifle liberty of discussion, can be a formidable fetter on freedom of opinion.

Criminal Libel

Libel may also be a criminal offence. Any defamatory writing can be the subject of a criminal prosecution; so also can be seditious or blasphemous or obscene writings or words. In practice prosecutions for defamation are confined to cases where the libel is aggravated by its intrinsic gravity or public nature. In the past prosecutions for libel were a powerful weapon in the hands of Governments in the eighteenth century to stifle opposition. Nowadays an action for political libel is rare, while prosecutions for criminal libel have almost disappeared. The reason for this is due less to a change in the law than to the attitude of the public to political controversy. For this there are several reasons, amongst which may be mentioned the improvement of political education which has accompanied each extension of the franchise. So long, however, as the law remains unaltered there is the possibility of a revival of the severity of its administration, against which the unwillingness of juries to convict is a principal safeguard. It is necessary therefore to go back some way in the history of this branch of the law in order to understand both its contents and the present attitude to its administration.

From the days of Elizabeth I printed matter was licensed before publication. Printing was then and continued until after 1688 to be the monopoly of members of the London Stationers' Company. At an earlier date printing presses had come under the supervision of the Star Chamber. In 1693 Parliament renewed for a final period of two years the Licensing Act, but the lapse of the Act in May, 1695, cannot be attributed to any vigorous public demand for a free Press. The causes of the failure to renew the Act were rather the exactions of the Stationers' Company and the eccentricities of licensing officials.[1] The result was that for the future the law of libel controlled the liberty of the Press. That branch of law developed in a period when it was considered that all authority had been delegated to the ruler and consequently comment on his actions was libellous.[2] As the Government of the day came in the eighteenth century to be substituted for the Monarch, the restriction upon liberty of discussion which such conception of authority made possible was opposed to current ideas of politics.[3] It was, however, not until later in the century (1771) that Parliament practically ceased

[1] See Dawson, *The Law of the Press* (1927), for a short account of the history of Press law.

[2] Holdsworth, *History of English Law*, Vol. VI (1924), p. 377; Vol. VIII (1926), p. 341; Vol. X (1938), p. 673.

[3] *Cf.* Holdsworth, *History of English Law*, Vol. X (1938), p. 72. Walpole could claim that his Government punished few political libels, despite much provocation.

to enforce its claim to prevent publication of debates. It was still in 1765 contempt of court to publish without licence of the judge a report of legal proceedings, even as a law report for the use of lawyers.[1]

The administration of the law of libel differed from the general rule of administration of the criminal law, in that a verdict on the general issue was not allowed to juries, who were asked to find a verdict only as to the fact of publication and the truth of any innuendo. It was, despite the exceptional precedent of the *Case of the Seven Bishops*,[2] for the judges to decide in cases of seditious and other libellous publications the issue of libel or no libel as a matter of law. Judges, then as now, were prone to be conservative in their outlook and it was not difficult to convict political extremists of sedition. The enactment of Fox's Libel Act 1792, the sequel to a long judicial controversy as to the function of judges in administering the law of libel,[3] enabled the jury in a prosecution for criminal (including a seditious) libel to return a verdict on the general issue. The measure coincided with the fears of revolution spreading across the Channel. At first convictions of political pamphleteers were as readily obtained from "twelve shopkeepers" as from a bench of judges bent upon repression, but later the new machinery established liberty of discussion within the framework of the common law with little further assistance from the legislature. It is only in times of crisis, when men's passions run high and reason is blurred, that the jury is as a rule willing to convict of seditious or other forms of criminal libel those who seek to disturb the existing order of government by attacking its defects and abuses. The offence of sedition cannot be made the subject of a successful prosecution in the absence of incitement to violence, though the breadth of its definition remains unaltered.[4] Juries are apt to refuse conviction when they are convinced of the unsuitability of the law. In the case of *The King* v. *Aldred*[5] there is to be found in the charge of Mr. Justice Coleridge to the jury a summary of the law of seditious libel which represents the modern attitude to this offence:

> You are entitled to look at all the circumstances surrounding the publication with a view to seeing whether the language used is calculated to produce the results imputed; that is to say you are entitled to look at the audience addressed, because language which

[1] Dawson, *op. cit.*, p. 2.
[2] (1688), 12 St. Tr. 183.
[3] Holdsworth, *History of English Law*, Vol. X (1938), pp. 676–88.
[4] *The King* v. *Caunt* (1947), reported verbatim in *An Editor on Trial* (Morecambe Press Ltd.); the case was tried at Liverpool Assizes.
[5] (1909), 22 Cox C.C.1.

would be innocuous, practically speaking, if used to an assembly of professors or divines might produce a different result if used before an excited audience of young and uneducated men. You are entitled to take into account the state of public feeling. Of course there are times when a spark will explode a magazine . . . A prosecution for seditious libel is somewhat of a rarity. It is a weapon that is not often taken down from the armoury in which it hangs, but it is a necessary accompaniment to every civilised government . . . The expression of abstract academic opinion in this country is free. A man may lawfully express his opinion on any public matter, however distasteful, however repugnant to others, if of course he avoids defamatory matter or if he avoids anything that can be characterised either as blasphemous or as an obscene libel. Matters of State, matters of policy, matters even of morals—all these are open to him. He may state his opinion freely, he may buttress it by arguments, he may try to persuade others to share his views. Courts and juries are not the judges in such matters. For instance, if he thinks that either a despotism or an oligarchy, or a republic, or even no government at all is the best way of conducting business affairs, he is at perfect liberty to say so. He may assail superstition, he may attack governments, he may warn the executive of the day against taking a particular course. . . . He may seek to show that rebellions, insurrections, outrages, assassinations and such like are the natural, the deplorable, the inevitable outcome of the policy which he is combating. All that is allowed because it is innocuous, but on the other hand if he makes use of language calculated to advocate or to incite others to public disorders, to wit, rebellions, insurrections, assassinations, outrages, or any physical force or violence of any kind, then whatever his motives, whatever his intentions, there would be evidence on which a jury might, on which I think a jury ought, to decide that he is guilty of a seditious publication.

It is more than a hundred years since a newspaper editor in Great Britain has been successfully prosecuted for sedition. In 1947, in *The King* v. *Caunt*, a case which was tried on circuit, there was a powerful illustration of the unwillingness of juries to convict a newspaper of seditious libel.

A provincial newspaper, at a time when feeling against Jews was running high in this country on account of atrocities committed against British troops in Palestine before the creation of the State of Israel, published a leading article attacking British Jewry in virulent terms. The article concluded with a suggestion that violence might be the only way of bringing British Jewry to its senses. Notwithstanding these words, which came very close to an incitement to violence, the defendant editor was acquitted.

It is possible to explain this case on the ground of anti-Semitism; in other words that the verdict of the jury was perverse. There is, however, little to justify this view in the verbatim report of the trial which was conducted by one of the greatest exponents of freedom of opinion among the judges of the present century, Lord Birkett.

Precedents then of an earlier age are not very helpful to an understanding of what is required to constitute the offence of sedition or seditious libel to-day. In contrast with the very wide definition of libels on Governments, which Mr. Justice Stephen gave in his *Digest of the Criminal Law* in the nineteenth century,[1] it is now established beyond doubt that the prosecution must prove an incitement to violence over and above the defamatory criticism of public affairs. That same definition included an intention to promote feelings of ill-will and hostility between different peoples and classes—a matter germane in the case of Caunt. If an incitement to violence were not an essential ingredient, it would be arguable that the speeches of opponents at any modern General Election might constitute the offence of sedition under this limb of the definition. Although prosecutions for sedition are rare in the United Kingdom, they are a more frequent occurrence in overseas territories, some of which are still without a jury system. Thus in 1954 there were a number of prosecutions for sedition in Uganda and Zanzibar. These were tried by a judge with two assessors.[2]

Akin to the definition of sedition are those of blasphemy and obscenity. Of the former the old precedents have ceased to be helpful. To-day even the fundamentals of religion may be attacked provided that the decencies of controversy are observed without a person being found guilty of blasphemous libel. Whatever advantages still accrue to the Church of England through its establishment, it derives no special protection from the law of blasphemy.[3] On the other hand the law relating to obscene publications which, like the law of blasphemy, derives from a less tolerant age is in some danger of being applied to prevent the publication of scientific, literary and artistic material which by modern standards is unobjectionable. This branch of the law of libel must therefore be examined in some detail.[4]

Civil Liability for Defamation

First it is desirable to look at the law of defamation in its ordinary sense of an attack on the reputation of the individual which may be

[1] Stephen, *Digest of the Criminal Law*, 9th edn., Articles 112, 114; Dicey, *Law of the Constitution*, 10th edn., pp. 243–44.

[2] For a case from the Gold Coast (now Ghana), see *Wallace-Johnson* v. *The King*, [1940] A.C. 231.

[3] See especially *Bowman* v. *Secular Society*, [1917] A.C. 406, and *The Queen* v. *Ramsay and Foote* (1883), 48 L.T. 733.

[4] Chap. 37.

calculated to bring him into hatred, ridicule or contempt. This branch of the law is divided into slander, *i.e.* defamation in a transitory form by word or gesture, and libel in a permanent form, such as the printed word or picture. By reason of the measure of publicity which it confers, the broadcasting of words by means of wireless telegraphy is treated as publication in permanent form as are dramatic performances in theatres. This is not the place to embark on a technical discussion of the law of defamation, but it is necessary to point out that there can be no defamation so far as liability for damages in a civil action is concerned, in the absence of publication to a third person. The basis of liability in criminal libel rests on a probability of a breach of the peace and therefore publication only to the person defamed suffices. Immunity from civil liability for defamation is granted to such occasions as the law allows to be privileged. As this privilege extends to judicial and parliamentary proceedings as well as to certain communications of an official character, it is necessary to examine it in some detail in relation to liberty of discussion of public affairs. With defamatory attacks in private life constitutional law is little concerned save to note that liberty of speech does not extend to unlicensed abuse of one's neighbour. But open criticism of public affairs is an essential attribute of a democratic community. In determining when such criticism is privileged, *i.e.* does not attract the ordinary civil liability for defamation, the law endeavours to balance the scales between private right and public interest. Accordingly privilege is divided into two kinds, (*a*) absolute, (*b*) qualified. The former confers complete immunity however virulent the criticism; the latter may be rebutted on proof of special malice, *i.e.* the privilege ceases to protect the defamer if he has sought the protection of privilege in order to vent his spite on the plaintiff. Parliament extended the scope of qualified privilege by the Defamation Act 1952 in favour of reporting matters of public interest.[1]

Parliamentary Proceedings; Absolute Privilege

Communications which are absolutely privileged include those made in the course of parliamentary proceedings. This was the earliest manifestation of freedom of speech. At first it served to protect members of Parliament from fine and imprisonment on account of criticism of the Crown. To-day it is the one substantial privilege which members of Parliament enjoy. The modern law derives from the provision of the Bill of Rights 1688, that

> freedom of speech and debates or proceedings in Parliament ought

[1] Pp. 520–2 ff., *post*.

not to be impeached or questioned in any court or place out of Parliament.

The exact scope of this provision is still uncertain. The House of Commons by a narrow majority as recently as 1958 resolved, contrary to a recommendation from its Committee of Privileges, that these words did not cover a letter from a member of Parliament to a Minister of the Crown containing material defamatory of a third party, a statutory corporation within the nationalised electricity industry, which the writer asserted to the Minister had been guilty of a business malpractice.[1] On the other hand disclosures made in Parliament whether in the form of questions to Ministers or in a speech ought not to be made the subject matter of a prosecution under the Official Secrets Acts 1911—1939.[2] The test seems to be that no member may be held liable for words spoken in the performance of his duty as a member of Parliament. And this extends to words spoken outside the precincts of the House of Commons if spoken in the essential performance of duty by a member. But the protection does not extend to the passing on of irresponsible criticism even if the mode of communication is a letter signed by a member of Parliament. So jealous is Parliament of its privilege that a member may not without the consent of the House give evidence as a witness in a court of law concerning what has passed in Parliament, and this extends to proceedings in Committees of either House.[3]

Qualified Privilege

Privilege also extends under the Parliamentary Papers Act 1840 to any publication made by authority of either House of Parliament. An action in respect of defamatory matter contained in such publication would be stayed on the production of a certificate from an officer of the relevant House. The same Act gives protection to the fair and accurate extracts from such publications, but this protection may be rebutted on proof of malice. Similarly in the absence of malice, unofficial reports of proceedings in Parliament are privileged if fair and accurate, as well as is honest and fair comment in any article which is founded on what has passed in Parliament.[4] The justification for these privileges is to be found in the view that the interest of the public is of more importance than inconvenience to individuals which may be occasioned by their exercise.

[1] P. 161, *ante*.
[2] Report from the Select Committee on Official Secrets Acts, H.C. 101 (1939).
[3] Chap. 10, for parliamentary privileges generally.
[4] *Wason* v. *Walter* (1868), L.R. 4 Q.B. 73; K. & L. 295.

In the nature of things these privileges are of particular benefit to newspapers and periodicals. By the Defamation Act 1952, s. 7 the qualified privilege enjoyed by newspapers and periodicals was considerably extended, provided that the matter reported or commented on is of public concern and is not otherwise prohibited by law. Thus a fair and accurate report of the proceedings of any other legislature in the Commonwealth enjoys privilege and there is in this case no obligation to publish any explanation or contradiction of statements which a plaintiff who complains of being defamed by the report may have requested by way of explanation or contradiction. Similar privilege is given to reports of the public proceedings of any international organisation of which the United Kingdom or its Government is a member or of any international conference to which that Government sends a representative.[1]

Judicial Proceedings privileged

Judicial proceedings enjoy absolute privilege. The immunity of judges for any acts done or words spoken in their judicial capacity in a court of justice is not conferred for the protection or benefit of the judges but "for the benefit of the public, whose interest it is that the judges should be at liberty to exercise their functions with independence and without fear of consequences." [2] It is as important that judges should be protected from harassing actions brought by disappointed litigants as it is that they should be free from the influence of the Executive; this is especially so in the case of judges of inferior courts and magistrates. But the immunity extends not merely to judges of all degrees but also to the parties, witnesses, counsel or solicitors in respect of words spoken in court and to juries as regards their verdicts.[3] Corruption, neglect of duty or misconduct in the execution of judicial duties can be punished under the criminal law, though instances of prosecutions are nowadays extremely rare and in the case of the higher judiciary unknown. In this context it is interesting to note that although a witness can be prosecuted, as can the parties to proceedings, for perjured evidence, no civil action lies in respect of injuries caused by the perjury. Thus if imprisonment results from perjured evidence the man who has been wrongfully imprisoned cannot sue the perjurer for damages. The reason for this is the need to protect those who give evidence in a court of law, while at the same time punishing those who commit deliberate perjury.

[1] Schedule, Part I.
[2] *Scott* v. *Stansfield* (1868), L.R. 3 Ex. 220, at p. 223.
[3] Chap. 23.

Reports of Judicial Proceedings [1]

Newspapers and periodicals enjoy privilege in respect of fair and accurate contemporary reports of any public proceedings of any court in the United Kingdom and also of any court exercising jurisdiction throughout any part of the Commonwealth outside the United Kingdom or of a court-martial held outside the United Kingdom under the disciplinary statutes of the Forces of the Crown. Similar protection is given to the report of any public proceedings of an international court. The privilege is usually regarded as absolute, but it can be rebutted by proof of malice. In any of the above cases there is no obligation on the defendant to publish any letter, explanation or statement in contradiction at the request of the plaintiff. Although in general privilege does not attach to fair and accurate reports of judicial proceedings in foreign courts, if the foreign report contains subject matter closely connected with the administration of justice in England an English newspaper reproducing defamatory material without malice may be protected.[2]

The position of reports of the proceedings of public inquiries is different. Where such inquiry is held within the United Kingdom and the admission of the public allowed, a fair and accurate report of the proceedings in a newspaper or periodical enjoys privilege, but the defence may be rebutted if it is proved that the defendant has refused or neglected to publish in the newspaper in which the original report was made, a reasonable letter or statement by way of explanation or contradiction. If on the other hand the inquiry is held on behalf of the government or legislature of any part of the Commonwealth outside the United Kingdom, the requirement to have published an explanation or contradiction is not available to a plaintiff. Presumably this discrimination was authorised by Parliament on the ground that it would be too difficult to check the accuracy of cabled reports from overseas and so the Press would be discouraged from reporting on important inquiries, say, in Australia, unless they could do so without being under any obligation other than to refrain from a malicious publication.

Extensions of Absolute Privilege

Absolute privilege has been given by recent legislation to the reports of the Parliamentary Commissioner for Administration and of communications by members of Parliament on matters relevant to his inquiries [3] and to the reports of the Prices and Incomes Board.

[1] Law of Libel Amendment Act 1888, s. 2 and Defamation Act 1952, s. 7 and Schedule.

[2] *Webb* v. *Times Publishing Co. Ltd.*, [1960] 2 Q.B. 535.

[3] P. 711, *post.*

Qualified Privilege; Administrative Action

Public inquiries are on the border line between judicial and administrative functions. When it comes to acts of the executive government and still more to the acts of the local authorities, the availability of qualified privilege is more restricted. The common law gives qualified privilege to communications passing between a Minister of the Crown and the Sovereign or between one Minister and another, as it does also to military reports or to any communication made in pursuance of a legal, social or moral duty to another person who has an interest in receiving the communication. There are no examples in the sphere of central administrative activity of statements by the Press being privileged without the obligation to publish an explanation or contradiction, if so requested, except in such matters as copies or extracts from any register which by law is open to inspection by the public and certain notices or advertisements published by authority of a court or judge. By statute[1] a fair and accurate report in a newspaper of proceedings of any meeting of any local authority or committee of such authority which is open to the public does enjoy qualified privilege, subject to the obligation to publish if requested a reasonable letter or statement by way of explanation or contradiction in the same paper in which the original report appeared. Similar protection extends to reports of proceedings before justices of the peace acting otherwise than as a court, as indeed it does to the reports of the proceedings of any public meeting held in the United Kingdom *bona fide* and for a lawful purpose and for furtherance or discussion of any matter of public concern, whether the admission of the public is general or restricted. In other words the special protection given to reports of administrative activity is more restricted.

So far as the officers and servants of central and local government authorities are concerned the protection which they enjoy is derived from the common law and Parliament has not seen fit to confer any special privilege upon them. This means that they must justify defamatory statements or letters by proving their truth or as regards matters of comment must rely on the defence that the comment was fair. But a statement made by a member of any public body at a meeting of the body, if material and pertinent to the matter under discussion, has qualified privilege, as being a matter in which the defendant and the person to whom it is made have a common interest.[2] In practice actions for defamation against such persons

[1] Defamation Act 1952, ss. 7, 16 and Schedule.
[2] Gatley, *Libel and Slander*, 5th edn., p. 234.

are very rare and it may be doubted whether a man who serves both as a justice of the peace and as an elected councillor, is really conscious that he enjoys virtually absolute immunity in one capacity and relatively little in the other. In this context it must be remembered that proof of malice rebuts the defence of fair comment even on a matter of public interest.

Special Press Law

In the course of discussing privilege mention has been made of some of the more important privileges which the Press enjoys. For this purpose the term "Press" covers those who are responsible for the publication not only of daily and weekly newspapers but also periodicals which are published either in parts or numbers at periods not exceeding thirty-six days. The other special protections which the Press enjoys are not extensive, but mention may be made of the safeguard which in practice secures that the law of criminal libel is seldom invoked. No prosecution can be instituted against the proprietor, publisher, editor or any person responsible for the publication of a newspaper for any libel contained therein without the order of a judge in chambers and before the order can be made the person accused must be given an opportunity of being heard.[1] Such prosecutions are nowadays very rare. This restriction, however, does not apply to an information laid by the Attorney-General in respect of attacks upon the Government. In civil matters mention has already been made of the tendency of juries to regard the proprietors of newspapers as possessed of unfathomable pockets from which huge damages may be drawn. A newspaper, like any other defendant, may however give evidence in mitigation of damages if the plaintiff has already recovered or has brought actions for damages or has otherwise been compensated in respect of a similar libel as that for which the current action is being brought.[2]

At one time the Press enjoyed a right of admission for their accredited representatives only to the meetings of certain public bodies. By the Public Bodies (Admission to Meetings) Act 1960 any meeting of a local authority or similar body (including education committees and regional hospital boards) exercising public functions, is open to the public; this secures admission for the Press who are for the first time also entitled to receive copies in advance of the agenda of meetings. It is possible to secure exclusion of the public, including the Press, by resolution of the meeting wherever publicity would be prejudicial to the public interest. It is thus possible for a

[1] Law of Libel (Amendment) Act 1888, s. 8.
[2] Defamation Act 1952, s. 12; *Lewis* v. *Daily Telegraph Ltd.*, [1964] A. C. 234.

local authority to meet in closed session to receive reports not merely from its committees but also from its officers. In the case of the Houses of Parliament, admission of members of the Press is the same as that for the general public who are admitted on sufferance. Moreover publication of the proceedings can be restricted as a matter of privilege. The practice however is very different and the Press is afforded special facilities for obtaining parliamentary news; secret sessions are confined to war time, and even then are rare. There have been occasions in the past when the general public has been excluded by reason of persistent misbehaviour on the part of a few individuals; the press gallery however has remained open on such occasions.

Unintentional Defamation

The general law relating to unintentional defamation was introduced following on one of the recommendations of the Committee on the Law of Defamation 1939–48.[1] Unintentional defamation does not provide a full defence but it can prevent the assessment of damages in the action coming before a judge or jury. The Defamation Act 1952, s. 4 provides that if a person who has published words alleged to be defamatory of another claims that the words were published by him innocently so far as that person is concerned, he may make an offer of amends. If the offer is accepted and is duly performed, the proceedings for libel or slander are stayed. The party aggrieved however may refuse to accept the offer and prefer to go on with the action. In that case it is a defence in any proceedings for libel or slander brought by him against the person making the offer for the defendant to prove that the words complained of were published by him innocently in relation to the plaintiff, if the offer of amends was made as soon as practicable after the defendant had notice that the words were or might be defamatory of the plaintiff and that such offer has not been withdrawn. An offer of amends must take the form of offering to publish a suitable correction of the words complained of and a sufficient apology to the aggrieved party: where copies of a book or other document containing the words have been distributed by the person making the offer or with his knowledge, he must also offer to take such steps as are reasonably practical on his part to notify any persons to whom copies have been distributed. Newspaper proprietors and other publishers on whose representations the Committee on Defamation was set up have

[1] Cmd. 7536 (1948).

without securing actual immunity, derived considerable pecuniary protection from its provisions. A newspaper will not normally be required to disclose the origin of its source of information.[1] This rule which is particularly relevant in the interlocutory proceedings in a civil action must in practice afford considerable protection to those who supply the Press with news and comment. It has no direct reference to the law relating to the offer of amends, but it may be thought that an editor, aware that under the present law the consequence of an action for defamation may not from a pecuniary point of view be serious to his paper, may be less likely to check the accuracy of the information with which he is supplied than was previously the case when unintentional defamation enjoyed no such protection and a newspaper, like any private individual, published at its risk.

Restrictions on Reporting

Despite this special defence and the other immunities enjoyed by the Press it is difficult to maintain that these provisions amount to a special law for the Press. The State has been content to leave the public expression of opinion to the working of the ordinary law and does not attempt censorship previous to publication in any shape or form with the exception that certain types of reports of judicial proceedings are restricted as to their contents. The Judicial Proceedings (Regulation of Reports) Act 1926 prohibits the publication in newspapers of indecent matter and medical, surgical or physiological details given in evidence in committal proceedings and in a trial, the publication of which are calculated to injure public morals; in the case of reports of matrimonial cases lawful publication is limited to the names of the parties, their legal advisers and witnesses, statements on the matter at issue, submissions and rulings on points of law and the judgment. These restrictions which at the time of their introduction were bitterly contested as savouring of censorship, are concerned solely with public morals. There are further restrictions in the Children and Young Persons Acts 1933 and 1963. A court may direct that no newspaper report of the proceedings shall reveal the name, address or school of any child or young person concerned and that no picture shall be published as being a picture of any such child. S. 49 of the Act of 1933 forbids similar publication in relation to any proceedings in a juvenile court, though the court has power to dispense with these provisions if it considers that it is in the interests of justice so to do; it is only rarely that a juvenile court will sit as examining justices, but the restrictions apply to all proceedings in that court.

[1] But cf. p. 542, *post*.

A court may prohibit the Press from publishing anything which would lead to the identity of a child or young person, *i.e.* under the age of 17 years, concerned in any court proceedings, as a witness.

Censorship of Plays and Films

For centuries dramatic and operatic performances at playhouses were subject to the censorship of an officer of the Royal Court, the Lord Chamberlain. By the Theatres Act 1968, which also extends to ballet, this former prerogative power which had been given parliamentary authority by the Licensing Act 1747 and the Theatres Act 1843 was abolished. In place of pre-performance censorship the presentation and direction of plays is subject to the criminal law of obscenity,[1] as well as to that relating to the incitement to racial hatred and provocation threatening a breach of the peace. Prosecutions for these offences require the consent of the Attorney-General, as does an offence at common law committed by publication of defamatory matter in the course of the performance of a play. Theatres are licensed by the principal local authorities, as are premises for the exhibition of films, but the latter control is based on safety regulations rather than on order and decency. Control may be exercised over actual films to be shown in licensed premises by making the licences conditional on the showing of films which carry the approval of the British Board of Film Censors, an official body maintained by the trade, which is usually presided over by a distinguished retired public servant.[2] Whether or not a film which lacks this approval can be exhibited depends on the discretion of the local licensing authority who may delegate their powers to the local justices of the peace.

Horror Comics

Another example is even more remote from the field of political censorship. The Children and Young Persons (Harmful Publications) Act 1955, commonly known as the Horror Comics Act, was enacted to prevent the dissemination of pictorial publications considered harmful to the young. Pictures, magazines and similar publications which are likely to fall into the hands of the young and consist wholly or mainly of stories told in pictures may not be

[1] The topic of obscenity is dealt with in Chap. 39.

[2] Cinematograph Act 1952, s. 3, which expressly authorises an authority to refer to the certification of films by the Board in its conditions relating to the admission of children which may be attached to the licence; *cf. Ellis* v. *Dubowski*, [1921] 3 K.B. 621, where such a condition was held *ultra vires* on the ground that a statutory duty may not be delegated to some other body.

printed, published or sold, under summary penalties, if the stories portray (*a*) the commission of crimes, or (*b*) acts of violence or cruelty, or (*c*) incidents of a repulsive and horrible nature in such a way that the work would tend to corrupt a child or young person into whose hands it might fall. It is a defence if the sale or loan of the book is without knowledge of its contents. No prosecution may be brought without the sanction of the Attorney-General. The court may order copies, plates and the like which are found in the possession or control of a convicted person to be forfeited. On information laid before a single justice, the police may obtain a warrant to search the premises on suspicion of containing publications covered by the Act. It is unnecessary to comment further on this welfare provision for the protection of the young. The only danger to liberty of opinion would seem to come from the fact that it does attempt censorship, however beneficial the form thereof.

The Official Secrets Acts [1]

The Official Secrets Acts 1911 to 1939 conferred drastic powers which can be used to prevent comment upon matters of general public interest. The principal purpose of this legislation is the prevention of espionage and the communication of any information which may be calculated to prejudice the safety of the State in the hands of a potential enemy.[2] In order to achieve this object it was considered necessary to frame the enactments in terms wide enough to prevent the publication of any communication made in confidence which it might be detrimental to the public interest to disclose. Accordingly some of the provisions of the Act can be used to stifle the discussion of information derived from official sources which has little or no bearing upon the safety of the State. The Atomic Energy Act 1946, s. 11 strengthens the provisions of the Official Secrets Acts in a field which is obviously related to national security. Legislation of this character has its effect beyond national boundaries, and, as has been the experience in the case of legislation in the United States, has hindered the interchange of scientific information between allies.

[1] *Not in the Public Interest*, by D. G. T. Williams (Hutchinson), esp. Pt. I, is a critical monograph on this subject.

[2] See *Chandler* v. *Director of Public Prosecutions*, [1964] A.C. 814, the Wethersfield Airfield prosecution of members of nuclear disarmament movements, which shows that the Act is wide enough to cover acts of sabotage as well as acts of espionage. An offence under s. 1 of the Act of 1911 is complete if the purpose of approaching a prohibited place is to cause obstruction or interference prejudicial to defence dispositions. The Crown alone by its prerogative powers can decide the disposition and order of the armed forces.

By the Official Secrets Act 1911, s. 2 (1):

> If any person having in his possession or control . . . any information . . . which has been entrusted in confidence to him by any person holding office under Her Majesty . . . (*a*) communicates the . . . information to any person other than a person to whom he is authorised to communicate it . . . that person shall be guilty of a misdemeanour.

The general character of this provision is obvious. The offence can be committed by disclosing information which bears no relation to matters of national importance since the language is wide enough to cover any information whatsoever which is given in confidence to anyone holding an office, however humble, under the Crown. There is, however, an important safeguard against the abuse by the Executive of this power to suppress information in that the consent of the Attorney-General is required to any prosecution under the Acts. Nevertheless much information which comes the way of a civil servant or member of the Forces in the course of duty is entrusted to that person in confidence. Thus it would be a breach of this section for an officer of the Board of Inland Revenue to disclose the contents of an income-tax return deposited in his office. A matter of first importance in the administration of justice is the publicity given by the press to trials and summary proceedings. A police constable takes an oath of office under the Crown and is therefore a person holding office under Her Majesty within the meaning of s. 2 (1) of the Act of 1911. If he discloses to a newspaper reporter information relating to an offence, even if it be of no particular public interest, both he and the reporter who makes use of the information as news are on the face of it guilty of offences. It was formerly the law that refusal on demand by an officer of the police not below the rank of inspector to disclose the source of information obtained in breach of the Official Secrets Acts constituted a misdemeanour,[1] but by the Official Secrets Acts 1939 this special power of interrogation is restricted to cases covered by s. 1 of the Official Secrets Act 1911 which relates to acts of espionage or sabotage of defence installations. Moreover, there is a further safeguard that except in cases of urgency the consent of a Secretary of State is a condition precedent to the exercise of this special power of interrogation.

It is clear then that whatever be the justification for putting Ministers, civil servants and members of the Forces of the Crown under restriction as to the information which they may disclose to the public, journalists, speakers and others who comment upon

[1] *Lewis* v. *Cattle*, [1938] 2 K.B. 454; but a constable is not for some other purposes a servant of the Crown, see p. 242, *ante*.

matters of public interest of which they may have learned from official sources could be prosecuted under the Acts. Moreover, there are wide powers of search upon mere suspicion of the commission of an offence under these Acts, and these powers are not limited by the requirement that a search warrant can only be issued by a judicial authority.[1]

It is true that such a warrant cannot be accurately described as a general warrant, but it is a means of enabling information to be obtained in circumstances where without action under the warrant there is insufficient evidence of the commission of an offence either having been or about to be committed. The enormous increase in governmental activities has meant that very large sections of the community have been brought within the provisions of the Official Secrets Acts by reason of their employment in the service of the Crown. Moreover, the wider governmental activity extends, the greater is the number of ordinary citizens who may be put in peril of prosecution for disclosing an "official secret." There is, however, very little evidence that the Executive has abused its wide powers. Any such abuse would hardly have escaped detection despite the fact that proceedings under the Acts may be held wholly or partly in camera, if the prosecution applies to the Court.

Incitement to Disaffection

There are several enactments on the Statute Book which are designed to prevent the spread of disaffection. These are mainly concerned with the protection of public servants, and more particularly members of the Armed Forces who may be exposed to attempts to seduce them from their duty or allegiance. The Aliens Restriction (Amendment) Act 1919,[2] prohibits an alien from causing sedition or disaffection among the civil population as well as among the Armed Forces of the Crown and those of its Allies, and provides for summary punishment for the promotion of, or interference in an industrial dispute by an alien in any industry in which he has not been engaged in the United Kingdom for at least two years immediately preceding. The Police Act 1964 [3] contains a prohibition on any acts which are calculated to cause disaffection among members of police forces. The Incitement to Disaffection Act 1934 which was intended to provide less harsh penalties than those under the unrepealed Incitement to Mutiny Act 1797 makes it an offence to seduce a member of the Forces from his duty or allegiance and contains stringent provisions for the prevention and detection of this

[1] P. 487, *ante*. [2] S. 3. [3] S. 53.

offence. There are wide powers of search on suspicion, but a warrant issued by a Judge of the High Court is required to authorise such search. Moreover, it is an offence for any person with intent to commit, or to aid, counsel or procure the commission of the principal offence to have in his possession or under his control any document of such a nature that the distribution of copies thereof among members of the Forces would constitute that offence. This measure arms the Government with a means of restricting the distribution of political propaganda; particularly it could be used to suppress the distribution of pacifist literature. It must be admitted that prosecutions are rare and that juries are reluctant to convict. But that there are risks over and above those contained in the ordinary law of defamation for all who may seek to persuade servants of the Government to betray, or even to deviate from their duty is apparent.[1]

Obstruction

A more subtle means of restricting freedom of discussion may be exercised by the police, who can by a strict enforcement of the law relating to obstruction of the highway hamper the distribution to the public of pamphlets, handbills and similar literature without any need to prove that the contents of the literature infringe any provision of the law. Since, as we shall see later, there is no legal right to use the highway for any purpose other than that of passage, a distributor of leaflets can be requested by a police constable to "move on," even in circumstances where there is no suspicion or likelihood of a breach of the peace occurring. Since it is the duty of the police to keep the highway clear of obstruction (and merely to stand on the highway may be treated as impeding the rights of others to pass and repass), any resistance may result in a charge of obstructing a police officer in the execution of his duty.[2]

Search and Seizure

There is no general power under which the police can seize a stock of literature other than on the authority of a search warrant; this can only be authorised in relation to the particular offence, on suspicion of the commission of which a judge, magistrate, or exceptionally a senior police officer, is authorised to issue such a warrant. In other words, there is no authority to seize anything which is not evidence of the commission of an offence under a particular statute which authorises the issue of the warrant.

[1] Pp. 513–6 ff., *ante*, for Sedition and Criminal Libel.
[2] Pp. 553–4, *post*.

But, while it is not possible to justify the wholesale seizure of the contents of premises unless they are evidence of the commission of a particular offence, there is some authority for saying that it does not matter by whom the offence has been committed, provided that the police have entered private premises for the purpose of making a lawful arrest.

> In *Elias* v. *Pasmore*,[1] where the police held a warrant for the arrest of an official of an organisation, entry was made into the offices of that organisation for the purpose of executing the warrant. The accused man was duly arrested but the police searched not only his person, which is a reasonable precaution, but also the whole premises and removed a large quantity of literature belonging to the organisation for purposes of examination at a police station. In an action for trespass brought against the police concerned it was held that upon the arrest by lawful process of an accused man the police can search the premises where the man is arrested and seize material which is relevant to the prosecution of any crime committed by any person, and not merely by the accused.

This decision stops short of justifying the wholesale seizure of contents of premises, and damages were awarded against the police in respect of taking away such of the material as was not used for the prosecution of anybody. Had the court decided otherwise, there would have been little left of the rule in *Entick* v. *Carrington*,[2] which declared illegal the issue of a general warrant as to the papers (unspecified) of a named person.

The Law and Radiocommunications

The attitude of the law towards modern means of influencing public opinion has not yet been fully explored. At one time legal opinion was divided on the question whether defamatory statements published by sound broadcasting constituted slander or libel. The Defamation Act 1952, s. 1 settled the doubts by providing that publication whether by sound broadcasting or television constituted publication in "permanent form" and so brought the publication of defamatory matter within the law of libel. That this view should have prevailed was perhaps inevitable, for it must be obvious that the damage to the reputation of the individual by the wide publicity given to a defamatory attack published by either of these methods can be far greater than an isolated publication to a third party. But there are other means than the law of libel for controlling the contents of a broadcast. So long as sound broadcasting remains a monopoly and television is limited to two agencies, it is inevit-

[1] [1934] 2 K.B. 164; p. 487, *ante*.

[2] (1765) 19 St. Tr. 1030; K. & L. 174; p. 486, *ante*, for seizure of goods suspected of being stolen property.

able that there will be controversy and allegations of partiality. The major political parties have solved this difficulty so far at all events as the facilities of the British Broadcasting Corporation are concerned by reaching agreement as to the amount of time allowed to each for uncensored political speeches or discussions. All other programmes are subject to the choice of the B.B.C. or, in the case of commercial television, the contracting companies. These companies are under the control of the Independent Television Authority upon which is placed responsibility for maintaining the standard of programmes by the companies.[1] This authority was set up by the Television Act 1954 and a main function is to ensure that there is no abuse of the facilities allowed by the Act for advertising. No Minister is responsible either for the B.B.C. or the I.T.A.; they are in effect as well as in law independent public corporations although their members are appointed by the Government of the day. These powerful agencies are in a position to suppress or encourage political controversy at their will. The B.B.C. at all events has shown its susceptibility to public criticism and in practice protects itself by a wide choice of speakers, including a great many members of Parliament of all parties, in any political discussion. There can, however, be little doubt that there are dangers in the present system; these are perhaps inevitable with any monopoly or quasi-monopoly organisation. Nevertheless it is difficult to overemphasise the importance of these modes of influencing public opinion and the tactics of broadcasting and television will doubtless play an increasingly important part in political education. As far back as 1931 it was possible to point to a particular broadcast as having a decisive effect on the results of an ensuing General Election. Today it seems that the highest offices in the Government are likely be to denied to those who cannot project their personality by the medium of television.

[1] Television Act 1964, ss. 1–8.

CHAPTER THIRTY-SEVEN

CONTEMPT OF COURT

Civil Contempt

CONTEMPT of court may take two forms. To disobey the order of a superior court of record which has made an order prescribing a certain course of conduct upon a party to an action may constitute civil contempt. Obedience to an order, which may equally be directed to a witness to compel his attendance, is secured by a power in the judge to commit to prison anyone who disregards any order which is binding upon him. It is in this way that decrees of specific performance and injunctions, as well as obedience to the writ of habeas corpus and to orders of certiorari, prohibition and mandamus, are enforced by the High Court; such jurisdiction is not connected with the topic of freedom of discussion, and the only suggestion for the improvement of the present law is that the actual order for committal might be made by a different judge from the one who issued the original order. In practice it would seem preferable that the judge who has cognizance of the whole demeanour and conduct of parties and witnesses throughout the proceedings should decide the question of contempt in this sense. Particularly is it important where the contempt arises out of the disregard of an order made in the interests of a child who is a ward of court that the offending parent or guardian should be under the compulsion of the same judge. For civil contempt the sole punishment is imprisonment. The Crown cannot grant a pardon.[1]

Criminal Contempt

The other type of commitment for contempt by a court is in the nature of a criminal proceeding. It may arise in two ways.

1. Conduct which scandalises the court, whether it be by one of the parties or by strangers.
2. Conduct which is calculated to prejudice a pending proceeding.

All superior courts of record have power to punish summarily by fine or imprisonment an act of violence committed or a threat uttered in face of the court. Under this head a judge of a superior court of record can punish an act of physical violence against himself

[1] For distinction between civil and criminal contempts, see 25 M.L.R. 179.

or anyone in court, and equally restrain the use of threatening words or scurrilous abuse whether directed at himself or any of his brother judges. The issue whether the alleged act constitutes the offence of contempt of court is for the judge alone. If the act is committed in his own court he is in a sense prosecutor, chief witness, judge and jury. There is clearly room for the abuse of such a power and it is perhaps for this reason that it has never been extended to justices of the peace. A county court judge has power to commit for contempt any person who wilfully insults the judge, a juror, witness or officer of the court, or wilfully interrupts the proceedings; the order for committal must be for a specified period not exceeding one month; alternatively the judge may impose upon the offender a fine not exceeding £20.[1] The restraint upon voicing an opinion in court which could result from an abuse of this power on the part of a judge is considerable. But against this may be weighed the fact that no action for defamation can lie as a result of anything said by party, counsel or witness, judge or jury in open court. This immunity, which is undoubtedly justified by the general requirements for the administration of impartial justice, may on occasions require action by a judge to ensure the orderly conduct of proceedings in his court. There is no jurisdiction for the court to discharge a person who is purging his contempt where committal is for a fixed period, *e.g.* committal by the Divisional Court for obstructing a county court bailiff.[2]

Sub Judice

It may be generally agreed that nothing should be allowed to prejudice the fair trial of a pending proceeding. Whenever a matter is *sub judice*, public discussion should be suspended. This rule is accepted by both Houses of Parliament, and is enforced against the Press and others by summary punishment at the hands of the High Court.[3] Here, then, is a definite restraint on freedom of discussion of a matter which may well be of public concern. A breach of the rule is treated as contempt of court and if it is adjudged to be an impediment to the administration of justice may be punished by any member of the High Court before whom the contempt is alleged. In practice if the proceedings are already being heard the matter may come before the trial judge. But if the hearing is pending, the normal procedure is by way of motion in the Divisional Court of the Queen's Bench Division before three judges. The Court has power to punish by fine or imprisonment, or both. In the case of a

[1] County Courts Act 1959, s. 157.
[2] *Attorney-General* v. *James*, [1962] 2 Q.B. 637.
[3] Innocent publication is protected by Administration of Justice Act 1960, s. 11.

pending trial for murder in 1949 such a court imposed upon the editor of a national newspaper a sentence of three months' imprisonment and fined the proprietors of the paper £10,000 on account of an article which suggested that the accused man had been responsible for the death of persons other than that of the victim for whose murder he was about to be tried.

It is obvious that public discussion of matters which are calculated to affect the result of a trial by jury must be prejudicial to an accused. But the rule applies with equal strictness to proceedings before a judge alone, and nowadays the vast majority of civil actions are so tried. Nevertheless, there is a strong body of opinion which inclines to the view that the trial of an issue for contempt ought itself to be determined as part of the ordinary criminal law by judge and jury. The offence has never been defined by statute and its limits are to some extent still uncertain. It is treated by the judges as a common law misdemeanour and as such punishable by a fine on which no limit has been imposed, or imprisonment at the pleasure of the court as a civil prisoner. This in practice means that committal lasts until such time as the judge who has inflicted the imprisonment considers that the contempt has been purged by a sufficient apology.

Past Proposals for alteration of Law

On five occasions between 1883 and 1908 unsuccessful attempts were made to deal with the subject of contempt of court by legislation.[1] There is historical evidence that criminal contempts committed by a stranger out of court by libelling the judge were at one time treated like any other trespass and tried by a jury.[2] This, however, does not seem ever to have extended to the punishment of conduct which is likely to prejudice a pending case. In 1906, and again in 1908, the House of Commons accepted resolutions which drew attention to the fact that the jurisdiction of the judges in dealing with contempt of court was practically arbitrary and unlimited. These resolutions expressed the opinion that action by Parliament was called for with a view to the definition and limitation of this jurisdiction.[3]

Committal Proceedings

A topic which in the opinion of some may be as prejudicial to a fair trial as comment in advance of the actual hearing is the reporting in the Press of the proceedings before examining magistrates. It is as a result of this preliminary enquiry that magistrates determine

[1] Fox, *History of Contempt of Court*, p. 3.
[2] *Op. cit.*, p. 4, 34 ff.
[3] 155 H.C. Deb. (4th Series), col. 614; and 185 H.C. Deb., col. 1432.

whether or not an accused person shall stand his trial. The proceedings are in no sense a trial of the issue, and the accused person is not put in peril thereby. The object of the enquiry is to decide whether the prosecution has made out a sufficient case to justify the accused being committed to stand his trial before judge and jury upon an indictment. The court or a single magistrate hears a statement by the prosecution of the circumstances of the alleged offence and this is supported by the evidence which is in the form of written depositions from the principal witnesses for the prosecution. When this has been completed and the court is of opinion that there is a case to answer, the accused is given an opportunity of giving evidence or making a statement in rebuttal and calling witnesses for his defence. He is not obliged to say anything at this stage and he is normally well advised to reserve his defence, if any, until his trial. The proceedings are heard in public. The admission of the public involves the presence of the Press.

In a murder trial which attracted international publicity in 1957 the presiding judge (Devlin, J.) referred to the wide publicity given to certain evidence which was investigated in the local magistrates' court but was not before the court at the trial. This evidence was wholly prejudicial to the accused, a doctor who was charged with the murder by poisoning of an elderly patient. In consequence a Departmental Committee was appointed "to consider and report whether it is necessary or desirable that any restrictions should be placed on the publication of reports of proceedings before examining magistrates."[1] An examination of the historical background to the practice of sitting in open court showed that it was the practice until the Indictable Offences Act of 1848 for the examining justice not to sit in public. The Act marked the turning point at which committal proceedings came normally to be taken in open court, and, at all events until 1957, the modern practice was for examining justices to sit in camera only when hearing evidence which ought to be kept secret in the interests of national security or from a witness who genuinely fears intimidation or when evidence has to be taken elsewhere than in a court, *e.g.* at the bedside of an injured person.

The history of reporting committal proceedings shows that prior to the Act of 1848 the courts did not recognise them as judicial proceedings for the purpose of applying the defence of privilege in libel. But by 1893 in consequence of the decision in *Kimber v. Press*

[1] *The Report of the Departmental Committee on Proceedings before Examining Magistrates* (Cmnd. 479, 1958) is reflected in the Criminal Justice Act 1967, Part I.

Association[1] it was clear that a fair and accurate report of committal proceedings would be privileged if published without malice.

The Present Law

A simplified committal procedure was introduced in 1968 under the provisions of Part I of the Criminal Justice Act 1967. It is only available when the accused is represented by a solicitor or counsel; it enables the committal to take place formally by consent on production to the examining justices of written statements by the prosecution. These statements must be served on the defence before the hearing; they are not read out in court nor considered by the justices unless the defence asks for prosecution witnesses to be called. A statement must contain a declaration that it is made with the knowledge that penalties akin to those for perjury may be incurred for any knowingly false information. The justices have to be satisfied that all the evidence in the form of written statements is before them. The defence may submit that there is not sufficient evidence to justify committal; in that event the proceedings must take the form of hearing the evidence and taking depositions, as under the procedure which has been outlined in the preceding paragraphs.

The advantage to the accused is that he is assured of legal representation throughout and the defence can be properly prepared at the outset. The hearing, as hitherto, takes place in open court, but it is usually a formality. There is thus nothing for the press to report beyond the decision to commit. When the accused is not represented or there is a submission that there is no case to answer, the evidence of the prosecution must be taken. The press then are subject to restrictions laid down by the Criminal Justice Act 1967. These restrictions forbid the publication of details of the evidence and allow only formal matters (name, age, address, offence charged, result of committal proceedings) to be published unless the accused asks that the restriction be lifted, as is usual when he opts for a full hearing of the evidence instead of the simplified procedure. Where two or more persons are charged with the same offence, the removal of the restrictions on reporting at the request of one of the accused involves the removal in respect of the proceedings against all.

Nature of Contempt

"Every libel upon a person about to be tried is not necessarily a contempt of court, but the applicant must show that something has been published which either is clearly intended, or at least is cal-

[1] [1893] 1 Q.B. 65.

culated to prejudice the trial which is pending."[1] The offence is based upon the idea of not allowing the jury to hear before the trial anything of the past character of the accused. There are, it is believed, no precedents of a newspaper being punished for contempt of court on account of references favourable to the accused being published contemporaneously with the pending proceedings. But there seems no reason for concluding that a deliberate write-up of his character inspired by his own prompting or that of his friends might not be treated as contempt, alleging interference with the due course of justice, if the attention of the court to the write-up was drawn by the prosecution.

The type of comment which will normally result in proceedings for contempt being brought against the author and his publisher is that which relates to the probable result of the trial—at all events if adverse to the accused or to the previous character of an accused or either of the parties to a civil action. Even the publication of a photograph of an accused person may constitute contempt of court where it is reasonably clear that a question of identity may arise and where the publication is calculated to prejudice a fair trial. Contempt of court is not confined to pending cases. It is not necessary that proceedings for contempt would be confined to matters published after legal process has actually begun. Where in the case of a man who was obviously about to be arrested on his return from abroad and tried on charges of gross fraud, a television interview of him had clearly for its object the establishment of his guilt and the interview was also published verbatim in a Sunday paper, both the interview and the report constituted contempt of court, in the opinion of the Court of Appeal (Criminal Division).[2] Victimisation of a witness, being an interference with the proper administration of justice in deterring potential witnesses in future cases, is contempt even after proceedings have finished. Victimisation aimed at punishing a witness for his evidence is contempt, even though the punishment was not the predominant motive.[3]

There is another type of conduct which may scandalise a court even after the trial and any consequential appeal have been concluded. It has been held to be a contempt to criticise a judgment or sentence if such criticism is regarded by the court as mere invective or otherwise tends to bring into ridicule or contempt the administration of justice. To attribute a particular decision to the personal

[1] *The Queen* v. *Payne and Cooper*, [1896] 1 Q.B. 577, at p. 580.

[2] *The Queen* v. *Savundranayagan and Walker*, [1968] 3 All E.R. 439; the appeal was, however, dismissed on its merits.

[3] *Attorney-General* v. *Butterworth*, [1963] 1 Q.B. 696.

weaknesses of the judge is to suggest that he is incapable of administering impartial justice in some circumstances. An allegation of incompetence or even serious infirmity of mind or body calculated to disable his judgment may amount to contempt, if not directly, by innuendo. The *New Statesman* once commented upon a judgment in a libel action and concluded with regrets that similar decisions might follow since "an individual owning to such views as those of . . . (the defendant) cannot apparently hope for a fair hearing in a court presided over by Mr. Justice Avory—and there are so many Avorys. . . ." Three colleagues of the judge in question, though they imposed no fine upon the editor, adjudged him to be guilty of contempt, for they considered that the article imputed to the judge in question partiality.[1] On the other hand, it is permissible to discuss the merits of a decision in law. Argument, or even expostulation, may be offered against any judgment, both on the ground that it was contrary to law or, though legally unexceptional, to the public good. The respectful submissions of contributors to professional periodicals may be tinged with sarcasm, but the writers are almost certainly protected if they confine their criticisms to the legal merits of a case. More dangerous may be, as witness the case of the *New Statesman*, comment upon the social implications of a judgment, especially if it be attributed to the judge showing in the course of the trial his disapproval of the defendant's conduct or beliefs. An imputation of partiality on the part of a single judge may well be treated by his brethren as a reflection upon the Bench as a whole, but the highest courts have encouraged criticism provided that there is no imputation of improper motives to those whose duty it is to administer justice. Thus it is permissible to criticise the inequality of contemporary sentences for similar offences. One of the best statements is contained in a judgment of the Judicial Committee of the Privy Council which was given by Lord Atkin.[2]

> Whether the authority and position of an individual judge, or the due administration of justice, is concerned, no wrong is committed by any member of the public who exercises the ordinary right of criticising, in good faith, in private or public, the public act done in the seat of justice. The path of criticism is a public way: the wrongheaded are permitted to err therein: provided that members of the public abstain from imputing improper motives to those taking part in the administration of justice, and are genuinely exercising a right of criticism, and not acting in malice or attempting to impair the

[1] *The King* v. *New Statesman* (*Editor*), *ex parte Director of Public Prosecutions* (1928), 44 T.L.R. 301.

[2] *Ambard* v. *Attorney-General for Trinidad and Tobago*, [1936] A.C. 323, at p. 335.

administration of justice, they are immune. Justice is not a cloistered virtue: she must be allowed to suffer the scrutiny and respectful, even though outspoken, comments of ordinary men.

This case arose out of a fine imposed on a journalist for contempt of a court in a colony. The alleged contempt consisted of criticism in an article of sentences imposed by two of the three judges who held him to be in contempt. The Judicial Committee advised that the conviction for contempt should be set aside.

Safeguards

It is a guarantee against an abuse of the power to commit for contempt that the power is only entrusted to professional judges who have attained their position after years of experience at the Bar. Nowadays the occasions are rare indeed when the High Court Bench comes under criticism in respect of partiality or competence. It is seldom that the court will be moved to commit for contempt unless serious cases of genuine contempt are in issue. Nevertheless, not even the holders of high judicial office are exempt from social prejudices. This might lead to action being taken to stifle criticism in the face of a contrary public opinion. A prominent member of the Bar, now dead, once expressed the view that from the pages of the law reports there could be produced evidence of the social background of members of the Bench. To publish the results of such a study might expose the author and publisher to some risk of being committed for contempt.

To-day the reputation of the Bench is as high as it has ever been, but earlier this century a trade union did not expect to receive justice in the courts. Much criticism was directed at the Judges and Law Lords who decided the *Taff Vale Railway Company Case* [1] in 1901, and the *Osborne Case* [2] in 1910.

Again, when a Chancery Judge in an interlocutory judgment condemned as illegal the General Strike of 1926 his impartiality was challenged.[3] It is perhaps significant that legislative action followed closely upon the decision in each of these cases. In the *Taff Vale Case* and the *Osborne Case*, the Trades Disputes Act 1906 and the Trade Union Act 1913 emancipated trade unions from the effects of the judgments, but the Trade Disputes and Trade Unions Act 1927 which was repealed in 1946, upheld the judge's view in *Reed's Case*. Both the Act of 1927 and the repealing Act of 1946 [4] clearly

[1] *Taff Vale Railway* v. *Amalgamated Society of Railway Servants*, [1901] A.C. 426 (tortious liability of trade union).

[2] *Osborne* v. *Amalgamated Society of Railway Servants*, [1910] A.C. 87 (use of funds for political purposes illegal).

[3] *National Sailors' and Firemen's Union* v. *Reed*, [1926] Ch. 536.

[4] Trade Disputes and Trade Unions Act 1946.

reflected contemporary political viewpoints. It seems inevitable that, given the traditional rule that the Bench should be recruited exclusively from the Bar, judges should be prone to regard sociological considerations as far less important than points of law in the strict sense. If ever we reverted to a state of affairs where the judges were identified with a particular Government, it would be open to the judges under the existing state of the law to stifle opposing voices, just as their predecessors by a harsh administration of the law relating to seditious libel [1] restrained the critics of Governments in a less sensitive era.

Comparison with Parliamentary Privilege

There have been allegations that judges have assumed new powers to punish for contempt of court newspapers which have incurred their displeasure.[2] The expression "contempt of court" suggests an affront to a court, but, as we have seen, it has long covered any conduct which is calculated to interfere with the due administration of justice. Definitions do not help very much, nor is it easy to determine the scope of the expression *sub judice*; yet any discussion of a case which may be held to be *sub judice* may be deemed to be an interference with the due administration of justice and be punished by the imposition of an unlimited fine or indefinite imprisonment. In this connection comparison may be made between the attitude of the courts to privilege of Parliament and contempt of court. Both confer immunities upon the claimant; both are justified as being necessary for the proper conduct of affairs. The courts are zealous to restrain any attempt by Parliament to enlarge the field of privilege. There is no corresponding movement to limit the contents of what may constitute contempt of court. There are historical reasons for this contrast. In the days when conciliar jurisdiction prevailed to punish an exceeding of power it fell to the Star Chamber to punish summarily for contempt. After its abolition the judges assumed the power to punish summarily and so contempt became a common law offence, punishable summarily. No such assumption of jurisdiction has ever taken place with regard to privilege. Here the struggle has been between Parliament and the courts, each asserting supremacy. It is thus not surprising to find that, while the judges reserve to themselves the right to determine the limit of privilege, they concede the jurisdiction to Parliament over a wide field.

[1] P. 513, *ante*.

[2] See *The Times*, Article, 17 June, 1958.

Examples of Contempt

With contempt of court there is nothing to restrain the judge's arbitrary discretion in the absence of any legislation by Parliament. As *The Times* has remarked,[1] "The pattern of case after case today is as familiar as it is squalid." Each case starts with abject apologies, and these usually succeed in keeping the editor out of prison, but invariably he is condemned as being in contempt.

In 1956 *The People*[2] was convicted of contempt in respect of a statement deemed to be prejudicial to pending criminal proceedings of which they did not even know the existence. In the following year the well-known firm of W. H. Smith and Sons was found by the Divisional Court to be guilty of gross contempt of court. The offence consisted of distributing copies of a foreign periodical printed and published abroad which commented on a murder trial then in progress at the Old Bailey. The disclosures which preceded the trial had received a wide publicity. Although innocent dissemination is a defence in a civil action for libel, it did not avail to secure the acquittal of W. H. Smith and Sons when charged with contempt of court for distributing copies of the periodical.[3]

About the same time the unauthorised disclosure of proceedings before a Chancery Judge sitting in Chambers was held to be contempt, although no question arose of prejudicing a fair trial.[4] In this connection, if the origin of the jurisdiction in contempt of court be found in the fear that a jury might be prejudiced in advance of the trial, it is to be observed that no jury is available in any circumstances in Chancery proceedings, while the proportion of civil actions tried with a jury, if one omits defamation and false imprisonment (wrongful arrest), has for many years been negligible.

In the course of an inquiry into the circumstances in which a person subsequently convicted of spying had been employed in the Admiralty, three journalists refused to disclose the source of their information when ordered to do so by the President of a Tribunal which was set up under the Tribunals of Inquiry (Evidence) Act 1921. Such a tribunal has the same power as a High Court to order a witness to give information. The cases established that there is no legal privilege to enable journalists to refuse to disclose their sources of information when ordered by the High Court or by a Tribunal

[1] *The Times*, 17 June, 1958.

[2] *The Queen* v. *Odhams Press Ltd.*, [1957] 1 Q.B. 173.

[3] *The Queen* v. *Griffiths, ex parte Attorney-General*, [1957] 2 Q.B. 194. The innocent disseminator is now protected; p. 544, *post*.

[4] *Alliance Perpetual Building Society* v. *Belrum Investments Ltd.*, [1957] 1 W.L.R. 720.

under this Act.[1] Thus the journalist, like the minister of religion, the doctor or the banker, commits contempt of court if he refuses to answer a question when ordered to do so by the court. The only exception is in favour of members of the legal profession who cannot be compelled to disclose against their will what passes between them and their clients.

The present procedure has sometimes been compared with summary trial in a criminal court, but unlike summary trial there was until 1960 no appeal, and therefore the law could not be considered by the Court of Appeal or the House of Lords. It is to be observed that the leading case was an opinion of the Judicial Committee [2] and that the appeal was allowed despite the strong terms used by the offending journalist in commenting on the inequality of sentences passed by the two judges whose sentences were under discussion. It was much the same in the eighteenth century when there was no appeal from convictions in criminal courts, and the judges condoned a savage use of prosecutions for seditious libel to coerce the equivalent element to the present-day opposition press.

Access to Court Papers

Early in 1959, in the course of litigation, counsel disclosed to the court the existence of a rule, now Order 63, Rule 4, which had been enacted by the Rules Committee of the Supreme Court seventy-five years earlier. The rule gives to every member of the public the right to inspect all the documents in a case which are filed at the Central Office of the Supreme Court. It would seem that the rule had long been superseded. At all events its existence must have been overlooked when the Masters of the Supreme Court not many years after the introduction of the rule stated by their own practice rules that only parties to an action should have access to the records of it. In practice the Masters allowed applicants with a personal interest in a case similar access but such interest did not extend to the inquiries of journalists in search of copy. The Masters' rule has now been repealed. It could not remain in stark contradiction to the Rules Committee enactment.

Of the many writs issued in the High Court only a tiny percentage result in open hearings in court. It is clear that if the Press make liberal use of this source of information, the law of contempt of court as well as the law of libel, will be resorted to, particularly by those

[1] *Attorney-General* v. *Clough*, [1963] 1 Q.B. 773; *Attorney-General* v. *Mulholland*, v. *Foster*, [1963] 2 Q.B. 477, p. 153, *ante*, for proposed modifications to law of contempt to the tribunals.

[2] P. 538, *ante*.

whose defences may be prejudiced by premature disclosures prior to trial in open court. In this context it has already been shown[1] that whenever a matter is *sub judice* public discussion should be suspended. If applications to commit for contempt of court become more frequent it may hasten the day when that branch of the law receives its long-delayed overhaul. It is questionable whether the right of the general public to inspect court documents is in the best interests of justice. Such documents are necessarily partial to the cause which they seek to promote. There can surely be no satisfactory substitute for the open hearing, certainly not if it takes the form of trial by newspaper. The free disclosure of the merits of only one side of the case in advance of the trial can only hamper the impartial administration of the law.

Proposed Reforms

The cases cited above were responsible for an investigation into jurisdiction by way of contempt of court. This investigation was conducted by a committee of members of Justice, the British Section of the International Commission of Jurists. The Report was published in April, 1959, and the principal recommendations may be summarised as follows:

A. SUBSTANTIVE LAW

1. *Basic principles:*

(*a*) The court should retain residuary power in all cases to prevent interference with the course of justice by punishment for contempt.

(*b*) Proceedings should be instituted only by the Attorney-General.

(*c*) There should be no conviction unless the court considers the interference is substantial and unjustifiable.

2. *Publications prejudicial to pending proceedings.* There should be a defence that there was no knowledge or no reason to suspect that a proceeding had begun. A distributor of published matter should be able to plead in defence that he had not examined the contents of the publication and had no reason to suspect that it contained matters in contempt of court. But distributors "should be astute to suspect contempt" especially if the publishers are not amenable to English law. Published matter relating to a suspect should be capable of being treated as contempt although published before arrest where (*a*) it is a matter of which the law forbids evidence being given, and (*b*) the publisher knew that an arrest was imminent.

3. Criticism of a judge should not be capable of amounting to contempt unless prejudice, corruption or other improper motive is alleged against him.

[1] P. 533, *ante*.

4. Proceedings in Chambers should not come within the law of contempt unless the publication is in breach of an order of the court prohibiting publication in a proceeding relating to an infant, lunatic, or secret process, or in interlocutory proceedings where publication might prejudice a fair trial.

B. PROCEDURE

1. There should be a right of appeal to the Court of Appeal against any conviction or sentence by the High Court in contempt of court.
2. No prosecution for criminal contempt outside the court should lie except by, or with the consent of, the Attorney-General.
3. Any application for attachment or committal for civil contempt should be heard in public. The accused should be entitled to give oral evidence in defence.
4. The powers of all courts to punish summarily for contempt in court should be limited in a way similar to county courts, *i.e.* limited to wilful insult to the judge, juror, witness, officer of the court or wilful interruption of proceedings.
5. There should be a power to certify contempt in face of the court for trial by another judge of the High Court.

Two important changes were made in relation to the law of contempt of court by the Administration of Justice Act 1960, although these do not go as far as the proposals summarised above. Section 11 protects the innocent disseminator by providing that no one shall be guilty of contempt of court on the ground that he has published any material likely to interfere with the course of justice in pending proceedings if at the time of publication he, having taken all reasonable care, did not know, and had no reason to suspect, that proceedings were either pending or imminent. This protection is also extended to the distributor. The defence is only available in that type of contempt of court where prejudice to a fair trial is involved. The second change is that it will no longer be contempt of court of itself to publish information relating to proceedings before any court sitting in private, but this protection does not apply to proceedings relating to wardship, adoption and guardianship, cases brought under the Mental Health Act 1959 before a review tribunal or a county court, or where a court sits in private for reasons of national security or where information relating to a secret process is in issue.[1]

The Committee suggested a right of appeal to the Court of Appeal against conviction by the High Court for contempt. The Act confers a right of appeal in cases of both civil and criminal contempt.[2] From an order for committal by an inferior court there is

[1] Ss. 11 and 12.
[2] S. 13.

a right of appeal to the Divisional Court, except that from a County Court the appeal is to the Court of Appeal. Appeals from orders or decisions of a Divisional Court or the Court of Appeal (Criminal Division) and the Courts Martial Appeal Court lie to the House of Lords provided that, if the appeal is a second appeal, a point of law has been certified as being of general public importance.

CHAPTER THIRTY-EIGHT

PUBLIC MEETINGS AND PROCESSIONS

Introductory

AT one time the law relating to public meetings and processions was closely associated with the conduct of election campaigns. Nowadays, when political meetings, even those attended by a leading member of the Government or Opposition, seldom attract large audiences, the operation of the law is rarely seen at the small meetings which candidates still feel it their duty to arrange throughout their constituencies at election times. We must look elsewhere in the field of television and sound radio for the control by the State of these means of influencing the electorate.

There are, however, other occasions when different sections of the public are likely to clash in circumstances which may lead to a breach of the peace. An obvious example is the resistance of pickets to attempts by strike breakers to enter industrial premises. In the political field the unpopularity of views is sometimes met by forceful resistance. This may come from hostility to some aspect of Government policy, or from resistance to those who advance provocative minority views, or through the activities of movements which practise civil disobedience. Issues of national security may arise even from pacifist demonstrations, *e.g.* by obstructing the approach to an airfield.[1] In recent years the arrival from other parts of the Commonwealth of large numbers of coloured workers and their families who have tended to concentrate in their own separate communities, has led to complaints and sometimes forcible resistance on the part of their near-neighbours. For the most part these clashes of rival factions which are confined to the poorer districts of large towns impose upon the police a severe local burden. The threat to the general public order from problems of racial discrimination has led to the enactment of the Race Relations Acts 1965 and 1968.[2]

The law which governs the method of the exercise of expression of opinion in public places is not entirely clear. In former days Governments felt it necessary to protect themselves from violence and there were evolved by the common law specific offences for which rioters

[1] P. 526, *ante*.
[2] P. 500–1, *ante*.

could be prosecuted; these were riot, rout, unlawful assembly and affray. But these offences are weapons ill-suited to the suppression of what is little more than provocative abuse. The intervention of the police for example at noisy street-corner meetings, will nowadays usually result in summary charges for the use of insulting words, or, if there is resistance from members of the public, of obstructing the police in the execution of their duty. Parliament enacted by s. 5 of the Public Order Act 1936 that:

> the use in public of threatening, abusive or insulting words or behaviour with intent to provoke a breach of the peace or whereby a breach of the peace was likely to be occasioned

should be a statutory offence punishable summarily.[1] In 1963 this offence was made punishable on indictment consequent upon an increase of disorder in public places through political or racial motives. The Race Relations Act 1965, s. 7, extended s. 5 of the Act of 1936 to the distribution or display of written matter.

Absence of Guaranteed Right

The attitude of a democratic State towards free expression of opinion by means of public speeches and demonstrations is partly responsible for the lack of clarity in the existing English law on this subject. The law does not expressly allow or forbid meetings as such. But it treats certain actions as criminal or tortious, if committed in the course of using the highway or any other place for assembling a meeting.[2] It is not always the case that a written constitution of the type which embodies a statement of fundamental rights will contain a guarantee of the right of public meeting. In the absence of such a guarantee public meetings may be left to police regulation. Any Government in the United Kingdom at the present time should be sufficiently aware of the need to listen to public protests without their attention having to be directed to the need for action by the use of force. But within the present century the suffragette movement demonstrated against the Government with a show of violence. Later in the century the Public Order Act 1936 was passed to meet the threat to public order from fascists and communists. This Act, it may be claimed, has effectively suppressed para-military and other uniformed bodies of demonstrators. Disorders arising out of demonstrations organised to protest against government policy have been increasing in intensity in the 1960s. The police are then called upon to protect the

[1] *Jordan* v. *Burgoyne*, [1963] 2 Q.B. 744, conviction for Jew-baiting under the section.

[2] *Cf.* Wills, J., in *Ex parte Lewis* (1888), 21 Q.B.D. 191, at p. 197.

persons of senior ministers and to secure access to public buildings. In the industrial sphere the problem of peaceful picketing has been solved by legalising such methods of persuasion and it is not often that strikes, however prolonged, occasion serious disorder. Industrial strife no longer leads to riots such as occurred at the Ackton Hall Colliery in 1893.[1] Until 1969 the armed forces of the Crown had not been required to supplement the police for some forty years, but disorders in Northern Ireland were the occasion of a substantial number of troops taking over from the local police the task of maintaining order. There remain problems of public order occasioned by the colour problem.[2]

Police Powers

What has been called the public nuisance aspect may result from freedom to speak and to demonstrate in public to the annoyance of one's neighbours. This is essentially a police problem. Some of the difficulty comes from the problem of administration of the present law rather than from doubts caused by its complexity. Police action can only be justified when there is evidence that a breach of the peace is likely to be committed. There will always be zealous police constables on the evidence of whose suspicions magistrates will be called upon to decide as to the probability of a breach of the peace. No matter how precisely the law may be formulated some discretion must be entrusted to the police and it can never be easy to decide at what point action will become necessary. A policeman may decide to intervene not as a matter of officiousness, but because he is over-cautious and envisages possible disturbances from the attitude of a crowd surrounding the advocate of an unpopular cause or from the presence of a handful of interrupters at a political meeting. It is the function of the police to prevent the commission of offences as well as to prosecute those who have actually offended. It can never be easy to reproduce in the witness box the scene as viewed by a constable in attendance on duty at a meeting or procession. From time to time the police are inevitably accused of using excessive force, and doubtless on occasions deplorable incidents may have happened. It is not, however, necessary to assume that even in such cases the police have abused their discretion. It is entirely in accordance with the law relating to public meetings, *i.e.* the right to meet without let or hindrance to advocate a cause, that the attention of the police should primarily be directed against those who seek to disrupt meetings. Their action in favouring a meeting first in the field rather

[1] See C.7234 reproduced in Dicey, *op. cit.*, 9th edn., pp. 620–24.
[2] P. 500, *ante*.

than a counter demonstration is strictly in accordance with the common law duty to prevent the disturbance by opponents of a meeting lawfully assembled. Justification for this view may be found in the famous charge to the Bristol Grand Jury [1] by Tindal, C.J., on the occasion of the Reform Bill riots in that city, and in the resulting case of *The King* v. *Pinney*.[2]

Processions

It is obvious that an appeal to reason which freedom of speech is designed to secure must be defeated if the appeal is made inaudible by counter demonstrations. It was doubtless with this in mind as well as traffic control that Parliament gave to chief officers of police special powers with regard to public processions. By s. 3 (1) of the Public Order Act 1936 such an officer may give directions to and impose conditions on the organisers of processions when it appears to him to be necessary for the preservation of public order, for example to prescribe a route in order to divert the procession from passing through a hostile district. These powers are reinforced under the following sub-section by a provision which enables a senior police officer to apply to the local borough or district council for an order prohibiting all or any class of public processions for a period not exceeding three months. Such an order can only be made by the council with the consent of the Secretary of State. In the case of the Metropolis the Commissioner of Police may issue a prohibition order with the consent of the Home Secretary and without applying to any local authority. It should be noted that this provision of the Public Order Act gives no power to the police or anyone else to forbid the holding of any meeting. Such a prohibition must await the event and can only be issued if and when a reasonable apprehension of a breach of the peace has arisen. A practice which has been encouraged by the Metropolitan Police in the 1960s is to advise organisers of demonstrations to inform the police in advance of the intended route and destination of the demonstrators. It is believed that prohibitions under s. 3 (2) of the Public Order Act have not been issued to control the epidemic of protesting bodies which has infected the central metropolitan area in this period.

No Rights to proscribe Meetings

The tradition of free speech remains so strong that there is no authority anywhere in the land which may proscribe in advance the holding of a meeting. True, the letting of a municipal building or of

[1] (1832), 5 Car. & P. 261; K. & L. 208.
[2] (1832), 9 B. & Ad. 947; K. & L. 211.

a private hall may be denied to the promoters of an unpopular cause and this may suffice to stifle their activity in a particular instance.[1] Some would advocate that the risk of disorder in the streets could be reduced by offering fuller facilities for the use of public buildings to all political organisations. At present it is only schools and similar buildings which are made available free of charge to candidates at election time. Further provision for the use of public buildings could do much to remove the risk of disorder by demonstrators in organised marches which so seldom achieve their purpose and which invariably prevent a reasonable use of the highway by the inhabitants of the district in which they are held. It must be confessed that motor traffic has done more than have the police to reduce street processions and meetings. It seems doubtful whether even now public opinion would tolerate the banning of meetings by a Minister of the Crown, though it has accepted in the past the exercise of the power of prohibition of processions in certain districts in London. These prohibitions have been successful in preventing clashes between Fascists and Communists as well as aggressive provocation from hangers-on, as may be seen from the charge sheets which result from police intervention on the occasion of big demonstrations. There is no complete solution to this problem. If we are agreed that the law should allow free expression on all points of view in public it must nevertheless retain the means of preventing outbreaks of disorder. There can be no freedom to provoke opposition to the point of disorder.

The Present State of the Law

The law of public meeting developed with the growth of the habit of petitioning Parliament. This and other forms of political agitation which marked the turn of the eighteenth century from about 1780 made public meetings common and emphasised their importance as a constitutional right. With the various movements for broadening the franchise, political and other forms of agitation have made the right of public meeting an important topic of constitutional law.[2] Apart from the Seditious Meetings Act 1817—a measure which, with the exception of a single provision relating to open-air meetings of a political character in the neighbourhood of the Houses of Parliament, was repealed later in the century—the Legislature made few if any important contributions to this branch of the law until the Public Order Act 1936. Just as the right of freedom of speech was in Dicey's view little more than the right to

[1] See note on p. 511, *ante*, as to Trafalgar Square, London.
[2] Holdsworth, *History of English Law*, Vol. 10, pp. 701 ff.

say anything which a jury of twelve shopkeepers thought it expedient to be said or written,[1] so in the view of the same writer "the right of assembling is nothing more than a result of the view taken by the courts as to individual liberty of person and individual liberty of speech." [2] This view does not recognise or afford any guaranteed right; rather does it throw upon an objector to the exercise of the so-called right of assembly the necessity of proving the breach of some provision of the criminal law or of the law of tort. The attitude of the law may be described as neutral. Just as it recognises no right of meeting, so it enforces no duty to allow a meeting any more than it recognises the right to forbid a meeting. As one judge put it in the nineteenth century, "Things are done every day in every part of the Kingdom, without let or hindrance, which there is not and cannot be a legal right to do, and not infrequently are submitted to with a good grace because they are in their nature incapable by whatever amount of user, of growing into a right." [3] At most there is a liberty to which the law gives no positive recognition but which it only restrains by certain prohibitions to act at one's peril in occupying any available unoccupied spaces in a public place for holding a meeting. The analogy of parking cars on the highway where there are no parking regulations in force is relevant.

Unlawful Assemblies

Such prohibitions as the criminal law provided in the nineteenth century were the offence of unlawful assembly and the similar crimes of rout and riot. At an earlier stage when there were no organised police forces magistrates were under a legal duty to take measures to disperse an unlawful assembly, and they were encouraged to take action since they were justified in using reasonable force in dispersing such a meeting. Apart from the criminal law the civil law of trespass put limitations on the places where meetings could lawfully be held, while the civil law relating to obstruction, later to be reinforced in 1835 by the Highway Act with its criminal penalties, prevented an abuse of the highway for the purpose of holding a public meeting and so obstructing the passage of those passing to and fro on their lawful occasions. It is significant that the Seditious Meetings Act 1817 was enacted at a time of serious unrest resulting from the dispersal of the Army after the Napoleonic Wars. This legislation virtually caused a total prohibition of public meetings unless the previous consent of two justices of the peace had been

[1] Dicey, *Law of the Constitution*, p. 246.
[2] Dicey, *op. cit.*, p. 271.
[3] *Ex parte Lewis* (1888), 21 Q.B.D. 191, at p. 197.

obtained for meetings held on enclosed premises, while other meetings of more than fifty persons without previous notice to the authorities on the part of at least seven householders resident in the place where it was proposed to hold the meeting were totally prohibited. But, as has been seen, this legislation was not of long duration. It fell to the courts to develop the definition of the term "unlawful assembly" and of the powers of the police in connection with the control or dispersal of such assemblies, a task which was not finally accomplished until the end of the century and which even to-day would cause difficulties of administration but for the fact that the offence has become infrequent in the face of different police methods for handling disorder, actual or potential, at meetings. An unlawful assembly at common law is an assembly of three or more persons for purposes forbidden by law, *e.g.* committing a crime by open force; or with intent to carry out any common purpose, lawful or unlawful, in such a manner as to endanger the public peace or to give firm and courageous persons in the neighbourhood reasonable grounds to apprehend a breach of the peace in consequence of it.[1]

The essence of the offence lies in determining not only the purpose of a meeting but also the manner of its assembling and the means used by the promoters and speakers. An assembly will, of course, be unlawful if it has gathered together for the commission of a crime involving violence or breach of the peace, or incitement thereto. But in the course of time the courts extended the offence to gatherings for a lawful purpose if those present at the meeting, whether speakers or audience, acted in such a way "as to give firm and rational men, having families and property there, reasonable ground to fear a breach of the peace." [2] But the law stopped short of holding to be unlawful a meeting which in itself gave rise to no such fear but was threatened by disturbances from an outside source.

In *Beatty* v. *Gillbanks*,[3] which arose out of opposition to the Salvation Army in its early days, the local Salvationists had been convicted of unlawful assembly and ordered to find sureties to keep the peace by a court of petty sessions. On appeal to the Divisional Court it was held that since the association was for religious exercises an assembly and procession in the streets was not in itself unlawful. The disturbance of the peace was caused by the opponents of the Salvationists (known as the Skeleton Army) who had on several occasions violently interfered with their activities. It was clear that, had the Salvationists not met in public and marched in procession, there would have been no disturbance of the peace. Moreover previous meetings had caused disorder so that the Salvationists knew

[1] Hawkins, *Pleas of the Crown*, c. 65, s. 9.
[2] *The Queen* v. *Vincent* (1839), 9 C. & P. 91, at p. 109.
[3] (1882), 9 Q.B.D. 308; K. & L. 198.

> that similar consequences were likely to ensue. But since the disturbances were caused by people antagonistic to the Salvationists and they themselves had committed no acts of violence, they could not be convicted of unlawful assembly and be bound over to keep the peace.

It was this case which warned the police that they could not take the easy course of dispersing an otherwise lawful assembly simply because they, the police, feared opposition from another body, and this doubtless led to the practice which has already been noted that the police favoured the meeting first in the field and directed their attention to preventing counter demonstrations. In time the law admitted that there might be circumstances in which a person in the course of his lawful occasions stirred up opposition or the threat of it to such an extent that only by ordering the dispersal of the meeting, or at least the abandonment of speech-making by such a person, could order be maintained. The wearing of provocative emblems, for example, may constitute an intention to incite a breach of the peace on the part of opponents to such an extent as to fill peaceful citizens with the fear that the peace will be broken. It is similar, of course, with provocative language.[1]

Less difficult is the situation where the speaker or promoter of the meeting has by his conduct on previous occasions caused disorder, for the attempt to hold a meeting on the part of such a person will occasion a reasonable belief on the part of the authorities of the likelihood of the repetition of disorder.[2]

Procession Distinguished

It is not easy to separate, apart from the provisions of s. 3 of the Public Order Act 1936,[3] the law relating to processions from that relating to meetings. Indeed *Beatty* v. *Gillbanks* [4] was itself a case of a public procession. If we accept the view that the topic must be discussed in relation to user of the highway, the distinction indeed becomes unnecessary. The law authorises user of the highway solely for the purpose of passing and re-passing. No person can claim to exercise this right by standing still and making a speech or listening to speeches. In practice the law relating to the right of free passage is only enforced when an obstruction is caused, and the case of *Ex parte Lewis* [5] shows that the right of public meeting is strictly

[1] *O'Kelly* v. *Harvey* (1883), 14 L.R. Ir. 105; *Humphries* v. *Connor* (1864), 17 Ir. C.L.R. 1, at pp. 8 and 9.
[2] *Wise* v. *Dunning*, [1902] 1 K.B. 167; K. & L. 201.
[3] P. 549, *ante*.
[4] P. 552, *ante*.
[5] P. 551, *ante*.

irreconcilable with the right of free passage, which while allowing reasonable rest and recreation by the wayside treats other user of the highway as a trespass.[1] A physical obstruction of the highway constitutes a nuisance if it is proved that there has been unreasonable use of the highway.[2] Misuser of the highway, whether it be a meeting or a procession which causes the obstruction, constitutes a trespass normally against the highway authority in which the surface of the highway is vested, but in practice civil proceedings are not used to keep the highway clear. It is, however, an offence punishable summarily under the Highways Acts[3] to obstruct passage; nor is it a defence to show that the obstruction only affected part of the highway leaving the other part clear.[4]

Scots Law

Nor is the law of Scotland more favourable to freedom of expression of opinion in public places. For the magistracy have a general power of preventing the misuser of the streets and prohibiting their use for any but primary public purposes. It is interesting to note that it is the magistracy and not the police who are the judges of the extent to which free speech can be exercised in open spaces and public places.[5] Scots law, indeed, denies to any individual a private right to make use of public streets for holding meetings, but at the same time accepts the right of the equal participation of all members of the public in the various uses for which the streets are kept open, of which free and unrestricted passage is the most important but not necessarily the most in use.[6] Scots and English law unite on the proposition that "the right of free speech is a perfectly separate thing from the question of the places where it is to be exercised."

Conclusion

So far as any valid distinction can be made between the legality of a procession as distinct from a meeting it may be admitted that a procession need amount to no more than the collective exercise of

[1] *Harrison* v. *Duke of Rutland*, [1893] 1 Q.B. 142; *Hickman* v. *Maisey*, [1900] 1 Q.B. 752.

[2] *The Queen* v. *Clark* (No. 2), [1964] 2 Q.B. 315.

[3] Highway Act 1835, ss. 72 and 78; Highways Act 1959, s. 121. The sections of the earlier Act remain in force, with amendments; 25th Sched.

[4] *Homer* v. *Cadman* (1886), 16 Cox C.C. 51.

[5] *M'Ara* v. *Magistrates of Edinburgh*, 1913 S.C. 1059. The powers given to police officers for the control of processions by s. 3 of the Public Order Act 1936 are in Scotland exercised by magistrates.

[6] *Aldred* v. *Miller*, 1924 J.C. 117; a case where there was evidence of obstruction contrary to the express terms of a local Police Act. *Cf. Burden* v. *Rigler*, [1911] 1 K.B. 337.

the right of passing and re-passing along the highway. It will depend upon the facts of each case whether this constitutes a reasonable use of the highway and whether other members of the highway are obstructed thereby. On the other hand, a public meeting, if stationary, *prima facie* constitutes an obstruction and is therefore unreasonable, *i.e.* unlawful use of the highway, but there are public places which in law have been dedicated as part of the highway where a meeting need not constitute an obstruction, such as wide verges.

The present state of the law with regard to the right of public meetings and processions is in need of clarification on several points. The tendency which has been noted of prosecuting summarily those whose conduct threatens or causes a breach of the peace has resulted in most of the authorities being found among the cases decided by a Divisional Court on a case stated from a court of Petty or Quarter Sessions. It is only since 1960 that an appeal has been allowed to the House of Lords from a Divisional Court,[1] and most of this branch of the law has hitherto lacked a ruling beyond the Divisional Court.

Dicey's Views

When Dicey penned his last words on the right of public meeting in the form of a long note to his Eighth Edition [2] he supplemented his original statement of the law (to which he devoted Chapter VII, dealing mainly with the case of *Beatty* v. *Gillbanks* and the other cases already cited above) and discussed four questions which he regarded as important. These were: (1) Is there any general right of meeting in public places? (2) What is the meaning of the term "an unlawful assembly"? (3) What are the rights of the Crown or its servants in dealing with such an assembly? (4) What are the rights of members of a lawful assembly when the meeting is interfered with or dispersed by force?

Liability of Spectator

His answers to the first three questions contain little more than an elaboration of the case law. In answering the fourth question he emphasises the position of an innocent spectator attending a meeting. Whether or not a spectator can be successfully prosecuted for the offence of unlawful assembly will depend upon his knowledge of the character of the meeting. His presence may be accidental; he may be ignorant of the purpose of the meeting; the meeting may have assembled for a lawful purpose but have changed its character by

[1] Pp. 304 and 306, *ante*.
[2] Dicey, *op. cit.*, 8th edn., Appendix, note v, pp. 497–512.

the production of weapons or the outbreak of actual disorder; even so the spectator may have taken no part. But the law would seem to be that it is no defence against a charge of taking part in the meeting to plead ignorance of the fact that it was or became an unlawful assembly if steps have been taken to bring to the attention of bystanders that the meeting is convened for a criminal object.[1] Bearing in mind that it is not within the power even of a Secretary of State, much less a magistrate or a policeman, to declare a meeting unlawful in advance of its assembling (unless it is advertised for the promotion of criminal activities) the difficulties of prosecuting for the offence of unlawful assembly are great, if it is decided to prosecute anyone other than the speakers whose conduct is responsible for imparting the unlawful character to the assembly. Yet magistrates, policemen, and indeed all citizens, are not merely entitled but are under a legal duty to disperse such an assembly and if necessary to use force in so doing. This duty is emphasised if a riot has broken out.

Disorder at Lawful Meeting

The situation is much more difficult for a policeman or a steward provided by the promoters when a meeting assembled for an ostensibly lawful purpose degenerates into disorder. The duty to disperse or otherwise intervene does not arise until the situation becomes so threatening that by no other means than dispersal or arrest can the peace be preserved. It will always be a nicely balanced question—at what stage ought force to be used to preserve the peace? Once that stage is reached, then resistance becomes punishable not only by prosecution for the offence of unlawful assembly but also for the statutory offence under the Prevention of Crimes Acts 1871 and 1885 of obstruction of a police officer in the execution of his duty. In either case the prosecution should succeed if a police witness can give evidence that he reasonably feared that a breach of the peace was likely. It is easy to say that the zeal or the anxiety of a single constable may lead to a mistaken belief in the threat to the peace. It is not easy for the defence to show that the formation of a belief in the constable's mind was unreasonable unless by subsequent action it is shown that the conduct of the policeman was due to panic-stricken fear or a similar obsession.

This situation can best be illustrated by reference to the much-discussed decision in *Duncan* v. *Jones*.[2]

[1] *The King* v. *Fursey* (1833), 6 C. & P. 80.
[2] [1936] 1 K.B. 218; K. & L. 203.

Mrs. Duncan, a woman speaker, was forbidden on her arrival by Jones, a police officer, to hold a meeting at a place opposite a training centre for the unemployed. Fourteen months previously Mrs. Duncan had held a meeting at the same spot which had been followed by a disturbance in the centre attributed by the superintendent of the centre to the meeting. Mrs. Duncan mounted a box to start the meeting but was taken into custody and charged under the Prevention of Crimes Acts 1871 and 1885 with obstructing a police officer in the execution of his duty. There was no allegation of obstruction of the highway or of inciting or provoking any person to commit a breach of the peace. Quarter Sessions found (*a*) that Mrs. Duncan must have known of the probable consequences of her holding the meeting, viz. a disturbance and possibly a breach of the peace, and was not unwilling that such consequences should ensue, (*b*) that Jones reasonably apprehended a breach of the peace, (*c*) that in law it therefore became his duty to prevent the holding of the meeting, (*d*) that by attempting to hold the meeting Mrs. Duncan obstructed Jones when in the execution of his duty. On appeal to the Divisional Court it was held that Mrs. Duncan had been rightly convicted.

On one view it would seem that the so-called right of public meeting disappears if the suspicions of a policeman on the spot are aroused. But the finding that Mrs. Duncan must have known of the probable consequences of her holding the meeting and was not unwilling that such consequences should ensue may possibly limit the authority of this decision to those cases where it can be shown that the defendant has been responsible of causing a disorder on a previous occasion. Even this is not satisfactory from the point of view of free expression of opinion because it means that speakers are being convicted for past misconduct irrespective of whether they have committed an offence on the occasion which has given rise to the charge. The members of the Salvation Army whose conduct was vindicated in *Beatty* v. *Gillbanks* would, on this view, still be protected because their previous conduct had led to a disturbance or breach of the peace not by the Salvationists or their supporters but only by their opponents. But any advocate of an unpopular cause who may once have fallen foul of the police, and in particular anyone who on a previous occasion has been bound over by a court to keep the peace, would seem to stand little chance of failing to arouse suspicion, and so reasonable fear, of a breach of the peace in the mind of any policeman who was aware of his identity. The threat to liberty contained in *Duncan* v. *Jones* comes from the finding as to Mrs. Duncan's knowledge of the consequences being reached without any allegation even of obstruction of the highway by her, much less of incitement or provocation by her of any person to commit a breach of the peace. Her conduct *on the occasion in question* seems to have been as impeccable as that of the Salvationists. It is also significant that both Quarter Sessions and the Divisional Court were in doubt whether the defendant's knowledge of the consequences was a material fact. If it was not, the conviction must have rested solely on the fact that the policeman reasonably apprehended a breach of the peace. It must, however, be admitted there there had been a disturbance in the nearby training centre on the first occasion when Mrs. Duncan had addressed a meeting at that particular spot, and that attempts to hold subsequent meetings had been frustrated by the police. This does go some way towards equating the position of the defendant to that of the Skeleton Army, who should have been proceeded against on the occasion of the clash which led to the decision in *Beatty* v. *Gillbanks*.[1]

Dilemma of Police

However much one sympathises with the wish to preserve freedom of expression of opinion, it must be agreed that the lot of the policeman, or exceptionally of the magistrate who has been called upon to intervene, as so often in the days before organised police forces, is a difficult one. If he fails to take steps to preserve order and to prevent injuries to person or property, he may be prosecuted, and, in the case of the policeman, is almost certain to incur the displeasure of his superiors and may possibly be dealt with under the police disciplinary code. If his belief is shown to be unreasonable and consequently no duty to disperse or otherwise intervene can have arisen, he may be sued for trespass and may be false imprisonment, or even malicious prosecution. The plea of superior orders is unlikely to be accepted if such orders were of a general character as distinct from a specific command to do something which was not necessarily or manifestly illegal.[2]

The ambiguity suggests that the right to hold a public meeting as the law stands to-day can only safely be exercised if prior police approval is obtained or, at least in the case of meetings held on private premises off the highway, if the services of a policeman have been engaged. It is most unlikely that a senior police officer would authorise a prosecution of the promoters of a meeting in such circumstances. If disorder actually broke out, proceedings would be taken against the opponents rather than the promoters. Promo-

[1] See T. C. Daintith, *Disobeying a Policeman, a Fresh Look at Duncan* v. *Jones*, [1966] *Public Law* 248, where it is argued that the statutory offence of obstructing the police was not framed to give extra powers in preserving public order.

[2] *Keighley* v. *Bell* (1866), 4 F. & F. 763; a case, however, which dealt with the liability of a soldier acting under the orders of an officer.

ters of unpopular causes are not usually willing to seek previous police approval, and there is certainly no legal requirement to compel them to do so. But it rests with the police to intervene, not merely on account of an actual or apprehended breach of the peace, but even for the minor offence of causing an obstruction on the highway if the meeting be held there. It may be suggested that this ambiguous situation could best be met by a more generous provision of facilities for public meetings, especially in areas where the hiring of halls is not possible. Just as London has its Hyde Park Corner where the policy of toleration is exemplified at its best, so similar facilities could be made available in all large towns. Is it too much to suggest that the free use of school premises for meetings of candidates at election time could be extended? It is easier to ensure that eloquence does not provoke disorder in circumstances where admission can be controlled, if need be, by ticket. The risk of an outdoor meeting attracting undesirable attention in any crowded district is obvious.

Admission to Meetings

Control of the right of admission to meetings has been the subject of statements by the authorities and findings by the judges on more than one occasion in the present century. At one time the official view in the Home Office was that "the law provides that, unless the promoters of a meeting ask the police to be present in the actual meeting, they cannot go in, unless they have reason to believe that an actual breach of the peace is being committed in the meeting." [1]

This statement was the sequel to disorder which occurred at a Fascist meeting in the Albert Hall, London, when the stewards of the promoters of the meeting inflicted physical violence on dissentients in the audience. No police were stationed on the premises, though large numbers had been assembled in nearby streets. Within a year the courts disapproved of the Home Office view of the law.

The facts in *Thomas* v. *Sawkins* [2] were that a meeting was advertised in a Welsh town for the purpose (1) of protesting against the Incitement to Disaffection Bill which was then before Parliament, and (2) to demand the dismissal of the Chief Constable of the County (Glamorgan). Admission to the meeting was open to the public without payment. In view of the second purpose of the meeting it was not surprising that the police arranged for some of their number to attend. The promoter requested the police officers to leave. A constable committed a technical assault on the promoter thinking that the promoter was on the point of employing force to remove a superior police officer from the room. There was no allegation that any

[1] 290 H.C. Deb., col. 1968.
[2] [1935] 2 K.B. 249.

criminal offence had been committed by any person at the meeting at any time or that any breach of the peace had occurred. The finding in the magistrates' court was that the police had reasonable grounds for believing that if they were not present at the meeting there would be seditious speeches and other incitement to violence and that breaches of the peace would occur; that the police were entitled to enter and remain in the hall throughout the meeting; and that consequently the constable did not unlawfully assault the promoter. On a case stated to the Divisional Court these findings were upheld. The Lord Chief Justice (Lord Hewart) was of opinion that the police have power to enter and to remain on private premises when they have reasonable grounds for believing that the commission of an offence is imminent; nor did he limit this statement to offences involving a breach of the peace. Mr. Justice Avory citing the many statutes which have given the police express powers of entry noted that these were all cases where a breach of the peace was not necessarily involved; hence the need for express statutory authority. If the former view is correct, there would seem no need for any statutory authorisation.

Although the second objective of the meeting in *Thomas* v. *Sawkins* was admittedly provocative to the local police, it did not suggest an incitement to violence which it is necessary to prove in order to succeed in a prosecution for sedition. Nor need a protest against a Bill punishing sedition necessarily involve a breach of the peace.

Apart from express statutory authorisation there is no other authority for extending the power of the police to enter premises where meetings are being held, unless an offence involving violence or a breach of the peace has occurred or is apprehended, but in the absence of a ruling by a higher court it does seem that the case has extended the common law which only enabled the police to enter private premises to deal with offences which endanger the public peace. Sedition or seditious libel is a common law offence and if Lord Hewart is right, the police can now enter on suspicion of the commission of any offence whether or not it involves a breach of the peace. Here is a situation where the law has been left in a state which calls for a clear restatement.

Attendance of Police

There is another aspect of the effect of the decision in *Thomas* v. *Sawkins* on liberty of discussion. The court, rejecting the view that the police cannot be present unless invited to attend, found that any meeting which is advertised as open to the public can be attended by all members of the public including members of the police force. But in this case the promoter specifically asked those particular members of the public to withdraw and thereby rescinded the open invitation. Did not this make the officers concerned trespassers on private premises from that point onwards? At all events, if a ticket holder who has not paid for admission has his invitation withdrawn, he can be ejected with reasonable force if he declines to leave. There is moreover a slightly later authority for the proposition that the power of entry by the police into private premises does not extend to cases where a summary offence which does not involve a breach of the peace has been committed, even if the offence took place on an adjacent highway.

In *Davis* v. *Lisle*[1] a lorry had been left on the highway outside a garage. A constable went into the garage to make enquiries about the obstruction which he thought had been caused by two employees of the owner of the garage. The constable had of course no warrant to enter, nor did he ask permission from the proprietor who told him to leave. The case came before a magistrates' court on a charge of assault against the proprietor who resisted the demand of the constable to remain. Lord Hewart was again a member of the Divisional Court which held that the constable became a trespasser as soon as he was asked to leave. He could accordingly be removed with no undue force and, as he was not acting in the execution of his duty, no charge of obstructing him could be sustained.

If the law is that the belief of a single policeman that a seditious speech (according to Lord Hewart, the commission of any offence) irrespective of an actual threat to the peace entitles him to remain on the premises, it is easy to see that a Chief Constable could assert a right of entry into most political meetings and probably all others where the purpose of the meeting was to advocate an unpopular cause; for it must be remembered that the definition of the offence of sedition is wide enough to include the promotion of feelings of ill will and hostility between different classes of the community.[2] This view however disregards the need to establish incitement to violence as an ingredient of the offence. This is certainly a long way from the conception of liberty which derives from the guarantee that no man can be punished unless he has committed some definitely assignable legal offence. It may be that preventive measures cannot be reconciled with this conception of liberty and thus that the real guarantee lies in the good sense of those who are responsible for the maintenance of order. It should however be remembered that the power to compel a person to enter into an undertaking to keep the peace or to be of good behaviour still lies, as it has done ever since

[1] [1936] 2 K.B. 434; for police entry on to private premises, see *Robson* v. *Hallett*, [1967] 2 Q.B. 939.

[2] P. 513, *ante*. Dicey, *op. cit.*, p. 244; Stephen, *Digest of the Criminal Law*, 9th edn., article 114.

1361, with the magistrates and there is naturally a reluctance to admit that such a power should be exercised by a policeman. But this power derives from long before the time of organised police forces.

Binding Over

Magistrates have a wide power to order any person, including witnesses in proceedings, to enter into a recognisance (undertaking) with or without sureties to keep the peace or to be of good behaviour either in general or to a particular person.[1] In the latter case reasonable apprehension of personal danger is not essential to the exercise of the power. On refusal to enter into a recognisance there may be imposed by a court of summary jurisdiction a committal to prison for a term not exceeding six months.[2] A person bound over must at least be told what is passing through the mind of the magistrate and given a chance of answering.[3] The origin of this power is obscure; it may rest upon the Justices of the Peace Act 1361 or may be inherent in the commission of the peace held by magistrates. It appears that it is not necessary to show that there has been anything done calculated to lead to violence.

In *The King* v. *Sandbach, ex parte Williams*,[4] the offender had despite warnings and previous convictions for obstructing the police repeatedly advised a street bookmaker of the approach of the police and so enabled him to avoid arrest. It was held that a magistrate may properly bind a man over whenever it is apprehended that he is likely to commit a breach of the peace or do something contrary to law.

It is curious that there is no firm definition of what constitutes a breach of the peace but on the analogy of the Queen's Peace it would certainly include every crime.[5] In Scotland it has been held to constitute a breach of the peace to peer into lighted windows after nightfall.[6] The definition of an affray, which is a crime, may be of some assistance, *i.e.* a public offence to the terror of the Queen's subjects, but there is no power to arrest after an affray is over unless there are reasonable grounds for apprehending its continuance. Whatever be the definition, a surety to keep the peace seems to be limited to potential breaches of the peace by assaults or threats including fear.

[1] *Lansbury* v. *Riley*, [1914] 3 K.B. 229.
[2] Magistrates' Courts Act 1952, s. 91.
[3] *Sheldon* v. *Bromfield*, [1964] 2 Q.B. 573.
[4] [1935] 2. K.B. 192.
[5] *Jordan* v. *Burgoyne*, [1963] 2 Q.B. 744, a case of a breach caused by the use of deliberately insulting words; see p. 547, *ante*.
[6] *Raffaelli* v. *Heatley*, 49 S.L.T. 284. There is no definition given in Archbold, *Criminal Pleading, Evidence and Practice*.

Since the making of an order to keep the peace does not constitute a conviction, there was until statutory provision was made in 1956 no right of appeal open to the person bound over.[1] In 1956, however, provision for appeal to Quarter Sessions against an order binding a person over was provided by the Magistrates' Courts (Appeals from Binding Over Orders) Act.

Riot and Affray

Riot is a common law offence punishable with imprisonment. The elements essential to constitute a riot are five in number: (1) the presence of not less than three persons, (2) a common purpose, (3) execution or attempted execution of the common purpose, (4) an intent to help one another, by force if necessary, against anyone who may oppose them in the execution of the common purpose, (5) force or violence displayed in such manner as to alarm at least one person of reasonable firmness.[2] It has been doubted whether it is necessary to prove the alarm of any person, at all events if the riot danger is obvious. On a charge of an affray direct evidence of such alarm is not necessary.[3] An affray which is a common law offence is a fight in a public place or on private premises between two or more persons to the terror of the Queen's subjects, *i.e.* of innocent third parties who neither participate nor encourage the fighting.[4] A rout is a similar offence, *i.e.* a disturbance of the peace by three or more persons who assemble with an intent to do something which if executed will amount to a riot and who actually make a move towards the execution of their common purpose.

Damage done by Rioters

Formerly compensation for damage done to property by rioters was payable by the Hundred, an ancient division of a county. The Riot (Damages) Act 1886 entitles property owners to recover compensation out of the county or borough funds (police expenses), thus throwing the burden on to the general body of the ratepayers. In a claim for compensation under this Act it was held that acts which constitute a riot when committed by civilians equally constitute a riot when committed by soldiers, notwithstanding that the acts may take place at a military camp in England during time of war.[5]

[1] *The King* v. *County of London Quarter Sessions Appeals Committee, ex parte Metropolitan Police Commissioner*, [1948] 1 K.B. 670, a case of binding over to be of good behaviour.

[2] *Field* v. *Receiver of the Metropolitan Police*, [1907] 2 K.B. 853.

[3] *The Queen* v. *Sharp and Johnson* (1957), 41 C.A.R. 86.

[4] Hawkins, *Pleas of the Crown*, c. 63, s. 1. *Button* v. *Director of Public Prosecutions*, *Swain* v. *D.P.P.*, [1966] A.C. 591.

[5] *Pitchers* v. *Surrey County Council*, [1923] 2 K.B. 57.

Duty to Disperse Unlawful Assemblies and Riots

It is the duty of every citizen and the special duty of magistrates and police officers to suppress unlawful and disorderly assemblies.[1] A magistrate or police officer must hit the exact line between excess and failure of duty and is guilty of criminal neglect if he fails to judge rightly.[2] Soldiers have the same duty as other citizens to suppress riots, but it is desirable that they, like civilians, should act in subordination to a magistrate and that an officer in charge of troops should not order recourse to arms on his own initiative, unless the danger is pressing and immediate.

[1] *Charge to the Bristol Grand Jury* (1832), 5 C. & P. 261; K. & L. 208.

[2] *The King* v. *Pinney* (1832), 5 C. & P. 254; K. & L. 211. It is not the practice to prosecute a private citizen for failure to take action on his own initiative.

CHAPTER THIRTY-NINE

THE LAW RELATING TO OBSCENITY

AT first sight it is not obvious that obscenity should be a subject of constitutional interest. The reason is that it illustrates well the clash between the right of the individual freely to express his opinions and the duty of the State to safeguard public morals. To put it another way, it is equally the duty of the State to safeguard freedom of expression by the individual and to see that youth is not corrupted.

The law relating to obscene publications, like the law of blasphemy, dates from a less tolerant age. To-day the enforcement of the law of blasphemy seems to be a matter of the past and in view of the decision in *Bowman* v. *Secular Society*[1] it has long been lawful to attack the fundamentals of any religion, provided that the decencies of controversy are observed, without fear of being found guilty of a blasphemous libel. Until 1959 the attitude of the law to obscenity failed to distinguish between noxious material which might possess scientific, literary or artistic merit and pornographic literature. By modern standards the inclusion of such material in, for example, scientific publications and, more doubtfully, works of literature or art is generally regarded as unobjectionable.

Nature of Offence

It was a common law misdemeanour to publish obscene matter. The Obscene Publications Act 1959 put the offence on a statutory footing, and provided that it may be punished either on indictment or summarily. Apart from some cases at Guildhall, there is no record of an obscene libel being punished at common law until 1727. The reason for this was that matters of obscenity, and indeed all matters concerning public morals, were originally within the jurisdiction of the ecclesiastical courts.[2]

History

The evidence given before the Select Committee on the Obscene Publications Bill 1957, which was the outcome of cases heard in 1954,[3] included a Memorandum on Obscenity submitted by

[1] [1917] A.C. 406.
[2] *Curll's Case*, 17 St. Tr. 153.
[3] P. 568, *post*.

Sir Alan Herbert on behalf of the Society of Authors.[1] From this it would seem that before the invention of printing in the fifteenth century the topic did not present a social problem, and so far as offences of this character were concerned they were punished by the ecclesiastical courts, but were treated as matters of minor importance compared with heresy. Control of the printing press for long continued to be a matter dealt with by the Executive under the prerogative. The monopoly of all printing which was granted by the Crown to the Stationers' Company in 1556 required the Company to seek out and suppress all printers of seditious and heretical works, but no mention is found of action being taken against obscenity before 1595, when a printer was punished for printing a lewd book. The Crown was throughout the Tudor period in a position to enforce its decrees with regard to matters falling under the Royal Prerogative through the Privy Council, and in particular the Court of Star Chamber. The jurisdiction of the Court of Star Chamber was abolished in 1640 by the Long Parliament, but there is hardly any reference right up to that date of any punishment having been imposed for obscenity. The control of printing so far as it had actually been relaxed was restored at the Restoration. The Licensing Act 1662 controlled the printing of books for the next thirty years. When Parliament failed to renew it in 1694, such control as remained was enforced through the criminal law, and particularly by prosecutions for seditious libel, but the ecclesiastical courts exercised their old jurisdiction in heresy and obscene offences. It was not until 1727 in *Curll's Case* [2] that the common law jurisdiction was decisively asserted and the court took the view that it was an offence at common law to publish a book which tended to corrupt morals and was against the King's peace. That peace could be broken in many instances without actual force if the act was against the civil government or against religion or against morality. It was not until *Hicklin's Case* one hundred and forty years later that any attempt was made to define obscenity, and no case of importançe seems to have been reported between the two dates. During this long interval a great change had come over the attitude towards matters of public behaviour. Although Victorianism to some extent antedated the accession of the Queen, no attack on serious literature was made by the law. The view, at all events, of the Society of Authors is that a most complete censorship was exercised by a prudish public opinion, as witness the outbursts which greeted not only Swinburne for his poems and ballads, but Tennyson for *Maud*, George Eliot for *Adam*

[1] H.C. 122 (1957), at pp. 91–96.
[2] 17 St. Tr. 153.

Bede, and Meredith for *Modern Love*. Prosecutions of serious literature as opposed to pornography only date from the 1880s, by which time public opinion was beginning to be less prudish.

The Hicklin Test

The principal difficulty derived from a decision of the courts in the middle of the last century which laid down the test for determining whether a publication constituted an obscene libel as

> whether the tendency of the matter charged as obscene is to deprave and corrupt those whose minds are open to such immoral influences and into whose hands a publication of this sort may fall.

This was the test propounded in *The Queen* v. *Hicklin* by Chief Justice Cockburn.[1]

Whatever the difficulties of applying the Hicklin test or any other definition the issue of corruption of public morals is for the jury and therefore to some extent the public is the judge of whether or not a publication exceeds the requirements of the public good, but prosecutions for the actual offence of publishing an obscene libel are, generally speaking, few and far between. The reason for this is to be found in the Obscene Publications Act 1857,[2] which conferred summary powers of seizure and destruction stopping short of the prosecution and consequent punishment on conviction of those responsible for the publication. By this statute a magistrates' court (two or more justices or a stipendiary magistrate), on receiving a complaint on oath that the complainant believed that obscene publications were kept for sale in any place and that one or more of such publications had been sold and on being satisfied that publication would constitute a misdemeanour (*i.e.* that of the misdemeanour of publishing an obscene libel) and proper to be prosecuted as such, was empowered to give authority to a constable to search the premises by day and to seize the publications and bring them before the court. No prosecution needed to ensue, but the occupier of the premises, who would not usually be the author or even the publisher of the offending material, had to be summoned to appear within seven days to show cause why the publications should not be destroyed. If the court was satisfied that the publications were obscene and were kept for the purpose of sale, it might order them to be destroyed; otherwise they would be returned to the occupier. It is to be noted that no one could be convicted of any offence under this Act, the only positive result being the destruction of obscene works.

[1] *The Queen* v. *Hicklin* (1868), L.R. 3 Q.B. 360, at p. 371.

[2] Repealed but re-enacted in amended form by Obscene Publication Acts 1959. See pp. 571–3, *post*.

Other provisions relate to publications harmful to children and young persons which have already been considered under the title of restrictions on reporting,[1] or to seizure by the Commissioners of Customs under the Customs and Excise Act 1952, s. 275 enforcing the prohibition under the Customs and Excise of indecent or obscene material which dates from the Customs Consolidation Act 1876, s. 42; there are similar provisions to prevent the use of the postal services for the transmission of such material.[2]

The difficulties of applying the Hicklin test were well illustrated by a series of cases which came before the courts in 1954. Thus in *The Queen* v. *Reiter* [3] the Court of Criminal Appeal took the view that a jury should direct their attention to the result of an obscene publication falling into the hands of young people, but a few months later Mr. Justice Stable in charging the jury in *The Queen* v. *Secker, Warburg Ltd.*[4] asked the jury to consider what the test meant: "Are we to take our literary standards as being the level of something that is suitable for the decently-brought-up female aged fourteen? Or do we go even further back than that and are we to be reduced to the sort of books that one reads as a child in the nursery?"

He answered these rhetorical questions in the negative. "A mass of literature, great literature from many angles, is wholly unsuitable for reading by the adolescent, but that does not mean that the publisher is guilty of a criminal offence for making those works available to the general public." In the same year another judge specifically referred to the effect a work might have on young persons, while yet another (Mr. Justice Devlin) said more than once in a summing up that what the jury had to consider was the effect of the work on the minds of ordinary men. The critical question is whether an intention to corrupt public morals is a necessary ingredient. Since the law presumes a person to intend the natural consequence of his act, it must be a formidable task to rebut the presumption, once the act of publication and the tendency of the matter to deprave and corrupt has been proved by the prosecution. There was until the Act of 1959 no authoritative decision that it was a defence to show that the publication of matter *prima facie* obscene was for the public good as being necessary or advantageous to religion, science, literature or art, provided that the manner and extent of the publication did not exceed what the public good required.

[1] Chap. 36, *ante*.
[2] Post Office Act 1953, ss. 11.
[3] [1954] 2 Q.B. 16.
[4] (1954), 38 C.A.R. 124, 128.

It was suggested that this alleged defence was no more than a facet of the ordinary law of obscenity to which attention was drawn in *Hicklin's Case* when Cockburn, C.J., said that a medical treatise may in a certain sense be obscene and yet not the subject of indictment, although it could not be exhibited for girls and boys to see; he said that immunity for such a work depended upon the circumstances of publication.[1] It is unnecessary to refer again in detail to the Children and Young Persons (Harmful Publications) Act 1955 [2] except to repeat that the test to be applied is much the same as that laid down in *Hicklin's Case*, save that the work is to be adjudged as a whole for the purpose of determining whether it would tend to corrupt a child or young person into whose hands it might fall. As the offence created by the Act is not punishable on indictment, it is for a magistrates' court (a stipendiary magistrate or two or more justices) to apply this test.

Summary Procedure

The Obscene Publications Act of 1857 (Lord Campbell's Act) followed on a number of prosecutions to check the flourishing business of pornography in the Victorian underworld. In commending the measure Lord Campbell said that it was designed to apply "exclusively to works written for the single purpose of corrupting the morals of youth and of a nature calculated to shock the common feelings of decency in a well-regulated mind." The summary procedure thus made available has not always been used to obtain the destruction of books which clearly come within this "single purpose," and there is no doubt that on occasions the censorship of the magistrates' court has not agreed with public opinion upon standards of morality. The present senior editor gave it as his view thirty years ago, "It is questionable whether such powers ought ever to be entrusted to a single magistrate or to justices of the peace whose judgment through bigotry or ignorance may thus imperil the destruction of scientific or other knowledge."[3] In this connection it should be noted that an order for destruction could, until 1959, only be made by a magistrates' court if the court was satisfied that the articles for which the order was sought were of such a character and description that their publication would be a misdemeanour proper to be prosecuted. The Act preceded by eleven

[1] Home Office Memorandum to Select Committee on the Obscene Publications Bill, 1957, H.C. 122 (1957), at p. 3.

[2] P. 525, *ante*.

[3] Dicey, *Law of the Constitution*, 9th edn., Appendix, Liberty of Discussion, p. 581.

years the Hicklin definition of what constituted the misdemeanour, and therefore it would appear that Parliament in 1857 was requiring the court to apply a test which had not been used for a prosecution since *Curll's Case* in 1727 where, as we have seen,[1] the court made no attempt to define obscenity. But over ninety years the Hicklin definition of obscenity applied as well to the misdemeanour as to destruction orders by summary process.

Literature v. *Pornography*

How far did this definition stand in the way of satisfying the requirement that there ought to be a distinction between pornography and literature? If the administration of the law was always wise enough to leave matters of literary taste to the judgment of the literary public and limit prosecutions to the purveyors of pornography, the definition might still serve. This definition [2] says nothing about the intention of the publisher. Primarily the test is the tendency to deprave and corrupt, irrespective of the motive of the publisher. Once a book is published there can be little or no control to prevent its falling into the hands "of those whose minds are open to immoral influences." If the offending matter is contained in a scientific, medical or other technical book or in a volume which could properly be classed as literature, it would be difficult to establish an intention in the publisher to commit the offence. But as the law has been interpreted the publisher's motive is irrelevant and his intention to commit the crime is inferred from the fact of publication. To require in any statutory definition a specific intent to deprave and corrupt would not meet the criticism satisfactorily because, in the words of Sir Alan Herbert, "No writer, publisher, printer or bookseller says to himself 'I am going to corrupt,' or even 'I am not going to corrupt my readers or customers.' " A serious author or artist is more concerned lest his work be criticised as inartistic rather than condemned as illegal. On the other hand the writer of pornography as well as the designer of smutty postcards knows that the commercial success of his work is dependent upon the creation of "inordinate and lustful desires." [3] One solution would be to omit from the definition all reference to the tendency to deprave and corrupt and in substitution state a dominant purpose or effect. If the author, publisher or artist can be made responsible for the publication of a book or picture, the dominant purpose or

[1] P. 566, *ante*. [2] P. 567, *ante*.
[3] H.C. 122 (1957), p. 146. Supplementary Memorandum by Sir Alan Herbert.

effect of which is to provoke lustful desires among those to whom it was intended to appeal, it should suffice to bring home the crime to those engaged in the business of pornography. At the same time, the serious writer at all events would escape attack on account of incidental passages of doubtful taste or worse, unless they could be shown to contaminate the whole volume and so destroy its artistic merits as a literary work. One can sympathise with the suggestion of Sir Alan Herbert that any legislation designed to redefine the offence of publishing an obscene libel should contain a preamble contrasting the purpose of those who produce works of art, literature, science and history with those who, for the sake of gain, deliberately publish matter injurious to morals.[1] The presence of such a preamble would at the least reduce the temptation for any judge to strain the statutory definition in the summing up to a jury who were asked to condemn a serious work on account of a few doubtful passages.

The Act of 1959

The Obscene Publications Act 1959 was introduced by a private member in the House of Commons. The definition now reads as follows:

> For the purposes of this Act an article (this includes a book) shall be deemed to be obscene if its effect or (where the article comprises two or more distinct items) the effect of any one of its items, is, if taken as a whole, such as to tend to deprave and corrupt persons who are likely, having regard to all relevant circumstances, to read, see or hear the matter contained or embodied in it (s. 1 (1)).

By way of comment it is still controversial, as it was before the Act, whether the price of the article, the place of purchase or the circumstances of publication should be taken into consideration. By reason doubtless of the strong feeling that there is need to suppress pornography the penalties upon those who publish, whether for gain or not, an obscene article may be severe. On summary conviction a fine not exceeding £100 or imprisonment for a term not exceeding six months may be imposed. A person convicted on indictment may be fined an unlimited amount or sentenced to imprisonment of up to three years, or may suffer both penalties. It is the intention that the Act shall supersede the common law, which has been open to so much criticism on account of the Hicklin test.[2] It is provided that no prosecution shall be brought for an offence at common law

[1] But see defence of public good: Obscene Publications Act 1959, s. 4.

[2] P. 567, *ante*. For the unsuccessful prosecution of D. H. Lawrence's *Lady Chatterley's Lover* see the reprint of the trial as a Penguin book, *The Trial of Lady Chatterley*.

consisting of the publication of any matter contained or embodied in an article where it is of the essence of the offence that the matter is obscene (s. 2 (4)). While this would seem to ensure the burial of the Hicklin test, there are a number of other statutes surviving, such as the Vagrancy Act 1824, s. 4, the Customs and Excise Act 1952, s. 44, to which the new definition does not apply until such time as the law of obscenity has been consolidated and codified.

The long title of the 1959 Act includes not only the amendment of the law relating to the publication of obscene matter, but also provision for the protection of literature and the strengthening of the law concerning pornography. There is no separate definition of pornography, and accordingly the test of obscenity must be applied. Section 3 strengthens the summary procedure under the Obscene Publications Act 1857 which is repealed. A warrant may be issued for seizure and search of premises, stalls or vehicles where it is suspected that obscene articles are kept for publication for gain. In order for the prosecution to secure a seizure and destruction order, it is no longer necessary to prove a sale. Accordingly the stocks of both wholesaler and retailer come under the summary procedure.[1] Evidence of likely use is to be regarded in determining what is obscene for the purposes of obtaining a summary order for destruction. The warrant to seize articles believed to be obscene also now empowers the seizure and removal of any documents found in the premises, stall or vehicle which relate to a trade or business carried on there. Formerly it was impossible to seize books of account to show the extent of the trade. It was a defect of the old procedure that the author was unable to appear before the summary court to show cause why alleged obscene articles should not be forfeited. Now cause against forfeiture may be shown by any person, in addition to the person summoned, being the owner, author or maker of the articles or a person through whose hands they have passed before being seized. In addition to a right of appeal to quarter sessions against an order for destruction, the making of the order may be challenged by way of case stated for the opinion of the High Court. This is the same machinery as under the Act of 1857. The court has power to award costs against an unsuccessful complainant on whose information the warrant for seizure has been issued. In this way the author who exercises his right of appearing before the court to show cause why his book should not be forfeited may, if successful in his submission, cover the cost of his appearance.

[1] Application for a warrant can only be made by the Director of Public Prosecution or by the police. A private citizen must prosecute under s. 2 for obscene publication, an offence triable by jury.

A significant change from the common law is given by s. 4 which provides the defence of public good. A conviction for an offence and an order for forfeiture under the Act shall not be made if it is proved that publication of the article is justified as being for the public good on the ground that it is in the interests of science, literature, art or learning or of other objects of general concern. A jury does not have to consider this defence until it has come to the conclusion that the publication is obscene taken as a whole as required by section 1 of the Act.[1] The opinion of experts as to such merit is admissible in any proceedings under the Act, either to establish or negative the defence. Hitherto there has been some doubt as to the admissibility of what is in reality the opinion of experts in cases of obscenity. There is no doubt that the campaign against pornography will be assisted by the new provisions for search and seizure. The other object of the Act, the protection of literature, science and art, is certainly assisted by that part of the definition which requires an article to be taken as a whole before judging whether it tends to deprave or corrupt. It is unlikely that the legislature in a matter of taste and morals can provide a complete solution which will satisfy those who would strive to the utmost for the protection of literature, and those, perhaps the narrower section of the community, who are alive to the evils which flow from trade in pornographic articles.

Operation of Act of 1959

It was not long before the Act of 1959 was shown to be deficient in certain particulars. In the first place it proved impossible to obtain a conviction for publishing an obscene article under the test of obscenity laid down in Section 1 in cases where the publication took place to police officers who from their long experience of handling such matters were not susceptible of corruption by the article.[2] It was further held that no offence was committed by the mere exposure of an obscene article for sale.[3] The Obscene Publications Act 1964 made it an offence under Section 2 of the 1959 Act, for a person to have an obscene article for publication for gain; the question whether an article is obscene is to be determined by reference to any publication which may reasonably be said to have been in the contemplation of the accused. The 1964 Act also extended the earlier Act to cover things intended to be used for the

[1] *The Queen* v. *Calder and Boyars Ltd.*, [1969] 1 Q.B. 151. The judgment of Salmon, L.J., shows the difficulty of interpreting this section.

[2] *The Queen* v. *Clayton*, [1963] 1 Q.B. 163.

[3] *Mella* v. *Monahan*, [1961] *Criminal Law Review* 175.

reproduction or manufacture of obscene articles, *i.e.* photographic negatives. These changes in no way detract from the defence that publication is in the interests of science, literature, art or learning, but are solely aimed at strengthening the law against the flood of pornographic trash.

Public Mischief

From time to time in the history of the common law the judges have enlarged by their decisions the category of crimes for which there was neither previous precedent nor statutory authority. An important example of this judicial legislation in the field of public morality is the offence known as public mischief. In the nature of things this offence is characterized by vagueness and uncertainty of definition.[1] In 1962 the House of Lords upheld a conviction for conspiracy to corrupt public morals as being an offence known to the common law.[2] At least one of the judges was prepared to support the proposition that the corruption of public morals is in itself a crime. Three others based their decision on the principle that a conspiracy to commit acts not in themselves criminal or tortious and which are nevertheless "unlawful" is a crime. In this case the prosecution was based on paid advertisements by prostitutes appearing in a magazine. This practice is not in itself illegal. Thus by using the crime of conspiracy it is possible for the judges to enlarge the category of unlawful acts, the commission of which, at all events by conspirators, can be punished under the criminal law. This decision seems to emphasise the function of the courts as custodians of morals. The difficulty is that there is no certainty as to what morally reprehensible conduct constitutes an offence against the law of the land. From the constitutional point of view the important principle is that an act is criminal only if prohibited by a law in force at the time of its commission. But there is something to be said in favour of the administration of justice relying upon the sentiments of a jury who may be expected to reflect the prejudices as well as the reasoned convictions of society in general.

[1] *The King* v. *Manley*, [1933] 1 K.B. 529—conviction for misleading the police by false allegations.

[2] *Shaw* v. *Director of Public Prosecutions*, [1962] A.C. 220—the Ladies' Directory case.

CHAPTER FORTY

SPECIAL SECURITY MEASURES[1]

The Security Service [2]

The Security Service is not established by statute nor is it recognised by common law. Thus there is no mention of its existence in such relevant statutes as the Official Secrets Acts,[3] which create offences relating to espionage. The cardinal principle of operations is that the Service is to be used solely for the purpose of the defence of the realm. It has been said that the Service does not exist to pry into any man's private conduct or business affairs nor into his political opinions except in so far as they are subversive, *i.e.* they would contemplate the overthrow of the Government by unlawful means. The members of the Service have no special powers of arrest or search such as the police have; indeed in the eyes of the law they are ordinary citizens with no powers greater than anyone else. In numbers the Service is comparatively small. It is essentially a professional organisation charged with the task of countering espionage, subversion and sabotage. The absence of special powers and the small size of the Service have made essential close co-operation with the police forces and in particular in London with the Special Branch of the Metropolitan Police. Elsewhere the co-operation is with Chief Constables. If, for example, a search warrant is required by a member of the Security Service, it is granted to a constable. The police alone are entrusted with executive power.

Ministerial Responsibility

In the past there has been considerable misapprehension about ministerial responsibility for this Service. Since the purpose of the Service is the defence of the realm, responsibility should lie on the Secretary of State for Defence or the Prime Minister as chairman of the Defence and Overseas Policy Committee of the Cabinet. As a result of the experience of the Second World War, ultimate

[1] See D. G. T. Williams, *Not in the Public Interest*, Part 2 for a critical survey of the Security Service, and *Individual Rights and National Security*, by David C. Jackson, 20 M.L.R. pp. 364–79.

[2] The principal source of information is contained in Part II of Lord Denning's Report, Cmnd. 2152 (1963).

[3] Pp. 526–8, *ante*.

responsibility was left with the Prime Minister, but the Security Service became the responsibility of the Home Secretary chiefly because the functions of the Service are more closely allied to those of the Home Office, which has the ultimate constitutional responsibility for defending the realm against subversive activities and for preserving law and order.[1] In 1964 there was set up by the Prime Minister a new Security Commission which is required for assistance to the Prime Minister to investigate and report upon the circumstances in which a breach of security is known to have occurred in the public services or there is good reason to believe that it has occurred (apart from court proceedings). It is the function of this Commission to examine any failure of departmental security arrangements and to advise whether any change is necessary or desirable. The first members of the Commission were a High Court Judge, a former Secretary to the Cabinet and a former First Sea Lord.

Application to Public Servants

Freedom of political belief is perhaps the most important aspect of liberty of opinion. Although it follows from the need to secure impartial service to succeeding Governments on the part of civil servants that they should be prohibited from accepting parliamentary candidature and should otherwise abstain from active participation in politics so long as they are in touch with Ministers of the Crown and those who work in close contact with them in the Departments, it has not until recently been found necessary to investigate the political beliefs of anyone in the public service.[2] But to-day the holding of a belief in communism or in fascism is regarded as endangering the stability of the State. Indeed a Communist Party member is commonly believed to be under an obligation to the Party to achieve the establishment of a communist regime, if necessary by force. If one accepts the view that force comprises cold war as well as hot war, it is easy to see why even in times of nominal peace it is necessary to exclude an active communist from the higher posts in many government departments and from other activities in any way related to national defence or security. Accordingly there has sprung up since the Second World War the practice of screening systematically candidates for the public services and serving officers in posts which involve the handling of security material. If, for example, an official serving in the Ministry of Defence is reported by the security services to be unreliable, he may, and usually will, be removed from his present post by the Head of

[1] Denning, *op. cit.*, Chapter XVIII.
[2] P. 223, *ante*.

his Department and either transferred to work of a less confidential character or called upon to resign. He will not normally be told the evidence upon which he has come under suspicion. Nor does he enjoy any form of trial in the sense of being entitled to meet his accusers. It is understandable that the security services cannot disclose even in private to a suspected person the sources of their information, if only because such sources would be valueless for the future. If a Minister rules that a *prima facie* case has been made out against an individual by the security services, the civil servant is told and sent on special leave. If he decides that the allegations of political unreliability have been made out, with the consequences indicated above, the "accused" person can, before the Minister makes a final decision, appeal to three advisers—the three wise men—to dispute the *prima facie* case against him. These advisers are drawn from the ranks of retired members of the public services; in the nature of things they must hear an appeal in camera, and the appellant is handicapped because he can never be confronted with his real accusers or refute evidence, the nature of which is unknown to him.

Conference of Privy Councillors

The system adopted in the United Kingdom was first outlined in a Treasury memorandum dated May 5, 1948, which was superseded by a memorandum dated March 1, 1957, in consequence of certain recommendations made by a conference of Privy Councillors.[1]

This conference made a close examination of the security procedures in the Public Services. The substance of the report included a number of specific recommendations but the full text could not be published. The conference stressed that the main risk was no longer espionage by the professional agents of foreign Powers but came from communists and others subject to communist influence. The communist faith over-rode a man's normal loyalty to his country. Thus the problem was to identify members of the British Communist Party and the wider body of those who were sympathetic to communism. All such persons should be prevented from having access to secret information. Security precautions should be more stringent in the Foreign Service, the field of defence, and the Atomic Energy Organisation. The conference dealt with the relation between security risks and defects of character and conduct, such defects being liable to expose a man to blackmail for instance by foreign agents. A further recommendation was that it should be recognised

[1] Statement on the Findings of the Conference of Privy Councillors on Security, Cmd. 9715 (1955).

that the fact that a public servant is a communist not only bars his employment on secret duties but may also in some departments affect his prospects of promotion. Association with communist sympathisers and in particular living with a wife or husband who is a communist or communist sympathiser may for that reason alone justify removal from secret work.

It is recognised that some security measures are alien to traditional practices, *e.g.* the withholding of evidence so as not to imperil sources of information, or refusal or employment without proof of grounds which would be acceptable in a court of law. The tribunal of the three advisers should be retained to convince public opinion that security measures will not be exercised unreasonably.

The conference rejected any addition through statutory powers for the detention of suspects or for preventing them leaving the country. They also reviewed the procedure for the security of secret government contracts involving persons outside government employment. They considered that persons subject to these procedures should, like persons in the public service, be allowed to have their case considered by the three advisers. This conference, all the members of which held or had held high office as Ministers or in the public service, had been set up in consequence of the dismissal of the assistant solicitor to Imperial Chemical Industries[1] at the request of the Minister of Supply. The request for dismissal was based upon the finding by the Minister that the solicitor was a security risk, and that accordingly certain government contracts could not be placed with the company so long as he remained a member of the legal staff.

Departmental Responsibility

Each Minister is responsible for designating the appointments in his Department which are concerned in work vital to the security of the State. If a person holding such an appointment is found by the Minister *prima facie* to be a member of the Communist Party or to be, or have recently been, sympathetic to communism in such a way as to raise reasonable doubts as to his reliability, or associated with communist sympathisers, or susceptible to communist pressure so as to cause legitimate doubts as to his reliability, he is normally to be sent on special leave with pay. He is informed under which of the above heads he is thought to come and given any particulars such as dates of his alleged meetings with communists as might enable him to clear himself. But he cannot be given any particulars which might involve the disclosure of the sources of evidence. A period of

[1] See 197 H.L. Deb., cols. 1226 and 1260.

fourteen days is allowed for a reply, and, if the Minister adheres to his original ruling, the suspended servant has a further seven days in which to decide whether or not to appear before the advisory body. The advisers are not required merely to give a definite answer—yes or no—to the question, is the servant a communist? In cases of doubt their task is simply to assess the evidence presented before them and to recommend accordingly. If the Minister upholds the recommendation that the servant should be treated as unreliable, he is given further opportunity to make representation to the Minister as indeed happens if he does not wish his case to go to the advisers. If and when the Minister finally decides that the servant is a security risk, he will either be transferred to a non-secret post or dismissed, unless he accepts the option of resigning. An employee of government contractors who is similarly charged with political unreliability is entitled to a hearing before the advisory body.

Atomic Energy Authority

There are mentions of security in the Statute Book, e.g. the Atomic Energy Act 1954, First Schedule, para. 7 (4) provides that the Authority shall not terminate on security grounds the employment of any of its officers or servants except with the consent of the Minister responsible to Parliament for the activities of the Atomic Energy Authority.[1] The expression "security grounds" are defined as being those for the time being applicable for dismissal from the Civil Service for reasons of national security.

Effect on Criminal Liability

It is to be observed that an adverse finding on unreliability in a civil servant is not a finding that he has committed an offence, such as a breach of the Official Secrets Act. The conference of Privy Councillors recognised that the State may be compelled to take measures to protect its security even though they are "in some respects alien to our traditional practices." It is contrary to such practices to convict a man solely on account of opinions which he is supposed to hold or even for opinions supposed to be held by his wife, as was alleged in the Imperial Chemical Industries case. Refusal of employment without proof of anything which would be accepted by a court of law as establishing an offence is similarly contrary to our traditions. But the overwhelming need for the security of the State makes counter-measures essential. Punishment for a specific offence is not sufficient safeguard. For it is the commission of the offence which constitutes the danger to security,

[1] In 1969 the Minister of Technology.

whereas the special security measures are designed to prevent the action arising out of which the offence could be committed.

Telephone Tapping

The monopoly of postal communications is historically based on the prerogative, although in modern times a series of Post Office Acts have regulated this branch of the public service. At least as far back as 1735, and probably much earlier, Parliament has always recognised that the Secretary of State, in practice the Home Secretary, had special powers to authorise by warrant the interception of letters. This power has been used mainly in recent times to assist in the detection of crime and of the evasion of customs. When, in 1957, the practice of telephone tapping was challenged in Parliament and elsewhere by reason of the disclosure by the Home Secretary to the Chairman of the Bar Council of information about the conduct of a barrister so obtained, the issue was referred to a Committee of Privy Councillors.

Their Report [1] disclosed that messages had been intercepted ever since the introduction of the telephone, and prior to 1937 the Post Office acted on the view that the power was not contrary to law. Accordingly no warrants were issued to authorise interception. When the position was reviewed in 1937 it was the policy rather than the legality of the practice which was in question. The Home Office then expressed the opinion that the power to authorise the interception of letters and telegrams on the authority of a warrant was wide enough to include the interception of telephone messages. Since that date interception has been limited to cases expressly authorised by warrant. It may be argued that the action taken in 1937 was an extension by the Executive of the scope of the royal prerogative and that there was no precedent for extending a power limited to letters to telephone messages. On the other hand, there is authority for treating a telephone conversation as a telegraphic communication,[2] and just as the Telegraph Act 1868, s. 20, empowered the Postmaster-General to intercept all telegraphic messages, so he must be deemed to have power to intercept telephone conversations. But modern legislation which has defined a postal packet to include a telegram and which expressly recognises the executive power of the Secretary of State to authorise the interception of postal packets by warrant does not extend to telephone communications. It is difficult to justify the interception of telephone

[1] Cmnd. 283 (1957)

[2] *Attorney-General* v. *Edison Telephone Co.* (1880), 6 Q.B.D. 244.

communications by reference to a prerogative power which in its application to all other forms of postal communications is recognised but not defined, by modern statutes.

In the United States of America the practice of telephone tapping raises constitutional issues related to the guarantee against trespass to private property which the Constitution confers. Thus it has been held that to drive a pin into a wall to fix a microphone was an actual intrusion into the constitutionally protected area and therefore illegal.[1] On the other hand, it was no trespass to attach a detectaphone to a wall surface.[2] Thus in both countries the problem has now become one of statutory interpretation but only in the United States can it raise a constitutional issue as such.

The Report of the Committee of Privy Councillors, 1957, to which reference has just been made emphasises the difficulty of determining the exact scope of a prerogative power in the absence of a formal inquiry. Powers are likely to remain undefined, in the absence of a challenge to their legality, if they assist the Executive. It is not, therefore, surprising that it requires an unusual use of power before its exact extent can be determined. It is established practice since 1957 not to give information on the subject of authorising tapping by warrant, but exceptionally the House of Commons was told by the Prime Minister in 1966 that there had been and would be no tapping of Members' telephones.[3]

'*D*' *Notices*

The Government, acting through a committee known as the Services, Press and Broadcasting Committee, may address a formal warning or request, known as a D Notice to newspaper editors, news editors in broadcasting, editors of periodicals concerned with defence information and publishers selected by the Committee acting through its secretary. The object is to request a ban on publication of certain subjects which bear upon defence or national security. The system is a voluntary one based on mutual trust and confidence between the Government and the press. There is no compulsion and there are no sanctions to enforce disregard of a notice. The Committee contains twice as many representatives of the press as of the government departments. D Notices originate from a department and are circulated to the Committee for comment after discussion by the department with the secretary. The notice is issued to the press by the secretary on behalf of the Committee, or in cases of urgency

[1] *Silverman* v. *U.S.* 365 U.S. 505 (1961).
[2] *Goldman* v. *U.S.* 316 U.S. 129 (1942).
[3] 736 H.C. Deb. cs. 634 ff.

on his own responsibility. His interpretation of a notice is unlikely to be departed from by a newspaper editor save after full discussion with him and a personal decision by the editor. In consequence of the publication in a national daily in 1967 of a statement which said that private cables and telegrams overseas were made available to the security authorities for scrutiny an investigation by three Privy Councillors [1] was made into the incident which was alleged to be a breach of D Notice procedure. The allegation was not upheld, but a number of details for improving the system were suggested. The Prime Minister later announced that in the event of differences of opinion between the Committee and the recipient of a notice there would in future be an appeal to a Privy Councillor.

[1] Cmnd. 3309 (1967).

PART III: Administrative Law

Report of the Committee on Ministers' Powers (H.M.S.O.,1932; Cmd. 4060).
Report of the Committee on Administrative Tribunals and Inquiries (H.M.S.O., 1957, Cmnd. 218).
Principles of Administrative Law, 4th edn., by J. A. G. Griffith and H. Street (Pitman)
Administrative Law, 2nd edn., by H. W. R. Wade (O.U.P.).
Judicial Review of Administrative Action, 2nd edn., by S. A. de Smith (Stevens).
Cases in Constitutional Law, 5th edn., by Sir David Keir and F. H. Lawson, Section V (O.U.P.).
The Law and the Constitution, 5th edn., by Sir Ivor Jennings, Chaps. V and VI (University of London Press).
Concerning English Administrative Law, by Sir Cecil Carr (O.U.P.).
Administrative Law, 2nd edn., by J. F. Garner (Butterworth).
A Source Book of English Administrative Law, by D. C. M. Yardley (Butterworth).
Law of the Constitution, 10th edn., by A. V. Dicey, Introduction (E. C. S. Wade) and Appendix, Section I (P. M. Gaudemet) (Macmillan).
Justice and Administrative Law, 3rd edn., by W. A. Robson (Stevens).
Governmental Liability, H. Street (C.U.P.).
Law and Orders, by Sir Carleton Allen, 3rd edn. (Stevens).
Executive Discretion and Judicial Control, by C. J. Hamson (Stevens).
Justice in the Welfare State, by H. Street (Stevens).

CHAPTER FORTY-ONE

DEVELOPMENT OF ADMINISTRATIVE LAW

ADMINISTRATIVE law is a branch of public law which is concerned with the composition, powers, duties, rights and liabilities of the various organs of government which are engaged on administration. The emphasis should be on the exercise of power as well as on its control. Nor is the control entrusted solely or indeed mainly to the courts; it is rather by higher administrative authority, itself directly responsible to Parliament through Ministers, that the actions of the Executive are reviewed.

The study of administrative law has for many years been influenced by the comparison which Dicey drew between the system of administrative jurisdiction (*contentieux administratif*) in France, under which a special hierarchy of administrative courts dealt with most legal disputes concerning the exercise of administrative power, and the common law system in England. The latter, as Dicey saw it, subjected executive actions to control by the same courts and according to the same principles as governed the relationships between private citizens. In concentrating on this single aspect of administrative law, Dicey concluded that the common law system gave the citizen better protection against arbitrary action by the Executive than the French system. Today we cannot come to this conclusion with anything like Dicey's certainty, but Dicey's influence is not the only reason why the lawyer tends to concern himself with administrative jurisdiction rather than administration as such. He is primarily interested in legislation as providing the source of power and adjudication as the means of determining disputes which may arise from the exercise of administrative powers. Legislation, and particularly delegated legislation, is the source of all modern administrative powers except for the comparatively few, though important, powers of the royal prerogative which in so far as they relate for the most part to foreign affairs and defence are normally outside the scope of judicial review.

Judicial control is conditioned by the limits which Parliament has placed upon it. It is an important aspect of the rule of law that administrative authorities should not enjoy immunity from civil or criminal liability. In this respect, the British approach, manifest both in case-law and in the Crown Proceedings Act 1947, has been to treat the organs of the Executive on much the same footing as private individuals. The enforcement of vicarious liability against public authorities is well established. Certain exceptions to liability and certain procedural advantages are enjoyed by some public agencies, but the legal liability of administrative authorities is so far as possible assimilated to that of private individuals.

Although general principles of contract and tort liability are applied to government agencies (albeit with certain unavoidable modifications), the same solution cannot be adopted in respect of the judicial control of administrative powers. Here the question is not one of money damages for an established tort or breach of contract, but of excess or abuse of power or a mistaken interpretation of the law on the part of the public authority. As the powers being exercised are generally not comparable with the powers of private citizens, special principles of law are necessary. In English law, these developed from the use of the old prerogative writs (which since 1938 have usually been known as prerogative orders) certiorari, prohibition and mandamus. More recently, use has been made of the action for a declaration of right and the injunction, remedies which today serve both private and public law purposes. But the application of these various remedies to the wide variety of administrative agencies which exists has not always been easy and often Parliament has provided an appeal to the court or an administrative tribunal as a means of controlling the exercise of jurisdiction. Following the recommendation of the Franks Committee on Administrative Tribunals and Inquiries, Parliament accepted the general principle that it should be possible to appeal from the decision of an administrative tribunal, first on the merits to a higher tribunal, and secondly on a point of law to the High Court and thence to the Court of Appeal.[1]

If one is to broaden the study of administrative law so as to cover topics other than legislation and adjudication, a profitable approach is to study a particular public service, preferably one like Education where the administration is shared between central government and local authorities. Thus a detailed examination of the current Education Acts gives a fairly complete picture of the organisation and working of a national service administered through the agency of local authorities. These Acts assume the existence of the central and local government structure, but provide the powers which are necessary if a public system of education is to exist. From the Acts can be drawn illustrations of legislation by statutory instrument and of machinery for the adjudication of disputes both by the Secretary for Education and, in the case of the independent schools, by an administrative tribunal. The study of such a service should leave little doubt that judicial control is not the most important aspect of public administration.

Nevertheless the ultimate control which courts can exercise to prevent an excess or abuse of power by statutory instrument or administrative action remains a constitutional safeguard of high importance. Today, resort to judicial control of the administration arises most often from the acquisition or control of the use of land by public authorities, and from a citizen's dissatisfaction with administrative decisions involving money claims either by the State against the individual (*e.g.* taxation) or by the individual against the State (*e.g.* social security, statutory compensation). So far as administration is concerned, the fundamental political rights of freedom of the person and freedom of speech are generally well accepted. But despite the acceptance in practice of political liberty, the very fact that the State nowadays makes provision for a great variety of public services of necessity means that there are many grounds which can give rise to disputes between citizen and authority. Many of these disputes may now be settled by administrative tribunals, but there are many areas of government in which no administrative tribunals exist. The public inquiry procedure provides a valuable safeguard for the citizen against ill-informed or unreasoned decisions. The creation of the office of Parliamentary Commissioner for Administration in 1967, to provide a further remedy for injustice caused

[1] Tribunals and Inquiries Act 1958, s. 9; pp. 594–5, *post*.

by the maladministration of central government, was itself a recognition that traditional legal methods did not provide the citizen with a remedy whenever he needed one.

Historical Development

To make an adequate study of administrative law it is first necessary to trace its historical development in this country. The fact that the constitution is unwritten makes it particularly difficult in Britain to separate administrative from constitutional law. Our position may be contrasted with that in France and in the U.S.A. In France, the succession of written constitutions has not prevented the continuing evolution of a system of administrative law applied quite separately from civil and penal law. In the United States the existence of the eighteenth-century constitution created against the background of the common law of England has hampered the growth of administrative law, more particularly since the Supreme Court, having assumed power to interpret the constitutionality of Acts of Congress, has been jealous to preserve the separation of the judicial power from the executive power. From these comparisons it is evident that separate courts are not an essential characteristic of a system of administrative law. Adherence to the doctrine of the separation of powers has secured this result in France. It has failed to secure it in the United States, where in practice the doctrine has hitherto exerted greater influence than in any European State.

Definitions are part of the history of the subject, showing as they do the reluctance of English nineteenth-century writers, Dicey in particular, to grant it recognition. In contrast, in the twentieth century the tendency is to go to the other extreme and to advocate for administrative law a separate system of adjudication, not only to take over the limited control of administration which is now exercised by the courts but also to provide remedies against maladministration irrespective of legal liability under the common law.

If, following definitions, the structure of the administration is examined, it will be appreciated that government does not merely mean administration by a central department under a Minister of the Crown. Some functions of central government are exercised by a great variety of authorities for which no Minister is, at all events directly, responsible. Local authorities in themselves present a complex picture, but one that must be understood if only for the reason that there are relatively few local government services where regulation or control by central government is not a feature; indeed in some cases the local authorities are little more than agents of the central government.

The third element in the administrative structure of government is provided by the modern public corporations which are responsible for the nationalised industries and other important services. Here constitutional interest lies primarily in the relationship between the public corporation and Parliament: to what extent is the Corporation answerable to Parliament, given that a Minister of the Crown has been vested with statutory powers of direction over the Corporation? [1] But at the level of administrative law, a consumer or competitor of a public corporation may look for legal remedies to ensure that its activities are conducted in accordance with the law.

The protection of the individual against the administration depends less upon the tribunal than, to quote Professor Borchard, "on the mores of a particular community as reflected in the political instruments it creates." [2] It is because systems have developed from varying historical foundations that different forms of control over those who exercise governmental powers have developed. Thus in France, after the revolution, the courts were suspect because they were successors of the *Parlements* which before 1789 were both courts of justice and administrative bodies. On the other hand, in England the courts came to be regarded as the guarantee against a return to the Tudor and Stuart despotism. The result was that a system of administrative jurisdiction was established in a comparatively short time in France, whereas in Britain there is no separate system of administrative courts and the growth of administrative tribunals has been piecemeal, though in the present century the development has been rapid.

The nature of administrative law in England—and since most of the recent development has been by statute law which applies in both jurisdictions, Scots law does not greatly differ except as regards the remedies available at common law and some of the related principles of private law—may be made clearer by considering developments after 1688. The Bill of Rights [3] effected a legal revolution. It resolved the conflict arising from the claims of the Stuarts who had failed to recognise that powers of government were passing into other hands than those of the sovereign and his courtiers; in particular the landed and commercial classes were growing in strength and making their influence felt through Parliament and in local government. The fundamental principles which governed constitutional power had remained undetermined after the civil war. The solution contained in the Bill of Rights, supplemented by the provisions of the Act of

[1] Chap. 21.
[2] 'A Symposium upon Administrative Law', 18 *Iowa Law Review* at p. 134.
[3] P. 8, *ante*.

Settlement which secured the independence of the judges, involved the restriction of prerogative powers without destroying the prerogative as an instrument of government. Parliament and the common lawyers had reconciled their claims to legal supremacy at the expense of the Crown. To this at an earlier stage Sir Edward Coke and the common law judges had contributed, as can be seen in the opinions given in the *Case of Proclamations* [1] and in the *Case of Shipmoney* [2]. If the prerogative had not been curtailed in 1688, our public law might have developed as a branch of the powers of the Sovereign. As ministerial responsibility to Parliament developed through the eighteenth century, the prerogative could still have been brought under the political control of Parliament, but there would have been no legal control through the courts. Even to-day in those comparatively rare cases where Parliament entrusts an absolute discretion to the Crown acting through Ministers, there is no room for the courts to intervene. As it was, the prerogative was curtailed and for the future governmental power could only be enlarged by Parliament. Accordingly it is Parliament which has authorised the great volume of public law relating to administration which now far exceeds in bulk those functions which still fall to be exercised under the royal prerogative.

Even in the eighteenth century Blackstone criticised the powers given by Parliament to the Commissioners of Customs and Excise.[3] Dr. Johnson's definition of excise nearly led to his prosecution for criminal libel.[4] Finance Acts imposed duties upon officials of the Exchequer long before the composite annual Act found its place in the Statute Book.

If one looks beyond what Maitland called "the showy parts of the Constitution," it is easy to see that in England there never has been a complete separation of the administration from the judiciary. For centuries in the person of the justice of the peace, administration and the maintenance of order through the criminal courts were inextricably blended. With the ending of control by the Privy Council, which did not revive at the Restoration in 1660, the justices of the peace exercised wide administrative powers for which sometimes in the eighteenth century there was no authority from Parliament. The rule of the justices in quarter sessions continued in rural England until nearly the end of the nineteenth century. Indeed Maitland deplored the removal of administrative

[1] Pp. 39–40, *ante*.
[2] P. 41, *ante*.
[3] 4 Bl. Comm. 281.
[4] Holdsworth, H.E.L., X, pp. 419, 454.

powers to the new county councils by the Local Government Act 1888, because he found virtue in the fact that the judicial discretion which was exercised on the local bench permeated the numerous administrative duties of the justices.[1] It is not surprising that the composition of a modern administrative tribunal which sits locally closely resembles that of a bench of magistrates. The justices were the chief administrators of the eighteenth and early nineteenth centuries. There was little, if any, administrative control over their activities, but their exercise of power could be challenged in the Court of King's Bench by recourse to the prerogative writs. When in the period of reform after 1832 the work of the justices, except in the criminal law, was largely transferred to untried elected bodies with salaried officials responsible for the actual work of administration, it became clearer that administrative law was something separate from justices' law. The creation of poor-law guardians, health boards, highway boards, school boards and burial boards followed in rapid succession. Even before the age of reform, local commissioners of sewers, improvement commissioners, turnpike trustees had pointed the way to more and more administrative tasks being sanctioned by Parliament. It was only gradually that the administrative chaos created partly by local and partly by general Acts of Parliament could be sorted out and a pattern of administrative law became discernible. The creation of modern local authorities by statute, or in the case of municipal corporations their reform by the same means, was followed by the creation of new departments of central government and the vesting in Ministers of powers which formerly fell within local government.

So it is that judicial control which was designed to check the powers of inferior courts, *i.e.* the justices of the peace, has been adapted to review the exercise of statutory powers first by local authorities and in this century also by Ministers of the Crown. It is a long step from reviewing the byelaws of a turnpike trust to interpreting statutory regulations of the Minister of Transport relating to the construction and use of motor vehicles, which bind the whole community as if they had been enacted by Parliament itself. Yet it is the same kind of control which the courts exercise to-day whether they are reviewing a narrow point of law raised in a magistrates' court or the excess of jurisdiction by a Minister of the Crown. That this development has hitherto sufficed is partly due to the growth of the political responsibility of Ministers to Parliament. But the judges have shown the adaptability of common law methods

[1] *The Shallows and Silences of Real Life*, Collected Papers, I, pp. 467 *et seq.*

to changing conditions in the functions of government. Not only has the *ultra vires* doctrine been refined to cope with more complex legislation; the rules of natural justice have also been developed and extended, though at times there have been reasons for fearing their judical restriction. On the other hand judicial review by itself would have proved inadequate, had there not been substituted for the old control of the Privy Council the answerability of Ministers to Parliament.

The responsibility, collective and individual, of government to the legislature for all its actions provides a political means for the redress of grievances but from the point of view of the individual it is less effective than a legal remedy which can be enforced by process in the courts. No matter what publicity may attach to the ventilation of grievances in the House of Commons, there is no assurance that even a favourable reply by a Minister to a question addressed to him on behalf of a constituent by a private member will provide a remedy. The importance of intervention by members of Parliament, whether by correspondence with a Minister, questions in the House, motions on the adjournment or other parliamentary devices, should not be underestimated. But the practical limitations on ministerial responsibility as a means of controlling the administration were one reason for the creation in 1967 of a British Ombudsman, a Parliamentary Commissioner for the redress of grievances, with power to investigate complaints of maladministration.[1] The appointment of this official has been of some value, but it has not altered the basic characteristics of administrative law in Britain.

Definitions

This short account of the historical development of administrative law in Britain may help to explain why, amongst British writers, it was not only Dicey who was reluctant to grant recognition to this subject as one deserving of separate study. The slow growth of public law can be explained on political grounds. It was the common law which had triumphed over the executive in the seventeenth century. Even in the nineteenth century academic writers hesitated to regard the growing powers of the executive as forming a separate body of law. A further reason lies in the fact that the courts retained ultimate control over the exercise of governmental power. It was natural that judges trained in the common law should be slow to recognise a possible rival to the individualistic traditions in which they were nurtured. Nevertheless as the nineteenth century advanced it must have become clear that criminal

[1] Chap. 47 C.

law, contract, tort and property law did not embrace the full jurisdiction of the courts. The fusion of law and equity in 1875 operated in the field of private law and did little to contribute to the recognition of administrative law.

In the definition of administrative law given at the beginning of this chapter, it is the powers of government rather than its rights and liabilities which are of primary importance. It is the exercise of power conferred upon public bodies but not shared with individual citizens which distinguishes governmental agencies. Accordingly administrative law is first and foremost concerned with the discretions which normally accompany the grant of power.[1]

It was Maitland in the famous course of lectures which he first delivered in Cambridge in 1887–8 who spoke of administrative law and drew attention to its content.

> I do consider it worth our while just to see that there are these vast tracts of modern constitutional law, though we can do little more than barely state their existence. I say of constitutional law, for it seems to me impossible so to define constitutional law that it shall not include the constitution of every organ of government whether it be central or local, whether it be sovereign or subordinate. It must deal not only with the king, the parliament, the privy council, but also with the justices of the peace, the guardians of the poor, the boards of health, the school boards, and again with the constitution of the Treasury, of the Education Department, of the courts of law. Naturally it is with the more exalted parts of the subject that we are chiefly concerned; they are the more intelligible and the more elementary: but we must not take a part for the whole or suppose that matters are unimportant because we have not yet had time to explore them thoroughly. Year by year the subordinate government of England is becoming more and more important. The new movement set in with the Reform Bill of 1832: it has gone far already and assuredly it will go farther. We are becoming a much governed nation, governed by all manner of councils and boards and officers, central and local, high and low, exercising the powers which have been committed to them by modern statutes.[2]

Maitland began his consideration of the definition of constitutional law by referring to those of Austin and Holland. Austin regarded administrative law as determining "the ends and modes to and in which the sovereign powers shall be exercised; shall be exercised directly by the monarch or sovereign member, or shall be exercised directly by the subordinate political superiors to whom portions of those powers are delegated or committed in trust." [3]

[1] *Cf.* Sir Ivor Jennings, *The Law and the Constitution*, Chap. VI, for the definition of the subject.

[2] See *Constitutional History of England* (1908), pp. 500–1.

[3] Austin, *Jurisprudence* (edn. 1873), Vol. I, p. 73.

It is clear that few of the functions of the political sovereign were embraced by the term, "administrative law." This is wider than the accepted scope of the subject to-day since it included Parliament and the courts as well as the Executive. Parliament is admittedly the source of the vast bulk of administrative law but the subject does not embrace the powers of Parliament nor those of the courts except so far as the latter control the exercise of powers of the Executive.

Holland [1] gave administrative law as one of his six divisions of public law, the first was constitutional law as dealing with structure, the second administrative law as being concerned with function. But Holland's ultimate opinion favoured the inclusion of some of the broader rules which included function under constitutional law; for example the royal prerogative was so treated and therefore excluded from administrative law. This treatment is commonly followed by modern writers, notwithstanding that there are a number of limited but important powers of the Executive which derive from the prerogative and therefore in conformity with the definition given above are appropriately treated as administrative law. No doubt it would be far fetched so to include most of the powers of the Foreign Office in the field of policy or of the Secretary for Defence in relation to the disposition of the Armed Forces of the Crown, but matters like the issue of passports and the admission of aliens clearly relate to the exercise of administrative power.

Turning to the twentieth century we find at first a tendency to narrow the definition. Port, writing in 1929, defined the scope of administrative law as coinciding with administrative powers and duties [2] but his detailed discussion of English administrative law was confined to delegated legislation and adjudication by administrative bodies. The first edition of Professor W. A. Robson's book, *Justice and Administrative Law*, published in 1927, gave to the term a meaning which was limited to jurisdiction of a judicial nature exercised by administrative agencies over the rights and property of citizens and corporate bodies. Sir David Keir and Professor F. H. Lawson in successive editions of their *Cases in Constitutional Law* have given increased attention to the judicial control of public authorities and proceedings against the Crown. While a substantial part of the section devoted to judicial control is occupied by a discussion of administrative adjudication and its review by the courts, no place is found for administrative law in the wider sense of the current definition. It was only after 1945 that administrative law at last

[1] Holland, *Jurisprudence*, 10th edn., pp. 138, 139 and 359-63.
[2] Port, *Administrative Law* (1929), Chap. I.

received full recognition, if not by the courts, at all events by text book writers, most of whom have accepted the broad definition of the subject as covering all administrative powers and duties.[1]

French writers influenced by the presence of a strong administrative court in the Conseil d'Etat have long since reduced the field of the law of government to a system upon which generalisation has been possible. Jèze defined administrative law as "l'ensemble des règles relatives aux services publics." [2] Gaudemet defines *droit administratif* as the part of internal public law which concerns the organisation of the administrative authorities and the relations of public authorities with the citizens.[3]

The overriding importance of the constitution in United States public law has sometimes led to administrative law being treated in American legal literature merely as a specialised branch of constitutional law. The federal constitution, with its emphasis on the separation of powers, made inevitable the development of government through independent regulatory commissions. The famous case book of Professor (later Mr. Justice) Frankfurter, was concerned particularly with the law covering the fields of legal control exercised by law-administering agencies other than courts and the field of control exercised by courts over such agencies. On the evidence afforded by more recent texts, there can be no doubt that the full recognition of administrative law in the American academic world preceded, if only by a short period, the recognition in the United Kingdom which has just been described.

Committees on Administrative Law

The development of administrative law in Britain since the First World War has been much influenced by two major governmental committees appointed by the Lord Chancellor to inquire into aspects of the subject. The Committee on Ministers' Powers was appointed in 1929 at a time when a storm of criticism was being directed against the departments by the Bench and Bar, by prominent academic lawyers at Oxford and a small group of lawyers and others in the House of Commons. The appointment of the Committee closely followed the publication of a strongly critical essay by the Lord Chief Justice, Lord Hewart,[4] who considered that the courts were

[1] See works listed on p. 583.
[2] *Les Principes généraux du Droit administratif* (3rd edn., 1925), p. 1.
[3] Dicey, *Law of the Constitution*, 10th edn., p. 475.
[4] *The New Despotism* (Benn).

losing their historic control over the activities of the Executive. The terms of reference to the Committee were

> to consider the powers exercised by, or under the direction of (or by persons or bodies appointed specially by), Ministers of the Crown by way of (*a*) delegated legislation, and (*b*) judicial or quasi-judicial decision, and to report what safeguards were desirable or necessary to secure the constitutional principles of the sovereignty of Parliament and the supremacy of the law.

The Committee, which vindicated the Civil Service from the charge of bureaucratic tyranny, analysed from the point of view of constitutional principle the legislative and judicial powers vested in Ministers and made many constructive recommendations on delegated legislation and administrative justice. Though no Government formally adopted its recommendations, its influence was seen in changes made in drafting Bills which conferred powers on departments and also in the establishment by the House of Commons in 1944 of a Select Committee to scrutinise delegated legislation.[1]

Twenty-three years after the Report of this Committee was published, at a time when the power of the governmental machine was again under attack from certain sections of political opinion,[2] the Committee on Administrative Tribunals and Inquiries was appointed to consider and make recommendations on:

> (*a*) The constitution and working of tribunals other than the ordinary courts of law, constituted under any Act of Parliament by a Minister of the Crown or for the purposes of a Minister's functions.
>
> (*b*) The working of such administrative procedures as include the holding of an inquiry or hearing by or on behalf of a Minister on an appeal or as the result of objections or representations, and in particular the procedure for the compulsory purchase of land.

This Committee, over which Sir Oliver Franks presided, reported in 1957.[3] Its terms of reference corresponded broadly to the second part of the terms of reference of the earlier Committee but, unlike that Committee, it found great difficulty in distinguishing formally between judicial and administrative decisions.[4] Adopting a more empirical approach than its predecessor, it examined one by one the tribunals which fell within its terms of reference and inquired how far the characteristics of openness, fairness and impartiality applied to each. It also made recommendations for strengthening the public inquiry as a protection for citizens affected by town planning

[1] Pp. 614–5, *post*.

[2] This attack was intensified by the disclosures made in the Crichel Down affair (pp. 89–90, *ante*).

[3] Cmnd. 218 (1957).

[4] Pp. 624–5, *post*.

and compulsory purchase. The Committee concluded that judicial control, whether by direct appeal to the courts or by review through the prerogative orders, should be maintained and where necessary extended. These recommendations led directly to the Tribunals and Inquiries Act 1958, which set up the Council on Tribunals, and to other legislative and administrative action designed to implement the Committee's report.[1]

The terms of reference of the Franks Committee confined its attention to areas where recourse to a tribunal or a public inquiry was already available. The Committee could not consider those areas of governmental power where neither safeguard existed.[2] Nor could the Committee consider the provision of a redress for individuals suffering from maladministration. These two problems were examined in 1961 by a non-governmental committee appointed by Justice.[3] The report, *The Citizen and the Administration*, recommended (*a*) that, except where there are overriding considerations of government policy, a citizen should be entitled to appeal from a departmental decision on a matter of discretion to an impartial tribunal. Rather than the creation of many new tribunals, a general tribunal should be created to hear miscellaneous appeals against discretionary decisions. (*b*) The appointment of a Parliamentary Commissioner to investigate complaints of maladministration. The appointment of a Parliamentary Commissioner for Administration was first made in 1967. Notwithstanding this innovation, the English and Scottish Law Commissions, after a preliminary survey of the whole field, recommended in 1969 that a Royal Commission be appointed to examine administrative law in both English and Scottish law.[4]

Importance of Powers

The exercise of administrative powers normally involves the choice between two or more possible courses of action on the part of the administrator. Only rarely is there placed upon him the duty of taking an imperative course of action; for example, once an outbreak of foot and mouth disease has been confirmed by an official of the Ministry of Agriculture, statute prescribes an imperative course of action, namely the declaration of an infected area within which the movement of certain classes of animals is prohibited. But in general

[1] See particularly Chap. 47.
[2] J. A. G. Griffith, *Tribunals and Inquiries*, (1959) 22 M.L.R. 125.
[3] For comment see [1962] Public Law 15 (I. M. Pedersen) and 24 (J. D. B. Mitchell) and [1962] C.L.J. 82 (A. W. Bradley). Justice is the British section of the International Commission of Jurists, p. 75, *ante*.
[4] Cmnd. 4059 (1969).

administrative action involves the exercise of discretion; and there are many important rules of administrative law which govern the exercise of a discretion. For administrative discretion, although it may be wide, is seldom, if ever, unlimited. Generally, the right to exercise a discretion is derived from statute. It is always possible to seek a remedy in the courts on the ground that a particular discretionary decision is beyond the authority of the relevant statute. Where the discretion is conferred directly by Act of Parliament, the provision in the Act cannot be challenged. But where the discretion is conferred by subordinate legislation, it may be possible to show that the subordinate instrument is outside the powers of legislation conferred by the parent Act.[1] Alternatively, the administrative act itself can be challenged as being in excess of statutory authority. This arises not only in the obvious case of an official embarking on a scheme which is wholly unlawful; it arises also where an official makes a decision which would otherwise be within his powers but where he has applied a wrong procedure or acted for a wrong purpose. In cases where there is no direct appeal against a discretionary decision, this ground for attacking the validity of administrative action is important.[2]

Common Law and the Administration

If a public authority is to fulfil the broad duties laid upon it by Parliament, *e.g.* the duty of the Minister of Health to promote the health of the people, or the duty of local housing authorities to abate overcrowding, the authority must necessarily be equipped with legal powers which may seriously affect the common law rights of individuals. When use of these powers is challenged in the courts, the authority will often rely on its broad statutory duty as a justification for the action which it has taken to the alleged detriment of an individual. The individual will seek to show that the administrative powers in question have not been exercised in a lawful manner. The court may thus be faced with a dilemma. It is not easy to reconcile action taken on behalf of the public at large with the interests of a single private individual whose liberty of action, including the free enjoyment of his property, may be affected by the exercise of the public power.[3] The court must avoid anything in the nature of reversing the policy which has been determined by the authority. At the same time it must protect the individual from any attempt to ride

[1] Pp. 609–11, *post*.
[2] Chap. 44, B.
[3] *E.g. Pride of Derby and Derbyshire Angling Association Ltd.* v. *British Celanese Ltd.*, [1953] Ch. 149.

roughshod over his legal rights except by due process of law. When, for example, land is compulsorily acquired for a statutory purpose, the court is not there to ensure that, for example, one man's land shall be taken but not that of his neighbour; that is a policy matter to be decided by the administrative agency. But it is the function of the court to see that if the land is to be compulsorily acquired, all the legal rules and procedures which apply to that acquisition are observed. Thus a judge who is reviewing the legality of executive action has a different constitutional function from that of the administrator responsible for a particular branch of government. It is true that there are factors of policy in many judicial decisions, particularly on new points of law and in the sentencing of convicted offenders. But the element of policy plays a much larger part in administrative decisions and the administrator is, in law, free either to follow his previous decisions or to ignore them. An administrator's decision cannot be challenged in a court on the ground that he has disregarded precedent or the weight of the evidence. The forum where his decision can be criticised is Parliament.[1] A further distinction between judge and administrator is that the judge must await a dispute to be referred to him before he can function at all. It is the duty of the administrator to conduct or to supervise the conduct of a particular branch of governmental activity. His is the discretion when to act and, usually, how to act.

Judicial Powers of the Administration

Although of great importance, the principles governing the exercise of discretionary power do not arise in every dispute between the State and the individual, for example where the issue is whether a citizen is entitled to a money payment from the State, or the amount of the citizen's tax liability. It is true that in deciding upon a citizen's claim to supplementary benefit, the official exercises some discretion, but his powers are governed by statutory rules laying down the relevant factors and prescribing scales on which benefits may be paid. Moreover, in the case of contributory schemes such as the national insurance and industrial injuries schemes, statutory rules provide that in certain circumstances the citizen is entitled to certain benefits. Under these schemes, a citizen whose claim is refused by a civil servant of the department concerned may appeal, first to a local tribunal and thence to the National Insurance Commissioners, who exercise exclusively judicial functions.[1] Why cannot the citizen take this dispute straight to the ordinary courts? In the past the courts were preferred

[1] *E.g. Franklin* v. *Minister of Town and Country Planning*, [1948] A.C. 87.
[2] Pp. 698–9, *post*.

and disputes over workmen's compensation were heard in the first instance in the county court with the judge acting as arbitrator between employer and employee. Today the basic liability for compensating workmen injured in industrial accidents is laid on the State and few even from the legal profession would advocate a return to the county court. The reason for excluding the courts is not that the disputes concern matters of departmental policy which must be left to the Minister to settle; indeed by setting up the tribunal structure the Minister has shown a desire to be rid of responsibility for individual decisions. The reason for preferring specialised tribunals is that they have procedural advantages over the ordinary courts which enable them to do the work more effectively.[1] Nonetheless, as matters of legal right may be as much in issue as in private litigation, the qualities of openness, fairness and impartiality which characterise the ordinary courts must be maintained; thus the members of the tribunals should not be subject to ministerial influence except through their duty to observe any regulations properly made by the Minister and forming part of the law.

Conclusion

The nature of our modern society explains in two ways the growth of administrative law. First, in the case of discretionary powers, the rules of administrative law seek to ensure that discretion is exercised according to the law. Secondly, the creation of new forms of public right and obligation give rise to new procedures of adjudication, which must observe certain basic qualities if just decisions are to be made.

The future development of administrative law can be expected to flow from the decisions of the ordinary courts, exercising their supervisory jurisdiction, but to an even greater extent from legislation by Parliament and Ministers improving machinery for adjudication of administrative disputes and providing new remedies. The need for further remedies arises in relation to those areas of discretion where no special adjudicative procedures exist and where accepted principles of judicial review stop short of providing the citizen with what he often wants, a review of the merits of the original decision itself.

[1] Chap. 47.

CHAPTER FORTY-TWO

ADMINISTRATIVE LAW—SOURCES

ADMINISTRATIVE law is mainly concerned with powers. It is necessary therefore to examine the source of power before considering in detail how power is controlled. In general, the sources of legal power are common law and statute, and so it is with administrative authority. So far as the central Government is concerned its common law powers fall under the royal prerogative; but the prerogative has no relevance to the activities either of local government authorities or modern statutory corporations, which include both ministerial departments, such as Housing and Local Government, Education, Health and Transport, as well as the nationalised undertakings. Since the latter are exclusively the creation of Parliament it follows that their powers are derived solely from the same source.

Royal Prerogative

The prerogative as a source of administrative power predominates in the sphere of foreign affairs. The Foreign and Commonwealth Office seldom makes claims on the Legislation Committee of the Cabinet for a place in the queue of parliamentary Bills. It is still competent for the Crown to legislate by Order in Council for colonial and other dependent territories but this power is relatively unimportant today. The prerogative too plays its part in sanctioning the activities of the Defence Department: such matters as pay, promotion and pensions for members of the Armed Forces are governed by prerogative. In the sphere of internal government, scales of pay for the Civil Service, as well as conditions of employment and rules of conduct, are laid down by Treasury warrant or other prerogative instrument. The only other spheres where the prerogative remains an important source of power are (1) the powers of patronage vested in the Crown, and (2) the prerogative of pardon which is exercised on the advice of the Home Secretary. For the vast areas of administrative activity which are required for the maintenance of the Welfare State, it is almost exclusively to statute that one must look for the source of power. Nevertheless, in so far as a statute does not otherwise provide, agencies of government exercise their powers subject to the common law. But this is a matter which can better be examined at a later stage under the head of legal liability.

Statute

Statute law is, then, a well-nigh exclusive source of administrative power. The term covers both Acts of Parliament and delegated legislation. Acts of Parliament comprise public general Acts and private or local Acts. Most delegated legislation, or as it is sometimes called, subordinate legislation, is made in the form of statutory instruments. The function of legislation in regard to the machinery of government is twofold. First, statutory authority is necessary to create new organs of government, whether elected local authorities, a new central department or a public corporation. An Act which is primarily concerned with this, like the Local Government Act 1933, may be called a constituent Act. It sets out the arrangements for the incorporation and composition of the new authorities, their methods of operation and financial arrangements, and also some basic general powers, like power to employ staff and acquire premises. Secondly, statutory authority is necessary for a particular public service to be provided. An Act which is primarily concerned with a particular service, like housing or education, may be called an enabling Act. Its aim is to equip existing public authorities with the powers necessary for providing the service. Although a constituent Act is likely to contain all the provisions which are essential if the authorities it creates are to be able to function, a modern enabling Act will often do no more than outline the main features of a public service, leaving the details to be filled out by subordinate legislation. In volume the bulk of statutory instruments is formidable. In 1968 there were enacted 77 Public General Acts which were contained in 2426 pages. In the same year the total of statutory instruments issued was 2077; although over half of these were local in effect, the published volumes of general instruments amounted to over 5500 pages.

Delegated Legislation: Historical Development

The formal process by which a Bill becomes an Act has never been the sole method of legislation. In the period before the legislative function of Parliament had become clearly established, it was difficult to distinguish between enactment by King in Parliament and legislation by the King in Council. Even when legislation by Parliament had become a distinct process, considerable power of legislation by proclamation remained with the Crown and in Tudor times these decrees were enforced through the agency of the Council and the Star Chamber. In 1539, by the Statute of Proclamations, royal power to issue proclamations "for the good order and governance" of the country was recognised to exist and such proclamations were to be observed and enforced as if made by Act of Parliament. One reason given for the Act was that sudden occasions might arise when speedy remedies were needed which could not wait for the meeting of Parliament; the Act contained saving words for the protection of the common law, life and property. The repeal of the Statute in 1547 made little difference to the Tudor use of proclamations and only in the seventeenth century were the limits of the prerogative power to legislate defined.[1]

The modern doctrine of the sovereignty of Parliament means that such prerogative powers of legislation as still exist have survived by grace of Parliament, and also that any other legislative powers exercised within the country must be derived from the authority of Parliament. From early times there are instances of Parliament granting the task of legislating in specialised fields to subordinate authorities. In 1531 Parliament granted legislative powers to the Commissioners of Sewers, the early counterpart of the modern Rivers and Land Drainage Boards. The county justices received power to legislate for their counties under various social and economic Acts and in the eighteenth century Quarter Sessions exercised legislative as well as judicial and administrative functions. After 1689 the annual Mutiny Acts delegated power to the Crown to make regulations for the better government of officers and soldiers (Articles of War), but in general it was not until the period of social reform in the nineteenth century that delegation of wide legislative power became common. The first modern Factories Act [2] in 1833 conferred power on the four factory inspectors appointed under the Act to make orders and regulations, breaches of which were punishable under the criminal law. Comparison should be made between this Act and the consolidating Factories Act 1961, which conferred well over one hundred legislative powers on the then Minister of Labour. A very wide power that remained law for over a century was the power, first vested in the Poor Law Commissioners, "to make and issue all such rules, orders and regulations for the management of the poor . . . and for carrying this Act into execution . . . as they shall think proper". [3]

[1] Pp. 39–40, *ante*.
[2] Labour of Children etc. in Factories Act 1833.
[3] Poor Law Amendment Act 1834, s. 15.

The late nineteenth century saw a great increase in the delegation of legislative power to government departments and other subordinate bodies, granted piecemeal as need arose. The resulting confusion of terms (including rules, regulations, orders, byelaws, schemes and directions), the variety of procedures by which the powers were exercised, and the great difficulty of discovering what the law was, led in 1890 to a system of official printing and publication and to the Rules Publication Act 1893. This introduced the general expression, "statutory rules and orders", helped to unify procedures and introduced a safeguard of prior publicity. During the First World War, the Defence of the Realm Acts granted power in very wide terms to the Government to make regulations for the conduct of the war.[1]

In the period between the World Wars many lawyers became acutely conscious of the wide legislative powers of government departments. The Committee on Ministers' Powers [2] concluded that unless Parliament was willing to delegate law-making powers, it would be unable to pass the kind or quantity of legislation which modern public opinion required. The Committee drew attention to certain dangers in delegated legislation and suggested the introduction of greater safeguards against abuse. Since then the Statutory Instruments Act 1946 has replaced the Rules Publication Act 1893 and has made possible a greater uniformity of procedure.[3] Parliamentary control of delegated legislation has been improved by the annual appointment since 1944 of a scrutinising committee of the House of Commons; and the Second World War and the welfare State have contributed to the present degree of subordinate legislation.

Justification of Delegated Legislation

Delegated legislation is an inevitable development in the modern State for the following reasons:

(1) *Pressure upon parliamentary time.* If Parliament attempted to enact all legislation itself, the parliamentary machine would break down, unless there was a radical alteration in the procedure for the consideration of Bills. The granting of legislative power to a department which is administering a public service can largely obviate the need for amending Bills. Although many statutory instruments are laid before Parliament, only rarely do they give rise to matters which need the consideration of either House, and in

[1] Chap. 48.
[2] P. 593, *ante*.
[3] P. 613, *post*.

practice Parliament spends less than one twentieth of its time on business connected with them.[1]

(2) *Technicality of subject-matter*. Legislation on technical topics necessitates prior consultation with experts and interests concerned.[2] The giving of legislative power to Ministers facilitates such consultation.[3] Bills are confidential documents and their actual text is not disclosed until they have been presented to Parliament and read a first time. Thereafter they can only be altered by formal amendment at the committee or report stages. No such secretive custom need impede the preparation of delegated legislation, unless security considerations arise. There is also a good reason for keeping out of the statute book highly technical provisions which do not involve questions of principle, and which only experts in the field concerned can readily understand.

(3) *The need for flexibility*. When a major new social service is being established it is not possible to foresee every administrative difficulty that may arise, nor to have frequent recourse to Parliament for amending Acts to make adjustments that may be called for after the scheme has begun to operate. Delegated legislation fills those needs. The National Insurance Act 1911 could not have come into operation, had it not been followed over a two-year period by delegated legislation amplifying its provisions. The present national insurance scheme was enacted by Parliament two years before it was brought into operation, a step which was preceded by a great volume of regulations made under the parent Acts. Changes in social habits, *e.g.* the increased use of motor cars, and technological developments, make necessary continual amendment of the law.

(4) *State of emergency*. In times of emergency, a government may need to take action quickly and in excess of its normal powers. Many written constitutions include provision in times of emergency for the suspension of formal guarantees of individual liberty. In the United Kingdom, Parliament both enlarges the discretionary powers of the Government by a general enabling Act and at the end of the emergency, if need be, protects its officers from liability in the courts by passing an Indemnity Bill legalising any illegalities committed *bona fide* during the period. Although the Crown still possesses an ill-defined residue of prerogative power capable of use in time of national danger, the Emergency Powers Act 1920 today makes permanent provision enabling the Executive to legislate

1 33 *Public Administration* 325.
2 Pp. 608–9, *post*.
3 M.P.R., Vol. II, Evidence, p. 120.

subject to parliamentary safeguards in the event of certain emergencies.[1] Following the unilateral declaration of independence by the Rhodesian government in 1965, Parliament granted exceptionally wide legislative powers enabling the Queen in Council to take all necessary steps to bring about the resumption of lawful government in Rhodesia.[2]

Exceptional Types of Delegated Legislation

Criticism centres upon particular types of delegated legislation.

(*a*) *Matters of principle.* There is a clear threat to parliamentary government if power is delegated to legislate on matters of general policy, or if so wide a discretion is conferred that it is impossible to be sure what limit the legislature intended to impose.[3] If power is delegated to legislate on matters of principle, it is essential to maintain parliamentary control over the exercise of the power. If the power of the courts to declare delegated legislation *ultra vires* is to be of any real value, the delegated power must obviously be defined with reasonable strictness. Critics of the departments are apt to forget that regulations must usually be drawn in such a way as to provide for all possible contingencies. Acts of Parliament conferring powers are frequently wide in their terms; regulations made under them usually avoid vague propositions and when they subdelegate powers, *e.g.* to local authorities, they do so in clear and exact terms. Indeed, the citizen is more troubled by the bulk and complexity than by the generality of delegated legislation.[4]

(*b*) *Delegation of taxing power.* We have seen how vital in the development of parliamentary control over the Executive has been the function of imposing taxation.[5] Nonetheless the responsibility for the national economy exercised by the Government today has made it necessary for Parliament to delegate certain taxing powers to the Government. In particular, the working of a tariff system has been found inpracticable without delegation of the power to vary and impose import duties from time to time.[6] Moreover since 1961 the Government has had power to vary certain classes of indirect

[1] Chap. 48, *post*.
[2] Southern Rhodesia Act 1965.
[3] See *e.g.* in Northern Ireland, the controversial Civil Authorities (Special Powers) Act 1922 which confers legislative powers on the Minister of Home Affairs at Belfast which would not be acceptable in Britain except in extreme emergency. See also M.P.R., p. 31, and Sir Cecil Carr, *Concerning English Administrative Law*, p. 38.
[4] See, however, *Blackpool Corporation* v. *Locker*, [1948] 1 K.B. 349, esp. at p. 362.
[5] Chap. 4.
[6] Pp. 133-4, *ante*. See now Import Duties Act 1958.

taxation by order of the Treasury.[1] Each of these powers is subject to special parliamentary control in that orders imposing import duties or varying indirect taxation cease to have effect unless they are confirmed by a resolution of the House of Commons within a limited time.

(*c*) *Sub-delegation.* **The technique of a delegate sub-delegating** the power to legislate was encouraged by the Emergency Powers (Defence) Act 1939, s. 1 (3), which expressly permitted Defence Regulations to be made authorising named authorities or officials to make orders, rules or byelaws for any of the purposes for which Defence Regulations could be made. On occasions this resulted in legislative action at four removes from the parent Act, as when general licences were authorised under directions issued, which directions were given under the authority of orders made under a Defence Regulation which in turn was made under the Act of 1939. Such sub-delegation has been condemned as tending "to postpone the formulation of an exact and definite law" and as encouraging "the taking of powers meanwhile in wider terms than may ultimately be required." [2]

Apart from express statutory provision for sub-delegation, it is doubtful whether an initial delegation of the power to legislate carries with it the power to authorise the making of other categories of instrument by the relevant Minister himself or by other bodies. Where such authority is assumed, control by the ordinary constitutional methods becomes difficult. The House of Commons Select Committee on Statutory Instruments has been quick to criticise unauthorised sub-delegation.[3]

(*d*) *Retrospective operation.* **In discussing the supremacy of Parliament mention has been made of legislation having retrospective operation.[4] To change the character of past transactions carried out** on the faith of the then existing law is repugnant to the conception of the rule of law. If on occasions retrospective legislation is considered necessary, as in the case of the War Damage Act 1965, this should be done by Parliament itself and not through the means of

[1] Finance Act 1961, s. 9, and Finance Act 1964, s. 8.

[2] *Third Special Report of the Select Committee on Statutory Rules and Orders*, H.C. 186 (1945–6), para. 16. See also pp. 644–5, *post*.

[3] On 20 April 1964 the House of Commons debated a motion relating to regulations made by the Minister of Health and the Secretary of State for Scotland, which seemed to the Select Committee to have the effect of sub-delegating legislative power to professional bodies outside Parliament: 693 H.C. Deb., cols. 1017 *et seq.*

[4] Pp. 46–7, *ante*.

delegated legislation, which Parliament itself cannot amend.[1] Such legislation can only be justified if Parliament has the opportunity of debating the matter as one of principle on second reading and of amending the proposal in committee, if need be.

(*e*) *Exclusion of the jurisdiction of the courts.* We shall see that the jurisdiction of the courts is confined to declaring delegated legislation *ultra vires.*[2] The real control over delegated legislation must be parliamentary and administrative. Parliament can define powers clearly and scrutinise through a small committee the regulations made in pursuance of delegated powers. Ministers can see that departments and subordinate bodies under their control act reasonably in the exercise of their powers. The courts can ensure only that powers are exercised *bona fide* and for the purposes defined in Acts of Parliament. None the less the control of the courts is important and should only exceptionally be excluded: it should never be for the Minister to determine the limits of his own powers.

(*f*) *Authority to modify an Act of Parliament.* Sometimes power is delegated to modify a statute. The passing of a complicated and far-reaching statute may involve minor alterations in numerous local Acts.[3] Particularly criticised has been the so-called "Henry VIII Clause" enabling a Minister to modify the Act itself so far as necessary for bringing it into operation.[4] The use of this clause has in practice been innocuous and its abandonment would mean that once an Act had been passed, no defect in its provisions could be modified without an amending Act. None the less the Committee on Ministers' Powers recommended that this type of clause should never be used except for the purpose of bringing an Act into operation and that it should be subject to a time limit of one year from the passing of the Act. It is clearly dangerous in principle to permit the Executive to change an Act of Parliament. One example of a very wide power to modify the parent Act is to be found in Part III of the Factories Act 1961, which makes general provision for the welfare of factory workers. Section 62 authorises the responsible Minister by special regulations to order steps to be taken "either in addition to, or in substitution for, or by way of extension or variation of, any of the foregoing provisions of this Part of this Act". Further, the Minister is authorised by regulations to "extend the matters to which this section applies so as to include other matters affecting the welfare of employed persons or any class of them".

[1] For some war-time illustrations, see *Law and Orders*, by Sir Carleton Allen, 3rd edn., p. 204.

[2] Pp. 609–11, *post.*

[3] Chap. 26, section B, *ante.*

[4] M.P.R., pp. 36–38; Carr, *op. cit.*, pp. 41–47.

Nomenclature

Despite the passing of the Statutory Instruments Act 1946, terminology is still at times confusing. The term, "statutory instrument", is a comprehensive expression to describe all forms of subordinate legislation subject to the 1946 Act. Within the scope of the Act are many legislative powers conferred on Ministers by Acts passed before the 1946 Act came into operation. As regards Acts passed after the 1946 Act came into operation, there are two categories of statutory instrument: (i) legislative powers conferred on the Queen in Council and stated to be exercisable by Order in Council; (ii) legislative powers conferred on a Minister of the Crown and stated to be exercisable by statutory instrument. The first of these, the statutory Order in Council, must be distinguished from prerogative Orders in Council, which are not technically statutory instruments at all, even though for convenience many of them are published as an appendix to the annual volumes of statutory instruments. One reason why some legislative powers are vested in the Queen in Council and others are vested in a named Minister is that some powers may need to be exercised by any department of the Government whereas others concern only one particular department; also the greater formality of an Order in Council is thought appropriate to some classes of legislation, even though the legal effect is the same. The expression, "statutory instrument", does not include local authority byelaws, nor does it include such acts as the confirmation of compulsory purchase orders by a Minister.

Although statutory instrument is the generic term, replacing the former expression, "statutory rules and orders",[1] a variety of names still apply to different kinds of statutory instrument: rules, orders, regulations, warrants, schemes and even licences and directions. Several of these terms may be used in a single Act to distinguish the different procedures applied to different powers.[2] The argument for uniform practice in nomenclature is based on convenience. In practice, the term "regulation" is used mainly for matters of general importance, such as the National Insurance regulations. Where the legislation deals with procedure, rules are generally enacted, *e.g.* the Rules of the Supreme Court. With the term "order" there is less uniformity; thus Order in Council may

[1] Thus the official abbreviation for delegated legislation made before 1 January, 1948 was S.R. & O.; thereafter S.I., followed in each case by the year of enactment and the number of the instrument, *e.g.* S.I., 1968, No. 252.

[2] The Factories Act 1961 refers to regulations, special regulations, rules and orders.

give effect to the judicial advice given to Her Majesty by the Judicial Committee of the Privy Council, or it may bring into effect a whole Act of Parliament, the operation of which was postponed at the time of enactment. A Royal Warrant may provide a code for pay or pensions of the Armed Forces; outside the legislative field, a warrant may denote the judicial order authorising the arrest of a suspected criminal, or the authority for repayment of income tax.

Control of Delegated Legislation

"There is now general agreement over the necessity for delegated legislation; the real problem is how this legislation can be reconciled with the processes of democratic consultation, scrutiny and control."[1] The process of subordinate legislation differs significantly from that of legislation by Bill; it is equally important that there should be effective forms of control. The existing means of control will be described under four headings: (1) consultation of interests, (2) challenge in the courts as to validity, (3) control through parliamentary procedures, (4) publication.

(1) *Consultation of Interests*

Unlike the procedure of legislation by Bill, whereby the proposals are considered publicly in principle and in detail as the Bill passes through both Houses, and are known in their final form even before the Royal Assent is given, most delegated legislation comes into force as soon as it is made public, either at once or after a short interval stated in the document itself. At one time the Rules Publication Act 1893 required forty days' notice to be given in the *London Gazette* of a proposal to make rules of a permanent character. But the Act was not very effective and its operation was frequently excluded by enabling Acts; it was repealed by the Statutory Instruments Act 1946.

There is therefore no general requirement of prior publicity, and an ordinary member of the public has little chance of getting to know about proposed statutory instruments.[2] But by an almost universal practice, the department proposing to make a new statutory instrument takes steps to ensure that the various interests particularly affected by the proposal are consulted. Some Acts of Parliament make this a legal requirement. Thus before making regulations under the Police Act 1964 the Home Secretary must take into account

[1] Memorandum of the late Aneurin Bevan, M.P., quoted in Report of Select Committee on Delegated Legislation, H.C. 310. 1953.

[2] J. F. Garner, *Consultation in Subordinate Legislation*, [1964] Public Law 105.

any recommendations made by the Police Council of Great Britain and must furnish the Council with a draft of the regulations.[1] National Insurance regulations must be submitted in draft to the National Insurance Advisory Committee, whose disagreements, if any, with the Minister must be reported to Parliament along with the regulations.[2] Another important example of obligatory consultation is that the Council on Tribunals must be consulted before rules of procedure for administrative tribunals and inquiries are made.[3] Several Acts do not specify the bodies to be consulted, leaving it to the Minister to consult with such associations and bodies as appear to him to be affected.[4] Even where there are no express statutory requirements, advantage may be gained from consultations with trade organisations or organised interests likely to be affected by the proposed legislation. Nor is there any objection to showing the actual draft of a regulation to outside bodies, unlike the position regarding the texts of proposed Bills.[5] Consultation helps to ensure that the contents of subordinate legislation are as acceptable as possible to the trade and professional interests concerned, and also secures for the Ministry the benefits of specialised knowledge from outside government. In one or two exceptional instances, the Ministry's legislative proposals must be published and the interests affected are given the right to present their objections before an inspector appointed by the Minister. But this form of inquiry is usually reserved for such matters as the ministerial confirmation of compulsory purchase orders.[6]

(2) *Challenge in the Courts*

If made in accordance with the prescribed procedure, and if it is within the powers conferred by the parent Act, a statutory instrument is as much part of the law as the statute itself: breach of a statutory instrument may give rise to the same liabilities as breach of a statute. The essential difference between statute and statutory instrument is that a Minister exercises a subordinate power of legislation and has not unlimited powers. Consequently, if a government department attempts to enforce a statutory instrument against an individual, whether by criminal or civil proceedings, the individual may as a defence question the validity of the instrument. The chances of such a defence succeeding depend primarily on the terms of the Act by which legislative power has been conferred. If a Minister

[1] Police Act 1964, s. 45; see p. 240, *ante*.
[2] National Insurance Act 1965, s. 108.
[3] Tribunals and Inquiries Act 1958, section 8 and 7A; see pp. 702–3, *post*.
[4] *E.g.* Agriculture Act 1957, sections 1 and 11.
[5] P. 603, *ante*.
[6] Garner, *op. cit.*, pp. 110–11.

is given power to make such regulations as appear to him to be necessary or expedient for achieving a particular purpose, the Minister is unlikely to be successfully challenged unless he uses the power for a totally different purpose. But even in such a case there are certain principles of interpretation which a court will apply; these have the effect of a judicial presumption that Parliament does not intend certain forms of legislation to be made unless by express words or by necessary implication it has clearly authorised them. The principles that no man should be deprived of access to the courts except by clear words of Parliament, and that there is no power to levy a tax without clear authority are illustrated by cases arising out of Defence Regulations made during the First World War.[1] That these basic constitutional principles can cut down the width of even such expressions as "power to make such regulations as seem to the Minister to be necessary" was illustrated in *Commissioners of Customs and Excise* v. *Cure and Deeley Ltd.*[2]

> The Finance (No. 2) Act 1940 empowered the Commissioners to make regulations providing for any matter for which provision appeared to them to be necessary for giving effect to the statutory provisions relating to purchase tax. Regulations were made under which, if proper tax returns were not submitted by manufacturers, the Commissioners might determine the amount of tax due, "which amount shall be deemed to be the proper tax due", unless within seven days the tax-payer satisfied the Commissioners that some other sum was due. *Held* that the regulation was invalid in that it purported to prevent the tax-payer proving in a court the amount of tax actually due, and substituted for the tax authorised by Parliament some other sum arbitrarily determined by the Commissioners.[3]

By similar reasoning it is possible that a court would declare invalid a statutory instrument which purported to have retrospective effect, or to sub-delegate legislative power, in the absence of clear authority from Parliament for such provisions.

In practice such opportunities for challenge rarely arise, for great care is taken in the drafting of departmental legislation by a Minister's legal advisers; a further inducement to caution is provided by the necessity to submit most statutory instruments to scrutiny in Parliament. The courts may take into account these parliamentary safeguards in considering the validity of subordinate legislation. Thus although byelaws may be challenged on the ground of unreasonable-

[1] *Attorney-General* v. *Wilts United Dairies Ltd.* and *Chester* v. *Bateson*, discussed at pp. 55–6, *ante* and 720, *post*.

[2] [1962] 1 Q.B. 340. Cf. *McEldowney* v. *Forde*, [1969] 2 All E.R. 1039: on appeal from Northern Ireland, House of Lords upheld ban on republican clubs imposed by the Minister for Home Affairs under the Civil Authorities (Special Powers) Act 1922 (N.I.).

[3] See now Purchase Tax Act 1963, s. 27 (2).

ness,[1] it is doubtful whether a statutory instrument could be challenged on this ground.

In *Sparks* v. *Edward Ash Ltd.*,[2] the Court of Appeal rejected a contention that pedestrian crossing regulations made by the Minister of Transport were invalid on grounds of unreasonableness.

A serious procedural error by the department concerned could lead to a statutory instrument being declared invalid, for example, if the Minister responsible for social security purported to make National Insurance regulations without consulting the National Insurance Advisory Committee. This does not mean that every minor procedural error would vitiate the statutory instrument; some procedural requirements are held to be directory (*i.e.* of such a kind that failure to comply with them does not invalidate the instrument) and not mandatory or imperative.

It was at one time generally believed that if the parent Act provided that regulations when made should have effect "as if enacted in this Act", the courts were precluded from inquiring into the validity of the regulations; but in 1931 the House of Lords were of the opposite opinion [3] and it is likely that this expression in the parent Act adds nothing to the binding effect of a properly made statutory instrument. Certainly it is undesirable that the power of a court to rule on the validity of a statutory instrument should be excluded. Although it is exercised on rare occasions only, this function of judicial control is important in maintaining the principle that government departments, no less than individuals, are bound by Act of Parliament.

(3) *Control by Parliament*

Parliamentary control of delegated legislation originates in the fact that legislative powers derive from statute. There is therefore always some opportunity of giving detailed consideration, at the Committee stage of a Bill, to those clauses delegating legislative power. It has at times been questioned how effective this control is. The Ministers' Powers Committee recommended that all Bills conferring power to legislate should in each House be referred to a small standing committee to report whether there were any objections of principle to the proposals.[4] This recommendation has never been adopted and in 1953 a Committee of the House of Commons considered that individual members and unofficial committees of

[1] P. 376 *ante*, p. 646 *post*.
[2] [1943] K.B. 223; see also *Taylor* v. *Brighton Corporation*, [1947] K.B. 736.
[3] *Minister of Health* v. *The King*, [1931] A.C. 494, p. 663 *post*.
[4] M.P.R., pp. 67–68.

members on each side of the House could be relied on to take close interest in any proposed delegation.[1]

A measure of general control over departmental legislation is provided by the political responsibility of a Minister to Parliament for the entire activity of his department. Thus responsibility for regulations made may be raised through questions to the Minister, by general debates relating to his department and motions on the adjournment. Parliament has also provided for additional means of control specially restricted to ministerial legislation. It must not, however, be forgotten that basic reasons for delegating legislative power are pressure on Parliament's time and the technical nature of the subjects; the very object of delegation would be frustrated if Parliament had to approve each statutory instrument in detail. The parliamentary procedure through which a statutory instrument must pass depends on the terms of the parent Act. The principal procedures are the following:

(i) laying before Parliament, with no further provision for control—in this case it seems that Parliament can take no formal action;
(ii) laying before Parliament of an instrument that takes immediate effect, subject to annulment by resolution of either House;
(iii) laying before Parliament of an instrument to come into effect only when approved by affirmative resolution of each House (in the case of financial instruments, of the House of Commons only);
(iv) laying of an instrument that takes immediate effect but requires approval by affirmative resolution within a stated period as a condition of continuance;
(v) laying in draft, subject to resolution that no further proceedings be taken—in effect a direction to the Minister not to "make" the instrument;
(vi) laying in draft, and requiring affirmative resolution before instrument can be "made".

In cases (i)–(iv), the instrument is formally made by the Minister before it is laid, but in cases (v) and (vi) the Minister is required to lay the draft instrument before Parliament before he has formally made it.

Of these procedures, by far the most common is number (ii) (the negative procedure); the most frequent of the positive procedures is number (vi). The main difference between negative and positive procedures is that, under the positive procedure, it is the Minister concerned who must secure the affirmative resolution and if necessary the Government must allot time for the resolution to be discussed in Parliament within the course of ordinary business; under the negative procedure, it is for any member who so wishes to "pray" that the instrument should be annulled. Consideration of

[1] Report of Select Committee on Delegated Legislation, H.C. 310, 1953.

"prayers" is exempted business and, subject to a closure time of 11.30 p.m.,[1] may be taken after the normal close of business. In practice, the positive procedure is reserved for particularly important measures, *e.g.* orders made by the Treasury varying indirect taxation or import duties [2] or regulations made under the Emergency Powers Act 1920.[3]

One feature common to all these procedures is that neither House has power to amend a statutory instrument. If this were possible, it might well involve the House too closely in detailed consideration of matters which Parliament has delegated to a Minister, and it would cause complications and delay if each House introduced different amendments. It seems better that if a House is not satisfied with an instrument as it stands, the Minister should withdraw it and start again.

The Statutory Instruments Act 1946 introduced some general provisions to promote uniformity of procedure. By section 4, where an instrument must be laid in Parliament after being made, it must in general be laid before it comes into operation; every copy of such an instrument must show on its face three dates, showing when it was made, laid, and came into operation respectively.[4] What constitutes laying before Parliament is governed by the practice or direction of each House [5] and an instrument may be laid even when Parliament is not sitting. By section 5 of the 1946 Act, where an instrument is subject to annulment, as in procedure (ii) above, there is a uniform period of forty days during which a prayer for annulment may be moved, exclusive of any time during which Parliament is adjourned for more than four days or is prorogued or dissolved. Where, as in procedure (v) above, a statutory instrument is laid in draft but subject to the negative procedure, there is a similar period of forty days during which the resolution may be moved. In the case of instruments which need an affirmative resolution before they can come into operation (procedure (iii) above), no set period is provided during which this must be done as it is for the Government in each case to decide how urgently the instrument is needed. Under procedure (iv) above, the length of time during which the affirmative resolution must be secured if the instrument is to continue in force is stated in the parent Act and varies from case to case. There are detailed rules contained in the Standing Orders of each House and reinforced by Treasury directions to government departments for ensuring that

[1] Report of Select Committee on Delegated Legislation, H.C. 310, 1953.
[2] P. 133, *ante*.
[3] P. 717, *post*.
[4] See specimen Statutory Instrument, printed in Appendix C, p. 734.
[5] Laying of Documents before Parliament (Interpretation) Act 1948.

statutory instruments are properly laid before Parliament. Each instrument usually contains an explanatory note to enable members and other readers to appreciate the aim of the new legislation and to indicate its general purport.

Although a parent Act may expressly confine parliamentary control of statutory instruments to the House of Commons, and this occurs in the case of fiscal measures, the House of Lords is usually granted the same powers of control as the House of Commons. Moreover, the procedure under the Parliament Acts 1911 and 1949 for by-passing the House of Lords applies only to Bills and not to statutory instruments. But it is extremely rare for the House of Lords to exercise its legal veto over subordinate legislation. When in 1968 the House rejected an order containing sanctions against the Rhodesian Government made under the Southern Rhodesia Act 1965 [1], this caused the Labour Government to propose that the power of the House of Lords to veto statutory instruments should be abolished.[2] Although the present power of veto could be abused for political reasons as a means of harassing a government unpopular with the House of Lords, it could become a valuable safeguard against misuse by the Executive of legislative powers provided that the composition of the House of Lords was itself reformed.

Scrutinising Committee

Every general statutory instrument which must be laid before Parliament, as well as certain other statutory orders, comes under scrutiny by the Select Committee on Statutory Instruments, a sessional committee of the House of Commons. Instruments which require an affirmative resolution from the House of Lords are also examined by the Special Orders Committee of the House of Lords. The House of Commons Committee is advised by the Speaker's Counsel. The Committee's duty is to consider whether the attention of the House should be drawn to a statutory instrument on any of the following eight grounds, namely:

(i) that it imposes a charge on the public revenues or contains provisions requiring payments to be made to the Exchequer or any government department or to any local or public authority in consideration of any licence or consent, or of any services to be rendered, or prescribes the amount of any such charge or payments;

[1] On 18 June 1968, the Southern Rhodesia (United Nations Sanctions) Order 1968 was rejected, but on 18 July 1968, an Order containing identical provisions was approved by the House of Lords without a division.

[2] See *House of Lords Reform*, Cmnd. 3799, 1969 pp. 22–3; Parliament (No. 2) Bill 1969, clauses 13–15.

(ii) that it is made in pursuance of an enactment containing specific provisions excluding it from challenge in the courts, either at all times or after the expiration of a specified period;

(iii) that it appears to make some unusual or unexpected use of the powers conferred by the statute under which it is made;

(iv) that it purports to have retrospective effect where the parent statute confers no express authority so to provide;

(v) that there appears to have been unjustifiable delay in the publication or in the laying of it before Parliament;

(vi) that there appears to have been unjustifiable delay in sending a notification to Mr. Speaker under the proviso to section 4 (1) of the Statutory Instruments Act 1946, where an instrument has come into operation before it has been laid before Parliament[1];

(vii) that for any special reason its form or purport calls for elucidation;

(viii) that the drafting of it appears to be defective.

It is not the function of this Committee to concern itself with the merits or policy of an instrument. These are matters which may be discussed by the whole House in a debate on an affirmative resolution or on a prayer for annulment. Although the Committee is not expressly invited to invoke the doctrine of *ultra vires*, it must comment on any unusual or unexpected use of the power conferred by the enabling Act; this may well disclose an *ultra vires* exercise of power—a matter exclusively for the courts to determine. Before an adverse report on an instrument is made to the House the government department concerned is given an opportunity to furnish orally or in writing such explanations as it may think fit. In practice, a senior official, and not the Minister, offers the necessary explanation. Very few instruments are reported to the House in proportion to the total output of subordinate legislation.[2] The report by the Committee on a particular instrument itself has no effect on the instrument, although it may encourage a member to table a prayer against the instrument. The Committee's report is not always available to the House within the period during which resolutions may be moved; the House of Lords has a preferable rule that no affirmative resolution can be considered until the report from the Special Orders Committee has been received. As well as its periodical reports to the House of Commons, the Committee has also issued a number of special reports which have led to improvements in the drafting of statutory instruments and in the publicity given to them.

(4) *Publicity*

Although in principle it is desirable that all legislation should be publicised before it takes effect, there are some matters, *e.g.* changes in

[1] P. 613, *ante*.

[2] *E.g.* in the three sessions 1960–63, the Committee examined a total of 1924 instruments and reported 11 to the House.

price control or rates of customs, where the object of the legislation would be defeated if it had to be made known to the public in advance of enactment. This is recognised by the Statutory Instruments Act, which allows that for essential reasons a statutory instrument may come into operation, even before it is laid before Parliament, with the safeguard that the Lord Chancellor and the Speaker must be furnished with an immediate explanation. Apart from this, publicity is now secured by the following rules. (1) A uniform procedure has been laid down for numbering, printing, publishing and citing statutory instruments.[1] An instrument classified as local by reason of its subject-matter and certain classes of general instrument certified by the authority which makes the instrument may be exempted from the requirements of printing and sale of the publication. (2) The rule that where an instrument has to be laid before Parliament it must be laid before it comes into operation has already been mentioned;[2] in practice a day's interval between laying and coming into operation is quite usual. (3) It is a defence in proceedings for contravention of a statutory instrument to prove that it had not been issued by H. M. Stationery Office at the date of the alleged contravention unless it is shown by the prosecutor that reasonable steps have been taken to bring the purport of the instrument to the notice of the public or of persons likely to be affected by it or of the person charged.[3] This means that ignorance of a statutory instrument is no defence but that failure to issue it may in certain circumstances be a defence. In practice the enforcement agency or the police are as likely as the offender to be ignorant of the change in the law for some time after it has been made. But the statutory defence is necessary because these instruments, unlike Acts of Parliament, may otherwise operate without any warning of their enactment. (4) Each year is published a collected edition of all statutory instruments, containing all general instruments made during the year which are still operative; the annual volumes contain numerical and classified lists of statutory instruments.

Byelaws

In chapter 26 above the powers of local authorities to make byelaws have been described. Byelaws are a form of delegated legislation where the legislative initiative is conferred on a local authority or some other public body. Central control is retained through the requirement of ministerial confirmation before a byelaw can take

[1] Statutory Instruments Act 1946, s. 2.

[2] P. 613, *ante*.

[3] Statutory Instruments Act 1946, s. 3 (2); *Simmonds* v. *Newell*, [1953] 2 All E.R. 38; *The Queen* v. *Sheer Metalcraft Ltd.*, [1954] 1 Q.B. 586.

effect; the courts have also exercised a greater degree of control over byelaws than over ministerial regulations.[1] Byelaws are not within the definition of statutory instrument, but copies are required to be available in the locality in which they operate.

Administrative Quasi-Legislation

A development is the growth of what has been described as "administrative quasi-legislation." [2] Government departments have adopted the practice of issuing pronouncements stating the official point of view on doubtful points in statutes, or announcing concessions that will be made in the application of statutes to individual cases. In 1944 the Chancellor of the Exchequer presented to Parliament a twenty-page list of extra-statutory war-time concessions given in the administration of inland revenue duties.[3] The Finance Acts remained on the statute book, but certain provisions ceased to represent the law as applied in practice. These extra-legal arrangements are clearly less satisfactory than formal changes in the law, even when they are brought to the notice of all those affected. Even if they were relevant to litigation, a court would generally be bound to disregard them.

An important field where ministerial decisions have an almost legislative effect is town and country planning. The Minister's decisions on appeals against the refusal of planning permission often embody reasons of policy or law which directly affect local authorities and private landowners. Selected decisions are published and since 1959 it has been possible to challenge the validity of the Minister's decisions in the High Court.[4] Ministerial circulars to local authorities sometimes contain statements of policy which have an effect akin to modifying the law; usually, but not always, these circulars are public documents. On important matters of general policy where controversial issues are involved, government by circular is not a satisfactory substitute for legislation. Thus in July 1965 the Secretary of State for Education and Science requested local authorities by circular to prepare schemes of comprehensive education. Amendment of the Education Act 1944 was not then considered necessary, although the new policy represented an important change in the structure of education envisaged in the 1944 Act.

[1] P. 376, *ante*.
[2] *Administrative Quasi-Legislation*, by R. E. Megarry, 60 L.Q.R., p. 125.
[3] Cmd. 6559 (1944).
[4] Town and Country Planning Act 1962, s. 179.

CHAPTER FORTY-THREE

THE NATURE AND CLASSIFICATION OF POWERS

IN every State during this century there has been a vast increase in the activities of government and therefore of the volume and importance of administrative law. It is in the field of discretionary powers over persons and property that disputes most frequently arise. The question, how far can the courts control the exercise of discretionary power, is one of the most difficult problems in administrative law. But equally important constitutional issues are raised by the relationship between Parliament and the various administrative agencies. Ministerial responsibility lies at the root of representative government; it may be impaired if too wide a scope is given to an independent agency. The authority of Parliament is weakened by the unrestricted delegation to the Executive of power to legislate. The independence of the judges becomes merely academic in importance if control over adjudication passes from their hands. The more rapidly government expands, the more important it is to safeguard principles which might otherwise be overlooked in the pressure to devise an expedient to overcome some urgent administrative problem. Not the least useful task of the lawyer is to watch the progress of legislation, whether by Bill or by statutory instrument, and to test new provisions by reference to established constitutional usage. Nor need such a task imply opposition to every innovation. Both Minister and civil servant may look impatiently upon the lawyer as obstructing the realisation of policy. Especially is this so, if the lawyer takes his stand in the past and is blind to changing social conditions. It is important that the lawyer of today should fill the role of a constructive critic in the process of reconciling individual liberty with the public interest. The rule of law is still the basis of political liberty, as it is understood in the Western World. But just as our legal forefathers in the seventeenth century helped to secure that liberty by their contribution to the parliamentary cause, so lawyers to-day can secure the survival of the rule of law by their insistence upon the impartial administration of government agencies, especially in the field where individual rights may appear to conflict with public interest.

The Lawyer and the Administrative Process

It is not easy for the lawyer trained in the common law system of rights and duties to reconcile the discretionary powers of the administrator, which may often seem to resemble arbitrary power, with the rule of law. The civil servant, with an eye always open to the political consequences of his acts for his Minister, may be as averse as the lawyer from a departure from precedent, though he may be less aware of the impact of administrative action on the individual. An understanding of the administrative process is as vital to the lawyer as an appreciation of the rule of law is for the public servant. Where disputes arise, it is the judicial approach to their solution which is the more likely to secure a feeling of justice done. But if the lawyer is to play his part in this it is necessary to understand the nature and limits of discretionary power. We must therefore examine the nature of powers conferred by Parliament upon public authorities before considering the extent of judicial review of their exercise.

Legal Powers

Legal rights in the strict sense are the benefits which are derived by the individual from legal duties imposed upon other persons. A legal power is the ability to affect the legal relations of other people. The exercise of its legal powers by a public authority may affect the rights of individual citizens, even though they are exercised for the good of the public in general. The acts of a public authority are lawful only so long as the authority does not exceed its powers. The capacity to challenge the exercise of a power belongs to those who may be adversely affected by it as individuals because their rights may be injured. This means that the power can be challenged by any one to whom the authority owes a duty not to exceed the power. If a power is exceeded, the excess may expose the authority to common law liability in tort; for example a government inspector who enters private premises without authorisation may be sued for damages for trespass by the occupier. But more often the remedy sought is not to redress tortious injury or actual loss to the plaintiff, but simply to restrain the unlawful exercise of power. Here difficult problems may arise concerning the standing of the individual to seek judicial review. Thus a ratepayer may challenge expenditure out of the rate fund of his local authority for a purpose not authorised by law because the authority is under a duty to him and to all the other ratepayers not to exceed its powers.

> In *Prescott* v. *Birmingham Corporation* [1] a ratepayer successfully challenged the validity of free municipal transport for certain classes of elderly residents at the expense of the general body of ratepayers.

Similarly a manufacturer may seek judicial review of a public corporation's decision to adopt a scheme of manufacture which affects his own business.[2] But unless his common law rights are affected, a land-owner may not seek review of planning decisions concerning his neighbour's land [3] and the payment of national taxes would not entitle a citizen to seek judicial review of central government decisions.

For the most part the conferment of a power on a public authority does not create any duty to the individual because powers are given to enable services to be provided for the good of the public as a whole. In general an individual cannot by litigation compel a public authority to exercise a power which has not been exercised when or as it should have been, unless he can show that the default constitutes a breach of duty owed to him as an individual.[4] Yet, unless by express words or by necessary inference a statute authorises injury to be inflicted upon the property or the person of an individual, the existence of a power does not *ipso facto* authorise the commission of a tort or breach of contract.[5] If a discretionary power can reasonably be exercised without infringing private rights, the courts will require the power to be so exercised *e.g.* without the commission of a nuisance at common law.[6] But where a statutory power clearly authorises interference with private rights, the individual may sue for the resulting loss only to the extent that acts of carelessness have occurred which have unnecessarily added to the injury.[7]

Challenge in the courts to the exercise of a power may be based on the ground that there is no such power, or that the power has been exceeded or used for an unauthorised purpose. Since most powers are exercisable at the discretion of the authority, the court may not substitute its own discretion for that of the authority. For this would

[1] [1955] Ch. 210, criticised in de Smith, *Judicial Review of Administrative Action*, pp. 478–9; and see p. 645, *post*. Existing concessions for old people were authorised retrospectively by the Public Service Vehicles (Travel Concessions) Act 1955; and see Travel Concessions Act 1964.

[2] *Charles Roberts & Co.* v. *British Railways Board*, [1965] 1 W.L.R. 396.

[3] *Gregory* v. *Camden Borough Council*, [1966] 1 W.L.R. 899.

[4] *East Suffolk Catchment Board* v. *Kent*, [1941] A.C. 74; K. & L. 486.

[5] *Geddis* v. *Proprietors of Bann Reservoir* (1878), 3 App. Cas. 430, 455.

[6] *Metropolitan Asylum District* v. *Hill* (1881), 6 App. Cas. 193; K. &. L. 29.

[7] *Hammersmith Railway Co.* v. *Brand* (1869), L.R. 4; H.L. 171.

defeat the intention of the statute which has entrusted the discretion to a particular agency. But a court may hold either that the discretion has not been exercised at all or that a proposed exercise is not a lawful exercise of the discretion because the authority has taken a wrong view in law of the nature of the discretion, *e.g.* by acting on irrelevant considerations;[1] or that it has been abused, *e.g.* from corrupt motives and, therefore, in effect has not been exercised; or, if the record of the proceedings so discloses, *e.g.* from the reasons given, that the exercise of the power has been carried out by an error in law. These propositions will be illustrated in the description of powers which follows and in the succeeding chapters which examine the relationship between the courts and public authorities.

It is necessary for Parliament when conferring a power to determine upon whom it should be conferred and what safeguards should be imposed on its exercise. Such a decision will largely be based on consideration of each particular power and the belief that it will best be exercised by some particular body or person, *e.g.* a Minister, a court of law or an independent statutory body. It is obvious that in a complex modern society powers and duties must be entrusted to public authorities which are not possessed by private individuals. "A sanitary inspector can enter my house to inspect my drains; my employer can not. A sheriff can summon me to serve on a jury; my friends can not."[2] The powers of public servants are usually exercised on behalf of the Crown or of Ministers or of local authorities; powers are rarely conferred by statute on subordinate officers themselves. But private citizens and public authorities and their officers alike must justify the exercise of a power in the same way; the power must be shown to have originated either from a statute or the common law and to be exercised according to law.

Powers of Private Citizens

If A.B. does an act which affects the rights of his neighbour, C.D., he must be able to justify his act, if need be, in a court of law. He must exercise his power in the manner prescribed by law, and for the purpose for which the law has sanctioned it. Suppose that A.B. wishes to remove a branch of C.D.'s tree overhanging his garden, he must first be sure that he is entitled by law to do so; he must then consider in what particular way the law permits him to do

[1] *The Queen* v. *Boteler* (1864), 4 B. & S. 959; K. & L. 443; p. 642, *post*.

[2] Jennings, *The Law and the Constitution*, 5th edn., p. 312.

it. Can he, if he wishes, enter his neighbour's garden for the purpose? Can he lop it off without notice? Sometimes the exercise of a power is optional; sometimes there is a legal duty to exercise it. A citizen has duties as a member of the public. Every man is under a duty to assist in quelling a breach of the peace, if called upon to aid a constable; he would, for example, be under a duty to assist a police officer who called upon him to assist in arresting a violent offender.[1]

Authority for acts of Public Authorities

If A.B. instead of being a private citizen is the holder of a public office, *e.g.* a collector of taxes, or a justice of the peace, his official acts must be justified in the same way. For every act performed in the course of a public duty there must be legal authority; or, as it is frequently put, a public authority or public servant must act *intra vires.* Just as it is from statute or common law that a power must be shown to originate, so also will statute or common law determine how and for what purposes the power must be exercised. The tax collector must be able to show, if challenged, that Parliament, or a body entrusted by Parliament with the levying of taxation, has conferred the power to collect taxes on holders of his office or on the department which he serves; further, he must collect them only in accordance with certain statutory rules. By accepting office he comes under a duty to collect taxes in the manner allowed by law. The same is true of the justice of the peace. In addition to powers and duties of an administrative character, he is in his judicial capacity responsible for enforcing much of the criminal law, within limits defined by Parliament. He is under a duty to exercise these powers if called upon to do so, and he can be controlled, if need be, by process in the courts compelling him to exercise his powers or not to exceed them.

Enforcement of Statutory Duty

There are many statutory duties, particularly those laid upon public authorities and private individuals alike, which create rights in other individuals; for example, if a factory worker is injured through his employer's breach of duty under the Factories Act 1961, the remedy will be an action in damages.[2] But there are many statutory duties, especially those laid only on public authorities, which cannot easily be discussed in terms of their enforceability in a court. Thus the Education Act 1944, s. 76, obliges a local education authority to pay regard

[1] P. 484, *ante*. [2] Pp. 636–9, *post*.

to the general principle that, so far as is compatible with the provision of efficient instruction . . . and reasonable public expenditure . . . pupils are to be educated in accordance with the wishes of their parents.

How far does this statutory duty create enforceable rights in the parents of children of school age?

In *Watt* v. *Kesteven County Council*,[1] the authority, which maintained no grammar school, secured places and paid fees for pupils entitled to secondary education at an independent school within their area. A Roman Catholic parent refused this facility and sent his two sons to a Catholic school in an adjacent county. The authority declined to pay the fees for attendance at this school, although it was recognised as efficient. *Held* by the Court of Appeal that the duty on the authority to make school places available was not enforceable by action by the parent, but only by the Minister of Education under his default powers.

However much the courts may strive to assimilate the duties of public authorities to the duties of individuals in private life, there will be some public duties from which it is impossible to deduce a right of private enforcement. This is particularly so where the duty is one which has no counterpart in the relations between two individuals, such as the statutory obligation of the Secretary of State for Education to promote education and the progressive development of educational institutions. This is not to say that there is no sanction to the duty; the sanction may be political, though the doctrine of ministerial responsibility, or it may take the form of higher administrative control. For example, a defaulting authority may in the last resort be replaced by a superior authority. But this may be small comfort to the citizen who, as in *Watt* v. *Kesteven C.C.*, seeks a judicial remedy to put right what he regards as an unreasonable decision which adversely affects him.

Classification of Powers—Legislative, Administrative and Judicial

Governmental powers may be classified in accordance with the three functions of government [2] *i.e.* legislative, administrative and judicial, though it is often impossible to distinguish clearly between legislative and administrative powers or between administrative and judicial powers.[3] The body upon which a power is conferred affords no reliable test of the nature of the power. The Queen in Council exercises legislative, administrative and judicial powers. Some of the

[1] [1955] 1 Q.B. 408, applied in *Bradbury* v. *London Borough of Enfield*, [1967] 3 All E.R. 434.
[2] Chap. 2.
[3] Jennings, *op. cit.*, App. I.

functions of the judiciary are administrative. It may be said that legislation is the making of general rules of conduct, but administration instructions may be general in scope, for example, Home Office instructions issued to all immigration officers.[1] Again, the legislative form may be used to deal with individual cases, *e.g.* an Act of Parliament indemnifying an individual from the consequences of an illegal act.[2]

Judicial Powers

The exercise of judicial functions involves investigation, deliberation and the making of findings and other pronouncements on the rights and liabilities of parties.[3] These rights and liabilities are determined by settled procedure and their content is in principle governed by an objective standard. The extent of the discretion which the court can exercise is usually strictly limited. But the administrator, even when he is engaged in settling a dispute, will normally not be so circumscribed. His discretion enables him to take what he thinks is the right course in all the circumstances, *i.e.* to decide according to policy, which may have more regard to public interest than private rights. The term quasi-judicial has been used to describe a process which is partly judicial as well as administrative.[4] That part of the process which has a judicial element may be described as "quasi-judicial," or the whole power may be described as a "quasi-judicial" power. Thus the exercise of an administrative power, *e.g.* the confirmation by a Minister of an order made by a local authority, must frequently be preceded by a public inquiry before an official appointed by the Minister. The holding of the inquiry involves the hearing of evidence, and this resembles the judicial process. It must be conducted in accordance with rules of natural justice. The decision whether or not to confirm the order involves the exercise of a discretion; the Minister must take into account the findings at the inquiry, as well as other relevant factors, *e.g.* general policy in regard to similar orders. Thus the Minister, while to some degree he may be acting as a judge, arrives at his decision not by applying any fixed rule of law, but by exercising his own judgment as to what in all the circumstances is fair and just, having regard to the public interest as well as the private rights of any

[1] *E.g.* Cmnd. 3830 (1968).
[2] *E.g.* Niall Macpherson Indemnity Act 1954.
[3] See *Administrative Tribunals and the Courts*, by D. M. Gordon, 49 L.Q.R. 94.
[4] See H. W. R. Wade, *Quasi-judicial and its Background*, (1949) 10 C.L.J. 216 which accepts the inevitability of this inelegant term to describe functions which lie on the borderline between judicial and administrative spheres.

objectors. "Though the act of affirming a clearance order is an administrative act, the consideration which must precede the doing of the act is of the nature of a quasi-judicial consideration."[1] In general it may be said that a power involves a judicial element whenever it involves the decision of a dispute. When the decision in resolving a dispute primarily involves the application of law to facts, it is a judicial process. When the final decision primarily involves an exercise of discretion based on policy, it is a quasi-judicial process.[2]

Another view is that a tribunal which bases its decision on policy or expediency is legislating and suggests that the true distinction is between a judicial tribunal which looks to law to guide it and an administrative one which is a law unto itself.[3] It has been suggested that a judicial decision is merely a decision which is made by the courts in accordance with strict legal procedure, whereas a quasi-judicial decision is given by an administrator or an administrative court entitled to follow its own procedure provided only that the rules of natural justice are observed.[4] Frequently it is determined only as a matter of expediency whether a decision shall be entrusted to a judge or to an administrator,[5] but it is submitted that when the law is being applied to facts for the purpose of settling a question of right or obligation (*e.g.* does a citizen fall within the definition of an injured person under a particular statute?) a strictly judicial function is exercised, whether it is in fact exercised by judge or administrator. If classification is by function or substance, we use the terms "judicial" and "quasi-judicial" as showing the nature of the decision to be given. If classification is by procedure, we use the term "judicial" when a decision is given by a judge following ordinary legal procedure, and the term "quasi-judicial" when a decision is given by an administrator after hearing the opposing parties. It must be emphasised that the classification of powers may vary depending on the purpose for which it is being made and no single scheme of classification would serve in all contexts.[6] Thus for the purpose of affording absolute protection from liability in tort to judges and magistrates in relation to their judicial powers, the concept of a judicial function is very broad indeed.

[1] *Errington* v. *Minister of Health*, [1935] 1 K.B. 249, at p. 273.

[2] *Cf. Franklin* v. *Minister of Town and Country Planning*, [1948] A.C. 87, p. 653, *post*.

[3] See 49 L.Q.R. 94 and 419 for article by D. M. Gordon, *Administrative Tribunals and the Courts*; see his definition of a judicial tribunal at p. 106.

[4] Jennings *op. cit.*, 5th edn., pp. 294–304.

[5] Pp 693-6, *post*.

[6] de Smith, *op. cit.*, p. 77.

The following examples illustrate some types of governmental powers:

Legislative Power conferred on the Sovereign in Council

1. Extradition Act 1870, s. 2:

> "When an arrangement has been made with any foreign state with respect to the surrender to such state of any fugitive criminals, Her Majesty may, by Order in Council, direct that this Act shall apply in the case of such foreign state.
>
> Her Majesty may, by the same or any subsequent order, limit the operation of the order, and restrict the same to fugitive criminals who are in or suspected of being in the part of Her Majesty's dominions specified in the order, and render the operation thereof subject to such conditions, exceptions, and qualifications as may be deemed expedient. . . ."

Legislative Power conferred on a Minister

2. Police Act 1964, s. 33 (1):

> "Subject to the provisions of this section, the Secretary of State may make regulations as to the government, administration and conditions of service of police forces."
>
> (The section then specifies certain matters, such as ranks, qualifications for appointment and promotion, hours of duty, leave and pay, on which regulations may be made, "without prejudice to the generality of subsection (1)").

The difference between legislation by Order in Council and legislation by a Minister is one of form, nor of substance. In each case the content of the legislation is framed by a department.[1]

Administrative Power conferred on a Department

3. Diseases of Animals Act 1950, s. 15:

> "The Ministry of Agriculture and Fisheries may if it thinks fit in any case cause to be slaughtered any animals affected by foot and mouth disease."

The Minister is empowered at his discretion to implement the statutory policy of slaughter to eradicate the disease; provided that the infection is confirmed, an order to kill the cattle cannot be challenged.

Quasi-Judicial Power conferred on a Minister

4. The Housing Act 1957, Part III and Fifth Schedule, deals with the submission of clearance orders in connection with housing schemes prepared by local authorities:

[1] P. 607, *ante*.

"(1) If no objection is duly made by any of the persons on whom notices are required to be served, or if objections so made are withdrawn, then, subject to the provisions of this Schedule, the Minister may, if he thinks fit, confirm the order with or without modification.

"(2) If any objection duly made is not withdrawn, the Minister shall, before confirming the order, either cause a public local inquiry to be held or offer to any person by whom an objection has been duly made as aforesaid and not withdrawn an opportunity of appearing before and being heard by a person appointed for the purpose, and, after considering any objection not withdrawn and the report of the person who held the inquiry or of the person appointed as aforesaid, may, subject to the provisions of this Schedule, confirm the order with or without modification." [1]

The public inquiry for the hearing of objections resembles a judicial process so far as it includes the requirement to hear evidence; the Minister must consider the objections and the report of the inspector appointed to conduct the inquiry before he makes up his mind on the policy issues involved. If there are no objections, the Minister is exercising a power which is purely administrative, and there is little scope for judicial review of his decision.[2]

Object of Classifying Powers

In countries like the U.S.A., with a written Constitution which formally embodies the doctrine of the separation of powers, it is necessary to examine the nature of the powers conferred on the administration to decide whether there is any infringement of the constitutional principle of separation. In English law the importance of classifying the powers vested in the administration has always lain in the object of establishing the degree of judicial control that may be exercised over them.[3] Thus the High Court can issue orders of certiorari and prohibition when there is a duty to act judicially in determining matters which affect rights of individuals. Chapter 41 has already described the growth of the jurisdictional control exercised by the Court of King's Bench over inferior tribunals through the prerogative writs, and also the extension of this control to many government agencies which were not inferior courts in the traditional sense, but were none the less said to be exercising judicial functions. A parallel development was seen in relation to the rules of natural justice, which were considered to be binding on administrative bodies when the latter were exercising judicial or quasi-judicial

[1] Fifth Schedule, para. 5 (1) and (2). *Cf.* the Acquisition of Land (Authorisation Procedure) Act 1946, First Schedule, Part I, para. 4.

[2] Pp. 652–3, *post*.

[3] de Smith, *op. cit.*, pp. 76–80.

functions. The duty to act judicially has often been seen as a pre-requisite of judicial control.

In *Nakkuda Ali* v. *Jayaratne*,[1] defence regulations prohibited trade in textiles in Ceylon without a licence. The government controller of textiles had power to revoke a licence where he had "reasonable grounds to believe that any dealer is unfit to be allowed to continue as a dealer". Nakkuda Ali's licence was revoked and he thereupon claimed that certiorari lay to quash the revocation order. The Judicial Committee held (*inter alia*) that certiorari did not lie because the controller was under no duty to act judicially, one reason for this being that the controller was not expressly required to give a hearing to the dealer before cancelling a licence.

But the line of cases of which *Nakkuda Ali* v. *Jayaratne* was the culmination was later authoritatively criticised by the House of Lords in *Ridge* v. *Baldwin*: [2] Lord Reid stated that in situations where officials and others had power to make decisions affecting the rights of individuals, the duty to act judicially could readily be inferred from the nature of the decision; it was not necessary to look for any express judicial element, such as the duty to give a formal hearing. An earlier decision of the House of Lords, *Franklin* v. *Minister of Town and Country Planning*,[3] had caused grave doubt to be cast on the meaning of the term, quasi-judicial, in its relation to Ministers' powers. In the light both of *Franklin's* case and of *Ridge* v. *Baldwin*, less emphasis need now be placed on the classification of a power as judicial or quasi-judicial in considering the possibility of judicial review. Unlike the Ministers' Powers Report (1932), which gave much attention to the classification of powers, the Report of the Franks Committee on Administrative Tribunals and Inquiries (1957), preferred to consider what practical changes would be valuable in the interests of openness, fairness and impartiality. If the courts likewise come to place less emphasis on the formal classification of powers, they will be able to develop more flexible principles of judicial review to take full account of the great variety of powers and procedures available to public authorities.

[1] [1951] A.C. 66.
[2] Pp. 641, 655–6, *post*.
[3] P. 653, *post*.

CHAPTER FORTY-FOUR

JUDICIAL CONTROL OF POWERS

Reasons for stressing Judicial Control

JUDICIAL control of the exercise of powers by administrators or by administrative tribunals raises some of the most difficult and fundamental problems of administrative law. The lawyer, bred in the common law system with its emphasis on the right of the individual to defend his rights in the courts, may watch critically the adjudication of disputes by tribunals and other official bodies. But it must not be supposed that adjudication is the main function of the Executive. Its task is to govern by providing and administering the public services. The establishment of a system of administrative courts to settle those justiciable issues which are now decided by administrators or by tribunals would still leave the bulk of administrative work to be performed, as at present, by the government departments and other bodies which enjoy a greater or less degree of autonomy in these matters. The main functions of administrators —planning for the future, co-ordinating the policies of different agencies, supervising the daily work of government, settling priorities in the allocation of resources—are not of a character susceptible of adjudication in court. Control of these functions is essentially a matter for administrative and political means, not for the courts.

Nevertheless, judicial control is important in reconciling the existence of wide administrative powers with the principle of the rule of law. In some administrative fields Parliament has provided for an appeal to the courts from an administrative decision. But in the absence of express rights of appeal, the courts exercise a residual controlling power. This seeks to ensure that the intentions of Parliament, as inferred by the courts from the words of the statute conferring the administrative power in question, are fulfilled, and that individual rights are not affected to a greater extent than that contemplated by Parliament. In a particular case, the extent of judicial control depends on a variety of factors: the nature of the power concerned; its statutory context; the agency on which the power is conferred; the existence of other means of appealing from or challenging the decision; the standing of the individual who seeks a remedy in the courts. Nonetheless certain general principles have emerged and these are discussed in this chapter. Although expressed in the form of legal principles, judicial control embodies a political attitude to governmental power which is at the heart of a democratic society.

Limitations of Judicial Control

Although the exercise of many discretionary powers may be questioned in the courts, this does not mean that the courts may substitute their own decision for that of the body or person to whom a discretion has been entrusted.

> In *Associated Provincial Picture Houses Ltd.* v. *Wednesbury Corporation* [1] the local authority gave the plaintiff company leave for Sunday cinema performances subject to the condition that no children under 15 should be admitted to Sunday performances, with or without an adult. The Sunday Entertainments Act 1932 gave a local authority power to sanction Sunday performances, "subject to such conditions as the authority saw fit to impose." The Court of Appeal held that the local authority had not acted unreasonably or *ultra vires* in imposing the condition.

When an authority has wide discretionary power and the court is asked to hold that it has acted unreasonably, the court can only investigate the action of the authority to see if it has taken into account any matters which ought not to be, or disregarded matters which ought to be, taken into account. In the absence of provision for an appeal the merits of a decision cannot be challenged in the courts. Indeed, the main control of discretionary powers is by administrative agencies. Senior officials control their subordinates and are themselves responsible to the Minister who presides over the department. It is always open to a person aggrieved to apply to the Minister for a review of a departmental decision. Sometimes it is specifically provided by statute that the decision requires ministerial confirmation or is subject to an appeal to the Minister concerned.[2] Nor is judicial review the sole or even the main external control. Persons aggrieved by administrative decisions will more frequently appeal to their member of Parliament than to the courts; by means of parliamentary questions and other opportunities for criticism the House of Commons is able to exercise a degree of control.[3] It must be borne in mind that it is the abnormal exercise of administrative power which is challenged in the courts. The most authoritative

[1] [1948] 1 K.B. 223; K. & L. 444.
[2] Chap. 47.
[3] Chap. 9.

account of judicial review in English law opens with the words: "In the broad context of the administrative process the role of judicial institutions is inevitably sporadic and peripheral. The administrative process is not, and cannot be, a succession of justiciable controversies".[1] When administrative action is challenged in the courts, the courts can intervene only if statutory power has been exceeded or if a discretion has been wrongfully exercised.[2] In practice it may be extremely difficult to discover the reasons that lie behind an administrative decision, and the findings of fact on which it is based. Indeed it may be virtually impossible to establish a wrongful exercise of discretion in the case of a public authority which cannot be required to disclose its administrative procedure or to produce its files in court.[3]

In some cases the language of the statute seems to confer an absolute discretion on the administrator; where this is so the powers of the court are very much reduced. Under the British Nationality Act 1948, the Home Secretary may grant a certificate of naturalisation to an alien who satisfies certain conditions. Even if these conditions are satisfied, his discretion is absolute and against his refusal there exists no appeal to a court of law.[4] During the Second World War power was given to the Home Secretary by a defence regulation [5] to detain anyone whom he had reasonable cause to believe came within one of the specified categories, which included persons of hostile origin or association.

In *Liversidge* v. *Anderson* [6] the plaintiff who had been detained under the regulation brought an action against the Home Secretary for false imprisonment. It was held by the House of Lords, Lord Atkin dissenting, that the court could not enquire into the grounds for the belief which led to the making of the detention order; the matter was one for executive discretion. In regard to a political and non triable issue an objective test of reasonableness could not be applied, but only a subjective test. The statement of his belief by the Home Secretary was accepted as conclusive. Lord Wright, however, appeared to accept the view expressed in an earlier case by Tucker, J. (as he then was), that the applicant for a writ of habeas corpus was entitled to challenge the *bona fides* of the Home Secretary by affirmative evidence.[7]

[1] S. A. de Smith, *Judicial Review of Administrative Action*, p. 3.
[2] Section B *post*.
[3] See pp. 687–90, *post* (Crown Privilege). See also G. Ganz, *A Voyage of Discovery into Administrative Action*, [1963] Public Law 76.
[4] British Nationality Act 1948, s. 10 (1) and Second Schedule.
[5] Defence Regulation 18B; see Chap. 48.
[6] [1942] A.C. 206. And see Chap. 48 and K. & L. 410.
[7] *Stuart* v. *Anderson and Morrison*, [1941] 2 All E.R. 665.

Perhaps this case may be regarded as an example of a discretion theoretically open to question but in practice absolute. The Home Secretary must have reasonable cause to believe, but the court cannot go behind his statement that he had such reasonable cause to believe. A comparable power was considered in *The Queen* v. *Governor of Brixton Prison, ex parte Soblen,*[1] where the Home Secretary's power to deport an alien whom he deemed it conducive to the public good to deport was upheld in terms which make it almost impossible effectively to challenge the Home Secretary's decision. In every case the degree of discretion conferred by a statute or regulation must be determined by reference to the statute or regulation in question. In *Nakkuda Ali* v. *Jayaratne,*[2] the Judicial Committee held that there was no general principle that a court could not examine whether reasonable grounds in fact existed. And in *Padfield* v. *Minister of Agriculture,*[3] the House of Lords held that the Minister had failed to exercise his discretion in accordance with the intention of the statute which conferred the power.

This means that the power of the courts to control the administration is subject to what Parliament has laid down; and Parliament may exclude the courts either expressly,[4] or indirectly by conferring discretions of such a kind that there is virtually no possibility of challenge. Even the most revered principles of statutory interpretation are subject to the express words of the legislature. Another characteristic of judicial control in English law, that which was considered by Dicey to be its strength, is that claims against the administration and challenge to official acts must be brought in the ordinary courts; there is no separate hierarchy of courts for this purpose as in France. Hence the general principles of judicial control have to be deduced from numerous judicial decisions interpreting and applying particular statutes by which common law rules may have been expressly or impliedly varied. In section A of this chapter is examined the extent to which officials and public authorities are bound by the private law rules of tort and contract. There is some justification for the view that, not only in this field but in the whole of our administrative law, we do not yet have a comprehensive and effective legal framework for the conduct of public administration.[5]

[1] [1963] 2 Q.B. 243; pp. 257–9, *ante*.
[2] [1951] A.C. 66; p. 628, *ante*.
[3] [1968] A.C. 997; p. 642, *post*.
[4] Pp. 673–7, *post*.
[5] See, for example, H. Street, *Governmental Liability*, pp. 76–80, and J. D. B. Mitchell, *The Contracts of Public Authorities*, pp. 220–44.

A. Liability in Tort and Contract

In English law, for historic reasons which are increasingly less appropriate to modern government, a distinction has been drawn between (*a*) the Crown, including departments of the central government, and (*b*) other public authorities—for example, local authorities and public corporations—which do not fall within the structure of central government. In this section will be discussed the common law liabilities of public authorities and their servants: the special position of the Crown will be considered in Chapter 46.

Individual Liability

In the absence of statutory immunity every individual is liable for the commission of wrongful acts and for such omissions of duty as give rise to actions in tort at common law or for breach of statutory duty.

> Thus in *Entick* v. *Carrington* [1] the King's Messengers were held liable in an action of trespass for breaking and entering the plaintiff's house and seizing his papers, even though they were acting in obedience to a warrant issued by the Secretary of State. This was no defence as the Secretary had no legal authority to issue such a warrant.

Obedience to orders does not normally constitute a defence [2] whether the orders are those of the Crown, a local authority,[3] a limited company or an individual employer. The constable who finds himself a defendant in an action for false imprisonment cannot plead that he was acting under the orders of his sergeant in effecting a wrongful arrest. It is, however, seldom that officials of public authorities are sued in tort in respect of acts done in the course of duty without the employing authority being joined as defendant. A plaintiff usually sues the authority because (*a*) the authority is a more substantial defendant, and (*b*) certain statutes [4] exempt the servants of a local authority from being sued in respect of acts done *bona fide* in the course of duty. Actions against servants of the Crown were formerly more common owing to the exemption of the Crown itself from liability for tort prior to the operation of the Crown Proceedings Act 1947. The general principle that superior

[1] (1765), 19 St. Tr. 1030; K. & L. 312; p. 486, *ante*.

[2] For the position of members of the armed forces under criminal law, see Chap. 25, B.

[3] *Mill* v. *Hawker* (1875), L.R. 10 Ex. 92.

[4] *E.g.* Public Health Act 1936, s. 305; Food and Drugs Act 1955, s. 128. Cf. Town and Country Planning Act 1968, s. 64 (6).

orders are no defence to an action in tort would, if unqualified, have placed an impossibly heavy burden on many subordinate officials and would have impeded the administration of justice and government. At common law an officer of the court, such as a sheriff, who executes a judgment or order of the court, is protected from personal liability unless the judgment or order is on its face clearly outside the jurisdiction of the court.[1] Moreover it has been found necessary to provide statutory protection for certain classes of official. Thus the Constables Protection Act 1751 protects constables who act in obedience to the warrant of a magistrate and do not exceed the authority of the warrant, even though the magistrate has acted without jurisdiction in issuing the warrant. Again, the Customs and Excise Act 1952, s. 280, affords revenue officers a considerable measure of protection where there is probable cause for the seizure and detention of property as liable to forfeiture. The liability of the individual official will therefore turn both on the common law powers which he may be able to exercise and also on the statutory powers, privileges and immunities on which he may rely.

Liability of Public Authorities

A public authority (now including, for most purposes, departments of the Central Government)[2] is, like any other employer, liable for the wrongful acts of its servants or agents committed in the course of their employment. It was established in 1866 that the liability of a public body whose servants negligently execute their duties is identical with that of a private trading company.

> In *Mersey Docks and Harbour Board Trustees* v. *Gibbs*,[3] a ship and its cargo were damaged on entering a dock by reason of a mud bank left negligently at the entrance. The Trustees were held liable on appeal to the Exchequer Chamber. They appealed to the House of Lords on the ground that they were not a company deriving benefit from the traffic, but a public body of trustees constituted by Parliament for the purpose of maintaining the docks. That purpose involved authority to collect tolls for maintenance and repair of the docks, for paying off capital charges and ultimately for reducing the tolls for the benefit of the public. It was held that these public purposes did not absolve the Trustees from the duty to take reasonable care that the docks were in such a state that those who navigated them might do so without danger.

In spite of the argument that a corporation should not be liable for a wrongful act, since a wrongful act must be beyond its lawful

[1] *The Case of the Marshalsea* (1613), 10 Co. Rep. 76a.
[2] Chap. 46.
[3] (1866), L.R. 1 H.L. 93; K. & L. 381.

powers and therefore not attributable to it, it is clear that a corporation is, like any other employer, liable for the torts of its employees acting in the course of their employment. Thus a hospital authority (now a regional hospital board) will be liable for negligence in the performance of their professional duties of those physicians and surgeons who are employed by the authority.[1] Even where the employee's act is *ultra vires* the corporation, the corporation may be vicariously liable.[2] Under general principles of tortious liability, a public authority is not liable for acts committed by an employee who is acting outside the course of his employment "on a frolic of his own". Moreover, even where an official is appointed and employed by a local authority, the authority is not liable for acts which he commits under the control of a central authority or in the exercise of a distinct public duty imposed on him by the law.

In *Stanbury* v. *Exeter Corporation*,[3] a local authority was held not liable for the negligence of an inspector, who, though appointed by it, was acting at the time under an order of the Board of Agriculture.

When a policeman makes an arrest, whether acting under common law or statutory powers, he does not in law act as the servant of the local police authority.[4] Formerly therefore the police authority were not liable for torts committed by the police such as wrongful arrest, but vicarious liability for wrongful acts of the police was imposed by the Police Act 1964.[5]

Statutory Justification

Where Parliament has expressly authorised something to be done, the doing of it cannot be wrongful. Compensation for resulting damage is usually provided by Parliament. Certain presumptions are, however, observed in the interpretation of statutes. In particular it is assumed that, when discretionary power is given to a public body to perform some administrative act, there is no intention to interfere with private rights, unless the power is expressed in such a way as to make interference inevitable.

In *Metropolitan Asylum District* v. *Hill*, hospital trustees were empowered by statute to build hospitals in London. A smallpox hospital was built at Hampstead in such a way as to constitute a

[1] *Cassidy* v. *Minister of Health*, [1951] 2 K.B. 343; and see *Clerk and Lindsell on Torts*, 13th edn., para. 212.
[2] See *Clerk and Lindsell on Torts*, *op. cit.*, paras. 169–170.
[3] [1905] 2 K.B. 838.
[4] *Fisher* v. *Oldham Corporation*, [1930] 2 K.B. 364.
[5] P. 242–3, *ante*.

nuisance at common law. *Held* in the absence of express words or necessary implication in the statute authorising the commission of a nuisance, the building of the hospital was unlawful. "Where the terms of the statute are not imperative, but permissive, when it is left to the discretion of the persons empowered to determine whether the general powers committed to them shall be put into execution or not, I think the fair inference is that the Legislature intended that discretion to be exercised in strict conformity with private rights and did not intend to confer licence to commit nuisance in any place which might be selected for the purpose." [1]

If, however, the exercise of a statutory power, and *a fortiori* of a statutory duty, inevitably involves injury to private rights, or if express powers are given to do something in a particular way which must involve injury, *e.g.* to construct a building upon a particular site for a particular purpose, there is no remedy unless the statute makes provision for compensation.[2] The negligent performance of a statutory duty or exercise of statutory powers may, however, be tortious; and where the exercise of a statutory power necessarily involves injury, care must none the less be taken to avoid aggravating the injury by negligent execution.[3] Where a statutory power can be exercised in a manner either hurtful to an individual or in a manner innocuous to an individual "that man or body will be held to be guilty of negligence if he chooses, or they choose, the former mode available to him or them." [4]

Thus in *Fisher* v. *Ruislip–Northwood Urban District Council*,[5] where a motorist had been injured through colliding with an unlit shelter, it was held that a statutory power to erect air-raid shelters on the highway could only be exercised subject to a duty to take reasonable care to safeguard the public user of the highway by such special lighting as was permissible, even though ordinary street lighting was at that time prohibited.

Statutory Duties

It was at one time the view that any person who could show that he had sustained harm from a failure to perform a duty imposed by Parliament could bring an action for damages against the person or body liable to perform it.[6] If this general principle applied today, it would be very important as a means of compelling public authorities

[1] (1881), 6 App. Cas. 193 at pp. 212–13 *per* Lord Watson; K. & L. 29.
[2] *Hammersmith Railway Co.* v. *Brand* (1869), L.R. 4 H.L. 171.
[3] *Geddis* v. *Proprietors of Bann Reservoir* (1878), 3 App. Cas. 430, at pp. 455–56.
[4] *Lagan Navigation Co.* v. *Lambeg Bleaching Dyeing and Finishing Co.*, [1927] A.C. 226, *per* Lord Atkinson at p. 243.
[5] [1945] K.B. 584.
[6] Dicta to this effect in *Couch* v. *Steel* (1854), 3 E. & B. 402 were disapproved in *Atkinson* v. *Newcastle Waterworks Co.* (1877), 2 Ex. D. 441.

to perform their statutory duties. But a remedy of damages is not available for every breach of statutory duty. One type of duty has already been discussed where the only means of enforcement is by political pressure on the authorities responsible.[1] Each case turns on the true construction of the statute and no action for damages will lie if the intention is that some other remedy, civil or criminal, shall be the only one available.[2] It is not always easy to determine whether a duty is owed to the State, *i.e.* to the public at large, or primarily to an individual and only incidentally to the State. Thus Parliament has imposed general obligations upon owners of factories which are enforceable by statutory penalties in the shape of fines imposed by the criminal courts, but this does not prevent an injured employee recovering damages which he has sustained through the failure of his employer to perform his statutory duty. If it is the intention of Parliament to exclude an injured individual from a civil remedy, the duty may be made enforceable only by criminal prosecution or by an action for an injunction at the suit of the Attorney-General. Moreover Parliament, though recognising a private right in an individual, may prescribe an alternative remedy to damages as the sole remedy available for breach.[3]

Where a statute creates a new duty without providing any express remedy for breach of it, the appropriate remedies may be either criminal or civil. A pecuniary penalty payable to the Crown will not normally exclude an action for damages for breach of a statutory duty which involves compensation to injured persons.[4] It is difficult to generalise on the question of whether an individual may seek compensation for breach of a statutory duty. Where a statutory duty resembles an existing common law duty, and the harm suffered by the individual consists of injury to person or property, a court may readily hold that damages may be claimed for the breach. In such cases, *e.g.* the duty on employers under the Factories Act 1961 to fence dangerous machinery, the matter is essentially one arising out of the employment relationship and the liabilities of a public authority as employer and those of a private employer should be the same. It is much more difficult to decide the appropriate remedy for an aggrieved individual in the case of statutory duties arising from

[1] P. 623, *ante*, *Watt* v. *Kesteven C.C.*, [1955] 1 Q.B. 408.

[2] *Winfield on Tort*, 8th edn., chap. 8; *Clerk and Lindsell on Torts*, *op. cit.*, chap. 21.

[3] *E.g. Atkinson* v. *Newcastle Waterworks Co.* (1877), 2 Ex D. 441, no liability where plaintiff's house and sawmill were burned down because of failure to maintain pressure in water pipes; *Saunders* v. *Holborn District Board*, [1895] 1 Q.B. 64, no liability where damage caused by failure to clear street refuse; cf. *Read* v. *Croydon Corporation*, [1938] 4 All E.R. 631.

[4] *Monk* v. *Warbey*, [1935] 1 K.B. 75.

public services or public powers of control. Here the comparison with private law remedies cannot easily be made and a court may hold that the duty is owed only to a higher public authority, and not to a private individual. In 1969 the English and Scottish Law Commissions recommended that the courts should in interpreting statutes assume that the remedy of damages is available for breach of statutory duty, unless Parliament expressly provides to the contrary.[1] Yet this recommendation seems not to take account of the characteristic relationships between government and the individual which are the concern of administrative law; in many of these instances the award of damages might not be an appropriate remedy.

The great variety of duties imposed by statute helps to explain why there is no single form of judicial proceedings for enforcing public duties and why different methods have been preferred at different periods of legal history. A breach of public duty was at one time punishable on indictment as a misdemeanour and this was appropriate to the enforcement of duties of an administrative nature at a time when Quarter Sessions exercised both criminal and local government functions. Today civil proceedings may be brought by the Attorney-General on behalf of the public interest.[2] Certain duties may be enforced by the prerogative order of mandamus.[3] In the case of the common law duty to repair the highway, which was transferred by statute from the inhabitants of a parish to the elected local highway authority, an action formerly lay against a highway authority for misfeasance,[4] (*e.g.* the imperfect filling of a trench) but not for non-feasance [5] (*i.e.* mere failure to repair). The historical origin of the non-feasance rule long preceded the development of the tort of negligence and the rule became unjustifiable in modern conditions. Under the Highways (Miscellaneous Provisions) Act 1961, liability was imposed on highway authorities for failure to maintain a highway maintainable at the public expense, subject to the defence of reasonable care having been taken. The remedy of indictment for non-repair of the highway had been abolished earlier by the Highways Act 1959, s. 59. Apart from these overdue statutory reforms, the courts had earlier shown their dislike for the non-feasance rule by their unwillingness to allow non-feasance to be a defence to actions concerning other public duties than the duty to repair highways.[6]

[1] H.C. (1968–69) 256, para. 38.
[2] Pp. 669–70, *post.*
[3] Pp. 658–9, *post.*
[4] *Shoreditch* (*Mayor of*) v. *Bull* (1904), 90 L.T. 210.
[5] *Cowley* v. *Newmarket Local Board*, [1892] A.C. 345.
[6] *Pride of Derby and Derbyshire Angling Association Ltd.* v. *British Celanese Ltd.*, [1953] Ch. 149; cf. *Smeaton* v. *Ilford Corporation*, [1954] Ch. 450.

Special protection in litigation was formerly given to many public authorities by the statutory rule that actions against public authorities and officials arising under statute or out of breach of duty had to be commenced within one year from the date on which the cause of action accrued. This special protection was abolished in 1954,[1] along with the rule that prosecutions for criminal proceedings against public authorities had to be started within six months. There are now no general immunities from criminal process available to public authorities, but departments of the central government share in the immunity of the Crown from prosecution; as individuals Crown servants can be prosecuted and cannot plead superior orders as a defence.

B. Excess and Abuse of Powers

Ultra Vires Rule

It has been shown that the main control of administrative powers is that exercised by higher administrative agencies and through ministerial responsibility to Parliament, but that the courts can exercise control when a power is exceeded or abused.[2] When a power is exceeded, any acts done in excess of the power are invalid as being *ultra vires*. The *ultra vires* doctrine cannot be used to question the validity of an Act of Parliament; but it is effective to control those who exceed the administrative discretion which an Act has given. The simplest instance of the *ultra vires* rule is where an act is done in excess of a power, or where jurisdiction to adjudicate upon a dispute is exceeded. Three examples may be given:

(1) In *Attorney-General* v. *Fulham Corporation* [3] the borough council of Fulham arranged to benefit the housewives of the borough by installing a municipal laundry with the latest contrivances worked by corporation officials. Under the Baths and Wash-houses Acts, 1846 and 1847, the council had power to establish a wash-house, where people could wash their own clothes. A ratepayer sought by an injunction to restrain the corporation from conducting the laundry as a business. *Held* that the statutory power was confined to the establishment of a wash-house and that it was *ultra vires* for the Fulham Corporation to establish something different. Thus were the women of Fulham deprived of the benefit of an up-to-date municipal laundry.

(2) Under the Housing Act 1925 [4] the Minister of Health was empowered to confirm improvement schemes submitted by local authorities in pursuance of the Act. The Act required schemes to

[1] Law Reform (Limitation of Actions, etc.) Act 1954, s.1, repealing the Public Authorities Protection Act 1893, as amended by the Limitation Act 1939.

[2] Pp. 619–21, *ante*.

[3] [1921] 1 Ch. 440.

[4] Since repealed. See now Housing Act 1957, Part III.

show how the compulsorily acquired land was to be developed. The Derby Corporation submitted a scheme for confirmation which contained no provisions showing how the land was to be developed, but left the Corporation free to develop, sell or lease the land for any purpose. The form of this scheme was one commonly used by local authorities and previously confirmed by the Minister. An owner of the land affected brought proceedings to restrain the Minister from confirming the scheme. *Held* that the Minister's jurisdiction was restricted to confirming schemes which were within the Act; the scheme was *ultra vires* and, had he confirmed it, the Minister would have acted in excess of his jurisdiction.[1]

(3) The Caravan Sites and Control of Development Act 1960 gave power to local authorities to grant licences for caravan sites "subject to such conditions as the authority may think it necessary or desirable to impose . . . in the interests of persons dwelling thereon in caravans. or of any other class of persons, or of the public at large". An appeal against unduly burdensome conditions lay to the local magistrates' court. Chertsey Urban District Council issued a licence subject to conditions (*inter alia*) that individual site rents should be agreed with the council and that no premiums should be charged on incoming dwellers, that the dwellers should be granted security of tenure similar to that under the Rent Acts for controlled tenancies, that dwellers should be free to choose where they did their shopping and should not be restricted in the callers they had or in the formation of tenants' or political associations. The site-owner challenged these conditions as *ultra vires*. *Held* by the House of Lords that the Act of 1960 was restricted to granting powers to impose conditions relating to the use of the site; these conditions related to the contents of the agreements for letting caravans made with individual dwellers; despite the apparently very wide terms of the enabling Act, all the conditions were *ultra vires* and void.[2]

The limits of an authority's power are not always obvious. Although, as the last example illustrates, the courts will sometimes cut down the scope of an apparently wide discretion, the powers of an authority may be held to include not only those expressly conferred by statute but also those which are reasonably incidental to those expressly conferred.

By the Housing Act 1957, the "general management, regulation and control" of council houses were vested in the local housing authority. At no cost to the general rate fund, a local authority arranged with an insurance company a scheme by which tenants could pay a small weekly premium, collected by the council together with the rent, for the insurance of their household goods. The scheme was held to be within the authority's statutory power of management.[3]

[1] *The King* v. *Minister of Health, ex parte Davis*, [1929] 1 K.B. 619.
[2] *Mixnam's Properties Ltd.* v. *Chertsey Urban District Council*, [1965] A.C. 735.
[3] *Attorney-General* v. *Crayford Urban District Council*, [1962] Ch. 575.

Abuse of Powers

The courts will intervene not only to prevent powers being exceeded, but also to prevent their being abused. Control of the improper exercise of powers may also be regarded as an application of the *ultra vires* doctrine. The exercise of a discretion without taking into account all relevant considerations is equivalent to a failure to exercise it. The exercise of a power for an improper purpose is not an exercise of a power conferred for purposes defined in the statute which confers it. Acts which are *prima facie* lawful may be invalidated if they are done for a wrong purpose or by a wrong procedure. It must, however, again be stressed that where a discretion is committed to an administrator, no appeal based solely on the merits of the decision lies to the courts. Provided that the discretion is exercised legitimately, the courts cannot substitute their discretion for his.[1] The only appeal is to higher administrative authority or by raising the matter in Parliament.

Incorrect Procedure

Where statute authorises a certain power to be exercised after a stated procedure has been followed, failure to observe the procedure may result in the purported exercise of the power being declared a nullity. This does not however mean that every minor procedural error will invalidate the decision as substantial compliance with the procedure may be considered sufficient.

> In *Ridge* v. *Baldwin*,[2] the Brighton watch committee had dismissed their chief constable following his trial at the Central Criminal Court on charges of conspiracy; his acquittal had been accompanied by serious criticism of his conduct by the trial judge. Disciplinary regulations made under the Police Act 1919 laid down a procedure by which formal inquiry had to be held into charges brought against a chief constable before he could be dismissed. The watch committee contended that this procedure did not apply to the power of dismissal which they were exercising under the Municipal Corporations Act 1882. *Held* (House of Lords) *inter alia* that the disciplinary regulations did apply in this case, and "inasmuch as the decision was arrived at in complete disregard of the regulations it must be regarded as void and of no effect"[3].

Irrelevant Considerations

Powers vested in a Minister, local authority or other public body must be exercised in accordance with the intention of Parliament as

[1] P. 630, *ante*.

[2] [1964] A.C. 40, discussed by A. W. Bradley in *A Failure of Justice and Defect of Police*, [1964] C.L.J. 83.

[3] *Per* Lord Morris of Borth-y-Gest at p. 117.

may be inferred from the Act in question. The scope of the Act limits the considerations which the authority may take into account.

In *The Queen* v. *Boteler* [1] justices refused to order a parish to contribute to the expenses of its poor law union because they disapproved of the Act of Parliament which had annexed the parish to the union. *Held* that the justices had not exercised their lawful discretion, since they based their decision on the ground that the operation of the Act of Parliament was unjust. Cockburn, C.J., said: "That is not a tenable ground on which this court can allow magistrates to decline to exercise their discretion according to law".

The same principle, albeit in a much refined form, has been used to review the discretionary decisions of central government.

Under the Agricultural Marketing Act 1958, statutory marketing schemes include a complaints procedure by which a committee of investigation examines any complaint made about the operation of the scheme "if the Minister in any case so directs". In *Padfield* v. *Minister of Agriculture*,[2] Padfield, a farmer in south-east England, complained about the scheme of prices paid to farmers in that region by the Milk Marketing Board. The Minister refused to direct that the complaint be referred to the committee of investigation, and claimed that he had an unfettered discretion in deciding whether or not to refer complaints to the committee. *Held* (House of Lords) the Minister would be directed to deal with the complaint according to law. The reasons given by the Minister for his refusal were not good reasons in law and showed that he had not exercised his discretion in a manner which promoted the intention and objects of the Act of 1958. "The policy and objects of the Act must be determined by construing the Act as a whole, and construction is always a matter of law for the court." (*Per* Lord Reid).[3]

The court's power to rule that certain considerations are irrelevant to a statutory discretion may severely limit the scope of general words in a statute. For example, in deciding whether to grant a caravan licence under public health legislation, a public health authority could not take into account matters of local amenity, as these were relevant to town planning law.[4] Nevertheless each situation turns on interpreting the statute in question, and the court does not always interpret statutory discretion so narrowly.[5]

[1] (1854), 4 B. & S. 969; K. & L. 443.

[2] [1968] A.C. 997.

[3] [1968] A.C. 997, 1030.

[4] *Pilling* v. *Abergele Rural District Council*, [1950] 1 K.B. 636; the relevant provisions of the Public Health Act 1936 were later replaced by the Caravan Sites and Control of Development Act 1960, under which the licensing power has also been narrowly interpreted by the courts: see *Mixnam's Properties Ltd.* v. *Chertsey Urban District Council*, [1965] A.C. 735, p. 640, *ante*.

[5] *E.g. Hanks* v. *Minister of Housing and Local Government*, [1963] 1 Q.B. 999, *Maurice* v. *London County Council*, [1964] 2 Q.B. 362, and *Iveagh* v. *Minister of Housing and Local Government*, [1964] 1 Q.B. 395.

Improper Purposes

The exercise of a power for an improper purpose is invalid as not being done *bona fide*. Improper purposes include, but are not restricted to, malice or personal dishonesty on the part of the officials or councillors making the decision; examples of this kind are rare and most instances of improper purpose have arisen out of a mistaken interpretation by a public authority of what it is empowered to do, sometimes contributed to by an excess of zeal in the public interest.

The Municipal Council of Sydney was empowered to acquire land compulsorily for the purpose of extending streets or improving the city. The council purporting to exercise this power acquired land, not for the purpose of an extension or improvement, but with the object of taking advantage of an anticipated increment of value. The acquisition of the land was an invalid exercise of the power.[1]

Difficulty arises when the authority is motivated both by lawful and unlawful purposes.

The Westminster Corporation was empowered to construct public conveniences but not to provide pedestrian subways. Underground conveniences were designed so that the subway leading to them provided a means of crossing a busy street. It was sought to restrain the Corporation from proceeding with the work on the ground that the real object was the provision of a crossing and not of public conveniences. The court refused to intervene. "It is not enough to show that the Corporation contemplated that the public might use the subway as a means of crossing the street. In order to make out a case of bad faith, it must be shown that the Corporation constructed the subway as a means of crossing the street under colour and pretence of providing public conveniences not really wanted." [2]

In such cases a distinction has sometimes been drawn between purpose and motive, so that where an exercise of power fulfils the purposes for which the power was given, it matters not that those exercising it were influenced by an extraneous motive. But the motive-purpose distinction is difficult to maintain, and it has sometimes given way to the test of what was the dominant purpose, or to the rather stricter rule, already outlined, that the presence of any extraneous or irrelevant considerations invalidates the decision.[3] Although the exercise of powers by an administrative organisation of a subordinate character may be challenged on the ground that it has acted for an inadmissible or ulterior purpose, such a challenge

[1] *Municipal Council of Sydney* v. *Campbell*, [1925] A.C. 338.

[2] *Westminster Corporation* v. *London and North Western Railway Co.*, [1905] A.C. 426, *per* Lord Macnaghten, at p. 432. Cf. *Webb* v. *Minister of Housing and Local Government* [1965] 2 All E.R. 193, noted in [1965] C.L.J. 1.

[3] See de Smith, *Judicial Review of Administrative Action*, pp. 304–17.

cannot succeed against a representative body whose function is legislative rather than administrative.

A seeds committee had issued general orders prohibiting the sale of seeds of certain descriptions; it was held that the *bona fides* of the committee in making the orders could be challenged, whereas in similar circumstances the good faith of a legislature could not be called in question in a court of law: *Arthur Yates & Co. Pty. Ltd.* v. *Vegetable Seeds Committee.*[1]

Discretion may not be delegated or surrendered

An authority to which the exercise of discretion has been entrusted by statute cannot delegate that exercise to another unless upon the construction of the relevant statute it is clear that the delegation is authorised.

Barnard v. *National Dock Labour Board*[2] concerned a statutory scheme for the registration of dock-workers, under which the disciplinary powers of the National Dock Labour Board had to be delegated to local dock boards. The London Dock Board purported to delegate its disciplinary function to the port manager, who during a trade dispute suspended Barnard from work. *Held*, that disciplinary powers could not be lawfully delegated to the port manager; the purported suspension was declared a nullity.

The rule against unauthorised delegation of powers might seem to require all powers vested in a Minister to be exercised by him personally. That the courts have accepted the exigencies of departmental administration was shown in *Local Government Board* v. *Arlidge*:[3] powers and duties conferred on a Minister may properly be exercised by officials in his department, whose decisions the Minister can control and for whom he is responsible to Parliament.[4]

A discretion may not be surrendered, whether the surrender takes the form of contracting in advance to exercise it in a particular way or of pre-judging the way in which it shall be exercised. Thus the licensing committees of the justices have full discretion in licensing matters, but it is their duty to hear all applications and to apply their minds in each case presented to them, whatever general policy they may have decided upon. Each applicant must have the opportunity of urging that the general policy should not be applied in the particular circumstances of his case. Even so extensive a discretion must be exercised in a judicial manner.[5]

[1] (1945), 72 C.L.R. 37; K. & L. 450.

[2] [1953] 2 Q.B. 18, K. & L. 432, p. 672, *post*; see also *Vine* v. *National Dock Labour Board,* [1957] A.C. 488.

[3] [1915] A.C. 120, p. 651, *post*.

[4] *Carltona Ltd.* v. *Commissioners of Works*, [1943] 2 All E.R. 560.

[5] *Sharp* v. *Wakefield,* [1891] A.C. 173.

Nor can a discretion be taken away by orders from a superior.

In *Simms Motor Units Ltd.* v. *Minister of Labour* [1] a National Service Officer, who had been given a war-time statutory power to reinstate dismissed employees at his discretion, failed to exercise his discretion, but applied instead a general instruction given to him by his Minister to the effect that he should reinstate in all cases of a particular type, thus negativing the exercise of the discretion.

Local Authority Discretions

While the above principles of judicial review apply to all administrative authorities, the courts are somewhat readier to cut down the width of discretions vested in local authorities than those vested in Ministers. In particular, discretions which appear on their face to be absolute or entirely subjective are held to be subject to limitations. Thus a town planning authority have power to grant planning permission "subject to such conditions as they think fit" [2]; although an appeal lies from the imposition of conditions to the Minister of Housing and Local Government, the courts have imposed limitations which appreciably reduce the scope of this power.[3]

One particular factor which must guide the decisions of a local authority lies in their financial responsibility to the ratepayers. Excessive expenditure upon a lawful object may be illegal: in *Roberts* v. *Hopwood* [4] the court held invalid a payment of wages by the Poplar Borough Council which fixed an arbitrary rate for wages without regard to existing labour conditions. But the courts will not interfere with the discretion of local authorities as to payment of wages, unless the authority has taken extraneous considerations into account in fixing the rate.[5] The general rate fund cannot be used to subsidise free municipal transport for elderly citizens at the expense of the ratepayer generally, in the absence of statutory authorisation.[6] In these cases, the local authority's duty to its ratepayers has directly influenced judicial interpretation of the authority's powers.

A similar attitude may be seen in the case of byelaws. Unlike other delegated legislation, byelaws made by subordinate bodies may be declared invalid on the ground that they are unreasonable.[7]

1 [1946] 2 All E.R. 201.

2 Town and Country Planning Act 192, s. 17 (1).

3 *Hall & Co. Ltd.* v. *Shoreham-by-Sea Urban District Council*, [1964] 1 All E.R. 1; see also the *Mixnam's Properties* case (p. 640, *ante*), and cf. *Westminster Bank Ltd.* v. *Beverley Borough Council*, [1969] 1 Q.B. 499.

4 [1925] A.C. 578. See also *Taylor* v. *Munrow*, [1960] 1 All E.R. 455.

5 *In re Decision of Walker*, [1944] K.B. 644.

6 *Prescott* v. *Birmingham Corporation*, p. 620, *ante*.

7 The court will not interfere with the exercise of legislative power by the Central Government, except on grounds of *vires: Attorney-General for Canada* v. *Hallet and Carey Ltd.*, [1952] A.C. 427.

The courts will not, however, treat the byelaws of a public authority as unreasonable unless they are manifestly oppressive, whereas the byelaws of a trading concern, such as a water company, will be rigorously scrutinised

> In *Kruse* v. *Johnson* [1] a byelaw of the Kent County Council prohibiting the playing of musical instruments or singing in the highway within fifty yards of a dwelling-house to the annoyance of the inmates was held to be good. The Court held that it should be slow to condemn as invalid on the ground of supposed unreasonableness any byelaw made by a body legislating under the delegated authority of Parliament within the extent of the authority given to the body to deal with matters which concerned it.

But a byelaw will be held *ultra vires* if it is repugnant to the general law of the land, for example if it attempts to make unlawful something which is expressly made lawful by statute.[2] Similarly a byelaw may be held to be void if it is unreasonable in its application.[3]

C. Natural Justice

The rule that certain powers must be exercised in accordance with natural justice is a most important principle of judicial review. The requirements of natural justice are essentially unwritten rules of the common law; on many matters they have been embodied in enacted law, for example by the provision of statutory procedures enabling an individual who disagrees with an official decision to appeal to a special tribunal. As an unwritten principle, natural justice evolved largely through the control exercised by the central courts over bodies of inferior jurisdiction.[4] This control applied not only to the justices of the peace but also to other bodies in relation to certain of their powers, *e.g.* the power of the governing body of a corporation to deprive persons of membership or corporate office, and the power of a bishop to take disciplinary action against clergy in his diocese. During the nineteenth century, the rules of natural justice were applied to the conduct of arbitrators, and to the disciplinary functions of professional bodies and voluntary associations. With the development of new governmental powers affecting an individual's property or livelihood, natural justice served to supplement the procedural shortcomings of Victorian legislation. Both local and central govern-

[1] [1898] 2 Q.B. 91, K. & L. 48.
[2] *Powell* v. *May*, [1946] K.B. 330.
[3] *Repton School Governors* v. *Repton Rural District Council*, [1918] 2 K.B. 133 (interference with private property right).
[4] Pp. 587–90, *ante*; de Smith, *op. cit.*, pp. 135–42.

ment authorities were bound to observe natural justice in many of their functions, but it was for the courts to determine the precise limits of this obligation. The achievement of the courts in this difficult task will be considered later in this section. It is convenient first to illustrate the two main rules of natural justice with examples drawn from the ordinary courts themselves.

The Rule against Bias: *No man a judge in his own cause*

The essence of a fair judicial decision is that it shall have been made by an impartial judge. The rule against bias laid down in *The Queen* v. *Rand* [1] is that disqualification of a judge from acting in a particular case can arise in two ways: (*a*) where he has any direct pecuniary interest, however small, in the subject matter of inquiry—thus a judge who is a shareholder in a company appearing before him as a litigant must decline to hear the case, save by consent of all the parties [2]; (*b*) where, apart from direct pecuniary interest, there is a real likelihood that the judge would have a bias in favour of one of the parties. Where bias is alleged, the reviewing court does not decide whether the decision was in fact biased, but whether in the circumstances a reasonable possibility of bias was established. *The King* v. *Sussex Justices, ex parte McCarthy* [3] is an extreme instance of the principle that justice should not only be done, but should manifestly and undoubtedly be seen to be done.

> The acting clerk to the justices was a member of a firm of solicitors who were to represent the plaintiff in civil proceedings pending as a result of a collision in connection with which the applicant was summoned for a motoring offence. The acting clerk retired with the bench but was not asked to advise the justices on their decision to convict the applicant. *Held* that, as the clerk's firm was connected with the case in the civil action, he ought not to advise the justices in the criminal matter and therefore could not, had he been required to do so, properly have discharged his duties as clerk. The conviction was accordingly quashed, despite the fact that the clerk had actually taken no part in the decision to convict.
>
> On the other hand, in *The Queen* v. *Rand*,[4] the Court of Queen's Bench refused to set aside a certificate given by justices in favour of the Bradford Corporation merely on the ground that two of the justices were trustees of societies which had invested funds in bonds of the Corporation.

To disqualify a person from acting in a judicial or quasi-judicial capacity a real likelihood of bias must appear, not only from the

[1] (1866), L.R. 1 Q.B. 230, approved in *The King* v. *Sunderland Justices*, [1901] 2 K.B. 357.
[2] *Dimes* v. *Grand Junction Canal* (*Proprietors of*) (1852), 3 H.L.C. 759.
[3] [1924] 1 K.B. 256.
[4] (1866), L.R. 1 Q.B. 230; K. & L. 516.

materials in fact ascertained but from such further facts as might readily be verified in the course of enquiries.[1] But if on all the facts there are grounds for a reasonable suspicion of bias on the part of one or more members of an adjudicating body, its decision must be set aside.

> In *Metropolitan Properties Ltd.* v. *Lannon*,[2] a rent assessment committee had fixed the rent for three flats in one block of flats. The chairman of the committee was a solicitor who lived with his father in a second block of flats owned by the same property group. The chairman's firm was negotiating about rents with the landlords on behalf of his father and other tenants in the second block. *Held* that the decision of the committee must be quashed. "No man can be an advocate for or against a party in one proceedings, and at the same time sit as a judge of that party in another proceeding." [3]

The Right to a Hearing: No man to be condemned unheard

It is equally fundamental to a just judicial decision that each party should have the opportunity of knowing the case against him and of stating his own case. Each party must have the chance to present his version of the facts and to make his submissions on the relevant rules of law. Each side must be able to comment on all material considered by the judge, and neither side must communicate with the judge behind the other's back. Although the written rules of court procedure are founded on these general principles, there is scope for the unwritten right to a hearing to operate even in the ordinary courts. Thus the High Court cannot order a solicitor personally to bear costs caused by his misconduct unless he is given an opportunity to meet the complaint,[4] nor can a witness to proceedings for assault in a magistrates' court be bound over to keep the peace unless the magistrates give him an opportunity of being heard on the point.[5] Yet, as will be seen to a much greater extent in the administrative field, the requirements of natural justice are not invariable; thus although a party to civil proceedings is normally entitled to know all the material considered by the judge, the nature of the Chancery Division's ancient jurisdiction over children is such that in exceptional cases the judge may take into account confidential medical reports on the children which are not disclosed to the parents.[6]

Natural Justice and Administrative Authorities

In what circumstances are bodies other than the courts bound to

[1] *The Queen* v. *Camborne Justices, ex parte Pearce*, [1955] 1 Q.B. 41; see also *The Queen* v. *Barnsley Licensing Justices*, [1960] 2 Q.B. 167.

[2] [1969] 1 Q.B. 577.

[3] *Per* Lord Denning, M.R., [1969] 1 Q.B. 577, 600.

[4] *Abraham* v. *Jutsun*, [1963] 2 All E.R. 402; see also Rules of the Supreme Court, Order 62, rule 8.

[5] *Sheldon* v. *Bromfield Justices*, [1964] 2 Q.B. 573.

[6] *In re K (Infants)*, [1965] A.C. 201.

observe the rules of natural justice? It would be an exaggeration to suggest that natural justice must be observed whenever an official or public body exercises a legal power. The duty arises in a variety of situations whenever it is particularly important to an individual directly affected by the decision that a fair procedure should be observed; therefore, if the exercise of power directly affects a man's rights, or his property, or his character, it is more likely to be subject to natural justice; so is a decision which follows a procedure involving the confrontation of two opposing views, in a manner comparable to that of litigation.[1] Thus a university could not deprive a senior member of his degrees without informing him of the charges brought against him and giving him an opportunity of answering them.[2] Nor can a trade union expel a member without giving him adequate notice of the charges giving rise to the penalty of expulsion.[3] Exactly the same principle was applied in the nineteenth century to action by a local authority under statutory powers directed against an individual's property.

> In *Cooper* v. *Wandsworth Board of Works*,[4] the plaintiffs recovered from the defendant Board damages in trespass for demolishing his partly-built house. He had failed to notify his intention to build the house to the Board, which by statute thereupon had power to demolish the building. *Held*, that the Board should have given a hearing to the plaintiff before exercising their statutory power of demolition. "Although there are no positive words in a statute requiring that the party shall be heard, yet the justice of the common law shall supply the omission of the legislature".[5]

The courts justified their intervention in cases such as these by describing the statutory power in question as being judicial in character:

> "In condemning a man to have his house pulled down, a judicial act is as much implied as in fining him £5; and as the local board is the only tribunal that can make such an order its act must be a judicial act, and the party to be affected should have a notice given him".[6]

In a similar manner the rule against bias has been applied to local authorities.

[1] For an elaboration of this approach, see note by R. B. Cooke in [1954] C.L.J. pp. 14–19.

[2] *Dr. Bentley's Case* (1723), 1 Stra. 557; see also *Ceylon University* v. *Fernando*, [1960] 1 All E.R. 631; and *The Queen* v. *Aston University Senate, ex parte Roffey*, [1969] 2 Q.B. 538. But cf. *Vidyodaya University Council* v. *Silva*, [1964] 3 All E.R. 865, discussed in [1965] C.L.J. 3.

[3] *Annamunthodo* v. *Oilfields Workers' Trade Union*, [1961] A.C. 945.

[4] (1863), 14 C.B. (N.S.) 180; K. & L. 518.

[5] *Per* Byles, J. at p. 194.

[6] *Per* Wills J. in *Hopkins* v. *Smethwick Local Board of Health* (1890), 24 Q.B.D. 713.

Thus a local authority's decision to grant planning permission for the development of certain land was quashed by certiorari on the ground that one of the councillors who had approved the granting of permission had acted as estate agent for the developer.[1]

In another case, a watch committee's resolution to confirm a chief constable's decision to dismiss a police sergeant was invalidated because the chief constable remained with the committee during its deliberation, after it had heard the sergeant's case against dismissal.[2]

The Content of Natural Justice

These illustrations will show the wide variety of situations to which the principle of natural justice has been applied. It is difficult to describe the content of natural justice when applied to administrative authorities except in very general terms, such as those used by Lord Selborne in *Spackman* v. *Plumstead Board of Works*[3]:

> "No doubt in the absence of special provisions as to how the person who is to decide is to proceed the law will imply no more than that the substantial requirements of justice shall not be violated. He is not a judge in the proper sense of the word; but he must give the parties an opportunity of being heard and stating their case and their view. He must give notice that he will proceed with the matter and he must act honestly and impartially and not under the direction of some other person or persons to whom the authority is not given by law. There must be no malversation of any kind. There would be no decision within the meaning of the statute if there were anything of that sort done contrary to the essence of justice."

More recently, a *dictum* of Tucker, L.J., has received approval:

> "There are in my view no words which are of universal application to every kind of inquiry and every kind of domestic tribunal. The requirements of natural justice must depend on the circumstances of the case, the nature of the inquiry, the rules under which the tribunal is acting, the subject-matter that is being dealt with and so forth.[4]"

Natural Justice and Ministers' Powers

Many instances of natural justice in the law reports date from the period before the development of the present administrative structure. Today the granting of new governmental power is usually accompanied by complex statutory procedures designed to reconcile administrative needs with democratic safeguards. To what extent is it desirable or possible for additional unwritten rules of procedure

[1] *The King* v. *Hendon Rural District Council, ex parte Chorley*, [1933] 2 K.B. 696. The councillor would now be liable for prosecution under the Local Government Act 1933, s. 76; p. 369, *ante*.

[2] *Cooper* v. *Wilson*, [1937] 2 K.B. 309.

[3] (1885), 10 App. Cas. 229.

[4] *Russell* v. *Duke of Norfolk*, [1949] 1 All E.R. 109 at 118; applied in *University of Ceylon* v. *Fernando*, [1960] 1 All E.R. 631 and *In re K (Infants)*, [1965] A.C. 201.

to be implied? Does the rule that no man should be judge in his own cause continue to be relevant if the settlement of disputes arising from the execution of policy is entrusted to the Minister whose department is itself responsible for maintaining that policy? The interest of the community at large in efficient administration is no less important than the rights of the individual objector or appellant. A dispute arising as an incident in the conduct of a public service cannot, by reason solely of prejudice to private rights, be isolated from the general responsibility of the department concerned. There are some instances of governmental power where there seems little scope for natural justice, notably the powers of the Home Secretary in relation to aliens.[1] In regard to many other departmental powers, the common law rules of natural justice may require little more from a department than the carrying out in good faith of its usual procedures. The leading case is *Local Government Board* v. *Arlidge*.[2]

The Hampstead Borough Council had made a closing order in respect of a house which appeared unfit for human habitation. The owner appealed to the Local Government Board in the manner prescribed by the Housing and Town Planning Act 1909.[3] This right of appeal replaced an earlier statutory right of appeal to Quarter Sessions. A public inquiry was held before a housing inspector of the Board and after receiving his report the Board confirmed the closing order. Arlidge applied to the court to declare the decision invalid, mainly on the grounds that the order of the Board did not disclose which of the officials of the Board actually decided the appeal; that he, the plaintiff, did not have an opportunity of being heard orally by that official; and that he was not permitted to see the report of the inspector who conducted the public inquiry on behalf of the Board. It was held by the House of Lords, reversing the Court of Appeal, that Arlidge could not object to the order on these grounds since Parliament having entrusted judicial duties to an executive body must be taken, in the absence of any declaration to the contrary, to have intended it to follow the procedure which was its own and was necessary if it was to be capable of doing its work efficiently. Furthermore, Parliament had empowered the Board to frame rules to regulate its own procedure. So long as the officials dealt with the question referred to them without bias, and gave the parties an opportunity of presenting the case in adequate form, the Board could follow its own established methods of procedure, even though that procedure did not follow meticulously that of a court of law.

[1] Pp. 256 ff., *ante*; *ex parte Venicoff*, [1920] 3 K.B. 72; *In re H.K.* (*an infant*), [1967] 2 Q.B. 617; *Schmidt* v. *Home Secretary*, [1969] 2 Ch. 149. The creation of the Immigration Appeals Tribunal would seem to have extended the scope for natural justice considerably (pp. 254–5, 258, *ante*).

[2] [1915] A.C. 120; K. & L. 521.

[3] For present appeal to the County Court, see Housing Act 1957, s. 20.

Similarly in *Board of Education* v. *Rice*,[1] Lord Loreburn laid it down that in disposing of an appeal the Board of Education was bound to act in good faith and to listen fairly to both sides, since that was a duty which lay on everyone who decided anything. The Board was not, however, bound to follow the procedure of a trial. It could obtain information in any way it thought best, always giving a fair opportunity to those who were parties in the controversy to correct or contradict any relevant statement prejudicial to their view.

The Housing Acts Cases

Notwithstanding these two decisions of the House of Lords, a government department was not thereby freed from the duty to observe the essentials of fair procedure, particularly when, as in *Arlidge's* case, the department had the task of weighing a local authority's proposal against objections to it raised by individuals. The courts have drawn a distinction between the department's duty in deciding the dispute in question, such a duty being regarded as quasi-judicial, and its overall responsibility for policy.

In *Errington* v. *Minister of Health*,[2] the court quashed an order of the Minister because of a failure to act quasi-judicially. The Minister was empowered under the Housing Act 1930[3] to confirm, after holding a public inquiry, clearance orders made by local housing authorities. The Minister was thus in the position of having to decide a contest between the owners of the property affected by the proposed order and the local authority. After an inquiry had been held, but before the order had been confirmed, there took place further communications on the subject-matter of the inquiry between the Ministry and the local authority without the knowledge of the owners who had objected to the order being confirmed. Furthermore, an official of the Ministry viewed the property in the company of officials of the local authority and formed an opinion upon it in the absence of the owners. It was held that an order made after an inquiry based on additional evidence obtained in the absence of the objectors was not within the powers of the Act.

Before, however, an objection was lodged, the Minister could make such enquiries as he thought fit, and this would not invalidate a subsequent confirmation order, even though an objection was lodged at a later date. In so far as the Minister dealt with the confirmation of a clearance order in the absence of objection by the owners, he would be acting in an administrative capacity and entitled to make such enquiries as he thought fit to enable him to make up his

[1] [1911] A.C. 179. And see *In re H.K.* (*an infant*), [1967] 2 Q.B. 617.
[2] [1935] 1 K.B. 249. For comment on this decision, see *Frost* v. *Minister of Health*, [1935] 1 K.B. 286, and Note by E. C. S. Wade in 51 L.Q.R. 417; see also *Robins & Son, Ltd.* v. *Minister of Health*, [1939] 1 K.B. 537; *Stafford* v. *Minister of Health*, [1946] K.B. 621.
[3] See now Housing Act 1957, Fourth Schedule.

mind.[1] Sometimes the Minister is faced with two duties and has to reconcile an executive duty under one section of an Act with a quasi-judicial duty under another. In one case, the fact that he had under consideration an objection to a clearance order did not debar the Minister from fulfilling his statutory duty to advise a local authority on handling overcrowding, despite the fact that the area involved by the clearance order was part of the area discussed in connection with overcrowding.[2] It would appear that the Minister may perform his executive duties without being restricted by the need to have both parties before him, although they overlap his quasi-judicial duties, but that he (or his officers) must act judicially when the act done (*e.g.* an interview) is specifically related to the subject-matter of quasi-judicial proceedings.

Scope of Rule

In these cases under the Housing Acts can be seen the application of the analysis of judicial and quasi-judicial powers made in the Ministers' Powers Report.[3] The basis of this approach was that, although the final decision was based on matters of policy, the department was exercising judicial functions at the public inquiry stage. This approach was called into question in *Franklin* v. *Minister of Town and Country Planning.*[4]

> The New Towns Act 1946 empowered the Minister, after consultation with local authorities, to make a draft order designating the site of a proposed new town. If objections were made and not withdrawn, the Minister was bound to arrange for a local public inquiry and to consider the report of the person holding the inquiry. While the Act was still a Bill, the Minister had made a public speech stating that Stevenage would be the first new town. When the Act had become law, he made a draft order designating Stevenage as a new town and a local inquiry was held into the objections received. Later the Minister confirmed the draft order. The validity of this confirmation was challenged in the High Court. The House of Lords held (1) that there was no evidence that the Minister had not genuinely considered the report of the inspector who held the inquiry; (2) that the inquiry was essentially into the objections received and the Minister was not bound to call evidence in favour of the scheme at the inquiry.

The striking feature of the decision is that the House of Lords considered that at no stage was any judicial or quasi-judicial duty

[1] *Frost* v. *Minister of Health*, [1935] 1 K.B. 286.

[2] *Offer* v. *Minister of Health*, [1936] 1 K.B. 40, which was also based on the fact that no objection had yet been lodged; *Horn* v. *Minister of Health*, [1937] 1 K.B. 146, where at the interview complained of the Minister did not discuss the particular site involved.

[3] Pp. 624–5, *ante*.

[4] [1948] A.C. 87.

imposed on the Minister, that his duty to consider the inspector's report was purely administrative and that talk of the rule against bias was irrelevant. It is difficult, if not impossible, to reconcile this reasoning with the Housing Act cases which have been discussed.[1] There is an obvious distinction in that the Housing Act procedure involves the confirmation by the Minister of a scheme initiated by the local authority, whereas it is for the Minister alone to take the initiative and decide the issue in selecting a new town. In this sense Parliament has expressly made the Minister judge in his own cause, and this necessarily means that the rule against bias must be modified. But the common law conception of natural justice which required a man to be heard in defence of his property never depended on the two-tier situation of one authority confirming the proposals of another. As has already been seen, the doctrine of natural justice was worked out by the courts long before central control of local authorities in its modern form developed.[2] Moreover, the analysis of quasi-judicial duties made in the Ministers' Powers Report accepted that in such cases the Minister could base his decision on reasons of national policy, just as the local authority could take factors of local policy into account. It may be best to explain the decision of the House of Lords in terms of a deliberate refusal to involve the courts in the task of assessing the merits of the pioneer project of a politically controversial new scheme of social control; for this responsibility must be owed to Parliament.[3]

It would be wrong to conclude from *Franklin's* case that the principle established in *Errington* v. *Minister of Health* no longer applies. In one instance, namely the consideration by the Minister of Housing and Local Government of development plans prepared by local planning authorities, consultation between the Ministry and the local planning authority is expressly allowed after the local inquiry.[4] Apart from this change in the law, there has been no indication that the departments responsible for confirming compulsory purchase orders and deciding town planning appeals do not still regard themselves as exercising quasi-judicial functions. Moreover, to a considerable extent the effect of natural justice on pro-

[1] See *Quasi-judicial and its Background*, by H. W. R. Wade, (1949) 10 C.L.J. 216; cf. *Wednesbury Corporation* v. *Ministry of Housing and Local Government*, [1966] 2 Q.B. 275.

[2] *E.g. Cooper* v. *Wandsworth Board of Works*, p. 649, *ante*; H. W. R. Wade, *The Twilight of Natural Justice?*, 67 L.Q.R. 103, at p. 110; *Ridge* v. *Baldwin*, [1964] A.C. 40, 72–73 (Lord Reid).

[3] Direct parliamentary control over orders designating new towns is now possible: New Towns Act 1965, s. 53 (5).

[4] Town and Country Planning Acts: 1962, s. 10 (3); 1968, s. 4 (4).

cedures involving a ministerial inquiry has become an academic question in view of the reforms strengthening the inquiry procedure made following the Franks Report on Administrative Tribunals and Inquiries. These reforms, brought about by legislative and governmental action and not by judicial decision, will be discussed in Chapter 47.

A Revival of Natural Justice?

Franklin's case was not the only decision of the courts which cast doubt on the scope of natural justice. Thus the revocation by a government official of a textile-dealer's licence was held by the Judicial Committee not to be subject to the duty to give a prior hearing to the dealer, *inter alia* on the ground that there was no express statutory requirement of a hearing.[1] To base the decision on the point on whether there was an express duty to give a hearing was not consistent with such earlier cases as *Cooper* v. *Wandsworth Board of Works.*[2] This narrowing in the scope of natural justice was arrested by the House of Lords in *Ridge* v. *Baldwin.*[3]

In this case the Court of Appeal had held that the watch committee were under no duty in natural justice to grant the chief constable a hearing before the committee exercised its power to dismiss "any constable whom they think negligent in the exercise of his duty or otherwise unfit for the same";[4] "in dismissing the plaintiff, the defendants were acting in an administrative or executive capacity just as they did when they appointed him".[5]

The House of Lords overruled this view: quite apart from the procedure laid down by the discipline regulations, natural justice required that a hearing should have been given before the watch committee exercised its power. On this point *Nakkuda Ali* v. *Jayaratne* could no longer be regarded as authoritative. The failure to give a hearing as required by natural justice invalidated the dismissal, and the subsequent hearing given to Ridge's solicitor did not cure the earlier defect.

In the course of his judgment, Lord Reid suggested that the difficulties over natural justice in the twentieth-century case-law had been caused partly by a failure to realise that the old common law principles could have only limited application to modern instances

1 *Nakkuda Ali* v. *Jayaratne*, [1951] A.C. 66; p. 628, *ante*, discussed by Professor H. W. R. Wade in *The Twilight of Natural Justice?*, 67 L.Q.R. 103; see also *The Queen* v. *Metropolitan Police Commissioner, ex parte Parker*, [1953] 2 All E.R. 717, discussed by D. M. Gordon in *The Cab-driver's Licence Case*, 70 L.Q.R. 203, and *Ex parte Fry*, [1954] 2 All E.R. 118.

2 P. 649, *ante*.

3 [1964] A.C. 40; p. 641, *ante*; and see A. W. Bradley, [1964] C.L.J. 83.

4 Municipal Corporations Act 1882, s. 191 (4).

5 [1963] 1 Q.B. 539, *per* Harman L. J., at p. 576.

of governmental power, particularly those vested in Ministers, and were often excluded by the exigencies of war-time legislation. But these difficulties should not affect the court's interpretation of the power of dismissal that was here in issue. One important emphasis made in *Ridge* v. *Baldwin* is that the mere description of a statutory function as "administrative", "judicial", "quasi-judicial", or even "quasi-administrative",[1] is not in itself enough to settle the requirements of natural justice. As Lord Hodson said:

> [The] answer in a given case is not provided by the statement that the giver of the decision is acting in an executive or administrative capacity, as if that was the antithesis of a judicial capacity. The cases seem to me to show that persons acting in a capacity which is not on the face of it judicial, but rather executive or administrative, have been held by the courts to be subject to the principles of natural justice.[2]

This emphasis could lead to a fruitful re-examination of the role of natural justice in protecting the individual from unfair exercise of certain powers which directly affect him. But it is still doubtful whether the common law principles of natural justice are yet sufficiently refined to enable the courts to assist effectively in the improvement of administrative procedures over the whole range of governmental power.[3]

[1] *In re K (Infants)*, [1965] A.C. 201, at p. 217.

[2] [1964] A.C. 40, 130; and pp. 627–8, *ante*.

[3] For vigorous criticism of natural justice in English law, see K. C. Davis, [1962] *Public Law* 139, 142–9. For decisions indicating a narrow use of *Ridge* v. *Baldwin*, see *Vidyodaya University Council* v. *Silva*, [1965] 1 W.L.R. 77, noted in [1965] C.L.J. 3; *Durayappah* v. *Fernando*, [1967] 2 A.C. 337, discussed by H. W. R. Wade, in (1967) 83 L.Q.R. 499; and *Re H.K.* (*An Infant*), [1967] 2 Q.B. 617.

CHAPTER FORTY-FIVE

METHODS OF JUDICIAL CONTROL[1]

HITHERTO we have considered the principles which regulate the review of administrative powers by the courts. There must now be examined the different procedures by which the jurisdiction of the courts can be invoked. A review may take place incidentally in the course of a prosecution for an offence under a statutory regulation, when it is a defence to show that the regulation is *ultra vires* and so invalid. Again, a civil action may be based on a claim for damages for an act which, unless justified by statutory authority, would be a wrongful act. Apart from review in the course of ordinary litigation, there are several means of directly invoking the jurisdiction of the courts to check excess or abuse of powers. Those deriving from common law will be described first, but their operation has often been affected by statute and in practice statutory methods of challenge are no less important.

Orders of Mandamus, Certiorari and Prohibition

At common law, in addition to remedies in contract and tort,[2] the principal machinery of review was provided by the prerogative writs —mandamus, certiorari and prohibition. These prerogative writs have now been replaced by judicial orders obtained by a more simple procedure of application to the Queen's Bench Division of the High Court.[3] The origin of these writs suggests special association with the King, but the earlier opinion that prerogative writs were issued only at the suit of the King has been challenged in recent years. Prohibition, like the better-known writ of habeas corpus, appears to have issued on the application of subjects from earliest times. When in the seventeenth and eighteenth centuries the term, "prerogative", was applied to the writs, this was because they were considered to be closely connected with the rights of the Crown; no doubt it was for this reason that they issued chiefly out of the King's Bench Court.[4]

[1] For a full treatment, see *Judicial Review of Administrative Action*, by S. A de Smith, Part III.

[2] Chap. 44, A.

[3] Administration of Justice (Miscellaneous Provisions) Acts, 1933, s. 5 and 1938, s. 7.

[4] de Smith, *op. cit.*, Chap. 8; see also Edith G. Henderson, *Foundations of English Administrative Law: Certiorari and Mandamus in the 17th Century* (Harvard).

Mandamus

Mandamus is a peremptory order, issuing out of the Queen's Bench Division of the High Court, commanding a body, or person, to do that which it is its, or his, duty to do. It lies to secure the performance of a public duty, in the performance of which the applicant has a sufficient legal interest. The issue of the order cannot be required as of right; it is entirely a matter for the discretion of the court, which "will render it as far as it can the supplementary means of substantial justice in every case where there is no other specific legal remedy for a legal right; and will provide as effectually as it can that others exercise their duty wherever the subject-matter is properly within its control." [1] The order does not lie against the Crown. If a government department is acting as agent of the Crown and is responsible only to the Crown, having no duty to the subject in the matter, it is not amenable to the orders of the court in the exercise of its prerogative jurisdiction in granting or refusing mandamus.[2] But mandamus will lie to enforce the performance of a public duty which has been imposed by statute on a department of government or its servants provided that the applicant can show that the duty is one which is owed to him and not merely to the Crown; in the latter case his remedy lies in having his grievance ventilated in the House of Commons, but he has no remedy in the courts.[3] The distinction turns upon the rule that no third party (the complainant) can compel an agent (the department) to perform a duty which is owed not to him, but solely to the principal (the Crown). Against other bodies or persons mandamus will only be granted where the duty is in the nature of a public duty and especially affects the rights of an individual, provided that there is no more appropriate remedy. Thus mandamus will not lie if there is an alternative remedy in a domestic tribunal.[4] The applicant must have demanded performance of the duty and been refused. Mandamus will not lie if the authority has complete discretion whether or not to act. But there may be a duty to exercise a discretion one way or another, such as the duty of a magistrates' court to hear and determine a case which falls within its jurisdiction. The exercise of such discretion is enforceable by mandamus.

[1] *Per* Lord Ellenborough, C.J., in *The King* v. *Archbishop of Canterbury* (1812), 15 East 117, 136.

[2] *The Queen* v. *Lords of the Treasury* (1872), L.R. 7 Q.B. 387. *Cf.* for a failure to enforce by action a duty owed to the Crown: *Gidley* v. *Lord Palmerston* (1822), 3 Brod. & B. 275.

[3] *The Queen* v. *Special Commissioners for Income Tax* (1888), 21 Q.B.D. 313, at p. 317.

[4] *The King* v. *Dunsheath, ex parte Meredith*, [1951] 1 K.B. 127.

It was held in *The King* v. *Housing Tribunal*[1] that mandamus lay against a tribunal to compel it to hear and determine an appeal. Its previous decision had been given without hearing the applicants and was accordingly brought up and quashed by certiorari.[2] Again, where a purported election for aldermen to a newly created borough council departed so seriously from the statutory procedure that in law there was no election at all, mandamus to hold a lawful election was the appropriate remedy.[3] Mandamus has also been obtained by a ratepayer to compel the production of the accounts of a local authority for inspection by his agent,[4] notwithstanding that the officers of the council concerned were liable to prosecution, which, even if successful, could only have resulted in a fine and could not have secured the production of the accounts. Where, however, a statute creates an obligation and provides a specific remedy for enforcing it, *e.g.* complaint to a Minister, mandamus will not generally lie.[5]

Today mandamus is available in a wide variety of situations. For example, many local Acts of Parliament oblige local authorities and public utility undertakings to carry out works for the benefit of individuals whose property has been affected by the grant of special powers: these duties are enforceable by mandamus at the instance of the person aggrieved. More generally, mandamus is an important means of ensuring that government is conducted according to law—whether by a Cabinet minister, a valuation officer or the Metropolitan Police Commissioner.[6]

Prohibition

An order of prohibition issues out of a superior court (Queen's Bench Division) primarily to prevent an inferior court from exceeding its jurisdiction, or acting contrary to the rules of natural justice, *e.g.* to restrain a judge from hearing a case in which he is personally interested. It does not matter that the inferior court administers a different law from that of the High Court; thus it lies against ecclesiastical courts and lay against the old Admiralty courts prior to the

[1] [1920] 3 K.B. 334.

[2] P. 661, *post*.

[3] *In re Barnes Corporation, ex parte Hutter*, [1933] 1 K.B. 668.

[4] *The King* v. *Bedwelty Urban District Council, ex parte Price*, [1934] 1 K.B. 333.

[5] *Pasmore* v. *Oswaldtwistle Urban District Council*, [1898] A.C. 387.

[6] See respectively *Padfield* v. *Minister of Agriculture*, [1968] A.C. 997; *The Queen* v. *Paddington Valuation Officer, ex parte Peachey Property Corpn.*, [1966] 1 Q.B. 380; *The Queen* v. *Metropolitan Police Commissioner, ex parte Blackburn*, [1968] 2 Q.B. 118.

Judicature Acts. For many years past it has also been granted against Ministers of the Crown and public authorities in general to control the exercise of judicial or quasi-judicial functions. It does not lie against non-statutory bodies, such as a social club, *e.g.* in relation to the expulsion of a member. It will not lie unless something remains to be done which a court can prohibit, *e.g.* a continuing excess of jurisdiction.

Scope of Remedy

It is not clear what are the precise limitations of the order; it is certain that it will lie against a body exercising public functions, but it cannot be used to restrain legislative powers or those powers which cannot be challenged in a court of law because they are purely executive in character. An attempt to invoke prohibition (together with certiorari) against the National Assembly of the Church of England and its legislative committee to restrain that body from proceeding with the Prayer Book Measure 1928 was unsuccessful, on the ground that neither the Assembly nor the committee was empowered to act, or did in fact attempt to act, judicially in matters affecting the interests of the subject.[1] Nevertheless in this as in other spheres of judicial review, the courts have generally interpreted in a wide sense their power of controlling any body of persons to whom has been entrusted a "judicial" power of imposing obligations upon others. The case of *The King* v. *Electricity Commissioners, ex parte London Electricity Joint Committee*,[2] is of particular interest:

> The Commissioners possessed statutory powers enabling them to draw up schemes for improving the existing organisation for the supply of electricity in districts. A scheme was not to become operative until a public inquiry had been held and the scheme confirmed by the Minister of Transport and approved by resolution of each House of Parliament. A writ of prohibition was granted to prevent the holding of an inquiry on the ground that the scheme to be presented at the inquiry was *ultra vires*. In discussing the scope of certiorari and prohibition, Atkin, L. J. said: "Wherever any body of persons, having legal authority to determine the rights of subjects and having the duty to act judicially, act in excess of their legal authority, they are subject to the controlling jurisdiction of the King's Bench Division exercised in these writs".[3]

In this case the Electricity Commissioners were not exercising the powers of a court of law; their functions seem rather to have

[1] *The King* v. *The Legislative Committee of the Church Assembly, ex parte Haynes-Smith*, [1928] 1 K.B. 411, p. 471, *ante*.
[2] [1924] 1 K.B. 171; K. & L. 427.
[3] [1924] 1 K.B. 171, 205.

been those of inquiry and recommendation prior to the exercise of delegated legislative powers. Nevertheless for the purpose of judicial review the Commissioners could be regarded as acting judicially in considering a scheme which if confirmed would affect the rights of the private electricity companies. In this sense judicial has a wide meaning not referable exclusively to what is done within a court of justice. Moreover, the common requirement of confirmation by a higher authority, even where the approval has to be that of the Houses of Parliament, does not put an order of a public authority outside the category of a judicial proceeding which can be restrained by means of prohibition. Atkin, L.J., said:

> In the provision that the final decision of the commissioners is not to be operative until it has been approved by the two Houses of Parliament I find nothing inconsistent with the view that in arriving at that decision the commissioners themselves are to act judicially and within the limits prescribed by Act of Parliament, and that the courts have power to keep them within those limits.

The case should also be studied in connection with certiorari.

Certiorari

Certiorari issues to remove a suit from an inferior court which administers the same law into the Queen's Bench Division of the High Court. The following are the uses to which the order can be put:

(i) to secure an impartial trial, *e.g.* where bias is alleged in the court;
(ii) to review an excess of jurisdiction or an *ultra vires* decision;
(iii) to quash a judicial decision arrived at in breach of natural justice;
(iv) to correct errors of law on the face of the record.

In none of these cases is the court entertaining a straight appeal and it is not empowered to substitute its own discretion for that of the court or other agency whose act is being reviewed. Certiorari does not lie to review the decisions of a court exercising separate jurisdiction in a limited sphere, such as an ecclesiastical court, though prohibition will lie to restrain such a court from exceeding its jurisdiction.[1] The reason for this distinction is that the High Court does not exercise ecclesiastical jurisdiction (apart from any special statutory provisions) and, therefore, is not competent to review a

[1] *The King* v. *Chancellor of St. Edmundsbury and Ipswich Diocese*, [1948] 1 K.B. 195.

decision on ecclesiastical law; it can, however, restrain a court which goes beyond the sphere of its own jurisdiction. Certiorari, like prohibition, will issue to statutory tribunals, *e.g.* magistrates' courts and administrative tribunals. A non-statutory domestic tribunal, *e.g.* the Stewards of the Jockey Club, from which no appeal lies to the courts, may be controlled by an action for a declaration and by an injunction.[1] But certiorari is available to review the decisions of a judicial but non-statutory board appointed under prerogative power to administer funds provided by Parliament for distribution to victims of criminal violence on an *ex gratia* basis.[2] Certiorari was formerly used before a trial to remove the case for trial to a higher court.[3] Today it is usually invoked to quash an order which has been made without jurisdiction or in defiance of the rules of natural justice. While it is only applicable to review a judicial act, "judicial" is again used in the widest sense. "The power of obtaining an order of certiorari is not limited to judicial acts or orders in a strict sense, that is to say, acts or orders of a court of law sitting in a judicial capacity. It extends to the acts and orders of a competent authority which has power to impose a liability or to give a decision which determines the rights or property of the affected parties."[4]

As illustrations of the wide scope of certiorari, three examples may be given.

> At the instance of an adjacent owner, certiorari was granted to quash a decision of a district council permitting development of land in an area where, under a town planning scheme, permission might have given rise later to a claim for compensation payable from the rates; the reason for quashing the decision was that a councillor voted for the permission who was the developer's estate agent.[5]
>
> Certiorari lay against a county council which purported to act under its statutory powers as a licensing authority by granting permission to a cinema proprietor to open his cinema on a Sunday at a time when the Sunday opening of places of entertainment was expressly forbidden by statute.[6]
>
> Certiorari lay to quash a decision of the General Medical Council removing a doctor's name from the medical register. The Council was under a statutory obligation to hold a "due inquiry" but had

[1] *Nagle* v. *Feilden*, [1966] 2 Q.B. 633.

[2] *The Queen* v. *Criminal Injuries Compensation Board, ex parte Lain*, [1967] 2 Q.B. 864.

[3] Removal of trial to another assize or quarter sessions court is now governed by the Administration of Justice (Miscellaneous Provisions) Act 1938, s. 11 (3).

[4] *Local Government Board* v. *Arlidge*, [1915] A.C. 120, at p. 140.

[5] *The King* v. *Hendon Rural District Council, ex parte Chorley*, [1933] 2 K.B. 696; for liability of the councillor, see p. 369, *ante*.

[6] *The King* v. *London County Council, ex parte Entertainments Protection Association Ltd.*, [1931] 2 K.B. 215.

refused to hear fresh evidence to dispute a finding in the Divorce Division of the High Court that the doctor had committed adultery with a patient.[1]

Prohibition and Certiorari Contrasted

As means of jurisdictional control prohibition and certiorari cover broadly the same ground. The main difference is that certiorari is a means of quashing an order or decision already given, and prohibition is a means of preventing an order or decision being made which if made would be subject to certiorari. The distinction is brought out by two Housing Act cases, both arising out of housing schemes prepared in terms which were not authorised by the Housing Act 1925.[2]

In *The King* v. *Minister of Health, ex parte Davis*,[3] a property owner in the area affected by the proposed scheme successfully applied for a writ of prohibition to prevent the Minister proceeding to consider the scheme with a view to confirmation. The scheme contained provisions *ultra vires* the Housing Act, and it would not have been within the jurisdiction of the Minister to confirm it.

In *The King* v. *Minister of Health, ex parte Yaffé*, a similar housing scheme had already been confirmed with modifications by the Minister and it was too late to prohibit confirmation. The Court of Appeal granted certiorari to quash the Minister's order even though the Housing Act provided that the Minister's order when made "should have effect as if enacted in the Act".[4] This decision was reversed by the House of Lords on a different interpretation of the housing scheme as confirmed, but the availability of certiorari was upheld.[5]

Both prohibition and certiorari may be sought in the same proceedings. This is convenient when a decision in excess of jurisdiction has already been made and other similar decisions have yet to be made.

Under the Furnished Houses (Rent Control) Act 1946, local authorities had statutory powers of referring furnished lettings to rent tribunals for review of the rent. One council decided that in the case of any property in respect of which at least two reductions in rent had been made by the tribunal, all other lettings in the property should be referred to the tribunal. In this case, the council referred over 300 flats in one large block of flats to the tribunal. At the time

[1] *General Medical Council* v. *Spackman*, [1943] A.C. 627. The Medical Act 1956, s. 33 (2), now prevents the re-trial of the issue of adultery, the Disciplinary Committee of the Council being bound to accept the decision of the High Court.

[2] For present procedure for challenging a clearance order or compulsory purchase order, see Housing Act 1957, Part III, and Fourth and Fifth Schedules; and see pp. 667–9, *post*.

[3] [1929] 1 K.B. 619; p. 640, *ante*.

[4] [1930] 2 K.B. 98.

[5] *Minister of Health* v. *The King*, [1931] A.C. 494.

proceedings were taken, the tribunal had reduced the rents of eight flats. *Held*, the Act required the council to make investigation or inquiry into individual lettings before referring them. In the absence of a valid reference to the tribunal, the tribunal had no jurisdiction to act; certiorari lay to quash the eight decisions made, and prohibition lay to restrain the tribunal from considering any other flats in the block.[1]

In appropriate cases certiorari and mandamus may be sought in the same proceedings, certiorari to quash a decision in excess of jurisdiction and mandamus to compel the tribunal to hear and determine the case according to law.[2]

Error of Law on the Face of the Record

One important use of certiorari, for which there is no equivalent in the case of prohibition, is as a means of ensuring that inferior tribunals and statutory bodies apply the law correctly, at least so far as the official record of their decision is concerned. This was laid down in modern law by the Court of Appeal in *The King* v. *Northumberland Compensation Appeal Tribunal, ex parte Shaw*.[3] In this case the tribunal, set up to hear appeals as to the compensation payable to local government officers made redundant through the introduction of the National Health Service, had not exceeded its jurisdiction but had given reasons for its decision which were bad in law due to a wrong interpretation of the relevant statute. Such an error of law can be reviewed by certiorari, provided that the error is disclosed on the record of the decision.[4] The availability of the remedy depends on the documents which form the record for this purpose.[5] The inferior tribunal need not be a court of record nor need the error go to jurisdiction. This is not to say that the High Court can substitute its own discretion for that of the body to which Parliament has entrusted the exercise of the power, nor can the decision be reviewed if no reasons have been given. A tribunal may well misdirect itself as to the law without disclosing error in the record. On the other hand, the record may disclose an error in law without expressly stating it, the error being revealed by inference from the decision reached; thus in the *Northumberland* case cited above, the

[1] *The King* v. *Paddington and St. Marylebone Rent Tribunal, ex parte Bell London and Provincial Properties Ltd.*, [1949] 1 K.B. 666.

[2] *The King* v. *Housing Tribunal*, [1920] 3 K.B. 334; p. 659, *ante*; and *The Queen* v. *Paddington Valuation Officer*, [1966] 1 Q.B. 380.

[3] [1951] 1 K.B. 711; [1952] 1 K.B. 388; K. & L. 464.

[4] This overruled an earlier decision of the Court of Appeal, *Racecourse Betting Control Board* v. *Secretary of State for Air*, [1944] Ch. 114, and followed *Walsall Overseers* v. *London North Western Railway Co.* (1879), 4 App. Cas. 30, 40.

[5] *Baldwin and Francis, Ltd.* v. *Patents Appeal Tribunal*, [1959] A.C. 663.

tribunal had assessed compensation on a scale which could only have been applied by a misreading of the Act authorising the compensation. The importance for this purpose of sufficiently full reasons being given, as well as the general desirability of reasoned decisions, was recognised in the Tribunals and Inquiries Act 1958. Section 12 imposes a duty on tribunals subject to the Act, and on Ministers where a public inquiry has been or could have been held, to state the reasons for their decisions if requested at the time to do so; any statement of reasons is deemed to be part of the record, so that certiorari lies if reasons which are wrong in law are given.[1]

A statutory provision that a decision of a tribunal "shall be final" does not exclude review by certiorari, whether for excess of jurisdiction or for error of law on the face of the record.[2] But the power of the court to review for error of law is more readily excluded than the power to review for excess of jurisdiction.[3] In accordance with the recommendation of the Franks Committee, Parliament accepted the general principle that there should be a right of appeal on law from administrative tribunals to the High Court.[4] Such an appeal gives the court wider scope than certiorari for error of law on the record; thus the practical effect of a statutory right of appeal on points of law is to supersede the use of certiorari for this purpose. However, in regard to certain tribunals from which there is still no appeal on law, *e.g.* under the National Insurance Acts,[5] the power by certiorari to correct errors of law on the record is still of practical importance.

Although in this context "error of law" generally refers to an error in applying principles of statute law or common law, it has been extended to include an error in applying a compensation scheme made under the prerogative, in the administration of which the compensation board is required to act judicially.[6]

Locus Standi

When an administrative body's decision is challenged by a private individual the question arises whether that individual has sufficient interest in the decision to justify the court's intervention. Some would wish the courts to entertain a challenge to the exercise of

[1] See *Re Poyser and Mills' Arbitration*, [1964] 2 Q.B. 467 (reasons given too vague, award set aside); and *Givaudan & Co.* v. *Minister of Housing*, [1966] 3 All E.R. 696.

[2] *The Queen* v. *Medical Appeal Tribunal, ex parte Gilmore*, [1957] 1 Q.B. 574.

[3] *Anisminic Ltd.* v. *Foreign Compensation Commission*, [1969] 2 A.C. 147, p. 675, *post*.

[4] Tribunals and Inquiries Act 1958, s. 9.

[5] Report of the Franks Committee, pp. 25–26; p. 699, *post*.

[6] *The Queen* v. *Criminal Injuries Compensation Board*, [1967] 2 Q.B. 864.

administrative discretion from any member of the public. But English law has always refused to entertain civil proceedings where there are no sufficient legal grounds for seeking a decision of the court. Thus a court will always refuse to answer a hypothetical question. In administrative law it is necessary for a complainant to have a peculiar grievance which is not suffered in common with the rest of the public. For example, a person deprived of an office or denied a licence clearly has a peculiar grievance against the relevant public authority. But membership of a special section of the community which has a grievance of its own may entitle an individual to seek relief. This question of *locus standi*, or standing to seek review, is of particular importance where certiorari or prohibition are sought. Since the remedies are discretionary, the meaning of a person aggrieved has been widened so that personal interest is less strictly required than, for example, in an action for damages. But the court may regard a personal interest as being too slight or too remote in a given case.[1]

The Importance of the Prerogative Orders

In principle, both certiorari and prohibition are available only in respect of tribunals and other public bodies which are required to act judicially. It has been seen already that the duty to act judicially has in general been widely interpreted.[2] *Ridge* v. *Baldwin* was not a case in which certiorari was sought, but Lord Reid's opinion that a duty to act judicially may readily be inferred where there is statutory authority to decide what an individual's rights should be, is as applicable to the prerogative orders as in the realm of natural justice.

In *The Queen* v. *Manchester Legal Aid Committee, ex parte R. A. Brand & Co. Ltd.*[3], a legal aid certificate had been granted to a bankrupt, but later was wrongly renewed in favour of his trustee in bankruptcy. In granting certiorari to quash the certificate, the Divisional Court held that the legal aid committee was under a duty to act judicially. Such a duty "may arise in widely different circumstances which it would be impossible, and, indeed, inadvisable, to attempt to define exhaustively. Where the decision is that of a court, then, unless, as in the case, for instance, of justices granting excise licences, it is acting in a purely ministerial capacity, it is clearly under a duty to act judicially. When, on the other hand, the decision is that of an administrative body and is actuated in whole or in part by questions of policy, the duty to act judicially may arise in the course of arriving at that decision. Thus, if, in order to arrive at the decision, the body concerned had to consider proposals and objections and consider

[1] de Smith, *op. cit.*, pp. 422–32; see also articles by D. C. M. Yardley in (1955) 71 L.Q.R. 388, and (1957) 73 L.Q.R. 534; and by S. M. Thio in [1966] Public Law 133. Cf. *Durayappah* v. *Fernando*, [1967] 2 A.C. 337.

[2] Pp. 655–6, *ante*.

[3] [1952] 2 Q.B. 413; K. & L. 475.

evidence, then there is the duty to act judicially in the course of that inquiry."[1]

But the rule that certiorari and prohibition lie only in respect of judicial functions is only one of the difficulties associated with the prerogative orders. One practical shortcoming is that although more than one prerogative order may be sought in the same proceedings, prerogative proceedings cannot be combined with the usual civil remedies *e.g.* action for damages, injunction or declaration; and in comparison with ordinary civil proceedings, there is virtually no interlocutory procedure in connection with the prerogative orders; thus in proceedings for certiorari it is not possible to obtain discovery of documents.[2]

In the opinion of an American critic of English administrative law, the prerogative orders are subject to such technicalities and limitations as means of securing judicial review of administrative decisions that they should be superseded by statutory methods of challenge or by an extended use of the court's power to make declaratory judgments.[3] It will be seen below that the declaratory remedy has several advantages over the prerogative orders and that in many fields Parliament has ousted the prerogative orders in favour of statutory methods of challenge and appeal. Yet as recently as 1958 Parliament extended the application of the prerogative orders.[4] Provided that convenient statutory procedures are available whenever they are needed, the prerogative orders have value as residual remedies. But that there is a need for procedural reform is incontestable.

Statutory Machinery for Challenge

It was formerly a frequent practice to provide by statute for the challenge by certiorari of orders or decisions which owing to the absence of a judicial element could not be challenged by certiorari at common law.[5] Today it is more usual to substitute a simpler statutory procedure which is available for a limited time after the making of an order or decision. A particularly important example of this is provided by the standard procedure for the compulsory purchase of land. After a compulsory purchase order has been made by the local authority, and, where objections have been raised by the owner concerned, an inquiry has been held by a

1. Per Parker, J., [1952] 2 Q.B., at pp. 428–29.
2. See *Barnard* v. *National Dock Labour Board*, [1953] 2 Q.B. 18; p. 672, *post*.
3. K. C. Davis, *The Future of Judge-Made Public Law in England*, 61 Columbia Law Review 201, 204; see also [1962] Public Law 139, 407 and [1963] Public Law; cf. H. W. R. Wade, *The Future of Certiorari*, [1958] C.L.J. 218.
4. Tribunals and Inquiries Act 1958, s. 11 (p. 676, *post*) and s. 12 (p. 665, *ante*).
5. *E.g.* Local Government Act 1888, s. 80: orders for payments out of county funds could be challenged by certiorari.

Ministry inspector, the Minister must decide whether to confirm the order. If he decides to confirm, there is a period of six weeks from the announcement of confirmation during which any person aggrieved by the compulsory purchase order may challenge the validity of the order in the High Court on two grounds: (a) that the order is not within the powers of the enabling Act; or (b) that the (procedural) requirements of the Act have not been complied with and that the objector's interests have been substantially prejudiced thereby.[1] If the order is not challenged in the High Court during the six week period, the order is statutorily protected from challenge in the courts,[2] and it would seem that any other form of judicial review is altogether excluded, whether before or after the confirmation of the order. This limited but effective method of challenge was first provided by the Housing Act 1930 at a time when there was strong feeling against the exclusion of Ministers' actions from judicial review. Today it is to be found in the Housing Act 1957 in regard to slum clearance orders and in many other statutes relating to land.[3] Resort to this statutory method of seeking judicial review has often enabled the High Court to give its entire attention to the principles of judicial review in issue, uncomplicated by the preliminary procedural and jurisdictional questions which may arise in regard to the prerogative orders.[4] The imposition of a time-limit on such a right of challenge is necessary in order that if no objection is taken promptly the authorities concerned can proceed to put the decision into effect. Other statutory rights of appeal to the courts include the right to appeal to the county court against the condemnation of an individual dwelling-house as unfit for human habitation,[5] the right to appeal to the High Court on matters of law from the decisions of many administrative tribunals,[6] and the many express procedures for recourse to the High Court in connection with town planning decisions.[7]

It is of course necessary for an applicant to the court to bring himself within the scope of the statutory procedure, and the question of *locus standi* depends on the statutory provisions. The six week right to challenge compulsory purchase orders is given to "any person

[1] Acquisition of Land (Authorisation Procedure) Act 1946, s. 1 and First Schedule, para. 15.

[2] Pp. 673–6, *post*.

[3] *E.g.* Town and Country Planning Act 1962, ss. 178–179.

[4] *E.g.* the Housing Act cases discussed at pp. 652–3, *ante*; *Franklin* v. *Minister of Town and Country Planning*, p. 653 *ante*; and *Webb* v. *Minister of Housing and Local Government*, [1965] 2 All E.R. 193.

[5] Housing Act 1957, ss. 11 and 20.

[6] Tribunals and Inquiries Act 1958, s. 9.

[7] Town and Country Planning Act 1962, Part XI.

aggrieved". This clearly includes the owner of the land affected, but, at least in town planning law, it does not include neighbouring owners, who are considered to have no legal interest that would render them aggrieved persons in the eyes of the court.[1] In general, pending reform of the prerogative orders and other common law remedies, the advantages of statutory rights of appeal are such that whenever comprehensive legislation introduces a new public service or form of public control, express provision for appeal to or review by the courts should be made.

Surcharge

An example of statutory machinery for judicial review of administrative decisions which is important within local government is the power of district auditors to disallow items of expenditure in local authority accounts and to surcharge them on the individual members of the council responsible.[2] A right of appeal from the district auditor's decision lies to the High Court, but an alternative right of appeal lies to the Minister of Housing and Local Government if the amount involved does not exceed £500. If appeal is taken to the Minister, he may be required to state a special case for the opinion of the High Court on a matter of law. An unsuccessful appeal to the High Court cannot be followed by an appeal to the Minister.[3] Whether or not he appeals, a person surcharged may apply to the Minister or the High Court for a declaration that he acted reasonably or in the belief that his action was authorised by law and the surcharge may then be remitted. *Roberts* v. *Hopwood* is the best-known example of judicial control through the machinery of surcharge.[4]

Injunctions [5]

An injunction may be claimed against a public authority by any individual who can show that he will suffer special damage as the result of contemplated illegal action, *e.g.* a public nuisance, or that he has suffered such special damage as the result of action which it is not too late to restrain. An injunction may be obtained to restrain any *ultra vires* act, *e.g.* to restrain an improper expenditure of borough funds.[6] An injunction can be obtained for these purposes by the Attorney-General, either at his own instance or at the instance

[1] *Buxton* v. *Minister of Housing and Local Government*, [1961] 1 Q.B. 278; cf. *Maurice* v. *London County Council*, [1964] 2 Q.B. 362.

[2] Chap. 26 C, *ante*.

[3] *The King* v. *Minister of Health, ex parte Dore*, [1927] 1 K.B. 765.

[4] [1925] A.C. 578; p. 645, *ante*.

[5] See generally de Smith, *op. cit.* Chap. 10.

[6] *Attorney-General* v. *Aspinall* (1837), 2 My. & Cr. 406.

of a relator (one who informs). A relator need have no personal interest in the subject-matter of the claim except his interest as a member of the public. The Attorney-General must be joined as a party where the individual complaining can show no special damage to himself. It is at the discretion of the Attorney-General whether or not to proceed. If the public body is doing an act which tends to injure the public, it is the right of the Attorney-General to intervene, and he will be successful, even though he cannot prove that injury will result from the act complained of. A relator action, as these proceedings are called, lies to restrain an illegal act, even though its validity could be tested by certiorari: [1] or though the infringement of public rights could be visited with other penalties.

Thus in *Attorney-General* v. *Sharp* [2] the defendant was the owner of a fleet of omnibuses in Manchester; he had been prosecuted 48 times for breach of local statutory regulations in plying for hire without a licence. The defendant continued to run his 'buses without a licence, since despite the fines, he found it profitable to do so. *Held* that, since the rights of the public were involved and as the remedies provided by the local Act had proved ineffective, there was jurisdiction to grant an injunction at the instance of the Attorney-General by way of ancillary relief. In somewhat similar circumstances, relator proceedings have been used to enforce town planning control against those who find it more profitable to evade it,[3] and also to secure compliance with provisions of a local Act.[4]

There are two cases where a person can sue without joining the Attorney-General: [5] (1) if interference with the public right also constitutes an interference with the plaintiff's private right, *e.g.* where an obstruction upon a highway is also an interference with a private right of access to the highway; [6] (2) where no private right of the plaintiff is interfered with, but he, in respect of his public right, suffers special damage peculiar to himself from the interference with a public right, *e.g.* where as a result of a public nuisance a plaintiff's premises have been rendered unhealthy and incommodious.[7]

The High Court may grant an injunction to restrain a person from acting in an office to which he is not entitled, and may also declare the office to be vacant. This procedure takes the place of the ancient procedure of an information in the nature of a writ of quo

[1] *Attorney-General* v. *Tynemouth Corporation*, [1899] A.C. 293.
[2] [1931] 1 Ch. 121.
[3] *Attorney-General* v. *Bastow*, [1957] 1 Q.B. 514; *Attorney-General* v. *Smith*, [1958] 2 Q.B. 173.
[4] *Attorney-General* v. *Harris*, [1961] 1 Q.B. 74.
[5] *Boyce* v. *Paddington Borough Council*, [1903] 1 Ch. 109.
[6] *Lyon* v. *Fishmongers Co.* (1876), 1 App. Cas. 662.
[7] *Benjamin* v. *Storr* (1874), L.R. 9 C.P. 400.

warranto,[1] but the principles which governed the former procedure still apply.[2] By this means those who have improperly assumed to exercise an office may be removed. Under the Local Government Act 1933, s. 84, a local government elector may initiate proceedings either summarily or in the High Court to question the right of a person to act as a member of a local authority. The High Court may declare that the office is vacant and order the payment of penalties. A court of summary jurisdiction may impose a fine not exceeding £50 for each conviction of a person who acts while disqualified.

Declaratory Judgments [3]

A declaratory judgment is one which is merely declaratory of the legal relationship of the parties and is not accompanied by any sanction or means of enforcement. The authority of a court's ruling on law is such that a declaratory judgment will normally serve to restrain both the Crown and public authorities generally from illegal conduct. Order 15, rule 16, of the Rules of the Supreme Court provides:

> No action or other proceeding shall be open to objection on the ground that a merely declaratory judgment or order is sought thereby, and the Court may make binding declarations of right whether or not any consequential relief is or could be claimed.

This "remedy" has enabled trade unions and their members to obtain relief, though they are prevented from directly enforcing certain contracts by the Trade Union Act 1871, s. 4. It is also an obvious convenience in a dispute between a ratepayer and his local authority or between two local authorities to be able to have the law determined in its application to a particular case without seeking a coercive remedy. Somewhat similar is the practice of local authorities agreeing to state a case on points of law for the decision of the court. An action for a declaratory judgment or the statement of a special case must be based on a concrete case which has arisen. The courts will not give answers to questions propounded in the form of hypothetical cases. Nor can the judges be asked to give advisory opinions on points of law.[4] The remedy by declaration has the advantage that it may be available when other remedies are spent.

[1] For examples, see *The King* v. *Speyer*, *The King* v. *Cassel*, [1916] 1 K.B. 595, and [1916] 2 K.B. 858; and *Darley* v. *The Queen* (1845), 12 Cl. & F. 520.

[2] Administration of Justice (Miscellaneous Provisions) Act 1938, s. 9.

[3] de Smith, *op. cit*., Chap. 11; I. Zamir, *The Declaratory Judgment* (Stevens).

[4] See *Consultation of the Judiciary by the Executive*, by E. C. S. Wade, 46 L.Q.R. 169; and p. 461, *ante*, for references to the Judicial Committee of the Privy Council.

In *Barnard* v. *National Dock Labour Board*,[1] (p. 644, *ante*) certiorari did not lie to quash an order which suspended certain dock workers because an application for that remedy would have been out of time. But the court, without laying down the bounds of its jurisdiction, expressed itself competent and willing to declare any injustice as unlawful in the absence of any available remedy and further to restrain that injustice by an injunction. The court stated that this discretionary relief would only be used sparingly, without defining the bounds of its application; it is, however, available against domestic as well as administrative tribunals.[2]

In *Pyx Granite Co. Ltd.* v. *Minister of Housing and Local Government* [3] the Minister challenged the jurisdiction of the court to grant a declaration, arguing that Parliament by the Town and Country Planning Act 1947, s. 17, had excluded the jurisdiction of the court by providing that the decision of the Minister on whether or not planning permission was needed for certain development should be final. The House of Lords held that there was nothing in the Act to exclude the jurisdiction of the court to grant declarations and that the section relied upon by the Minister merely provided an alternative method of having the question determined.

Although the relevant statutory provisions have now been amended,[4] the last case shows the value of an action for a declaration as a means of upholding the principle that recourse to the courts for the determination of rights of the subject is not to be excluded except by clear words.

As a means of judicial review, the declaration is often both alternative to and preferable to the prerogative orders; thus the judgment of an inferior tribunal may be declared to be invalid as being in excess of jurisdiction.[5] But the declaration cannot be used as a means of appealing against the decision of an administrative tribunal on matters of fact or law which do not affect the validity of the decision. Thus decisions of the National Insurance Commissioners [6] may be quashed by certiorari for error of law on the face of the record, but after the time for seeking certiorari has expired, the court has no jurisdiction to grant a declaration that the decision of a Commissioner is wrong in law.[7] Where a statute confers both a right and a means of deciding the extent of the right, the court may have no jurisdiction

[1] [1953] 2 Q.B. 18. For an important and early example of this jurisdiction, see *Dyson* v. *Attorney-General*, [1912] 1 Ch. 158, where a declaration was granted against the Crown. Other leading examples are *Vine* v. *National Dock Labour Board*, [1957] A.C. 488 and *Ridge* v. *Baldwin*, p. 641, *ante*.

[2] *Lee* v. *Showmen's Guild*, [1952] 2 Q.B. 329.

[3] [1960] A.C. 260.

[4] Town and Country Planning Act 1962, s. 43 and s. 181.

[5] *Anisminic Ltd.* v. *Foreign Compensation Commission*, p. 675, *post*.

[6] P. 699, *post*.

[7] *Punton* v. *Ministry of Pensions* (No. 2), [1964] 1 All E.R. 448.

to decide the same question.[1] Moreover, where neither statutory nor common law rights are in issue, the court may refuse to grant a declaration of right to an individual who is in fact seriously prejudiced by an *ultra vires* decision of a public authority.[2]

Scope of Injunction and Declaration

It is only in comparatively recent times that either the injunction or the declaratory order has played much part in English public law. The declaratory action even now has found more favour in those parts of the Commonwealth where federal constitutions call for interpretation. Nevertheless, as the technicalities which derive largely from judicial precedent confuse the development of certiorari and prohibition, the declaration and the injunction seem to offer greater flexibility. For example, the test of what is a judicial act, which must be overcome if certiorari is sought, may be avoided altogether in declaratory proceedings, which could, for example, be brought to test the validity of a legislative order. A further advantage of declaratory proceedings is that they may be coupled with an action for damages; the usual interlocutory procedure permits discovery of documents in declaratory proceedings,[3] whereas this is not so in the case of the prerogative orders; moreover, the usual periods of limitation apply to declaratory proceedings, while an order of certiorari must be sought within six months of the decision challenged. It is true that a declaratory action, unless coupled with an enforceable remedy, does not result in an enforceable judgment. This defect is less important than might at first sight appear. Although no committal for contempt can result from a disregard of a declaratory order, as distinct from the grant of an injunction, it is unlikely that responsible public authorities will disregard a finding by the High Court on the matter in dispute. This is certainly true when the dispute is between two public authorities and makes the remedy appropriate for interpreting federal constitutions. But even where the applicant is a private individual, public opinion would restrain any disregard of a declaratory order by a government agency.

Statutory Exclusion of Judicial Control

There is a strong presumption that the legislature does not intend

[1] *Argosam Finance Co. Ltd.* v. *Oxby*, [1965] Ch. 390.

[2] *Gregory* v. *Camden Borough Council*, [1966] 1 W.L.R. 899, criticised in [1966] C.L.J. 156; cf. *Buxton* v. *Minister of Housing and Local Government*, p. 669, *ante*.

[3] *Barnard* v. *National Dock Labour Board*, p. 644, *ante*.

access to the courts to be denied.[1] But where Parliament has appointed a specific tribunal for the enforcement of new rights and duties, it is necessary to resort to that tribunal in the first instance. Unless a right of appeal to the ordinary courts is provided by the statute, their jurisdiction is limited to the methods already discussed in this chapter. But many statutes have contained words designed to oust the jurisdiction of the ordinary courts. Such provisions have been interpreted by the courts so as to leave, if at all possible, the supervisory powers of the courts intact. At one time it was customary for the prerogative orders to be excluded by name but even the express exclusion of certiorari may not be effective against a manifest defect of jurisdiction or fraud committed by a party procuring an order of the court.[2] One frequently found clause was that a particular decision should be final, but it is settled law that such a clause does not restrict the power of the court to issue certiorari to quash, either for jurisdictional defects or for error of law on the face of the record.[3] Such a clause means simply that there is no right of appeal from the decision.

Another instance of a clause which does not deprive the courts of their supervisory jurisdiction is where it is stated that a statutory order when made shall have effect as if enacted in the Act which authorised it; the court may nonetheless hold the order to be invalid if it conflicts with the provisions of the Act.[4]

It is then only by an exceptionally strongly worded formula that Parliament can effectively deprive the High Court of its supervisory jurisdiction over inferior tribunals and other public authorities. Exclusion clauses today frequently accompany the granting of an express right to challenge the validity of an order or decision during a limited time. Thus the statute which permits challenge of a compulsory purchase order within six weeks of its confirmation continues: "Subject to the provisions of the last foregoing paragraph, a compulsory purchase order . . . shall not, either before or after it has been confirmed, made or given, be questioned in any legal proceedings whatsoever. . . ."[5]

In *Smith* v. *East Elloe Rural District Council* the plaintiff, whose land had been taken compulsorily for the building of council houses

[1] de Smith, *op. cit.*, Chap. 7, for a full treatment of this subject.

[2] *Colonial Bank of Australasia* v. *Willan* (1874), 5 P.C. 417.

[3] *The Queen* v. *Medical Appeal Tribunal, ex parte Gilmore*, [1957] 1 Q.B. 574.

[4] *Minister of Health* v. *The King*, [1931] A.C. 494, p. 663, *ante;* cf. *Institute of Patent Agents* v. *Lockwood*, [1894] A.C. 347. See also *The Parliamentary Powers of English Government Departments*, by John Willis (Harvard University Press), 1933, and Note in 60 L.Q.R. 325, by Sir Carleton Allen.

[5] Acquisition of Land (Authorisation Procedure) Act 1946, s. 1 and First Schedule, Para. 16. See also Town and Country Planning Act 1962, ss. 176, 177.

nearly six years previously, alleged that the making of the order had been caused by wrongful action and bad faith on the part of the council and its clerk. She submitted that the exclusion clause did not apply to exclude the court's power in cases of fraud and bad faith. On this preliminary point of law, the House of Lords held by a bare majority that the effect of the Act was to protect compulsory purchase orders from judicial review except by statutory challenge during the six-week period. Although the validity of the order could no longer be challenged, the action against the clerk of the council for damages could proceed.[1]

A different attitude towards the scope of an exclusion clause was taken by the House of Lords in 1968 in a decision which some considered to mark a return to older principles of judicial review.

In *Anisminic Ltd.* v. *Foreign Compensation Commission*,[2] the Foreign Compensation Act 1950, s. 4 (4), provided that the determination by the Commission of any application made to them under the Act "shall not be called in question in any court of law". The Commission was a judicial body responsible for distributing funds supplied by foreign governments as compensation to British subjects. It rejected a claim for compensation made by Anisminic Ltd. on the ground that the company were not eligible to claim under a scheme applying to British subjects who had lost property in Egypt. *Held*, by a majority in the House of Lords, section 4 (4) of the 1950 Act did not debar a court from inquiring whether the Commission had made in law a correct decision on the question of eligibility to claim. "Determination" meant a real determination, not a purported determination. By taking into account a factor which in the view of the House of Lords was irrelevant to the Egyptian compensation scheme, the Commission's decision was a nullity. Lord Wilberforce said, "What would be the purpose of defining by statute the limit of a tribunal's powers, if by means of a clause inserted in the instrument of definition, those limits could safely be passed?" [3]

This decision is a particularly striking example of the ability of the courts to interpret privative clauses in such a way as to maintain the possibility of judicial review. Although the authority of *Smith* v. *East Elloe R.D.C.* was questioned in the *Anisminic* case, the former decision was not overruled: indeed, the issues involved in considering the finality which should be given to a compulsory purchase order are different from those involved in considering how far an award of compensation should be subject to review. As an immediate sequel to the *Anisminic* case, the Government proposed an amendment to the Act of 1950 to reverse the decision prospectively but were

[1] [1956] A.C. 736; see also *Woollett* v. *Ministry of Agriculture*, [1955] 1 Q.B. 103.
[2] [1969] 2 A.C. 147.
[3] *Ibid.*, p. 208.

persuaded by legal opinion to accept instead an express right of appeal on points of law from the Foreign Compensation Commsision to the Court of Appeal.[1]

Tribunals and Inquiries Act 1958, *s.* 11

The Franks Committee recommended that no statute should contain words purporting to oust the prerogative orders [2] and this recommendation was embodied in the Tribunals and Inquiries Act 1958. Section 11 provided that

> any provision in an Act passed before the commencement of this Act that any order or determination shall not be called into question in any court, or any provision in such an Act which by similar words excludes any of the powers of the High Court, shall not have effect so as to prevent the removal of the proceedings into the High Court by order of certiorari or to prejudice the powers of the High Court to make orders of mandamus.

It may be assumed from this section that words of exclusion will not lightly be introduced into future enactments. There is a corresponding provision to restrict exclusion of the supervisory jurisdiction of the Court of Session. This extension of supervisory power does not apply in three cases, namely (1) to discretionary decisions of the Secretary of State under s. 26 of the British Nationality Act 1948, (2) to an order or determination of a court of law, or (3) where an Act makes special provision for application to the High Court within a specified time limit *e.g.* the power to challenge the validity of a compulsory purchase order within six weeks of its confirmation. This means that section 11 of the 1958 Act has no effect on the decision in *Smith* v. *East Elloe Rural District Council.*

Much will depend on the interpretation to be placed by the court on the meaning of the words "order or determination." To take one example from the Parliament Act 1911, section 3 provides that "any certificate of the Speaker of the House of Commons . . . shall be conclusive for all purposes and shall not be questioned in any court of law." Such a certificate would seem to be a determination within the meaning of s. 11 of the Tribunals and Inquiries Act. But is the latter statute to be construed as setting aside the common law rule which prevents the courts from inquiring into any matter which is internal to the proceedings of the House of Commons? [3]

[1] Foreign Compensation Act 1969, s. 3. H.L. Debates, 4th Feb. 1969 cols. 11–72; 13th Feb. 1969 cols. 640–54. And see [1969] C.L.J. 161 and (1969) 85 L.Q.R. 198.

[2] Cmnd. 218, p. 27.

[3] Pp. 166–8, *ante*.

The section admittedly extends the supervisory powers of the High Court only in cases where certiorari or mandamus is the appropriate remedy. There is no precedent for challenging the action of the Speaker by either of these procedures. It is, however, arguable that the Speaker in deciding whether or not to certify a Bill is under a duty to act judicially since he can only make up his mind by applying the statutory definition of a money Bill as provided in the Parliament Act itself. Perhaps guidance is to be found in the First Schedule to the Act where for other purposes than s. 11 are listed the tribunals which come within the various provisions of the Act. These seem to have one characteristic in common; they are concerned with official action affecting the rights of the individual and not with such public matters as the passage of legislation by Parliament.

There is one common form of statutory provision which is not affected by section 11 of the 1958 Act. The jurisdiction of the courts may be restricted indirectly if a statutory power is conferred upon an authority in terms which allow it to act "if it is satisfied," "if it thinks fit," "if it appears to it," or "if in its opinion." Most of these expressions had their origin in war-time legislation when the resistance of the courts to an encroachment of their jurisdiction was understandably weak. There is thus a contrast in the attitude of the courts to the statutory formulae under discussion. The courts have always sought to retain their supervisory jurisdiction in face of statutes purporting to exclude their powers of review. On the other hand, they have sometimes been content to interpret literally words conferring discretionary powers on Ministers.[1] More recent decisions suggest a trend away from war-time and post-war decisions towards a more positive doctrine of judicial review.[2]

[1] de Smith, *op. cit.*, pp. 271–80; and see *e.g. Robinson* v. *Minister of Town and Country Planning*, [1947] K.B. 702.

[2] *Commissioners of Customs and Excise* v. *Cure and Deeley Ltd.*, [1962] 1 Q.B. 340, p. 610, *ante*; *Padfield* v. *Minister of Agriculture*, p. 642, *ante*; *Durayappah* v. *Fernando* [1967] 2 A.C. 337.

CHAPTER FORTY-SIX

PROCEEDINGS BY AND AGAINST THE CROWN

THERE were two main rules which until 1948 governed the complicated law relating to the liability of the Crown and its servants: (1) the rule of substantive law that the King could do no wrong; (2) the procedural rule that the King could not be sued in his own courts—a rule derived from days when a feudal lord could not be sued in his own court.

What is the Crown?

With the development of modern government, it became increasingly anomalous that these rules applied to the activities of the central government. Formerly, unless a statute provided otherwise,[1] a Minister of the Crown retained the immunity of the Crown when as agent of the Crown he or his departmental officials exercised his statutory functions. The shield of the Crown extended to what was described not very satisfactorily as the general government of the country.[2] The immunity of the Crown was enjoyed neither by local authorities nor by autonomous public corporations outside the structure of central government.[3] In some cases, however, bodies acted on behalf of the Crown notwithstanding their corporate personality: modern examples would be the Land Commission or the Supplementary Benefits Commission. With the passing of the Crown Proceedings Act 1947, the Crown and central departments lost their general immunity from being sued, but there are still other reasons why it may be necessary to decide whether a public authority shares the position of the Crown.[4] If the question arises, it is necessary to examine the Act of Parliament which established the body concerned, but this does not always give a direct answer. It is possible for a public

[1] P. 686, *post*.

[2] *Liability for Acts of Public Servants*, by Sir W. Harrison Moore, 23 L.Q.R., p. 12. *Mersey Docks Trustees* v. *Cameron* (1861), 11 H.L.C. 443, at p. 508.

[3] See the *Mersey Docks* case, p. 634 *ante*.

[4] *E.g.* liability to taxation and the criminal law; extent of Crown privilege (*post*, p. 687); whether staff are Crown servants. Modern cases include *Tamlin* v. *Hannaford*, [1950] 1 K.B. 18; *Nottingham Hospital Management Committee* v. *Owen*, [1958] 1 Q.B. 50; *Pfizer Corporation* v. *Ministry of Health*, [1965] A.C. 512; *B.B.C.* v. *Johns*, [1965] Ch. 32. And see Chap. 21.

agency to be regarded as "the Crown" for some purposes but not for others.

Contractual Liability before 1948: Petition of Right

Notwithstanding the immunity of the Crown from being sued, it was essential that the subject should be able to obtain judicial redress under a contract made with a government department. The petition of right was originally a remedy available only for the recovery of property from the Crown, but it became available to enforce any contractual obligation. The practice was governed by the Petitions of Right Act 1860. A petition of right lay in respect of any claim arising out of contracts by which the Crown could be bound, but not in respect of claims arising out of tortious acts. It lay also for the recovery of real property, for damages for breach of contract,[1] and to recover compensation under a statute.[2] It probably lay for recovery of a chattel.[3] It was a condition precedent to the hearing of a petition by the court that it should be endorsed with the words *fiat justitia* by the Crown on the advice of the Home Secretary, who acted on the opinion of the Attorney-General. There was no appeal against the refusal of the *fiat*. A judgment in favour of a suppliant on a petition of right took the form of a declaration of the rights to which the suppliant was entitled and, being always observed by the Crown, was as effective as a judgment in an ordinary action, though execution could not be levied against Crown property.

The Law since 1948

The Crown Proceedings Act 1947,[4] which came into force on January 1, 1948, enables the appropriate government department, or in the alternative where no department is named for the purpose of legal process the Attorney-General, to be sued both in the High Court and in a county court by ordinary process under rules of court in all those cases where a petition of right or a special statutory procedure (some of these were of great antiquity and extreme complexity) had hitherto been required. The ordinary rules of agency apply; thus an agent need only have ostensible authority to bind the Crown and there is no rule requiring the actual authority of the Crown. Those who make contracts on behalf of the Crown, as its agents, are in accordance with the general rule not liable personally.[5]

1 *Thomas* v. *The Queen* (1874), L.R. 10 Q.B. 31.
2 *Attorney-General* v. *De Keyser's Royal Hotel*, [1920] A.C. 508; K. & L. 118.
3 Winfield, *Law of Tort*, 5th edn., p. 84.
4 For text, see K. & L. 349–59. Section 1 relates to contracts.
5 *Macbeath* v. *Haldimand* (1786), 1 T.R. 172.

But it is not every contract entered into by the Crown which gives a right to redress for its breach. Thus, if the contract expressly provides that money payments thereunder are to be made out of monies provided by Parliament, such provision is a condition precedent to liability under the contract, but it is not necessary that specific appropriations shall be made in advance to meet the obligations of the Crown. Any damages awarded against the Crown will, however, be recoverable only if appropriation is made by Parliament in the usual way.[1] This applies whether the liability is in contract or in tort; nor, as will be seen, can execution to enforce a judgment be levied against Crown property. There is, moreover, a rule of law, the exact extent of which it is not easy to determine, that the Crown cannot bind itself so as to fetter its future executive action.

In *Rederiaktiebolaget Amphitrite* v. *The King* [2] a Swedish steamship company, Sweden being a neutral in the First World War, was aware that neutral ships were liable to be detained in British ports. They obtained an undertaking from the British Government that a particular ship, if sent to this country with a special class of cargo, would not be detained. Accordingly the ship was sent with such a cargo, but the Government withdrew their undertaking and refused clearance for the ship. On trial of a petition of right, which nowadays would take the form of an action for breach of contract, it was held that the undertaking of the Government was not enforceable as the Crown was not competent to make a contract which would have the effect of limiting its power of executive action in the future.

It has been suggested that the defence of executive necessity only "avails the Crown where there is an implied term to that effect or that is the true meaning of the contract" [3]; or again that the defence has no application to ordinary commercial contracts made by the Crown. A preferable view seems to be that the *Amphitrite* case illustrates a general principle that the Crown, or any other public authority, cannot be prevented by an existing contract from exercising powers which are vested in it either by statute or common law for the protection of the public interest.[4]

In *Commissioners of Crown Lands* v. *Page*, the Crown sued for arrears of rent due under a lease of Crown land that had been assigned to the defendant. The defence was that the land had been requisitioned by a government department and that this constituted eviction by the Crown as landlord. The Court of Appeal held that the arrears were

[1] See H. Street, *Governmental Liability*, pp. 84–92. For Appropriation, see p. 144, *ante*.

[2] [1921] 3 K.B. 500; K. & L. 361.

[3] *Robertson* v. *Minister of Pensions*, [1949] 1 K.B. 227, at p. 231.

[4] Street, *op. cit.*, pp. 98–99; J. D. B. Mitchell, *The Contracts of Public Authorities*, pp. 27–32, 52–65, and (1960) 23 M.L.R., pp. 672–74.

payable. Devlin L. J. said: "When the Crown, in dealing with one of its subjects, is dealing as if it too were a private person, and is granting leases or buying and selling as ordinary persons do, it is absurd to suppose that it is making any promise about the way in which it will conduct the affairs of the nation".[1]

There are many other problems arising from government contracts to which the accepted principles of English law provide no answer.[2]

Service under the Crown

Service under the Crown is another instance of the special contractual position of the Crown; for it is part of the prerogative that the Crown employs its servants at its pleasure, whether in the civil service or the armed forces. The Crown relies on its freedom to dismiss its servants at will in the public interest; thus it seems that the relationship between the Crown and its servants is unilateral and in the absence of statutory provision [3] no Crown servant has a remedy for wrongful dismissal.

In *Dunn* v. *The Queen*,[4] Dunn claimed that he had been engaged as a consular agent in Crown service by the Consul General for the Niger Protectorate for a term of three years certain. His claim for damages for premature dismissal failed. Lord Herschell said:

"Such employment being for the good of the public, it is essential for the public good that it should be capable of being determined at the pleasure of the Crown, except in exceptional cases where it has been deemed to be more for the public good that some restriction should be imposed on the power to dismiss its servants."

Having failed in his petition of right, Dunn sued the servant of the Crown who had engaged him, for damages for breach of warranty of authority. It was held that no action lies against a Crown servant for breach of warranty of authority, but the decision can be supported on the narrower ground that Dunn must be deemed to have known that the officer who had engaged him had no power in law to engage him for a fixed period: *Dunn* v. *Macdonald*.[5]

The Crown's power to dismiss its servants at pleasure has sometimes been explained on the basis that a term to this effect is implied into every contract of employment made by the Crown. If this were so, the Crown's power to dismiss at pleasure could be excluded by an express term in the contract of employment, but the court may well

[1] [1960] 2 Q.B. 274, at p. 292; see also *William Cory & Son, Ltd.* v. *City of London*, [1951] 2 K.B. 476.

[2] See *e.g.* C. C. Turpin, (1968) 31 M.L.R. 241.

[3] *E.g.* the statutory provision that judges hold office during good behaviour, p. 329, *ante*; see also *Gould* v. *Stuart*, [1896] A.C. 575, where the New South Wales Civil Service Act 1884 was held to override the general rule.

[4] [1896] 1 Q.B. 116; K. & L. 360.

[5] [1897] 1 Q.B. 401. Discussed in K. & L., p. 335.

disregard any such attempt to depart from the normal rule as a clog or fetter on the overriding power of the Crown.[1]

But although a civil servant has no tenure of office as a matter of law, in practice he has a very high degree of security. This security depends upon convention rather than law.[2] The agreements as to wages and other conditions of service reached between the Treasury and representatives of the staffs of government departments in joint councils (Whitley Councils) [3] and afterwards confirmed by the Treasury do not give rise to contractual rights.[4] No remedy exists where an officer appointed under statutory authority loses his office through its premature termination by Act of Parliament without compensation, since the agreement has become impossible of performance.[5] But is Crown service a contractual relationship at all? Members of the armed forces cannot sue for arrears of pay, for no engagement between the Crown and members of the armed forces can be enforced by a court of law.[6] It has been held that no debt is owed by the Crown to a civil servant in respect of his salary.[7] But it is hard to see why this need be so and in one House of Lords case petition of right proceedings to determine the entitlement of a former civil servant to supplementary payments were successful.[8] It has been suggested *obiter* that arrears of salary would be recoverable on a *quantum meruit*,[9] but the main question remains open.

Tortious Liability: the Law before 1948

Before 1948 the Crown could be sued neither in respect of wrongs expressly authorised by the Crown nor in respect of wrongs committed by servants of the Crown in the course of their employment.

> In 1834 the Speaker of the House of Commons had his official house burned down in the fire which destroyed the two Houses of Parliament. He subsequently brought a petition of right to recover the value of his personal effects which had been destroyed in the fire. It was alleged that the fire was caused by burning the old tallies

[1] *Terrell* v. *Secretary of State for the Colonies*, [1953] 2 Q.B. 482.

[2] P. 218, *ante*.

[3] P. 221, *ante*.

[4] *Rodwell* v. *Thomas*, [1944] K.B. 596.

[5] *Reilly* v. *The King*, [1934] A.C. 176.

[6] *Leaman* v. *The King*, [1920] 3 K.B. 663; *Kynaston* v. *Attorney-General* (1933), 49 T.L.R. 300.

[7] *Lucas* v. *Lucas and High Commisioner for India*, [1943] P. 68, but see *A Civil Servant and his Pay*, by D. W. Logan, 61 L.Q.R. 240. See also *Dudfield* v. *Ministry of Works, The Times*, 24 January 1964, where a civil servants' union attempted unsuccessfully to get an authoritative ruling on this point.

[8] *Sutton* v. *Attorney-General* (1923), 39 T.L.R. 294.

[9] *Per* Goddard, L.C.J., in *Commissioners of Inland Revenue* v. *Hambrook*, [1956] 2 Q.B. 641.

(receipts for Exchequer payments) in the stoves used for warming the House of Lords in so negligent and careless a way that the fire was caused by the stoves being over-heated. It was held that even assuming the negligence the Sovereign was not responsible for its consequences: *Viscount Canterbury* v. *Attorney-General.*[1]

The rigour of the Crown's immunity was eased in practice by the fact that the Treasury Solicitor usually defended an action against a subordinate official and the Treasury, as a matter of grace, paid damages if he was found liable. In 1942 the Lord Chancellor appointed an independent person to certify (if the plaintiff so desired) whether a subordinate was acting in the course of his employment. This enabled the plaintiff before proceeding with his action against the actual tortfeasor to determine whether or not he could expect the Crown to stand behind the defendant and meet any damages which the court might award to him against the defendant personally. In some cases, the Crown was willing to nominate a defendant on whom the writ could be served, even though the defendant nominated could not have been personally responsible for the alleged tort. Disapproval of this practice by the House of Lords in *Adams* v. *Naylor* [2] caused great hardship to litigants until the law was changed.

In this case the court refused to give judgment against an army officer who had been nominated to accept service of the writ in respect of injuries to children in a derelict minefield on the coast. As the officer in charge of the area at the time of the accident to the children, he was in no way responsible for having laid any of the mines which caused the injuries. No negligence could be proved against him personally and the case was dismissed, leaving the injured parties without any legal redress against the Crown, the real occupier.

It was therefore urgently necessary for the law to be changed to allow tort actions against the Crown. As early as 1927, a draft Bill had been recommended by the Crown Proceedings Committee [3] but this had been seriously opposed by some government departments, in particular the Service Departments and the Post Office. The Ministers' Powers Report referred to the "lacuna in the rule of law" caused by the law on Crown proceedings, but the Administration of Justice (Miscellaneous Provisions) Act 1933, while improving the Crown's position as a litigant (*e.g.* allowing proceedings by the Crown in the County Court, allowing the Crown to recover debts due to it by ordinary writ of summons and allowing costs to be awarded to or against the Crown in any civil proceedings to which the Crown was a party [4]), did not

[1] (1842), 1 Ph. 306.
[2] [1946] A.C. 543. See also *Royster* v. *Cavey*, [1947] 1 K.B. 204.
[3] *Crown Proceedings Committee Report* (Cmd. 2842), 1927.
[4] If the Crown seeks leave to appeal to the House of Lords, leave may be conditional on payment of the respondent's costs of the appeal in any event; see *e.g.* *Marriott* v. *Minister of Health*, [1937] 1 K.B. 128, at p. 143.

remove the Crown's immunity in tort. The Limitation Act 1939 made the ordinary periods of limitation for bringing an action applicable to proceedings by and against the Crown with one exception.[1] One argument against a Crown Proceedings Bill was that juries would award excessive damages to successful plaintiffs, but any validity in the argument was largely discounted by the decline in the use of juries in civil trials after the Second World War. The need to remove the general immunity of the Crown was increased by the fact that various statutes had allowed proceedings to be brought against particular departments, and the varying methods adopted caused great perplexity.[2]

Tortious Liability: the Present Law

With certain important exceptions, the Crown Proceedings Act 1947 established the principle that the Crown is subject to the same liabilities in tort as if it were a private person of full age and capacity, in particular (*a*) in respect of torts committed by its servants or agents, (*b*) in respect of the duties which an employer at common law owes to his servants or agents, and (*c*) in respect of any breach of the common law duties of an owner or occupier of property (s. 2 (1)). The Crown is therefore now vicariously liable for the torts of its servants or agents, *e.g.* negligent driving by a Crown servant while in the course of his employment.

The Crown was also made liable for breach of a statutory duty, provided that the statute is one which binds the Crown, as well as private persons (s. 2 (2)) such as the Occupiers' Liability Act 1957 and the Factories Act 1961. The Act of 1947 imposes no liability enforceable by action in the case of statutory duties which bind only the Crown or its officers, such as the duty placed upon the Secretary for Education and Science by s. 1 of the Education Act 1944, to promote the education of the people.[3]

Although the general principle of Crown liability in tort is established, the Act of 1947 elaborates this in some detail. Thus the vicarious liability of the Crown is restricted to the torts of its officers as defined in the Act (s. 2 (6)). This definition requires that the officer shall (*a*) be appointed directly or indirectly by the Crown and (*b*) be paid in respect of his duties as an officer of the Crown at the

[1] Previously there was no period of limitation for actions by the Crown, except that for the recovery of land the period was 60 years. For this type of action it is now 30 years, instead of the ordinary period of 12 years.
[2] See *Minister of Supply* v. *British Thomson-Houston Co., Ltd.*, [1943] K.B. 478.
[3] P. 623, *ante*.

material time wholly out of the Consolidated Fund,[1] moneys provided by Parliament, the Road Fund or a fund certified by the Treasury. This excludes, for example, the police.[2] There is also no vicarious liability for acts done by officers acting in a judicial capacity or in execution of judicial process (s. 2 (5)), nor for acts or omissions of a Crown servant unless apart from the Act the servant would have been personally liable in tort (s. 2 (1)). The general law relating to indemnity and contribution applies to the Crown as if it were a private person (s. 4) The Act does not authorise proceedings to be brought against the Sovereign in his personal capacity (s. 10 (1)) and does not abolish any prerogative or statutory powers of the Crown, in particular those relating to the defence of the realm and the maintenance of the armed forces (s. 11 (1)).

The principal exception from liability in tort relates to the armed forces. Neither the Crown nor a member of the armed forces is liable in tort in respect of acts or omissions causing death or personal injury which are committed by a member of the armed forces while on duty, where the injured or killed was himself (*a*) a member of the armed forces on duty at the time or, if not on duty as such, was on any land, premises, ship, aircraft or vehicle which was being used for the purposes of the armed forces, and (*b*) the injury is certified by the Secretary of State for the Social Services as attributable to injury for purposes of pension entitlement (s. 10). This certificate does not however guarantee an award of a pension unless the conditions for entitlement are fulfilled.[3]

A similar exception from liability formerly applied to the Post Office. The Act of 1947 provided that neither the Crown, nor an officer of the Crown (save at the suit of the Crown) could be held liable in tort for any act or omission in relation to a postal packet (unless it was a registered inland packet) or to a telephonic communication (s. 9). Nor was there any liability in contract.[4] When in 1969, the Post Office ceased to be a department of the central government and became a public corporation with a status like that of a nationalised industry, the existing limitations on the liability of the Post Office were continued, even though the Post Office is no longer part of the Crown.[5]

Although the Act of 1947 in principle assimilated the tortious liabilities of the Crown to those of a private person, the duties of the central government may well give rise to issues of liability which

[1] P. 143–6, *ante*.
[2] Pp. 242–3, *ante*.
[3] *Adams* v. *War Office*, [1955] 1 W.L.R. 1116.
[4] *Triefus & Co. Ltd.* v. *Post Office*, [1957] 2 Q.B. 352.
[5] Post Office Act 1969, ss. 6 (5), 29, 30.

would hardly arise in the case of a private person, and may not easily be resolved by applying legal principles which relate to the acts of private individuals.

Thus in *Dorset Yacht Co.* v. *Home Office*,[1] the Home Office were sued for the value of a yacht which had been taken away from its moorings and wrecked by Borstal boys who had absconded at night from a Borstal summer camp. It was argued for the Home Office that the system of open Borstals and prisons would be jeopardised if liability was imposed on the government for the acts of any who escaped. *Held* (Court of Appeal) that the Home Office would be liable if the plaintiff could establish that negligence on the part of the Borstal authorities had led to the escape.

But it is doubtful whether in such a case the plaintiffs are in a position to establish negligence on the part of the Home Office, or indeed whether liability should depend on proof of negligence at all.[2]

Application of Statutes

The rule that Acts of Parliament do not bind the Crown, *i.e.* that the Crown is not to be prejudiced as to its prerogatives, unless the particular statute so enacts either by express words or by necessary implication, has an important bearing on the liability of the Crown for breach of statutory duty.[3] It is by the operation of this rule that Crown property is exempt from local rates and income tax. Here, again, the term "the Crown" includes all those departments which can be regarded as exercising functions which form part of the general government of the country, but the mere fact that premises are used for public purposes does not result in exemption. Thus exemption from income tax was accorded in respect of a building used for Assizes and as a county police station [4] but exemption from rates was not accorded to the outfall works of a county council acting as sewerage authority.[5] Where a statute does not apply to the Crown or its servants acting in the course of duty, there is no liability on the part of the individual servant for a breach of the statute, for he has committed no offence.[6]

[1] [1969] 2 Q.B. 412; upheld by the House of Lords, [1970] 2 All E.R. 294.
[2] [1969] C.L.J. 273, 276; [1969] Public Law 269.
[3] *Food Controller* v. *Cork*, [1923] A.C. 647; *Bank Voor Handel en Scheepvaart N.V.* v. *Administrator of Hungarian Property*, [1954] A.C. 584. It has been held that when a statute is enacted "for the public good," the Crown is not bound by implication, unless to exclude the Crown would wholly frustrate the purpose of the Act: *Province of Bombay* v. *Municipal Corporation of Bombay*, [1947] A.C. 58.
[4] *Coomber* v. *Justices of Berkshire* (1883), 9 App. Cas. 61.
[5] *L.C.C.* v. *Erith (Churchwardens) and Dartford Union Assessment Committee*, [1893] A.C. 562.
[6] *Cooper* v. *Hawkins*, [1904] 2 K.B. 164. And now see Road Traffic Act 1960, s. 250.

Procedure

Where the Crown Proceedings Act 1947 enables proceedings to be brought against the Crown, whether in tort or contract or for the recovery of property, in principle the normal procedure of litigation applies. The action is brought not against the Crown as such but against the appropriate government department, the Minister for the Civil Service being responsible for publishing a list of the departments and naming the solicitor for each department to accept process on its behalf; in cases not covered by the list, the Attorney-General may be made defendant. The trial follows that of an ordinary High Court or County Court action except that:

(*a*) judgment against the department cannot be enforced by the ordinary methods of levying execution or attachment; but the department is required to pay the amount certified to be due as damages and costs (s. 25);

(*b*) in place of an injunction or a decree of specific performance, remedies which are sanctioned by imprisonment for default, and therefore inappropriate, the court makes an order declaring the rights of the parties (s. 21); [1]

(*c*) similarly, there can be no order for restitution of property but the court may declare the plaintiff entitled as against the Crown (s. 21).

An action for a declaration [2] may be brought against the Crown without claiming any consequential relief, *e.g.* where a wrong is merely threatened [3] but not to determine purely hypothetical questions which may never arise; *e.g.* as to whether there is a contingent liability to a tax.[4] Formerly the scope of this remedy in Crown proceedings was doubtful and it could not be used to prejudge an issue which might have had to be adjudicated in a petition of right for breach of contract or detention of property by the Crown.[5]

Crown Privilege

Discovery of documents, an important interlocutory proceeding to enable a party to inspect all documents in the possession or control

[1] Unsuccessful attempts to obtain injunctions against Ministers of the Crown were made in *Merricks* v. *Heathcoat-Amory*, [1955] Ch. 567 and *Harper* v. *Secretary of State for Home Department*, [1955] Ch. 238. An interim declaration in lieu of an interim injunction may not be made: *International General Electric Co.* v. *Commissioners of Customs and Excise* [1962] Ch. 784.

[2] Pp. 671–3, *ante*, for the scope of relief by declaratory judgments.

[3] *Dyson* v. *Attorney-General*, [1912] 1 Ch. 158.

[4] *Argosam Finance Co. Ltd.* v. *Oxby*, [1965] Ch. 390.

[5] *Bombay and Persia Steam Navigation Co.* v. *Maclay*, [1920] 3 K.B. 402, at p. 408.

of his opponent which relate to the matters in dispute in the action, could formerly not be used against the Crown. By section 28 of the 1947 Act the Court may order discovery against the Crown and may also require the Crown to answer interrogatories, *i.e.* written questions to obtain information from the other party on material facts. But the Act expressly preserves the existing rule of law that the Crown may refuse to disclose any document or to answer any question on the ground that this would be injurious to the public interest; the Act even protects the Crown from disclosing the mere existence of a document on the same ground. Crown privilege, the power of the Crown to withhold documentary evidence from the courts, is not restricted to proceedings to which the Crown is a party and applies equally to civil proceedings between private individuals. The need for some power to protect documents from publication in the interests of state security was well illustrated by *Duncan* v. *Cammell Laird & Co. Ltd.*[1] What is more difficult is to determine the precise extent of Crown privilege, the grounds on which it may be claimed, and the power of the court to control the Executive in exercising this privilege. Subsequent history shows that these matters were not finally settled by the House of Lords in *Duncan* v. *Cammell Laird & Co. Ltd.*, as was once thought.

> Early in 1939 a new naval submarine sank while on trial with the loss of 99 lives, including civilian workmen. A large number of actions in negligence were brought by the personal representatives against the respondents, who had built the submarine under contract with the Admiralty. In a test action, the respondents objected to the production of several documents relating to the design of the submarine. The First Lord of the Admiralty had directed the company not to produce the documents on the ground of Crown privilege, since disclosure would be injurious to national defence.
>
> Viscount Simon L.C., giving judgment on behalf of a strong House of Lords, held that the documents should not be disclosed. Although a validly taken objection to disclosure was conclusive, and should be taken by the Minister himself, the decision ruling out such documents was that of the judge. In deciding whether it was his duty to object, a Minister should only withhold production where the public interest would otherwise be damnified, *e.g.* where disclosure would be injurious to national defence, or to good diplomatic relations, "or where the practice of keeping a class of documents secret is necessary for the proper functioning of the public service".[2]

On the basis of this judgment particular documents may be withheld *either* because the contents of those documents must be kept secret (as in *Duncan* v. *Cammell Laird & Co. Ltd.* itself) *or* on the much

[1] [1942] A.C. 624.
[2] At p. 642.

wider ground that they belong to a class of documents which must as a class be treated as confidential, *e.g.* civil service memoranda and minutes, to guarantee freedom and candour of communication on public matters. Following these *dicta* of Viscount Simon, the practice developed of withholding documents simply on the Minister's assertion that they belonged to a class of documents which it was necessary in the public interest for the proper functioning of the public service to withhold.[1] Where documents were withheld, oral evidence of their contents could not be given; and it seemed that the courts could not overrule the Minister's objection if taken in correct form.

Conflict between unduly wide claims of Crown privilege and the public interest in the administration of justice was to some extent eased by government concessions. In 1956 the Lord Chancellor stated that privilege would no longer be claimed in certain types of litigation where the litigants' interest was clearly prejudiced by non-disclosure of certain kinds of documents in a government department's possession; these included factual reports about accidents involving government employees or government premises and, where the Crown or a Crown employee was being sued for negligence, medical reports by Service or prison doctors. Again in 1962 the Government agreed that statements made to the police during criminal investigations would not be withheld where the police were sued for malicious prosecution or wrongful arrest, and that in other civil proceedings the question of whether statements made to the police should be withheld would be left to the trial judge, subject in each case to the names of police informers not being revealed.[2] These statements of future government policy were not accompanied by any change in the law, and it was still considered that in English law, unlike Scots law, the courts were bound by the Minister's objection. It was already established in Scotland that a court must take account of the Minister's decision but is not bound by it and in exceptional circumstances may overrule it if the interests of justice so require.[3]

Following several decisions of the English Court of Appeal which cast increasing doubt on the conclusiveness of the Minister's objection,[4] in 1968 the House of Lords overruled an objection taken by

[1] See *Ellis* v. *Home Office*, [1953] 2 Q.B. 135 and *Broome* v. *Broome*, [1955] P. 190, for illustrations of the harsh operation of Crown privilege.

[2] See 197 H.L.Deb. 741–48 (6 June 1956) and 237 H.L.Deb. 1191 (8 March 1962).

[3] *Glasgow Corporation* v. *Central Land Board*, 1956 S.C. (H.L.) 1: *Whitehall* v. *Whitehall*, 1957 S.C. 30.

[4] *Merricks* v. *Nott-Bower*, [1965] 1 Q.B. 57, *In re Grosvenor Hotel, London* (No. 2), [1965] Ch. 1210, and *Wednesbury Corporation* v. *Ministry of Housing and Local Government*, [1965] 1 W.L.R. 261. See also D. H. Clark, (1967) 30 M.L.R. 489.

the Home Secretary to the production of certain police reports, so establishing the principle that it is for the court to hold the balance between the public interest in the administration of justice and the public interest in the withholding of documents whose disclosure would be injurious to the conduct of government.

In *Conway* v. *Rimmer* [1] a former probationary constable sued a police superintendent for malicious prosecution following an incident of a missing electric torch which had led to the acquittal of the plaintiff on a charge of theft and to his later dismissal from the police. The Home Secretary claimed Crown privilege for (*a*) probationary reports on the plaintiff and (*b*) the defendant's report on the investigation into the incident. He certified that these were confidential reports within a class of documents production of which would be injurious to the public interest. *Held*, the court has jurisdiction to order the production of documents for which Crown privilege is claimed. The court will give full weight to a Minister's view, but this need not necessarily prevail if the relevant considerations are such that judicial experience is competent to weigh them.

The House of Lords thus departed from the wide rule laid down in *Duncan* v. *Cammell Laird*,[2] which it accepted had been properly decided on the facts. English law was thereby brought into line with Scots law, Lord Reid considering there to be no rational justification for the law on such a matter of public policy being different in the two countries. Although cases are likely to be rare in which a court may properly question a Minister's objection to production based on a document's contents, it seems that the powers of the court are wider when the objection is based on the class into which a document falls.

The "formula of compromise" between Executive and courts laid down in *Conway* v. *Rimmer* still has to be worked out in detail. Cabinet papers, foreign office despatches, high level inter-departmental minutes and documents concerning the administration of the armed forces will continue to be privileged and the same may apply to all civil service minutes and internal memoranda. Where the court decides to overrule the Minister, it will first order the documents to be produced for inspection by the court before they are made available to the parties—even though it is contrary to a basic principle of justice that the judge should see documents which are not disclosed to the parties. Although *Conway* v. *Rimmer* arose from an incident within the police, most police documents relating to the detection and prevention of crime will probably continue to be privileged.[3]

[1] [1968] A.C. 910.
[2] *Ante*, p. 688.
[3] Cf. *Auten* v. *Rayner* (No. 2), [1960] 1 Q.B. 669; *McKie* v. *Scottish Motor Traction Co.*, 1952 S.C. 206.

Scotland

The Crown Proceedings Act applies to Scotland with the substantial variations which are caused by the differences in Scots law and civil procedure. Thus the liability of the Crown in tort is reproduced in Scotland by liability in reparation; the Lord Advocate is the proper person to sue and be sued on behalf of the Crown or a department of government; the sheriff's court replaces the county court. The procedure by petition of right never had any application in Scotland, but the ordinary forms of actions for payment or declarator are, as hitherto, used against the Lord Advocate in cases of contractual liability. As already mentioned, there is an inherent right in the Court of Session founded on public interest to overrule a ministerial refusal to produce documents required in the course of litigation. The Court is not called upon to decide whether a Minister's objection is justified or not on grounds of public policy, but to decide whether the interests of justice are paramount.[1]

[1] *Glasgow Corporation* v. *Central Land Board*, 1956 S.C. (H.L.) 1.

CHAPTER FORTY-SEVEN

ADMINISTRATIVE JUSTICE

In this chapter will be examined the characteristics and functions of those administrative bodies which exercise powers of adjudication, and also the various procedures designed to assist in the settlement of disputes between the citizen and the administration. For many centuries Britain has had specialised courts in addition to the courts of general jurisdiction. Medieval merchants had their courts of pie poudre; the tin miners of Devon and Cornwall had their courts of Stannaries. The growth of governmental activities and State services associated with the Welfare State and the mixed economy has led to the creation of many special procedures for the settlement of disputes. Thus the National Insurance Act of 1911, which created the first large scale social insurance scheme, provided for the adjudication of disputes by specially created administrative agencies. The present social security scheme includes a complex and virtually self-contained structure for the settlement of disputes concerning the benefit or pension payable to claimants. Many public services and controls, *e.g.* housing, highways, town planning and rent control, necessarily involve interference with individuals' property rights in the interests of the community.

There are three main ways in which disputes arising out of State services and controls may be settled: (*a*) by conferring new jurisdiction on one or other of the ordinary courts; (*b*) by creating *ad hoc* machinery in the form of special tribunals; (*c*) by empowering the appropriate Minister to make the decisions. In the latter case, Parliament may be content with the normal process of departmental decision or may require the Minister to observe a special procedure, *e.g.* to hold a public inquiry, before the decision is made. In Section A of this chapter several specialised tribunals will be considered in outline, together with certain problems of control and procedure which would not have arisen if Parliament had chosen merely to enlarge the jurisdiction of existing courts. In Section B will be examined the public inquiry procedure: to what extent does this protect the individual against an arbitrary or ill-informed exercise of power? By contrast with the period of the Ministers' Powers

Report, the distinction between tribunals and inquiries is now well accepted, and this was reflected in the report of the Franks Committee.[1] But the distinction is still liable to be misunderstood. On the one hand, the appearance of tribunals as part of the whole administrative structure is deceptive, for the typical tribunal exercises functions which are essentially judicial in character, although of a specialised nature. Indeed most administrative tribunals could well be regarded as specialised courts. As the Franks Committee stated, "We consider that tribunals should properly be regarded as machinery provided by Parliament for adjudication rather than as part of the machinery of administration. The essential point is that in all these cases Parliament has deliberately provided for a decision outside and independent of the Department concerned".[2] On the other hand, the public inquiry, while it grants citizens affected by official proposals and decisions a legal safeguard against ill-informed and unreasoned decisions, is essentially a step in a complex process which leads to a departmental decision for which a Minister is responsible to Parliament. Granted the distinction between tribunals and public inquiries, why should they still be treated together under a single heading of administrative justice? Probably the best answer, based on the general conclusions of the Franks Committee, is that both with tribunals and inquiries the ordinary departmental procedures are not considered enough to protect the individual's interests. All powers of government should be exercised fairly—but principles of openness, fairness and impartiality must be maintained with especial care whenever Parliament does not leave it to a department to make its decision in the manner it thinks best.

Further problems arise in those areas of administrative power to which neither tribunals nor public inquries extend. A partial solution is now provided by the Parliamentary Commissioner for Administration, whose office is described in Section C of this chapter. Section D deals briefly with some outstanding problems of administrative justice.

Reasons for Administrative Justice

The creation of special tribunals has at times been considered to endanger the position of the judiciary and the influence of the law as applied in the ordinary civil and criminal courts. Modern problems cannot, however, be solved by a rigid application of the

[1] P. 594, *ante*.
[2] Cmnd. 218, p. 9.

doctrine of separation of powers; there must be considered what Lord Greene called the functional capacity of the judicial machine.[1] Constitutional machinery must be suited to its intended product and must be able to satisfy the demands made upon it.[2] The right of access to the courts is indeed a safeguard of our liberties, but its preservation will not be assisted if the judiciary is asked to undertake tasks which fall outside its proper sphere. It is true that many tasks performed by the judiciary involve the exercise of discretion, for example in the settling of hitherto undecided points of law and in the sentencing of convicted criminals. But modern government gives rise to many disputes which cannot be solved by applying objective legal principles or standards and depend ultimately on what is desirable in the public interest as a matter of social policy. Although there is a danger in over-simplifying the distinction between law and policy, decisions which depend on broad issues of national policy should be made by Ministers responsible for their decisions to Parliament; but where it is possible to formulate the relevant criteria of decision as a body of statutory principles, it may be desirable to vest the power to decide either in the ordinary courts or in a specially created tribunal. The setting up of the Restrictive Practices Court in 1956 [3] was accompanied by a keen division of opinion. On the one hand, it was argued that the decisions to be made by the Court were essentially political and should therefore be made by the Government of the day. On the other hand, the Government considered that economic, social and political factors involved could be formulated in such terms that power to apply them in a particular case should be vested in a branch of the High Court specially constituted to include economic and other experts.[4] In some fields, particularly town planning, housing and new towns, the general policy of Governments has been to retain power to decide in the hands of the Minister concerned; in other fields, such as social security, the principles applicable have been laid down in statutes or in statutory instruments, and the duty of applying them has been vested in a hierarchy of agencies, for whose decisions no Minister is politically responsible, and

[1] *Law and Progress*, Haldane Memorial Lecture, published in 94 *Law Journal*, October 28, November 4 and November 11, 1944; and Lord Greene's judgments in *Johnson* (*B.*) *& Co.* (*Builders*), *Ltd.* v. *Minister of Health*, [1947] 2 All E.R. 395 and in *Robinson* v. *Minister of Town and Country Planning*, [1947] K.B. 717.

[2] Lord Greene, *op. cit*.

[3] P. 311, *ante*.

[4] 549 H.C.Deb. col. 1927 ff. (March 6 1956). See also G. Marshall, *Justiciability*, in Oxford Essays in Jurisprudence, ed. Guest, 1961, pp. 282–87, and R. Stevens, *Justiciability*: *the Restrictive Practices Court Re-examined*, [1964] Public Law 221.

which the Government can control only by amending the relevant statutory rules. Here the relationship between Minister and tribunal approaches that which exists between the Government and the ordinary judiciary. If this is so, why is it that so many special tribunals have been created in preference to enlarging the jurisdiction of the ordinary courts?

There is no single answer. Under the legislation establishing rent control, for example, some additional jurisdiction was conferred on the county courts, but it was also thought desirable to establish Rent Tribunals with a wide discretion to control the rents of furnished lettings. Factors that have favoured the setting up of special tribunals include the following: the desire for a procedure which avoids the formality of the ordinary courts, on the ground that litigious procedure does not produce the right atmosphere for the working of a social insurance scheme; the need, in implementing a new social policy, for the speedy, cheap and decentralised determination of a very large number of individual cases; the need for expert and specialised knowledge on the part of the tribunal which a court with a wide general jurisdiction might not acquire; and the danger of imposing too many additional burdens on the ordinary courts. Moreover some judges, influenced by the principle of interpretation that the common law can only be changed by express words or necessary intendment,[1] have interpreted the social legislation of the present century too narrowly and have failed to adapt the individualistic tradition of the common law to the conception of liberty as it is understood in the Welfare State. In this respect the accepted principles of statutory interpretation often do not give a sufficient guide to the court in determining the intention of Parliament.[2] The essential differences in training and approach between lawyer and administrator help to explain why disputes arising from social legislation have been entrusted to tribunals rather than to the courts. The difficulty has been well put by Professor Jackson: "Social legislation can rarely be comprehended by seeing its effects as solely an issue between two individuals, but the isolated issue is the centre of traditional common law technique".[3] The department responsible for administering a social policy has often preferred special machinery for the adjudication of disputes, controllable by subordinate legislation, rather than have disputes settled in the ordinary courts entirely separated from the department.

[1] See, however, p. 55, *ante*, note 4.
[2] See the English and Scottish Law Commissions' paper, "The Interpretation of Statutes", H.C. 256 (1968–69).
[3] R. M. Jackson, *The Machinery of Justice*, 5th edn., p. 301.

Merits of the Ordinary Courts

The necessity for administrative justice must not however lead to under-rating the merits of the traditional legal system. In the view of the Franks Committee, "a decision should be entrusted to a court rather than to a tribunal in the absence of special considerations which make a tribunal more suitable".[1] Moreover, granted the need for specialised tribunals, the merits of the traditional system should so far as is practicable be incorporated in the new. The Franks Committee emphasised that tribunals are more properly regarded as machinery for adjudication than as part of the machinery of administration. The desire of a department to control its own system of tribunals must not be permitted to conflict with the principle of an independent judiciary administering the law in open court. In particular, the independence of the tribunal is not protected if appointment and dismissal of members are solely in the hands of the Minister concerned. Again, there is danger as well as merit in the informality of procedure; one safeguard lies in the appointment of legally qualified chairmen, another in maintaining in all cases the right to legal representation—although if this right is to benefit those who most need it, the legal aid scheme must be extended to tribunals. A further safeguard is the right of appeal either to a higher tribunal or to the ordinary courts; in particular it should always be possible to challenge in the superior courts a tribunal's ruling on points of law. And, if the right of appeal is to be at all valuable, tribunals must give reasons for their decisions. Since the Franks Report of 1957 acceptance of many of these principles has removed much earlier distrust of special tribunals. Similarly, executive and legislative action has improved many aspects of the public inquiry procedure, but here the analogy with the ordinary courts is much less close, for the reason already given that ultimately the decision may depend on matters of governmental policy.

A. Administrative Tribunals [2]

It is not easy to classify the many different tribunals which exercise judicial functions in relation to a specialised branch of government. The Franks Committee grouped tribunals under five heads, namely

[1] Cmnd. 218, p. 9.

[2] See Report of the Franks Committee, Cmnd. 218 (1957), Parts II and III; W. A. Robson, *Justice and Administrative Law*, 3rd edn., Chap. 3; R. M. Jackson, *The Machinery of Justice*, 5th edn., Chap. VI; Sir Carleton Allen, *Administrative Jurisdiction*, [1956] Public Law 13; J. F. Garner, *Administrative Law*, Chaps. 7 and 8.

(1) land and property, (ii) national insurance, national assistance and family allowances, (iii) the national health service, (iv) military service, and (v) transport; but tribunals outside this classification included the General and Special Commissioners of Income Tax and the Independent Schools Tribunal.

A convenient list of tribunals under the supervision of the Council on Tribunals [1] is published annually as an Appendix to the Council's report to Parliament. This includes tribunals relating to agriculture, air transport, the betting levy, children's voluntary homes, independent schools, forestry, industry, land valuation, mental health, milk and dairies, mines and quarries, national insurance and supplementary benefits, the national health service, patents designs and trade marks, pensions, performing rights, rent assessment and rent control, revenue, road traffic, transport and wireless telegraphy. It is only possible to describe in outline some of these tribunals.

General Considerations

Tribunals are concerned with a wide range of activities but certain questions are of general application. (*a*) What is the composition of the tribunal? Tribunals are seldom composed of government officials: in general they are constituted of lay member of the public, but in certain tribunals specialist qualifications are required and membership may involve a full-time salaried appointment; frequently provision is made for a legally qualified chairman. (*b*) Who appoints the members of the tribunal and who has power to dismiss? Usually appointments are made for a fixed period of years, either by the Minister concerned, by the Lord Chancellor, or by both Minister and Lord Chancellor jointly; in general dismissal now requires the concurrence of the Lord Chancellor.[2] (*c*) What are the powers and jurisdiction of the tribunal? In particular, how extensive is the tribunal's discretion? Many tribunals, like the Lands Tribunal and the Commissioners of Income Tax, exercise strictly judicial functions. Some, like the Transport Tribunal, base their decisions on wider aspects of policy, in effect exercising administrative functions in a judicial form. (*d*) What procedure is followed by the tribunal and how formal is it? Are hearings in public or in private, and do individuals appearing before it have the right of legal representation? (*e*) Are the tribunal's decisions final, or is there the right to appeal, whether on law, on fact, or on the merits? The Franks Committee considered that the ideal appeal structure took the form of a general appeal from

[1] P. 703, *post*.

[2] Tribunals and Inquiries Act 1958, s. 5.

the tribunal of first instance to an appellate tribunal; that as a matter of principle appeal should not lie from a tribunal to a Minister; and that all decisions of tribunals should be subject to review by the courts on points of law.[1] The structure of appeals under the national insurance scheme complies with this pattern but many other tribunals depart from it. (*f*) Are the tribunal's decisions published and, if so, do they have authority as binding or persuasive precedents for other tribunals?

Commissioners of Income Tax

Appeals against rulings of inland revenue officials on income tax liability lie either to the General Commissioners of Income Tax or to the Special Commissioners of Income Tax. The General Commissioners in England and Wales are appointed and may be removed by the Lord Chancellor;[2] they are often magistrates. The Special Commissioners are whole-time officials appointed by the Treasury and hold office during pleasure; they are appointed either from officials already within the Inland Revenue Department or from barristers who have specialised in taxation work. Both General and Special Commissioners sit in private. Their function is simply to apply the income tax law to the facts of individual tax-payers' circumstances. They may be required to state a case for the opinion of the High Court on a point of law. Of the Special Commissioners the Committee on Ministers' Powers stated: "By common consent this tribunal gives general satisfaction by its impartiality, in spite of the fact that its members are not only appointed by the Treasury but may, when not performing judicial duties, actually act as administrative officials. All we can say about it is that it is a standing tribute to the fair-mindedness of the British Civil Service; but the precedent is not one which Parliament should copy in other branches of administration".[3] The Franks Committee received no evidence to suggest that this tribunal had ceased to give general satisfaction. The Special Commissioners who exercise judicial functions are now not required to undertake any administrative duties.

National Insurance Appeals [4]

Claims for benefit under the National Insurance Act 1965 are submitted to an insurance officer appointed by the Secretary of State for the Social Services; he is a full-time civil servant and

[1] Cmnd. 218, p. 25.
[2] Tribunals and Inquiries Act 1958, s. 7.
[3] M.P.R., pp. 86–87.
[4] See Street, *Justice in the Welfare State*, ch. 1.

in addition to his powers of adjudication may have ordinary administrative duties. From his decision there is a right of appeal to a local tribunal; this includes two members, each drawn from a representative panel, one of persons representing employers and insured persons other than those who are in employment, the other of employed persons, together with a chairman who is a lawyer, selected by the Secretary of State from a panel of persons appointed by the Lord Chancellor. From the tribunal's decision there is a full right of appeal to the National Insurance Commissioners, who are senior barristers appointed by the Crown. Normally an appeal is heard by a single Commissioner, but the Chief Commissioner may direct that an appeal involving a question of law of special difficulty should be heard by a tribunal of three Commissioners.[1] There is no right of appeal either on law or fact from a Commissioner's decision, but certiorari will lie to review it.[2] Some questions of a technical character, but not a direct claim to benefit, are reserved for decision by the Secretary of State, who may, if he wishes, refer the matter to a single judge of the High Court; from a decision of the Secretary of State on these questions there is a right of appeal to the High Court judge whose decision is final. The same system of adjudication also deals with industrial injuries; but questions concerning the extent of disablement due to an industrial injury are decided first by a medical board of two doctors, with an appeal to a medical appeal tribunal, consisting of two doctors sitting with a lawyer as chairman; from the medical appeal tribunal appeal lies on a point of law to a National Insurance Commissioner. Selected decisions of the Commissioners are officially published and bind all insurance officers and local tribunals.

Lands Tribunal

The Lands Tribunal Act 1949 authorised two Lands Tribunals, one for Scotland and one for the rest of the United Kingdom. No Tribunal has, however, been established in Scotland. The Tribunals are given jurisdiction over a variety of matters relating to the valuation of property, including the assessment of compensation for compulsory acquisition of land and rating appeals from the local valuation courts.[3] The jurisdiction can be enlarged by Order in Council. The President of the Lands Tribunal, who must have held

[1] National Insurance Act 1965, s. 9.

[2] *E.g. The Queen* v. *Deputy Industrial Injuries Commissioner*, [1965] 1 Q.B. 456. But the High Court cannot declare the Commissioner's decision to be wrong in law, *Punton* v. *Minister of Pensions* (No. 2), [1964] 1 All E.R. 448.

[3] P. 378, ***ante***.

judicial office or be a barrister of standing, is like the other members appointed by the Lord Chancellor. These members must be barristers, solicitors or persons qualified by professional experience in the valuation of land. There is no fixed composition for the Tribunal; this is varied according to the particular case as the President may determine. Thus a single surveyor may sit or the President together with members who are lawyers and surveyors. On the application of any party a case may be stated on a point of law for determination of the Court of Appeal; otherwise the decision of the Lands Tribunal is final.

The establishment of the Lands Tribunal is of great interest because the decision of disputes on a variety of kindred matters is vested in a single court, thereby establishing a single consistent jurisdiction which combines legal and technical valuation experience. One solution to the problem of administrative justice might be on the lines of a series of higher administrative courts, each covering a range of specialised but related jurisdictions. The Franks Committee examined various proposals for amalgamation of first instance tribunals, but did not accept that a policy of amalgamation would improve the quality of adjudication. The Committee considered that complete integration of tribunals serving different functions was not possible and did not wish to increase the burden on part-time lay members of tribunals; the Committee rejected the general principle that tribunal service should be whole-time or salaried, although recognising that membership of the Lands Tribunal must be an exception.

Industrial Tribunals

Industrial tribunals were first established under the Industrial Training Act 1964, s. 12, to determine disputes arising from the imposition on certain industries of a levy to meet the expenses of industrial training boards. They have rapidly acquired a jurisdiction which may be compared in scope with that of the Lands Tribunal. This now includes jurisdiction over disputed claims under the Redundancy Payments Act 1965 (over 10,000 appeals were heard in Britain in 1968) certain disputes arising from the Contracts of Employment Act 1963, and disputes arising out of the Selective Employment Payments Act 1966. An industrial tribunal consists of a legally qualified chairman sitting with two members drawn from panels representing employers and employed persons. An appeal lies to the High Court on a point of law. Selected decisions of industrial tribunals are published in the Industrial Tribunals Reports.

The industrial tribunals are centrally organised but sit in local centres accessible to parties from both sides of industry.

Rent Tribunals [1]

First appointed in 1946, rent tribunals are now appointed under the Rent Act 1968, Part VI, with the primary purpose of settling certain disputes between landlord and tenant of furnished dwelling accommodation subject to control. In particular, the tribunal must determine what is a reasonable rent in return for the facilities and services provided by the landlord. The discretion of the tribunal to determine what is a reasonable rent is very wide, and no appeal on fact or merits lies from their decisions; since 1958 an appeal on a point of law has lain to the High Court. The chairman of the tribunal is selected by the Minister of Housing and Local Government from a panel of persons appointed by the Lord Chancellor, and the remaining members are appointed by the Minister of Housing. The rent tribunals were strongly criticised in the evidence given to the Franks Committee; in a number of instances procedural abuses had been corrected by means of the prerogative orders.[2] But with changes in the scope of rent control, with improvements made by the Tribunals and Inquiries Act 1958, and with the attention which the Council on Tribunals has given them,[3] the working of the rent tribunals improved.

When in 1965 rent control of many unfurnished dwellings was re-imposed, the Government preferred to set up new machinery for the purpose rather than extend the powers of rent tribunals. Part IV of the Rent Act 1968 now provides for a scheme of registration for regulated tenancies under which a rent officer must initially assess a "fair rent", if possible with the approval of both landlord and tenant. Disputes are referred to a rent assessment committee, which may fix a fair rent after hearing both parties and the rent officer. The chairmen and members of rent assessment committees are drawn from panels nominated respectively by the Lord Chancellor and by the Minister for Housing. Appeal lies to the High Court on a point of law. The difficult jurisdictional issues that may arise in drawing the line between furnished and unfurnished accommodation and other practical considerations suggest that it would be sensible if the rent tribunals and assessment committees were amalgamated.[4]

[1] Street, *op. cit.*, chap. 2.

[2] *E.g. The King* v. *Paddington and St. Marylebone Rent Tribunal*, p. 664, *ante*.

[3] Annual Reports on Council on Tribunals for 1959–62.

[4] Cf. D. C. M. Yardley, *Rent Tribunals and Rent Assessment Committees*, [1968] Public Law 135, 152–3.

Professional Tribunal: Discipline Committee (Solicitors)

The Discipline Committee appointed under the Solicitors Act 1957 is an example of a tribunal which exercises disciplinary powers over a profession under the authority of statute.[1] It is a committee established for the purpose of hearing applications against solicitors, either to strike them off the roll or to compel them to answer allegations made against them by clients. Solicitors are officers of the court and, therefore, are properly subjected to a disciplinary code of conduct by State machinery. This committee is appointed by the Master of the Rolls. For hearing of applications there sits a board of at least three members who are practising solicitors. The committee has power to order a solicitor to be struck off the roll, to suspend him from practice or to order him to pay costs. It acts as a judicial body hearing formally applications by complainants, administering oaths and generally conducting its procedure as a court of law. Every order made by the committee must be prefaced by a statement of the findings in relation to the facts of the case. An appeal from an order of the committee lies to the High Court.

Tribunals and Inquiries Act 1958

The main conclusions of the Franks Committee on the status of administrative tribunals have already been mentioned. The Committee also made detailed recommendations for improving existing tribunals, which were largely adopted. Thus in the national insurance field, the right of legal representation was recognised in all cases and the general principle of public hearings was established. Other recommendations were implemented by the Tribunals and Inquiries Act 1958: the chairmen of certain tribunals are now selected by the Minister concerned from a panel of persons approved by the Lord Chancellor (s. 3), a provision that helps to ensure that chairmen are either legally qualified or have suitable alternative experience; in the case of most tribunals the Minister's power to terminate membership of a tribunal can only be exercised with the concurrence in England and Wales of the Lord Chancellor, and in Scotland of the Lord President of the Court of Session (s. 5); appeals on points of law are provided from certain tribunals to the High Court (s. 9); and all tribunals are under a duty, if requested, to give reasons for their decision, such reasons whether written or oral being deemed to form part of the record for the purpose of review by certiorari (s. 12).[2]

[1] Pp. 67–8, *ante*.
[2] P. 665, *ante*.

Council on Tribunals

The Tribunals and Inquiries Act 1958 also established the Council on Tribunals.[1] The members of the Council (in number between ten and fifteen) are appointed by the Lord Chancellor and the Secretary of State for Scotland, and the Council has a Scottish Committee (s. 1). The Council is under a duty to keep under review the constitution and working of a large number of tribunals *i.e.* those originally named in the First Schedule to the 1958 Act and also those subsequently included by statutory instrument made by the Lord Chancellor and the Secretary of State for Scotland (s. 10). The Lord Chancellor and the Secretary of State have power to ask the Council to consider and report on matters concerning any tribunal other than ordinary courts of law. In one instance, concerning those administrative procedures which involve the holding of a statutory inquiry, the Council may itself take the initiative on a matter determined to be of special importance.[2] The Council's functions are essentially advisory; they have no power to interfere with the decision of a tribunal in a particular case, although they may comment on the circumstances in which it was made. The Council has no executive powers: the Franks Committee's recommendation that members of tribunals should be appointed by the Council was not accepted by the Government, and the Council merely has power to make to the appropriate Minister general recommendations on the appointment of tribunal members (s. 4).

The Council make an annual report to the Lord Chancellor and the Secretary of State for Scotland, and other reports by the Council are made to these Ministers. The Council may take the initiative in reporting on any tribunal placed under its general supervision, but it does not follow that any action will be taken on the report to the Lord Chancellor. The Council has no rule-making powers but must be consulted before any procedural rules are made for any tribunals subject to their supervision (s. 8) [3] or for any procedures involving a statutory inquiry.[4] Sometimes the Council is consulted by the Government on proposed legislation to create new tribunals.[5]

[1] H. W. R. Wade, [1960] Public Law 351, and J. F. Garner [1965] Public Law 321.

[2] P. 704, *post*.

[3] *E.g.* Mental Health Review Tribunal Rules, 1960 (S.I. 1960 No. 1139) and p. 489, *ante*.

[4] Tribunals and Inquiries Act 1958, s. 7A, added by Town and Country Planning Act 1959, s. 33.

[5] J. F. Garner, *op. cit.*, pp. 327–31.

B. Public Inquiries

In Chapter 44, section C, the legal rules affecting the public inquiry as part of the administrative process have been discussed in the context of natural justice. It was seen, particularly from the Housing Acts cases, that the application of common law principles to this frequent governmental device caused considerable difficulties, particularly over the extent to which the holding of a public inquiry could be regarded as a judicial or quasi-judicial function. The Franks Committee rejected the extreme "administrative" and "judicial" interpretations of the public inquiry; in the Committee's view, the objects of the inquiry procedure were (*a*) to protect the interests of the citizens most directly affected by a governmental proposal by granting them a statutory right to be heard in support of their objections; and (*b*) to ensure that thereby the Minister would be better informed of the whole facts of the case before the final decision was made.[1] To ensure a reasonable balance between the conflicting interests concerned, and to see that Parliament's intention in requiring the public inquiry procedure to be observed was fulfilled, the Committee recommended (*a*) that the individual should know in good time before the inquiry the case he would have to meet; (*b*) that any relevant lines of policy laid down by the Ministry should be disclosed at the inquiry; (*c*) that the inspectors who conduct inquiries should be under the control of the Lord Chancellor, and not under that of the Minister directly concerned with the subject-matter of their work; (*d*) that the inspector's report should be published together with the letter from the Minister announcing the final decision; (*e*) that the decision letter should contain full reasons for the decision, including reasons to explain why the Minister had not accepted recommendations of the inspector; (*f*) that it should be possible to challenge a decision made after a public inquiry in the High Court, on the grounds of jurisdiction and procedure.[2]

Except for the recommendation that the corps of inspectors should be transferred from the Ministry of Housing to the Lord Chancellor's Department, these recommendations were accepted by the Government and initially brought into force by administrative action.[3] Moreover, the Council on Tribunals was given power to consider and report on matters arising out of the conduct of statutory inquiries; this allows an individual who is dissatisfied with some aspect of a

[1] Cmnd. 218, p. 59.
[2] Cmnd. 218, Part IV.
[3] Ministry of Housing and Local Government, Circular no. 9/58, dated February 27 1958; and see Council on Tribunals Annual Report, 1963, App. A.

particular inquiry to complain to the Council. In this context, "statutory inquiry" originally meant an inquiry or hearing held by or on behalf of a Minister in pursuance of a duty imposed by any statutory provision. But it now may include an inquiry initiated by a Minister other than in pursuance of a statutory duty.[1]

Rules of Procedure for Public Inquiries

The Town and Country Planning Act 1959 gave the Lord Chancellor power, after consulting the Council on Tribunals, to make rules regulating the procedure at statutory public inquiries. Rules have now been made to govern procedure at inquiries held for many statutory purposes, including inquiries into local authorities' compulsory purchase orders and into appeals against the refusal of planning permission.[2] In the case of compulsory purchase inquiries, at least forty-two days' notice of the inquiry must be given to the local authority and to every owner of an interest in the land affected who has objected to the making of the compulsory purchase order. At least twenty-eight days before the inquiry, the local authority must send to every objector a written statement of the reasons for the order. Both objectors and the local authority have a right to appear at the inquiry and to be represented, either by a lawyer or some other person. Provision is made for enabling objectors to be informed of the views of any government departments which support the order, and departmental representatives may be required to attend the inquiry in order that they may be questioned about departmental policy. Some observance is paid to the traditional doctrine of ministerial responsibility by the provision that the inspector may disallow a question put to such a representative if in the inspector's opinion it is "directed to the merits of government policy". Procedure at the inquiry is to be determined by the inspector. The degree of formality may be expected to depend on the circumstances of the inquiry, particularly the extent of legal representation. The inspector is empowered to visit the land alone before or during the inquiry, but if he visits it after the inquiry, notice must be given to the local authority and to the objectors, who have the right to accompany him. The inspector's report must include his findings of fact and his recommendations, if any; it will be published when the Minister's decision is notified to the parties.[3]

[1] Tribunals and Inquiries Acts: 1958, s. 14 (1); 1966, s. 1; and see S.I. 1967 No. 451, which brings many discretionary inquiries within the scope of the 1958 Act.

[2] See *e.g.* S.I. 1962 No. 1424 and S.I. 1965 No. 473.

[3] This embodies what had been departmental practice since Circular no. 9/58. Whenever these rules apply, the decision in *Local Government Board* v. *Arlidge*, p. 651, *ante*, is to this extent reversed.

One particularly important rule deals with the situation where the Minister, after considering the inspector's report, either differs from the inspector on a finding of fact, or, after the close of the inquiry, "receives any new evidence, including expert evidence on a matter of fact, or takes into consideration any new issue of fact, not being a matter of government policy, which was not raised at the inquiry". In such a case, if the Minister proposes not to follow the inspector's recommendation because of this new material, the local authority and objectors must be informed and they have the right to require the inquiry to be re-opened. The background to this lies in what was known as the Chalk-pit affair.[1]

At an inquiry into a local planning authority's refusal of permission for the digging of chalk in North Essex, neighbouring owners brought evidence to show that their land would be seriously harmed if this were permitted. On the strength of this evidence the inspector recommended that permission should not be given. Subsequently the Ministry of Housing consulted privately with the Ministry of Agriculture about this, and later granted planning permission, *inter alia* on the ground that the chalk workings would not harm neighbouring land. The neighbouring owners tried unsuccessfully to seek a remedy in the High Court,[2] and then complained to the Council on Tribunals about this apparent abuse of the inquiry procedure. Although the Government, through the Lord Chancellor, refused to admit that anything improper had occurred, following pressure from the Council on Tribunals the Lord Chancellor finally accepted the Council's view on the point of principle in making the rules of procedure already quoted.

The effect of the statutory rules for inquiries is to give the individuals most closely affected by compulsory purchase and town planning proposals better protection, in that the provisions of the rules are enforceable in the courts. In circumstances such as those in *Errington* v. *Minister of Health*,[3] the landowner could now base his challenge to the compulsory purchase order on the failure to comply with the statutory rules. But the statutory rules are of direct assistance only to the owners of legal interests in the land subject to the local authority's proposals; neighbouring owners receive no rights under the rules, even if, as in the Chalk-pit affair, they have taken an active part in the inquiry proceedings.[4]

The part played by the Council on Tribunals in the preparation of these rules and the steps it has taken to secure the more frequent award of costs to those taking part in inquiries, particularly to owners

[1] See J. A. G. Griffith, *The Council and the Chalkpit*, (1961) 39 Public Administration 369.
[2] *Buxton* v. *Minister of Housing and Local Government*, [1961] 1 Q.B. 278.
[3] P. 652, *ante*.
[4] Cf. the *Packington Estate* case, discussed in [1966] Public Law 1–7.

who successfully object to the compulsory purchase of their land, indicate the value of the Council in continuing the work begun by the Franks Committee. But in circumstances of serious abuse, the courts have the power to give an effective remedy to an owner which the Council lacks.[1] Furthermore, as the courts have frequently emphasised, the public inquiry procedure is not a form of litigation; the ultimate decision has still to be based on the Ministry's own assessment of the needs of policy, and not on any question of legal right.

Recent changes in town planning inquiries

Three important changes affecting the use of public inquiries in town planning were made in 1968.[2] Extreme pressure on the public inquiry as an instrument of planning policy in the period following the Franks Report had led to delays and over-centralisation of decisions on many local issues and yet did not always guard against ill-considered decisions on national issues. First, new arrangements for development plans were made, designed to eliminate many extremely lengthy inquiries. In future the approval of central government would be needed only for outline or 'structure' plans; detailed development planning would be left to local planning authorities, who would themselves hold public inquiries into their own local plans. Public participation in the planning process at an earlier stage than the public inquiry was also encouraged. Secondly, the Minister was authorised to delegate responsibility for deciding certain categories of planning appeals to the inspector. Already in the great majority of small planning appeals, the Minister in practice accepted the inspector's recommendation. Judicial review lies in the case of an inspector's decision as it does in the case of decisions made by the Minister, but the Minister will not be responsible to Parliament for the decision. Thirdly, the Minister may now appoint an *ad hoc* Planning Inquiry Commission to inquire into matters of such national or regional importance, or involving technical and scientific matters of such a kind, that normal planning procedures would not be adequate to deal with them. The need for such commissions was illustrated by the Government's controversial decision, later withdrawn, that Stansted should become the third London airport.[3]

[1] *E.g. Webb* v. *Minister of Housing and Local Government*, [1965] 2 All E.R. 193.

[2] Town and Country Planning Act 1968, discussed by A. Samuels in [1969] Public Law 119.

[3] See *e.g.* Report for 1967 by Council on Tribunals, Appendix A.

C. The Parliamentary Commissioner for Administration

Until 1967, the main safeguards for the citizen against oppressive or faulty government were the following: judicial review of administrative action, through remedies described in chapter 45; the right of appeal to a tribunal against an administrative decision; the opportunity of taking part in a public inquiry held before a Ministry's decision was made; redress by parliamentary means with the aid of an M.P.; the request for administrative review of an existing decision. Although, as we have seen, each may be effective in particular situations, each has its limitations.[1] For example, many discretionary decisions affecting the individual are made without the possibility of recourse to a tribunal or inquiry. Judicial review is often uncertain, expensive, and liable to be too cumbrous in procedure; it is more effective in protecting established common law rights than in protecting interests which arise from social or economic legislation. Parliamentary procedures may not be well suited to the impartial finding of facts or to the resolution of disputes according to sound principles of administration. It follows from ministerial responsibility to Parliament that civil servants are not directly responsible to Parliament and that Parliament depends for its information about official decisions on what the Minister tells it.

To give further protection to the citizen, the office of Parliamentary Commissioner for Administration was created in 1967. Although it derives from the Ombudsman in Scandinavian countries and in New Zealand,[2] the British model was designed to fit within existing British institutions. While the Parliamentary Commissioner has close links with the Executive, the office is designed as an extension of Parliament; significantly it has virtually no links with the judicial system or the legal profession. The aim of the Parliamentary Commissioner Act 1967 is to improve the effectiveness of Ministerial responsibility to Parliament, without detracting from established parliamentary procedures.

Status and jurisdiction [3]

The Parliamentary Commissioner for Administration is appointed by the Crown and holds office during good behaviour, although he

[1] Cf. *The Citizen and the Administration* (the Whyatt Report) p. 595, *ante*. See also Cmnd. 2767 (1965).

[2] On comparative aspects, see *The Ombudsman*, ed. Rowat, 2nd edn. (Allen and Unwin); and *Ombudsmen and Others*, Walter Gellhorn (O.U.P.).

[3] References in the text are to the Parliamentary Commissioner Act 1967.

may be removed by the Crown following addresses by both Houses (s. 1). His constitutional status closely resembles that of the Comptroller and Auditor-General. His salary is fixed by statute and is charged on the Consolidated Fund (s. 2). He appoints his own staff, subject to Treasury consent as to numbers and conditions of service (s. 3). The practice of the first Commissioner (himself a former Comptroller and Auditor-General) has been to recruit exclusively from experienced civil servants.

The main task of the Commissioner is to investigate the complaints of citizens who claim to have suffered injustice in consequence of maladministration by government departments in the exercise of their administrative functions (s. 5). His area of jurisdiction is closely defined by the 1967 Act, the Second Schedule of which lists the departments of central government subject to investigation. This list may be amended by Order in Council (s. 4)—a power which must be exercised whenever departments are abolished or created.

The Commissioner has no jurisdiction over authorities which are not departments of the central government, for example, local authorities, the police, and the nationalised industries, the reason given for this being that Ministers are not responsible to Parliament for the decisions of these authorities. The Commissioner may, however, investigate complaints about the way in which Ministers have discharged their functions in these various fields. The Commissioner's jurisdiction is further limited by the exclusion of many matters for which Ministers are responsible to Parliament (s. 5 (3) and Third Schedule). They include:

(1) action taken in matters certified by a Secretary of State to affect relations or dealings between the U.K. Government and any other government, or international organisation;

(2) action taken outside the U.K. by any officer representing or acting under the authority of the Crown (*e.g.* a British consul abroad);

(3) the administration of colonial or dependent territories outside the U.K.;

(4) action taken by a Secretary of State under the Extradition Act 1870 or the Fugitive Offenders Act 1967;

(5) action taken by or with the authority of the Secretary of State for investigating crime or protecting the security of the State;

(6) the commencement or conduct of civil or criminal proceedings before any court in the U.K., court martial or international court;

(7) any exercise of the prerogative of mercy;

(8) action taken on behalf of the central government by regional hospital boards and other authorities in the National Health Service;

(9) matters relating to contractual or other commercial transactions on the part of central government; [1]

(10) appointments, discipline and other personnel matters in relation to the civil service and the armed forces;

(11) the grant of honours, awards or privileges within the gift of the Crown.

In respect of each restriction, different policy considerations arise. It was these restrictions which led in Parliament to criticism that the Parliamentary Commissioner Bill sought to carve up areas of possible grievances in an arbitrary way.[2] Those restrictions which have been most criticised are in (8), (9) and (10) above. The Government has power by Order in Council to revoke any of these restrictions but not to add to them (s. 5 (4)).

Another limitation is that the Commissioner may not normally investigate any action in respect of which the complainant has or had a right of recourse to a tribunal or a remedy by proceedings in any court of law, although he may do so if in a particular case the citizen could not reasonably be expected to exercise his right (s. 5 (2)). If a citizen is dissatisfied with a decision about a social security benefit, or an award of compensation on a compulsory purchase of land, he clearly should appeal to the relevant tribunal. But in some circumstances a judicial remedy may be so uncertain that he cannot reasonably be expected to embark on litigation.

There is also a time bar: the Commissioner may investigate a complaint only if it is made to an M.P. within twelve months from the date when the citizen first had notice of the matter complained of, except where special circumstances justify the Commissioner in accepting a complaint made after a longer interval (s. 6 (3)).

Although it is for the Commissioner to determine whether a complaint is duly made under the Act (s. 5 (5)), it is submitted that the Act does not protect the Commissioner if he takes up a complaint on a matter clearly outside his jurisdiction. Thus if he began to investigate a complaint about the dismissal of a civil servant, or the actions of a local authority, it is doubtful whether any person could be held liable for obstruction or contempt for refusing to supply information to the Commissioner (s. 9).

[1] This is subject to an exception for transactions relating to compulsorily purchased land and other land bought under the threat of compulsory powers. But for this exception, a latter-day Crichel Down Affair (p. 89, *ante*) would have been outside the Commissioner's jurisdiction.

[2] Mr. Quintin Hogg, H.C. Deb., 18th October 1966, col. 67.

Procedure

One important feature of the Ombudsman idea is the ease with which the citizen may refer a grievance to the Ombudsman. But in Britain the citizen has no right to present his complaint to the Parliamentary Commissioner. In the first instance, a complaint of maladministration must be addressed by the person who claims to have suffered injustice to an M.P. (s. 5 (1)). It is for the M.P. to decide whether or not to refer the complaint to the Commissioner. Usually a citizen will send the complaint to the M.P. for his own constituency but the Act does not require this. When the Commissioner receives a complaint from an M.P. he must first decide whether it falls within his jurisdiction. If so, and if he decides to conduct an investigation, he must give the department concerned and any person named in the complaint an opportunity of commenting on any allegations made (s. 7 (1)). The investigation must be carried out in private (s. 7 (2)); normally an officer of the Commissioner's staff examines the relevant departmental files. The Commissioner has wide powers of compelling Ministers and officials to produce documents and has the same powers as the High Court in England or the Court of Session in Scotland to compel any witness to give evidence before him (s. 8). The Commissioner's investigation is not restricted by the doctrine of Crown privilege (s. 8 (3)). The only documents which are statutorily privileged are those certified by the Secretary of the Cabinet, with the approval of the Prime Minister, to relate to proceedings of the Cabinet or a committee of the Cabinet (s. 8 (4)).

When the investigation is complete, the Commissioner must send to the M.P. concerned a report of the results of the investigation (s. 10 (1)). If the Commissioner considers that injustice was caused through maladministration and has not been remedied, he may lay a special report before Parliament (s. 10 (3)). A Minister has no power to veto an investigation, but he may give notice to the Commissioner that publication of certain documents or information would be prejudicial to the safety of the State or against the public interest and this notice binds the Commissioner in making his report (s. 11 (3)).

The Commissioner has no executive powers. Thus he cannot alter a departmental decision or award compensation to a citizen, although he may suggest an appropriate remedy. But a Minister will be under a strong obligation to accept the Commissioner's findings and take necessary corrective action. Circumstances might arise in which a report by the Commissioner would have such controversial political or administrative implications that a Minister could come under pressure not to accept the recommendations. To give support to the Commissioner in such a situation, and to watch over the work of the Commissioner, a Select Committee is appointed by the House of Commons each session to examine the reports he lays in Parliament. This committee may take evidence from the departments concerned and may report to the House on the Commissioner's work.

The Commissioner's case-work

What is meant by the phrase, "injustice caused to the person aggrieved in consequence of maladministration" (s. 10 (3))? No definition and no illustrations of maladministration and injustice are given in the Act. Maladministration includes such defects as "neglect, inattention, delay, incompetence, ineptitude, perversity, and arbitrariness" [1] but further examples of maladministration will arise from the case-work of the Commissioner. Even if maladministration is found to have occurred, this does not in itself mean that injustice has thereby been caused to the individual. Conversely, injustice or extreme hardship may be found to exist which has not been caused by maladministration, but, for example, by an Act of Parliament or a judicial decision.

One difficult matter which is not yet solved has been the relation between maladministration and discretionary decisions. It is a basic principle of judicial review that a court may not substitute its own decision for the discretionary decision of a Minister, provided the Minister has acted within the four corners of his discretion. Unlike the New Zealand Ombudsman, who is empowered to find that a discretionary decision was wrong, the Commissioner is prohibited from questioning the merits of a discretionary decision taken without maladministration (s. 12 (3)). Where administrative errors have been made in the procedures leading to a discretionary decision, the Commissioner can report accordingly. But what is the position where a discretionary decision has caused manifest hardship to the individual, but no identifiable administrative defect has occurred in the procedures leading up to it? Despite initial hesitation, the Commissioner is now willing in such a case to infer an element of maladministration from the very decision itself. Similarly he is now prepared to inquire into harsh decisions which may have been based on the over-rigorous application of departmental policies.[2]

Although the Commissioner's reports to Parliament must be read if the nature of his case-work is to be appreciated, one example of his

[1] Mr. R. H. S. Crossman, H.C. Deb., 18th October, 1966, col. 51.

[2] First Report of P.C.A. (1968–69) H.C. 9; Second Report from Select Committee on P.C.A. (1967–68) H.C. 350.

investigations may be given, the Sachsenhausen case, which was the first occasion on which he found a government department to be seriously at fault.[1]

> Under the Anglo-German Agreement of 1964, the German government provided £1 million for compensating U.K. citizens who suffered from Nazi persecution during the Second World War. Distribution of this money was left to the discretion of the U.K. Government and in 1964 the Foreign Secretary (then Mr. Butler) approved rules for the distribution. Later the Foreign Office withheld compensation from twelve persons who claimed to be within the scope of these rules because of their detention within the Sachsenhausen concentration camp. Pressure from many M.P.s failed to get this decision reversed and a complaint of maladministration was referred to the Parliamentary Commissioner. By this time the whole of the £1 million fund had been distributed to other claimants. After extensive investigations, the Commissioner reported that there were defects in the administrative procedure by which the Foreign Office reached its decisions and subsequently defended them, and that this maladministration had damaged the reputation of the claimants. When the Commissioner's report was debated in the House of Commons, the Foreign Secretary (Mr. George Brown) assumed personal responsibility for the decisions of the Foreign Office, which he maintained were correct. He was nonetheless prepared to make available an additional £25,000 in order that the claimants might receive the same rate of compensation as successful claimants on the fund.[2]

It may be commented that at no time were any legal rights of the claimants involved, for the Foreign Offices rules were not enforceable in law, and there was no possibility of a judicial remedy.[3] Parliamentary pressure alone, without the report of the Commissioner, would not have been successful. Indeed, the Commissioner's report was based on information about the Foreign Office decisions which traditional parliamentary procedures could not have discovered. The case well illustrates the fact that the Commissioner has jurisdiction to investigate the conduct of Ministers as well as civil servants (s. 4 (4)). In retrospect, it appears that the Foreign Office erred in deciding to distribute the money itself, rather than entrusting this to the Foreign Compensation Commission, a judicial body for whose decisions the Foreign Secretary is not responsible.[4]

[1] Third Report of P.C.A. (1967–68) H.C. 54; First Report from Select Committee on P.C.A. (1967–68) H.C. 258.

[2] H.C. Deb., 5th February, 1968, cols. 105–17.

[3] See *Rustomjee* v. *The Queen* and *Civilian War Claimants' Association* v. *The King* (p. 266, *ante*).

[4] Report from Select Committee on P.C.A. (1968–69) H.C. 385, para. 19. And see *Anisminic Ltd.* v. *Foreign Compensation Commission* (p. 675, *ante*) and [1968] C.L.J. 42.

The Commissioner's recent annual reports suggest that over 1100 complaints are referred by M.P.s each year. Of these over half are rejected as being outside his jurisdiction (*e.g.* because no central government department was involved, or because a personnel matter from the civil service or armed forces was involved). In about 10 per cent of the cases which are fully investigated, elements of maladministration are found to exist. The remedies which departments provide include the payment of *ex gratia* compensation; special arrangements for collecting arrears of social security contributions or income tax; administrative review of the original decision; and revised procedures to prevent a repetition of the error. In general the Commissioner has revealed minor administrative defects rather than major instances of bias, corruption or oppressive conduct.

D. Outstanding Problems

In previous editions of this book it was said that the future of administrative justice was uncertain. Some of that uncertainty was removed by action following the Franks Report; in particular, the constitutional status and functions of the tribunal and inquiry procedures were clarified. Yet in the period between 1964 and 1969 there were indications that the use of public inquiries had reached its limit both in town planning,[1] and in the reform of local government.[2] Moreover these same years saw a resurgence of judicial activity in the field of administrative law, manifest particularly in a series of decisions of the House of Lords.[3] These decisions are associated primarily with Lord Reid, whose dictum in *Ridge* v. *Baldwin* is pertinent: "We do not have a developed system of public law—perhaps because until fairly recently we did not need it".[4] The creation of the Parliamentary Commissioner for Administration in 1967 with strictly limited jurisdiction has at most provided an additional remedy. Even if the Ombudsman idea is extended to other fields such as the police, local government and the National Health Service, basic questions about the legal control of administraton remain.

In the past proposals based on the need for a general system of

[1] P. 707, *ante*.
[2] P. 341, *ante*.
[3] *Ridge* v. *Baldwin*, [1964] A.C. 64; *Conway* v. *Rimmer*, [1968] A.C. 910; *Padfield* v. *Minister of Agriculture*, [1968] A.C. 997; *Anisminic Ltd.* v. *Foreign Compensation Commission*, [1969] 2 A.C. 147.
[4] [1964] A.C., p. 72.

administrative justice received scant consideration. Suggestions for a comprehensive system of administrative tribunals were rejected both by the Committee on Ministers' Powers and by the Franks Committee.[1] One proposal, associated particularly with Professor W. A. Robson, was for the creation of a general administrative appellate tribunal, outside the framework of the ordinary courts, with jurisdiction to hear appeals from tribunals and from decisions of Ministers following a statutory inquiry, and also with power to review harsh or unfair decisions from any branch of government. Another proposal was for an Administrative Division of the High Court, with appellate jurisdiction over administrative tribunals and with controlling powers over administrative decisions generally. Moreover the Franks Committee recommended the extension of judicial remedies such as certiorari and mandamus, without adequately considering the case for reform of the law relating to these remedies.[2]

More recently it has been argued that Britain needs a comprehensive system of public law to govern the Executive in all its relations with individuals, such as there is in France.[3] Weight is given to this argument by the formidable task which United Kingdom membership of the European Economic Community would present to British lawyers and civil servants in adapting to a continental approach to law and government.

The conservative nature of British institutions, as well as the great strength of some aspects of the present law, may make unlikely the introduction of a comprehensive system of public law. Yet at a time when local government is undergoing radical reform, when new techniques of training and management are being developed within the Civil Service, and when the inherited relationship between Parliament and the Executive is being questioned, there could hardly be a more suitable time for reassessing the role of the law in controlling administration. The recommendation by the English Law Commission for a royal commission on administrative law is timely.[4] More could yet be done to prevent and redress the unnecessary harm to individuals which actions and omissions of public authorities may inflict. It would be wrong to expect a judicial solution for every matter in dispute between an individual and a public authority;

[1] M.P.R., pp. 110–12; Cmnd. 218, pp. 28–9.

[2] Cmnd. 218, pp. 27–8.

[3] See articles by J. D. B. Mitchell in [1962] Public Law 24, [1965] Public Law 95, (1966) 15 I.C.L.Q. 133, [1967] C.L.J. 46, and [1968] Public Law 201. Cf. L. L. Jaffe [1968] Public Law 119 and H. W. R. Wade [1968] *Current Legal Problems* 75. See also L. N. Brown and J. F. Garner, *French Administrative Law* (Butterworth) and P. Weil [1965] C.L.J. 242.

[4] Cmnd. 4059, 1969.

but, through our constitutional institutions, we should be alert to recognise the harm that may be done by government action to individual and minority interests. Whatever the form that judicial intervention takes, ministers, civil servants, Members of Parliament and local officials alike must recognise the need for clearly defined powers, fair procedures, and informed and reasoned decisions.

CHAPTER FORTY-EIGHT

EMERGENCY POWERS IN PEACE AND WAR

A. Emergency Powers Act 1920

In times of grave national emergency, normal constitutional principles must if necessary give way to the overriding need to deal with the emergency. By the Emergency Powers Act 1920, Parliament has authorised government by regulation in exceptional circumstances. But the operation of the Act is subject to the safeguard of parliamentary control, which distinguishes it from old claims by the Crown to legislate independently of Parliament by virtue of necessity. The special power to govern by regulation arises only when a state of emergency has been declared by the Executive.[1]

State of Emergency

Before it is lawful to declare a state of emergency there must have occurred, or be on the point of occurrence, events of such a nature and on so extensive a scale as to be calculated to deprive the community, or any substantial portion of it, of the essentials of life by interfering with the supply and distribution of food, water, fuel or light, or with the means of locomotion. The present definition of emergency is wide enough to cover events such as serious flooding not due to human action.[2] The state of emergency is declared by proclamation, which can remain in force only for one month, though in practice the period may be continued thereafter by the issue of a new proclamation. The proclamation must be forthwith communicated to Parliament. If Parliament is not sitting, it must be summoned within five days. So long as the proclamation is in force, regulations may be made by Order in Council for securing the essentials of life to the community. Such powers may be conferred on government departments and on the police as may be deemed necessary for the purpose of preserving peace or for securing and regulating the supply and distribution of necessities and maintaining the means of transport. But the regulations must stop short of imposing compulsory military service or industrial conscription,

[1] The text of the Act is given in K. & L., pp. 221–3.
[2] See the Emergency Powers Act 1964, s. 1.

and no regulation may make it an offence for anyone to take part in a strike or peacefully to persuade others to do so. Regulations may provide for the trial by courts of summary jurisdiction of persons guilty of offences against the regulations, subject to maximum penalties. The regulations must be laid before Parliament and expire after seven days, unless a resolution is passed by both Houses providing for their continuance. The Act does not suspend the writ of habeas corpus and expressly prohibits the alteration of any existing procedure in criminal cases or the conferring of any right to punish by fine or imprisonment without trial. The Trade Disputes and Trade Unions Act 1927, which was passed as a direct result of the General Strike of 1926, aimed at preventing a repetition of such an event by making illegal sympathetic strikes or lock-outs, if conducted on a scale calculated to coerce the Government, by persons in trades not affected by any existing dispute. The Act was, however, wholly repealed in 1946.

There has been only one adequate opportunity of considering the effectiveness of the Act of 1920,[1] but the occasion was so important, namely, the General Strike and the Coal Strike, 1926, that the Act may be regarded as having provided an effective means of dealing with internal disorder on a large scale. In 1948 a state of emergency was declared in consequence of a dockers' unofficial strike in London and elsewhere, but the strike ended at once and no regulations under the Act were made. On July 11, 1949, for the same cause an emergency was again declared and regulations came into force; these enabled the Government to take over the working of those London docks which were affected by the strike.

The Emergency Powers Act 1964 gives permanent authority to the Government to employ troops on agricultural or other work of national importance.

B. Emergency Powers in Time of War

It has always been recognised that times of grave national emergency demand the grant of special powers to the Executive. At such times arbitrary arrest and imprisonment may be legalised by Act of Parliament. Modern war demands the abandonment of personal liberty in that the duty of compulsory national service necessarily takes away for the time being the right of the individual to choose his occupation. It was not, however, until the present century that conscription, even in time of war, was introduced in Great Britain.

[1] In time of war far wider powers are needed: see Section B, *post*.

Former Legislative Practice

In former times it was the practice in times of danger to the State to pass what were popularly known as Habeas Corpus Suspension Acts.[1] These Acts in effect prevented the use of the writ of habeas corpus for the purpose of insisting upon speedy trial or the right to bail in the case of persons charged with treason or other specified offences. They did not suspend generally the use of habeas corpus proceedings and, as soon as the period of suspension in relation to particular crimes was passed, anyone who for the time being had been denied the assistance of the writ could seek his remedy in the courts by an action for false imprisonment or malicious prosecution. Suspension did not legalise illegal arrest; it merely suspended a particular remedy in respect of particular offences.

Accordingly it was the practice at the close of the period of suspension to pass an Indemnity Act, in order to protect officials concerned from the consequences of any incidental illegal acts which they might have committed under cover of the suspension of the prerogative writ. During a period of emergency many illegalities might have been committed by the Executive in its efforts to deal with a critical situation. All such illegalities could be retrospectively legalised by the Indemnity Act.

First World War

Neither during the First nor Second World Wars was there any direct suspension of habeas corpus. The Defence of the Realm Acts, 1914–15, empowered the Executive to make regulations by Order in Council for securing the public safety or for the defence of the realm. It was held that this general power was wide enough to support a regulation authorising imprisonment without trial.

In *The King* v. *Halliday, ex parte Zadig*,[2] the House of Lords held that a regulation was valid which authorised the Secretary of State to detain a British subject on the grounds of his hostile origin or association. It was contended on behalf of Zadig, who was a naturalised British subject, that some limitation must be put upon the general words of the statute delegating power to the Executive; that there was no provision for imprisonment without trial, and indeed the Defence of the Realm Act 1915 had expressly provided for the trial of British subjects in a civil court by a jury; that general words in a statute could not take away the vested right of a subject or alter the fundamental law of the Constitution; that the statute being penal in nature must be strictly construed and that no construction should be adopted which was repugnant to the constitutional tradition of the country.

[1] Dicey, *op. cit.*, pp. 229–37.
[2] [1917] A.C. 260; K. & L. 39.

The majority of the court swept aside these arguments and held that on the construction of the Act the Executive had unrestricted powers. Lord Shaw of Dunfermline delivered a strong dissenting speech; he declined to infer from the delegation of a power to make regulations for public safety and defence that Zadig could be detained without a trial and indeed without being accused of any offence, save that he was of hostile origin or association as defined by the regulation; Parliament had not expressly said in words any one of these things.

A person detained under a valid regulation giving unrestricted power to detain cannot subsequently bring an action for false imprisonment in order to test the merits of his detention. Thus, though habeas corpus proceedings are not suspended, there is a greater infringement of liberty in giving the Executive unrestricted power to detain than in suspending habeas corpus proceedings in respect of particular charges.

Wide, however, as were the powers of the Executive, it was still practicable to challenge a regulation in the courts. Two cases deserve mention.

In *Attorney-General* v. *Wilts United Dairies, Ltd.* [1] an attempt by the Food Controller to impose a charge was held invalid on the ground that the regulation challenged conferred no express power to impose charges upon the subject. Doubt was also expressed whether a regulation conferring such a power would have been within the general power to make regulations for the public safety or the defence of the realm.

In *Chester* v. *Bateson* [2] there was held invalid a regulation which deprived a citizen of the right of access to the courts. The regulation empowered the Minister of Munitions to declare an area in which munitions were manufactured, stored or transported to be a special area. The effect of such declaration was to prevent any person without the consent of the Minister from taking proceedings for the recovery of possession of, or for the ejectment of a tenant of, any dwelling-house in the area, if a munition worker was living in it and duly paying rent. It was held that Parliament had not deliberately deprived the citizen of resort to the courts and accordingly that a regulation framed to forbid the owner of property access to legal tribunals was invalid, unless it could be shown to be a necessary or even reasonable way of securing the public safety or the defence of the realm.

Despite the wide powers conferred by the Defence of the Realm Acts numerous illegalities were undoubtedly committed and after the war there were passed the wide Indemnity Act 1920, and a separate Act relating to illegal charges, the War Charges Validity Act 1925.

[1] (1921), 37 T.L.R. 884; K. & L. 55. P. 55, *ante*.
[2] [1920] 1 K.B. 829; K. & L. 44.

Second World War

The legislators of 1939 took pains to close the gaps left in 1914–15 and specific powers were taken to avoid the effects of all the decisions of the First World War (except *Chester* v. *Bateson, ante*), which had restricted the powers of the Executive. No attempt was made to prohibit access to the courts, but the powers given were so wide that such a precaution was unnecessary. The Emergency Powers (Defence) Act 1939 empowered the making of regulations by Order in Council which appeared necessary or expedient for the public safety, the defence of the realm, the maintenance of public order, the efficient prosecution of any war in which His Majesty might be engaged and the maintenance of supplies and services essential for the life of the community. There followed a list of particular purposes for which regulations could be made without prejudice to the generality of the five general purposes; these included power to make provision for the trial of offenders against the regulations[1] and for the detention of persons by the Secretary of State in the interests of the public safety or the defence of the realm (a tribute to the dissenting judgment of Lord Shaw in *The King* v. *Halliday, ante*), and for authority to enter and search any premises. The case of *Attorney-General* v. *Wilts United Dairies, Ltd.* (*ante*), was not overlooked and the Treasury was empowered to impose charges in connection with any scheme of control under Defence Regulations. Treasury regulations imposing charges required confirmation by an affirmative resolution of the House of Commons. Other regulations had to be laid before Parliament "as soon as may be" after they were made and could be annulled by negative resolution within twenty-eight days. Orders made on the authority of Defence Regulations were not subject to any special form of parliamentary control. In addition to the Emergency Powers (Defence) Act there were passed within a few weeks of the outbreak of war some sixty temporary Acts, most of which suspended or amended provisions of permanent Acts relating to various public services.

The Emergency Powers (Defence) Act 1939 expressly forbade the imposition by regulations of any form of compulsory military service or industrial conscription. Compulsory service was imposed by separate National Service Acts.[2] The ban on the imposition by Defence Regulations of industrial conscription was removed by the Emer-

[1] For trial by court-martial and war zone courts, see Chap. 29.
[2] Chap. 27.

gency Powers (Defence) No. 2 Act 1940. This Act expressly authorised the making of defence regulations to establish a scheme of direction of labour, or industrial conscription.[1] Moreover regulations were made imposing strict government control over those who wished to change their employment. Some of these special powers were continued in the immediate post-war period.[2]

The Courts during the Second World War

Although access to the courts was not barred, the scope for judicial review of executive action was limited. Thus the courts could not consider whether a particular regulation was necessary or expedient for the purposes of the Act which authorised it. The question of necessity or expediency was one for the Government to decide.[3] The court could, however, hold an act to be illegal as being not authorised by the regulation relied upon to justify it.

> Thus in *John Fowler & Co. (Leeds), Ltd.* v. *Duncan* [4] it was held that an order authorising a controller to control financial transactions in connection with an undertaking did not authorise him to direct the undertaking to increase its bank overdraft.

Regulation 18B

Most relevant of all the Defence Regulations to personal liberty was Regulation 18B. We have seen [5] that Parliament expressly empowered the Executive to make regulations for detention without trial in the interests of public safety or the defence of the realm. Under Regulation 18B the Home Secretary was empowered to detain anyone whom he had reasonable cause to believe came within specified categories of suspects (including persons of hostile origin or association) and that by reason thereof it was necessary to exercise control over him. Facilities were given to persons detained to make objections to an advisory committee appointed by the Home Secretary. The Home Secretary was obliged to report to Parliament monthly the number of persons detained and the number of cases in which he had not followed the advice of the advisory committee. It was open to the subject to challenge detention by application for a writ of habeas corpus, but such applications had little chance of success in view of the decision of the House of Lords

[1] See *e.g.* Defence Regulation 58A made under the Act of 1940.

[2] See the Control of Engagement Orders, reimposed from 1947 until March 1950, and also pp. 723–4, *post*.

[3] *The King* v. *Comptroller-General of Patents, ex parte Bayer Products*, [1941] 2 K.B. 306. See also *Progressive Supply Co.* v. *Dalton*, [1943] Ch. 54.

[4] (1941), 57 T.L.R. 612.

[5] P. 721, *ante*.

in *Liversidge* v. *Anderson.*[1] In spite of a powerful dissenting judgment by Lord Atkin the House of Lords took the view that the power to detain could not be controlled by the courts, if only because considerations of security forbade proof of the evidence upon which detention was ordered. The words "had reasonable cause to believe" only meant that the Home Secretary must direct personal attention to the matter. It was sufficient for him to have a belief which in his mind was reasonable. The courts would not enquire into the grounds for his belief, although apparently they might examine positive evidence of *mala fides* or mistaken identity.[2] Stress was laid upon the high position of the Home Secretary and his responsibility to Parliament. Indeed, the House of Lords appeared to go very near to upholding the doctrine of State necessity so decisively rejected in the eighteenth century in *Entick* v. *Carrington.*[3] In another case decided at the same time the House of Lords held that a mistake on the part of the advisory committee in failing, as was required by the regulation, to give the appellant correct reasons for his detention did not invalidate the detention order.[4] In only one case did a person who had been detained under the regulation secure his release by means of habeas corpus proceedings. An order was made for the detention of the applicant on the ground that he was connected with a fascist organisation. He was wrongly informed that the order had been made on the ground of his being of hostile association. The Divisional Court ordered his release. His triumph was, however, short-lived, as the Home Secretary made a new order for his detention.[5]

Emergency Powers since 1945

Although the Emergency Powers (Defence) Acts 1939–40 expired in February 1946, and most defence regulations were revoked soon after the end of hostilities, post-war conditions did not permit all the war-time powers to be ended, in particular those which authorised

[1] [1942] A.C. 206. P. 631, *ante*.

[2] *Per* Lord Wright, at p. 261, approving the judgment of Tucker, J., in *Stuart* v. *Anderson*, [1941] 2 All E.R. 665. In the United States the Supreme Court took the view that the test to be applied in any judicial review of action taken to meet the war emergency was whether the action was necessary for that purpose. Thus, however wide was the general protective measure against persons of enemy origin and association it did not justify detention of a person admitted by the Government to be a loyal citizen of the United States, albeit of Japanese ancestry; *Hirabayashi* v. *United States*, 320 U.S. 81 (1943); *Ex parte Endo*, 323 U.S. 283 (1944).

[3] P. 486, *ante*; see Sir Carleton Allen, 58 L.Q.R. 232 and R.F.V. Heuston, 86 L.Q.R. 33.

[4] *Greene* v. *Secretary of State for Home Affairs*, [1942] A.C. 284.

[5] *The King* v. *Home Secretary, ex parte Budd*, [1942] 2 K.B. 14. See also *The Times*, 28 May, 1941.

rationing schemes and the control of industry. Economic difficulties in the late 1940s and the Korean War in 1951 caused the government to retain and even extend its powers under a series of Supplies and Services Acts.[1] These Acts authorised the government to make regulations to maintain and control essential supplies and services for a number of wide purposes *e.g.* to secure a sufficiency of essential supplies and services and their equitable distribution and their availability at fair prices; to promote the productivity of industry, commerce and agriculture; for redressing the balance of trade, and generally for assuring that the whole resources of the community were available for use in a manner best calculated to serve the interests of the community. These powers were so wide that in law the economy could have been entirely reorganised by government regulation alone. In fact these powers were used for relatively narrow purposes and today only a few such powers survive. The Land Powers (Defence) Act 1958 replaced the Defence Regulations which authorised the requisition of land and made permanent provision for the use of land for military purposes. Under the Emergency Laws (Re-enactment and Repeals) Act 1964, certain powers were made permanent, principally those dealing with the control of hire-purchase, credit-sale and other like transactions, and certain exchange transactions outside the scope of the Exchange Control Act. As these powers may be needed by any peace-time government, it is now merely a matter of history that these controls originated in the special conditions of war-time. In the event of an extreme national emergency occurring which could not adequately be dealt with under the Emergency Powers Acts 1920 and 1964, it is probable that Parliament would rapidly be asked to pass fresh legislation on the lines of that used in the Second World War.

[1] Supplies and Services (Transitional Provisions) Act 1945, Supplies and Services (Extended Purposes) Act 1947, Supplies and Services (Defence Purposes) Act 1951.

INDEX TO APPENDICES.

APPENDIX A. LEGISLATIVE FORMS.

APPENDIX B. NOTE ON DOCUMENTS ISSUED BY THE CROWN

APPENDIX C. FORMS OF PREROGATIVE AND STATUTORY INSTRUMENTS.

APPENDIX D

APPENDIX A.

Legislative Forms.[1]

Short title.

TREATY OF PEACE ACT 1919.

CHAPTER 33.

Long title. Date of Royal Assent.

AN Act for carrying into effect the Treaty of Peace between His Majesty and certain other Powers.

[31*st July*, 1919]

Preamble.

WHEREAS at Versailles, on the twenty-eighth day of June, nineteen hundred and nineteen, a Treaty of Peace (including a protocol annexed thereto), a copy of which has been laid before each House of Parliament, was signed on behalf of His Majesty, and it is expedient that His Majesty should have power to do all things as may be proper and expedient for giving effect to the said Treaty:

Enacting Clause.

BE it enacted by the King's most Excellent Majesty, by and with the advice and consent of the Lords Spiritual and Temporal, and Commons, in this present Parliament assembled, and by the authority of the same as follows:

Delegated Powers.

1. (1) His Majesty may make such appointments, establish such offices, make such Orders in Council, and do such things as appear to him to be necessary for carrying out the said Treaty, and for giving effect to any of the provisions of the said Treaty.

(2) Any Order in Council made under this Act may provide for the imposition, by summary process or otherwise, of penalties in respect of breaches of the provisions thereof, and shall be laid before Parliament as soon as may be after it is made, and shall have effect as if enacted in this Act, but may be varied or revoked by a subsequent Order in Council and shall not be deemed to be a statutory rule within the meaning of section one of the Rules Publication Act, 1893:[2]

Method of Parliamentary Control of Delegated Power.

Provided that, if an address is presented to His Majesty by either House of Parliament within the next twenty-one days on which that House has sat after any Order in Council made under this Act has been laid before it praying that the Order or any part thereof may be annulled, His Majesty in Council may annul the Order or such part thereof, and it shall thenceforth be void, but without prejudice to the validity of anything previously done thereunder.

[1] Excluding Statutory Instruments.
[2] P. 602, *ante*.

(3) Any expenses incurred in carrying out the said Treaty shall be defrayed out of moneys provided by Parliament.

2. This Act may be cited as the Treaty of Peace Act 1919. Citation.

ENACTING CLAUSE (SUPPLY BILL).

Most Gracious Sovereign,

We, Your Majesty's most dutiful and loyal subjects, the Commons of the United Kingdom in Parliament assembled, towards raising the necessary supplies to defray Your Majesty's public expenses, and making an addition to the public revenue, have freely and voluntarily resolved to give and grant unto Your Majesty the several duties hereinafter mentioned: and do therefore most humbly beseech Your Majesty that it may be enacted, and be it enacted by the Queen's most Excellent Majesty, by and with the advice and consent of the Lords Spiritual and Temporal, and Commons, in this present Parliament assembled, and by the authority of the same, as follows:

VOTE FOR SUPPLY SERVICES.

Appropriation Act 1962.

Schedule (B), Part 10.

Civil—Class II.

Schedule of sums granted and of the sums which may be applied as appropriations in aid in addition thereto, to defray the charges of the several Civil Services herein particularly mentioned, which will come in course of payment during the year ending on the 31st day of March 1963, viz.:—

	Sums not Exceeding	
	Supply Grants.	Appropriation in Aid.
Vote.		
1. For the salaries and expenses of the Department of Her Majesty's Secretary of State for Foreign Affairs; for sundry services; and for certain grants in aid (including a Supplementary sum of £50,000)	23,155,000	3,163,000
2. For sundry grants and services connected with Her Majesty's Foreign Service, including subscriptions to certain international organisations and certain grants in aid (including a Supplementary sum of £90,000)	18,803,000	2,000
3. For a grant in aid of the British Council . .	3,952,000	—
Carried forward	56,910,000	3,165,000

	Sums not Exceeding	
	Supply Grants.	Appropriation in Aid.
Brought forward	56,910,000	3,165,000
Vote.		
4. For the salaries and expenses of the Department of Her Majesty's Secretary of State for Comonwealth Relations; for sundry services; and for certain grants in aid (Revised sum) (including a Supplementary sum of £245,000) . .	9,725,000	149,000
5. For sundry Commonwealth services, including subscriptions to certain international organisations and certain grants in aid (including a Supplementary sum of £4,178,000) . .	14,845,000	—
6. For schemes made under the Colonial Development and Welfare Act 1959 for development in Central Africa (Revised sum) . . .	2,075,000	—
7. For the salaries and expenses of the Department of Her Majesty's Secretary of State for the Colonies; for sundry services; and for grants in aid (Revised sum) (including a Supplementary sum of £240,000)	9,284,000	1,145,000
8. For sundry Colonial Services including subscriptions to certain international organisations and certain grants in aid (Revised sum) (including a Supplementary sum of £1,263,000) . .	14,683,000	75,000
9. For schemes made under the Colonial Development and Welfare Act 1959 for development in territories for which the Colonial Office is responsible (Revised sum)	21,000,000	—
10. For the salaries and expenses of the Department of the Secretary for Technical Co-operation; for sundry foreign, Commonwealth and Colonial services; for a subscription to an international organisation; for certain grants in aid; and for certain expenditure on schemes made under the Colonial Development and Welfare Act	28,398,000	2,292,000
11. For a grant in aid of the Commonwealth War Graves Commission and certain other expenses	1,175,000	—
12. For the salaries and expenses of the Central African Office; for sundry services; a loan, and grants in aid	1,796,000	17,000
Total, Civil, Class II. . . £	148,891,000	6,843,000

TITLE OF PROVISIONAL ORDER CONFIRMATION ACT.

25 and 26 GEO. 5. c. XLV.

An Act to confirm a Provisional Order of the Minister of Transport under the Portsmouth Corporation Act 1930 relating to Portsmouth Corporation Trolley Vehicles.

APPENDIX B.

Note on Documents issued by the Crown.[1]

SOME appreciation of the wide activities of government may best be gathered from a consideration of documents issued by the Crown and Ministers. These fall into two main classes: (1) instruments executed by, or in the name of the Queen, many of which bear Her Majesty's signature, and (2) departmental instruments. The latter category is so vast that, beyond a reproduction in Appendix C of some specimen orders, no attempt can be made to enumerate the documents which issue from the departments in the course of their administrative activities.

Royal instruments fall under three heads:

(1) Orders in Council.

(2) Warrants, Commissions, Instructions to Colonial Governors and Orders under the Sign Manual.

(3) Proclamations, Writs, Letters Patent, Charters, Grants and other documents under the Great Seal.

Orders in Council.

(1) By means of Orders made by the Sovereign, by and with the advice of the Privy Council, are exercised the prerogative and statutory powers of the Crown. As an example of a prerogative Order in Council may be cited colonial legislation, such as the Mauritius (Legislative Council) Order in Council 1947, reconstituting the Legislative Council of the Colony, or the Order in Council commanding the issues of writs for the calling of a new Parliament, which accompanies the Proclamation dissolving Parliament. The statutory powers of the Crown are normally exercised by Order in Council, if they are conferred upon the Crown, as under the Foreign Jurisdiction Act 1890, and not upon a specified Minister. The judgments attendant on appeals to the Judicial Committee are promulgated in this manner, the Queen in Council making an Order on the advice tendered by the Committee. While legal responsibility for Orders in Council rests upon the members of the Privy Council in attendance at the meeting (usually not more than four or five), other than the Sovereign, political responsibility rests with the Minister, in whose department the draft Order is framed.

Warrants, Commissions and Orders under the Sign Manual.

(2) Documents under the Sign Manual relate both to prerogative and statutory powers. They are used to authorise administrative acts and to make appointments to office or to commissioned ranks in the Forces. Instructions to Colonial Governors, as well as their Commissions of Appointment, are examples of documents so executed. The term, Sign

[1] Halsbury, *Laws of England* (3rd edn.), Vol. 7, pp. 331 ff., should be consulted on this subject. See also, Anson, *Law and Custom of the Constitution*, 4th edn., Vol. 2, Part I, pp. 62–72.

Manual, is applied to the execution by signature of instruments which require the Queen's own hand. Either the Seal of the Secretary of State concerned or the counter-signature of such Secretary or other responsible Minister is required.

The Great Seal.

(3) The Great Seal is employed for the issue of writs for parliamentary elections and to summon peers to sit in Parliament, for treaties, for Letters Patent constituting the office of Governor of a Colony and making provision for the Government thereof and for all public instruments and orders of State which relate to the whole Kingdom. It is brought into use by a Warrant under the Sign Manual, signed by the Queen's own hand and counter-signed either by the Lord Chancellor, a Secretary of State, or two Lords Commissioners of the Treasury, but in some cases it may be employed by order of the Lord Chancellor without previous authorisation by Sign Manual Warrant: Great Seal Act 1884. Proclamations may only be issued by authority of the Crown under the Great Seal; no private person may issue a proclamation. Proclamations are valid in law on publication in the *London Gazette*; they receive judicial notice and are of the same validity as Acts of Parliament, though their lawful use is restricted to prerogative acts and to calling attention to provisions of existing law: *Case of Proclamations* (1611).[1]

Letters Patent are used (*inter alia*) to constitute an office, to confer a title, to appoint a Royal Commission enquiring into an important problem of the day and to provide for the government of a colony. They must be distinguished from a Patent conferred by statutory authority under the seal of the Patent Office, granting a monopoly of making, using and selling an article of manufacture new within the realm to the first and true inventor, a purely departmental matter under the Board of Trade.

Grants and Charters confer franchises, create corporations and grant prerogative privileges, many of which are now regulated by statute.

[1] Pp. 39-40, *ante*.

APPENDIX C.

Forms of Prerogative and Statutory Instruments.

THE object of this Appendix is to present the reader with specimens of some of the executive documents to which reference has been made from time to time. Both documents issued in the name of the Queen and specimens of departmental statutory instruments, which are a leading feature of present-day administration, are included. The authors desire to acknowledge the assistance of the Departments of State in facilitating the reproduction of certain documents and the courtesy of the Comptroller of H.M. Stationery Office in allowing the reproduction in an unofficial work of documents, the copyright of which is vested in the Crown. For the accuracy of reproduction the authors alone are responsible.

Royal Proclamation.

BY THE KING.

A PROCLAMATION.

For Dissolving the Present Parliament, and Declaring the Calling of another.
GEORGE R.I.[1]

WHEREAS We have thought fit, by and with the advice of Our Privy Council, to dissolve this present Parliament which stands prorogued[2] to Friday, Twenty-fourth day of May instant; We do, for that End, publish this Our Royal Proclamation, and do hereby dissolve the said Parliament accordingly: And the Lords Spiritual and Temporal, and the Knights, Citizens, and Burgesses, and the Commissioners for Shires and Burghs, of the House of Commons, are discharged from their Meeting and Attendance on the said Friday, the Twenty-fourth day of May instant: And We being desirous and resolved, as soon as may be, to meet Our People, and to have their Advice in Parliament, do hereby make known to all Our loving Subjects Our Royal Will and Pleasure to call a new Parliament: And do hereby further declare, that, by and with the advice of Our Privy Council, We have given Order that Our Chancellor of Great Britain and Our Governor of Northern Ireland do respectively, upon Notice thereof, forthwith issue out Writs, in due Form and according to Law, for calling a new Parliament: And We do hereby also, by this Our Royal Proclamation under Our Great Seal of Our Realm, require Writs forthwith to be issued accordingly by Our said Chancellor and Governor respectively, for causing the Lords Spiritual and Temporal and Commons who are to serve in the said Parliament to be duly returned to, and give their

[1] Until 1947 the King's Title included Emperor (Imperator) of India
[2] The Prorogation ceremony may be dispensed with, as in September 1964.

Attendance in, Our said Parliament on Tuesday, the Twenty-fifth day of June next, which Writs are to be returnable in due course of Law.

Given at Our Court of Saint James, this Tenth day of May, in the year of Our Lord One thousand nine hundred and Twenty-nine, and in the Twentieth year of Our Reign.

GOD SAVE THE KING.

A Proclamation followed commanding all the peers of Scotland to meet at the Palace of Holyroodhouse, Edinburgh, at noon on Friday, May 31, to choose the 16 peers to sit and vote in the House of Lords in the next Parliament.

Orders in Council were also gazetted as follows:

The Lord High Chancellor of Great Britain and the Governor of Northern Ireland were ordered forthwith to cause writs to be issued for the calling of a new Parliament, to meet on Tuesday, June 25.

The Convocations of Canterbury and York were forthwith dissolved, and the Lord Chancellor was to cause writs to be issued for electing new members of the Convocations. The writs were to be returnable on Wednesday, July 10.

STATUTORY INSTRUMENT, ROAD TRAFFIC ACT 1960

1963 No. 1553

THE MOTOR VEHICLES (INVALID CARRIAGES) REGULATIONS 1963

Made	10*th September* 1963
Laid before Parliament	16*th September* 1963
Coming into Operation	30*th September* 1963

The Minister of Transport, in exercise of his powers under sections 99, 113 and 253 of the Road Traffic Act 1960 [1] (hereinafter referred to as "the Act"), and of all other powers enabling him in that behalf, and after consultation with representative organisations in accordance with the provisions of section 260 (2) of that Act, hereby makes the following Regulations:—

1.—(1) These Regulations shall come into operation on the 30th September 1963, and may be cited as the Motor Vehicles (Invalid Carriages) Regulations 1963.

(2) The Interpretation Act 1889 [2] shall apply for the interpretation of these Regulations as it applies for the interpretation of an Act of Parliament.

(3) In these Regulations references to the Act shall be construed as references to that enactment as amended or applied by or under any subsequent enactment.

2. For the purposes of Part II of the Act and all regulations thereunder (which relate to the minimum age for driving motor vehicles and the licensing of drivers thereof) the maximum weight specified in subsection (5) if section 253 (which subsection defines the expression "invalid carriage" or the purposes of the Act) shall be varied from five hundredweight to six hundredweight.

3. Paragraph (*b*) of section 99(5) of the Act (which provides for certain tests of competence to drive to be taken as sufficient for the granting of licences authorising the driving of particular classes or descriptions of vehicles) shall apply to invalid carriages the weight of which unladen exceeds five hundredweight but does not exceed six hundredweight (as respects a test of competence to drive vehicles of a class or description comprised in Group 10 of the groups of vehicles set out in the first column in Schedule 5 to the Motor Vehicles (Driving Licences) Regulations 1963 [3] passed before the coming into operation of these Regulations).

Given under the Official Seal of the Minister of Transport the 10th September 1963.

(L.S.)

Ernest Marples,
The Minister of Transport.

[1] 8 & 9 Eliz. 2. c. 16.
[2] 52 & 53 Vict. c. 63.
[3] S.I. 1963/1026 (1963 II, p. 1730).

EXPLANATORY NOTE [1]

(*This Note is not part of the Regulations, but is intended to indicate their general purport.*)

These Regulations vary the maximum weight in the definition of invalid carriage from 5 cwt. to 6 cwt. for the purposes of Part II of the Road Traffic Act 1960 and all regulations thereunder, which relate to the minimum age for driving motor vehicles and the licensing of drivers thereof. In particular group 10 in Schedule 5 to the Motor Vehicles (Driving Licences) Regulations 1963 will be extended to include invalid carriages up to 6 cwt. and persons at present entitled to a licence enabling them to drive invalid carriages up to 5 cwt. will become entitled to a licence enabling them to drive invalid carriages up to 6 cwt.

[1] An explanatory note is not an operative part of a statutory instrument and may not, therefore, be used to assist interpretation of the instrument by a court of law.

(2) Demolition Order, Form of, under Housing Act, 1957, s. 17 (1). Schedule to Housing Act (Form of Orders and Notices) Regulations.

ORDER FOR DEMOLITION OF A HOUSE.

Whereas the [Council of] (hereinafter referred to as "the Council") being satisfied that the house known as is unfit for human habitation, and is not capable at a reasonable cost of being rendered so fit, have complied with the provisions of s. 16 of the Housing Act, 1957, in relation to the house:

Now Therefore the Council in pursuance of section 17 of the Housing Act, 1957, hereby order as follows:—

(1) the house shall be vacated within days from the date on which this Order becomes operative:

(2) the house shall be demolished within six weeks after the expiration of the last-mentioned period, or if the house is not vacated before the expiration of that period, within six weeks after the date on which it is vacated.

Dated this day of 19

(To be sealed with the Common Seal of the Local Authority.)

NOTE.

Any person aggrieved by a demolition order .... may within 21 days after the date of the service of the Order appeal to the County Court.................. No proceedings may be taken by the local authority to enforce any order against which an appeal is brought, before the appeal has been finally determined...................

Letters Patent. Form for creation of Baron.

PATENT FOR CREATION OF AN HEREDITARY PEER.

ELIZABETH THE SECOND by the Grace of God of the United Kingdom of Great Britain and Northern Ireland and of her other realms and territories. Queen, Head of the Commonwealth, Defender of the Faith, To all Lords Spiritual and Temporal and all other Our Subjects whatsoever to whom these Presents shall come Greeting Know Ye that We of Our especial grace certain knowledge and mere motion do by these Presents advance create and prefer Our to the state degree style dignity title and honour of Baron of in Our County of And for Us Our heirs and successors do appoint give and grant unto him the said name state degree style dignity title and honour of Baron to have and to hold unto him and the heirs male of his body lawfully begotten and to be begotten Willing and by these Presents granting for Us Our heirs and successors that he and his heirs male aforesaid and every of them successively may have hold and possess a seat place and voice in the Parliaments and Public Assemblies and Councils of Us Our heirs and successors within Our United Kingdom amongst other Barons And also that he and his heirs male aforesaid successively may enjoy and use all the rights privileges pre-eminences immunities and advantages to the degree of a Baron duly and of right belonging which other Barons of Our United Kingdom have heretofore used and enjoyed or as they do at present use and enjoy.

In Witness, &c.

APPOINTMENT OF AMBASSADOR.

(L.S.)

ELIZABETH R.

ELIZABETH, by the Grace of God, of the United Kingdom of Great Britain and Northern Ireland, and of her other realms and territories Queen, Head of the Commonwealth, Defender of the Faith

To All and Singular to whom these Presents shall come, Greeting!

Whereas it appears to Us expedient to nominate some Person of approved Wisdom, Loyalty, Diligence, and Circumspection to represent Us in the character of Our Ambassador Extraordinary and Plenipotentiary to

Now Know Ye that We, reposing especial trust and confidence in the discretion and faithfulness of Our (Right) Trusty and Well-beloved (Counsellor) (Sir).. have nominated, constituted and appointed, as We do by these Presents nominate, constitute and appoint him the said

to be Our Ambassador Extraordinary and Plenipotentiary to

as aforesaid. Giving and Granting to him in that character

all Power and Authority to do and perform all proper acts, matters and things which may be desirable or necessary for the promotion of relations of friendship, good understanding and harmonious intercourse between our Realm and

and for the protection and furtherance of the interests confided to his care; by the diligent and discreet accomplishment of which acts, matters and things aforementioned he shall gain Our approval and show himself worthy of Our high confidence.

And We therefore request all those whom it may concern to receive and acknowledge Our said

as such Ambassador Extraordinary and Plenipotentiary as aforesaid and freely to communicate with him upon all matters which may appertain to the objects of the high Mission whereto he is hereby appointed.

Given at Our Court of Saint James, the day of in the year of Our Lord One Thousand Nine Hundred and and in the Year of Our Reign.

By Her Majesty's Command.

(Countersigned by One of Her Majesty's Principal Secretaries of State.)

FREE PARDON.

ELIZABETH THE SECOND, by the Grace of God, of the United Kingdom of Great Britain, and Northern Ireland and of her other realms and territories Queen, Head of the Commonwealth, Defender of the Faith. To all to whom these Presents shall come, Greeting!

WHEREAS A.B. was convicted of and was thereupon sentenced to

NOW KNOW YE that We in consideration of some circumstances humbly represented to Us are graciously pleased to extend Our Grace and Mercy to the said A.B. and to grant him Our Free Pardon in respect of the said conviction, thereby pardoning, remitting and releasing unto him all pains penalties and punishments whatsoever that from the said conviction may ensue; and We do hereby command the Judges, Justices and others whom it may concern that they take due notice hereof; and We do require and direct the Governor of any Prison in which the said A.B. may be detained in respect of the said conviction to cause him to be forthwith discharged therefrom;

And for so doing this shall be a sufficient Warrant.

Given at Our Court at St. James's the day of 19 in the year of Our reign.

By Her Majesty's Command.

(Countersigned by One of Her Majesty's Principal Secretaries of State.)

APPENDIX D.

THE FOLLOWING IS A LIST OF MEMBERS OF THE GOVERNMENT FORMED BY MR EDWARD HEATH IN JUNE 1970

The Cabinet

Prime Minister and First Lord of the Treasury
Secretary of State for the Home Department
Secretary of State for Foreign and Commonwealth Affairs
Chancellor of the Exchequer
Lord Chancellor
Lord President of the Council and Leader of the House of Commons
Secretary of State for Defence
Secretary of State for Social Services
Chancellor of the Duchy of Lancaster
Minister of Technology
Secretary of State for Employment and Productivity
Secretary of State for Education and Science
Secretary of State for Scotland
Lord Privy Seal and Leader of the House of Lords
Minister of Housing and Local Government
Secretary of State for Wales
Minister of Agriculture, Fisheries and Food
President of the Board of Trade

Ministers not in the Cabinet

Minister of Overseas Development
Minister of Public Building and Works
Minister of Transport
Paymaster General
Attorney General
Lord Advocate
Solicitor General
Solicitor General for Scotland
Ministers of State, Home Office
Minister of State for Foreign and Commonwealth Affairs
Chief Secretary to the Treasury
Minister of State, Treasury
Minister of State, Ministry of Defence
Minister of State, Health and Social Security
Ministers of State, Ministry of Technology (2)

Minister of State, Department of Employment and Productivity
Minister of State, Scottish Office
Minister of Posts and Telecommunications
Minister of State, Welsh Office
Minister of State, Board of Trade

Her Majesty's Household

Lord Commissioner of Her Majesty's Treasury and Parliamentary Secretary, Civil Service Department
Treasurer
Comptroller
Vice-Chamberlain
Captain, Gentlemen at Arms
Captain, Yeoman of the Guard
Lords in Waiting

THE MAIN PROPOSALS OF THE ROYAL COMMISSION ON ASSIZES AND QUARTER SESSIONS 1966–69 WERE:[1]

(1) *Creation of a single new higher criminal court*

This would be called the Crown Court, would have jurisdiction throughout England and Wales, and sit when and where required.

It would absorb the criminal jurisdiction of present courts of Assize, the Central Criminal Court, and Lancashire Crown Courts, and borough and county quarter sessions.

The Crown Court would be served by two tiers of judges, the upper tier consisting of High Court judges as now, and the lower tier by a new bench of full-time judges, called Circuit judges, supported by some part-time recorders.

The bench of Circuit judges would consist of about 175 judges dealing with both criminal and civil cases. It would comprise the 32 judges now dealing with criminal work in the higher courts, the 101 county-court judges, and 40 new full-time appointments.

Existing part-time recorders, chairmen, and deputy chairmen of quarter sessions should be replaced by 120 new part-time appointments for which the name of recorder should be kept.

The commission proposed that two High Court judges should be assigned to each circuit to supervise the running of the courts. These would be known as Presiding judges.

The Lord Chancellor should have the power to open certain Crown courts to solicitors. The majority of the commission said that solicitors should be eligible for appointment to the circuit bench or to recorderships.

[1] Cmnd. 4153, 1969.

Cases would be allocated to the two tiers to ensure that, in general, High Court judges tried only cases which required their level of judicial talent.

(2) *Civil courts*

Civil business would be separated completely from criminal cases to ensure that civil work did not suffer as now, by the priority given to criminal cases.

The High Court would have jurisdiction to deal with civil cases throughout the country, sitting when and where required.

Normally, cases would be tried by High Court judges. But to avoid delay where there was a heavy case load, Circuit judges could be brought in to try simpler actions.

No changes were recommended in the structure of the county courts except that their jurisdiction in actions of contract and tort would be increased from £750 to £1,000.

HEADQUARTERS CITIES

(3) *Location of the courts*

Courts would be administered from headquarters cities in six regions or circuit areas.

These circuit areas (with the administrative centres in brackets) would be: Midland (Birmingham), North-Eastern (Leeds), Northern (Manchester), South-Eastern (London), Wales and Chester (Cardiff) and Western (Bristol).

There would be three different types of court centre within each administrative circuit.

At High Court and Crown Court centres visiting High Court judges would sit either continuously or for long periods to take the more important and difficult civil and criminal cases.

They would be assisted by Circuit judges who would hear less serious or less complex cases, now taken by High Court judges at assizes, and types of crime now tried at quarter sessions.

At some towns Crown courts would be held, served by both High Court and Circuit judges. These would differ from the first category only in that no High Court civil work would be taken there.

At the third type of court centre, only Circuit judges would normally sit, dealing with quarter-session-type cases. Only rare visits would be made by High Court judges.

As a result of the commission's proposals, High Court judges would no longer normally visit 33 of the present 61 assize towns. They would sit, however, at seven towns not now visited.

The commission proposes the creation of a unified court administrative service, appointed and paid by the Lord Chancellor and organised on a circuit basis.

(4) *Administration of the Courts*

In proposing that the Lord Chancellor should assume Ministerial responsibility for running the higher courts, the commission said that the administration of justice should be recognised as a central Government responsibility.

Court services should be financed by the Exchequer instead of indirectly as now.

Responsibility for the courts is shared now by the Lord Chancellor's office, the Home Office, the Ministry of Works, and local authorities.

TERMS OF REFERENCE OF THE ROYAL COMMISSION ON THE CONSTITUTION APPOINTED 1969

To examine the present functions of the central legislature and government in relation to the several countries, nations and regions of the United Kingdom;

To consider, having regard to developments in local government organisation and in the administrative and other relationships between the various parts of the United Kingdom, and to the interests of the prosperity and good government of Our people under the Crown, whether any changes are desirable in those functions or otherwise in the present constitutional and economic relationships;

To consider, also, whether any changes are desirable in the constitutional and economic relationships between the United Kingdom and the Channel Islands and the Isle of Man.

GENERAL INDEX

A

PAGES

PAGES

PAGES

E

F

G

PAGES

H

I

M

N

PAGES

Q

R

U

PAGES

V

W